# GOVERNMENT AND BUSINESS

# GOVERNMENT AND BUSINESS

*Second Edition*

by

RONALD A. ANDERSON

Member of the Pennsylvania and Philadelphia Bars

Professor of Law and Government, Drexel Institute of Technology

Coauthor of *Business Law, Fifth Edition*
*Business Law Principles and Cases, Second Edition*

Author of *Anderson Pennsylvania Civil Practice*
*Anderson Pennsylvania Civil Practice Forms*
*Purdon's Pennsylvania Forms*
*Couch's Cyclopedia of Insurance Law (2nd Edition)*
*Jones' Chattel Mortgages and Conditional Sales Supplement*
*Wharton's Criminal Evidence (12th Edition)*
*Wharton's Criminal Law and Procedure (1st Edition)*

Consulting Editor of the *Pennsylvania Law Encyclopedia*

Published by

SOUTH-WESTERN PUBLISHING COMPANY

Cincinnati 27 Chicago 5 San Francisco 3 Dallas 2 New Rochelle, N. Y.

H55

Library of Congress Catalog Card Number: 60-5826

H160

Printed in the United States of America

# PREFACE

As stated in the preface of the first edition, one of the most significant trends in the last one hundred years has been the growth in the extent to which government regulates business and the economy. This trend has many implications and raises great problems with which our leaders and our voters must be familiar. This book has been written and revised to meet the need for a text at the college level that would give a complete presentation of the problems involved. *Government and Business*, Second Edition, may be used for advanced study in a sequence of political science courses, economics courses, or business administration courses.

Since the subject of government regulation of business raises the question of "which government" as well as "what business," the first part of the book is devoted to a summary of the distribution of powers within our multi-unit system of government. The second part of the book deals with the constitutional limitations that restrict government in regulating business. The third part then treats specifically the different powers of the governments and the regulations that have been imposed under their authority. The fourth part of the book deals with the actual problems of administration. The success or the failure of government regulation of business may depend to a very large degree on the powers and the abilities of the administrators who make or apply the regulations.

Both the textbook method and the casebook method of presentation have been employed, the nature of the material determining in each instance which method would be followed. Source materials have been liberally edited and correlated so as to stress the fundamental principles and problems. At the end of each chapter there are discussion questions that not only call for an understanding of the text but also call upon the student to do original thinking.

A number of significant decisions have been rendered by the United States Supreme Court since the appearance of the first edition. This growth of the law accounts for the addition of 34 opinions of that court. In order to round out the development of the law, 8 Supreme Court opinions decided prior to the first edition have also been included.

The physical arrangement of the book has been improved by dividing each chapter into numbered sections. These sections are themselves subdivided under lettered headings calling attention to the particular topic and opinion which are there set forth. At the beginning of each chapter appears a table of contents setting forth all the sections and subsections of the chapter and the names of the cases. These should prove helpful both in initial orientation and in checking for review.

The table of contents for the entire book has been expanded to include the full titles of all sections, as well as the chapter titles. The table of cases has been expanded to include not only the opinions set forth in the book but also the more important cases cited in the text or footnotes. These changes will facilitate locating material in the book.

The content of many chapters has been expanded, and two new chapters have been added: Chapter 12, Regulation of Pricing Practices, and Chapter 30, Administrative Investigation.

As one reads the book, the political platforms of many parties both past and present come to mind. This resemblance is not purely accidental, for the greater part of the regulations and the problems discussed either were or still are matters of political controversy. This book, however, has not been written with the view or hope of persuading the reader. Its only goal has been an understandable presentation of the problems that confront society when government regulates business.

The importance of such an understanding need hardly be stressed when the Supreme Court of the United States brings home to the reader the recognition of these facts: (1) that the power of governments generally to regulate business is, in a sense, without limit; (2) that between Federal and local governments the power of the Federal has been increased until in the very words of the Court that power is as broad as the economic needs of the nation; (3) that this vast power of the governments to regulate business is administered by persons who are not directly subject to the voters and whose decisions are to a very large degree not subject to effective review by the courts; and (4) that the changed technology, the era of industrialization, and the impact of the twentieth century economy upon the Constitution—not foreign ideologies or domestic political theory—have been the cause of this change in the American way of government. Perhaps the pages of the past may guide us in the changes that await tomorrow.

Ronald A. Anderson

# CONTENTS

# TABLE OF CASES



* (C) refers to cases cited within the text or within a footnote.

# PART I. THE FEDERAL SYSTEM

## Chapter 1

## THE DIVISION OF POWER



### § 1:1. The National Powers

#### *(a) The problem*

Regulation of business in the United States always raises a legal or a constitutional question. Because our American governmental system is based upon written constitutions, every government, whether national, state, or local, finds that its power to regulate business, as well as to take any other action, is restricted in some way by either the national constitution or a state constitution, or by both.

This problem does not arise in an unlimited monarchy in which there is no restraint on governmental power. In such a state the power to regulate business exists without any limitation, and the only question that faces the sovereign is whether there should be such regulation and how it should be enforced. The ruler is concerned only with questions of policy and plan.

In contrast with this, the regulation of business in the United States raises the preliminary question of whether the governing body has the authority, under the applicable constitutional provisions, to make the regulation at all. It is therefore a three-fold problem of power, policy, and plan. It is to the questions of power and of plan that the present book is directed. The question of policy is only incidentally raised, as such a question involves underlying problems of economics, sociology, and political expediency.

### *(b) The historical background*

Returning to consideration of the question of power, its analysis in the United States is made more complicated by the fact that power is divided among different governments. Even the statement that power is divided is not strictly accurate, for some powers are shared by different governmental bodies. Examination of the historical development of governmental system will explain this.

The states that formed the United States in 1789 had come into being as colonies of England. By the long war of the Revolution, they obtained their independence; but, even before the formal declaration of that war, the colonies regarded themselves as independent. Pursuant to the call of the Continental Congress of May 15, 1776, the colonies drew up state constitutions, many of which were merely adaptations of their colonial charters.

These revolutionary state constitutions must be kept in mind because they and the succeeding state constitutions remain in the picture of governmental power from those days on. The effect or the purpose of a state constitution was to prescribe the structure and the power of the state government and to set forth the limitations of that power. In addition, such state constitutions, or later state constitutions adopted in their place, set forth the powers of the political subdivisions of states (towns, cities, boroughs, and counties) or merely authorized the legislatures to pass laws to specify the powers and the structure of such political subdivisions. On top of this pattern of state constitutions and state laws, all prescribing the powers and the structure of state and local governments, is added the national constitution.

The first national written constitution was the Articles of Confederation, which came into effect in 1781 and remained until displaced by the present Constitution of the United States in 1789. The central government under the Confederation was in substance a league or group to which the ex-colonies belonged but by which they could not be controlled. Differences between the states led to clashes on questions of boundaries and commerce. These became so numerous that finally a series of meetings was called to endeavor to remedy this evil.

The third of these meetings was the Philadelphia Convention, which, although officially called "to take into consideration the situation of the United States, to devise such further powers as shall appear to them necessary to render the Constitution of the federal government adequate to the exigencies of the union," soon turned its attention to drafting an entirely new constitution. This new constitution, which is the one by which we are now governed, specifies the structure and the power of the national government and contains limitations on the powers of both national, state, and local governments.

The effect of the adoption of the national constitution was to take certain powers away from the states and to give them to the national government. Thus the power to wage war was exclusively given to the national government. Other powers given to the national government could be exercised concurrently by the states. For instance, the power to tax granted to the federal government did not destroy the state power to tax, even though both governments were to tax the same subject or base. In addition, some powers may be exercised by the states only so long as they are not exercised by the national government. Thus state safety appliance laws may apply to interstate trains until a federal law on the subject is adopted. Other powers are denied to all governments, such as the passage of ex post facto laws making criminal an act already committed that was not criminal when committed or increasing the penalty for an act already committed above the penalty in force at the time it was committed.

### *(c) Delegation of power*

Speaking generally, we are concerned with three types of government: the government of the United States, the government of the states, and the government of the political subdivisions of the states. By the term "political subdivision" is meant any county, city, borough, township, or district that is created by a state. The national government may exercise only those powers expressly enumerated in the Constitution as being delegated to it and such powers as may be construed as reasonably necessary and proper to carry into execution the expressly granted powers. The power of the national government is based upon the power of the President and the Senate to execute treaties, of the executive to conduct foreign relations generally, and of Congress to exercise the following powers expressly enumerated in Article 1, Section 8, of the Constitution:

The Congress shall have Power To lay and collect Taxes, Duties, Imposts and Excises, to pay the Debts and provide for the common Defence and general Welfare of the United States; but all Duties, Imposts and Excises shall be uniform throughout the United States;

To borrow money on the credit of the United States;

To regulate Commerce with foreign Nations, and among the several States, and with the Indian Tribes;

To establish an uniform Rule of Naturalization, and uniform Laws on the subject of Bankruptcies throughout the United States;

To coin Money, regulate the Value thereof, and of foreign Coin, and fix the Standard of Weights and Measures;

To provide for the Punishment of counterfeiting the Securities and current Coin of the United States;

To establish Post Offices and post Roads;

To promote the Progress of Science and useful Arts, by securing for limited Times to Authors and Inventors the exclusive Right to their respective Writings and Discoveries;

To constitute Tribunals inferior to the supreme Court;

To define and punish Piracies and Felonies committed on the high Seas, and Offenses against the Law of Nations;

To declare War, grant Letters of Marque and Reprisal, and make Rules concerning Captures on Land and Water;

To raise and support Armies, but no Appropriation of Money to that Use shall be for a longer Term than two Years;

To provide and maintain a Navy;

To make Rules for the Government and Regulation of the land and naval Forces;

To provide for calling forth the Militia to execute the Laws of the Union, suppress Insurrections and repel Invasions;

To provide for organizing, arming, and disciplining the Militia, and for governing such Part of them as may be employed in the Service of the United States, reserving to the States respectively, the Appointment of the Officers, and the Authority of training the Militia according to the discipline prescribed by Congress;

To exercise exclusive Legislation in all Cases whatsoever, over such District (not exceeding ten Miles square) as may, by Cession of particular States, and the acceptance of Congress, become the Seat of the Government of the United States, and to exercise like Authority over all Places purchased by the Consent of the Legislature of the State in which the Same shall be, for the Erection of Forts, Magazines, Arsenals, dock-Yards, and other needful Buildings;—And

To make all Laws which shall be necessary and proper for carrying into Execution the foregoing Powers, and all other Powers vested by this Constitution in the Government of the United States, or in any Department or Officer thereof.

In reading this list of powers, one is inevitably impressed by the silence respecting many matters that are today the subject of federal regulation. To a large extent this book is the story of the expansion of Article 1, Section 8, into the Constitution of today.

### § 1:2. Interpretation of the Federal Powers

Almost from the outset of national existence, it was recognized that the federal powers should be liberally construed. As stated by Story, J., in *Martin* v. *Hunter's Lessee,* 1 Wheat. (U. S.) 304 (1816):

"The constitution unavoidably deals in general language. It did not suit the purposes of the people, in framing this great charter of our liberties, to provide for minute specifications of its powers, or to declare the means by which those powers should be carried into execution. It was foreseen that this would be a perilous and difficult, if not an impracticable, task. The instrument was not intended to provide merely for the exigencies of a few years, but was to endure through a long lapse of ages, the events of which were locked up in the inscrutable purposes of Providence. It could not be foreseen what new changes and modifications of power might be indispensable to effectuate the general objects of the charter; and restrictions and specifications, which, at the present, might seem salutary, might, in the end, prove the overthrow of the system itself. Hence its powers are expressed in general terms, leaving to the legislature, from time to time, to adopt its own means to effectuate legitimate objects, and to mold and model the exercise of its powers, as its own wisdom and the public interest should require. . . ."

This liberal or broad interpretation has not always been adhered to, and much of the subsequent history of the Constitution is concerned with defining the limits of the powers of government.

#### *(a) Incorporation of a national bank*

McCULLOCH v. MARYLAND

4 Wheat. 316 (1819)

The first bank of the United States was chartered for twenty years in 1791 and again in 1816. Hostile state legislation attempted to drive it out of existence. In 1818, Maryland adopted a law imposing a tax on bank notes issued by any bank not chartered by the state legislature. McCulloch, the cashier of the Baltimore branch of the National Bank, issued bank notes on which this tax had not been paid. Suit was brought by the State of Maryland against him to recover the statutory penalties imposed for violation of the statute. The opinion of the Supreme Court is the classic statement of the right of the federal government to exercise powers not expressly granted to it by the Constitution.

OPINION BY MARSHALL, C. J.

The first question . . . is, has Congress power to incorporate a bank? . . .

This government of the Union . . . is acknowledged by all to be one of enumerated powers. . . .

Among the enumerated powers, we do not find that of establishing a bank or creating a corporation. . . . A constitution, to contain an accurate detail of all the subdivisions of which its great powers will admit, and of all the means by which they may be carried into execution, would partake of the prolixity of a legal code, and could scarcely be embraced by the human mind. It would probably never be understood by the public. Its nature, therefore, requires, that only its great outlines should be marked, its important objects designated, and the minor ingredients which compose those objects be deduced from the nature of the objects themselves. . . .

Although, among the enumerated powers of government, we do not find the word "bank" or "incorporation," we find the great powers to lay and collect taxes; to borrow money; to regulate commerce; to declare and conduct a war; and to raise and support armies and navies. The sword and the purse, all the external relations, and no inconsiderable portion of the industry of the nation, are intrusted to its government . . . a government, intrusted with such ample powers, on the due execution of which the happiness and prosperity of the nation so vitally depends, must also be intrusted with ample means for their execution. The power being given, it is the interest of the nation to facilitate its execution. It can never be their interest, and cannot be presumed to have been their intention, to clog and embarrass its execution by withholding the most appropriate means. Throughout this vast republic, . . . revenue is to be collected and expended, armies are to be marched and supported. The exigencies of the nation may require that the treasure raised in the North should be transported to the South, that raised in the East conveyed to the West, or that this order should be reversed. Is that construction of the Constitution to be preferred which would render these operations difficult, hazardous, and expensive? Can we adopt that construction (unless the words imperiously require it) which would impute to the framers of that instrument, when granting these powers for the public good, the intention of impeding their exercise by withholding a choice of means? If, indeed, such be the mandate of the Constitution, we have only to obey; but that instrument does not profess to enumerate the means by which the powers it confers may be executed; nor does it prohibit the creation of a corporation, if the existence of such a being be essential to the beneficial exercise of those powers. It is, then, the subject of fair inquiry, how far such means may be employed. . . .

The government which has a right to do an act, and has imposed on it the duty of performing that act, must, according to the dictates of reason, be allowed to select the means; and those who contend that it may not select any appropriate means, that one particular mode of effecting the object is excepted, take upon themselves the burden of establishing that exception. . . .

But the Constitution of the United States has not left the right of Congress to employ the necessary means, for the execution of the powers conferred on the government, to general reasoning. To its enumeration of powers is added that of making "all laws which shall be necessary and proper, for carrying into execution the foregoing powers, and all other powers vested by this Constitution, in the government of the United States, or in any department thereof."

. . . This provision is made in a constitution intended to endure for ages to come, and, consequently, to be adapted to the various crises of human affairs. To have prescribed the means by which government should, in all future time, execute its powers, would have been to change, entirely, the character of the instrument, and give it the properties of a legal code. It would have been an unwise attempt to provide, by immutable rules, for exigencies which, if foreseen at all, must have been seen dimly, and which can be best provided for as they occur. [The Court rejected the contention that "necessary" means "absolutely necessary."] . . . Sound construction of the Constitution must allow to the national legislature that discretion, with respect to the means by which the powers it confers are to be carried into execution, which will enable that body to perform the high duties assigned to it, in the manner most beneficial to the people. Let the end be legitimate, let it be within the scope of the Constitution, and all means which are appropriate, which are plainly adapted to that end, which are not prohibited, but consist with the letter and spirit of the Constitution, are constitutional.

. . . It can scarcely be necessary to say, that the existence of state banks can have no possible influence on the question. No trace is to be found in the Constitution of an intention to create a dependence of the government of the Union on those of the states, for the execution of the great powers assigned to it. . . . The choice of means implies a right to choose a national bank in preference to state banks, and Congress alone can make the election.

## § 1:3. State Powers

All powers not delegated to the Congress of the United States nor prohibited are expressly reserved to the states by the Tenth Amendment. This provision merely confirmed the fact that the states had only surrendered to the national government those powers expressly delegated by the Constitution. Among the powers thus retained by the states is the police power, the power to tax, the power to take private property by eminent domain, and the power to own and operate businesses. Of these four powers, the police power confers the broadest ability to control business. The police power is in a general sense the power or right to govern. It is defined as the power of a state to enact laws for the health, safety, morals, and general welfare.

### *(a) Prosecution by different governments*

UNITED STATES v. LANZA

260 U.S. 377 (1922)

The defendant was fined under the state law of Washington for the illegal possession of liquor. He was then indicted and tried in the federal courts for violating the federal law against manufacturing, transporting, and possessing liquor. He asserted that the second prosecution put him in jeopardy for the same offense for which he had already been tried in the state court, since the same illegal acts were charged in both proceedings. The decision of the Supreme Court emphasizes the fact that the states continue to exist as sovereign governments in spite of their cession of power to the national government.

OPINION BY TAFT, C. J.

. . . The defendants insist that two punishments for the same act, one under the National Prohibition Act and the other under a state law, constitute double jeopardy under the Fifth Amendment; and in support of this position it is argued that both laws derive their force from the same authority,—the second section of the [prohibition] amendment,—and therefore that, in principle, it is as if both punishments were in prosecutions by the United States in its courts. . . .

To regard the amendment as the source of the power of the states to adopt and enforce prohibition measures is to take a partial and erroneous view of the matter. Save for some restrictions arising out of the federal Constitution, chiefly the commerce clause, each state possessed that power in full measure prior to the amendment, and the probable purpose of declaring a concurrent power to be in the states was to negative any possible inference that, in vesting the national government with the power of country-wide prohibition, state power would be excluded. In effect the second section of the Eighteenth Amendment put an end to restrictions upon the state's power arising out of the federal Constitution, and left her free to enact prohibition laws applying to all transactions within her limits. To be sure, the first section of the amendment took from the states all power to authorize acts falling within its prohibition, but it did not cut down or displace prior state laws not inconsistent with it. Such laws derive their force, as do all new ones consistent with it, not from this amendment, but from power originally belonging to the states, preserved to them by the Tenth Amendment, and now relieved from the restriction heretofore arising out of the federal Constitution. . . .

We have here two sovereignties, deriving power from different sources, capable of dealing with the same subject-matter within the same territory. Each may, without interference by the other, enact laws to secure prohibition. . . . Each government, in determining what shall be an offense against its peace and dignity, is exercising its own sovereignty, not that of the other.

It follows that an act denounced as a crime by both national and state sovereignties is an offense against the peace and dignity of both, and may be punished by each. The Fifth Amendment, . . . applies only to proceedings by the federal government . . . and the double jeopardy therein forbidden is a second prosecution under authority of the federal government after a first trial for the same offense under the same authority. Here the same act was an offense against the state of Washington, because a violation of its law, and also an offense against the United States under the National Prohibition Act. The defendants thus committed two different offenses by the same act, and a conviction by a court of Washington of the offense against that state is not a conviction of the different offense against the United States, and so is not double jeopardy. . . .

## § 1:4. Local Powers

The police power of the state may also be exercised to some extent by the political subdivisions of the state, subject to the constitutional or public law limitations of each particular state in addition to those imposed by the Federal Constitution on the states.

### *(a) Protection of public safety*

BARBIER v. CONNOLLY
113 U.S. 27 (1885)

OPINION BY FIELD, J.

In this case we can only consider whether the fourth section of the ordinance of the city and county of San Francisco is in conflict with the Constitution or laws of the United States. . . .

That fourth section . . . was simply a prohibition to carry on the washing and ironing of clothes in public laundries and wash-houses, within certain prescribed limits of the city and county, from ten o'clock at night until six o'clock on the morning of the following day. The prohibition against labor on Sunday is not involved. The provision is purely a police regulation within the competency of any municipality possessed of the ordinary powers belonging to such bodies. . . . It may be a necessary measure of precaution in a city composed largely of wooden buildings like San Francisco, that occupations, in which fires are constantly required, should cease after certain hours at night. . . . Neither the [Fourteenth] amendment—broad and comprehensive as it is—nor any other amendment, was designed to interfere with the power of the State, sometimes termed its police power, to prescribe regulations to promote the health, peace, morals, education, and good order of the people, and to legislate so as to increase the industries of the State, develop its resources, and add to its wealth and prosperity. From the very necessities of society, legislation of a special character, having these objects in view, must often be had in certain districts, such as for draining marshes and irrigating arid plains. . . .

## § 1:5. Comparison of National, State, and Local Powers

The power of the states to regulate business differs from that of the national government. In the case of a state regulation, the court begins with the assumption that the law is within the power of the state to enact. If the power of the state is to be successfully challenged, it is necessary to show that the law in question cannot be adopted because of some constitutional limitation or the surrender or prohibition of the power to adopt the law.

By contrast, in order to sustain a federal law it must be shown at the outset that the law comes within the type of law expressly covered by one of the powers delegated to the national government. If it is not within such express grant of power and cannot be reasonably implied from an express grant, then the federal law is unconstitutional as going beyond the power of the federal government.

As respects the states, the political subdivisions occupy a position similar to that of the national government. Like the national government, the political subdivisions can only exercise such powers as have been delegated to them. In the case of the political subdivisions, it will be found that the state constitution or a law passed by the state legislature has created the subdivision in question and defined what powers it can exercise. Generally these powers are more limited in scope than the powers of the state and are ordinarily confined in operation to the geographic area over which the subdivision is given control; that is, a city would be given power to run affairs within the city, but ordinarily would not have any power to regulate matters extending outside the city limits. As a practical matter also, the authority generally given a subdivision is more likely to be confined to minor details or matters directly affecting the actual physical health and safety of the people.

Because of these three classes of governments in the United States, a law calling for the regulation of business raises the question as to which of the three governments, if any, has the power to adopt the particular law. The situation is also complicated by the fact that business problems are no respecters of geography. City problems in many areas have ceased to become merely citywide in scope and have become metropolitan, reaching out beyond the city limits into neighboring suburbs and territories. Many social economic problems that formerly were merely local or state problems have risen to national significance. Big business has become national and international in scope. The history of the regulation of business has been that of a constant drive towards national legislation to keep pace with the nationalization of the economy.

## Questions for Discussion

1. (a) What is a constitution? (b) What is its purpose? (c) What is the test of a good constitution? (d) Does the Federal Constitution differ from a state constitution?

2. What was the first constitution of the United States?

3. What steps led to the adoption of the present constitution of the United States?

4. What effect did the adoption of the national constitution have on the states? on the national government?

5. Assume that the federal government imposed a 50% tax on the sales price of oleomargarine colored to resemble butter. (a) Could a state also impose a 50% tax on the sales price of oleomargarine colored to resemble butter? (b) What would the answer be if each government imposed a 60% tax on the sales price of colored oleomargarine?

6. The state of Pennsylvania adopted a law regulating the type of steps for railroad trains. Congress adopted a law establishing different specifications for such steps. The X Railroad conformed to the state law and was prosecuted for violating the federal law. The X Railroad claimed that it was incorporated under the laws of Pennsylvania and must therefore abide by those laws. Is this contention correct?

7. J, a meat dealer in M city, sold meat from diseased cattle. On July 10, 1958, a number of persons became seriously ill from diseased meat that they had purchased from him that day. On July 15 the City Council adopted an ordinance imposing a $100 fine on anyone selling diseased meat. J was prosecuted for violating this ordinance and was fined $100. He appealed the case, claiming that he could not be convicted under the ordinance. Was he correct?

8. (a) What is the source of the powers of the national government? of the state governments? of the governments of the cities and counties? (b) How does this affect the question of the constitutionality of an ordinance or law?

9. How are provisions of a constitution to be interpreted? What meaning is to be given to its words?

10. (a) To what extent does "necessity" affect the meaning of the Constitution? (b) To what extent was "necessity" relied upon in the *McCulloch* case?

11. (a) Should a constitution be drawn in broad general language or in detailed specific terms? (b) What are the advantages and the disadvantages of each method?

12. What is the constitutional basis for a national bank?

13. What is the constitutional basis for creating national corporations?

14. (a) Does the Constitution prescribe the means by which the powers of the national government are to be exercised? (b) What choice must be made when several means are available for executing a power of Congress?

15. May the same act be a crime against both state and national laws? May it violate city, state, and national laws? Give illustrations.

16. To which governments do the amendments of the Constitution apply?

17. What is the police power? Give five illustrations of its application.

18. If you were making a constitution for the United States, would you give the national government more or fewer powers than are given by Article I, Section 8, of the Constitution?

19. If there is a difference between your constitution and Article I, Section 8: (a) What is the difference? (b) Why did not the framers draw the Constitution the way you believe it should be?

20. Louis XIV of France is famed for his statement, "I am the state." Can the Congress or the President of the United States assert that they are the nation?

21. Has the nationalization of economic and social problems made our state-national system of government obsolete?

22. Is Congress expressly given power to adopt laws on the subjects listed below? If not, can the power be implied from the express powers? Does the Constitution prohibit a national law on any of these subjects?

(a) Raise and maintain armies.
(b) Print paper money.
(c) Impose a tax on imports.
(d) Impose a tax on exports.
(e) Establish a depository bank for the safekeeping of treasury funds.
(f) Maintain post offices.
(g) Maintain military posts.
(h) Grant money for public relief.
(i) Create private business corporations.

23. Make a list of five of the most important national laws. What is the constitutional basis for each of these laws?

24. Make a list of five of the most important measures pending before Congress. What is the constitutional basis for each of these measures?

25. What would have been the result in the *Lanza* case if he had been acquitted in the state court before he was prosecuted in the Federal court for the same act?

26. It is a Federal crime to plan to overthrow the Federal government by force. A state adopts a law making it a state crime to plan to overthrow the state or Federal government by force. X plans to overthrow the Federal government by force and is prosecuted in the state court for that crime. Does X have any defense?

## Chapter 2

# THE COURTS AS GUARDIANS OF THE CONSTITUTION



### § 2:1. Supremacy of the Constitution

Because the powers of government are either conferred or limited by constitutions, the question is always present whether a particular statute comes within the constitutional authority. In the case of a federal law, it must conform to the Federal Constitution. In the case of a state law, the law must conform to both the state constitution and to the Federal Constitution. As between the Federal Constitution and the state constitutions, the Federal Constitution is supreme. In the case of an ordinance or a regulation adopted by a political subdivision, it must conform to the charter or the statute giving the political subdivision authority and also to both the federal and the state constitutions. Who is to determine whether a law or an ordinance conforms to the constitutional requirements?

### § 2:2. The Supreme Court as the Final Interpreter of the Constitution

During the early years of our national existence, there was strong controversy as to whether there was any umpire or referee to decide whether the rules of the constitutional game were being observed. In *Marbury* v. *Madison,* 1 Cranch 137 (1803), Chief Justice Marshall established the right of the Supreme Court of the United States to perform this function. Speaking for the Court, he declared that it could declare void an act of Congress that went beyond the limitations imposed by the Federal Constitution. He reasoned that since, as a judge, he was bound to recognize the Constitution as the supreme law of the land, he must necessarily ignore a law that conflicted with that Constitution.

### *(a) Judicial review*

MARBURY v. MADISON

1 Cranch 137 (1803)

Marbury was appointed a justice of the peace for the District of Columbia, but the commission by which his appointment would become effective was not delivered to him. He brought an action to compel the Secretary of State, Madison, to deliver the commission. This action was brought in the Supreme Court, which had been given authority to hear such cases by the Judiciary Act of 1789. The Constitution did not permit the bringing of actions of this nature in the Supreme Court. The Supreme Court therefore had to consider whether the Constitution or the statute was the superior authority.

OPINION BY MARSHALL, C. J.

That the people have an original right to establish, for their future government, such principles as, in their opinion, shall most conduce to their own happiness, is the basis on which the whole American fabric has been erected. . . .

This original and supreme will organizes the government, and assigns to different departments their respective powers. It may either stop here, or establish certain limits not to be transcended by those departments.

The government of the United States is of the latter description. The powers of the legislature are defined and limited; and that those limits may not be mistaken, or forgotten, the Constitution is written. To what purpose are powers limited, and to what purpose is that limitation committed to writing, if these limits may, at any time, be passed by those intended to be restrained? The distinction between a government with limited and unlimited powers is abolished, if those limits do not confine the persons on whom they are imposed, and if acts prohibited and acts allowed are of equal obligation. It is a proposition too plain to be contested, that the Constitution controls any legislative act repugnant to it; or, that the legislature may alter the Constitution by an ordinary act.

Between these alternatives there is no middle ground. The Constitution is either a superior paramount law, unchangeable by ordinary means, or it is on a level with ordinary legislative acts, and, like other acts, is alterable when the legislature shall please to alter it.

If the former part of the alternative be true, then a legislative act contrary to the Constitution is not law; if the latter part be true, then written constitutions are absurd attempts, on the part of the people, to limit a power in its own nature illimitable.

Certainly all those who have framed written constitutions contemplate them as forming the fundamental and paramount law of the nation, and, consequently, the theory of every such government must be, that an act of the legislature, repugnant to the constitution, is void. . . .

If an act of the legislature, repugnant to the Constitution, is void, does it, notwithstanding its invalidity, bind the courts, and oblige them to give it effect? Or, in other words, though it be not law, does it constitute a rule as operative as if it was a law? . . .

It is emphatically the province and duty of the judicial department to say what the law is. . . . If two laws conflict with each other, the courts must decide on the operation of each.

So if a law be in opposition to the Constitution; if both the law and the Constitution apply to a particular case, so that the court must either decide that case conformably to the law, disregarding the Constitution, or conformably to the Constitution, disregarding the law, the court must determine which of these conflicting rules governs the case. This is of the very essence of judicial duty.

If, then, . . . the Constitution is superior to any ordinary act of the legislature, the Constitution, and not such ordinary act, must govern the case to which they both apply. . . .

Why does a judge swear to discharge his duties agreeably to the Constitution of the United States, if that Constitution forms no rule for his government? . . .

It is also not entirely unworthy of observation, that in declaring what shall be the supreme law of the land, the Constitution itself is first mentioned; and not the laws of the United States generally, but those only which shall be made in pursuance of the Constitution, have that rank.

Thus, the particular phraseology of the Constitution of the United States confirms and strengthens the principle, supposed to be essential to all written constitutions, that a law repugnant to the Constitution is void; and that courts, as well as other departments, are bound by that instrument. . . .

## § 2:3. Extent of Review by the Supreme Court

The right of the Supreme Court to invalidate all laws conflicting with the Federal Constitution was firmly established by subsequent decisions, which held that the Court could declare unconstitutional a state law that conflicted with the Constitution and could hear appeals from state supreme courts in order to determine such questions.

It should be noted that the Supreme Court enforces only the Federal Constitution, although it may enforce it as against national law, or state constitution or law, or local ordinance or regulation. The picture of judicial review, as this process of examining the constitutionality of a law is called, is not complete, however, without noting that, in addition to the right of the Supreme Court to make such decisions, any lower federal court may make such decisions subject to review by the Supreme Court of the United States. In addition, any state court may declare a state law or local ordinance unconstitutional because it violates the federal or the state constitution. With respect to a violation of the state constitution, the supreme court of the state is the final arbiter; but, with respect to a violation of the Federal Constitution, the final decision is made by the Supreme Court of the United States. Any state court may also declare a federal law unconstitutional because it is in violation of the federal constitution, although in this instance the Supreme Court of the United States will have the final word in the matter.

## § 2:4. Criticism of Judicial Review

Numerous attacks have been made from the first on the power of judicial review. Andrew Jackson stated that every branch of the government was bound to recognize the Federal Constitution as supreme and therefore must follow its own conviction as to what the Constitution meant, rather than be bound to accept what the Supreme Court said it meant. Objection was repeatedly made that the American system of government was based on a division of executive, judicial, and legislative functions into coordinate branches and that this system was destroyed by judicial review which raised the court above the other two branches. The fact that the power of judicial review was not expressly conferred, that decisions could be rendered by a one-man majority, and that, until comparatively recent times, the general attitude of the court was conservative, also brought the doctrine under general attack.

As a practical matter, the doctrine of judicial review is now so firmly entrenched that a direct attack on that doctrine seems futile.

As a question of political science or the art of government, the power of judicial review must be lodged in someone or in some branch of the government. Just as a game cannot be played without an umpire or a referee, a government of limited powers cannot be run without some arbiter to determine whether its limitations are being observed. This problem does not arise in an unlimited monarchy, for there is no requirement in such a state that the government stay within any boundaries. We must therefore conclude that, if we wish to retain a constitutionally limited government, we must accept the fact that there must be an umpire and that, when he decides against the interest of the particular group or class to which we belong, we should not condemn him or his decision.

### § 2:5. Proposals for Change

It has been suggested that, in place of judicial review by the courts, the public should be allowed to express its wishes at the polls. This suggestion is based on the thought that, since the judges of the Supreme Court of the United States are not elected by the people of the United States, it is in conflict with the principle of government through popularly elected representatives to permit the Court to nullify a law enacted by the representatives of the people in Congress. Such a proposal is open to the theoretical but nevertheless real objection that the limitations contained in the constitutions would cease to be legal barriers and could be ignored when the will of a sufficient number of voters so desired. The proposal thus converts a legal problem into a political issue. Another very practical objection to such a plan is that modern legislation relates to matters of such complexity that it is unreasonable to expect the great mass of voters to have acquired sufficient knowledge of the subject matter and of the relative merits and demerits of the law in question to enable them to cast an intelligent vote.

### § 2:6. Inherent Difficulties of the Problem

The problem of government under constitutional limitations is further complicated by the fact that the constitution, or book of rules, which the court, or umpire, applies is, in the case of the Federal Constitution and of most state constitutions, a very vague guide. While a number of state constitutions are unusually long and detailed, they remain basically vague in many points. It will be noted in the discussion of the "due process" clause in Chapter 4 that it is inevitable and impossible to interpret and apply such general vague provisions to our modern life without the umpire's decision being colored by his individual concept of what is socially, morally, and economically proper.

The only way to avoid the personal factor in interpretation is by the adoption of a specific detailed constitution that would cover every situation which would arise and that would be inflexibly applied. The impossibility of drafting such a constitution and securing its adoption, the inability to foresee the future and to provide for it in such a constitution, and the inability of such a constitution to change with the arrival of new eras indicate that such an alternative, while theoretically a solution, is not a practical cure.

The need for an umpire cannot be avoided. The solution for what are termed "bad" decisions is a constant demand by the public that competent and sincere judges be appointed. It is obvious that the better the courts, the better the decisions. In a democracy the ultimate responsibility for securing good judges rests upon "we, the people."

## Questions for Discussion

1. (a) Does the decision in *Marbury* v. *Madison* indicate the theory on which the government of the United States is based? (b) What is the authority of the people with respect to the creation of a government? (c) In whom is vested the ultimate sovereignty?

2. What is the nature of the government of the United States?

3. Why was the Constitution of the United States adopted?

4. Does the Constitution authorize the Supreme Court to determine whether a law is constitutional?

5. The power of the Supreme Court to declare laws void because they are contrary to the Constitution has been attacked as creating a one man tyranny. Explain.

6. What plan could be adopted in place of judicial review by the Supreme Court?

7. Can the Supreme Court declare a state law void if it conflicts with the national constitution?

8. A federal law provides that an appeal may be taken from the highest court of any state to the United States Supreme Court when a federal question is involved. X is convicted in a state court for doing a particular act. He claims that he is authorized to do the act by virtue of federal law. The state supreme court denies that the federal law gives him the authority to do the act, affirms the conviction, and then refuses to permit the case

to go on appeal to the Supreme Court of the United States. Can the United States Supreme Court compel the state supreme court to allow the appeal?

9. Z is required to pay a tax imposed by a state statute. He claims that the statute is contrary to the state constitution because a quorum as required by the state constitution was not present in the state legislature when the tax law was adopted. The state supreme court holds that there was a quorum within the meaning of the state constitution and that the state law is constitutional. X appeals to the United States Supreme Court and asks the court to review the decision of the state court. What decision will the Supreme Court make?

10. How would you answer Andrew Jackson's argument against the doctrine of judicial review?

11. Which of the following provides the greatest protection against arbitrary or tyrannical government:

(a) Division of powers into several branches, as executive, legislative and judicial.
(b) Popular elections.
(c) Judicial review.

12. Which of the following systems is preferable and why:

(a) Judicial review by the courts.
(b) A referendum system under which a law that is declared unconstitutional may be passed over the court's decision if three fourths of the voters approve the law at a later election.
(c) No power of judicial review, but power given to the voters to call a special election to repeal any law that is unsatisfactory to them.

13. (a) When there is a conflict between state and federal constitutions, which prevails? (b) Would your answer be affected by whether the state constitution had been adopted before or after the national constitution?

## Chapter 3

# CHANGING THE POWERS OF GOVERNMENT



### § 3:1. Amendment of the National Constitution

The scope and the division of powers established by the Constitution may be changed by express amendment or by a change in the judicial construction of the existing constitutional provisions.

Article V of the Constitution of the United States provides that the Constitution may be amended in the following manner:

> The Congress, whenever two-thirds of both Houses shall deem it necessary, shall propose Amendments to this Constitution, or, on the Application of the Legislatures of two-thirds of the several States, shall call a Convention for proposing Amendments, which, in either Case, shall be valid to all Intents and Purposes, as part of this Constitution, when ratified by the Legislatures of three-fourths of the several States, or by Conventions in three-fourths thereof, as the one or the other Mode of Ratification may be proposed by the Congress; Provided that no Amendment which may be made prior to the Year One thousand eight hundred and eight shall in any Manner affect the first and fourth Clauses in the Ninth Section of the first Article; and that no State, without its Consent, shall be deprived of its equal Suffrage in the Senate.

Are there any limits today on the nature of amendments that can be adopted? No limitation is specified by the Constitution other than the prohibition against destroying the equality of the states in voting in the Senate. Is there a spirit or a plan behind the Constitution that places an unwritten limitation on amendments? The Eighteenth, or Prohibition, Amendment was attacked on the ground that it was unconstitutional because it regulated local consumption, which was a matter reserved to the states. The Nineteenth, or Women's Suffrage, Amendment was attacked because it made a fundamental change in the body of voters within each state and was therefore unconstitutional. The Supreme Court held that both amendments were constitutional because adopted in the manner prescribed by the Constitution and that there was no unwritten spirit in the Constitution that restricted the kind of amendments that could be adopted.

The amending power therefore confers the right to make any change in the structure or powers of the national government if the amendment is adopted according to the prescribed procedure. It is immaterial how far-sweeping the economical, political, or social effects of the amendment may be or how novel or radical its purpose. The fact that the Constitution may be amended to provide anything that a sufficient majority of the public desires emphasizes the importance of an intelligent and active electorate.

Amendment of the Constitution by formal change under Article V is a slow and difficult process, as evidenced by the small number of amendments that have been adopted when compared with the number of years of our national life under the Constitution or the number of amendments proposed during that time.

### § 3:2. Amendment of State Constitutions

The amending of the state constitutions is a simpler matter in view of the fact that the approval of the voters of only one state is required. The amendment of the charter or the statute conferring authority upon political subdivisions may be a matter of action either by the state legislature or by the political subdivision, or both, depending upon the degree to which home rule is recognized for the subdivision. The area of permissible amendment of state constitutions and charters or laws of a subdivision is less than that of the Federal Constitution. This is due to the fact that in making amendments to state constitutions and state laws, it is necessary to conform to the limitations imposed by the Federal Constitution. Thus it is impossible for a state to amend its constitution so as to authorize something that the Federal Constitution would prohibit it from doing.

### § 3:3. Amendment by Judicial Construction

The greatest change in the Federal Constitution has been made not by amendment but by judicial interpretation. According to the classical school of thought, the judge merely declares what the law is and does not make the law, because to do the latter would usurp the function of the legislative branch. By this theory, a decision of the court cannot be regarded as amending the Constitution. It is true that, in a great many cases, judges merely apply a recognized or accepted rule of law to a set of facts. In such a case, the judge is merely declaring the law. When, however, the court is faced with a set of facts that do not come within the scope of any previously recognized or established rule of law, there is no law for him to declare.

To illustrate, consider the problem presented when the first suit was brought to recover damages against an air transport company for the death of a passenger in an airplane crash. The court was faced with the problem of deciding how the liability of an air carrier should be determined. Since this was, by hypothesis, the first case of its kind, there would be nothing in the law books or decisions determining or stating what the rule of law was. The judge was nevertheless required to decide the case, and in so doing he made new law because before that time there was no law applicable to those facts. If it is contended that he did not make the law, but merely declared pre-existing law, difficult questions arise. How did he find out the pre-existing law, if such a case had never been decided before? If he was merely declaring the law, when did it come into existence? Did it spring into being the minute the Wright Brothers defied the law of gravity for twelve fateful seconds in 1903, or did the principle of the liability of air carriers come down to the courts before the air carrier was invented? If so, how long before? The concept of principles of law floating about in some rarefied atmosphere until, at some later date, a judge, faced with a new fact situation, draws the principle from the clouds in the manner of a judicial Franklin is not one that appeals to common sense.

The fact must be accepted that a judge, when faced with a new situation, makes new law, just as though the legislature or the Congress had adopted a new statute. To be sure, the new law may draw on past law for support or analogy, and the court will desire to make it conform to the prior law or the policy of the prior law as far as is practical and reasonable. Nevertheless, when a rule of law results from a decision where there was no rule of law before, it is obvious that the court has made law.

The Supreme Court of the United States has therefore been a very powerful factor in the making of law and the decisional amendment of the Constitution of the United States, an effect that will become apparent in the subsequent chapters of this book.

The state courts have also, but to a lesser degree, been active in revising their constitutions through decisional interpretation. To a large extent the action of the state supreme courts has been merely to follow the federal decisions in construing similar provisions of their own state constitutions.

## Questions for Discussion

1. What provision does the Constitution of the United States make for amendment? Compare it with the provision for amending the constitution of your own state.

2. Would an amendment to the United States Constitution be valid that deleted the present Article V and in its place provided that an amendment could be adopted by a majority of those voting at a presidential election?

3. Would an amendment to the United States Constitution be valid that deleted the "proviso" at the end of Article V?

4. Can the Constitution be amended:
   (a) To authorize Congress to prohibit the sale of narcotics?
   (b) To authorize Congress to purchase all coal mines from their owners?
   (c) To abolish the office of the President of the United States?
   (d) To abolish the guarantee of uniformity of indirect taxes?

5. To what extent can an amendment to the United States Constitution remove or destroy the guarantees of:
   (a) Free speech.
   (b) Freedom of the press.
   (c) Trial by jury.
   (d) Due process of law.
   (e) Right to life, liberty, and property.

6. (a) Does the amending process established by the Federal Constitution encourage or discourage amendments to the Constitution? (b) Should the process be made easier or more difficult?

7. (a) What has been the nature of the amendments to the United States Constitution? (b) Can they be classified as to nature or object?

8. Compare the process of amending the charter of a corporation with the process of amending the National Constitution.

9. Are there any limits on the power to amend a state constitution?

10. What effect have decisions of the Supreme Court had on the growth of the Constitution?

11. Does a judge make or does he declare law?

12. When a judge makes a decision in a case that has never been decided before, what weight should he give to the following:
   (a) Logic.
   (b) Economic effect of his decision.
   (c) Social effect of his decision.
   (d) Effect of his decision on the administration of government.
   (e) Will of the voters.

13. What objection is there to having judges make the law? Does the process of judge-made law conflict with the principle of responsibility to the people?

14. One man in the Supreme Court can change the course of national events for years. Is this correct?

15. Does a judge violate his oath to maintain the Constitution when he changes its meaning by a decision?

16. Can a judge be impeached for openly disregarding the Constitution? For interpreting it so that its meaning is changed?

17. The Constitution was adopted to define the powers and the scope of government. Like any contract, it should be interpreted so as to give it the meaning in which its provisions were used by the framers who drafted it and the states that ratified it. Discuss the correctness and the advisability of following this view.

# PART II. CONSTITUTIONAL LIMITATIONS

## Chapter 4

## DUE PROCESS OF LAW



### § 4:1. Guarantees of Individual Right

The Federal Constitution contains limitations on what the national government may do. These limitations, or so-called "bill of rights," guarantee to the individual certain basic freedoms that were considered most vital at the time the constitutional provisions were adopted. The demand for these guarantees was so great that the ratification of the Federal Constitution could not be secured until it was agreed by the Federalists that, if the Constitution was ratified, a bill of rights would be adopted. This was done by the First Congress under the new Constitution, and in 1791 the first ten amendments of the new Constitution became effective.

These first ten amendments applied only to actions of the federal government. Later amendments dealt with action by state governments. In addition, during recent years the Supreme Court has regarded the Fourteenth Amendment, which applies to the states, as including in its general "due process" clause the more fundamental of the specific guarantees contained in the first ten amendments.

In addition to the guarantees contained in the Federal Constitution, the constitution of each state contains various guarantees, frequently employing the same wording as the Federal Constitution. As a starting point, the United States Supreme Court is the final interpreter of the meaning of the guarantees contained in the Federal Constitution, and the supreme court of each state is the final judge of the guarantees contained in its constitution. There is a natural tendency, however, for a state supreme court to follow a decision of the Federal Supreme Court in interpreting a provision that is the same as or similar to a provision of the Federal Constitution.

### § 4:2. Due Process as Guarantee of Historical Procedure

The guarantee of the Fifth Amendment and Fourteenth Amendment that neither Congress nor any state may deprive any person of "life, liberty, or property without due process of law" has had a long history and has been the subject of changing interpretations. The provision is based upon the Magna Charta by which the nobles at Runnymede in 1215 compelled King John of England to agree that he would respect their feudal rights and would not take any action against them except by the "law of the land."

This phrase became synonymous with "due process of law," and both were regarded as requiring that the ordinary procedure be followed before anyone could be subjected to liability or punishment. At first, the interpretation was given the due process clause that it merely guaranteed observance of the procedure that was customary at the time of the formation of the colonies. In *Murray's Lessee* v. *Hoboken Land & Improvement Co.,* 18 How. 272 (1855), the Supreme Court stated:

". . . The Constitution contains no description of those processes which it was intended to allow or forbid. It does not even declare what principles are to be applied to ascertain whether it be due process. . . . To what principles, then, are we to resort to ascertain whether this process, enacted by Congress, is due process? To this the answer must be twofold. We must examine the Constitution itself, to see whether this process be in conflict with any of its provisions. If not found to be so, we must look to those settled usages and modes of proceeding existing in the common and statute law of England, before the emigration of our ancestors, and which are shown not to have been unsuited to their civil and political condition by having been acted on by them after the settlement of this country. . . ."

## § 4:3. Due Process as Guarantee of Reasonable Procedure

The interpretation noted in the last section had the obvious disadvantage of perpetuating for all future ages the procedure as it existed during the era of discovery and colonization. The normal course of judicial history has been for men to change procedure in the endeavor to further the administration of justice. If due process was to be limited to the procedure permitted at the time of colonization, a dead hand would indeed be laid upon further procedural reform.

The Supreme Court met this challenge by expanding the concept of due process so that, instead of requiring the exact procedure of the colonization era, it was sufficient if the new procedure satisfied the basic standards of the old procedure.

In *Twining* v. *New Jersey,* 211 U.S. 78 (1908), the court stated: ". . . It does not follow, however, that a procedure settled in English law at the time of the emigration, and brought to this country and practiced by our ancestors, is an essential element of due process of law. If that were so the procedure of the first half of the seventeenth century would be fastened upon the American jurisprudence like a straight-jacket, only to be unloosed by constitutional amendment. . . ."

The existence of authority to sustain a new procedure on the ground that it was basically fair and just, and conversely the power to declare a procedure invalid if it was not, opened the door to a great expansion of the power of the courts. From that time on, instead of merely playing the part of the historian, the court could interpose its independent judgment as to whether a new procedure was basically fair.

### *(a) Prosecution on information*

HURTADO v. CALIFORNIA

110 U.S. 516 (1884)

At the common law a person could not be tried for a felony unless he had first been accused or indicted by a grand jury. Under the Fifth Amendment to the Federal Constitution a grand jury indictment or presentment is required in the case of every "capital, or otherwise infamous crime." The State of California adopted a law which provided that, whenever the prosecuting attorney believed that a person had committed certain types of crimes, the prosecuting attorney could bring the offender to trial by filing a complaint or information with a local magistrate. Hurtado was brought to trial for a crime in this manner and claimed that the procedure denied him due process in depriving him of the protection of a grand jury. The Supreme Court considered whether a state was bound by the concept of due process or any other provision to provide for a grand jury indictment in all cases.

OPINION BY MATTHEWS, J.

. . . There is nothing in *Magna Charta,* rightly construed as a broad charter of public right and law, which ought to exclude the best ideas of all systems and of every age; and as it was the characteristic principle of the common law to draw its inspiration from every fountain of justice, we are not to assume that the sources of its supply have been exhausted. On the contrary, we should expect that the new and various experiences of our own situation and system will mould and shape it into new and not less useful forms. . . .

It follows that any legal proceeding enforced by public authority, whether sanctioned by age and custom, or newly devised in the discretion of the legislative power, in furtherance of the general public good, which regards and preserves . . . principles of liberty and justice, must be held to be due process of law. . . .

### *(b) Burden of disproving disqualification*

SPEISER v. RANDALL
357 U.S. 513 (1958)

The Constitution of California prohibits allowing a tax exemption to anyone advocating the unlawful overthrow of the government of the United States or of any state. A California tax statute provided that anyone claiming an exemption must sign a declaration on his tax return stating that he did not engage in the prohibited activity. If the tax assessor did not believe that the claimant was entitled to an exemption, he could disallow the exemption and the burden was then upon the taxpayer to prove that he was entitled to the exemption. Speiser and Prince were honorably discharged veterans, who applied for the state veterans' tax exemption. When they were refused the exemption because the assessor believed that they advocated the unlawful overthrow of the government, they appealed from his decision and finally to the United States Supreme Court on the ground that the statute deprived them of due process of law.

OPINION BY BRENNAN, J.

. . . The question remains whether California has chosen a fair method for determining when a claimant is a member of that class to which the California court has said the constitutional and statutory provisions extend. . . .

To experienced lawyers it is commonplace that the outcome of a lawsuit—and hence the vindication of legal rights—depends more often on how the factfinder appraises the facts than on a disputed construction of a statute or interpretation of a line of precedents. Thus the procedures by which the facts of the case are determined assume an importance fully as great as the validity of the substantive rule of law to be applied. And the more important the rights at stake the more important must be the procedural safeguards surrounding those rights. . . . When the State undertakes to restrain unlawful advocacy it must provide procedures which are adequate to safeguard against infringement of constitutionally protected rights—rights which we value most highly and which are essential to the workings of a free society. . . .

The principal feature of the California procedure . . . is that the appellants, "as taxpayers under state law, have the affirmative burden of proof, in Court as well as before the Assessor. . . . [I]t is their burden to show that they are proper persons to qualify under the self-executing constitutional provision for the tax exemption in question—i.e., that they are not persons who advocate the overthrow of the government of the United States or the State by force or violence or other unlawful means or who advocate the support of a foreign government against the United States in the event of hostilities. . . .

It is of course within the power of the State to regulate procedures under which its laws are carried out, including the burden of producing evidence and the burden of persuasion, "unless in so doing it offends some principle of justice so rooted in the traditions and conscience of our people as to be ranked as fundamental.". . . "[O]f course the legislature may go a good way in raising . . . [presumptions] or in changing the burden of proof, but there are limits. . . . [I]t is not within the province of a legislature to declare an individual guilty or presumptively guilty of a crime.". . . The legislature cannot "place upon all defendants in criminal cases the burden of going forward with the evidence. . . . [It cannot] validly command that the finding of an indictment, or mere proof of the identity of the accused, should create a presumption of the existence of all the facts essential to guilt. This is not permissible. . . ."

In civil cases too this Court has struck down state statutes unfairly shifting the burden of proof.

It is true that due process may not always compel the full formalities of a criminal prosecution before criminal advocacy can be suppressed or deterred, but it is clear that the State which attempts to do so must provide procedures amply adequate to safeguard against invasion speech which the Constitution protects. . . . It is, of course, familiar practice in the administration of a tax program for the taxpayer to carry the burden of introducing evidence to rebut the determination of the collector. . . . But while the fairness of placing the burden of proof on the taxpayer in most circumstances is recognized, this Court has not hesitated to declare a summary tax-collection procedure a violation of due process when the purported tax was shown to be in reality a penalty for a crime. . . . The underlying rationale of these cases is that where a person is to suffer a penalty for a crime he is entitled to greater procedural safeguards than when only the amount of his tax liability is in issue. Similarly it does not follow that because only a tax liability is here involved, the ordinary tax assessment procedures are adequate when applied to penalize speech. . . .

Due process commands that no man shall lose his liberty unless the Government has borne the burden of producing the evidence and convincing the factfinder of his guilt. . . . Where the transcendent value of speech is involved, due process certainly requires in the circumstances of this case that the State bear the burden of persuasion to show that the appellants engaged in criminal speech. . . .

The vice of the present procedure is that, where particular speech falls close to the line separating the lawful and the unlawful, the possibility of mistaken factfinding—inherent in all litigation—will create the danger that the legitimate utterance will be penalized. The man who knows that he must bring forth proof and persuade another of the lawfulness of his conduct necessarily must steer far wider of the unlawful zone than if the State must bear these burdens. . . . How can a claimant whose declaration is rejected possibly sustain the burden of proving the negative of these complex factual elements? In practical operation, therefore, this procedural device must necessarily produce a result which the State could not command directly. It can only result in a deterrence of speech which the Constitution makes free. . . .

We hold that when the constitutional right to speak is sought to be deterred by a State's general taxing program due process demands that the speech be unencumbered until the State comes forward with sufficient proof to justify its inhibition. The State clearly has no such compelling interest at stake as to justify a short-cut procedure which must inevitably result in suppressing protected speech. . . .

### § 4:4. Due Process as Inapplicable to Substance

While the judicial development above noted was proceeding, an economic change was taking place that was soon to compel a further extension of the due process clause. Spurred by the Civil War and the expansion of transportation, the industrial revolution began to appear in earnest in the United States. In the wake of this change came numerous social and economic problems that gave rise to legislation regulating wages and hours of labor, establishing workmen's compensation, prohibiting food and drug adulteration, prohibiting conspiracies in restraint of commerce, and regulating rates of carriers and trade practices.

To the spirit of free enterprise of the last century, such interference with the natural operation of the laws of economics was unreasonable, contrary to nature, and therefore deemed unlawful. But, to declare a statute unconstitutional, it is necessary to point to some provision of the constitution and say that the statute conflicts with it. Which provision of the Federal Constitution could be summoned forth to support the claim that an "uneconomic" law was unconstitutional? No express provision was available, for the Constitution, drafted in an era long before the rise of the new economy, naturally contained no reference to the various regulatory statutes now coming into existence. Efforts were made to induce the court to hold that such economically unsound or unfair laws must violate due process. These efforts at first failed, as the Supreme Court refused to extend this clause beyond a guarantee of procedure.[1]

### § 4:5. Due Process as Guarantee of Freedom of Contract

Gradually, however, the Supreme Court adopted the view that the guarantee of a fair procedure is a meaningless gesture if the legislature or Congress is permitted, as long as it follows the proper procedure, to adopt a law the substance of which is unfair, capricious, or unsound. Accordingly, the guarantee of due process was expanded to guarantee not merely procedural fairness, but also that the substance of the statutes themselves be fair and reasonable.

---

[1] Davidson v. New Orleans, 96 U.S. 97 (1877).

But who is to be judge of what is reasonable and fair? It should be obvious that these are not fixed, immutable values but flexible concepts that change in the light of the personal history and philosophy of each individual.

For many years, the same conservative spirit that brought forth the concept of due process as a weapon against the new regulatory legislation held in effect that free enterprise was the criterion of reasonableness and fairness.

As an application of this view, it was held by the Supreme Court in *Adkins* v. *Children's Hospital,* 261 U.S. 525 (1923), that minimum wage laws violated the guarantee of due process because they interfered with the freedom of adult persons to make any contracts they saw fit. The Court said:

". . . The statute in question . . . forbids two parties having lawful capacity—under penalties as to the employer—to freely contract with one another in respect of the price for which one shall render service to the other in a purely private employment where both are willing, perhaps anxious, to agree, even though the consequences may be to oblige one to surrender a desirable engagement and the other to dispense with the services of a desirable employee. . . .

"It has been said that legislation of the kind now under review is required in the interest of social justice, for whose ends freedom of contract may lawfully be subjected to restraint. The liberty of the individual to do as he pleases, even in innocent matters, is not absolute. It must frequently yield to the common good. . . . But, nevertheless, there are limits to the power, and when these have been passed, it becomes the plain duty of the courts in the proper exercise of their authority to so declare. To sustain the individual freedom of action contemplated by the Constitution is not to strike down the common good but to exalt it; for surely the good of society as a whole cannot be better served than by the preservation against arbitrary restraint of the liberties of its constituent members. . . ."

### *(a) Criticism of the view*

That such cases were decided on the basis of economic belief rather than a rule of law is evident from a study of the cases involving government regulation of business. This criticism was very well stated in the dissenting opinions in *Lochner* v. *New York,* 198 U.S. 45 (1905). The State of New York had enacted a law limiting the hours of employment for men in bakeries. This was held unconstitutional on the ground that it was unreasonable to limit the freedom of employers and employees in a nonhazardous business to contract as they chose respecting hours of employment.

The conservative judicial attitude of the Court in regarding itself as the protector of society against the encroachments of radical and evil-minded legislatures is seen from the following statement in that case:

". . . It is impossible for us to shut our eyes to the fact that many of the laws of this character, while passed under what is claimed to be the police power for the purpose of protecting the public health or welfare, are, in reality, passed from other motives. We are justified in saying so when, from the character of the law and the subject upon which it legislates, it is apparent that the public health or welfare bears but the most remote relation to the law. The purpose of a statute must be determined from the natural and legal effect of the language employed; and whether it is or is not repugnant to the Constitution of the United States must be determined from the natural effect of such statutes when put into operation, and not from their proclaimed purpose. . . ."

These views were not shared by Justice Harlan who, in a dissenting opinion, recognized the basic conflict between the individual and public interests, stating:

". . . I find it impossible, in view of common experience, to say that there is here no real or substantial relation between the means employed by the State and the end sought to be accomplished by its legislation.

"We judicially know that the question of the number of hours during which a workman should continuously labor has been, for a long period, and is yet, a subject of serious consideration among civilized peoples, and by those having special knowledge of the laws of health. . . . What is the true ground for the State to take between legitimate protection, by legislation, of the public health and liberty of contract is not a question easily solved, nor one in respect of which there is or can be absolute certainty. . . .

". . . It is enough for the determination of this case, and it is enough for this court to know, that the question is one about which there is room for debate and for an honest difference of opinion. There are many reasons of a weighty, substantial character, based upon the experience of mankind, in support of the theory that, all things considered, more than ten hours steady work each day, from week to week, in a bakery or confectionary establishment, may endanger the health and shorten the lives of the workmen, thereby diminishing their physical and mental capacity to serve the State and to provide for those dependent upon them.

"If such reasons exist that ought to be the end of this case, for the State is not amenable to the judiciary, in respect of its legislative enactments, unless such enactments are plainly, palpably, beyond all question, inconsistent with the Constitution of the United States. . . ."

Two other justices joined in this dissent, and another dissenting opinion was filed by Justice Holmes in which he directly charged:

"This case is decided upon an economic theory which a large part of the country does not entertain. If it were a question whether I agreed with that theory, I should desire to study it further and long before making up my mind. But I do not conceive that to be my duty, because I strongly believe that my agreement or disagreement has nothing to do with the right of a majority to embody their opinions in law. . . .

"The Fourteenth Amendment does not enact Mr. Herbert Spencer's Social Statics. . . . A constitution is not intended to embody a particular economic theory, whether of paternalism and the organic relation of the citizen to the State or of laissez faire. It is made for people of fundamentally differing views, and the accident of our finding certain opinions natural and familiar or novel and even shocking ought not to conclude our judgment upon the question whether statutes embodying them conflict with the Constitution. . . .

". . . I think that the word 'liberty' in the Fourteenth Amendment is perverted when it is held to prevent the natural outcome of a dominant opinion, unless it can be said that a rational and fair man necessarily would admit that the statute proposed would infringe fundamental principles as they have been understood by the traditions of our people and our law. It does not need research to show that no such sweeping condemnation can be passed upon the statute before us. A reasonable man might think it a proper measure on the score of health. Men whom I certainly could not pronounce unreasonable would uphold it as a first instalment of a general regulation of the hours of work. Whether in the latter aspect it would be open to the charge of inequality I think it unnecessary to discuss."

The same view was expressed by Justice Stone in his dissenting opinion in the minimum wage case of *Moorehead* v. *New York ex rel. Tipaldo,* 298 U.S. 587 (1936):

"In the years that have intervened since the *Adkins* case we have had opportunity to learn that a wage is not always the resultant of free bargaining between employers and employees. . . .

"It is not for the courts to resolve doubts whether the remedy by wage regulation is as efficacious as many believe, or is better than some other, or is better even than the blind operation of uncontrolled economic forces. The legislature must be free to choose unless government is to be rendered impotent. The Fourteenth Amendment has no more embedded in the Constitution our preference for some particular set of economic beliefs than it has adopted, in the name of liberty, the system of theology which we may happen to approve."

In speaking of the then prevailing view that a minimum wage law violated the freedom of contract guaranteed by the due process clause, Justice Stone observed:

"... There is grim irony in speaking of the freedom of contract of those who, because of their economic necessities, give their services for less than is needful to keep body and soul together. . . ."

### § 4:6. Due Process as Guarantee of Nonarbitrary Substance

As the result of continuous and growing pressure by the labor class, the farmers, and the social reformers, and the changing philosophy encouraged by international wars and depressions, a new view of freedom and of due process came to be adopted. Instead of considering every individual as a legal being fully the equal of every other, with the same power to make contracts as everyone else, the courts departed from the concept of Adam Smith to a new consciousness of the stake of society in the making of what were formerly considered private contracts and of the possible need of protecting one of the parties to such a contract from exploitation by the other and of protecting society itself from the ultimate effect of such exploitation.

The right of the lawmaker to seek what he hoped would be economic and social salvation was no longer to be restrained because the court did not share his social and economic views. Even before the so-called "New Deal revolution" appeared in the Supreme Court, that body had adopted the new social philosophy. In *Nebbia* v. *New York*, 291 U.S. 502 (1934), the Court sustained a minimum resale price law for milk. As against the argument that price-fixing limited freedom of contract and thus violated the due process clause, the Court stated:

"... The due process clause makes no mention of sales or of prices any more than it speaks of business or contracts or buildings or other incidents of property. The thought seems nevertheless to have persisted that there is something peculiarly sacrosanct about the price one may charge for what he makes or sells, and that, however able to regulate other elements of manufacture or trade, with incidental effect upon price, the state is incapable of directly controlling the price itself. This view was negatived many years ago. *Munn* v. *Illinois*, 94 U.S. 113."

This new view was permanently established by the decision in the *West Coast Hotel* case in which the Court considered a state law imposing minimum wages for women and children.

### *(a) Minimum wage laws*

WEST COAST HOTEL CO. v. PARRISH

300 U.S. 379 (1937)

OPINION BY HUGHES, C. J.

. . . The Constitution does not speak of freedom of contract. It speaks of liberty and prohibits the deprivation of liberty without due process of law. In prohibiting that deprivation the Constitution does not recognize an absolute and uncontrollable liberty. . . . But the liberty safeguarded is liberty in a social organization which requires the protection of law against the evils which menace the health, safety, morals and welfare of the people. Liberty under the Constitution is thus necessarily subject to the restraints of due process, and regulation which is reasonable in relation to its subject and is adopted in the interests of the community is due process. . . .

This power under the Constitution to restrict freedom of contract has had many illustrations. That it may be exercised in the public interest with respect to contracts between employer and employee is undeniable. . . .

We think that the . . . decision in the *Adkins* case was a departure from the true application of the principles governing the regulation by the State of the relation of employer and employed. . . .

. . . What can be closer to the public interest than the health of women and their protection from unscrupulous and overreaching employers? And if the protection of women is a legitimate end of the exercise of state power, how can it be said that the requirement of the payment of a minimum wage fairly fixed in order to meet the very necessities of existence is not an admissible means to that end? The legislature of the State was clearly entitled to consider the situation of women in employment, the fact that they are in the class receiving the least pay, that their bargaining power is relatively weak, and that they are the ready victims of those who would take advantage of their necessitous circumstances. The legislature was entitled to adopt measures to reduce the evils of the "sweating system," the exploiting of workers at wages so low as to be insufficient to meet the bare cost of living, thus making their very helplessness the occasion of a most injurious competition. The legislature had the right to consider that its minimum wage requirements would be an important aid in carrying out its policy of protection. The adoption of similar requirements by many States evidences a deep-seated conviction both as to the presence of the evil and as to the means adapted to check it. Legislative response to that conviction cannot be regarded as arbitrary or capricious, and that is all we have to decide. Even if the wisdom of the policy be regarded as debatable and its effects uncertain, still the legislature is entitled to its judgment.

There is an additional and compelling consideration which recent economic experience has brought into strong light. The exploitation of a class of workers who are in an unequal position with respect to bargaining power and are thus relatively defenceless against the denial of a living wage is not only detrimental to their health and well being but casts a direct burden for their support upon the community. What these workers lose in wages the taxpayers are called upon to pay. The bare cost of living must be met. We may take judicial notice of the unparalleled demands for relief which arose during the recent period of depression and still continue to an alarming extent despite the degree of economic recovery which has been achieved. . . . The community is not bound to provide what is in effect a subsidy for unconscionable employers. The community may direct its law-making power to correct the abuse which springs from their selfish disregard of the public interest. . . .

Our conclusion is that the case of *Adkins* v. *Children's Hospital*, *supra*, should be, and is, overruled. . . .

### *(b) Confirmation of due process as guarantee of non-arbitrary substance*

The new view has also been stated by Justice Frankfurter in *Osborn* v. *Ozlin*, 310 U.S. 53 (1940): "It is equally immaterial that such state action may run counter to the economic wisdom either of Adam Smith or of J. Maynard Keynes, or may be ultimately mischievous even from the point of view of avowed state policy. . . ."

The same justice has also stated this view at greater length in his concurring opinion in *A. F. of L.* v. *American Sash & Door Co.*, 335 U.S. 538 (1949):

". . . [In the 19th century] Adam Smith was treated as though his generalizations had been imparted to him on Sinai and not as a thinker who addressed himself to the elimination of restrictions which had become fetters upon initiative and enterprise in his day. Basic human rights expressed by the constitutional conception of liberty were equated with theories of laissez faire. The result was that economic views of confined validity were treated by lawyers and judges as though the framers had enshrined them in the constitution. . . .

"The attitude which regarded any legislative encroachment upon the existing economic order as infected with unconstitutionality led to disrespect for legislative attempts to strengthen the wage-earner's bargaining power. . . . But when the tide turned, it was not merely because circumstances had changed and there had arisen a new order with new claims to divine origin. . . . [It was because] of increased deference to the legislative judgment. . . .

"The rationale of the . . . legislation . . . is founded on a . . . resolution of conflicting interests. Unless we are to treat as unconstitutional what goes against the grain because it offends what we may strongly believe to be socially desirable, that resolution must be given respect. . . .

"Even where the social undesirability of a law may be convincingly urged, invalidation of the law by a court debilitates popular democratic government. Most laws dealing with economic and social problems are matters of trial and error. . . .

"But there is reason for judicial restraint in matters of policy deeper than the value of experiment: it is founded on the recognition of the gulf of difference between sustaining and nullifying legislation. . . . As history amply proves, the judiciary is prone to misconceive the public good by confounding private notions with constitutional requirements, and such misconceptions are not subject to legitimate displacement by the will of the people except at too slow a pace. . . . Matters of policy . . . are by definition matters which demand the resolution of conflicts of value, and the elements of conflicting values are largely imponderable. Assessment of their competing worth involves differences of feeling; it is also an exercise in prophesy. Obviously the proper forum for mediating a clash of feelings and rendering a prophetic judgment is the body chosen for those purposes by the people. Its functions can be assumed by this court only in disregard of the historic limits of the Constitution."

The conflict of the decisions has passed and in *Williamson* v. *Lee Optical of Oklahoma,* 348 U.S. 483 (1955), the Court declared: "The day is gone when this Court uses the Due Process Clause of the Fourteenth Amendment to strike down state laws, regulatory of business and industrial conditions, because they may be unwise, improvident, or out of harmony with a particular school of thought. . . . 'For protection against abuses by legislatures the people must resort to the polls, not to the court.'"

***(c) Relation of modern interpretation of due process to judicial review***

Does this new viewpoint mean that the Court is returning to the days when it refused to use the due process clause as a weapon against regulatory legislation? This does not seem to be the case. What is happening seems rather to be that the Court is continuing to decide what is fair and reasonable, a decision that necessarily calls into play the Court's social and economic predilections. The difference lies in the fact that the social and economic philosophy of the Justices approves of government regulation and planning, and therefore a regulatory statute is not automatically regarded as capricious and arbitrary because it attempts to regulate free enterprise.

The language of the Court actually goes further than this, for, in stating that the Court will not impose its economic beliefs on the lawmakers, the Court would appear to be stating the doctrine that, even when it was opposed to the economics of a law, it would not declare that law a violation of due process. The real test would arise if a law were based on some radical economic principle of which a majority of the Justices disapproved. Would the Court hold that the law had no relation to a proper legislative purpose and was therefore arbitrary and unreasonable? Would it merely say that the lawmaker believed in the economic basis of the statute and then hold that this was sufficient to sustain the act even though the Court regarded it as unsound and without merit?

The solution to these questions must await the future. The answers are not without significance in view of the many economic panaceas that from time to time seize the imagination of a particular class of society or section of the country.

### Questions for Discussion

1. Are the first ten amendments of the Federal Constitution necessary?

2. What was the original meaning of the guarantee of due process of law?

3. Discuss the present day meaning of due process of law. Does it mark a retreat of the doctrine of judicial review?

4. What was the reason for the rise of the present day meaning of due process of law?

5. Who is the final interpreter of the meaning of the due process clause?

6. One of the Western states provides that a person may be convicted on a verdict rendered by two thirds or more of the jury and that a unanimous verdict is not required. X is tried for stealing and is found guilty by ten of the twelve jurors. He is convicted under the statute described above. He then claims that the law is unconstitutional as he is denied due process of law if the protection is removed of requiring that a unanimous verdict be rendered in order to sustain conviction. Is he correct?

7. A law provides that, when 5 per cent of the voters so request, a special election may be held to determine whether a change should be made in the tax law. If a majority of the voters voting at the election approve the tax proposal, it becomes effective as a law. Assume that such a referendum law has been adopted. A tax law is then adopted under this referendum. A taxpayer objects that the law was not adopted according to due process. Is the taxpayer's objection correct?

8. A tax law is adopted at a popular election pursuant to such a referendum statute. Three quarters of the public are eligible to vote. Of these, approximately two thirds voted at the election. A little more than one half voted in favor of the tax, which was then declared adopted. A taxpayer objects that the law deprives him of due process as it was not approved by a majority of the people or a majority of those eligible to vote. Is the taxpayer's objection correct?

9. A tax law is adopted by Congress over the objection of the representatives and the senators from the more heavily populated states. On the basis of the population represented by them, the bill was not supported by the congressmen representing a majority of the population. A taxpayer objects that the law therefore violates due process. Is the taxpayer's objection correct?

10. If the change in the national economy during the 19th and early 20th centuries induced a change in the interpretation of the Constitution, is it likely that there will be any further change in its meaning because of future changes in the economy?

11. As a matter of political science, should a constitution, either by amendment or interpretation, change as the economy changes or should principles of constitutional law remain fixed regardless of the change in the economy?

12. What is the basis or source of law? Does it rest on divine gift? social compact? force? habit?

13. What is the test of whether a law is good or bad?

14. Assume that it is decided that there are too many doctors in your state. A law is passed providing that no additional doctors shall be admitted to practice for the next ten years. A graduate from a medical school, otherwise eligible for practice, applies for a license to practice medicine and is refused because of this law. (a) Is he denied due process? (b) Would it affect your answer if the law had been adopted before the graduate had begun medical school?

15. Would it affect your answer to Question 14 if the state licensing board was permitted to admit in any one year "such number of applicants as it should deem proper"?

16. Does due process protect everything included within the concept of inalienable rights of "life, liberty and the pursuit of happiness"?

17. Does the due process clause prevent the adoption of a law regulating the hours of employment or wages of adult males in nondangerous occupations?

18. (a) What economic school of thought is adopted by the United States Constitution? (b) What school of thought existed when the Constitution was adopted?

19. (a) What is the constitutional basis for adopting a minimum wage law? (b) Does it make any difference if it is a federal or a state law?

20. (a) Does a minimum wage law violate due process? (b) Is the nature of the employment material? (c) Is it material whether the workers whose wages are regulated are men, women, or children?

21. (a) How are the worker, the industry, and society affected by the payment of unreasonably low wages? (b) What is the test of the "reasonableness of a wage"?

22. Does a law violate the due process clause if the Supreme Court believes that the law is socially undesirable or economically unwise?

23. What provision of the Constitution guarantees freedom of contract?

24. What is the test to determine whether a regulatory law satisfies the requirement of due process?

25. (a) Is the Supreme Court bound to follow earlier decisions that it has made? (b) Does it do so?

26. Why is it important whether or not a particular party has the burden of proof in litigation?

27. Human rights are more highly protected than property rights. Does the interpretation of the procedural aspects of due process support this statement?

# Chapter 5

## EQUAL PROTECTION OF THE LAW



### § 5:1. The Guarantee

The Fourteenth Amendment to the Federal Constitution prohibits the states from depriving any person of equal protection of the laws. No such limitation is placed upon Congress, although the broadening interpretation of the due process clause has to a large extent read the equal protection limitation into the Fifth Amendment.

The guarantee of the equal protection of the laws may be invoked on behalf of anyone, whether a natural person or a corporation, a citizen or an alien. As in the case of other constitutional guarantees, the limitation can only be invoked as against governmental action. It must be shown that the discrimination complained of is made by or under the authority of a law or an ordinance of a state or a political subdivision or of an agency, board, or court acting under governmental authority. The guarantee does not protect an individual from discrimination by other private individuals or groups or clubs. "Civil rights" laws have been adopted in a number of jurisdictions to protect individuals from discrimination by private persons. Such laws are held constitutional although they restrain the individual's liberty in prohibiting him from making a discrimination that he would otherwise make.

### § 5:2. Classification

The equal protection clause does not require that all persons be protected or treated equally. Reasonable classification is permitted, and a law is valid even though it does not apply to everyone or everything. Whether a classification is reasonable depends on whether the nature of the classification made bears a reasonable relation to the evil to be remedied or to the object to be attained by the law. In determining this, the courts have been guided generally by considerations of historical treatment in the past and by the logic of the situation. The trend is to permit the classification to stand unless it is clear that the lawmaking body has been arbitrary or capricious. Particularly wide latitude is allowed the lawmaker in the field of tax law.

#### *(a) Tax law exemption*

STEWARD MACHINE CO. v. DAVIS

301 U.S. 548 (1937)

The Federal Social Security law imposes taxes upon employers and employees in order to create a fund from which to pay the social security benefits. Certain classes of employers are exempt from this tax as is set forth in the portion of the opinion that follows. It was claimed that this exemption made the law unconstitutional.

OPINION BY CARDOZO, J.

. . . The excise is not invalid under the provisions of the Fifth Amendment by force of its exemptions.

The statute does not apply, as we have seen, to employers of less than eight. It does not apply to agricultural labor, or domestic service in a private home or to some other classes of less importance. Petitioner contends that the effect of these restrictions is an arbitrary discrimination vitiating the tax.

The Fifth Amendment unlike the Fourteenth has no equal protection clause. . . . But even the states, though subject to such a clause, are not confined to a formula of rigid uniformity in framing measures of taxation. . . . They may tax some kinds of property at one rate, and others at another, and exempt others altogether. . . . They may lay an excise on the operations of a particular kind of business, and exempt some other kind of business closely akin thereto. . . . If this latitude of judgment is lawful for the states, it is lawful, a fortiori, in legislation by the Congress, which is subject to restraints less narrow and confining. . . .

The classifications and exemptions directed by the statute now in controversy have support in considerations of policy and practical convenience that cannot be condemned as arbitrary. The classifications and exemptions would therefore be upheld if they had been adopted by a state and the provisions of the Fourteenth Amendment were invoked to annul them. . . . The act of Congress is therefore valid, so far at least as its system of exemptions is concerned, and this though we assume that discrimination, if gross enough, is equivalent to confiscation and subject under the Fifth Amendment to challenge and annulment. . . .

### *(b) Labor law exemption*

DOMINION HOTEL, INC. v. ARIZONA

249 U.S. 265 (1919)

An Arizona statute regulating the hours of employment of women exempted railroad restaurants. A hotel convicted of violating the statute claimed that the statute violated the Fourteenth Amendment.

OPINION BY HOLMES, J.

. . . The equal protection of the laws does not mean that all occupations that are called by the same name must be treated in the same way. . . . [The legislature] may do what it can to prevent what is deemed an evil and stop short of those cases in which the harm to the few concerned is thought less important than the harm to the public that would ensue if the rule laid down were made mathematically exact. The only question is whether we can say on our judicial knowledge that the legislature of Arizona could not have had any reasonable ground for believing that there were such public considerations for the distinction made by the present law. The deference due to the judgment of the legislature on the matter has been emphasized again and again. . . . Of course, this is especially true when local conditions may affect the answer, conditions that the legislature does but that we cannot know. . . .

Presumably, or at least possibly, the main custom of restaurants upon railroad rights of way comes from the passengers upon trains that stop to allow them to eat. The work must be adjusted to the hours of the trains. This fact makes a practical and, it may be, an important distinction between such restaurants and others. If in its theory the distinction is justifiable, as for all that we know it is, the fact that some cases, including the plaintiff's, are very near to the line makes it none the worse. That is the inevitable result of drawing a line where the distinctions are distinctions of degree; and the constant business of the law is to draw such lines. "Upholding the act as embodying a principle generally fair and doing as nearly equal justice as can be expected seems to import that if a particular case of hardship arises under it in its natural and ordinary application, that hardship must be borne as one of the imperfections of human things.". . . We cannot pronounce the statute void. . . .

### (c) *Traffic regulation exemption*

RAILWAY EXPRESS AGENCY, INC. v. NEW YORK

336 U.S. 106 (1949)

A traffic regulation of New York City prohibited the operation on any street of "an advertising vehicle; provided that nothing . . . shall prevent the putting of business notices upon business delivery vehicles, so long as such vehicles are engaged in the usual business or regular work of the owner and not used merely or mainly for advertising." The Railway Express Agency is a nationwide express business, operating about 1,900 trucks in New York City. It sold the space on the exterior sides of the trucks for advertising unconnected with its own business. It was fined for violating the traffic regulation against advertising vehicles, and it appealed.

OPINION BY DOUGLAS, J.

. . . The Court of Special Sessions concluded that advertising on vehicles using the streets of New York City constitutes a distraction to vehicle drivers and to pedestrians alike and therefore affects the safety of the public in the use of the streets. We do not sit to weigh evidence on the due process issue in order to determine whether the regulation is sound or appropriate; nor is it our function to pass judgment on its wisdom. . . . We would be trespassing on one of the most intensely local and specialized of all municipal problems if we held that this regulation had no relation to the traffic problem of New York City. It is the judgment of the local authorities that it does have such a relation. And nothing has been advanced which shows that to be palpably false.

The question of equal protection of the laws is pressed more strenuously on us. It is pointed out that the regulation draws the line between advertisements of products sold by the owner of the truck and general advertisements. It is argued that unequal treatment on the basis of such a distinction is not justified by the aim and purpose of the regulation. It is said, for example, that one of appellant's trucks carrying the advertisement of a commercial house would not cause any greater distraction of pedestrians and vehicle drivers than if the commercial house carried the same advertisement on its own truck. Yet the regulation allows the latter to do what the former is forbidden from doing. It is therefore contended that the classification which the regulation makes has no relation to the traffic problem since a violation turns not on what kind of advertisements are carried on trucks but on whose trucks they are carried.

That, however, is a superficial way of analyzing the problem, even if we assume that it is premised on the correct construction of the regulation. The local authorities may well have concluded that those who advertise their own wares on their trucks do not present the same traffic problem in view of the nature or extent of the advertising which they use. It would take a degree of omniscience which we lack to say that such is not the case. If that judgment is correct, the advertising displays that are exempt have less incidence on traffic than those of appellants.

We cannot say that that judgment is not an allowable one. Yet if it is, the classification has relation to the purpose for which it is made and does not contain the kind of discrimination against which the Equal Protection Clause affords protection. It is by such practical considerations based on experience rather than by theoretical inconsistencies that the question of equal protection is to be answered. . . . And the fact that New York City sees fit to eliminate from traffic this kind of distraction but does not touch what may be even greater ones in a different category, such as the vivid displays on Times Square, is immaterial. It is no requirement of equal protection that all evils of the same genus be eradicated or none at all. . . .

### § 5:3. Improper Discrimination

Laws that make distinctions in the regulation of business, the right to work, and the right to use or enjoy property in terms of race or alienage or religion are generally invalid.[1] A law prohibiting the ownership of land by aliens has been traditionally regarded as an exception to this rule, as the danger of large alien holdings of land is considered such a social evil as to justify legislation directly prohibiting such holding, although it appears that in course of time this discrimination may be declared invalid.[2]

### *(a) Alienage*

### TORAO TAKAHASHI v. FISH & GAME COMMISSION

334 U.S. 410 (1948)

A Japanese who had been born in Japan lawfully entered the United States and became a resident of California in 1907. Under the federal naturalization laws he was ineligible for United States citizenship. The California Fish and Game Code prohibited the issuance of fishing and hunting licenses to persons ineligible to citizenship. The plaintiff satisfied all the requirements of the Fish and Game Code but was refused a license to engage in commercial fishing in the California coastal waters because he was ineligible to citizenship. He then brought an action of mandamus to compel the issuance of a license.

OPINION BY BLACK, J.

. . . The question presented is whether California can, consistently with the Federal Constitution and laws passed pursuant to it, use this federally created racial ineligibility for citizenship as a basis for barring [the plaintiff] from earning his living as a commercial fisherman in the open waters off the coast of California. . . .

. . . It does not follow, as California seems to argue, that, because the United States regulates immigration and naturalization in

---

[1] Kotch v. Board of River Port Pilot Commissioners, 330 U.S. 552 (1947).

[2] The alien land laws have been held unconstitutional by the supreme courts of California, Montana, and Oregon, as violating the Fourteenth Amendment of the United States Constitution. Sei Fujii v. State, 38 Cal. 2d 718, 242 P. 2d 617 (1952); Montana v. Oakland, 129 Mont. 347, 287 P. 2d 39 (1955); Kenji Namba v. McCourt, 185 Ore. 579, 204 P. 2d 569 (1949). Earlier decisions of the Supreme Court of the United States had sustained the California and Washington statutes. Porterfield v. Webb, 263 U.S. 255 (1923); Terrace v. Thompson, 263 U.S. 197 (1923). Note, however, that in Oyama v. California, 332 U.S. 633 (1948), the Supreme Court held invalid a procedural provision of the California alien land law, the result of which decision was to impair greatly the efficacy of that act. In addition, four of the Justices expressed the opinion that the California land law was itself unconstitutional as excluding aliens.

The problem has also been met from another tangent in that the Nationality Act of 1952 provides that the right of a person to become a naturalized citizen of the United States shall not be denied or abridged because of race. It is thus possible for the alien to become a citizen and remove himself from any bar against aliens that may constitutionally be raised.

part on the basis of race and color classifications, a state can adopt one or more of the same classifications to prevent lawfully admitted aliens within its borders from earning a living in the same way that other state inhabitants earn their living. The Federal Government has broad constitutional powers in determining what aliens shall be admitted to the United States, the period they may remain, regulation of their conduct before naturalization, and the terms and conditions of their naturalization. . . . Under the Constitution the states are granted no such powers; they can neither add to nor take from the conditions lawfully imposed by Congress upon admission, naturalization and residence of aliens in the United States or the several states. State laws which impose discriminatory burdens upon the entrance or residence of aliens lawfully within the United States conflict with this constitutionally derived federal power to regulate immigration, and have accordingly been held invalid. . . .

### *(b) Currency exchange regulation*

MOREY v. DOUD

354 U.S. 457 (1957)

The Illinois Community Currency Exchanges Act requires that anyone providing a check cashing service or selling or issuing money orders in his own name must obtain a state license and be subject to state regulation. In the case of money orders, that statute does not apply to the United States Post Office, the American Express Company, the Postal Telegraph Company, or the Western Union Telegraph Company. Doud and his partners sold money orders in Illinois through the proprietors of drug and grocery stores who acted as their agents. The American Express Company, organized in 1868, conducts a world-wide business that includes the sale of money orders. In Illinois, American Express also sold money orders locally in the same manner as Doud and his partners. Doud and his partners sought an injunction to prevent Morey from enforcing the Illinois statute against them by requiring that they obtain a license, pay the fee, and comply with regulations under the statute.

OPINION BY BURTON, J.

. . . During the early 1930's, the closing of many banks in the Chicago area led to the development of simple banking facilities called currency exchanges. The principal activities of these exchanges were the cashing of checks for a fee and the selling of money orders. The fact that many of these exchanges went into business without adequate capital and without sufficient safeguards to protect the public resulted in the enactment of the Illinois Community Currency Exchanges Act in 1943.

This Act and its amendments provide a comprehensive scheme for the licensing and regulation of currency exchanges. . . .

The American Express Company, on the other hand, because its money orders are excepted, is relieved of these licensing and regulatory requirements, and appears to be exempt from any regulation in Illinois. . . .

The purpose of the Act's licensing and regulatory provisions clearly is to protect the public when dealing with currency exchanges. Because the American Express Company is a world-wide enterprise of unquestioned solvency and high financial standing, the State argues that the legislative classification is reasonable. It contends that the special characteristics of the American Express Company justify excepting its money orders from the requirements of an Act aimed at local companies doing local business. . . .

That the Equal Protection Clause does not require that every state regulatory statute apply to all in the same business is a truism. For example, where size is an index to the evil at which the law is directed, discriminations between the large and the small are permissible. Moreover, we have repeatedly recognized that "reform may take one step at a time, addressing itself to the phase of the problem which seems most acute to the legislative mind." . . . On the other hand, a statutory discrimination must be based on differences that are reasonably related to the purposes of the Act in which it is found. *Smith* v. *Cahoon,* 283 U.S. 553, involved a state statute which required motor vehicles, operating on local highways as carriers for hire, to furnish bonds or insurance policies for the protection of the public against injuries received through negligence in these operations. The Act excepted motor vehicles carrying specified products. This Court held that the exception violated the Equal Protection Clause since the statutory purpose of protecting the public could not reasonably support a discrimination between the carrying of exempt products like farm produce and of regulated products like groceries. " 'Such a classification is not based on anything having relation to the purpose for which it is made.' ". . .

. . . The provisions in the Illinois Act, such as those requiring an annual inspection of licensed community currency exchanges by the State Auditor, make it clear that the statute was intended to afford the public *continuing* protection. The discrimination in favor of the

American Express Company does not conform to this purpose. The exception of its money orders apparently rests on the legislative hypothesis that the characteristics of the American Express Company make it unnecessary to regulate their sales. Yet these sales, by virtue of the exception, will continue to be unregulated whether or not the American Express Company retains its present characteristics. On the other hand, sellers of competing money orders are subject to the Act even though their characteristics are, or become, substantially identical with those the American Express Company now has. Moreover, the Act's blanket exception takes no account of the characteristics of the local outlets that sell American Express money orders, and the distinct possibility that they in themselves may afford less protection to the public than do the retail establishments that sell competing money orders. That the American Express Company is a responsible institution operating on a world-wide basis does not minimize the fact that when the public buys American Express money orders in local drug and grocery stores it relies in part on the reliability of the selling agents.

The effect of the discrimination is to create a closed class by singling out American Express money orders. . . .

Taking all of these factors in conjunction—the remote relationship of the statutory classification to the Act's purpose or to business characteristics, and the creation of a closed class by the singling out of the money orders of a named company, with accompanying economic advantages—we hold that the application of the Act to appellees deprives them of equal protection of the laws. . . .

Dissenting Opinion by Black, J.

. . . Only recently this Court held that "the prohibition of the Equal Protection Clause goes no further than the invidious discrimination." . . . And, here, whatever one may think of the merits of this legislation, its exemption of a company of known solvency from a solvency test applied to others of unknown financial responsibility can hardly be called "invidious." Unless state legislatures have power to make distinctions that are not plainly unreasonable, then the ability of the States to protect their citizens by regulating business within their boundaries can be seriously impaired. . . .

I think state regulation should be viewed quite differently where it touches or involves freedom of speech, press, religion, petition, assembly, or other specific safeguards of the Bill of Rights. It is the duty of this Court to be alert to see that these constitutionally preferred rights are not abridged. But the Illinois statute here does not involve any of these basic liberties. And since I believe that it is not "invidiously discriminatory," I would not hold it invalid.

DISSENTING OPINION BY FRANKFURTER, J., in which Harlan, J. concurs.

. . . As is usually true of questions arising under the Equal Protection Clause, the answer will turn on the way in which that clause is conceived. . . . The great divide in the decisions lies in the difference between emphasizing the actualities or the abstractions of legislation.

. . . Law reflects distinctions that exist in fact or at least appear to exist in the judgment of legislators—those who have the responsibility for making law fit fact. . . . To recognize marked differences that exist in fact is living law; to disregard practical differences and concentrate on some abstract identities is lifeless logic. . . .

. . . It is suggested that the American Express Co. may not continue to retain "its present characteristics," while sellers of competing money orders may continue to be subject to the Act, even though their characteristics become "substantially identical with those the American Express Co. now has." What is this but to deny a State the right to legislate on the basis of circumstances that exist because a State may not in speculatively different circumstances that may never come to pass have such right? Surely there is time enough to strike down legislation when its constitutional justification is gone. Invalidating legislation is serious business and it ought not to be indulged in because in a situation not now before the Court, nor even remotely probable, a valid statute may lose its foundation. The Court has had occasion to deal with such contingency more than once. Regulatory measures have been sustained that later, in changed circumstances, were found to be unconstitutional. . . .

Sociologically one may think what one may of the State's recognition of the special financial position obviously enjoyed by the American Express Co. Whatever one may think is none of this Court's business. In applying the Equal Protection Clause, we must be fastidiously careful to observe the admonition of Mr. Justice Brandeis, Mr. Justice Stone, and Mr. Justice Cardozo that we do not "sit as a super-legislature." . . .

## § 5:4. Discrimination by Court Action

The act of a state court in enforcing a discriminatory agreement or awarding money damages for its breach is regarded as state action within the prohibition of the equal protection clause.[1] The state courts are therefore subject to the same limitation as the state legislatures. Neither by court order nor by legislative mandate may equal protection be denied.

### *(a) Racial restrictive covenants*

SHELLEY v. KRAEMER

334 U.S. 1 (1948)

OPINION BY VINSON, C. J.

These cases present for our consideration questions relating to the validity of court enforcement of private agreements, generally described as restrictive covenants, which have as their purpose the exclusion of persons of designated race or color from the ownership or occupancy of real property. . . .

. . . It cannot be doubted that among the civil rights intended to be protected from discriminatory state action by the Fourteenth Amendment are the rights to acquire, enjoy, own and dispose of property.

. . . It is likewise clear that restrictions on the right of occupancy of the sort sought to be created by the private agreements in these cases could not be squared with the requirements of the Fourteenth Amendment if imposed by state statute or local ordinance.

. . . Since the decision of this Court in the Civil Rights Cases, 1883, . . . the principle has become firmly embedded in our constitutional law that the action inhibited by the first section of the Fourteenth Amendment is only such action as may fairly be said to be that of the States. That Amendment erects no shield against merely private conduct, however discriminatory or wrongful.

We conclude, therefore, that the restrictive agreements standing alone cannot be regarded as a violation of any rights guaranteed to petitioners by the Fourteenth Amendment. So long as the purposes of those agreements are effectuated by voluntary adherence to their terms, it would appear clear that there has been no action by the State and the provisions of the Amendment have not been violated.

. . . But here there was more. These are cases in which the purposes of the agreements were secured only by judicial enforcement by state courts of the restrictive terms of the agreements.

. . . That the action of state courts and of judicial officers in their official capacities is to be regarded as action of the State within

[1] Barrows v. Jackson, 346 U.S. 249 (1953).

the meaning of the Fourteenth Amendment, is a proposition which has long been established by decisions of this Court.

. . . We hold that in granting judicial enforcement of the restrictive agreements in these cases, the States have denied petitioners the equal protection of the laws and that, therefore, the action of the state courts cannot stand. We have noted that freedom from discrimination by the States in the enjoyment of property rights was among the basic objectives sought to be effectuated by the framers of the Fourteenth Amendment. That such discrimination has occurred in these cases is clear. Because of the race or color of these petitioners they have been denied rights of ownership or occupancy enjoyed as a matter of course by other citizens of different race or color.

### § 5:5. Discrimination by Administrative Action

While a government under a constitution has often been extolled as guaranteeing a government of laws and not of men, it must be remembered that laws have no effect until they are enforced, that is, until men apply them to other men. If the administrative officials or officers charged with the enforcement of the laws are so minded, it is often possible for them to discriminate against certain individuals or to grant favors to others. Thus a law that is fair and nondiscriminatory on its face may in actual application be applied unfairly and unequally. This raises the problem whether the guarantee that the law be on its face equal in application, subject to reasonable classification, is to be defeated by the discriminatory practices of the administrators. The Supreme Court has held that it will look beyond the surface or the face of the law to determine what the actual application has been and will hold unconstitutional state action denying an equal treatment although the state law is itself a fair or proper law.

For practical purposes, however, it would seem that this doctrine will be decreasing in importance as the trend continues for government regulation to become increasingly discretionary in character. Under much of modern-day regulation, it is difficult if not impossible to determine whether there is a right or a wrong, so that it cannot be determined whether the official has in fact abused his judgment or discretion for the purpose of making a discriminatory decision.

## Questions for Discussion

1. Must a state statute afford equal protection of the laws? Must a federal statute?

2. (a) Does equal protection prevent classification? (b) When is classification proper?

3. Why was the classification sustained in:
   (a) *Steward Machine Co.* v. *Davis.*
   (b) *Dominion Hotel, Inc.* v. *Arizona.*

4. What weight does the Supreme Court attach to local conditions?

5. Is the burden of proof on the party claiming the law is constitutional or upon the person claiming it is unconstitutional?

6. Decide the constitutionality of a law prohibiting an alien from:
   (a) Running a grocery store.
   (b) Owning land.
   (c) Owning more than one house.
   (d) Driving an automobile.
   (e) Flying an airplane.
   (f) Working in a government shipyard.
   (g) Working in an atomic energy laboratory.

7. How would your answer to Question 6 be affected if the alien were a national of an enemy nation?

8. (a) How would your answer to Question 6 be affected if the law applied to the American-born children of aliens who were ineligible for citizenship? (b) Would it make any difference in this case if the United States was at war with the nation of which the parents were nationals?

9. The state of A sells public lands to B. The deed from the state to B contains a provision that the land will never be resold to Negroes or to aliens. After a number of years B attempts to sell the land to a Negro society to use as an orphanage. The state begins proceedings to stop the sale. Can it prevent the sale?

10. Does a state law prohibiting the employment of aliens on public works violate the equal protection clause?

11. Is a federal law prohibiting the employment of aliens on public works constitutional?

12. (a) Is a law constitutional which provides that no employer may employ more aliens than 20 per cent of his total number of employees? (b) Would it affect your answer if the percentage were 10 per cent? 40 per cent? 50 per cent? 70 per cent?

13. Is a state law constitutional that prohibits the employment of naturalized citizens in port and harbor facilities?

14. A state law provides that no one believing in the overthrow of government by force may be employed. Is this law constitutional?

15. A state statute prohibits an employer from discriminating in the employment of persons on the ground of color, race, or creed. A railroad refuses to employ an alien and claims that the law is unconstitutional. (a) Is the railroad's claim correct? (b) Does it affect your answer if the alien is a naturalized citizen of the United States? if the alien is a national or subject of a country with which the United States may soon be at war?

16. In *Morey* v. *Doud* what factors were present which would justify the classification made by the statute?

17. Appraise the reasoning of the Court in the *Morey* case based upon consideration of the fact that the financial stability of the American Express Company might change?

18. Was the Community Currency Exchanges Act discussed in the *Morey* case adopted as the result of economic or political philosophies?

19. Appraise the distinction made by Justice Frankfurter in his dissenting opinion in the *Morey* case.

20. Which of the following exemptions, if any, are valid as against the claim that equal protection is denied?

(a) The exemption of businesses in which the average sums received for safekeeping or transmission is more than $500 from a licensing statute designed to protect small depositors.

(b) The exemption of railroads less than 50 miles in length from a statute regulating the heating of railroad passenger cars and the placing of guards and guard posts on railroad bridges.

(c) The exemption of hotels with less than 50 rooms from a statute requiring hotelkeepers to take certain fire precautions.

## Chapter 6

## PRIVILEGES AND IMMUNITIES



### § 6:1. The Guarantee

The Fourteenth Amendment, among other things, prohibits the states from abridging the privileges and immunities of citizens of the United States. This provision, linked with the introductory statement of the Fourteenth Amendment that all persons born or naturalized in the United States and subject to the jurisdiction thereof are citizens of the United States and of the state wherein they reside, suggests that the framers of the amendment intended to place under federal custody the vast range of rights that the Declaration of Independence would have described as part and parcel of the inalienable rights of man. Of this there can be no doubt when the provision of the amendment is placed against its historical setting and it is appreciated that this was one of the three amendments by which the Northern Reconstructionists intended to bind into the Constitution the victory of the Civil War and to guarantee that the freedmen would be able to enjoy their newly acquired rights.

This expectation was soon defeated, for the Supreme Court construed the clause as merely guaranteeing as against state activity those rights that were conferred upon individuals by virtue of their federal citizenship. Under this interpretation, it did not protect the ordinary civil rights of man, it did not guarantee the protection of those rights guaranteed by the first eight amendments to the federal constitution, and it could not be invoked on behalf of one who was not a citizen of the United States.

### *(a) Status of state-based rights*

## SLAUGHTER-HOUSE CASES

16 Wall. 36 (1873)

A Louisiana statute granted a corporation a 25-year exclusive right to maintain a slaughter house. This monopoly was attacked as a violation of the Fourteenth Amendment. The court considered whether the statute was constitutional.

OPINION BY MILLER, J.

. . . Within the last eight years three other articles of amendment of vast importance have been added by the voice of the people to that now venerable instrument. [Const. amends. 13-15] . . . No one can fail to be impressed with the one pervading purpose found in them all, lying at the foundation of each, and without which none of them would have been even suggested; we mean the freedom of the slave race, the security and firm establishment of that freedom, and the protection of the newly-made freeman and citizen from the oppressions of those who had formerly exercised unlimited dominion over him. It is true that only the fifteenth amendment, in terms, mentions the negro by speaking of his color and his slavery. But it is just as true that each of the other articles was addressed to the grievances of that race, and designed to remedy them as the fifteenth.

We do not say that no one else but the negro can share in this protection. Both the language and spirit of these articles are to have their fair and just weight in any question of construction. . . .

The first section of the fourteenth article . . . to which our attention is more specially invited, opens with a definition of citizenship—not only citizenship of the United States, but citizenship of the states. . . . "All persons born or naturalized in the United States, and subject to the jurisdiction thereof, are citizens of the United States and of the state wherein they reside.". . .

It is quite clear, then, that there is a citizenship of the United States, and a citizenship of a state, which are distinct from each other. . . .

. . . The next paragraph of this same section, which is the one mainly relied on by the plaintiffs . . . , speaks only of privileges and immunities of citizens of the United States, and does not speak of those of citizens of the several states. . . .

. . . If there is a difference between the privileges and immunities belonging to a citizen of the United States as such, and those belonging to the citizen of the state as such, the latter must rest for their security and protection where they have heretofore rested. . . .

. . . Up to the adoption of the recent amendments, no claim or pretence was set up that those rights depended on the federal government for their existence or protection, beyond the very few express limitations which the federal Constitution imposed upon the states—such, for instance, as the prohibition against ex post facto laws, bills of attainder, and laws impairing the obligation of contracts. But with the exception of these and a few other restrictions, the entire domain of the privileges and immunities of citizens of the states, as above defined, lay within the constitutional and legislative power of the states, and without that of the federal government. . . .

One of [the privileges and immunities of citizens of the United States is] the right of the citizen of this great country, protected by implied guarantees of its Constitution, "to come to the seat of government to assert any claim he may have upon that government, to transact any business he may have with it, to seek its protection, to share its offices, to engage in administering its functions. He has the right to free access to its seaports, through which all operations of foreign commerce are conducted, to the sub-treasuries, land offices, and courts of justices in the several states." . . .

Another privilege of a citizen of the United States is to demand the care and protection of the federal government over his life, liberty, and property when on the high seas or within the jurisdiction of a foreign government. Of this there can be no doubt, nor that the right depends upon his character as a citizen of the United States. The right to peaceably assemble and petition for redress of grievances, the privilege of the writ of habeas corpus, are rights of the citizen guaranteed by the federal Constitution. The right to use the navigable waters of the United States, however they may penetrate the territory of the several states, all rights secured to our citizens by treaties with foreign nations, are dependent upon citizenship of the United States, and not citizenship of a state. One of these privileges is conferred by the very article under consideration. It is that a citizen of the United States can, of his own volition, become a citizen of any state of the Union by a bona fide residence therein, with the same rights as other citizens of that state. To these may be added the rights secured by the thirteenth and fifteenth articles of amendment, and by the other clause of the fourteenth. . . .

## § 6:2. Civil Rights

While there have been occasional indications of a broader interpretation of the privileges and immunities clause than that set forth in the preceding section, the narrow interpretation of the clause has been reaffirmed so as to exclude the protection of civil rights from the protection of the Fourteenth Amendment.

### *(a) Racial discrimination in public places*

CIVIL RIGHTS CASES
109 U.S. 3 (1883)

An Act of Congress prohibited persons operating hotels, public carriers, theatres, and other places of public amusement from making any distinction in the use of their accommodations and privileges on the basis of race, color, or previous condition of servitude. Violation of this statute was made a crime. The law was attacked as unconstitutional.

OPINION BY BRADLEY, J.

. . . Has congress constitutional power to make such a law? . . .

The first section of the fourteenth amendment . . . declares that "no state shall make or enforce any law which shall abridge the privileges or immunities of citizens of the United States; nor shall any state deprive any person of life, liberty, or property without due process of law; nor deny to any person within its jurisdiction the equal protection of the laws." It is state action of a particular character that is prohibited. Individual invasion of individual rights is not the subject-matter of the amendment. . . . It does not invest congress with power to legislate upon subjects which are within the domain of state legislation. . . . It does not authorize congress to create a code of municipal law for the regulation of private rights. . . .

An inspection of the law shows that it makes no reference whatever to any supposed or apprehended violation of the fourteenth amendment on the part of the states. . . . It steps into the domain of local jurisprudence, and lays down rules for the conduct of individuals in society towards each other, and imposes sanctions for the enforcement of those rules, without referring in any manner to any supposed action of the state or its authorities.

If this legislation is appropriate for enforcing the prohibitions of the amendment, it is difficult to see where it is to stop. Why may not congress, with equal show of authority, enact a code of laws for the enforcement and vindication of all rights of life, liberty, and property? . . .

When a man has emerged from slavery, and by the aid of beneficient legislation has shaken off the inseparable concomitants of that state, there must be some stage in the progress of his elevation when he takes the rank of a mere citizen, and ceases to be the special favorite of the laws, and when his rights as a citizen, or a man, are to be protected in the ordinary modes by which other men's rights are protected. . . .

### § 6:3. Taxes and License Fees

The most frequent application of the privileges and immunities clause has been to invalidate license and tax laws discriminating against nonresidents. For example, a license fee of $2,500 imposed on nonresident shrimp fishermen violates the clause when the fee charged resident fishermen is only $25, for the clause bars "discrimination against citizens of other states where there is no substantial reason for the discrimination beyond the mere fact that they are citizens of other states." [1] The fact, however, that a distinction is made in terms of activity within and activity outside a state does not violate the clause. Thus a tax has been sustained that was five times as great on money deposited in banks outside the state as on money deposited in banks within the state, on the theory that there is no federal privilege to carry on business beyond the boundaries of one's own state.[2]

#### *(a) Tax exemption of residents*

TRAVIS v. YALE & TOWNE MANUFACTURING CO.

252 U.S. 60 (1920)

A New York income tax law granted certain exemptions to residents that were not given to nonresidents. A taxpayer brought an injunction action to prevent the enforcement of this tax law on the ground that it was unconstitutional because the exemption provision violated the privileges and immunity clause.

OPINION BY PITNEY, J.

. . . The District Court . . . held that the act, in granting to residents exemptions denied to nonresidents, violated the provision of section 2 of article 4 of the federal Constitution:

---

1 Toomer v. Witsell, 334 U.S. 385 (1948).
2 Madden v. Kentucky, 309 U.S. 83 (1940).

"The citizens of each state shall be entitled to all privileges and immunities of citizens in the several states." . . . We are constrained to affirm the ruling. . . .

"It was undoubtedly the object of the clause in question to place the citizens of each state upon the same footing with citizens of other states, so far as the advantages resulting from citizenship in those states are concerned. It relieves them from the disabilities of alienage in other states; it inhibits discriminating legislation against them by other states. . . .

"Beyond doubt those words are words of very comprehensive meaning, but it will be sufficient to say that the clause plainly and unmistakably secures and protects the right of a citizen of one state to pass into any other state of the Union for the purpose of engaging in lawful commerce, trade, or business without molestation; to acquire personal property; to take and hold real estate; to maintain actions in the courts of the state; and to be exempt from any higher taxes or excises than are imposed by the state upon its own citizens."

The nature and effect of the crucial discrimination in the present case are manifest. Section 362, in the case of residents, exempts from taxation $1,000 of the income of a single person, $2,000 in the case of a married person, and $200 additional for each dependent. A non-resident taxpayer has no similar exemption; but by section 363, if liable to an income tax in his own state, including income derived from sources within New York and subject to taxation under this act, he is entitled to a credit upon the income tax otherwise payable to the state of New York by the same proportion of the tax payable to the state of his residence as his income subject to taxation by the New York act bears to his entire income taxed in his own state; "provided, that such credit shall be allowed only if the laws of said state . . . grant a substantially similar credit to residents of this state subject to income tax under such laws."

In the concrete, the particular incidence of the discrimination is upon citizens of Connecticut and New Jersey, neither of which states has an income tax law. A considerable number of complainant's employees, residents and citizens of one or the other of those states, spend their working time at its office in the city of New York, and earn their salaries there. The case is typical; it being a matter of common knowledge that from necessity, due to the geographical situation of that city, in close proximity to the neighboring states, many thousands of men and women, residents and citizens of those states, go daily from their homes to the city and earn their livelihood there.

They pursue their several occupations side by side with residents of the state of New York—in effect competing with them as to wages, salaries, and other terms of employment. Whether they must pay a tax upon the first $1,000 or $2,000 of income, while their associates and competitors who reside in New York do not, makes a substantial difference. . . . We are unable to find adequate ground for the discrimination, and . . . hold that it is an unwarranted denial to the citizens of Connecticut and New Jersey of the privileges and immunities enjoyed by citizens of New York. This is not a case of occasional or accidental inequality due to circumstances personal to the taxpayer . . . but a general rule, operating to the disadvantage of all nonresidents including those who are citizens of the neighboring states, and favoring all residents . . . of the taxing state. . . .

### § 6:4. Present Evaluation of the Guarantee

As the result of narrowing interpretation, the privileges and immunity clause has in effect become a lost or forgotten clause of the Constitution. The reluctance to give it a broader meaning is based in part upon the fear that there would be no way of limiting a broader meaning and that such a broader meaning would destroy the balance of power between the nation and the state. This concept that the Court must maintain a balance between the states and the nation regardless of what the Constitution says is seen time and again in the opinions of the Court, although for the present it is apparently repudiated as a guide to construction.

"The reason for this reluctance to enlarge the scope of the clause has been well understood since the decision of the *Slaughter-House* cases. If its restraint upon state action were extended more than is needful to protect relationships between the citizen and the national government, and it did more than duplicate the protection of liberty and property secured to persons and citizens by the other provisions of the Constitution, it would enlarge judicial control of state action and multiply restrictions upon it to an extent difficult to define, but sufficient to cause serious apprehension for the rightful independence of local government. That was the issue fought out in the *Slaughter-House* Cases, with the decision against the enlargement." [3]

"This court has not been timorous about giving concrete meaning to such obscure and vagrant phrases as 'due process,' 'general welfare,' 'equal protection,' or even 'commerce among the several states.'

[3] Stone, J., dissenting in Colgate v. Harvey, 296 U.S. 404 (1935).

But it has always hesitated to give any real meaning to the privileges and immunity clause lest it improvidently give too much." [4]

## Questions for Discussion

1. Upon which government is the privileges and immunities clause binding?

2. (a) In what part of the Constitution is the privileges and immunities clause found? (b) When was it adopted? (c) What was its purpose?

3. What rights are protected by the privileges and immunities clause?

4. Can the benefit of the privileges and immunities clause be claimed by:

   (a) A person born and living since childhood in the city of New York?

   (b) An alien who has become a naturalized citizen of the United States?

   (c) An alien going to school within the United States?

   (d) A corporation the stock of which is held by ten American citizens?

5. (a) How is state citizenship determined? (b) Does state citizenship confer any rights different from those conferred by federal citizenship?

6. In the *Slaughter-House* cases the Supreme Court avoided a particular construction of the privileges and immunities clause because the rejected interpretation "would constitute this Court a perpetual censor upon all legislation of the states, on the civil rights of their own citizens, with authority to nullify such as it did not approve as consistent with those rights. . ." Compare this attitude with the attitude of the Supreme Court in interpreting and applying the due process clause. Is the attitude of the Court the same in each case? Explain.

7. Classify the following rights as derived from federal or state citizenship or both:

   (a) Right to bring a law suit.

   (b) Right to vote for mayor of the city.

   (c) Right to protection when traveling abroad.

   (d) Right of free transit through air space by airplane.

   (e) Right to bear arms.

   (f) Right to vote for United States Senator.

   (g) Right to mine coal.

   (h) Right to protection when coming home late at night from a local club meeting.

   (i) Right that all taxes be equal.

   (j) Right of free speech.

   (k) Right to sell an automobile.

---

[4] Jackson, J., concurring in Edwards v. California, 314 U.S. 160 (1941).

(l) Right to travel on navigable waterways.
(m) Right to enter or leave a state.
(n) Right to own property.

8. A state law prohibits persons operating hotels, public carriers, theatres, and other public places from making any distinction in the use of their accommodations and privileges on the basis of race or color. (a) Is this law constitutional? (b) What is the effect of the *Civil Rights* cases with respect to this law?

9. Assume the existence of a state law as stated in Question 8. D owns a hotel and discriminates against a group of people because of their race. He is prosecuted under the state law. He defends on the ground that the hotel is his property and that the due process clause guarantees his right to use the property in any nondangerous way that he sees fit. He claims that the law is unconstitutional. Decide.

10. A state law provides that it shall be a criminal offense for the operator of a public place of any nature "to discriminate against any person or class of persons without reasonable cause." M operates a hotel and excludes all members of a particular religious sect. He is prosecuted for violating this statute. He claims that it is unconstitutional. Decide.

11. (a) How does the decision in the *Civil Rights* cases compare with the decision in the *Slaughter-House* cases? (b) Is the reasoning of the Court the same in both?

12. (a) Does Congress have power to "enact a code of laws for the enforcement and vindication of all rights of life, liberty, and property"? Do the states? (b) If either Congress or the states do not have such a power, should they?

13. The state of New York adopted a law making it unlawful for any labor union to exclude an applicant for membership on the ground of race or creed. X, a Negro, applied for membership in the union. He was refused solely on the ground of race. He brought an action to compel his admission as a member. The union defended on the ground that it was a voluntary association and could choose its own members. X claimed that the statute limited the right of the union to choose. The union claimed that the law was unconstitutional. Is X entitled to be admitted to the union? Decide. *Railway Mail Ass'n.* v. *Corsi*, 326 U.S. 88 (1945).

14. A state law provides that whenever a corporation is placed in receivership and its property sold in order to pay the claims of creditors, a preference should be given to resident creditors in the payment of debts. X is a creditor of Z Corporation, the property of which has been sold by a receiver in order to pay the debts of Z Corporation. X is a nonresident of the state. The proceeds from the sale are used to pay creditors in the state. As the result of this priority, no money is left for X. X claims that the law is unconstitutional in giving this preference to the other creditors who happen to reside within the state. Decide.

15. (a) Do you agree with the reasoning of *Travis* v. *Yale & Towne Mfg. Co.*? (b) Would it have made any difference in that case if the state of New York had a sales tax and it was shown that the average resident paid sales taxes in the course of a year in excess of the amount of the exemption given by the income tax law and that nonresidents paid practically no sales taxes since they made their purchases at their homes in other states?

16. Draft a constitutional amendment that would state what you think the privileges and immunities clause should expressly provide.

17. A state law provides that a nonresident cannot begin a law suit without first giving security or filing a bond with the court promising that he will pay all the costs that may be entered in the action against him. X, a nonresident, attempts to begin a law suit in the state but is denied the privilege of so doing because he has not given security or filed a bond. He claims that he cannot be required to do so because it is not required of resident plaintiffs. Decide.

18. Is there any relation between the equal protection clause and the privileges and immunities clause?

19. A state law requires every nonresident engaging in local business to appoint the Secretary of Revenue of the state as his agent to accept service of process in any action brought against the nonresident. Is the law constitutional?

20. A state law requires every nonresident engaging in the business of selling securities to file a bond to protect any persons injured by his business activities. Is the law constitutional?

21. Would it affect your answer to Question 20 if the state law applied to all forms of business?

22. In *Toomer* v. *Witsell*, 334 U.S. 385 (1948), the Court stated "... one of the privileges which the [privileges and immunities] clause guarantees to the citizens of State A is that of doing business in State B on terms of substantial equality with the citizens of that state." In *Madden* v. *Kentucky*, 309 U.S. 83 (1940), the Court stated "... we think it quite clear that the right to carry out an incident to a trade, business or calling, such as the deposit of money in banks, is not a privilege of national citizenship." Are these two statements in harmony?

## Chapter 7

## OBLIGATION OF CONTRACTS



### § 7:1. The Guarantee

The framers of the Constitution were familiar with state laws passed to prevent the collection of debts. These debtor relief and stay laws were regarded as inconsistent with sound business. The framers of the Constitution, concerned with the advancement of commerce and business, therefore sought to protect contracts that formed the basis for commerce from being set aside by law.

It was accordingly provided by Article 1, Section 10, Clause 1, that no state could impair the obligation of contracts. Curiously enough, no such prohibition was placed upon the national Congress. This omission has, however, been corrected by the Supreme Court, which has read the obligation of contract clause into the guaranty of due process.

### § 7:2. The Contracts Protected

All contracts between private individuals are protected. This was the class of contracts that the framers had in mind. In addition, the protection of the contract clause has been extended by decision to grants and charters given by a state to a corporation or a person. If the state has granted a charter or made a land grant, it is an impairment of the obligation of contracts for the state to revoke such grant. But if the grant is not by its terms an exclusive grant, the contract clause does not prohibit the state from giving to another corporation or person a similar grant even though the competition from the second grant will impair the first grant or even make it worthless.

The inviolability of state grants has been to a large degree offset by the recognition of a right of the state to include in the charter or the grant the reservation of a power to make future changes in its terms. When this has been done, a later modification is not in most instances regarded as an impairment of the contract. This statement is qualified by the phrase "in most instances" because it has been held that, even though such reservation is made, the state does not have a completely free hand in changing the grant or the charter.

A reservation of the right to change may also be included or exist in the general corporation law under the terms of which the particular corporation has been incorporated. In such cases, the corporation receives its charter subject to the provisions of the corporation law, and therefore the state has the same right to change its provisions as above stated.

### § 7:3. The Police Power

Independently of the existence of a reservation of the right to change, the effectiveness of the contract clause has been gradually and increasingly restricted as to both private and corporate contracts by giving the police power greater latitude in restricting contracts in the interest of the common good. This latter doctrine has seen its greatest application in the host of debtor relief laws inspired by the depression following 1929. Efforts at voluntary debt reduction or forbearance had met with but slight success. The legislatures and the Congress therefore came to the aid of the debtors in much the same manner as the colonial and early state legislatures had adopted stay laws for the protection of the farmer and debtor classes. In order to protect both home owners and farmers from virtual economic destruction by mortgage foreclosure, numerous laws were passed either prohibiting the foreclosure of mortgages for a stated period or limiting the rights of the mortgagee in some manner or restricting the amount of the deficiency judgment that could be entered against the debtor. The validity of these limiting laws raised a question of social policy in conflict with the letter of the Constitution. There could be no question of the propriety and validity of the mortgages; the law recognized them as lawful, and they were contracts protected by the constitutional guarantee. On the other hand, there were the personal, humanitarian and community economic arguments that it was no time in which to stand on legal rights and that mortgagees must forbear the assertion of their legal rights or else general disaster would come upon both the individual mortgagors and the community, including the mortgagees as members of the community.

The Supreme Court solved the dilemma by applying the test of reasonableness. The Supreme Court held that, when the rights of the creditor were too seriously impaired, the law was void as a violation of the contract clause in the case of a state law or a violation of the due process clause in the case of a federal law. On the other hand, wherever the law merely delayed the creditor for a reasonable time and gave him just compensation for his loss or merely prevented him from obtaining an unreasonable profit at the expense of the debtor, the law was constitutional.

### *(a) State mortgage moratorium*

HOME BUILDING & LOAN ASSN. v. BLAISDELL

290 U.S. 398 (1934)

OPINION BY HUGHES, C. J.

Appellant contests the validity of . . . the Minnesota Mortgage Moratorium Law, as being repugnant to the contract clause. . . .

The Act provides that, during the emergency declared to exist, relief may be had through authorized judicial proceedings with respect to foreclosures of mortgages, and execution sales, of real estate; that sales may be postponed and periods of redemption may be extended. . . .

[A state cannot] . . . adopt as its policy the repudiation of debts or the destruction of contracts or the denial of means to enforce them. But it does not follow that conditions may not arise in which a temporary restraint of enforcement may be consistent with the spirit and purpose of the constitutional provision and thus be found to be within the range of the reserved power of the State to protect the vital interests of the community. It cannot be maintained that the constitutional provision should be so construed as to prevent limited and temporary interpositions with respect to the enforcement of contracts if made necessary by a great public calamity such as fire, flood, or earthquake. . . . The reservation of state power appropriate to such extraordinary conditions may be deemed to be as much a part of all contracts, as is the reservation of state power to protect the public interest in the other situations to which we have referred. And if state power exists to give temporary relief from the enforcement of contracts in the presence of disasters due to physical causes such as fire, flood or earthquake, that power cannot be said to be non-existent when the urgent public need demanding such relief is produced by other and economic causes. . . .

It is manifest . . . that there has been a growing appreciation of public needs and of the necessity of finding ground for a rational compromise between individual rights and public welfare. The settlement and consequent contraction of the public domain, the pressure of a constantly increasing density of population, the interrelation of the activities of our people and the complexity of our economic interests, have inevitably led to an increased use of the organization of society in order to protect the very bases of individual opportunity. Where, in earlier days, it was thought that only the concerns of individuals or of classes were involved, and that those of the State itself were touched only remotely, it has later been found that the fundamental interests of the State are directly affected; and that the question is no longer merely that of one party to a contract as against another, but of the use of reasonable means to safeguard the economic structure upon which the good of all depends.

It is no answer to say that this public need was not apprehended a century ago, or to insist that what the provision of the Constitution meant to the vision of that day it must mean to the vision of our time. . . .

1. An emergency existed in Minnesota which furnished a proper occasion for the exercise of the reserved power of the State to protect the vital interests of the community. . . .

2. The legislation was addressed to a legitimate end, that is, the legislation was not for the mere advantage of particular individuals but for the protection of a basic interest of society.

3. In view of the nature of the contracts in question—mortgages of unquestionable validity—the relief afforded and justified by the emergency, in order not to contravene the constitutional provision, could only be of a character appropriate to that emergency and could be granted only upon reasonable conditions.

4. The conditions upon which the period of redemption is extended do not appear to be unreasonable. . . .

5. The legislation is temporary in operation. It is limited to the exigency which called it forth. . . .

DISSENTING OPINION BY SUTHERLAND, J.

The present exigency is nothing new. From the beginning of our existence as a nation, periods of depression, of industrial failure, of financial distress, of unpaid and unpayable indebtedness, have alternated with years of plenty . . . and the attempt by legislative devices to shift the misfortune of the debtor to the shoulders of the creditor without coming into conflict with the contract impairment clause has been persistent and oft-repeated.

The defense of the Minnesota law is made upon grounds which were discountenanced by the makers of the Constitution and have many times been rejected by this court. That defense should not now succeed, because it constitutes an effort to overthrow the constitutional provision by an appeal to facts and circumstances identical with those which brought it into existence. . . .

A statute which materially delays enforcement of the mortgagee's contractual right of ownership and possession does not modify the remedy merely; it destroys, for the period of delay, *all* remedy so far as the enforcement of that right is concerned. The phrase, "obligation of a contract," in the constitutional sense imports a legal duty to perform the specified obligation of *that* contract, not to substitute and perform, against the will of one of the parties, a different, . . . obligation. . . .

### *(b) Federal mortgage moratorium*

LOUISVILLE JOINT STOCK LAND BANK v. RADFORD

295 U.S. 555 (1935)

The Frazier-Lemke Act of 1934 provided, in part, that a bankrupt farmer could obtain a stay of proceedings of the foreclosure of a mortgage for a period of five years, during which time he could remain in possession of the mortgaged property and pay a reasonable rental that would be distributed among his creditors both secured and unsecured.

OPINION BY BRANDEIS, J.

. . . For centuries efforts to protect necessitous mortgagors have been persistent. . . . No instance has been found, except under the

Frazier-Lemke Act, of either a statute or decision compelling the mortgagee to relinquish the property to the mortgagor free of the lien unless the debt was paid in full.

This right of the mortgagee to insist upon full payment before giving up his security has been deemed of the essence of a mortgage. . . . Although each of our national bankruptcy acts followed a major or minor depression, none had, prior to the Frazier-Lemke amendment, sought to compel the holder of a mortgage to surrender to the bankrupt either the possession of the mortgaged property or the title, so long as any part of the debt thereby secured remained unpaid. . . .

. . . The bankruptcy power, like the other great substantive powers of Congress, is subject to the Fifth Amendment. Under the bankruptcy power Congress may discharge the debtor's personal obligation, because, unlike the States, it is not prohibited from impairing the obligation of contracts. . . . But the effect of the Act here complained of is not the discharge of Radford's personal obligation. It is the taking of substantive rights in specific property acquired by the Bank prior to the Act. . . .

. . . The controlling purpose of the Acts is to preserve to the mortgagor the ownership and enjoyment of the farm property. . . . It has taken from the Bank. . . .

1. The right to retain the lien until the indebtedness thereby secured is paid.

2. The right to realize upon the security by a judicial public sale.

. . . The province of the Court is limited to deciding whether the Frazier-Lemke Act as applied has taken from the Bank without compensation, and given to Radford, rights in specific property which are of substantial value. . . . As we conclude that the Act as applied has done so, we must hold it void. For the Fifth Amendment commands that, however great the Nation's need, private property shall not be thus taken even for a wholly public use without just compensation. If the public interest requires, and permits, the taking of property of individual mortgagees in order to relieve the necessities of individual mortgagors, resort must be had to proceedings by eminent domain; so that, through taxation, the burden of the relief afforded in the public interest may be borne by the public.

### *(c) Mortgage deficiency judgments*

GELFERT v. NATIONAL CITY BANK

313 U.S. 221 (1941)

A mortgagee foreclosed his mortgage and purchased the property at the foreclosure sale. At the time when the mortgage had been executed, the law of the state provided that a mortgagee was entitled to a deficiency judgment against the mortgagor for the balance of the mortgage debt remaining unsatisfied after the mortgagor was credited with the net proceeds of the foreclosure sale. At the time when the mortgage was foreclosed, the state law provided that the court in fixing the amount of the deficiency judgment should "determine, upon affidavit or otherwise as it shall direct, the fair and reasonable market value of the mortgaged premises" and should deduct from the amount of the debt the "market value as determined by the court or the sale price of the property whichever shall be higher. . . ." The mortgagee objected to the application of this statute in determining the amount of his deficiency judgment on the ground that it impaired the obligation of the mortgage contract.

OPINION BY DOUGLAS, J.

. . . We are concerned here solely with the application of this statute to a situation where the mortgagee purchases the property at foreclosure sale. We intimate no opinion of its constitutionality as applied to the case where the mortgagee is not the purchaser. . . .

The formula which a legislature may adopt for determining the amount of a deficiency judgment is not fixed and invariable. That which exists at the date of the execution of the mortgage does not become so imbedded in the contract between the parties that it cannot be constitutionally altered. . . . "Not only are existing laws written into contracts in order to fix obligations as between the parties, but the reservation of essential attributes of sovereignty is also read into contracts. . . ." . . .

The control of judicial sales of realty by courts of equity and by legislatures in order to prevent sacrificial prices has a long history. . . . For about two centuries there has been a rather continuous effort . . . to prevent the machinery of judicial sales from becoming an instrument of oppression. . . . Numerous devices have been employed to safeguard mortgagors from sales which will or may result in mortgagees collecting more than their due. . . . Underlying that change has been the realization that the price which property commands at a forced sale may be hardly even a rough measure of its value. The paralysis of real estate markets during periods of depression, the wide discrepancy between the money value of property to the mortgagee and the cash price [received at such a] sale . . . reflect the considerations which have motivated departures from the theory that competitive bidding in this field amply protects the debtor.

Mortgagees are constitutionally entitled to no more than payment in full. . . . They cannot be heard to complain on constitutional grounds if the legislature takes steps to see to it that they get no more than that. . . . There is no constitutional reason why in lieu of the more restricted control by a court of equity the legislature cannot substitute a uniform comprehensive rule designed to reduce or to avoid in the run of cases the chance that the mortgagee will be paid more than once. . . . Certainly under this statute it cannot be said that more than that was attempted. The "fair and reasonable market value" of the property has an obvious and direct relevancy to a determination of the amount of the mortgagee's prospective loss. . . . The fact that men will differ in opinion as to the adequacy of any particular yardstick of value emphasizes that the appropriateness of any one formula is peculiarly a matter for legislative determination. . . . The fact that an emergency was not declared to exist when this statute was passed does not bring [the mortgage] within the protective scope of the contract clause. . . .

Respondent points out that earlier decisions of this court have struck down under the contract clause, as respect contracts previously made, a state statute requiring judicial sale to bring two-thirds of the amount of the appraised value of the property. . . . We cannot permit the broad language which those early decisions employed to force legislatures to be blind to the lessons which another century has taught.

## § 7:4. The Effect of a Chronic Emergency

A significant extension of this power to impair the obligation of contracts was recognized in *East New York Savings Bank* v. *Hahn*, 326 U.S. 230 (1945), in which the Supreme Court sustained a debtor relief law in 1944, although it had originally been designed to correct evils existing in 1933, on the basis that the repeal or the invalidation of that law in 1944 would cause a revival of the conditions that gave rise to the law in 1933. The full implication of this decision may be that an emergency law can be sustained indefinitely if the repeal of the law would cause the emergency to revive.

### *(a) Continuing temporary impairment*

EAST NEW YORK SAVINGS BANK v. HAHN

326 U.S. 230 (1945)

OPINION BY FRANKFURTER, J.

This was an action begun in 1944 to foreclose a mortgage on real property in the City of New York for non-payment of principal that had become due in 1924. The trial court held that the foreclosure proceeding was barred by the applicable New York Moratorium Law. . . . This Law, Chapter 93 of the Laws of New York of 1943, extended for another year legislation first enacted in 1933, whereby the right of foreclosure for default in the payment of principal was suspended for a year as to mortgages executed prior to July 1, 1932. Year by year (except in 1941 when an extension for two years was made) the 1933 statute was renewed for another year. . . .

Since *Home Bldg. & L. Ass'n* v. *Blaisdell*, . . . there are left hardly any open spaces of controversy concerning the constitutional restrictions of the Contract Clause upon moratory legislation referable to the depression. . . . The *Blaisdell* case and decisions rendered since . . . yield this governing constitutional principle: when a widely diffused public interest has become enmeshed in a network of multitudinous private arrangements, the authority of the State "to safeguard the vital interests of its people". . . is not to be gainsaid by abstracting one such arrangement from its public context and treating it as though it were an isolated private contract constitutionally immune from impairment.

. . . This "protective power of the state" . . . may be treated as an implied condition of every contract and, as such, as much part of the contract as though it were written into it, whereby the State's exercise of its power enforces, and does not impair, a contract. A more candid statement is to recognize . . . that the power "which, in its various ramifications, is known as the police power, is an exercise of the sovereign right of the government to protect the . . . general welfare of the people, and is paramount to any rights under contracts between individuals. . . ."

Applying these considerations to the immediate situation brings us to a quick conclusion. In 1933, New York began a series of moratory enactments to counteract the virulent effects of the depression upon New York realty which have been spread too often upon the records of this Court to require even a summary. Chapter 793 of the Laws of 1933 gave a year's grace against foreclosures of mortgages, but it obligated the mortgagor to pay taxes, insurance, and interest. The validity of the statute was sustained. . . . The moratorium has been extended from year to year. When the 1937 reenactment was questioned, the New York Court of Appeals again upheld the legislation. . . . This decision was rendered after a joint legislative committee had made a thorough study and recommended continuance of the moratorium. New York Legislative Document (1938) No. 58. In 1941, the Legislature reflected some changes in economic conditions by requiring amortization of the principal at the rate of 1% per annum, beginning with July 1, 1942. The same legislature established another joint legislative committee to review once more the New York mortgage situation. "After a most exhaustive study of the moratorium," a report was submitted recommending its extension for another year. New York Legislative Document (1942) No. 45. The Governor of New York urged such legislation [New York Legislative Document (1943) No. 1, p. 9] and the Law now under attack was enacted. It is relevant to note that the New York Legislature in subsequent extensions of the moratorium again took note of changed economic conditions by increasing the amortization rate to 2% in 1944 (L. 1944, C. 562) and to 3% in 1945 (L. 1945, C. 378).

Appellant asks us to reject the judgment of the joint legislative committee, of the Governor, and of the Legislature, that the public welfare, in the circumstances of New York conditions, requires the suspension of mortgage foreclosures for another year. On the basis of expert opinion, documentary evidence, and economic arguments of which we are to take judicial notice, it urges such a change in economic and financial affairs in New York as to deprive of all justification the determination of New York's legislature of what New York's welfare requires. We are invited to assess not only the range and incidence of what are claimed to be determining economic conditions insofar as they affect the mortgage market—bank deposits and war savings bonds; increased payrolls and store sales; available mortgage money and rise in real estate values—but also to resolve controversy as to the causes and continuity of such improvements, namely the effect of the war and of its termination, and similar matters. Merely to enumerate the elements that have to be considered shows that the place for determining their weight and their significance is the legislature not the judiciary. . . . here there was no "studied indifference to the interests of the mortgagee or to his appropriate protection." Here the Legislature was not even acting merely upon the pooled general knowledge of its members. The whole course of the New York moratorium legislation shows the empiric process of legislation at its fairest: frequent reconsideration, intensive study of the consequences of what has been done, readjustment to changing conditions, and safeguarding the future on the basis of responsible forecasts. The New York Legislature was advised by those having special responsibility to inform it that "the sudden termination of the legislation which has dammed up normal liquidation of these mortgages for more than eight years might well result in an emergency more acute than that which the original legislation was intended to alleviate." New York Legislative Document (1942) No. 45, p. 25. It would indeed be strange if there were anything in the Constitution of the United States which denied the State the power to safeguard its people against such dangers. There is nothing. Justification for the 1943 enactment is not negatived because the factors that induced and constitutionally supported its enactment were different from those which induced and supported the moratorium statute of 1933. . . .

## § 7:5. Change of Procedure

The procedure in the courts of the several states is prescribed by common law, custom, statute, or rule. When changes are made to the procedure, it is generally not regarded as an impairment of the existing contracts that must thereafter be enforced by a different procedure. If, however, the effect of the change in procedure is such as to materially reduce the value of the obligation, it is held that the change in procedure effects an impairment of the obligation of the contract.

### *(a) Procedure for service of process*

McGEE v. INTERNATIONAL LIFE INSURANCE CO.
355 U.S. 220 (1957)

Franklin, of California, obtained a policy of insurance from the International Life Insurance Company, a Texas Corporation, naming McGee as beneficiary. Some time thereafter, California adopted a statute permitting suit to be brought in California against a foreign insurance company on local policies of insurance even though the company was not within the state, service being made by registered mail to the insurer at its home office. After Frankin's death, McGee brought suit on the policy in California against the insurance company and served it by mail at its Texas office.

OPINION BY BLACK, J.

. . . The California statute became law . . . after respondent [insurance company] had entered into the agreement with Franklin. . . . Respondent contends that application of the statute to this existing contract improperly impairs the obligation of the contract. We believe that contention is devoid of merit. The statute was remedial, in the purest sense of that term, and neither enlarged nor impaired respondent's substantive rights or obligations under the contract. It did nothing more than to provide petitioner [McGee] with a California forum to enforce whatever substantive rights she might have against respondent. At the same time respondent was given a reasonable time to appear and defend on the merits after being notified of the suit. Under such circumstances, it had no vested right not to be sued in California. . . .

## § 7:6. Change of Judicial Decisions

While the contract clause is a guarantee that the state or the national government may not pass a law directly aimed at changing the contract between the two parties, it does not prevent the courts of the state or the nation from changing their interpretation of the law governing contracts. The net effect of such change of decision is to change the scope or meaning of the obligation of the contract. Since any change in the meaning of a contract results in one party receiving more and in the other party receiving less or in one party being subject to a greater or a smaller liability, such a change of construction is in a practical sense an impairment or alteration of the contract as it originally stood. This type of change or impairment is not, however, prohibited by the Constitution.

### Questions for Discussion

1. Which governments are bound by the obligation of contracts clause?

2. What contracts are protected by the obligations of contracts clause?

3. A state granted a company a charter to operate a toll bridge across a particular river. Thereafter the state granted a similar charter to another corporation. The second corporation built a bridge several hundred feet away from the first. Because of the competition of the second bridge, the profits of the first corporation were materially reduced. The first corporation brought an action to prohibit the second corporation from operating within the area of the first bridge. Decide. *Charles River Bridge* v. *Warren Bridge,* 11 Peters 420 (1837).

4. Compare the approach of the Supreme Court to the question of freedom of contract under the due process clause and the obligation of contracts under the obligation of contracts clause.

5. Can a state change the terms of a charter that has already been given to a corporation?

6. (a) What kind of debtor relief laws were adopted during the 1929 depression? (b) Were the laws similar to those adopted during the Colonial period? (c) What was the attitude of the framers of the Constitution with respect to such laws?

7. Under what power of government were the debtor relief laws of 1929 adopted?

8. (a) What is a mortgage moratorium law? (b) Why is it so called? (c) Is such a law constitutional?

9. (a) When an emergency law is adopted, does the Supreme Court make up its own mind as to whether there is a "sufficient" emergency or does the Court accept the finding or statement of the lawmaker that there is an emergency? (b) Is the Court qualified to determine whether an emergency exists or that a particular remedy is an appropriate remedy for the evil?

10. In *Home B. & L. Assn.* v. *Blaisdell,* the Court reasons that the right to give temporary relief from the enforcement of contracts during a period of disaster due to physical causes includes the right to give such relief when disaster is due to "other and economic causes." (a) Were there in fact any causes other than economic present in this case? (b) Does the majority opinion dispose of the objection raised by the dissenting opinion?

11. "The decision in *Home B. & L. Association* v. *Blaisdell* is bad law but good statemanship." Do you agree with this statement in whole or in part? Explain.

12. What limitations on the powers of the state are recognized in *Home B. & L. Association* v. *Blaisdell*?

13. A state adopts a law providing that any debtor who owes more debts than he can pay may deliver whatever money or property he owns to a receiver appointed by the court and, if the court is convinced that the debtor has acted honestly, the court may enter a decree discharging the debtor from all his debts without regard to whether his creditors have been paid in full. D, a debtor, obtains a release under this statute. X, a creditor of D, is not paid in full and sues D for the amount of his debt. D claims that he is discharged from the debt because of the statute. X claims that the statute is unconstitutional and that D still owes him the money. Decide.

14. Compare *Louisville Joint Stock Land Bank* v. *Radford* with *Gelfert* v. *National City Bank.* (a) What is the difference between them? (b) Is

there a real difference between the legal effect of the statutes considered in each case?

15. Would the statute held void in *Louisville Joint Stock Land Bank* v. *Radford* have been constitutional if the mortgagor had been required to pay the mortgagee a reasonable rental during the period that a foreclosure sale was postponed?

16. (a) What effect does a deficiency judgment act of the kind considered in *Gelfert* v. *National City Bank* have on the mortgagee's rights? (b) Would such an act be valid if applied when the property was purchased by a third person instead of by the mortgagee?

17. In considering the validity of a mortgage deficiency judgment act, does the Supreme Court determine whether the standard for determining the value of the property that is set off against the mortgage debt is a fair standard? Does it accept the decision of the lawmaker as to what is the fair method of determining value? Does it substitute its own judgment for that of the lawmaker?

18. In *East New York Savings Bank* v. *Hahn,* the Court stresses the study made by the legislature prior to the adoption of the law in question. Does this have any bearing on the question of the legality or the constitutionality of the law as apart from its social necessity?

19. Is *East New York Savings Bank* v. *Hahn* consistent with *Louisville Joint Stock Land Bank* v. *Radford*?

20. Does *East New York Savings Bank* v. *Hahn* meet the objection raised by the dissenting opinion in *Home B. & L. Assn.* v. *Blaisdell*?

21. In determining the legal effect of operation of a mortgage stay law, should the Court consider the over-all picture of a stay law annually extended or merely the current extension and dispose of the validity of the law on the basis of its staying enforcement for one year?

22. A and B make an oral contract for the sale of standing timber. Under the local statute of frauds law as then interpreted, such a contract is valid. After the contract is made, the state supreme court decides a case between C and D in which it holds that a contract for the sale of standing timber must be in writing in order to satisfy the requirements of the statute of frauds. A sues B on the oral contract. B defends on the ground that the decision of the court made after the A-B contract was executed requires the court to hold that the contract is void because not in writing. A replies that the decision between C-D cannot affect the A-B contract and that if it is held that it does apply, the guarantee against the impairment of contracts is violated. Decide.

## Chapter 8

# FREEDOM OF SPEECH, PRESS, ASSEMBLY, AND PETITION



### § 8:1. The Guarantee

The First Amendment provides that "Congress shall make no law . . . abridging the freedom of speech or of the press; or the right of the people peaceably to assemble, and to petition the Government for a redress of grievances." Historically, the rights protected were those of the citizen as against the government. These political guarantees have been expanded to include the protection of economic rights of the individual and thus have become significant in the government regulation of business.

At the same time that the guarantee of the First Amendment has been expanded to include economic rights, the Supreme Court has also held that these guarantees are so fundamental that they are included in the guarantees of the due process clause imposed on the states by the Fourteenth Amendment.

### § 8:2. Limitations upon Free Speech

As stated by Justice Holmes, "The most stringent protection of free speech would not protect a man in falsely shouting fire in a theater and causing a panic." [1] Since some limitation may be imposed,

[1] Schenck v. United States, 249 U.S. 47 (1919).

the question resolves itself into one of degree. In order to protect speech from unreasonable limitation, it has been declared in many instances that it may be restrained or suppressed only when there is a "clear and present danger" that a substantive evil would result if the speech were not controlled. There is uncertainty at present as to the exact status of the clear and present danger rule, for there is authority that a probable danger is sufficient.[2] There is also uncertainty as to whether the evil to which the speaker's words will lead must be an act committed by his listeners upon other persons, or may include threatened unlawful acts directed by the listeners against the speaker himself. In accord with the view that the harm must be threatened to third persons, it has been held that the fact that an angry and turbulent crowd gathered outside the place where the defendant was speaking did not give rise to such a clear and present danger as would justify restraining the speaker's freedom, since the crowd's hostility to the speaker should not be permitted to abridge his right to speak.[3] In contrast, it was later held that the danger that persons in the speaker's audience would be aroused because of hostility to the speaker to commit a breach of the peace directed against the speaker was such a clear and present danger as justified suppressing the speaker's right to speak.[4]

### § 8:3. Private Solicitation and Mass Meetings

The peaceful and private solicitation of workers to join a union cannot be prohibited and is protected as free speech. Similarly, a peaceful mass meeting for the purpose of persuading workers to join a union cannot be prohibited and is protected under the right of assembly.[5] A law that requires a union organizer to obtain a license before he can make a unionization speech or privately solicit workers is an unconstitutional restriction of freedom of speech.

#### *(a) Union solicitation*

STAUB v. CITY OF BAXLEY

355 U.S. 313 (1958)

An ordinance of Baxley, Georgia, made it a criminal offense to solicit persons to join a labor union unless a license was first obtained by applying to the mayor and the city council. Under the ordinance,

---

[2] See § 8:5.
[3] Terminello v. Chicago, 337 U.S. 1 (1949).
[4] Feiner v. New York, 340 U.S. 315 (1951).
[5] Thomas v. Collins, 323 U.S. 516 (1945).

the application could be refused if the mayor and the council did not approve of the organizer or of the organization or believed that the growth of the organization would be harmful to the general welfare of the city. Staub was employed as an organizer by the International Ladies' Garment Workers Union. She visited Baxley and spoke of joining the union to a number of workers in their homes. She had no license and was prosecuted for violating the ordinance. From a conviction for violating the ordinance, she appealed ultimately to the United States Supreme Court, raising the objection that the licensing ordinance violated her right to free speech.

OPINION BY WHITTAKER, J.

. . . It will be noted that appellant was not accused of any act against the peace, good order or dignity of the community, nor for any particular thing she said in soliciting employees of the manufacturing company to join the union. She was simply charged and convicted for "soliciting members for an organization without a Permit." This solicitation, as shown by the evidence, consisted solely of speaking to those employees in their private homes about joining the union.

It will also be noted that the permit is not to be issued as a matter of course, but only upon the affirmative action of the Mayor and Council of the City. They are expressly authorized to refuse to grant the permit if they do not approve of the applicant or of the union or of the union's "effects upon the general welfare of citizens of the City of Baxley." These criteria are without semblance of definitive standards or other controlling guides governing the action of the Mayor and Council in granting or withholding a permit. . . . It is thus plain that they act in this respect in their uncontrolled discretion.

It is settled by a long line of recent decisions of this Court that an ordinance which, like this one, makes the peaceful enjoyment of freedoms which the Constitution guarantees contingent upon the uncontrolled will of an official—as by requiring a permit or license which may be granted or withheld in the discretion of such official—is an unconstitutional censorship or prior restraint upon the enjoyment of those freedoms. . . .

## § 8:4. Picketing

Peaceful picketing has held a fluctuating constitutional status. After a number of years, peaceful picketing was recognized as lawful but was subject to prohibition by statute. In 1940, however, the United States Supreme Court purported to declare that peaceful picketing was constitutionally protected as free speech, on the theory that it was a means of communication between pickets and third persons to inform the latter of the existence of a labor dispute. The Supreme Court then modified this view in a number of material respects as by holding that pickets must confine their activities within the geographic area in which the labor dispute exists,[6] that picketing loses its constitutional immunity when designed to induce the commission of an unlawful act; [7] and finally by 1957 it virtually reversed its former position in holding that peaceful picketing was not constitutionally protected when contrary to a specific local public policy.

While the removal of the constitutional immunity of picketing permitted state courts to enjoin such activity, a decision of the Supreme Court in the following year denied the state courts the power to issue any injunction against peaceful picketing conducted in connection with any labor activity that is within the jurisdiction of the National Labor Relations Board, without regard to whether such picketing was protected or prohibited by the Federal statute. That is, peaceful picketing in such cases is clothed with an immunity from state control because the control, if any, must be imposed under the Federal statute.[8] This concept has been qualified by the Labor-Management Reporting and Disclosure Act of 1959, which authorizes state action when the national board has refused to exercise its jurisdiction.

### *(a) Peaceful picketing*

#### THORNHILL v. ALABAMA

310 U.S. 88 (1940)

A state law made picketing a misdemeanor. Thornhill was convicted of violating this statute. He appealed, claiming that the statute was unconstitutional as it deprived him of freedom of speech.

OPINION BY MURPHY, J.

. . . The freedom of speech and of the press, which are secured by the First Amendment against abridgment by the United States, are among the fundamental personal rights and liberties which are secured to all persons by the Fourteenth Amendment against abridgment by a state.

---

[6] Carpenters & Joiners Union of America v. Ritter's Cafe, 315 U.S. 722 (1942).

[7] Gibboney v. Empire Storage & Ice Co., 336 U.S. 490 (1949).

[8] Hotel Employees Union Local No. 255 v. Sax Enterprises, 358 U.S. 270 (1959).

The safeguarding of these rights to the ends that men may speak as they think on matters vital to them and that falsehoods may be exposed through the processes of education and discussion is essential to free government. Those who won our independence had confidence in the power of free and fearless reasoning and communication of ideas to discover and spread political and economic truth. Noxious doctrines in those fields may be refuted and their evil averted by the courageous exercise of the right of free discussion. Abridgment of freedom of speech and of the press, however, impair those opportunities for public education that are essential to effective exercise of the power of correcting error. . . .

It is apparent that [the state law prohibits] every practicable method whereby the facts of a labor dispute may be publicized in the vicinity of the place of business of an employer. . . . In sum, whatever the means used to publicize the facts of a labor dispute, whether by printed sign, by pamphlet, by word of mouth or otherwise, all such activity without exception is within the inclusive prohibition of the statute so long as it occurs in the vicinity of the scene of the dispute.

The freedom of speech and of the press guaranteed by the Constitution embraces at the least the liberty to discuss publicly and truthfully all matters of public concern without previous restraint or fear of subsequent punishment. . . . Freedom of discussion, if it would fulfill its historic function in this nation, must embrace all issues about which information is needed or appropriate to enable the members of society to cope with the exigencies of their period.

In the circumstances of our times the dissemination of information concerning the facts of a labor dispute must be regarded as within that area of free discussion that is guaranteed by the Constitution.

### *(b) Peaceful picketing and public policy*

INTERNATIONAL BROTHERHOOD OF TEAMSTERS v. VOGT
354 U.S. 283 (1957)

Under the Wisconsin Labor Relations Act, it is an unfair labor practice for an employee individually or in concert with others to coerce an employer to interfere in any way with the rights of his employees or to do an act that would constitute an unfair labor practice if committed by him on his own initiative. Vogt owned and operated a gravel pit where he employed 15 to 20 men. The International Brotherhood of Teamsters attempted to organize the men. On failing to do so, they picketed the pit with signs reading "The men on this job are not 100% affiliated with the A.F.L.," thereby seeking to coerce Vogt to cause his men to join the union. Several trucking companies refused to cross the picket lines. Vogt sought an injunction against the picketing. The state court granted an injunction. The Union appealed.

OPINON BY FRANKFURTER, J.

. . . Courts began to find in one of the aims of picketing an aspect of communication. This view came to the fore in *Senn* v. *Tile Layers Union,* 301 U.S. 468, where the Court held that the Fourteenth Amendment did not prohibit Wisconsin from authorizing peaceful stranger picketing by a union that was attempting to unionize a shop and to induce an employer to refrain from working in his business as a laborer.

. . . Three years later, in passing on a restrictive instead of a permissive state statute, the Court made sweeping pronouncements about the right to picket in holding unconstitutional a statute that had been applied to ban all picketing, with "no exceptions based upon either the number of persons engaged in the proscribed activity, the peaceful character of their demeanor, the nature of their dispute with an employer, or the restrained character and the accurateness of the terminology used in notifying the public of the facts of the dispute." *Thornhill* v. *Alamaba,* 310 U.S. 88, 99. As the statute dealt at large with all picketing, so the Court broadly assimilated peaceful picketing in general to freedom of speech, and as such protected against abridgment by the Fourteenth Amendment.

These principles were applied by the Court in *A. F. of L.* v. *Swing,* 312 U.S. 321, to hold unconstitutional an injunction against peaceful picketing, based on a State's common-law policy against picketing when there was no immediate dispute between employer and employee. On the same day, however, the Court upheld a generalized injunction against picketing where there had been violence because "it could justifiably be concluded that the momentum of fear generated by past violence would survive even though future picketing might be wholly peaceful. *Milk Wagon Drivers Union* v. *Meadowmoor Dairies,* 312 U.S. 287, 294.

Soon, however, the Court came to realize that the broad pronouncements, but not the specific holding, of *Thornhill* had to yield "to the impact of facts unforeseen," or at least not sufficiently appreciated. . . . Cases reached the Court in which a State had designed a remedy to meet a specific situation or to accomplish a particular social policy. These cases made manifest that picketing, even though "peaceful," involved more than just communication of ideas and could not be immune from all state regulation. "Picketing by an organized group is more than free speech, since it involves patrol of a particular locality and since the very presence of a picket line may induce action of one kind or another, quite irrespective of the nature of the ideas which are being disseminated." . . .

The implied reassessments of the broad language of the *Thornhill* case were finally generalized in a series of cases sustaining injunctions against peaceful picketing, even when arising in the course of a labor controversy, when such picketing was counter to valid state policy in a domain open to state regulation. The decisive reconsideration came in *Giboney* v. *Empire Storage & Ice Co.*, 336 U.S. 490. A union, seeking to organize peddlers, picketed a wholesale dealer to induce it to refrain from selling to nonunion peddlers. The state courts, finding that such an agreement would constitute a conspiracy in restraint of trade in violation of the state antitrust laws, enjoined the picketing. . . .

The following Term, the Court decided a group of cases applying and elaborating on the theory of *Giboney*. In *Hughes* v. *Superior Court*, 339 U.S. 460, the Court held that the Fourteenth Amendment did not bar use of the injunction to prohibit picketing of a place of business solely to secure compliance with a demand that its employees be hired in percentage to the racial origin of its customers. . . .

On the same day, the Court decided *Teamsters Union* v. *Hanke*, 339 U.S. 470, holding that a State was not restrained by the Fourteenth Amendment from enjoining picketing of a business, conducted by the owner himself without employees, in order to secure compliance with a demand to become a union shop. . . .

A third case, *Building Service Employees* v. *Gazzam*, 339 U.S. 532, was decided the same day. Following an unsuccessful attempt at unionization of a small hotel and refusal by the owner to sign a contract with the union as bargaining agent, the union began to picket the hotel with signs stating that the owner was unfair to organized labor. The State, finding that the object of the picketing was in violation of its statutory policy against employer coercion of employees' choice of bargaining representative, enjoined picketing for such purpose. . . .

A similar problem was involved in *Plumbers Union* v. *Graham*, 345 U.S. 192, where a state court had enjoined, as a violation of its "Right to Work" law, picketing that advertised that nonunion men were being employed on a building job. This Court found that there was evidence in the record supporting a conclusion that a substantial purpose of the picketing was to put pressure on the general contractor to eliminate nonunion men from the job and, on the reasoning of the cases that we have just discussed, held that the injunction was not in conflict with the Fourteenth Amendment.

This series of cases, then, established a broad field in which a State, in enforcing some public policy, whether of its criminal or its civil law, and whether announced by its legislature or its courts, could constitutionally enjoin peaceful picketing aimed at preventing effectuation of that policy. . . .

The whole series of cases discussed above allowing, as they did, wide discretion to a State in the formulation of domestic policy, and not involving a curtailment of free speech in its obvious and accepted scope, led this Court, without the need of further argument, to grant appellee's motion to dismiss the appeal in that it no longer presented a substantial federal question. . . .

. . . The highest state court drew the inference from the facts that the picketing was to coerce the employer to put the pressure on his employees to join the union, in violation of the declared policy of the State. . . . The cases discussed above all hold that, consistent with the Fourteenth Amendment, a State may enjoin such conduct.

Of course, the mere fact that there is "picketing" does not automatically justify its restraint without an investigation into its conduct and purposes. State courts, no more than state legislatures, can enact blanket prohibitions against picketing. *Thornhill* v. *Alabama* and *A. F. of L.* v. *Swing, supra.* The series of cases following *Thornhill* and *Swing* demonstrate that the policy of Wisconsin enforced by the prohibition of this picketing is a valid one. . . .

DISSENTING OPINION BY DOUGLAS, J., in which Warren, C. J., and Black, J., concur.

The Court has now come full circle. In *Thornhill* v. *Alabama,* 310 U.S. 88, 102, we struck down a state ban on picketing on the ground that "the dissemination of information concerning the facts of a labor dispute must be regarded as within that area of free discussion that is guaranteed by the Constitution." Less than one year later, we held that the First Amendment protected organizational picketing on a factual record which cannot be distinguished from the one now before us. *A. F. of L.* v. *Swing,* 312 U.S. 321. Of course, we have always recognized that picketing has aspects which make it more than speech. *Bakery Drivers Local* v. *Wohl,* 315 U.S. 769, 776-777 (concurring opinion). That difference underlies our decision in *Giboney* v.

*Empire Storage & Ice Co.*, 336 U.S. 490. There, picketing was an essential part of "a single and integrated course of conduct, which was in violation of Missouri's valid law." . . . Speech there was enjoined because it was an inseparable part of conduct which the State constitutionally could and did regulate.

But where, as here, there is no rioting, no mass picketing, no violence, no disorder, no fisticuffs, no coercion—indeed nothing but speech—the principles announced in *Thornhill* and *Swing* should give the advocacy of one side of a dispute First Amendment protection.

The retreat began when, in *Teamsters Union* v. *Hanke,* 339 U.S. 470, four members of the Court announced that all picketing could be prohibited if a state court decided that that picketing violated the State's public policy. The retreat became a rout in *Plumbers Union* v. *Graham,* 345 U.S. 192. It was only the "purpose" of the picketing which was relevant. The state court's characterization of the picketers' "purpose" had been made well-nigh conclusive. Considerations of the proximity of picketing to conduct which the State could control or prevent were abandoned, and no longer was it necessary for the state court's decree to be narrowly drawn to prescribe a specific evil. . . .

Today, the Court signs the formal surrender. State courts and state legislatures cannot fashion blanket prohibitions on all picketing. But, for practical purposes, the situation now is as it was when *Senn* v. *Tile Layers Union,* 301 U.S. 468, was decided. State courts and state legislatures are free to decide whether to permit or suppress any particular picket line for any reason other than a blanket policy against all picketing. I would adhere to the principle announced in *Thornhill.* I would adhere to the result reached in *Swing.* I would return to the test enunciated in *Giboney*—that this form of expression can be regulated or prohibited only to the extent that it forms an essential part of a course of conduct which the State can regulate or prohibit. I would reverse the judgment below.

## § 8:5. Reform and Revolutionary Propaganda

A law making it a crime to urge the overthrow of the government cannot be applied to prohibit the printing and the distribution of books pointing out social defects and calling upon the public to change such evils by adopting necessary remedial laws. A meeting called to advocate "corrective" legislation cannot be barred, regardless of whether such laws are regarded as unwise, undesirable, or "dangerous."

The act of knowingly conspiring to teach and advocate the overthrow of the government by force and violence or to organize the Communist Party for that purpose has been held to present a clear and present danger, justifying suppression, even though only action at an indefinite future date was contemplated, and the danger to that extent probable rather than clear and present.[9] In sustaining the provision of the National Labor Management Relations Act, that requires the filing of an anti-Communist affidavit by union leaders, the Court has also declared that "when the effect of a statute or ordinance upon the exercise of First Amendment freedoms is relatively small and the public interest to be protected is substantial, it is obvious that a rigid test requiring a showing of imminent danger to the security of the Nation is an absurdity." [10] In contrast, however, when there is merely an advocacy of ideas, it has been held that no clear and present danger is present although such ideas embrace the overthrow of the government.

### *(a) Advocacy of Communism*

YATES v. UNITED STATES
354 U.S. 298 (1957)

Yates and others were indicted under the Federal Smith Act for the crime of advocating and teaching the forcible overthrow of the government of the United States. They appealed from their conviction for that offense on the ground that the trial judge did not instruct the jury that they could not be guilty of the offense of "advocacy" if they were merely urging the adoption of an idea and that to be guilty it was necessary to prove that their advocacy was such as to incite persons to action.

OPINION BY HARLAN, J.

. . . Petitioners contend that the instructions to the jury were fatally defective in that the trial court refused to charge that, in order to convict, the jury must find that the advocacy which the defendants conspired to promote was of a kind calculated to "incite"

---

[9] Dennis v. United States, 341 U.S. 494 (1951).
[10] American Communications Association, C.I.O. v. Douds, 339 U.S. 382 (1950).

persons to action for the forcible overthrow of the Government. It is argued that advocacy of forcible overthrow as mere *abstract doctrine* is within the free speech protection of the First Amendment; that the Smith Act, consistently with that constitutional provision, must be taken as proscribing only the sort of advocacy which incites to illegal *action*; and that the trial court's charge, by permitting conviction for mere advocacy, unrelated to its tendency to produce forcible action, resulted in an unconstitutional application of the Smith Act. The Government . . . takes the position, however, that the true constitutional dividing line is not between inciting and abstract advocacy of forcible overthrow, but rather between advocacy as such, irrespective of its inciting qualities, and the mere discussion or exposition of violent overthrow as an abstract theory. . . .

We are . . . faced with the question whether the Smith Act prohibits advocacy and teaching of forcible overthrow as an abstract principle, divorced from any effort to instigate action to that end, so long as such advocacy or teaching is engaged in with evil intent. We hold that it does not.

The distinction between advocacy of abstract doctrine and advocacy directed at promoting unlawful action is one that has been consistently recognized in the opinions of this Court. . . .

In failing to distinguish between advocacy of forcible overthrow as an abstract doctrine and advocacy of action to that end, the District Court appears to have been led astray by the holding in *Dennis* that advocacy of violent action to be taken at some future time was enough. It seems to have considered that, since "inciting" speech is usually thought of as something calculated to induce immediate action, and since *Dennis* held advocacy of action for future overthrow sufficient, this meant that advocacy, irrespective of its tendency to generate action, is punishable, provided only that it is uttered with a specific intent to accomplish overthrow. In other words, the District Court apparently thought that *Dennis* obliterated the traditional dividing line between advocacy of abstract doctrine and advocacy of action.

This misconceives the situation confronting the Court in *Dennis* and what was held there. Although the jury's verdict, interpreted in light of the trial court's instructions, did not justify the conclusion that the defendants' advocacy was directed at, or created any danger of, immediate overthrow, it did establish that the advocacy was aimed at building up a seditious group and maintaining it in readiness for action at a propitious time. In such circumstances, said Chief Justice

Vinson, the Government need not hold its hand "until the *putsch* is about to be executed, the plans have been laid and the signal is awaited. If Government is aware that a group aiming at its overthrow is attempting to indoctrinate its members and to commit them to a course whereby they will strike when the leaders feel the circumstances permit, action by the Government is required. . . ." The essence of the *Dennis* holding was that indoctrination of a group in preparation for future violent action, as well as exhortation to immediate action, by advocacy found to be directed to "action for the accomplishment" of forcible overthrow, to violence as "a rule or principle of action," and employing "language of incitement,". . . is not constitutionally protected when the group is of sufficient size and cohesiveness, is sufficiently oriented towards action, and other circumstances are such as reasonably to justify apprehension that action will occur. This is quite a different thing from the view of the District Court here that mere doctrinal justification of forcible overthrow, if engaged in with the intent to accomplish overthrow, is punishable *per se* under the Smith Act. That sort of advocacy, even though uttered with the hope that it may ultimately lead to violent revolution, is too remote from concrete action to be regarded as the kind of indoctrination preparatory to action which was condemned in *Dennis*. As one of the concurring opinions of *Dennis* put it: "Throughout our decisions there has recurred a distinction between the statement of an idea which may prompt its hearers to take unlawful action, and advocacy that such action be taken.". . . There is nothing in *Dennis* which makes that historic distinction obsolete. . . .

*Dennis* was . . . not concerned with a conspiracy to engage at some future time in seditious advocacy, but rather with a conspiracy to advocate presently the taking of forcible action in the future. It was action, not advocacy, that was to be postponed until "circumstances" would "permit." . . .

The essential distinction is that those to whom the advocacy is addressed must be urged to *do* something, now or in the future, rather than merely to *believe* in something. . . .

We recognize that distinctions between advocacy or teaching of abstract doctrines, with evil intent, and that which is directed to stirring people to action, are often subtle and difficult to grasp, for in a broad sense, . . . "Every idea is an incitement."

## Questions for Discussion

1. (a) Why was the First Amendment adopted? (b) What governments are bound by it?

2. (a) What did freedom of speech mean to the men of the period when the Constitution was adopted? (b) Does it have the same meaning in the present decisions of the Supreme Court? If not, should the same meaning be given as it had when adopted?

3. (a) Does the Supreme Court accept the decision of a state legislature that conditions justify or require a limitation of the freedom of speech? (b) Is there any difference in the Court's treatment of the decision of a state legislature that economic conditions are such as justify a law impairing existing contracts or limiting the freedom of contract?

4. Could the *Staub* case have been decided differently on the basis of any other recognized legal principle?

5. A state adopts a law which recites that "agitators" have been causing much public unrest and that investigation by the legislature shows that many "agitators" have been inspired by "improper motives." The law then provides that no one may make a speech in any public place or street without first registering with the local police department his name, address, occupation, subject matter of the speech, whether any funds will be solicited, and whether the speaker is paid by anyone for making the speech and if so by whom. The law expressly states that the police department does not have the right to deny any applicant the right to register nor to refuse him the right to make the speech after he has registered unless the object and the effect of the speech is to incite to the commission of a crime. Is such a law constitutional?

6. A state law provides that no union organizer may collect money for the union without first registering his name, address, and position with the union, the name and a general description of the union and its purposes, and the names and the addresses of the principal officers of the union. Is the law constitutional?

7. Should a speaker be prohibited from speaking when persons in his audience threaten to injure him if he continues?

8. (a) May a state make it illegal to urge the adoption of a law providing for government ownership of industries? (b) May the national government make it illegal?

9. May a state make it illegal to persuade others to amend the Constitution to abolish state governments?

10. What are the practical difficulties with the concept of picketing as constitutionally-protected free speech?

11. Is the reconciliation of the *Thornhill* case made in the *Vogt* case valid?

12. What is the distinction between the immunity of picketing in the *Thornhill* case and that in the *Hotel Employees* case cited in § 8:4, footnote 8?

13. A speaker stirs the emotions of a crowd to such an extent that they destroy and burn down the local bank, which holds the mortgages on their property. The speaker had not suggested or hinted at the use of violence in any manner but merely described the number of mortgages that the bank had foreclosed and the subsequent economic misfortunes of those persons whose property had been foreclosed. Is the speaker liable for the damage done?

14. Would it make any difference in your answer to Question 13 if a state law made it illegal to incite to riot or acts of violence?

15. Would it make any difference in your answer to Question 13 if the chairman of the meeting addressed by the speaker had told the speaker beforehand that the crowd was in such a mood that they would be likely to burn down the bank if not held back?

16. (a) Could the local police authorities refuse to permit the speaker in Question 13 from speaking on this subject? (b) Would it make any difference if the speaker had spoken a week earlier in another city and mob violence had followed his speech in that city?

17. How does the Supreme Court distinguish the *Dennis* case in the opinion in the *Yates* case?

18. Can the exercise of the right to criticize the government be restricted geographically to any particular area?

19. Does picketing have the same scope as free speech in criticizing the government?

20. Would the decision in the *Staub* case have been different if the ordinance specified that a license would be granted in every case except to a person soliciting members for labor unions?

21. De Jonge attended a meeting that was held under the auspices of the Communist Party. The meeting was public and orderly and was held for a lawful purpose, and although it was held under the auspices of the Communist Party, no unlawful conduct was taught or advocated by anyone present at the meeting or by the persons running the meeting. De Jonge was indicted for "criminal syndicalism" under a statute that defined "criminal syndicalism" as "the doctrine which advocates crime, physical violence, sabotage, or any unlawful acts or methods as a means of accomplishing or effecting industrial or political change or revolution." Should De Jonge be convicted under this statute? *De Jonge* v. *Oregon,* 299 U.S. 353 (1937).

# PART III. REGULATION OF BUSINESS

## Chapter 9

## REGULATION OF COMMERCE



### § 9:1. The Federal Power

By Article I, Section 8, Clause 3, of the Constitution, power is given to the Congress of the United States "to regulate commerce with foreign nations, and among the several states, and with the Indian Tribes." This power is known as the commerce power. Few provisions of the Constitution have been the cause of as much litigation, and no other provision today confers as much power upon the federal government. The scope of the power cannot be stated precisely, particularly because the decisions of the Supreme Court since 1937 have given to the commerce clause a broader interpretation than was formerly accepted.

The necessity for defining the scope of the commerce clause has arisen in two types of cases. The first in point of time to come before the Supreme Court raised the question of whether an activity was interstate commerce so as to exclude state regulation. At a later date it was recognized that the mere fact that an activity was interstate commerce did not necessarily exclude state regulation because there was held to exist a concurrent power on the part of both the states and the federal government to regulate a certain sphere of interstate commerce.[1]

The second class of cases raised the question of whether Congress could regulate a particular activity on the ground that such an activity was interstate commerce.

### § 9:2. Interstate Commerce as Trade

Trade, trafficking in goods, buying and selling—in short, commerce—was very important to the business interests of the day when the Constitution was framed and adopted. The merchants then held the position of social and economic importance now held by the great industrialists, and the adoption of the Constitution was largely inspired by them. In fact, it was in part to free trade from governmental restrictions that the Revolutionary War had been waged. A new government established under the Articles of Confederation had proven unable to protect trade from the harmful restrictions and rivalries of the states. These in turn taxed and raised barriers of one nature or another against the trade from each other. The efforts made at the Annapolis and Alexandria Conventions to protect trade and the business interests led to the conclusion that the Articles of Confederation should be revised, and the call went out for the meeting of a convention in Philadelphia in 1787. It was there that the new Constitution was drafted.

Against this background of efforts to protect commerce and trade from the harmful effects of state regulations and tariffs, it is apparent that the framers of the Constitution regarded the power to regulate interstate commerce as the power to regulate interstate trade.

To constitute "trade" within the concept that interstate trade is interstate commerce, it is not now necessary that there be a sale of goods. Accordingly the concept of interstate commerce now includes the interstate sale of insurance; the interstate promotion of professional football and boxing; the interstate producing, booking, and presenting of theatrical performances; but not the interstate promotion of professional baseball.

#### *(a) Professional football*

RADOVICH v. NATIONAL FOOTBALL LEAGUE
352 U.S. 445 (1957)

The members of the National Football League use a standard player contract that prohibits a player from signing with another

[1] See generally Chapter 17.

club without the consent of the club holding his contract. A violation of this provision is punished by blacklisting the player and by imposing severe penalties on any club that employs the player in violation of the provision. Radovich played for the Detroit Lions, a National League Club. He asked for a transfer to the Los Angeles club because of the illness of his father. The transfer was refused. Radovich then broke his contract and played for the Los Angeles Dons, a club of the All-America Conference. The National League blacklisted him, and another Club then revoked an offer it had made to him to be a player-coach. Radovich sued the National Football League and others, claiming that they had violated the Sherman Anti-Trust Act.

OPINION BY CLARK, J.

. . . As part of its football business, the respondent league and its member teams schedule football games in various metropolitan centers, including New York, Chicago, Philadelphia, and Los Angeles. . . . As a further "part of the business of professional football itself" and "directly tied in and connected" with its football exhibitions is the transmission of the games over radio and television into nearly every State of the Union. This is accomplished by contracts which produce a "significant portion of the gross receipts" and without which "the business of operating a professional football club would not be profitable." The playing of the exhibitions themselves "is essential to the interstate transmission by broadcasting and television" and the actions of the respondents against Radovich were necessarily related to these interstate activities.

In the light of these allegations respondents . . . say the business of organized professional football was not intended by Congress to be included within the scope of the antitrust laws. . . .

Respondents' contention, . . . is that agreements similar to those complained of here, which have for many years been used in organized baseball, have been held by this Court to be outside the scope of the antitrust laws. They point to *Federal Baseball* [259 U.S. 200] and *Toolson* [346 U.S. 356], both involving the business of professional baseball, asserting that professional football has embraced the same techniques which existed in baseball at the time of the former decision. . . . In *Toolson* we continued to hold the umbrella over baseball that was placed there some 31 years earlier by *Federal Baseball.* The Court did this because it was concluded that more harm would be done in overruling *Federal Baseball* than in upholding a ruling which at best was of dubious validity. Vast efforts had gone into the development and organization of baseball since that decision and enormous capital had been invested in reliance on its permanence. Congress had chosen to make no change. All this, combined with the flood of litigation that would follow its repudiation, the harrassment that would ensue, and the retroactive effect of such a decision, led the Court to the practical result that it should sustain the unequivocal line of authority reaching over many years.

The Court was careful to restrict *Toolson's* coverage to baseball, following the judgment of *Federal Baseball* only so far as it "determines that Congress had no intention of including the business of baseball within the scope of the federal antitrust laws." . . . We now specifically limit the rule there established to the facts there involved, *i. e.*, the business of organized professional baseball. As long as the Congress continues to acquiesce we should adhere to—but not extend—the interpretation of the Act made in those cases. We did not extend them to boxing or the theater because we believed that the volume of interstate business in each—the rationale of *Federal Baseball*—was such that both activities were within the Act. Likewise, the volume of interstate business involved in organized professional football places it within the provisions of the Act.

If this ruling is unrealistic, inconsistent, or illogical, it is sufficient to answer, aside from the distinctions between the businesses, that were we considering the question of baseball for the first time upon a clean slate we would have no doubts. But *Federal Baseball* held the business of baseball outside the scope of the Act. No other business claiming the coverage of those cases has such an adjudication. We, therefore, conclude that the orderly way to eliminate error or discrimination, if any there be, is by legislation and not by court decision. Congressional processes are more accommodative, affording the whole industry hearings and an opportunity to assist in the formulation of new legislation. The resulting product is therefore more likely to protect the industry and the public alike. The whole scope of congressional action would be known long in advance and effective dates for the legislation could be set in the future without the injustices of retroactivity and surprise which might follow court action. Of course, the doctrine of *Toolson* and *Federal Baseball* must yield to any congressional action and continues only at its sufferance.

### § 9:3. Interstate Commerce as Crossing a State Line

Although the interstate commerce clause was originally designed as a protection to trade between the states, the Supreme Court gradually expanded the concept of interstate commerce to include any crossing of a state line of persons or goods, whether for profit or not. For example, this concept of interstate commerce includes all movement across a state line by any means, whether on foot or by vehicle, and without regard to whether the vehicle was known or in use at the time the Constitution was adopted. Thus a person walking across a state line moves in interstate commerce, as well as persons or goods moving across a state line by any means of transportation, whether on land, water, or in the air.

All forms of communication, such as telegraph, wireless, and radio, are forms of commerce and when such communication crosses a state line they are interstate commerce. "The powers . . . [over commerce and postal mails] are not confined to the instrumentalities of commerce, or the postal system known or in use when the Constitution was adopted, but they keep pace with the progress of the country, and adapt themselves to the new developments of time and circumstances. They extend from the horse with its rider to the stage, from the sailing vessel to the steamboat, from the coach and the steamboat to the railroad, and from the railroad to the telegraph, as these new agencies are successively brought into use to meet the demands of increasing population and wealth. They were intended for the government of the business to which they relate, at all times and under all circumstances." [2]

It is not necessary for passengers or goods to be in actual motion at every moment to give them the character of moving in interstate commerce. Questions may arise as to when goods are deemed to be "in interstate commerce."

### *(a) Goods intended for transit*

COE v. ERROL

116 U.S. 517 (1886)

A taxpayer named Coe owned two sets of logs. One set of logs had been cut and placed in the town of Errol, New Hampshire, on the bank of a stream to be floated down the river in the spring to another state. The second set of logs had been placed in the same river above the town of Errol and had floated down and was frozen in the river within the boundaries of the town of Errol. The town tax collector taxed Coe for both sets of logs. The taxpayer appealed.

---

[2] Pensacola Telegraph Co. v. Western Union Telegraph Co., 96 U.S. 1 (1877).

OPINION BY BRADLEY, J.

The question for us to consider . . . is, whether the products of a State (in this case timber cut in its forests) are liable to be taxed like other property within the State, though intended for exportation to another State, and partially prepared for that purpose by being deposited at a place of shipment. . . .

Do the owner's state of mind in relation to the goods, that is, his intent to export them, and his partial preparation to do so, exempt them from taxation? This is the precise question for solution.

There must be a point of time when they cease to be governed exclusively by the domestic law and begin to be governed and protected by the national law of commercial regulation, and that moment seems to us to be a legitimate one for this purpose, in which they commence their final movement for transportation from the State of their origin to that of their destination. When the products of the farm or the forest are collected and brought in from the surrounding country to a town or station serving as entrepot from that particular region, whether on a river or a line of railroad, such products are not yet exports, nor are they in process of exportation, nor is exportation begun until they are committed to the common carrier for transportation out of the State to the State of their destination, or have started on their ultimate passage to that State. Until then it is reasonable to regard them as not only within the State of their origin, but as a part of the general mass of property of that State, subject to its jurisdiction, and liable to taxation there. . . .

### *(b) Goods in transit*

NEW YORK, NEW HAVEN & HARTFORD RAILROAD COMPANY v. NOTHNAGLE

346 U.S. 128 (1953)

Nothnagle purchased a ticket from the New York, New Haven & Hartford Railroad Company for a journey from Meriden, Connecticut, to Fall River, Massachusetts, via New Haven, Connecticut. When the Meriden train reached New Haven, she gave her suitcase to a station porter to hold and take to the Fall River train. The porter failed to return the suitcase, and Nothnagle sued the Railroad in a Connecticut court. The appellate court of that state held that the liability of the Railroad was governed by Connecticut law on the theory that the journey in interstate commerce had been broken and that the transaction as to the suitcase and the porter was intrastate. The Railroad appealed, claiming that the Federal Interstate Commerce Act governed.

OPINION BY CLARK, J.

. . . We have little doubt that the transaction was incident to an interstate journey within the ambit of the Interstate Commerce Act. Neither continuity of interstate movement nor isolated segments of the trip can be decisive. "The actual facts govern. For this purpose, the destination intended by the passenger when he begins his journey and known to the carrier, determines the character of the commerce." In this case respondent undertook a journey from Connecticut to Massachusetts, with a temporary stopover for transfer along the way. And it goes unchallenged here that the redcap to whom she entrusted her baggage was a railroad employee performing functions, whether viewed as services in connection with an interrupted through trip from Meriden to Fall River or with the second unquestionably interstate leg of respondent's journey, incident to interstate travel and reached by the terms of the Interstate Commerce Act. . . . The Interstate Commerce Act, therefore, must control to whatever extent its provisions apply. . . .

### § 9:4. The Commerce Power and the General Welfare

Until 1937, the Supreme Court adhered to the concept that interstate commerce requires interstate movement and that the mere fact that it was intended to ship goods in interstate commerce in the future did not place the production of those goods within the reach of the interstate commerce power. During this period, Federal control was limited to the regulation of the facilities of interstate commerce and matters that were regarded as directly affecting the facilities or the interstate transit of goods, persons, or communications. Under this view of the commerce power, it is held that laws requiring safety devices on trains or limiting the hours of employment of trainmen on interstate trains are valid. A slightly less direct regulation of commerce but still clearly within the general area of regulation is the Federal Employers' Liability Act, which regulates the liability of employers engaged in interstate commerce when sued by employees for damages for industrial accidents arising out of their employment in interstate commerce.

With the decision of *National Labor Relations Board* v. *Jones & Laughlin Steel Corp.*,[3] the Supreme Court abandoned the limitation

[3] 301 U.S. 1 (1937).

of the early cases and then gradually expanded the concept of interstate commerce until it is now held to confer upon the Federal government the power to regulate any activity that has an effect on the national economic welfare. Instead of looking to see whether there is a crossing of a state line or any activity that directly affects persons or goods going across a state line, the Supreme Court now looks at the over-all national picture to see if the activity in question has an effect upon or is part of the national economic welfare or a significant segment thereof. Under this view, the power conferred by the interstate commerce power is now as broad as the economic needs of the nation.[4]

Does the right to "regulate" include the power to "prohibit"? Can Congress state that a particular article may no longer be sent in interstate channels? The argument was advanced that to regulate an activity required the continued existence of the activity, and that, while the activity might be restricted or qualified, it could not be stopped completely.

The Supreme Court rejected this argument and held that the power to regulate included the power to prohibit, since to regulate was to limit or restrict in some way and prohibition was merely the maximum or utmost limitation or restriction. The Supreme Court accordingly sustained federal statutes prohibiting the interstate shipment of articles that could cause harm if permitted to reach their destination or where the transportation was an essential step in the furthering of a wrong. The Court sustained federal laws prohibiting the interstate shipment of lottery tickets, impure or misbranded food and drugs, filled milk, obscene literature, women transported for an immoral purpose, stolen automobiles, and kidnapped persons. In adopting these statutes Congress was in effect exercising its commerce power to promote the health, safety, morals, and general welfare of the people. It could not do this directly and openly, for no police power to legislate for such ends is given to the Congress.

In 1916, Congress endeavored to end the evil of child labor by prohibiting the interstate shipment of the products of those factories and mines that had employed child labor at any time during the thirty days prior to the time the goods were offered for shipment. This Act was held unconstitutional in *Hammer* v. *Dagenhart,* 247 U.S. 251 (1918), by five of the nine justices, the Court holding that since the child labor-made goods were themselves harmless and since the harm of the employment of child labor had already been com-

[4] American Power & Light Co. v. S.E.C., 329 U.S. 90 (1946).

pleted before the goods were delivered for interstate shipment, the statute was not a regulation of commerce but was an attempt to regulate production, which was a matter reserved to the states.

Later, with the changing concept of the interstate commerce power so as to permit the regulation of activities within the production area on the ground that they affected interstate commerce, the *Hammer* decision was definitely undermined. Congress therefore again attempted to regulate production by specifying maximum hours and minimum wages and by prohibiting child labor. The constitutionality of this Fair Labor Standards Act came before the Court in *United States* v. *Darby,* reported below. Not only is this case significant in itself, but it is interesting to contrast it with the *Hammer* decision above, noting the way in which the dissenting minority view of the earlier case became the majority view, and also the ease with which the doctrine of the *Hammer* case is rejected as erroneous in spite of the ring of finality and confidence in its correctness found in this *Hammer* opinion.

## § 9:5. The Power to Prohibit Interstate Commerce

### *(a) Fair Labor Standards Act*

UNITED STATES v. DARBY

312 U.S. 100 (1941)

OPINION BY STONE, J.

The Fair Labor Standards Act set up a comprehensive legislative scheme for preventing the shipment in interstate commerce of certain products and commodities produced in the United States under labor conditions as respects wages and hours which fail to conform to standards set up by the Act. Its purpose . . . is to exclude from interstate commerce goods produced for the commerce and to prevent their production for interstate commerce, under conditions detrimental to the maintenance of the minimum standards of living necessary for health and general well-being; and to prevent the use of interstate commerce as the means of competition in the distribution of goods so produced, and as the means of spreading and perpetuating such substandard labor conditions among the workers of the several states. . . .

While manufacture is not of itself interstate commerce, the shipment of manufactured goods interstate is such commerce and the prohibition of such shipment by Congress is indubitably a regulation of the commerce. The power to regulate commerce is the power "to prescribe the rule by which commerce is governed.". . . It extends not only to those regulations which aid, foster and protect the commerce, but embraces those which prohibit it. . . . It is conceded that the power of Congress to prohibit transportation in interstate commerce includes noxious articles . . . stolen articles . . . kidnapped persons . . . and articles such as intoxicating liquor or convict-made goods, traffic in which is forbidden or restricted by the laws of the state of destination. . . .

But it is said that the present prohibition falls within the scope of none of these categories; that while the prohibition is nominally a regulation of the commerce its motive or purpose is regulation of wages and hours of persons engaged in manufacture, the control of which has been reserved to the states and upon which Georgia and some of the states of destination have placed no restriction; that the effect of the present statute is not to exclude the proscribed articles from interstate commerce in aid of state regulation . . . but instead, under the guise of a regulation of interstate commerce, it undertakes to regulate wages and hours within the state contrary to the policy of the state which has elected to leave them unregulated.

. . . Congress, following its own conception of public policy concerning the restrictions which may appropriately be imposed on interstate commerce, is free to exclude from the commerce articles whose use in the states for which they are destined it may conceive to be injurious to the public health, morals or welfare, even though the state has not sought to regulate their use. . . .

The motive and purpose of the present regulation are plainly to make effective the Congressional conception of public policy that interstate commerce should not be made the instrument of competition in the distribution of goods produced under substandard labor conditions, which competition is injurious to the commerce and to the states from and to which the commerce flows. The motive and purpose of a regulation of interstate commerce are matters for the legislative judgment upon the exercise of which the Constitution places no restriction and over which the courts are given no control. . . . Whatever their motive and purpose, regulations of commerce which do not infringe some constitutional prohibition are within the plenary power conferred on Congress by the Commerce Clause. Subject only to that limitation, . . . we conclude that the prohibition of the shipment interstate of goods produced under the forbidden substandard labor conditions is within the constitutional authority of Congress.

In the more than a century which has elapsed since the decision of *Gibbons* v. *Ogden,* these principles of constitutional interpretation have been so long and repeatedly recognized by this Court as applicable to the Commerce Clause, that there would be little occasion for repeating them now were it not for the decision of this Court twenty-two years ago in *Hammer* v. *Dagenhart,* 247 U.S. 251. In that case it was held by a bare majority of the Court over the powerful and now classic dissent of Mr. Justice Holmes setting forth the fundamental issues involved, that Congress was without power to exclude the products of child labor from interstate commerce. The reasoning and conclusion of the Court's opinion there cannot be reconciled with the conclusion which we have reached, that the power of Congress under the Commerce Clause is plenary to exclude any article from interstate commerce subject only to the specific prohibitions of the Constitution.

*Hammer* v. *Dagenhart* has not been followed. The distinction on which the decision was rested, that Congressional power to prohibit interstate commerce is limited to articles which in themselves have some harmful or deleterious property—a distinction which was novel when made and unsupported by any provision of the Constitution—has long since been abandoned. . . . The thesis of the opinion that the motive of the prohibition or its effect to control in some measure the use or production within the states of the article thus excluded from the commerce can operate to deprive the regulation of its constitutional authority has long since ceased to have force. . . .

The conclusion is inescapable that *Hammer* v. *Dagenhart* was a departure from the principles which have prevailed in the interpretation of the Commerce Clause both before and since the decision and that such vitality, as a precedent, as it then had, has long since been exhausted. It should be and now is overruled. . . .

## Questions for Discussion

1. Assume that the taxpayer in *Coe* v. *Errol* had placed a raft of logs in the river but, on learning of a log jam downstream, had pulled the logs back onto his land for the winter. Would the logs be subject to local taxation?

2. Would it make any difference in your answer to Question 1 if, after the logs had been pulled back on land, they remained there for two months, after which they were cut by the owner and used to build fences around the land?

3. A federal law prohibits interstate commerce in intoxicating liquor. A person buys a bottle of intoxicating liquor in Kentucky, puts it in his pocket, and then gets in a trolley car to ride from Kentucky to West Vir-

ginia. He is indicted for violating the federal statute prohibiting interstate commerce in intoxicating liquor. Is he guilty? *United States* v. *Simpson,* 252 U.S. 465 (1920).

4. A federal law prohibited exporting in foreign commerce munitions of war to countries where domestic violence existed. Such conditions existed in Mexico. Chavez carried 200 rounds of rifle ammunition from El Paso, Texas, to Mexico. He was prosecuted for violating the Act. He claimed that the Act was not applicable since he was carrying the property on his person. Was his defense good? *United States* v. *Chavez,* 228 U.S. 525 (1913).

5. The goods of a manufacturer had been taken from the factory loading platform and placed in the manufacturer's truck for delivery to another state. The truck after being loaded was sealed, the bill of lading was made out, and the truck was moved above two blocks from the loading platform and parked in a public street. The driver then removed the keys and took them to the garage where they were to be picked up by the drivers who were to take the truck on its interstate run. Before the two drivers reached the truck, the truck was broken open by the defendants and the contents were stolen. The defendants were prosecuted under a federal statute making it a crime to steal from any carrier or truck goods "moving as or which are part of an interstate shipment of freight." The defendants claimed that the shipment was not within the statute. Decide. *United States* v. *Gollin,* 176 F.2d 889 (CCA 3d, 1949).

6. A federal law provides that all aircraft must be licensed under the federal law. The owner and operator of a jet-propelled plane refuses to obtain a federal license on the ground that such planes were unknown when the Constitution was framed and that the Constitution does not delegate to Congress the power to regulate such planes. (a) Is he correct? Decide. (b) How does the Tenth Amendment affect your answer?

7. A federal law is adopted providing that no one may operate a television station without a federal license. Is the statute constitutional?

8. (a) Does the national government have power to adopt laws for the general welfare? (b) Can you object to a statute adopted under the commerce power on the ground that the purpose of the statute is to regulate the general welfare?

9. Is the Fair Labor Standards Act regarded in *United States* v. *Darby* as a commerce law or a welfare law?

10. Name five instances in which the federal commerce power has been used to advance health, welfare, morals, or safety. Why was it necessary to have a federal law on the subject?

11. The object of the framers of the Constitution in conferring the commerce power upon the national government was to protect that commerce from being throttled at the hands of the states. The power to regulate must therefore be construed to mean the power to foster and to pro-

tect, but not to include the power to prohibit the interstate shipment of any article not harmful in itself to those things surrounding it. Is this statement correct? Explain.

12. What is the practical justification for the view of the *Nothnagle* case?

13. The Byrnes Act of 1936, as amended in 1938, makes it a federal offense to "transport or cause to be transported in interstate or foreign commerce any person who is employed . . . for the purpose of obstructing on interfering by force or threats with:

> "1. Peaceful picketing by employees during any labor controversy affecting wages, hours or conditions of labor;
>
> "2. The exercise by employees of any of the rights of self-organization or collective bargaining."

Is this law constitutional?

14. A national law prohibits the shipments of deceptive, fraudulent, or harmful foods and drugs in interstate commerce. A shipment of eggs was sent by the Hippolite Egg Company to a bakery in another state. The shipment was seized by the federal authorities on the ground that it violated this law. The Hippolite Egg Company claimed that the federal authorities could not touch this shipment as it had already reached the person to whom it was sent and had thus left the channels of interstate commerce. Was this a good defense? *Hippolite Egg Co.* v. *United States*, 220 U.S. 45 (1911).

15. In *United States* v. *Appalachian Electric Co.*, 311 U.S. 377 (1940), the Court sustained the authority of the Federal Power Commission over hydroelectric projects on navigable waters. The Court stated: "In our view, it cannot properly be said that the constitutional power of the United States over its waters is limited to control for navigation. By navigation respondent means no more than operation of boats and improvement of the water-way itself. In truth the authority of the United States is the regulation of commerce on its waters. Navigability, in the sense just stated, is but a part of this whole. Flood protection, water-shed development, recovery of the cost of improvements through utilization of power are likewise parts of commerce control . . . that authority is as broad as the needs of commerce. . . ." (a) Does this case mark the end of the distinct identity of the power of Congress over navigable waters? (b) From what provision of the Constitution did the Congress derive its power over navigable waters? (c) Is the interpretation quoted above in harmony with the express language of the Constitution?

16. Is there a valid distinction between football and baseball with respect to whether they constitute interstate commerce?

17. Are national league football and baseball interstate commerce under the present decisions of the United States Supreme Court?

## Chapter 10

## REGULATION OF CARRIERS AND COMMUNICATIONS



### § 10:1. The Pattern of Regulation of Carriers

The history of the regulation of carriers by rail, highway, water, and air has tended to pass through three phases. There was first a period of uncontrolled competition and development. If government took any part in this period, it was for the purpose of encouraging the growth of the carriers. For example, national and local governments made free grants to railroads of more than two million acres of land and gifts of nearly $200,000,000. During this period of expansion, unfair trade practices developed until they reached such a point that pressure was brought to bear on government to correct the abuses. This introduced the second period of government action —a period of reform. In the course of time, the necessity for reform was either reduced or was regarded as less important and a rising consciousness of the need of adequate transportation facilities to further the general welfare developed. This brought in the third phase —encouragement subject to regulation—which in effect was a synthesis of the two preceding stages.

As the rate of invention and utilization of invention varied with the different types of carriers now known to us, it is only natural to find that the different phases were entered into at different times for the different classes of carriers. The political historian can also note that the speed with which a particular stage was passed or reached was influenced by the pressure that the friends or the foes of regulation were able to bring to bear upon the lawmaker. As a further modification, regulation adopted within recent decades tends to telescope the earlier stages into the later stage. This is a natural tendency, since the lawmaker has the advantage of the experience of the preceding years to guide him.

At present all carriers—rail, land, water, and air—are regulated by the national government and to a varying degree by the state governments. In general, the federal power is supreme wherever interstate commerce or traffic on navigable water is involved, and the field of intrastate commerce is left to the states for regulation. The dividing boundary line is not as clear cut as it may seem, and there is a substantial section of interstate commerce regulation that relates to details of such a local nature that the individual states may regulate them in the absence of a federal law on the subject.

The trends in the regulation of carriers have been a growing control by the national government and, within the national government, a growing control by the Interstate Commerce Commission. For many years, the placing of all transportation regulation in the hands of the Interstate Commerce Commission has been advocated. It must be recognized, however, that concentrating greater power in the hands of the Interstate Commerce Commission is not in itself a solution, but merely a step toward the solution, of the national transportation problem. Many difficulties arise in the way of reaching a single national policy.

## § 10:2. Regulation of Rail Carriers

Congress began its first regulation of carriers by rail by the Act of 1887, which created the Interstate Commerce Commission. Subsequent amendments have enlarged the Commission in size and in powers. It is now composed of eleven commissioners, each serving a ten-year term, who are appointed by the President with the advice and consent of the Senate. The jurisdiction of the Commission now extends over interstate railroads, including parlor car, sleeping car, and express car companies, bridges, ferries and lighters, interstate bus and motor truck transports, pipe lines carrying any product except water or natural gas, shipments partly by water and partly by other means, nonocean commodity transportation, and freight forwarders.

The Commission has power to regulate generally the services of the carriers subject to its jurisdiction. It has the authority to prohibit rebates and other discriminatory practices in order to enforce the duty to afford equal service. It may make regulations to secure the furnishing of car and terminal facilities upon an equal basis. It enforces the long and short haul clause, which is aimed at preventing geographic discrimination by carriers, by making it illegal for them "to charge or receive any greater compensation in the aggregate for the transportation of passengers or like kind of property for a shorter than for a longer distance over the same line, in the same direction, the shorter being included within the longer distance."

Because of its character as a common carrier, a public railroad can neither expand nor extend its facilities nor abandon any part or all of its operation without government approval. The Interstate Commerce Commission is given jurisdiction to approve such expansion or abandonment. It also has jurisdiction over the consolidation or merger of existing railroads.

In order to prevent the defrauding of the public through the sale of watered stock, the Commission is given jurisdiction over the issue of new securities.

The Commission is given the task of valuing the railroads. This has proved to be a very difficult and expensive job. Coupled with the valuation of the rail lines is the authority of the Commission to prescribe uniform accounting methods. Both of these powers serve in turn to aid the Commission in performing its rate-making function. The Commission is given authority to prescribe the rates for interstate railroads and may even go to the extent of directing the increase of intrastate state rates where the fact that they are lower than the interstate rate causes a discrimination against interstate commerce.

The Interstate Commerce Commission is given supervision over carriers to insure that they conform to safety appliance requirements. Beginning with the Federal Safety Appliance Act of 1893, Congress adopted a number of laws requiring certain types of safety devices on interstate carriers. At first these statutes expressly specified what appliances or devices were required. The Act of 1920 adopted a more liberal plan of merely giving the Commission authority to determine what safety devices should be used. This form of regulation is preferable to the earlier kind. Under the Act of 1920 the Commissioners may require the use of a new safety device without waiting for Congress to pass a law on that subject.

The power of the federal government to prescribe safety devices is not limited to the railroads that run in interstate commerce but also applies to intrastate trains making use of tracks on which run interstate trains.

A significant change in the policy of regulation was found in the Act of 1920, which can be regarded as bringing railroads into the third era of regulation. This Act authorized the Commission to prepare plans for the consolidation of existing rail lines into a fewer number of larger lines under a co-ordinated national railway system. Much has been done by investigation to further the consolidating of rail lines into fewer and larger systems of lines, but serious opposition has been encountered. The more prosperous lines and their stockholders and creditors are opposed to joining their good lines with other economically weaker lines. Consolidation is also opposed by the railroad employees. The combination of different lines by consolidation would reduce the number of jobs available for workers. Accordingly they oppose consolidation in the same manner that they generally oppose technological change.

The Act of 1920 also significantly gave the Commission power to approve agreements for freight pooling and division of earnings between competing railroads, thus exempting such agreements from the operation of the Sherman Antitrust Law. The scope of these exempt agreements was further extended by later legislation.

Another significant change in the powers of the Interstate Commerce Commission is based, not upon a change in the statute law, but in the present policy of the Supreme Court that it will accept as true findings of fact made by the Commission if they are supported by evidence appearing in the record. This changed the earlier rule that the Court could re-examine the case and make up its own mind on the basis of the record before it without regard to what the Commission had found.

### § 10:3. Regulation of Motor Carriers

The powers of the Interstate Commerce Commission were extended by the Act of 1935 to common and contract motor carriers. This distinction between the common and the contract carrier does not arise in the case of railroads, for all railroads that deal with the public are common carriers. In the case of motor carriers, however, some offer their services to the general public without discrimination. This is typically illustrated by the passenger bus, which makes its facilities available to any member of the public able to pay his fare as long as bus facilities are available. There is also the contract carrier, which carries in accordance with the contract that it makes with its customer. The contract carrier, however, is not bound to serve the public and can make or refuse to make a contract as it chooses. The contract carrier is illustrated by the moving-van company. This company ordinarily will try to have as much business as possible, but there is no requirement that it accept a moving job from everyone who seeks to obtain its services. The moving company can refuse to carry goods as it chooses.

In addition to these, there is the private carrier, illustrated by a manufacturing company that has its own fleet of trucks to do its own carrying rather than to make use of either a common or a contract carrier operated by someone else.

Because of these distinctions between the types of motor carriers, the authority of the Interstate Commerce Commission over them is not exactly the same as over railroads. As in the case of railroads, the Commission can prescribe accounting methods, safety devices, and traffic control, and can pass upon consolidations and mergers and the issuance of securities.

In the case of the common carrier, the Commission requires a certificate of convenience and public necessity; that is, the Commission will not permit an interstate common carrier to operate unless it is able to show that the services rendered by existing carriers to the public are inadequate and that the applicant has the ability to render the services needed by the public. In the case of the contract carrier, the Commission requires the obtaining of a permit, but this permit must be granted when the carrier establishes its fitness to perform the purposes in question. A contract carrier cannot be refused a permit on the ground that public convenience and necessity do not require the licensing of additional carriers.

The distinction between the types of carriers is also seen in the rate-making power. Here, by reason of the provisions of the statute, the Commission may fix minimum and maximum rates for common carriers but can set only minimum rates for the contract carriers. The Commission is expressly prohibited from fixing intrastate rates for the purpose of removing discrimination against interstate transportation. It has this power in the case of railroads, but not in the case of motor transports.

### *(a) Certificate of public convenience and necessity*

SCHAFFER TRANSPORTATION COMPANY v. INTERSTATE COMMERCE COMMISSION

355 U.S. 83 (1957)

The Schaffer Transportation Company, a motor carrier, applied to the Interstate Commerce Commission for a certificate of public convenience and necessity, which would authorize it to carry granite between designated states. The Commission refused to grant a certificate on the ground that there was railway service between the points in question and that such service was adequate. Schaffer appealed.

OPINION BY WARREN, C. J.

. . . The National Transportation Policy . . . requires the Commission to administer the Act so as to "recognize and preserve the inherent advantages" of each mode of transportation. . . . When a motor carrier seeks to offer service where only rail transportation is presently authorized, the inherent advantages of the proposed service are a critical factor which the Commission must assess. . . .

Rather than evaluate the benefit that Schaffer's proposed motor service might bring to the public, the Commission cast its first principal conclusion in terms of the adequacy of existing rail service, finding that service to be "reasonably adequate." . . . Of course, adequacy of rail service is a relevant consideration, but . . . "relative or comparative adequacy" of the existing service is the significant consideration when the interests of competition are being reconciled with the policy of maintaining a sound transportation system. The record here does not disclose the factors the Commission compared in concluding that existing rail service is "reasonably adequate." For example, the Commission has not determined whether there are benefits that motor service would provide which are not now being provided by the rail carriers, whether certification of a motor carrier would be "unduly prejudicial" to the existing carriers, and whether on balance the public interest would be better served by additional competitive service. To reject a motor carrier's application on the bare conclusion that existing rail service can move the available traffic, without regard to the inherent advantages of the proposed service, would give one mode of transportation unwarranted protection from competition from others. . . .

The Commission's second basic conclusion from the record was that the main purpose of the witnesses in supporting the application was the prospect of obtaining lower rates. For this reason the Commission discounted the testimony of these witnesses, apparently without even evaluating the claimed advantages of the proposed service other than reduced rates. We think this approach runs counter to the National Transportation Policy. The ability of one mode of transportation to operate with a rate lower than competing types of transportation is precisely the sort of "inherent advantage" that the congressional policy requires the Commission to recognize. . . .

### § 10:4. Regulation of Water Carriers

In the case of regulation of water transportation, the power of the Interstate Commerce Commission is similar to its power over motor carriers, although the federal power reaches further into the states because it is based not only on the commerce power but also on the power of Congress over navigable waters. With the exception of ocean transportation between the United States and a foreign country or possessions of the United States and the exception of bulk carriers such as tankers carrying not more than three classes of commodities, the Interstate Commerce Commission is given general jurisdiction over water transportation. It has the power to require the filing of reports and the following of standard methods of accounting. It can prohibit discrimination, rebates, and other improper business practices. It may fix maximum and minimum rates for common carriers and require of them certificates of public convenience and necessity. In the case of contract carriers, the Commission may fix only minimum rates and may require only permits.

### § 10:5. Regulation of Air Carriers

While control of water, air, and motor transportation has been brought under the power of the Interstate Commerce Commission, control of air commerce is still under a separate body called the Civil Aeronautics Board. This board is given power over air transports similar to the powers given to the Interstate Commerce Commission over motor transports. It requires that all planes be licensed as airworthy and that all pilots be licensed as qualified operators. Common carriers by air operating on scheduled runs must also obtain certificates of convenience and necessity. This is not required of other air carriers. The Civil Aeronautics Board is given the power to eliminate discrimination between carriers and to prescribe the rates that they may charge.

## § 10:6. State Regulation of Carriers

Within the area of intrastate commerce and the local fringes of interstate commerce or commerce upon navigable waters, the states may exercise their regulatory power. In consequence of this, each state has a railroad commission, a utilities commission, or another board that has as its purpose the exercise of powers similar to the Interstate Commerce Commission or to the Civil Aeronautics Board within the limited area in which the state may regulate commerce. As in the case of the federal agencies, these local agencies can prescribe methods of accounting, eliminate improper practices, pass upon security issues, pass upon the extension or the abandonment of operations or the consolidation or merger of carriers, and make rate and licensing regulations for common carriers and for contract carriers. A few states have even regulated private motor carriers, although these are generally not the subject of regulation.

The exact boundary line between federal and state regulatory power cannot be definitely drawn. In addition to the complexity of the constitutional problem of defining the boundary, Congress itself has established a nonuniform boundary line by authorizing the Interstate Commerce Commission to require the raising of intrastate rates in order to avoid discrimination against interstate rates in the case of railroads but prohibiting such control over intrastate rates in the case of motor carriers.

State regulation of railroads has not caused too much concern because such regulation has generally been restricted to local details that the state may regulate in the absence of congressional action, such as the adoption of safety appliances or the quarantine of shipments to permit health inspection. While these regulations, as in the case of any regulation, impose some degree of a burden on interstate commerce, the burden has not proven unduly great and has come to be accepted.

The motor carriers find themselves in a less fortunate position under state regulation. The motor carriers do not run on their own roadbed and their own right of way as do the railroads. The motor carrier must use a highway that does not belong to it. This gives the state a degree of control over motor traffic that it does not have over a railroad. In addition, since the highways are maintained and constructed by the state, there is the practical consideration that the carriers making use of those roads and contributing to their destruction by wear should in turn be subjected to regulations either to prevent such wear and tear or to make the carriers pay for some of the damage caused by use of the road.

Based upon these technical and practical considerations, the Supreme Court has gone a long way in sustaining state regulations of weight, size, construction, lighting, and other physical details of motor carriers and state forms of taxation and licensing. If the law of a state intentionally discriminates against interstate commerce, it is of course invalid; but, if it is fair on its face and applied to all alike, it is difficult to determine just where the boundary line of constitutionality is to be drawn. In addition, route regulation has also been sustained. Thus it is constitutional for a state to refuse permission to an interstate carrier to use a particular route through the state on the ground that that route is so heavily used that unreasonable traffic congestion would result. A number of states have also adopted a port of entry system under which carriers from another state are required to stop at designated border stations to be examined to see that they conform to state laws.

The combination of these different types of regulation has resulted in imposing upon the interstate motor carrier a very heavy burden. This in turn is giving rise to a demand that a federal law be adopted regulating such transportation. A great stumbling block to a federal program of motor transport regulation is the fact that the present state control is made the basis for obtaining money used in the maintenance of the roads. If the federal plan of regulation would not leave the states free to impose taxes or charges upon interstate carriers, it can be seen that the revenue sources of the states would be seriously affected. Whether this problem can be met by a system of federal subsidy or federal refund to the states of part of the federal license fees collected remains to be determined.

While analytically the regulation of aircraft presents a situation similar to that of motor transport in that there is the distinction between common and contract carriers, we do not find a burdensome system of state regulation of aircraft. While the states have power to prescribe regulations within a certain area, they have generally either stated that the federal law applied or have repeated word for word the provisions of the federal statute. Thus, apart from duplicate licensing in some instances, there has not proved to be any real burden upon air transport.

The existence of state regulations has not proved to be particularly burdensome in the case of water transportation. Here the state laws relate to local details of commerce that, while within the scope of the federal regulatory power, may also be regulated by the states as long as Congress does not act.

### § 10:7. Government Aid to Carriers

The picture of the regulation of carriers would not be complete without reference to the varied forms in which state and national governments have given aid to carriers.

Material aid is given motor transport by the roadbuilding activities of the states. These are sometimes financed by the state alone, or by the state with a federal subsidy. It is true that the various taxes and licenses paid by the carrier contribute more or less directly to the building of these highways. The cost of constructing the modern road is, however, far out of proportion to the contribution that each individual carrier makes for that purpose. Government may therefore be regarded as a real partner in motor transport, furnishing the roadbed while the carrier furnishes the moving stock.

Facilities are also supplied by government to aid water transport and air transport. The construction of harbors and landing fields, safety devices, beacon lights, and similar equipment is a necessary aid to such commerce.

The various carriers are also aided by government activities supplying them with information. Illustrations of this can be found in the service rendered by the United States Weather Bureau, the Coast and Geodetic Survey, the Hydrographic Office, the Naval Observatory, the Bureau of Standards, the Bureau of the Census, the Bureau of Foreign Commerce, the Bureau of Marine Inspection Navigation, the Bureau of Lighthouses, and other inspection or improvement-making or information-obtaining bureaus of the government. These services are of the greatest value to air and water carriers; if they were not furnished by the government, it would be necessary for carriers to obtain them at their own expense.

The carriers are to some extent aided by being given a partial legal monopoly. Refusal of government to issue a certificate of convenience and necessity to a newcomer in the transport field is an assurance to existing carriers in that field that they will not be faced with new competition so long as they render adequate service. While the fact that the carrier's rates are subject to regulation prevents them from making misuse of this monopoly power, the fact that they have such monopoly does enable them to operate more profitably than they could if such outside competition could not be excluded.

In the case of inland and coastal waters of the United States, this monopoly is placed on a national basis. Foreign vessels are not permitted to trade in these waters.

A common aid to carriers is the loaning of money to them. The R.F.C. and the P.W.A. have made extensive loans to railroads during depression years. In some respects this is merely a revival of the earlier government policy of encouraging railroad development by money and land grants.

The carriers have also been aided by gifts of government money made to them upon condition that they adhere to certain standards or perform certain services. These conditional gifts or subsidies may sometimes be concealed or indirect. This was the case with the contracts let by the United States Government for the carriage of air mail. It was commonplace that the contract price paid for such carriage was far in excess of the actual cost of performing the service. This differential between the cost of the service performed and the payment received was a subsidy to the carrier performing the contract. The modern trend is away from such indirect subsidies and toward the making of direct subsidies.

The greatest extension of this direct subsidy system is found in the provisions of the Merchant Marine Act, which, in the effort to further the development of an American merchant marine, has authorized the payment of both constructional and operational subsidies. As vessels may be constructed at a lower cost in foreign shipyards, it is provided that, if the vessel is built in an American yard and conforms to government regulations, the owner will be given a sum of money, subject to certain maximum limits, equal to the saving that he would have made if the vessel were constructed in a foreign yard. The vessels of foreign merchant marine are also operated at a lower cost, primarily because of the lower wages paid their seamen. To offset this, it is provided that a shipper whose vessel is operated in conformity with government regulations may receive from the government a sum of money equal to the difference between his operating costs and the costs of operating the vessel under a foreign registry. These two subsidies place the operator of the merchant marine vessel in a far better competitive position than he would hold if he had to face the direct competition of the lower construction and lower operating costs of foreign marine carriers.

Private ownership of carriers subject to regulation by the government has been the norm. This has been departed from in times of emergency. During World War I the railroads were operated by the government, and during World War II transportation generally was placed under the direction of a co-ordinator. Whether the future holds in store a system of government operation or ownership of carriers depends to a large degree upon the general economic conditions and the extent to which mere government regulation can cure such evils as the economic conditions then existing will bring.

There has been one notable exception to the rule that the federal government has not owned carriers. As a result of World War I, the United States Government found itself the owner of a number of inland waterway barges. Congress created the Inland Waterway Corporation to manage and operate them.

## § 10:8. Regulation of Communications

Communications were at first regulated by the states. Communications by wire, the telephone and the telegraph, were then placed under the Interstate Commerce Commission. When it made its appearance, communication by radio was placed under a Federal Radio Commission. The logical development then took place of transferring all communications by wire or wireless, including radio, to a single commission, the Federal Communications Commission, which now has such jurisdiction.

Apart from the differences in regulation made necessary because of the differences in the character of business regulated, the jurisdiction of the Federal Communications Commission is similar to that of the Interstate Commerce Commission. In the case of telephone and telegraph, the Federal Communications Commission is given jurisdiction to maintain the rates at a "just and reasonable" level and to eliminate discrimination between customers or geographical areas. The approval of the Commission is required for extensions, consolidations, or abandonment of lines.

The nature of radio communication has resulted in a number of special regulations. No one may broadcast without obtaining a federal license unless he is engaged only in intrastate broadcasting and his broadcast will not interfere with interstate transmission by other broadcasters. In order to obtain a license, it must be established that the granting of the license will further the "public interest, convenience, or necessity." The Commission can only grant a license for a limited period, and there is no assurance that it will be renewed at the expiration of that period.

The Commission is given power to determine the location of radio stations, to assign frequency bands to each station, to determine what services should be furnished by the station, and to prescribe the qualifications of the station operators.

While the federal act prohibits improper language or the advertising of lotteries and gift schemes, the Federal Communications Commission cannot set itself up as a censor of what is said over the air.

The Commission is given the difficult task of maintaining competition among radio broadcasters. This aim is furthered by denying the broadcasting chains the right to acquire more than one station in each service or broadcast area. In this respect the Federal Communications Commission contrasts with the Interstate Commerce Commission, which can permit certain combinations and agreements which would otherwise violate the antitrust law.

Further regulation is placed upon cable communication by the requirement that the President of the United States must approve the linking by cable of the United States with any other part of the world.

### *(a) Radio broadcasting*

#### FEDERAL COMMUNICATIONS COMMISSION v. SANDERS BROS. RADIO STATION

309 U.S. 470 (1940)

The Telegraph Herald applied for permission to construct a broadcast station. The respondent held a broadcasting station license and had operated a station for several years in the same city. It opposed granting an additional license on the ground that there was not sufficient advertising revenue or talent within the area to justify an additional station and that an additional station was not required by the public interest, convenience, or necessity. The proceeding was finally appealed by the Commission as petitioner to the Supreme Court.

OPINION BY ROBERTS, J.

. . . The respondent's proof showed that its station had operated at a loss; that the area proposed to be served by the Telegraph Herald was substantially the same as that served by the respondent and that, of the advertisers relied on to support the Telegraph Herald station, more than half had used the respondent's station for advertising.

. . . The Court of Appeals . . . entertained the appeal and held that one of the issues which the Commission should have tried was that of alleged economic injury to the respondent's station by the establishment of an additional station and that the Commission had erred in failing to make findings on that issue. It decided that, in the absence of such findings, the Commission's action in granting the Telegraph Herald permit must be set aside as arbitrary and capricious.

The petitioner's contentions are that under the Communications Act economic injury to a competitor is not a ground for refusing a broadcasting license. . . .

*First.* We hold that resulting economic injury to a rival station is not, in and of itself, and apart from considerations of public convenience, interest, or necessity, an element the petitioner must weigh, and as to which it must make findings, in passing on an application for a broadcasting license.

Section 307(a) of the Communications Act . . . directs that "the Commission, if public convenience, interest, or necessity will be served thereby, subject to the limitations of this Act, shall grant to any applicant therefor a station license provided for by this Act." This mandate is given meaning and contour by the other provisions of the statute and the subject matter with which it deals. The Act contains no express command that in passing upon an application the Commission must consider the effect of competition with an existing station. Whether the Commission should consider the subject must depend upon the purpose of the Act and the specific provisions intended to effectuate that purpose.

The genesis of the Communications Act and the necessity for the adoption of some such regulatory measure is a matter of history. The number of available radio frequencies is limited. The attempt by a broadcaster to use a given frequency in disregard of its prior use by others, thus creating confusion and interference, deprives the public of the full benefit of radio audition. Unless Congress had exercised its power over interstate commerce to bring about allocation of available frequencies and to regulate the employment of transmission equipment the result would have been an impairment of the effective use of these facilities by anyone. The fundamental purpose of Congress in respect of broadcasting was the allocation and regulation of the use of radio frequencies by prohibiting such use except under license.

In contradistinction to communication by telephone and telegraph, which the Communications Act recognizes as a common carrier activity and regulates accordingly in analogy to the regulation of rail and other carriers by the Interstate Commerce Commission, the Act recognizes that broadcasters are not common carriers and are not to be dealt with as such. Thus the Act recognizes that the field of broadcasting is one of free competition. The sections dealing with broadcasting demonstrate the Congress has not, in its regulatory scheme, abandoned the principle of free competition, as it has done in the case of railroads, in respect of which regulation involves the suppression of wasteful practices due to competition, the regulation of rates and charges, and other measures which are unnecessary if free competition is to be permitted.

An important element of public interest and convenience affecting the issue of a license is the ability of the licensee to render the best practicable service to the community reached by his broadcasts. That such ability may be assured the Act contemplates inquiry by the Commission, . . . into an applicant's financial qualifications. . . .

But the Act does not essay to regulate the business of the licensee. The Commission is given no supervisory control of the programs, of business management or of policy. In short, the broadcasting field is open to anyone, provided there be an available frequency over which he can broadcast without interference to others, if he shows his competency, the adequacy of his equipment, and financial ability to make good use of the assigned channel.

The policy of the Act is clear that no person is to have anything in the nature of a property right as a result of the granting of a license. Licenses are limited to a maximum of three years' duration, may be revoked, and need not be renewed. Thus the channels presently occupied remain free for a new assignment to another licensee in the interest of the listening public.

Plainly it is not the purpose of the Act to protect a licensee against competition but to protect the public. Congress intended to leave competition in the business of broadcasting where it found it, to permit a licensee who was not interfering electrically with other broadcasters to survive or succumb according to his ability to make his programs attractive to the public.

This is not to say that the question of competition between a proposed station and one operating under an existing license is to be entirely disregarded by the Commission, and indeed, the Commission's practice shows that it does not disregard that question. It may have a vital and important bearing upon the ability of the applicant adequately to serve his public; it may indicate that both stations,—the existing and the proposed—will go under, with the result that a portion of the listening public will be left without adequate service; it may indicate that, by a division of the field, both stations will be compelled to render inadequate service. These matters, however, are distinct from the consideration that, if a license be granted, competition between the licensee and any other existing station may cause economic loss to the latter. If such economic loss were a valid reason for refusing a license this would mean that the Commission's function is to grant a monopoly in the field of broadcasting a result which the Act itself expressly negatives, which Congress would not have contemplated without granting the Commission powers of control over the rates, programs, and other activities of the business of broadcasting.

We conclude that economic injury to an existing station is not a separate and independent element to be taken into consideration by the Commission in determining whether it shall grant or withhold a license.

### § 10:9. Regulation of Communication by Mail

Congress is authorized by the Constitution "to establish post offices and post roads" (Art. I, Sec. 8, Cl. 7). Under this power, Congress has entered the field of communication through the transportation of mail and the field of merchandise transportation through the carriage of parcels. In the case of the mail, transmission by the federal government has been made a monopoly. This has not been done in the case of parcel delivery.

In the exercise of the postal power, Congress may classify the various services according to their nature, impose different charges for each service, establish flat rates or zone rates, and deny persons the use of the mail for an improper purpose, such as the delivery of obscene, seditious, or fraudulent matter, lottery tickets, or illegally killed game. Denial of the use of the mail is also employed to enforce regulations of other phases of business, such as the denial of the use of the mails to interstate public utility holding companies failing to register with the Securities Exchange Commission.

The guarantee of freedom of the press, which is construed to include freedom of distribution of printed matter, does not bar the federal government from prohibiting the use of the mail in the above situations.

The fact that matter sent in the mail is physically in the possession of agents of the federal government does not give the federal government any greater right to open sealed letters or packages than it would have if they were in the sender's own possession. They are protected from unreasonable searches and seizures in the same manner as other documents and property. The federal government may and does charge a cheaper rate for unsealed mail, which may be opened by the postal authorities for inspection to determine whether the contents come within the classification of mail entitled to such lower rate.

## Questions for Discussion

1. At present, the regulation of interstate railroads, motor carriers, water carriers, freight forwarders, and pipe lines other than water or gas comes within the jurisdiction of the Interstate Commerce Commission; telephones, telegraphs, cables, and radio, within the jurisdiction of the Federal Communications Commission; electricity, gas, and pipe lines of natural gas under the Federal Power Commission; aviation under the Civil Aeronautics Board; shipping under the United States Maritime Commission; and gas and electric holding companies under the Securities and Exchange Commission. To what extent should these commissions be consolidated? Should all of them be combined into one commission? If not, why not?

2. It has been proposed to establish a new department in the federal government having control over transportation. Can a new secretary with cabinet rank and a new department be created by an act of Congress? Would the act be constitutional?

3. (a) Do you believe that railroads should be consolidated into several major systems? (b) Can Congress compel such consolidation?

4. (a) What is the present national policy towards carriers? (b) Is it the same with respect to each type of carrier?

5. What trend can be seen in the development of the administrative agencies having supervision over the various kinds of carriers?

6. (a) Is a railroad a public, private, or contract carrier? (b) What is the difference between these types of carriers? (c) What kind of carrier is a motor carrier? an air carrier? a water carrier?

7. Describe the organization and the powers of the Interstate Commerce Commission.

8. A stockyard owned a section of railroad trackage that it leased to an interstate railroad. By the terms of the lease the stockyard reserved the right to prohibit the railroad from transporting articles over the trackage. The Interstate Commerce Commission claimed that this authority to exclude was a violation of the Interstate Commerce Act. The stockyard claimed that it had the right to insert any terms in its lease since it was not

a carrier and was not subject to the Interstate Commerce Act. Is the claim of the company valid? *United States* v. *Baltimore & Ohio R.R.*, 333 U.S. 169 (1948).

9. What is the basis for the authority of the Interstate Commerce Commission with respect to (a) carriers by rail, (b) carriers by motor vehicle, and (c) carriers by water?

10. Would it be practical for the Interstate Commerce Commission to establish the same type of regulations for all motor carriers?

11. What pattern has been followed by the federal law requiring safety appliances on interstate commerce carriers? Appraise the merit of this trend.

12. (a) What is a "certificate of public convenience"? (b) When is it required and why? (c) How does it differ from a "certificate of fitness to operate"?

13. (a) What is the Civil Aeronautics Board? (b) What are its powers?

14. (a) To what extent do the states regulate carriers? (b) What is the constitutional basis for such regulation?

15. State A requires all motor vehicles entering the state to enter on certain designated roads and to stop at specified inspection stations. M operates a fleet of interstate trucks that ordinarily pass through State A without stopping. M objects to going along the designated routes as they are longer than the route that his trucks ordinarily follow, and he objects to stopping for inspection as this takes from one to four hours, depending upon the number of cars to be inspected. M claims that the state law is an unreasonable burden on interstate commerce and therefore void. Decide.

16. Compare the granting of the right to operate a railroad with the right to operate a radio station.

17. What is the constitutional basis for the national regulation of communications?

18. What pattern has been followed in the regulation of communications?

19. Describe the organization and the powers of the Federal Communications Commission.

20. (a) Does the Federal Communications Commission have control of rates, programs, and business activities of radio stations? (b) How does this compare with the control of the Interstate Commerce Commission over interstate railroads?

21. In *Federal Communications Commission* v. *Sanders Bros. Radio Station*, 309 U.S. 470 (1940), Justice Roberts stated: "In contradistinction to communication by telephone and telegraph, which the Communications

Act recognizes as a common carrier activity and regulates accordingly . . . the Act recognizes that broadcasters are not common carriers and are not to be dealt with as such. . . ." Why is this distinction made?

22. (a) For what reason can the use of the mails be denied? (b) Is this an interference with freedom of the press?

23. (a) What is the constitutional basis for the Merchant Marine Act of 1936? (b) Are its subsidy provisions valid?

24. (a) What subsidies are provided by the Merchant Marine Act? (b) Are they direct or indirect?

25. What aid is given to carriers by (a) the national government, (b) state governments, and (c) your own state?

26. (a) Should the national government subsidize interstate railroads? (b) Should it own them?

27. Should adequacy of existing service be the criterion of determining whether an application to operate as a common carrier should be refused? Is your answer affected by whether the applicant is the same type of carrier as existing carriers or a different type?

28. Are witnesses supporting an application for a license of a common carrier worthy of belief when they urge that the application be granted because it will result in lower rates to them?

## Chapter 11

# REGULATION OF COMBINATIONS

### Division A. The Sherman Act and Supplementary Legislation

§ 11:1. Federal Regulation
- (a) Parallel action—
  Theatre Enterprises v. Paramount Film Distributing Company

§ 11:2. Area of Application of the Sherman Act
- (a) Local transaction relating to transportation—
  United States v. Yellow Cab Co.
- (b) Local transaction relating to production—
  Mandeville Island Farms v. American Crystal Sugar Co.

§ 11:3. The Rule of Reason
- (a) The relevant market—
  United States v. E. I. du Pont de Nemours & Company

§ 11:4. Bigness and the Rule of Reason

### Division B. Tying and Interlocking Arrangements

§ 11:5. Tying Contracts
- (a) Tying of unrelated enterprises—
  Northern Pacific Railway Company v. United States

§ 11:6. Stock and Director Control
- (a) Stock ownership of customer corporation—
  United States v. E. I. du Pont de Nemours & Company

### Division C. Corporate Ownership and Structure

§ 11:7. Ownership of Property by Corporations
- (a) Limitations on ownership—
  Asbury Hospital v. Cass County

§ 11:8. Holding Companies
- (a) Dissolution of holding companies—
  American Power & Light Co. v. Securities and Exchange Commission

## Division A. The Sherman Act and Supplementary Legislation

### § 11:1. Federal Regulation

The rise of the modern American antitrust attitude dates from the period following the Civil War when the industrial and territorial expansion of the United States was accompanied by the cutthroat competition of "captains of industry." It is true that an earlier antimonopoly spirit can be seen, but this was opposition to royal monopoly. The special privileges given by the English crown to its favorites or to the famous trading companies did little to make monopolies popular with the general public. This attitude was not altered when England, as punishment for the Boston Tea Party, gave to the famous East India Company a monopoly over tea importation into the colonies. This early spirit of opposition to the royal monopolies can be seen in provisions of some of the state constitutions, such as the provision in the Constitution of Maryland of 1776 that "monopolies are odious, contrary to the spirit of free government and the principles of commerce, and ought not to be suffered."

It was after the Civil War, however, that the private monopoly appeared as a menace to the public welfare. Fortunes were made as industrial empires rose, often by means that were not merely unethical but actually unlawful. So widespread and corrupt were the practices of free enterprise that the adoption of a law to control business became a vital political issue in the 80's.

Finally, in 1890, the Sherman Act was adopted, declaring: "Every contract, combination in the form of trust or otherwise, or conspiracy, in restraint of trade or commerce among the several states, or with foreign nations, is hereby declared to be illegal." (Sec. 1) The Act also made it illegal for any person to "monopolize, or attempt to monopolize, or combine or conspire with any other person or persons, to monopolize any part of the [interstate or foreign] trade or commerce." (Sec. 2) The statute further provided that any person violating the law was guilty of a crime, that an injunction could be issued by the courts to stop his illegal acts, and that any person injured by his conduct could sue him for treble damages. This changed the common law under which an agreement in restraint of trade was unenforceable by the parties to the agreement but under which, as long as the parties continued to co-operate, neither the government nor any person injured had any legal basis for complaint.

The Sherman Act illustrates both the difficulties of government regulation of business and the defects in the drafting of a statute for that purpose. The statute in vague terms condemned combinations in "restraint" of interstate commerce and activities which monopolized that commerce. Without qualification, these were condemned in every instance without regard to whether or not the power created by the combination or monopoly was in fact exercised for the purpose or with the result of doing harm. Moreover, no recognition was given by the statute to the possibility that the public might have an interest in the continuation of a particular large-scale enterprise or combination.

The failure to recognize and make provision for these considerations led to judicial decisions that in effect whittled away substantial portions of the statute. In 1914 Congress adopted the Clayton Act in an effort to remedy this. In addition to these efforts to clarify or restate the object of the law, there have also been strong countercurrents that have as their object either the total abolition of antitrust legislation or the making of exceptions to the law in favor of particular groups or a particular practice. This countermovement has been fed by the necessity for mass production engendered by war. A great depression has also lent encouragement to the view that business should be left alone to work out its own problems free from antitrust prosecution, as seen in the provisions of the N.R.A. Codes that the antitrust laws should not be applicable. The rise of the international cartels and governmental commodity agreements have also added their arguments and their complications. The former effect restraints on competition which are beyond the power of any one nation to reach; while the latter are limitations on free competition approved by the very government, in the case of the United States, which declares restraints on trade to be illegal.

### *(a) Parallel action*

THEATRE ENTERPRISES v. PARAMOUNT FILM DISTRIBUTING COMPANY

346 U.S. 537 (1954)

Theatre Enterprises was a suburban motion picture theatre. It sued the Paramount Film Distributing Corporation and others, claiming that they violated the Sherman Anti-Trust Law by conspiring to restrict, for unreasonable periods, "first-run" pictures to downtown theatres. Theatre Enterprises proved that the defendants followed common or parallel practices in connection with the distribution of films.

OPINION BY CLARK, J.

. . . Petitioner approached each respondent separately, initially requesting exclusive first-runs, later asking for first-runs on a "day and date" basis. But respondents uniformly rebuffed petitioner's efforts and adhered to an established policy of restricting first-runs in Baltimore to the eight downtown theatres. Admittedly there is no direct evidence of illegal agreement between the respondents. . . . The various respondents advanced much the same reasons for denying petitioner's offers. . . .

The crucial question is whether respondents' conduct toward petitioner stemmed from independent decision or from an agreement, tacit or express. To be sure, business behavior is admissible circumstantial evidence from which the fact finder may infer agreement. . . . But this Court has never held that proof of parallel business behavior conclusively establishes agreement or, phrased differently, that such behavior itself constitutes a Sherman Act offense. Circumstantial evidence of consciously parallel behavior may have made heavy inroads into the traditional judicial attitude toward conspiracy; but "conscious parallelism" has not yet read conspiracy out of the Sherman Act entirely. . . .

## § 11:2. Area of Application of the Sherman Act

The Sherman Act is based upon the power of Congress to regulate interstate commerce. It therefore follows that monopolies or restraints of trade which are not "in interstate commerce" do not come within the condemnation of the federal act. While the great majority of states have enacted state antitrust laws, it is obvious that as a practical matter the state laws cannot cope with monopolies organized on a national basis.

At first the operation of the Sherman Act was severely handicapped when the Supreme Court held that a monopoly of manufacturing was not within the statute because manufacturing was a change of form and commerce was a change of place and the federal law could only operate upon monopolies affecting the latter. This concept and the distinction between manufacturing and commerce have been abandoned and it is now held that local transactions which will have a monopoly effect upon subsequent interstate transactions come within the operation of the Sherman Act.

### *(a) Local transaction relating to transportation*

UNITED STATES v. YELLOW CAB CO.
332 U.S. 218 (1947)

The Yellow Cab Company was charged with violating the Sherman Act through agreements relating to the transportation of (1) through passengers using taxi service to change from one train to another, and (2) passengers using taxi service between their homes and the railroad station.

OPINION BY MURPHY, J.

. . . It is said that the appellees have agreed that Yellow and Cab Sales will not compete with Parmalee for contracts with railroads or railroad terminal associations to transport passengers and their luggage between railroad stations in Chicago. . . . A great majority of the persons making interstate railroad trips which carry them through Chicago must disembark from a train at one railroad station, travel from that station to another some two blocks to two miles distant, and board another train at the latter point. The railroads often contract with the passengers to supply between-station transportation in Chicago. Parmalee then contracts with railroads and the railroad terminal associations to provide this transportation by special cabs carrying seven to ten passengers. Parmalee's contracts are exclusive in nature.

The transportation of such passengers and their luggage between stations in Chicago is clearly a part of the stream of interstate commerce. When persons or goods move from a point of origin in one state to a point of destination in another, the fact that a part of that journey consists of transportation by an independent agency solely within the boundaries of one state does not make that portion of the trip any less interstate in character. . . . That portion must be reviewed in its relation to the entire journey rather than in isolation. So viewed, it is an integral step in the interstate movement.

. . . Any attempt to monopolize or to impose an undue restraint on such a constituent part of interstate commerce brings the Sherman Act into operation. . . . The complaint accordingly states a violation of the Sherman Act in this respect. . . .

Finally, it is said that the appellees have conspired to control the principal taxi-cab operating companies in Chicago and to exclude others from engaging in transportation of interstate travellers to and from Chicago railroad stations. . . .

. . . Interstate commerce is an intensely practical concept drawn from the normal and accepted course of business. . . . We believe that the common understanding is that a traveller intending to make an interstate rail journey begins his interstate movement when he boards the train at the station and that his journey ends when he disembarks at the station in the city of destination. What happens prior or subsequent to that rail journey, at least in the absence of some special arrangement, is not a constituent part of the interstate movement. The traveller has complete freedom to arrive at or leave the station by [any means]. . . . Taxi-cab service is thus but one of the many that may be used. . . . From the standpoints of time and continuity, the taxi-cab trip may be quite distinct and separate from the interstate journey. To the taxi-cab driver, it is just another local fare. . . .

We do not mean to establish any absolute rule that local taxi-cab service to and from railroad stations is completely beyond the reach of the federal power or beyond the scope of the Sherman Act. . . .

All that we hold here is that when local taxi-cabs merely convey interstate train passengers between their homes and the railroad station in the normal course of their independent local service, that service is not an integral part of interstate transportation. And a restraint on or monopoly of that general local service, without more, is not proscribed by the Sherman Act. . . .

### *(b) Local transaction relating to production*

MANDEVILLE ISLAND FARMS v. AMERICAN CRYSTAL SUGAR CO.
334 U.S. 219 (1948)

Three California sugar refiners agreed among themselves to pay California sugar-beet farmers a uniform price for their crops. The refined sugar would be sold by the refiners in interstate markets. The petitioners, sugar-beet farmers, sued one of the refiners for treble damages under the Sherman Act on the theory that the agreement between the refiners was an illegal trust in violation of the Act.

OPINION BY RUTLEDGE, J.

. . . Petitioners' farms are located in northern California. . . . The only practical market available to beet farmers in that area was sale to one of three refiners. Respondent was one of these. Each season growers contract with one of the refiners to grow beets and to sell their entire crops to the refiner under standard form contracts drawn by it. Since prior to 1939 petitioners have thus contracted with respondent.

The refiners control the supply of sugar beet seed. Both by virtue of this fact and by the terms of the contracts, the farmers are required to buy seed from the refiner. The seed can be planted only on land specifically covered by the contract. Any excess must be returned to the refiner in good order at the end of the planting season.

. . . Sometime before the 1939 season the three refiners entered into an agreement to pay uniform prices for sugar beets. . . . The refiners adopted identical form contracts and began to compute beet prices on the basis of the average net returns of all three rather than the separate returns of the purchasing refiner.

. . . Since the refiners controlled the seed supply and the only practical market for beets grown in northern California, when the new contracts were offered to the farmers, they had the choice of either signing or abandoning sugar beet farming. . . . Because beet prices were determined for the three seasons with reference to the combined returns of the three refiners, the prices received by petitioners for those seasons were lower than if respondent, the most efficient of the three, had based its prices on its separate returns. . . .

[The respondent claimed that the growing, purchasing, and refining of sugar beets were local activities and not within the reach of the Sherman Act and that no illegal practice occurred in the subsequent interstate distribution of the refined sugar.]

. . . The broad form of respondent's argument cannot be accepted. It is a reversion to conceptions formerly held but no longer effective to restrict either Congress' power . . . or the scope of the Sherman Act's coverage. The artificial and mechanical separation of "production" and "manufacturing" from "commerce," without regard to their economic continuity, the effects of the former two upon the latter, and the varying methods by which the several processes are organized, related and carried on in different industries or indeed within a single industry, no longer suffices to put either production or manufacturing and refining processes beyond reach of Congress' authority or of the statute.

It is true that the first decision under the Sherman Act applied those mechanical distinctions with substantially nullifying effects for coverage both of the power and of the Act. *United States* v. *E. C. Knight Co.*, 156 U.S. 1. That case involved the refining and interstate distribution of sugar. But because the refining was done wholly within a single state, the case was held to be one involving "primarily" only "production" or "manufacturing," although the vast part of the sugar produced was sold and shipped interstate, and this was the main end of the enterprise. The interstate distributing phase however was regarded as being only "incidentally," "indirectly" or "remotely" involved; and to be "incidental," "indirect" or "remote" was to be, under the prevailing climate, beyond Congress' power to regulate, and hence outside the scope of the Sherman Act.

. . . The *Knight* decision made the statute a dead letter for more than a decade and, had its full force remained unmodified, the Act today would be a weak instrument, as would also the power of Congress, to reach evils in all the vast operations of our gigantic national industrial system antecedent to interstate sale and transportation of manufactured products.

. . . It is clear that the agreement is the sort of combination condemned by the Act, even though the price-fixing was by purchasers, and the persons specially injured under the treble damage claim are sellers, not customers or consumers. And even if it is assumed that the final aim of the conspiracy was control of the local sugar beet market, it does not follow that it is outside the scope of the Sherman Act. For monopolization of local business, when achieved by restraining interstate commerce, is condemned by the Act. . . . And a conspiracy with the ultimate object of fixing local retail prices is within the Act, if the means adopted for its accomplishment reach beyond the boundaries of one state.

. . . The statute does not confine its protection to consumers, or to purchasers, or to competitors, or to sellers. Nor does it immunize the outlawed acts because they are done by any of these. . . . The Act is comprehensive in its terms and coverage, protecting all who are made victims of the forbidden practices by whomever they may be perpetrated.

. . . Nor is the amount of the nation's sugar industry which the California refiners control relevant, so long as control is exercised effectively in the area concerned. . . .

. . . Under the facts characterizing this industry's operation and the tightening of controls in this producing area by the new agreements and understandings, there can be no question that their restrictive consequences were projected substantially into the interstate distribution of the sugar. . . .

Even without the uniform price provision and with full competition among the three refiners, their position is a dominating one. The growers' only competitive outlet is the one which exists when the refiners compete among themselves. There is no other market. The farmers' only alternative to dealing with one of the three refiners is to stop growing beets. They can neither plant nor sell except at the refiners' pleasure and on their terms. The refiners thus effectively control the quantity of beets grown, harvested and marketed, and consequently of sugar sold from the area in interstate commerce, even when they compete with each other. They dominate the entire industry. And their dominant position, together with the obstacles created by the necessity for large capital investment and the time required to make it productive, makes outlet through new competition practically impossible. . . . A tighter or more all-inclusive monopolistic position hardly can be conceived.

. . . Those monopolistic effects not only deprived the beet growers of any competitive opportunity for disposing of their crops by the immediate operation of the uniform price provision; they also tended to increase control over the quantity of sugar sold interstate; and finally by the tie-in provision they interlaced those interstate effects with the price paid for the beets.

These restrictive and monopolistic effects, resulting necessarily from the practices allegedly intended to produce them, fall squarely within the Sherman Act's prohibitions. . . .

### § 11:3. The Rule of Reason

The general approach of the Supreme Court to the trust problem has been that an agreement or a contract is not automatically or *per se* to be condemned as a restraint of interstate commerce merely because it creates a power or a potential to monopolize interstate commerce. It is only when the restraint actually imposed on interstate commerce is unreasonable that the practice is unlawful. In applying this "rule of reason," it is obvious that the court enters upon a controversial field. The establishing of the restraint by the parties to the restraining agreement may be regarded by them as an essential step in the stabilization of their industry and as a matter of enlightened self-interest. To the competitors or the general public who might be adversely affected by the application of this restraint, the restraint is "unreasonable."

The court has also sought to strengthen its application of the "rule of reason" by considering that it should not literally apply the statute in every case if to do so would harm the public interest or public welfare. This is not a separate, independent reason. It is merely a restatement of the rule of reason and, like that rule, turns upon the consideration of whether the public would be better or worse off if the restraint in question were prohibited or allowed.

The decision of these points is not one of law but one of applied economics or the science of governing. It hinges on one's attitude toward large-scale enterprise, free enterprise, the rights of the small producer, the rights of the consumer, and other equally vague and nonmeasurable standards.

In some instances the court has not followed this principle of the rule of reason and of public welfare but has adopted the direct approach that a certain type of transaction is illegal regardless of the circumstances or the consequences of such agreement. Thus a price-fixing agreement was held by the court to be illegal, although the court recognized the right of a seller to indicate to his buyer that, unless the buyer maintained a certain resale price, the seller would not sell to him in the future. As will be discussed, this prohibition against resale price maintenance has by statute been partly repealed.

### *(a) The relevant market*

UNITED STATES v. E. I. DU PONT DE NEMOURS & COMPANY
351 U.S. 377 (1956)

The United States sued du Pont to enjoin it from monopolizing the cellophane market in violation of Section 2 of the Sherman Anti-Trust Act. Du Pont contended that its domination of cellophane was not the criterion since there were substitutes for cellophane, and that accordingly it did not violate the Act unless it was found to dominate the general market for flexible packaging materials.

OPINION BY REED, J.

. . . If cellophane is the "market" that du Pont is found to dominate, it may be assumed it does have monopoly power over that "market." Monopoly power is the power to control prices or exclude competition. It seems apparent that du Pont's power to set the price of cellophane has been limited only by the competition afforded by other flexible packaging materials. Moreover, it may be practically impossible for anyone to commence manufacturing cellophane without full access to du Pont's technique. However, du Pont has no power to prevent competition from other wrapping materials. The trial court consequently had to determine whether competition from the other wrappings prevented du Pont from possessing monopoly power in violation of § 2. . . .

If a large number of buyers and sellers deal freely in a standardized product, such as salt or wheat, we have complete or pure competition. Patents, on the other hand, furnish the most familiar type of classic monopoly. As the producers of a standardized product bring about significant differentiations of quality, design, or packaging in the product that permit differences of use, competition becomes to a greater or less degree incomplete and the producer's power over price and competition greater over his article and its use, according to the differentiation he is able to create and maintain. A retail seller may have in one sense a monopoly on certain trade because of location, as an isolated country store or filling station, or because no one else makes a product of just the quality or attractiveness of his product, as for example in cigarettes. Thus one can theorize that we have monopolistic competition in every nonstandardized commodity with each manufacturer having power over the price and production of his own product. However, this power that, let us say, automobile or soft-drink manufacturers have over their trademarked products is not the power that makes an illegal monopoly. Illegal power must be appraised in terms of the competitive market for the product.

Determination of the competitive market for commodities depends on how different from one another are the offered commodities in character or use, how far buyers will go to substitute one commodity for another. For example, one can think of building materials as in commodity competition but one could hardly say that brick competed with steel or wood or cement or stone in the meaning of Sherman Act litigation; the products are too different. . . . On the other hand, there are certain differences in the formulae for soft drinks but one can hardly say that each one is an illegal monopoly. Whatever the market may be, we hold that control of price or competition establishes the existence of monopoly power under § 2. Section 2 requires the application of a reasonable approach in determining the existence of monopoly power just as surely as did § 1. . . .

. . . Where there are market alternatives that buyers may readily use for their purposes, illegal monopoly does not exist merely because the product said to be monopolized differs from others. If it were not so, only physically identical products would be a part of the market. To accept the Government's argument, we would have to conclude that the manufacturers of plain as well as moistureproof cellophane were monopolists, and so with films such as Pliofilm, foil, glassine, polyethylene, and Saran, for each of these wrapping materials is distinguishable. . . .

The "market" which one must study to determine when a producer has monopoly power will vary with the part of commerce under consideration. The tests are constant. That market is composed of products that have reasonable interchangeability for the purposes for which they are produced—price, use and qualities considered. While the application of the tests remains uncertain, it seems to us that du Pont should not be found to monopolize cellophane when that product has the competition and interchangeability with other wrappings. . . .

### § 11:4. Bigness and the Rule of Reason

The question of whether bigness is in itself illegal has caused the court much difficulty in applying Section 2 of the Sherman Act. In view of the marked trend toward concentration of economic power, few questions have greater bearing on business and on the national economy in general.

Unlike the first section of the Act, Section 2 does not require an agreement between two or more persons to establish a violation of the law. Under Section 2, one man or corporation may violate the law if he or it monopolizes or attempts to monopolize interstate commerce.

If monopoly means merely such control of a large portion of production as enables the producer to set his own price without fear of competition, the law automatically condemns the man who is the first to manufacture a particular commodity or the man who is the only producer of a given commodity within a particular competitive area. It would be an undesirable law that would make such a monopoly illegal without requiring proof of something harmful to the public.

The Supreme Court recognized this problem in *United States* v. *Griffiths*, 334 U.S. 100 (1948), in which it stated: "Any one who owns and operates the single theatre in a town, or who acquires the exclusive right to exhibit a film, has a monopoly in the popular sense. But he usually does not violate § 2 of the Sherman Act unless he has acquired or maintained his strategic position, or sought to expand his monopoly, or expanded it by means of those restraints of trade which are cognizable under § 1."

Thus interpreted, Section 2 is unnecessary since bigness is not an offense under Section 2 unless the big company has committed acts that would be unlawful under Section 1 regardless of the size of the wrongdoer.

In *United States* v. *Paramount Pictures*, 334 U.S. 131 (1948), the court held that the legality of vertical integration of companies engaged in different levels of production and distribution did not automatically violate the Sherman Act because of bigness, but that the legality "turns on (1) the purpose or intent with which it [the integration] was conceived, or (2) the power it creates and the attendant purpose or intent. . . ." This provides still a different test and makes bigness illegal only if coupled with intent. Analytically this intent may be an intent to do acts that are illegal under Section 1, in which case the standard is the same as recognized in *United States* v. *Griffiths*. It might also be an intent to exclude competition, not through any improper practices, but merely through an economically superior position.

Both of these cases recognized that Section 2 would be violated by the mere existence of the power, although not exercised, to exclude competition when it was desired to do so "provided it is coupled with the purpose of intention to exercise that power." If the proviso means that bigness becomes unlawful when it intends to make use of its natural position of economic superiority to dominate a market, the rule is absurd. If it has this meaning, it is in effect a command that no enterprise may grow beyond the point where it controls more than an unspecified percentage of the total product sold within the particular marketing area. If the intent must be an intent to use improper means, there is then an intention to violate Section 1.

After seventy years of litigation, the question remains substantially unanswered as to whether bigness, unattended by unlawful acts or purposes, is a violation of the antitrust law. The decision in the

*Columbia Steel Company* case,[1] in which both vertical and horizontal integration were held not to violate the Sherman Act, is a strong indication that the Supreme Court has turned away from the possibility of condemning bigness per se. Where bigness is achieved by horizontal or vertical integration, as distinguished from other forms of growth, the decisions here noted have been changed by statute. Section 7 of the Clayton Act has been amended to provide that "no corporation subject to the jurisdiction of the Federal Trade Commission shall acquire the whole or any part of the assets of another corporation engaged also in commerce, where in any line or commerce in any section of the country, the effect of such acquisition may be substantially to lessen competition, or to tend to create a monopoly." [2]

## Questions for Discussion

1. What was the origin of the antimonopoly movement?

2. (a) Can you explain why monopolies are prohibited at the same time that government gives public utilities a monopoly? (b) Can the argument in favor of the public utility monopoly be extended to basic industries? Would it affect your answer if the nation were at war?

3. What is the constitutional basis for the Sherman Act?

4. In *Appalachian Coal Inc.* v. *United States,* 288 U.S. 344 (1933), the Supreme Court stated that the Sherman Act possessed "a generality and adaptability comparable to that found in constitutional provisions. . . ." How does this compare with the rule that a statute proscribing a crime is unconstitutional unless it specifically states just what is prohibited so that a reasonable man will be able to know what act is unlawful and not permitted?

5. Does the decision in the *Mandeville* case depend upon the price at which the beet sugar was sold in interstate markets?

6. In the *Mandeville* case the Court states: "Because beet prices were determined for the three seasons with reference to the combined returns of the three refiners, the prices received by petitioners for those seasons were lower than if respondent, the most efficient of the three, had based its prices on its separate returns." Would the decision have been different if the respondent had been the least efficient?

---

[1] United States v. Columbia Steel Co., 334 U.S. 495 (1948). See also concurring opinion of Douglas, J., in Standard Oil Company v. United States, 337 U.S. 293 (1949).

[2] 15 U.S.C. § 18. In the light of the modern interpretation of the commerce power, see § 9:4, this provision is applicable to corporations that deal in, or manufacture products that move in interstate commerce and is not limited to transportation companies.

7. Assume that the three refiners in the *Mandeville* case were able to show that the prices they paid the beet farmer were still higher than prices paid to such farmers in other states. Would this have affected the decision of the Court?

8. What is the difference between determining the applicability of the commerce clause in terms of "substantial" relation of the object regulated to interstate commerce and in terms of "direct" or "proximate" effect upon interstate commerce of the activity to be regulated?

9. Does the *Mandeville* case give to the Sherman Act the same meaning that it had at the time of its adoption?

10. By the end of the nineteenth century, twenty-six trusts controlled 80% or more of the production within the several industries. The American Can Company, American Sugar Refining Company, The American Tobacco Company, The Corn Products Refining Company, The International Harvester Company, The National Cash Register Company, The Standard Oil Company, and The United Shoe Machine Company each controlled 90% or more of the production in its field. (a) To what extent was the appearance of these powerful combinations the result of the decision of the United States in *United States* v. *E. C. Knight*? (b) What would have been the effect on the American economy if the case of *United States* v. *Mandeville Farms* had been decided in 1895 instead of 1947? Would this have been better for the peacetime economy? For preparedness in time of war?

11. (a) What is the concept of the Congress power that is followed in the *Mandeville* case? (b) When may Congress regulate a local activity in the light of this decision?

12. Is the Sherman Act limited to agreements between sellers raising the price at which commodities are sold to the public?

13. Assume that a traveler through Chicago must go from one station to another in order to catch his connecting train. Is such a person moving in interstate commerce when he stops in a railroad restaurant to have lunch during the delay in connecting train service?

14. Would it make any difference in your answer to Question 13 if the traveler went to a motion-picture house near the railroad station to spend the time until his connecting train should arrive?

15. How does the decision in the *Yellow Cab* case compare with *Coe* v. *Errol*, page 99?

16. Is vertical integration by one enterprise legal?

17. Is the purchase of a competitor's business illegal on the ground that it removes competition and is therefore a restraint of trade?

18. What is the relationship between the rule of reason and the concept of the "relevant market?"

19. Does large-scale enterprise make savings that it passes on to the consumer?

20. Is large-scale enterprise as efficient as it theoretically could be?

21. What determines the boundaries of the "relevant market?"

22. Assume that size or "bigness" is the economic evil to be prevented. Draft a sentence defining what is to be outlawed. Examine your draft to see if it is clear and precise or if it is capable of more than one meaning.

23. Could Congress amend the Sherman Act so as to make mere size illegal?

24. What determines when conduct is per se unreasonable or a violation of the Sherman Act and when the answer depends upon the circumstances of the case?

25. What is the administrative advantage of determining that a practice is per se a violation of the Sherman Act?

26. In order to prove the existence of an illegal monopoly, is it necessary to show (a) that interstate commerce throughout the United States is affected or (b) that a substantial portion of the national production of the commodity concerned is affected?

27. The National Dairy Products Corporation was organized in 1923 and the Borden Company in 1938. They controlled the produce of over three million dairy farms and dominated the distribution of milk products throughout the country. When the earlier company was formed in 1923, the dairy farmer received 52¢ and the distributor 48¢ of every dollar paid by the consumer public for milk. In 1933 the share of the farmer had dropped to 35¢, while that of the distributor had increased to 65¢. While retail prices dropped 20%, the price received by the farmers from the distributors of milk dropped 50%. The hearings of the National Economic Committee revealed that National Dairy made a 13% profit during the depth of the depression, when other industries were suffering loss, and that the salaries paid the officials in the distributor companies exceeded those paid in other food commodities. (a) Does this situation present a case coming within the Sherman Act? (b) Can the rule of reason be applied here?

28. Is it unlawful for one producer or manufacturer to fix the prices that he charges and for other producers and manufacturers to follow his price schedule without any prior agreement to do so?

29. "The inevitable trend of business is toward monopoly." (a) If you agree, what should be done to the Sherman Act? (b) If the Sherman Act is repealed, can any safeguard be devised to take its place?

30. Is there any practical difference between the result of parallel action and concerted action?

## Division B. Tying and Interlocking Arrangements

### § 11:5. Tying Contracts

The Clayton Act prohibits the tie-in sale or tie-in lease by which the person buying or renting goods agrees that he will only use with such goods other materials sold or leased by the other party. The Act also prohibits exclusive dealer agreements by which a dealer agrees not to handle a competitor's articles. These tie-in and exclusive dealer arrangements are not absolutely prohibited, but only where their effect "may be to substantially lessen competition or tend to create a monopoly in any line of commerce." By virtue of this qualification, a provision that a person leasing machinery shall use only the materials furnished by the lessor is a lawful restriction if the nature of the materials and the machine is such that the machine will not operate with the materials produced or offered by any other person. Where, however, the materials furnished by any other competitor would be equally satisfactory, the agreement is illegal. Thus an agreement that the lessee of office machinery should only use the paper sold by the lessor for that type of office machine was illegal where it was shown that any other seller could supply paper of suitable quality.

The partial prohibition of the tie-in and exclusive dealer agreements is expressly stated by the statute to be limited by the right of any seller to "select [his] own customers in bona fide transactions and not in restraint of trade." There has also been a judicial trend to approve such agreements where the seller did not hold a dominant position in the market.

#### *(a) Tying of unrelated enterprises*

NORTHERN PACIFIC RAILWAY COMPANY v. UNITED STATES

356 U.S. 1 (1958)

The Northern Pacific Railway Company owns large tracts of land which it had received as federal grants to aid its original construction. It sold and leased several million acres of this land by deeds and leases that contained "preferential routing clauses" by which the grantees and lessees agreed to ship any of their produce or manufactured goods on the Northern Pacific as long as it offered rates and services equal to any competing carrier. The United States government brought suit against the Railroad to have the "preferential routing clauses" declared void as violations of the Sherman Anti-Trust Act.

Opinion by Black, J.

. . . There are certain agreements or practices which because of their pernicious effect on competition and lack of any redeeming virtue are conclusively presumed to be unreasonable and therefore illegal without elaborate inquiry as to the precise harm they have caused or the business excuse for their use. This principle of per se unreasonableness not only makes the type of restraints which are proscribed by the Sherman Act more certain to the benefit of everyone concerned, but it also avoids the necessity for an incredibly complicated and prolonged economic investigation into the entire history of the industry involved, as well as related industries, in an effort to determine at large whether a particular restraint has been unreasonable—an inquiry so often wholly fruitless when undertaken. Among the practices which the courts have heretofore deemed to be unlawful in and of themselves are price fixing, . . . division of markets, . . . ; group boycotts, . . . ; and tying arrangements, *International Salt Co.* v. *United States,* 332 U.S. 392. . . .

For our purposes a tying arrangement may be defined as an agreement by a party to sell one product but only on the condition that the buyer also purchases a different (or tied) product, or at least agrees that he will not purchase that product from any other supplier. Where such conditions are successfully exacted competition on the merits with respect to the tied product is inevitably curbed. Indeed "tying agreements serve hardly any purpose beyond the suppression of competition. . . ." They deny competitors free access to the market for the tied product, not because the party imposing the tying requirements has a better product or a lower price but because of his power or leverage in another market. At the same time buyers are forced to forego their free choice between competing products. For these reasons "tying agreements fare harshly under the laws forbidding restraints of trade. . . ." They are unreasonable in and of themselves whenever a party has sufficient economic power with respect to the tying product to appreciably restrain free competition in the market for the tied product and a "not insubstantial" amount of interstate commerce is affected. . . . Of course where the seller has no control or dominance over the tying product so that it does not represent an effectual weapon to pressure buyers into taking the tied item any restraint of trade attributable to such tying arrangements would obviously be insignificant at most. As a simple example, if one of a dozen food stores in a community were to refuse to sell flour unless the buyer also took sugar it would hardly tend to restrain competition in sugar if its competitors were ready and able to sell flour by itself.

In this case we believe the district judge was clearly correct in entering summary judgment declaring the defendant's "preferential routing" clauses unlawful restraints of trade. We wholly agree that the undisputed facts established beyond any genuine question that the defendant possessed substantial economic power by virtue of its extensive landholdings which it used as leverage to induce large numbers of purchasers and lessees to give it preference, to the exclusion of its competitors, in carrying goods or produce from the land transferred to them. Nor can there be any real doubt that a "not insubstantial" amount of interstate commerce was and is affected by these restrictive provisions. . . .

. . . The "preferential routing" clauses conferred no benefit on the purchasers or lessees. While they got the land they wanted by yielding their freedom to deal with competing carriers, the defendant makes no claim that it came any cheaper than if the restrictive clauses had been omitted. In fact any such price reduction in return for rail shipments would have quite plainly constituted an unlawful rebate to the shipper. So far as the Railroad was concerned its purpose obviously was to fence out competitors, to stifle competition. While this may have been exceedingly beneficial to its business, it is the very type of thing the Sherman Act condemns. In short, we are convinced that the essential prerequisites for treating the defendant's tying arrangements as unreasonable "*per se*" were conclusively established below and that the defendant has offered to prove nothing there or here which would alter this conclusion. . . .

## § 11:6. Stock and Director Control

The Clayton Act, as amended, also prohibits the purchase by a corporation of the stock of another corporation engaged in commerce where the effect may be to lessen competition substantially or tends to create a monopoly. The Act states that this does not prohibit purchase merely for the purpose of investment or purchase where there is no lessening of competition. This section does not prohibit the creation of a subsidiary corporation; nor the acquisition of stock in another company, which, though manufacturing or selling the same or a similar article, does not sell within the same price range or within the same geographic market.

The Clayton Act does not prohibit the holding of stock in competing corporations by the same person. It is possible for a group of individuals to control several corporations by virtue of the fact that they hold the controlling shares in each of them. As far as any formal action is concerned, these corporations would be separate and independent; but as they would all be run following the pattern established by the individuals holding the controlling shares in each of them, it is obvious that the same control would be present as though the corporations had joined in a prohibited monopoly. While the Clayton Act prohibits the director of one corporation from being a director of another competing corporation engaged in commerce, this prohibition is not effective in checking the monopoly potential of interlocking private stockholding.

### *(a) Stock ownership of customer corporation*

UNITED STATES v. E. I. DU PONT DE NEMOURS & COMPANY
353 U.S. 586 (1957)

In 1917 to 1919, du Pont acquired a 23 per cent stock interest in General Motors. During the following years, General Motors bought all its automotive finishes and fabrics from du Pont. In 1949, the United States claimed the effect of the stock acquisition had been to lessen competition in interstate commerce on the theory that the sales to General Motors had not been the result of successful competition but were the result of the stock ownership, and therefore such stock ownership violated the Clayton Act. The United States brought an action against du Pont, General Motors, and others. From a decision in their favor, the United States appealed.

OPINION BY BRENNAN, J.

. . . The primary issue is whether du Pont's commanding position as General Motor's supplier of automotive finishes and fabrics was achieved on competitive merit alone, or because its acquisition of the General Motors' stock, and the consequent close intercompany relationship, led to the insulation of most of the General Motors' market from free competition, with the resultant likelihood, at the time of suit, of the creation of a monopoly of a line of commerce [contrary to § 7 of the Clayton Act]. . . .

Section 7 is designed to arrest in its incipiency not only the substantial lessening of competition from the acquisition by one corporation of the whole or any part of the stock of a competing corporation, but also to arrest in their incipiency restraints or monopolies in a relevant market which, as a reasonable probability, appear at the time of suit likely to result from the acquisition by one corporation of all or any part of the stock of any other corporation. The section is violated whether or not actual restraints or monopolies, or the substantial lessening of competition, have occurred or are intended. Acquisitions solely for investment are excepted, but only if, and so long as, the stock is not used by voting or otherwise to bring about, or in attempting to bring about, the substantial lessening of competition. . . .

The first paragraph of § 7 plainly is framed to reach not only the corporate acquisition of stock of a competing corporation, where the effect may be substantially to lessen competition between them, but also the corporate acquisition of stock of any corporation, competitor or not, where the effect may be either (1) to restrain commerce in any section or community, or (2) tend to create a monopoly of any line of commerce. . . .

We hold that any acquisition by one corporation of all or any part of the stock of another corporation, competitor or not, is within the reach of the section whenever the reasonable likelihood appears that the acquisition will result in a restraint of commerce or in the creation of a monopoly of any line of commerce. Thus, although du Pont and General Motors are not competitors, a violation of the section has occurred if, as a result of the acquisition, there was at the time of suit a reasonable likelihood of a monopoly of any line of commerce. . . .

Appellees argue that there exists no basis for a finding of a probable restraint or monopoly within the meaning of § 7 because the total General Motors market for finishes and fabrics constituted only a negligible percentage of the total market for these materials for all uses, including automotive uses. It is stated in the General Motors brief that in 1947 du Pont's finish sales to General Motors constituted 3.5 per cent of all sales of finishes to industrial users, and that its fabrics sales to General Motors comprised 1.6 per cent of the total market for the type of fabric used by the automobile industry.

Determination of the relevant market is a necessary predicate to a finding of a violation of the Clayton Act because the threatened monopoly must be one which will substantially lessen competition "within the area of effective competition." Substantiality can be determined only in terms of the market affected. The record shows that automotive finishes and fabrics have sufficient peculiar characteristics and uses to constitute them products sufficiently distinct from all other finishes and fabrics to make them a "line of commerce" within the meaning of the Clayton Act. . . . Thus, the bounds of the relevant market for the purposes of this case are not coextensive with the total market for finishes and fabrics, but are coextensive with the automobile industry, the relevant market for automotive finishes and fabrics.

The market affected must be substantial. . . . Moreover, in order to establish a violation of § 7 the Government must prove a likelihood that competition may be "foreclosed in a substantial share of . . . [that market]." Both requirements are satisfied in this case. The substantiality of a relevant market comprising the automobile industry is undisputed. The substantiality of General Motors' share of that market is fully established in the evidence.

General Motors . . . accounts annually for upwards of two-fifths of the total sales of automotive vehicles in the Nation. . . . Du Pont supplied 67 per cent of General Motors' requirements for finishes in 1946 and 68 per cent in 1947. In fabrics du Pont supplied 52.3 per cent of requirements in 1946, and 38.5 per cent in 1947. Because General Motors accounts for almost one-half of the automobile industry's annual sales, its requirements for automotive finishes and fabrics must represent approximately one-half of the relevant market for these materials. Because the record clearly shows that quantitatively and percentagewise du Pont supplies the largest part of General Motors' requirements, we must conclude that du Pont has a substantial share of the relevant market.

The appellees argue that the Government could not maintain this action in 1949 because § 7 is applicable only to the acquisition of stock and not to the holding or subsequent use of the stock. This argument misconceives the objective toward which § 7 is directed. The Clayton Act was intended to supplement the Sherman Act. Its aim was primarily to arrest apprehended consequences of intercorporate relationships before those relationships could work their evil, which may be at or any time after the acquisition, depending upon the circumstances of the particular case. . . . The Government may proceed at any time that an acquisition may be said with reasonable probability to contain a threat that it may lead to a restraint of commerce or tend to create a monopoly of a line of commerce. . . .

We agree with the trial court that considerations of price, quality, and service were not overlooked by either du Pont or General Motors. Pride in its products and its high financial stake in General Motors' success would naturally lead du Pont to try to supply the best. But the wisdom of this business judgment cannot obscure the fact, plainly revealed by the record, that du Pont purposely employed its stock to pry open the General Motors market to entrench itself as the primary supplier of General Motors' requirements for automotive finishes and fabrics.

Similarly, the fact that all concerned in high executive posts in both companies acted honorably and fairly, each in the honest conviction that his actions were in the best interests of his own company and without any design to overreach anyone, including du Pont's competitors, does not defeat the Government's right to relief. It is not requisite to the proof of a violation of § 7 to show that restraint or monopoly was intended.

The statutory policy of fostering free competition is obviously furthered when no supplier has an advantage over his competitors from an acquisition of his customer's stock likely to have the effects condemned by the statute. We repeat, that the test of a violation of § 7 is whether, at the time of suit, there is a reasonable probability that the acquisition is likely to result in the condemned restraints. The conclusion upon this record is inescapable that such likelihood was proved as to this acquisition. . . .

## Questions for Discussion

1. N leases electrically driven drill equipment to B. By the terms of the lease, B is required to lubricate the drills with "N" brand oil sold by N. N is prosecuted for violation of the Clayton Act. Is he guilty? Compare *International Salt Company* v. *United States*, 332 U.S. 392 (1947).

2. The Radio Corporation of America, distributing 70 to 95 per cent of the radio tubes in the country, licensed manufacturers to use its patented circuits and specified that they must buy their tubes from RCA. Was this an unfair trade practice? *Lord* v. *RCA*, 24 F.2d 565 (1928), affirmed in 28 F.2d 257 (1928).

3. The General Motors Corporation requires its Buick and Chevrolet agents to use only General Motors replacement parts. The effect is to lessen competition of other parts manufactured. Is the General Motors Corporation guilty of an unfair trade practice? *Peck Manufacturing Co.* v. *General Motors Corp.*, 80 F.2d 641 (1935), affirmed in 299 U.S. 3 (1936).

4. The M Company made and distributed two-fifths of all dress patterns made in the country. It sought to require dealers buying patterns from it to enter into exclusive agreements that they would not handle the patterns made by any other company. Would such an agreement be an unfair trade practice? *Standard Fashion Co.* v. *Magrine-Houston Co.*, 258 U.S. 346 (1922).

5. In order to prove that a tying contract is a violation of the Sherman Act, what additional facts must be shown?

6. What is the difference, if any, between the policy of the Sherman Act and that of the Clayton Act?

7. Compare the legality of vertical and horizontal stock ownership control.

8. Are the circumstances surrounding the acquisition of stock in another corporation the determining factors as to whether the stockholding violates the Clayton Act?

9. In determining whether the Clayton Act has been violated, is it material that the public has been supplied with a good product?

## Division C. Corporate Ownership and Structure

### § 11:7. Ownership of Property by Corporations

From the early days of corporation law, various limitations have been imposed on corporate ownership and, in more recent times, on corporate structure. All states impose some limitation regulating the formation of corporations and the kinds of stock that may be issued. Limitations may also be imposed on the amount of land that a corporation may own. In view of the modern trend toward commercial as distinguished from subsistence farming, restrictions on the acreage that may be held by a farming corporation are a strong weapon of the small farmer.

#### *(a) Limitations on ownership*

ASBURY HOSPITAL v. CASS COUNTY

326 U.S. 207 (1945)

OPINION BY STONE, J.

The challenged statute [of North Dakota] declares, §§ 2, 3, that corporations both domestic and foreign, which "now own or hold rural real estate, used or usable, for farming or agriculture, except such as is reasonably necessary in the conduct of their business, shall dispose of the same within ten years from the date that this Act takes effect. . . ." . . . Farming land in the state owned by any corporation in violation of the statute is, by § 5, made subject to escheat to the county in which it is located, by suit instituted by the county attorney. The county is required to dispose of the land at public auction to the highest bidder within one year after escheat, and to pay the proceeds, less the expenses of sale, to the former corporate owner.

Appellant alleges in its amended complaint that prior to the enactment of the statute it had acquired a tract of land . . . in . . . North Dakota, in satisfaction of a mortgage indebtedness, and that it has since leased the property out to farmers who have used it as farm land, . . . that since the enactment of the statute appellant has constantly attempted to sell this tract, and that it has been and will be unable to sell it for an amount equal to the original mortgage debt before the expiration of the statutory ten year period; that any sale which the county, proceeding under the statute, might be able to make, would be for substantially less than the amount appellant has invested in the land and the costs of sale. . . .

The Fourteenth Amendment does not deny to the state power to exclude a foreign corporation from doing business or acquiring or holding property within it. . . . While recognizing the unqualified power of the state to preclude its entry into the state for these purposes, appellant points out that the state has permitted it to enter and to invest its money in obligations secured by mortgage on land within the state, in consequence of which it lawfully acquired the land free of restrictions. Appellant argues that the state may not, by later legislation, force a sale of the land thus innocently acquired, under conditions which do not allow recovery of the original investment. But a state's power to exclude a foreign corporation, or to limit the nature of the business it may conduct within the state, does not end as soon as the corporation has lawfully entered the state and there acquired immovable property. Subsequent legislation excluding such a corporation from continuing in the state has been sustained as an exercise of the general power to exclude foreign corporations which does not offend due process. . . . Similarly, this Court has upheld legislation imposing burdens greater than those to which such corporations were subject at the time of their entry on the ground that the state might exclude them altogether at a later date. . . . Appellant, even if its activities in North Dakota are now restricted to the ownership of farm land within the state, stands in no better position to invoke the protection of the Fourteenth Amendment. The total exclusion of a corporation owning fixed property within a state requires it to sell or otherwise dispose of such property. Appellant must do no more. While appellant is not compelled by the present statute to cease all activities in North Dakota, the greater power includes the less.

. . . The North Dakota Supreme Court held that the statute's exception from its operation, of lands owned and held by corporations whose business is dealing in farm lands, (§ 2), and of the lands belonging to cooperative corporations, seventy-five percent of whose members or stockholders are farmers residing on farms, or depending principally on farming for their livelihood, (§ 4), did not deny the equal protection claimed. We agree.

. . . We cannot say that there are no differences between corporations generally and those falling into the excepted classes which may appropriately receive recognition in the legislative application of a state policy against the concentration of farming lands in corporate ownership. . . .

## § 11:8. Holding Companies

The rise of big business was accompanied by the development of the holding company and the pyramiding of corporations. By the Securities and Exchange Act, it was provided that holding companies may be ordered to dissolve where they serve no economic purpose and are merely devices for the control and the regulation of operating corporations.

### *(a) Dissolution of holding companies*

AMERICAN POWER & LIGHT CO. v. SECURITIES AND EXCHANGE COMMISSION

329 U.S. 90 (1946)

The Securities and Exchange Act directed the Securities and Exchange Commission as soon as practicable after January 1, 1938, "to require by order, after notice and opportunity for hearing, that each registered holding company, and each subsidiary company thereof, shall take such steps as the Commission shall find necessary to insure that the corporate structure or continued existence of any company in the holding-company system does not unduly or unnecessarily complicate the structure, or unfairly or inequitably distribute voting power among security holders, of such holding-company system. . . ." Proceedings were begun before the Commission to obtain the dissolution of the Bond and Share holding company system.

OPINION BY MURPHY, J.

. . . The Bond and Share system including American and Electric, possesses an undeniable interstate character . . . this vast system embraces utility properties in no fewer than 32 states . . . as well as in 12 foreign countries. . . . The proper control and functioning of such an extensive multi-state network of corporations necessitates continuous and substantial use of the mails and the instrumentalities of interstate commerce. Only in that way can Bond and Share, or its subholding companies or service subsidiary, market and distribute securities, control and influence the various operating companies, negotiate inter-system loans, acquire or exchange property, perform service contracts, or reap the benefits of stock ownership. . . .

Congress, of course, has undoubted power under the commerce clause to impose relevant conditions and requirements on those who use the channels of interstate commerce so that those channels will not be conduits for promoting or perpetuating economic evil. . . . It may compel changes in the voting rights and other privileges of stockholders. It may order the divestment or rearrangement of properties. It may order the reorganization or dissolution of corporations. . . .

Since the mandates of [the statute] are directed solely to public utility holding-company systems that use the channels of interstate commerce, the validity of that section under the commerce clause becomes apparent. It is designed to prevent the use of those channels to propagate and disseminate the evils which had been found to flow from unduly complicated systems and from inequitable distributions of voting power among security holders of the systems. Such evils are so inextricably entwined around the interstate business of the holding-company systems as to present no serious question as to the power of Congress under the commerce clause to eradicate them.

In the extensive studies which preceded the passage of the Public Utility Holding Company Act . . . it had been found that "the most distinctive characteristic, and perhaps the most serious defect of the present holding-company organization is the pyramided structure which is found in all of the important holding-company groups examined." The pyramiding device in its most common form consisted of interposing one or more subholding companies between the holding company and the operating companies and issuing, at each level of the structure, different classes of stock with unequal voting rights. Most of the financing of the various companies in the structure occurred through the sale to the public of bonds and preferred stock having low fixed returns and generally no voice in the managements. Under such circumstances, a relatively small but strategic investment in common stock (with voting privileges) in the high levels of a pyramided structure often resulted in absolute control of underlying operating companies with assets of hundreds of millions of dollars. A tremendous "leverage" in relation to that stock was thus produced;

the earnings of a top holding-company were greatly magnified by comparatively small changes in the earnings of the operating companies. The common stock of the top holding company might quickly rise in value and just as quickly fall, making it a natural object for speculation and gambling. In many instances this created financially irresponsible managements and unsound capital structures.

Public investors in such stock found themselves the innocent victims. . . . Those who supplied most of the capital through the purchase of bonds and preferred stock likewise suffered in addition to being largely disfranchised. Prudent management of the operating companies became a minor consideration, with pressure being placed on them to sustain the excessive capitalization to the detriment of their service to consumers. Reduction of rates was firmly resisted. A conclusion was accordingly reached by those making the studies that the highly pyramided system "is dangerous and has no justification for existence" and "represents the holding-company system at its worst." . . .

[The] pyramided structures and the resulting abuses, like . . . other characteristics [of the holding-company systems], rests squarely upon an extensive use of the mails and instrumentalities of interstate commerce. . . .

To deny that Congress has power to eliminate evils connected with pyramided holding-company systems . . . which have been found to be promoted and transmitted by means of interstate commerce, is to deny that Congress can effectively deal with problems concerning the welfare of the national economy. We cannot deny that power. Rather we reaffirm once more the constitutional authority resident in Congress by virtue of the commerce clause to undertake to solve national problems directly and realistically, giving due recognition to the scope of state power. That follows from the fact that the Federal commerce power is as broad as the economic needs of the nation. . . .

## Questions for Discussion

1. Is the statute in the *Asbury Hospital* case constitutional with respect to a domestic corporation as well as a foreign corporation?

2. Why did the Court in the *Asbury Hospital* case conclude that the equal protection clause was not violated by the exemptions referred to in the opinion?

3. Is equal protection denied by the fact that a statute does not limit the amount of land that an individual can hold but only that which a corporation can hold?

4. (a) Under what power was the statute in the *Asbury Hospital* case adopted? (b) Would it have made any difference if it were a federal instead of a state statute?

5. (a) To what extent did the Bond and Share holding company engage in interstate commerce? (b) Was this interstate commerce the primary object of the holding company or merely incidental to its operations? (c) Is it material which it was?

6. What is the constitutional basis for the Federal Securities and Exchange Commission Act?

7. How do you define the commerce power after reading the *American Power & Light Company* case? In the opinion the Court stated: "we reaffirm . . . the constitutional authority resident in Congress . . . to solve national problems . . . giving due recognition to the scope of state power." What importance do you find in the phrase "giving due recognition to the scope of state power"?

## Division D. Patents, Copyrights, and Trade-marks

### § 11:9. Patents

Congress is authorized by the Constitution to "promote the progress of science and useful arts, by securing for limited times to authors and inventors the exclusive right to their respective writings and discoveries" [Art. I, Sec. 8, Cl. 8].

It is now provided that a patent may be obtained for "any new and useful art, machine, manufacture, or composition of matter, or any new and useful improvements thereof" or for "any distinct and new variety of plant." A patent will be refused for anything that is dangerous or injurious to health or morals.

In the mechanical field, the fact that a device is new does not make it patentable. If the device is fundamentally the same as a former device to which improvements have been made, a patent cannot be obtained if the improvement is nothing more than might be made by any skilled craftsman operating or familiar with the machine. A combination of already existing parts, units, or techniques is not patentable where each element performs an old and well-known function and the novelty is based only upon the fact that the various functions are performed at the same time. The fact that such a combination is more useful is not a basis for granting a patent. The fact that the final product is more efficient, convenient, cheaper, better looking, or in any other way more useful does not remove it from the operation of this rule. It is only if a new effect or resultant is derived from the combination over and beyond the functions independently performed by the various elements that a patent can be granted.

A patent must be sought in terms of the composition or the organization of the patented article. The patent does not cover the function, that is, the work that the patented device does. A patent will be rejected if it is stated merely in terms of what it does as distinguished from what it is. To take an extreme case as an illustration, a patent would not be granted for a device "to clean floors," whereas a patent could be granted for a newly invented device to clean floors where the patent described in detail how the device was constructed. The reason for this distinction is that, if a patent could be obtained in terms of a function, a person with one invention could obtain a blanket patent that would cover any machine thereafter invented that would do the same work or even do it better.

New recipes or formulas for cooking food that involve the addition or the elimination of common ingredients or treating them in ways that differ from the former practice do not amount to invention merely because no one else ever did the particular thing upon which the applicant asserts his right to a patent. There is nothing patentable unless the applicant produces a new, unexpected, and useful function.

Printed matter is not patentable. . . . "Patents cannot issue for the discovery of the phenomena of nature. . . . The qualities . . . of the sun, electricity, or the qualities of metals, are part of the storehouse of knowledge of all men. They are manifestations of laws of nature, free to all men and reserved exclusively to none. He who discovers a hitherto unknown phenomenon of nature has no claim to a monopoly of it which the law recognizes. If there is to be invention from such a discovery, it must come from the application of the law of nature to a new and useful end." [3]

## § 11:10. Patent Rights and the Antitrust Law

The holder of a patent is given the exclusive right to manufacture, use, or sell the article or material covered by the patent for a period of seventeen years. This is a legally authorized monopoly. The holder of the monopoly may refrain from making any use of his right if he so chooses. This is frequently done in industries where the utilization of new articles covered by patents held by particular manufacturers would cause a serious dislocation of the industry or

[3] Funk Bros. Seed Co. v. Kalo Inoculant Co., 333 U.S. 127 (1948).

require the scrapping of large amounts of equipment because the new inventions would make existing equipment obsolete.

Under the combination of the present patent law and our system of free enterprise, the holder of the patent cannot be required to make use of his patent on the theory that he is improperly withholding from the public the benefits of modern science. Whether he does so is for him to decide, and the government cannot commandeer or expropriate the monopoly given by the patent. There has been much criticism of the patent system on this score, and the proposals made range from abolition of patent monopoly to some flexible system that would permit the compulsory licensing of a patent upon the payment of reasonable royalty to the patentholder. Such a system of compulsory licensing has in effect been followed by the United States Government in time of war. The TVA has also been authorized to use privately held patents without regard to the consent of the holders of the patents upon the payment of a reasonable royalty to them.

While the holder of a patent is given a legally protected monopoly, this right, prior to the fair trade acts, did not give him any greater power to control the resale price of his product than that of any other manufacturer or distributor. He could refuse to sell or could sell on any terms he chose; but it was not until the fair trade acts that he could require the purchaser of the patented articles and subsequent distributors of them to observe a specified minimum resale price.

In the case of the licensing of another person to manufacture under the patent, the holder may specify the price at which the licensee's product will be sold. This is based upon the nature of the license and not on the fair trade acts. Licensing agreements are illegal where the patentee by means of such agreements endeavors to require the purchaser of the patented article to use a particular nonpatented article although any other article would be just as satisfactory. Here the patentholder is in effect using his patent as a weapon to compel observance of a restraint in the trade of the unpatented article.

While the patentholder now has the right to make vertical price agreements, the extent to which horizontal price agreements can be made is not clear. It is common for persons holding different patents to pool the patents and to permit all the members of the pool to make use of those patents. A similar device is found in cross-licensing, in which the holders of different patents license each other to make use of their own patents. Such patent pools and cross-licensing arrangements are lawful unless it is found by the court that the purpose of the arrangement is to restrain competition rather than to engender a bona fide advancement through interchange of patents. It is also lawful for different firms holding noncompeting patents to consolidate or merge and for the merged or consolidated corporation thus to hold all the patents. The fact that this gives the final corporation a strong economic position does not make the combination of the patents under a single control a restraint of trade.

### *(a) Cross licensing*

UNITED STATES v. LINE MATERIAL CO.

333 U.S. 287 (1948)

OPINION BY REED, J.

. . . The ultimate question for our decision on this appeal may be stated . . . whether . . . two or more patentees in the same patent field may legally combine their valid patent monopolies to secure mutual benefits for themselves through contractual agreements between themselves and other licensees, for control of the sale price of the patented devices. . . . In the absence of patent or other statutory authorization, a contract to fix or maintain prices in interstate commerce has long been recognized as illegal per se under the Sherman Act. This is true whether the fixed price is reasonable or unreasonable. It is also true whether it is a price agreement between producers for sale or between producer and distributor for resale.

It is equally well settled that the possession of a valid patent or patents does not give the patentee any exemption from the provisions of the Sherman Act beyond the limits of the patent monopoly. By aggregating patents in one control, the holder of the patents cannot escape the prohibitions of the Sherman Act. . . . During its term, a valid patent excludes all except its owner from the use of the protected process or product. . . . This monopoly may be enjoyed exclusively by the patentee or he may assign the patent "or any interest therein" to others. . . . As we have pointed out, a patentee may license others to make and vend his invention and collect a royalty therefor. Thus we have a statutory monopoly by the patent. . . . The Sherman Act was enacted to prevent restraints of commerce but has been interpreted as recognizing that patent grants were an exception.

. . . Nothing in the patent statute specifically gives a right to fix the price at which a licensee may vend the patented article. . . . While . . . a patentee may, under certain conditions, lawfully control the price the licensee of his several patents may charge for the patented device, no case of this Court has construed the patent and anti-monopoly statutes to permit separate owners of separate patents by cross-licenses or other arrangements to fix the prices to be charged by them and their licensees for their respective products. Where two or more patentees with competitive, non-infringing patents combine them and fix prices on all devices produced under any of the patents, competition is impeded to a greater degree than where a single patentee fixes prices for his licensees.

. . . There is no suggestion in the patent statutes of authority to combine with other patent owners to fix prices on articles covered by the respective patents. As the Sherman Act prohibits agreements to fix prices, any arrangement between patentees runs afoul of that prohibition and is outside the patent monopoly.

. . . The argument of respondents is that if a patentee may contract with his licensee to fix prices, it is logical to permit any number of patentees to combine their patents and authorize one patentee to fix prices for any number of licensees. . . . It seems to us, however, that such argument fails to take into account the cumulative effect of such multiple agreements in establishing an intention to restrain. . . . Even where the agreements to fix prices are limited to a small number of patentees, we are of the opinion that it crosses the barrier erected by the Sherman Act against restraint of trade though the restraint is by patentees and their licensees.

### § 11:11. Copyrights and Trade-marks

Copyrights and trade-marks do not raise the same problem respecting the administration of the antitrust laws. A copyright gives the author, composer, or artist the exclusive right to use what he has written, drawn, painted, composed, or photographed, for a period of 28 years with the privilege of renewing for a like period.

Trade-marks include all marks and symbols used to identify the product of a particular producer or manufacturer. Under the police power the states may regulate the use and the registration of trade-marks. The federal government has no direct regulatory power over trade-marks such as it has over patents and copyrights. Congress can regulate trade-marks only to the extent that they are used in interstate or foreign commerce. Under the present federal law trade-marks may be registered, and provision is made for the cancellation of the registration and for the determination of disputes between rival claimants to the right to use a particular trade-mark.

The fact that a name cannot be made a technical trade-mark in a particular case does not deprive the user of that name of all protection. If a person has used a trade name for so long a time that it has acquired a secondary meaning of identifying him or his product, the courts will protect him in the use of that name and will enjoin others seeking to make use of it. He may also obtain damages caused him by the unfair competition of others improperly using his name.

### Questions for Discussion

1. (a) What is the difference between a patent, a copyright, and a trade-mark? (b) Can they be regulated by Congress? by the states?

2. Draft a statute revising the patent laws so as to prevent the freezing of patents by the holder.

3. Draft a statute specifying the extent to which the holder of a patent may fix prices, either restating the law as it now exists or changing it. In either case give reasons for your selection.

4. M devises a system of writing music in which the notes are represented by different colors. M applies for a patent. Is he entitled to a patent? *Kieferle* v. *Kingsland,* 178 F.2d 728 (App.D.C. 1949).

5. K manufactures an electric fan that uses a plastic blade instead of a metal blade. K applies for a patent. Is he entitled to a patent?

## Division E. Exceptions to the Antitrust Laws

### § 11:12. Statutory and Judicial Exceptions

At the same time that the antitrust policy has been extended in certain directions, Congress has made several significant exceptions to its operation. In addition to removing resale price maintenance agreements from its operation in certain cases, Congress has authorized freight pooling and revenue division agreements between railroad carriers provided the approval of the Interstate Commerce Commission is obtained.

By virtue of statutory exemptions, traffic and freight agreements otherwise prohibited by the antitrust law may be made by ocean carriers, and interstate railroads and telegraph companies may consolidate upon obtaining the approval of the government commission having jurisdiction over them. Marine insurance associations are exempted from the Sherman Act.

By the Webb-Pomerene Act of 1918 authorization was given to exporters to form associations engaged solely in exporting that could make agreements in foreign trade without regard to the antitrust laws so long as those agreements did not restrain trade within the United States or did not restrain the export trade of any United States exporter. The premise underlying this statute is that foreign trade is subject to such a high degree of monopoly control that it is impossible for American exporters to secure their fair share of the world trade if they are required to deal as individuals and are not permitted to combine to fight monopoly with monopoly.

In 1922 the farmers and dairymen were given authority by the Capper-Volstead Act to form co-operatives for purchasing and selling without regard to the antitrust laws. This statute is not a blanket exemption to farmers and dairymen from the antitrust laws. If their co-operatives combine with other persons not members of the co-operatives to fix prices, they are subject to the antitrust laws. As long as they keep within the normal co-operative functions and do not attempt to fix prices by agreement with third persons, the antitrust laws are not applicable. Here again the exception to the antitrust law is based upon the belief that a policy of free competition is not desirable and that the farmers and dairymen can operate more profitably to themselves and to the community at large if they are permitted to combine, even though the prices at which they sell their goods are thus indirectly controlled or enhanced.

The policy of aiding the farmer by exemption from the antitrust law is further seen in the Agricultural Adjustment Act. The Secretary of Agriculture is authorized, after notice and hearing, to enter into marketing agreements with "processors, producers, associations of producers, and others engaged in the handling of any agricultural commodity or product." These agreements, subject to certain qualifications, are exempt from the operation of the antitrust law.

In consequence of the decision of the Supreme Court in *United States* v. *South-Eastern Underwriters' Association,* 322 U.S. 533 (1944), holding that interstate insurance is commerce and subject to the antitrust law, Congress adopted a law, which exempts insurance companies from the Sherman Act and federal regulation to the extent that there are state laws that regulate the insurance companies.

In addition to the statutory exemptions from the Sherman Act, it is also to be noted that the Supreme Court has construed statutes that did not expressly exempt labor from the Sherman Act as having that effect as long as labor did not conspire with nonunion groups or persons.

It is significant that the statutes making exceptions to the antitrust law have been adopted over a period of years. There is accordingly every likelihood that other groups in the future will seek exemption from the antitrust laws. It should also be noted with respect to most of the statutory exceptions that the exempting statute has not removed the exempted enterprise from all control, but has given it permission to engage in what would otherwise be prohibited provided the approval of a government official or commission has been obtained. This may well be an indication of the pattern of future regulation; that is, prohibiting certain forms of conduct that have a possibility or potential of causing harm, but providing that such conduct will be permitted if the parties can show the government that the possible harm will not in fact result.

### § 11:13. Significance of Exceptions

The narrowing down of the scope of the antitrust law both by court decision and by statutory exceptions has, in the minds of some, cast serious doubt upon the validity of antitrust legislation. It is claimed that both national and world economy evidence a relentless march toward greater concentration of capital and that increasingly bigger businesses, rather then free competition between small businesses, is the order of the times. By some, this is accepted as an inevitable evil, and the objective of antitrust legislation is approved but its attainment is deemed futile. Others approve of this increasing concentration of economic power on the ground that it would permit a greater stability and a greater realization of the economies of large-scale enterprise. Opposed to these are those who regard the maintenance of the small business and the small enterprise as essential to what has become known as the American way of life. To them the potential of evil found in large capitalization is not worth the savings that it can bring. To them small-scale production and free competition are worth preserving at any cost. Others go further and claim that large-scale economy keeps its savings for itself.

The difficulty of scientifically measuring the merit of the arguments advanced and the realization that much depends upon the applied ethical standards of the persons involved makes the selection of a steady course most difficult. The solution of the problem is not in any way aided by the fact that certain groups and practices are not subject to the antitrust control to which the remainder of the economy is subject. The advocates of consistency decry this split policy and claim that the exceptions are either the fruit of political pressure or the recognition that the general rule is not workable. In the one case, the exception should be removed; in the other, the general rule should itself be abolished and the exception made the general principle. Those who are not troubled by the need for formal consistency may be able to reconcile the existence of exceptions to the general rule. This, however, is not without its own difficulties, for a clear dividing line cannot be maintained between the excepted areas and those that are not excepted. It is quite possible that exporters who are permitted to combine for export trade purposes may in some instances carry over their policies of "co-operation" into the domestic trade within the United States, contrary to both the spirit and the letter of the antitrust laws.

## Questions for Discussion

1. Does an export association organized under the Webb-Pomerene Act violate the Sherman Act if it becomes a member of an international cartel?

2. It has been charged that the antitrust laws have failed to prevent the growth of economic concentration. Was that the purpose of the antitrust laws?

3. Antitrust legislation is typical of an immature, growing economy but it is not suited to a mature economy and cannot withstand the strains placed upon the economy by depressions and wars. Is this statement correct?

4. Senator O'Mahoney, the Chairman of the Temporary National Economic Committee, favored a compulsory federal incorporation of all companies engaging in business on a national scale. He claimed that monopoly practices increased because the state governments did not supervise the use made of the charters and that, if the companies operated under federal charters, the national government could take effective action to prevent the development of monopolies and monopoly practices. (a) What do you think of this proposal? (b) Is the enforcement of the antitrust law hampered by the fact that most business corporations are organized under state charters rather than national charters? (c) How would a proceeding against a corporation for misuse of its federal charter by engaging in monopoly practices differ from present proceedings under the Sherman Act?

5. Draft an antitrust law specifying the extent to which "trusts" are unlawful. Either restate the existing law or set forth what you believe it should be. Give reasons for your choice in either case.

6. With the expansion of the railroads there appeared the development of rate pools by which the railroads eliminated rate-cutting by forming groups to divide traffic or earnings among the members of the pool. Such agreements were prohibited by the Interstate Commerce Act of 1887. The railroads then formed traffic association agreements that provided for the division of traffic but also fixed the rates to be charged. These agreements were in turn held to violate the Sherman Antitrust Act of 1890. These decisions then spurred the movement for consolidation of separate lines, a trend that was hastened by the railroad failures in the great panic of 1893. Control by the bankers further accelerated the disappearance of competition between the railroads. It has been claimed that this development, among other things, shows the impossibility of avoiding the development of monopoly and concentration of economic power. Suggest the plan of a law that would prevent the march toward concentration of economic power and that would preserve independent competing of carriers.

## Chapter 12

## REGULATION OF PRICING PRACTICES



### § 12:1. Price Discrimination

The Clayton Act prohibits price discrimination between different buyers of commodities "where the effect of such discrimination may be substantially to lessen competition or tend to create a monopoly in any line of commerce." This is not an absolute prohibition of discrimination but a prohibition only where discrimination has a monopolizing effect. Discrimination is expressly authorized where it can be justified on the basis of: (1) difference in grade, quality, or quantity involved; (2) the cost or the transportation involved in making the sale; or (3) when the sale is made in good faith in order to meet competition.

The vagueness of these standards is apparent, and Congress in 1936 passed the Robinson-Patman Act to clarify these provisions. The latter Act permits price differentials based on differences in the cost of manufacturing, selling, and delivering caused by differences in methods or quantities. The Federal Trade Commission is significantly authorized to limit the quantity discounts that can be given if it finds that there are so few large quantity purchasers that a quantity reduction, even though justified by cost differential, gives too great an advantage to the large purchaser or tends to create a monopoly. Price differentials are also permitted because of deterioration of goods or where the seller in good faith is making a close-out sale of a particular line of goods. The Robinson-Patman Act reaffirms the right of a seller to select his customers and to refuse to deal with anyone he chooses as long as he is acting in good faith and not for the purpose of restraining trade. The problem of determining comparative costs after making proper allowance for differences in methods of accounting and differences in subsidiary costs in different areas and the problem of determining the intention of the parties really brought greater difficulties to an already difficult problem.

The federal law prohibits the furnishing of advertising or other services that, when rendered to one purchaser but not to the other, will have the effect of granting the former a price discrimination or lower rate. It is made illegal for a seller to accept any fee or commission in connection with the sale except for services actually rendered and unless his services are equally available to all on the same terms. The Act makes either the giving or the receiving of any illegal price discrimination a criminal offense.

### *(a) Local discrimination*

MOORE v. MEAD'S FINE BREAD COMPANY

348 U.S. 115 (1955)

Moore ran a bakery in Santa Rosa, New Mexico. His business was wholly intrastate. His competitor, Mead's Fine Bread Company, was one of several corporations held under interlocking ownership and management and engaged in an interstate business. Mead cut the price of bread in half in Santa Rosa but made no price cut in any other place in New Mexico or any other state. As the result of this price cutting, Moore was driven out of business. He then sued Mead for damages for violation of the Clayton and Robinson-Patman Acts. Mead claimed that the price cutting was purely intrastate and therefore did not constitute a violation of the federal statutes.

OPINION BY DOUGLAS, J.

. . . Respondent is engaged in commerce, selling bread both locally and interstate. In the course of such business, it made price discriminations, maintaining the price in the *interstate* transactions and cutting the price in the *intrastate* sales. The destruction of a competitor was plainly established, as required by . . . the Clayton Act; and the evidence to support a finding of purpose to eliminate a competitor, as required by § 3 of the Robinson-Patman Act, was ample.

We think that the practices in the present case are . . . included within the scope of the antitrust laws. We have here an interstate industry increasing its domain through outlawed competitive practices. The victim, to be sure, is only a local merchant; and no interstate transactions are used to destroy him. But the beneficiary is an interstate business; the treasury used to finance the warfare is drawn from interstate, as well as local, sources which include not only respondent but also a group of interlocked companies engaged in the same line of business; and the prices on the interstate sales, both by respondent and by the other Mead companies, are kept high while the local prices are lowered. If this method of competition were approved, the pattern for growth of monopoly would be simple. As long as the price warfare was strictly intrastate, interstate business could grow and expand with impunity at the expense of local merchants. The competitive advantage would then be with the interstate combines, not by reason of their skills or efficiency but because of their strength and ability to wage price wars. The profits made in interstate activities would underwrite the losses of local price-cutting campaigns. No instrumentality of interstate commerce would be used to destroy the local merchant and expand the domain of the combine. But the opportunities afforded by interstate commerce would be employed to injure local trade. Congress, as guardian of the Commerce Clause, certainly has power to say that those advantages shall not attach to the privilege of doing an interstate business. . . .

It is, we think, clear that Congress by the Clayton Act and Robinson-Patman Act barred the use of interstate business to destroy local business, outlawing the price cutting employed by respondent. . . .

### *(b) Discrimination to meet competition*

STANDARD OIL COMPANY v. FEDERAL TRADE COMMISSION
340 U.S. 231 (1951)

Standard Oil Company sold gasoline in Detroit to four large "jobber" customers at a lower price than it did to many smaller buyers in the same area. The Federal Trade Commission ordered it to stop such price discrimination. Standard Oil claimed that it had granted the large jobbers the lower price in order to retain them as customers by meeting the prices of Standard Oil's competitors. The Commission rejected this as a defense. Standard Oil Company appealed.

OPINION BY BURTON, J.

. . . Since the effective date of the Robinson-Patman Act, June 19, 1936, petitioner has sold its Red Crown gasoline to its "jobber" customers at its tank-car prices. Those prices have been 1½¢ per gallon less than its tank-wagon prices to service station customers for identical gasoline in the same area. In practice, the service stations have resold the gasoline at the prevailing retail service station prices. Each of petitioner's so-called "jobber" customers has been free to resell its gasoline at retail or wholesale. Each, at some time, has resold some of it at retail. One now resells it only at retail. The others now resell it largely at wholesale. As to resale prices, two of the "jobbers" have resold their gasoline only at the prevailing wholesale or retail rates. The other two, however, have reflected, in varying degrees, petitioner's reductions in the cost of the gasoline to them by reducing their resale prices of that gasoline below the prevailing rates. The effect of these reductions has thus reached competing retail service stations in part through retail stations operated by the "jobbers" and in part through retail stations which purchased gasoline from the "jobbers" at less than the prevailing tank-wagon prices. The Commission found that such reduced resale prices "have resulted in injuring, destroying, and preventing competition between said favored dealers and retail dealers in respondent's [petitioner's] gasoline and other major brands of gasoline. . . ."

The heart of our national economic policy long has been faith in the value of competition. . . . Congress did not seek by the Robinson-Patman Act either to abolish competition or so radically to curtail it that a seller would have no substantial right of self-defense against a price raid by a competitor. For example, if a large customer requests his seller to meet a temptingly lower price offered to him by one of his seller's competitors, the seller may well find it essential, as a matter of business survival, to meet that price rather than to lose the customer. It might be that this customer is the seller's only available market for the major portion of the seller's product, and that the loss of this customer would result in forcing a much higher unit cost and higher sales price upon the seller's other customers. There is nothing to show a congressional purpose, in such a situation, to compel the seller to choose only between ruinously cutting its prices to all its customers to match the price offered to one, or refusing to meet the competition and then ruinously raising its prices to its remaining customers to cover increased unit costs. There is, on the other hand, plain language and established practice which permits a seller . . . to retain a customer by realistically meeting in good faith the price offered to that customer, without necessarily changing the seller's price to its other customers.

In a case where a seller sustains the burden of proof placed upon it to establish its defense . . . we find no reason to destroy that defense indirectly, merely because it also appears that the beneficiaries of the seller's price reductions may derive a competitive advantage from them or may, in a natural course of events, reduce their own resale prices to their customers. It must have been obvious to Congress that any price reduction to any dealer may always affect competition at that dealer's level as well as at the dealer's resale level, whether or not the reduction to the dealer is discriminatory. Likewise, it must have been obvious to Congress that any price reductions initiated by a seller's competitor would, if not met by the seller, affect competition at the beneficiary's level or among the beneficiary's customers just as much as if those reductions had been met by the seller. . . . We . . . conclude that Congress meant to permit the natural consequences to follow the seller's action in meeting in good faith a lawful and equally low price of its competitor. . . .

### § 12:2. Horizontal Price Fixing

Horizontal price fixing, that is, the fixing of prices between competitors, is a violation of the Sherman Act without regard to the reasonable or unreasonable character of the price that is fixed. It is immaterial whether this fixing of the price is made pursuant to a formal plan adopted by all producers involved or is merely a gentlemen's agreement among them.

In *United States* v. *Trenton Potteries Co.*, 273 U.S. 392 (1927), the Court declared "the aim and result of every price-fixing agreement, if effective, is the elimination of one form of competition. The power to fix prices, whether reasonably exercised or not, involves power to control the market and to fix arbitrary and unreasonable prices. The reasonable price fixed today may, through economic and business changes, become the unreasonable price of tomorrow. Once established it may be maintained unchanged because of the absence of competition secured by the agreement for a price reasonable when fixed. Agreements which create such potential power may well be held in themselves to be unreasonable or unlawful restraint, without the necessity of minute inquiry, whether a particular price is reasonable or unreasonable as fixed, and without placing on the government in enforcing the Sherman law the burden of ascertaining from day to day whether it has become unreasonable through the mere variation of economic conditions. Moreover, in the absence of express legislation requiring it, we should hesitate to adopt a construction making the difference between legal and illegal conduct in the field of business relations depend upon so uncertain a test as whether prices are reasonable—a determination which can be satisfactorily made only after a complete survey of our economic organization and a choice between rival philosophies."

### § 12:3. Basing-Point and Zone-Delivered Pricing Systems

The producer's problem of maintaining price stability is given an additional complication when a geographic distribution of markets is involved. In such a case, in addition to the other competitive factors, each seller will be faced by a transportation cost of taking his goods to the market, and this cost may be different than that of his competitors whose plants are located at different geographical points.

In such cases, manufacturers have often sought to establish a standard price for convenience in advertising or in keeping their books or for the purpose of enabling them to assert a better control over the market. Sometimes sales are made at a price f.o.b. the manufacturer's plant; that is, regardless of where the purchaser would be located, he would pay the same price at the manufacturer's plant and then would pay his own cost in transporting the article from the manufacturer's plant to wherever he wanted it. If the manufacturer should sell at each point at a price determined by his own f.o.b. factory price plus his cost of taking the goods to the buyer's point, the manufacturer would be selling at variable prices. Some manufacturers have followed a plan of selling at a fixed price regardless of where the buyer was located and of absorbing part or all of the freight to such point. Sometimes the fixed delivery price system would be divided into uniform zones so that all buyers in a particular zone would be sold at the same price, the manufacturer possibly bearing some of the transportation cost in computing the price at which he would sell within that zone.

Such a price control system, however, is merely the price control of the individual manufacturer for the disposal of his own goods. In contrast with this, there developed a basing-point system of establishing a fixed price for the goods of all manufacturers within a given line of production. Thus, from 1900 to 1926, the steel industry used the single basing-point plan or the "Pittsburgh Plus Plan" under which the price of steel of any producer to any purchaser anywhere in the United States was quoted as the price of steel at Pittsburgh plus freight from Pittsburgh to the point of delivery, regardless of the route actually followed by the shipment. Under this plan, a person purchasing steel in California from a plant ten miles away from him would be required to buy at a price equal to what it would cost if he had bought the steel at Pittsburgh and had paid transportation of the steel from Pittsburgh to the place of purchase. This single basing-point system was later replaced by a multiple basing-point system in which, instead of all deliveries being priced at Pittsburgh plus, the country was zoned so that each purchaser would pay as of a certain city within his zone plus the cost of transportation as though the shipment had come from that city.

This multiple basing-point fixed price delivery system became fairly common in many of the bulk commodity industries. Here, because of the standardized quality of the product, there is little room for competition except as to price. The transportation factor looms high because these products have great bulk that gives rise to a high transportation cost but yet sell at a relatively low price per unit volume. Unless the selling price can be made uniform, the industry is subject to continual price warfare. The same factors that have led the large commodity industries to establish monopolies and cartels have induced them to adopt multiple basing-point systems.

Such systems have the economic disadvantage of retarding the development of producers at points other than the basing point. A new producer coming into a new area nearer the consumer would not secure any competitive advantage by locating at that point if he is required to sell at a basing-point figure. In addition, the basing-point price system also prevents the purchaser from reaping an economic advantage from the fact that he is purchasing from an existing nearby producer.

Both single and multiple basing-point systems have been condemned by the Supreme Court as illegal wherever they are based upon collusion between producers. The exact extent to which they are to be regarded as collusive is not clear. The Supreme Court has also sustained the action of the Federal Trade Commission in prohibiting the concerted use of a zone-pricing system, although it reserved the question whether such a system is a prohibited price discrimination when adopted individually and independently of others.[1]

### § 12:4. Vertical Price Fixing and Due Process of Law

Vertical price fixing or an agreement as to the resale price made by a manufacturer with his distributor or by a wholesaler with a retailer was originally illegal under the antitrust laws of both the nation and the states. Then first the states and later Congress authorized such price-fixing agreements. While at first glance such a price-fixing agreement seems harmful to the consumer in that it deprives him of the advantages of a price-cutting war, such statutes protect both the public and the manufacturer against the unfair trade use of a "loss leader." Under this "loss leader" practice a dealer sells a few well-known articles at a substantially reduced price. All his other merchandise consists of lesser known or inferior brands that are actually more expensive than well-known brands either because the dealer adds a few extra cents to the purchase price, or because he packages the articles so that the purchaser is buying less although he appears to be paying no more than the general price, or because the purchaser is buying an inferior product. Unless the purchaser is trained in marketing, he is not likely to detect these differences and fails to realize that the few pennies he saves on the "loss leader" are offset many times by the loss he suffers in purchasing other articles from such a dealer.

Price-fixing statutes also protect the manufacturer or the distributor who has spent much time and money in advertising his product. If price fixing were not permitted, dealers who did not care to cut the price might not handle the product of the manufacturer or the distributor, whose sales volume would therefore be decreased. It is true that the sales of the merchant cutting the price might increase, but it is not probable that this increase would be sufficient to offset the loss of sales to a number of other merchants.

The problems of maintaining a resale price could be avoided by other means of marketing and distribution. If the manufacturer sells his goods directly to the public through agents or outlet stores or if he sells to dealers on consignment, he has the power to fix the price at which the sale to the public shall be made. These alternative methods of distribution, however, have the disadvantage of placing a large administrative and capital investment burden on the manufacturer. For these reasons, such other devices are not practical, and

[1] Federal Trade Commission v. National Lead Co., 352 U.S. 419 (1957).

the direct approach of adopting laws permitting the maintenance of vertical resale prices offered the only satisfactory solution. Today such laws have been enacted by a large majority of the states.

These "fair trade acts" have been sustained even as applied to a remote dealer who had not made a price maintenance agreement directly with the manufacturer or the distributor, although in some states it is held unconstitutional to provide that a nonsigner is bound by the fair trade agreement. Under that view, the fair trade act has no greater operation than to protect the parties to the resale price maintenence agreement from liability under the applicable anti-trust law. It is not effective to bind anyone else to comply with its terms.

### *(a) Federal view*

OLD DEARBORN DISTRIBUTING CO. v. SEAGRAM DISTILLERS CORP.

299 U.S. 183 (1936)

OPINION BY SUTHERLAND, J.

These appeals bring here for decision the question of the constitutional validity of sections 1 and 2 of the Fair Trade Act of Illinois.

The Illinois statute constitutes a legislative recognition of a rule which has been accepted by many of the state courts as valid at common law. This rule was based upon the distinction found to exist between articles of trade put out by the manufacturer or producer under and identified by patent, copyright, trade-mark, brand, or similar device and articles of like character put out by others and not so identified. The same rule was followed for a time by some of the lower federal courts; but their decisions were upset by this court. . . . This court held that a system of contracts between manufacturers and wholesale and retail merchants which sought to control the prices for sales by all such dealers by fixing the amount which the consumer should pay, amounted to an unlawful restraint of trade, invalid at common law and, so far as interstate commerce was affected, invalid under the Sherman Anti-Trust Act . . . and it was held that the rule applied to such agreements notwithstanding the fact that they related to proprietary medicines made under a secret process and identified by distinctive packages, labels, and trade-marks. The argument that since the manufacturer might make and sell or not as he chose, he could lawfully condition the price at which subsequent sales could be made by the purchaser, was rejected.

*First.* In respect of the due process of law clause, it is contended that the statute is a price-fixing law, which has the effect of denying to the owner of property the right to determine for himself the price at which he will sell. . . .

We find nothing in this situation to justify the contention that there is an unlawful delegation of power to private persons to control the disposition of the property of others. . . .

Nor is section 2 so arbitrary, unfair or wanting in reason as to result in a denial of due process. We are here dealing not with a commodity alone, but with a commodity plus the brand or trade-mark which it bears as evidence of its origin and of the quality of the commodity for which the brand or trade-mark stands. Appellants own the commodity; they do not own the mark or the good will that the mark symbolizes. And good will is property in a very real sense, injury to which, like injury to any other species of property, is a proper subject for legislation. Good will is a valuable contributing aid to business—sometimes the most valuable contributing asset of the producer or distributor of commodities. And distinctive trade-marks, labels and brands, are legitimate aid to the creation or enlargement of such good will. It is well settled that the proprietor of the good will "is entitled to protection as against one who attempts to deprive him of the benefits resulting from the same, by using his labels and trade-marks without his consent and authority.". . . Section 2 of the act does not prevent a purchaser of the commodity bearing the mark from selling the commodity alone at any price he pleases. It interferes only when he sells with the aid of the good will of the vendor; and it interferes then only to protect that good will against injury. It proceeds upon the theory that the sale of identified goods at less than the price fixed by the owner of the mark or brand is an assault upon the good will. . . . There is nothing in the act to preclude the purchaser from removing the mark or brand from the commodity—thus separating the physical property, which he owns, from the good will, which is the property of another—and then selling the commodity at his own price, provided he can do so without utilizing the good will of the latter as an aid to that end.

There is a great body of fact and opinion tending to show that price cutting by retail dealers is not only injurious to the good will and business of the producer and distributor of identified goods, but injurious to the general public as well. The evidence to that effect is voluminous; but it would serve no useful purpose to review the evidence or to enlarge further upon the subject. True, there is evidence, opinion and argument to the contrary; but it does not concern us to determine where the weight lies. We need say no more than that the question may be regarded as fairly open to differences of opinion. The legislation here in question proceeds upon the former and not the latter view; and the legislative determination in that respect, in the circumstances here disclosed, is conclusive so far as this court is concerned. Where the question of what the facts establish is a fairly-debatable one, we accept and carry into effect the opinion of the Legislature. . . .

### § 12:5. Vertical Price Fixing and Federal Laws

These state fair trade acts were restricted to sales made locally and could not apply to interstate transactions. This inability to meet the problems on a national scale was met by the enactment by Congress of the Miller-Tydings Resale Price Maintenance Act.

This Act provides that nothing in the Sherman Act "shall render illegal, contracts or agreements prescribing minimum prices for the resale of a commodity which bears, or the label or container of which bears, the trademark, brand or name of the producer or distributor of such commodity and which is in free and open competition with commodities of the same general class produced or distributed by others, when contracts or agreements of that description are lawful as applied to intrastate transactions . . . in any state . . . in which such resale is to be made, or to which the commodity is to be transported for such resale." The exception created by this Act was applicable only when two conditions were satisfied: first, the article was a trade-mark or brand-name article, and second, the law of the state where the resale or shipment was to be made permitted such type of agreements. This Act permitted vertical price maintenance agreements only and prohibited horizontal price maintenance agreements, such as agreements between manufacturers or between wholesalers, brokers or other persons who were competing in the same stage or level of manufacturing or distribution.

The Act was also inapplicable when the purchaser has done work on the purchased article prior to making the resale.

Fourteen years after the adoption of the Miller-Tydings Act, the United States Supreme Court examined its provisions and discovered that, contrary to the common understanding of the object of the Act, it did not in fact contain any provision making fair trade agreements binding upon nonsigners but only made them valid as between the parties to the agreements.[2] This decision was thereafter overruled by statute, the Congress adopting the McGuire Act,[3] which provides that such agreements do not violate any federal law if they are valid in the state of resale, and that such agreements bind nonsigners if that state law so provides.

As an aftermath of this change in federal decision and statute, a number of state courts have declared that their fair trade acts did not bind nonsigners on the ground that the local act did not expressly, or could not constitutionally, do so. Most states, however, have continued to sustain the validity of their fair trade acts. Apart from the validity of such acts, widespread violation of fair trade agreements is found in some areas.

### § 12:6. Fixing of Price for Services

No distinction is made under the Sherman Antitrust Act between the regulation of the price of goods and the regulation of the price of services. It is necessary of course that the services or the agreements relating to the services be such as to constitute interstate commerce. Thus it has been held that an agreement between a state-wide medical society and various county medical societies not to compete with each other in furnishing prepaid medical care on a contract basis through nonprofit organizations, related only to intrastate commerce and was therefore not a restraint of trade in violation of the Sherman Act.[4]

#### *(a) Real estate brokers*

UNITED STATES v. NATIONAL ASSOCIATION OF REAL ESTATE BOARDS

339 U.S. 485 (1950)

The United States brought an action to enjoin the National Association of Real Estate Boards, the Washington Real Estate Board, and others, from violating the Sherman Anti-Trust Act by fixing by agreement the rates to be charged by member brokers for their services. The defendants contended that the commission-fixing agreements did not violate the Sherman Act because their business was not subject to the Act. From a judgment in favor of the defendants, the United States appealed.

---

[2] Schwegman Brothers v. Calvert Distillers Corp., 341 U.S. 384 (1951).
[3] 15 U.S.C. § 45(5).
[4] United States v. Oregon State Medical Society, 343 U.S. 326 (1952).

OPINION BY DOUGLAS, J.

. . . The prescribed rates are used in the great majority of transactions, although in exceptional situations a lower charge is made. But departure from the prescribed rates has not caused the Washington Board to invoke any sanctions. Hence the District Court called the rate schedules "non-mandatory."

. . . Price fixing is per se an unreasonable restraint of trade. It is not for the courts to determine whether in particular settings price fixing serves an honorable or worthy end. An agreement, shown either by adherence to a price schedule or by proof of consensual action fixing the . . . price, is itself illegal under the Sherman Act, no matter what end it was designed to serve. . . . And the fact that no penalties are imposed for deviations from the price schedules is not material. . . . Subtle influences may be just as effective as the threat or use of formal sanctions to hold people in line.

. . . The critical question is whether the business of a real estate agent is included in the word "trade" within the meaning of § 3 of the Act. . . . The fact that the business involves the sale of personal services rather than commodities does not take it out of the category of "trade" within the meaning of § 3 of the Act. . . .

> . . . Wherever any occupation, employment, or business is carried on for the purpose of profit, or gain, or a livelihood, not in the liberal arts or in the learned professions, it is constantly called a trade. . . .

It is in that broad sense that "trade" is used in the Sherman Act. That has been the consistent holding of the decisions. The fixing of prices and other unreasonable restraints have been consistently condemned in case of services as well as goods. Transportation services . . . , cleaning, dyeing, and renovating wearing apparel . . . , the procurement of medical and hospital services . . . , the furnishing of news or advertising services . . .—these indicate the range of business activities that have been held to be covered by the Act.

## Questions for Discussion

1. (a) Why is horizontal price-fixing declared illegal without regard to whether the price is reasonable? (b) How does this rejection of "reasonable price" compare with the rule applicable to determining the rates to be allowed public utilities and carriers?

2. Manufacturers A, B, C, and D are prosecuted for violating the Sherman Act. The only evidence which the government produces shows that

every time the four manufacturers made a bid to supply the government with materials, the bid presented by each manufacturer was identical in amount with the bids presented by the others. No proof was presented by the government that there was any prearranged plan or agreement that identical bids should be submitted. Are the manufacturers guilty of violating the antitrust law?

3. The major oil companies selling gasoline in a particular section of the country agreed to buy up the gasoline produced by independent refiners for the purpose of eliminating their product as a competitor on the market and thus making it possible for them to maintain their own prices. They were prosecuted for violating the Sherman Act. The defense was made that, by purchasing the "surplus" gasoline, ruinous price competition could be removed from the business and stability could be maintained. Is this a good defense? *United States* v. *Socony-Vacuum Oil Co.,* 310 U.S. 150 (1940).

4. A group of manufacturers representing nearly all of the manufacturers making a particular product, form an association that acts as a clearinghouse for information supplied to it by the members. Each member makes a daily report to it of all sales, including prices, his supply of goods on hand, and estimated production. Any member losing a sale may ask the other members if they made the sale and the price at which it was made. This association is prosecuted for violating the antitrust law. The association claims that it is not guilty because there is no agreement to maintain price or to suppress competition. Is it guilty? *United States* v. *American Linseed Oil Company,* 262 U.S. 371 (1923).

5. The Standard Oil Company of New Jersey, General Motors, and DuPont jointly owned the Ethyl Gasoline Corporation, which is the owner of the patent for the production of tetraethyl lead fluid used in manufacturing high-test gasoline. The major gasoline refiners are licensed by the Ethyl Gasoline Corporation to mix Ethyl with their gasoline, but they are permitted to sell only to jobbers licensed by Ethyl Gasoline Corporation. The Ethyl Gasoline Corporation in licensing jobbers requires them to maintain a stated price differential between the regular and the Ethyl gasoline. Jobbers' licenses could be canceled at any time by the Ethyl Gasoline Corporation and were in fact canceled if the jobbers did not adhere to the selling standard agreement. The United States prosecuted the Ethyl Gasoline Corporation for violating the Sherman Act. Was it guilty? *Ethyl Gasoline Corp.* v. *United States,* 309 U.S. 436 (1940).

6. Eight major producing-distributors and their trade association, the Motion Picture Producers and Distributors of America, dominate the motion picture industry through their production of four fifths of the feature films and their control of one half of the theaters in the country. These distributors agreed that they would not lease feature pictures to any distributor who did not sign a standard form of contract providing for compulsory arbitration of trade disputes. The provisions of this standard contract had been approved by a fair trade practice conference held under

the sponsorship of the Federal Trade Commission and had been approved by the Commission as a Group II Rule. A, an exhibitor, seeks an injunction to compel these producer-distributors to lease films to him without his signing such a contract. Should the injunction be granted? *Paramount Famous Laskie Corp.* v. *United States*, 282 U.S. 30 (1930).

7. The standard contract referred to in Question 6 also had the effect of prohibiting double-feature programs and of requiring minimum admission prices for second-run pictures. Y, an exhibitor, seeks an injunction against these provisions so that he may run double features and charge a lower admission price. Y claims that the standard contract is invalid under the Sherman Act. Is Y correct? *Vitograph* v. *Perelman*, 90 F.2d 142 (1936); *United States* v. *Interstate Circuit Inc.*, 20 F.Supp. 868 (1937), affirmed in 306 U.S. 208 (1939).

8. (a) What is the legal difference between price-fixing by the agreement of the parties and price-fixing by the legislature? (b) What is the economic or social difference? (c) Does it make any difference if the agreement fixing the price is a one-sided agreement in which one party is forced to deal on the terms stipulated by the other party?

9. Does it make any difference if the person reselling an article at a cut price does not know that there has been an agreement to fix or maintain the retail price?

10. Can a resale price maintenance agreement bind persons not parties to it?

11. Are the fair trade acts in harmony or in conflict with the basic antitrust concept?

12. Is the distinction made by the fair trade acts between trade-mark or brand-name goods and other goods a lawful classification?

13. Is the purchaser of a commodity subject to a fair trade price-fixing agreement bound by that agreement if he removes the trade-mark or identifying label from the commodity and sells it as an unidentified commodity?

14. Does the Court in the *Old Dearborn* case determine as a fact that vertical price fixing is socially and economically desirable?

15. How does the court in the *Old Dearborn* case meet the objection that the fair trade acts deny equal protection of the laws by creating a distinction between patented and trade-marked goods and goods that are not so identified?

16. The McGuire Act is unconstitutional because it depends for its effect upon the law of the states. Do you agree? Explain.

17. A is famous for a particular brand of leather. A sells this leather to B under an agreement fixing the resale price. C purchases the leather from B and then offers it for public sale as "A" brand leather but at a

price less than that provided for in the A-B agreement. A sues C under a fair trade statute to compel C to raise his price. Decide.

18. Would it make any difference in your answer to Question 17 if C dyed the leather and then sold it at a price less than that specified by the A-B agreement, in spite of the fact that he had done the additional work of dying the leather?

19. The plaintiff sued to enjoin a competitor from selling below the minimum price set by fair trade agreements. It was shown that the plaintiff had violated the same agreements with respect to other articles sold by him. The defendant claimed that the plaintiff was not entitled to an injunction. Decide. *Fogel* v. *Bolet*, 91 N.Y.Supp. 2d 642 (1949).

20. B, a druggist, advertises that a gift will be given to any person entering his drug store regardless of the amount purchased by him. He is sued by manufacturers of trade-marked articles on the ground that this offer violates the fair trade act prohibiting sales below a fixed minimum agreed to by the manufacturer. Decide. Would it affect your answer if B had advertised that the gift would be given to anyone making a purchase of $2 or more? *Bernhard* v. *Savall Drug Store*, 82 N.Y.Supp. 2d (1948).

21. D, a manufacturer, sold cosmetics to certain stores in different states, including the plaintiff's store. D supplied some of the stores with "demonstrators" whose salaries were paid in whole or in part by D. D refused to supply such a demonstrator to the plaintiff's store. P, the plaintiff, claimed that this was a discrimination in violation of the Robinson-Patman Act and sued for treble damages, claiming that the advantage given to his competitors who were furnished demonstrators diverted customers from his store to theirs. D claimed that as P conducted a purely intrastate business the federal law did not apply. Decide. *Sun Cosmetic Shoppe* v. *Elizabeth Arden Sales Corp.*, 178 F.2d 150 (CCA 2d 1949).

22. D owned and operated a number of ice plants throughout the state. He sold ice at these plants at a standard price. P opened an ice plant in one of the cities in which D operated a plant. D then reduced his prices in that city below his price in other cities in order to undersell P. P sued to enjoin D under the Robinson-Patman Act from cutting his price in this manner. D defended on the ground that the great bulk of his sales were for local consumption and only a very small percentage was sold to refrigerated railroad cars or interstate motor trucks. Decide. *Atlantic Co.* v. *Citizens Ice & Coal Storage Co.*, 178 F.2d 453 (CCA 5th 1949).

23. "Because the Robinson-Patman Act is based upon the interstate commerce power, it follows that the prohibited discriminations must be directed against interstate transactions." Appraise this statement.

24. Is it a violation of the Robinson-Patman Act to give one customer a special price when he threatens to go elsewhere if he is not given the reduced price?

25. What is embraced by "trade" in the phrase "restraint of trade?"

## Chapter 13

# REGULATION OF BUSINESS PRACTICES



## § 13:1. The Background

To some extent a person who is injured or who suffers loss because of fraud or unfair business practices of another may be entitled to recover money damages from him in a suit at law or to obtain an injunction in a court of equity to cause him to stop such practices. There are numerous limitations on these remedies as to many business practices that, though harmful, do not give rise to any legal liability. Even when liability exists, the individual injured may often be unwilling to undertake the expense and the burden of a law suit because the injury to him is comparatively small. A person who purchases a sweater that is falsely labeled as all wool would probably not desire to go to the expense of suing the manufacturer who falsely labeled the goods, particularly where the manufacturer may be in another state halfway or more across the country.

As the business world expanded following the period of the Civil War and as cutthroat competition brought in many fraudulent practices and get-rich-quick schemes, the individual soon realized that the customary procedures of law were inadequate to cope with such menaces to sound business.

The result was a demand for government to step in and to begin an era of regulation to prevent fraudulent practices and unfair methods of competition. As regards the federal government, such laws were generally based upon the commerce clause, and thus their sphere of operation was limited to what was deemed interstate commerce. To a lesser extent federal regulation might be based upon the power of the federal government to regulate weights and measures and to prohibit counterfeiting. In the case of the states, the police power furnished an ample basis for regulating such practices; but here the difficulty arose that each state was limited to activities within its own borders and was unable to cope with practices in interstate business. It was this latter factor that gradually brought the federal government into the field of regulation. In addition to the federal and state governments, the local governments, particularly the towns and cities, either by virtue of their charters or state laws, regulated business to prevent the use of false weights and measures and the sale of diseased or harmful food or drug products.

### § 13:2. Weights and Measures

From early colonial times government had embarked upon the program of preventing fraudulent business practices through use of false weights and measures. Devices such as scales adjusted to register heavy weight and measuring baskets with a false bottom so that they contained or would hold less merchandise than they appeared to hold were common fraudulent practices. From an early date, the attempt was made to drive these practices out of existence. It is to be noted how hardy a variety of fraud is involved, because such practices still continue today and governments, primarily local, have the very substantial task of checking all weighing and measuring machines used for the sale of all types of commodities. With the rise of the new economic order, the number of weighing and measuring machines has increased greatly. For example, the simple gasoline pump appearing at the numerous gasoline stations in itself creates a full-time job of inspection in many areas.

In addition to this type of regulation, the weight regulation is also found in the form of a requirement that the label or the container state the exact weight or content of the container. A package containing breakfast food or a wrapped loaf of bread may be required to state a minimum weight on the outside wrapper. Closely related to this type of regulation is a requirement that certain commodities be sold in specified bulks. In colonial times it was common to specify the size and the weight of a loaf of bread. Such detailed regulation is generally not common in modern times except in times of emergency when such regulation is adopted as a near relation to rationing.

Although not generally considered a regulation of business, it is proper to regard the various laws prohibiting the use of counterfeit money or making the passing of counterfeit money a crime as being regulations of business. The history of counterfeit and debased currency and coin is as old as the history of money itself. Government, particularly the federal government, has a difficult and continuing task in the elimination of fraudulent money practices.

### § 13:3. Impure and Misbranded Articles

The public also demanded protection from the following improper practices: selling articles, principally foods or drugs, that contain deadly substances or substances harmful or irritating to the user; selling materials or foods made from impure substances; selling foods containing harmful preservatives or dyed in order to make them look fresh; selling foods and other materials containing harmless adulterants or fillers, such as chicory in coffee or flour in sausage; using false labels on articles which do not disclose that they are harmful or adulterated in the above manner; and using labels that either clearly or by natural suggestion cause the consumer to think that the article which he is buying is something other than it really is, such as using the word "wool" in the name of cotton fabric.

These unfair practices came in for early regulation by the states. With the rise of the interstate flow of goods, the federal government began regulation under the commerce power. The statutes of the last century were directed at specific articles by name. Thus milk from diseased cows, or filled milk, or diseased cattle and poultry were specifically excluded from interstate commerce. Later statutes have adopted a broader approach of specifying a standard for exclusion or condemnation rather than attempting to name the particular articles that are condemned. The Pure Food and Drug Act of 1906 as amended in 1938 prohibits the interstate shipment of misbranded or adulterated foods, drugs, cosmetics, and therapeutic devices. These categories are broadly defined by the statute, and the Federal Commissioner of Foods and Drugs is authorized to prescribe standards and classifications to implement these broad standards.

The federal statute provides that goods, particularly where designed for human consumption, shall bear a label stating the content with particular reference to any drug or coloring matter included and the name and the address of the manufacturer. Criticism has been made of the federal law for its failure to carry this method of labeling into the field of cosmetics.

Under the Pure Food and Drug Act, an article is deemed "misbranded" if its "labeling" is false or misleading. The term "labeling" is defined to include written or printed matter that appears either upon the article or container itself or which accompanies the article.

Truthful labeling was also advanced by the Federal Wool Products Labeling Act of 1940, which makes the misbranding of woolen fabrics an unfair trade practice. Under this Act, woolen fabrics must be labeled to indicate the weight of the wool and its condition, whether new, processed, or reclaimed, and the weight of any other material in the cloth that is not wool, together with the name of the manufacturer. Similar steps against deception have been taken by the Federal Fur Labeling Act of 1951 and the Federal Textile Fibre Products Identification Act of 1958.

A new step was taken by the 1938 amendment to the Federal Pure Food and Drug Act in requiring that the Commissioner of Food and Drugs approve a new drug before it could be marketed. This type of government control is similar to that which had already been used in the case of the issuance of corporate securities. While this procedure goes a great way beyond government's merely standing by to see that articles are properly labeled, the direct intervention of government to approve the distribution beforehand has been shown to be highly desirable by the harmful effects that have attended the indiscriminate use of certain of the modern drugs.

The Food Additives Amendment of 1958 to the Pure Food, Drug, and Cosmetics Act further protects the public from food additives that have not been adequately tested to establish their safety.

Protection from physical injury is provided by the Federal Flammable Fabrics Act of 1953.

The far reach of the federal power is seen in *United States* v. *Sullivan*, 332 U.S. 689 (1948), decided under the Federal Food, Drug and Cosmetics Act, which provides that an article is misbranded when the label does not contain adequate directions and warnings as to use and which also prohibits the misbranding of drugs that are held for sale after they have come within a state through the channels of interstate commerce. From a properly labeled container, a druggist transferred sulpha tablets to small pill boxes for public resale. These small boxes were merely labeled "sulfathiazole." It was held that this was a "misbranding" in violation of the federal statute and that the statute was applicable regardless of how long after shipment in interstate commerce the misbranding occurred or how many intrastate sales had intervened or who had received the articles at the end of the interstate shipment. As against the claim that this invaded the reserved powers of the states, the court said the "purpose [of the statute] was to safeguard the consumer by applying the Act to articles from the moment of their introduction into interstate commerce all the way to the moment of their delivery to the ultimate consumer."

## § 13:4. Unfair Competitive Practices

The most significant development in the government regulation and prohibition of unfair competitive practices is found in the creation in 1914 of the Federal Trade Commission. This Commission is authorized to enforce certain specific prohibitions of the Clayton Act of 1914, which were designed to supplement the Sherman Act, and to enforce specific prohibitions of certain other federal statutes, most important of which is the declaration made by the Federal Trade Commission Act, as amended by the Wheeler-Lea Act, that "unfair methods of competition in commerce, and unfair or deceptive acts or practices in commerce, are hereby declared unlawful." Under this later Act, false advertising is made a crime if the article will injure the health if used as advertised or if the false advertising was made with the intent to defraud or mislead.

The Federal Trade Commission is also charged with the enforcement of the antitrust provisions of the Clayton Act directed against price discrimination, tie-in contracts and exclusive dealer agreements, and interlocking directorates and intercorporate stockholding.

The authority under the Federal Trade Commission Act to outlaw unfair trade practices to some extent conflicts with the authority to advance free competition. The elimination of unfair trade practices is to some extent an elimination of free competition by holding that certain forms of competition can no longer be engaged in. The distinction between activity that violates the antitrust laws because it restricts competition and activity that is unfair trade practice because it is too free a form of competition has tended to become obscured. This has been due in part to the fact that the Supreme Court has come to regard anything violatory of the antitrust legislation as being in itself an unfair trade practice.

During the course of the years the Federal Trade Commission has established certain categories of unfair trade practices that are unlawful, although in the last analysis the Supreme Court of the United States is the final judge as to whether a practice comes within the statutory condemnation.

Among the many forms of unfair trade practices that are condemned is the use of false endorsements or testimonials that an article has been approved by or is used by a particular person, government, or agency. In one instance, the deceptive practice went to the extent of naming a nonexisting association as having approved the article. It is illegal to misrepresent the products or the methods of a competitor. A false statement that one's competitors are using unsanitary, antiquated production methods is an unfair trade practice. Various harassing tactics are condemned, such as impeding the delivery of a competitor's goods, interfering with his advertising, secretly adulterating his product, or selling a harmful article under an imitation of the competitor's label so that the public believes that it is the competitor's product. The sending of spies into a competitor's store or factory to learn his trade secrets, causing his product to be boycotted, or forming a price conspiracy against him are likewise condemned.

The use of lotteries in connection with the sale of products is held an illegal trade practice. It is unlawful for the manufacturer of penny candy to provide for the sale of his goods on a lottery plan by which the purchaser of the lucky pieces of candy are refunded their purchase price.

Any false statement as to the seller's character is an unfair trade practice, such as a statement that the seller is a manufacturer and that the public by purchasing from him eliminates the middleman, when in fact the seller is a middleman and not a manufacturer. Falsely telling a purchaser that he is being given a special price or is being grouped in a category of purchasers who are given a special price when in fact there is no special price or category is also an unfair trade practice.

The use of a deceptively similar trade-mark is also made illegal.

The use of the name of a competitor or of a name deceptively similar to the competitor's name or the name of his product is an unfair trade practice that may be stopped by injunction. The person injured by this unfair competition may also sue for money damages to compensate for the injury through the diversion from him of sales that he would otherwise have had.

Where the name "borrowed" from the competitor is his own name or the special name that he has created for his product, the problem is basically one of proof of the effect of the practice and the extent of damages. An additional difficulty is added where the name of the competitor is a geographical name. Confined to its primary meaning, a geographical name is regarded as merely descriptive of the merchandise and is not capable of exclusive appropriation by any dealer. If the words have, however, been used so long and so exclusively by a particular manufacturer or dealer that they are generally understood by the public to refer to his particular product, the geographic name acquires a secondary meaning which justifies that manufacturer or dealer in preventing any one else from using that name. The question turns on whether there is a likelihood to confuse the competitor's article with the article that for years has gone under that particular name.

## § 13:5. State Securities Regulation

The phenomenal rise of industrial empires and modern corporations following the Civil War created a public mood favorable to the sale of corporate stocks and bonds. Dishonest manipulators took millions of dollars from a gullible public, which saw in the fancy engraved stock certificate or bond and in the name of "corporation" a magic assurance for the safety and the welfare of their investment. Different devices were employed. Sometimes the corporation whose stock or bonds were being sold did not exist. In some cases there was a corporation that consisted of an office of one room, but the giant plant or gold mine that it was supposed to operate did not exist. Slightly less illegal but nevertheless defrauding the public were the issues of securities in corporations that did exist but whose assets were greatly overvalued. In other cases a bona fide corporation would issue a large part of its stock to those on the inside without receiving from them any payment, as a result of which the assets acquired by the payments of members of the investing public were watered or thinned out since they were not matched by assets that the insiders should have contributed by payment for their stock. In some instances the manipulators of the stock would publish financial newspapers giving advice as to what securities were desirable for purchase when in fact they were praising securities in which they had a direct interest.

Often these manipulators would attempt to create the impression of great trading activity in their stock by means of wash sales. A wash sale is a fictitious sale that, although not in fact made, appears to the public as a bona fide transfer. Such a wash sale creates a false impression of trading activity and tends to make the price of the security rise. After the rise occurs, the manipulator sells his securities and obtains the profits resulting from the sale at the artificially-enhanced price. A similar device was that of placing matched orders. In this case the manipulator would employ two brokers, without informing one of the activity of the other, instructing one to sell a certain security at a certain price and the other to buy the same security at the same price. This again would appear to be a bona fide activity that would tend to make the price rise. In addition to these practices, the rigging of the market by means of false rumors and "inside tips" was also common.

The turn of the century saw such an expansion of these illegal trade practices that both state and national governments entered the field of regulation.

Many of the states adopted "blue-sky" laws of one variety or another. Some of these laws require that securities be approved by a state commission before they can be sold publicly or that dealers in securities be licensed. Other statutes merely provide that it is a criminal offense to engage in fraudulent stock practices and that an injunction may be obtained to prevent their continuation. These state laws were held constitutional by the Supreme Court of the United States but suffered from the defect of being limited in their sphere of operation. The fact that they could not reach the absentee dealer and transactions in interstate commerce made it imperative that the federal government enter the field of regulation.

### § 13:6. Federal Securities and Exchange Regulation

Federal regulation, in the form of investigation and publicity, had already been begun by the creation of the Bureau of Corporations in 1903. It was not, however, until the period of the great depression that the federal legislation assumed the proportions of a comprehensive plan.

By the Federal Securities Act of 1933 it is made unlawful for any issuer, underwriter, or dealer in securities to send either the securities or the prospectus for them through interstate commerce or in the mails without having first registered the security issue with the Securities Exchange Commission. In registering, full information must be given the Commission about capitalization, stockholder's rights, corporate debt, proposed selling price of the securities, and all commissions, discounts, and expenses of sale. In addition the Commission must be supplied with a balance sheet and with profit and loss statements. The information that is submitted to the Commission may be examined by the public.

The registration of securities with the Commission is not an approval by the Commission or by the government of the security nor any guarantee of the safety of the investment. The only effect of registration is to secure a full and adequate disclosure of information of which private investors may avail themselves.

A criminal penalty is imposed for failure to register or for the making of false statements to the Commission. The Commission may enjoin any practices that violate the Act, and the persons injured by the violation of the Securities Act may bring suit for civil damages against the violator.

There are a number of exceptions to the applicability of the Securities Act of 1933. It does not apply to the ordinary purchase and sale of stock by private individuals, nor does it apply to security issues under $100,000; the state laws remain operative as to these issues. A number of other exceptions are also made in terms of the body issuing the security, as securities issued by the government, or in terms of whether the issuer is already subject to some other form of regulation, as by the Interstate Commerce Commission in the case of interstate commerce carriers.

While the Securities Act of 1933 applies generally to all classes of securities, subject to the exceptions above indicated, it is merely a publicity-providing statute. The Transportation Act of 1920 conferred upon the Interstate Commerce Commission a much narrower jurisdiction, limited to the securities of interstate commerce carriers, but within that area gave the Commission a much greater power than possessed by the Securities Exchange Commission. Under the Transportation Act it is unlawful for any railroad to issue stock, bonds, or evidence of debt or assume any obligation until the Commission has investigated "the purposes and uses of the proposed issue and the proceeds thereof, or of the proposed assumption of obligation" and "authorizes such issue or assumption." In addition to an unlimited discretion to grant or refuse permission to issue a security, the Interstate Commerce Commission is also given the power to impose conditions or limitations upon such issuance.

In addition to the evils arising from the issuing and floating of securities, a number of evils were due to the practices at security exchanges. To some extent, improper exchange practices had been outlawed by state laws or by the voluntary action of the members of the various organized exchanges. The Securities and Exchange Act of 1934 carried further this regulation of exchanges. Certain practices, such as wash sales, matched orders, and circulation of false rumors and tips, are made unlawful and prohibited. Other practices that can be used either for a lawful trading or an unlawful manipulating purpose are subjected to the regulation of the Security Exchange Commission so that the Commission may see that they are used only for a legitimate purpose. Speculative activity in exchanges is restricted by giving the Commission power to fix the margin on which trading can be conducted and to restrict the extent to which money can be borrowed to finance stock transactions. Provision is made for giving the public complete information about securities listed on exchanges. In order to secure such a listing, it is necessary to file a registration statement containing information about the corporate and financial structure and management. Control of corporations by insiders is checked by requiring that solicitations for proxies state the identity and the interest of the solititor and what action is to be passed upon at the corporate meeting for which the proxy is solicited. Corporate insiders are also prohibited under certain circumstances from making a secret profit on the basis of information that they had as insiders but that the general public could not have.

Later statutes provide for the registration of interstate utility holding companies with the SEC and authorize the Federal Power Commission to regulate the rates of interstate shipments of natural gas and electric power. In registering, the holding company must file detailed information as to its corporate structure and financing. Authority is given to the SEC to order the dissolution of holding companies that have been created merely for the purpose of corporate manipulation and that serve no actual economic interest. If a holding company does not register as required by law, it is illegal for it to engage in any interstate business transactions. A holding company that has registered is subjected to various restrictions as to financing and security issue, and the Commission is given supervisory powers over the company's financial records.

## Questions for Discussion

1. (a) What remedies does a person defrauded by an unfair trade practice have at common law? (b) What are the limits on these remedies?

2. Is government regulation of unfair trade practices consistent with the principle of free enterprise and freedom of contract?

3. What is the constitutional basis for a state statute prohibiting unfair trade practices? for a federal statute?

4. What was the reason for the adoption of federal laws relating to unfair trade practices?

5. Describe three kinds of regulations designed to prevent the use of improper weights or measures.

6. What change has occurred in the pattern of the laws designed to control or prohibit unfair trade practices?

7. List five unfair trade practices that have been condemned under the federal law. State who is harmed by the practice that is prohibited and in what way.

8. Draft a food and drug act specifying the extent to which improper practices are condemned. Either restate the existing law or set forth what you believe it should be. Give reasons for your choice in either case.

9. Draft a "false labeling" act, specifying the extent to which labeling is regarded as false and is prohibited.

10. A dealer sends out several shipments of the same therapeutic device and at a later date sends a shipment of advertising literature describing the device. All the devices and the literature are sent to the same person. The devices are seized on the ground that the literature is false and that the devices are therefore falsely labeled within the meaning of the Federal Food, Drug and Cosmetics Act. The shipper defends on the ground that the literature, though describing the devices, was not part of the interstate shipment of the devices themselves, which were therefore not falsely labeled. Do you agree with the shipper? Discuss.

11. Does it make any difference in your answer if the devices in Question 10 are sent to one person and the advertising literature to another person?

12. A dealer distributed food products and then 18 weeks later sent to the persons who had received the products pamphlets describing them. The distributor was prosecuted on the ground that the statements were false and that the goods were accordingly misbranded. The defendant claimed that under the law the articles were misbranded only if there were false or misleading statements written on the article or the container itself or "accompanying" the article. Was he guilty of violating the Act? *Kordel* v. *United States*, 333 U.S. 872 (1948).

13. In view of such decisions as *United States* v. *Sullivan*, the power to pass laws against misbranding and false labeling should be exercised by the federal government alone. (a) Do you agree? (b) To what extent may state authority now be exercised?

14. (a) What is the Federal Trade Commission? (b) What powers does it have?

15. How does the Federal Trade Commission practice compare with the methods of enforcing the Sherman Act?

16. Is every unfair trade practice a violation of the antitrust law? If not, name three practices that are unfair but that are not violations of the antitrust law.

17. Is there any law against false advertising?

18. A dealer sold cabinets that, according to their printed instructions, had certain therapeutic qualities. The cabinets were seized by federal officers as falsely labeled. The dealer claimed that the goods were not "labeled" falsely because the instructions that contained the alleged false statements were not attached to the articles but were delivered separately with the article to the purchaser. Decide. *United States* v. *Four Devices*, 176 F.2d 652 (CCA 10th 1949).

19. The Federal Trade Commission ordered the Raladam Company, which was selling "Marmola," to cease advertising it as "a scientific remedy for obesity" and from advertising it without stating that it should only be taken upon prescription of a doctor. The company claimed that, whether or not the method of advertising was unfair, it could not be condemned as an unfair method of competition because it had not been shown by the Commission that any competitors were harmed by such advertising. Is the defense of the Company valid? *Federal Trade Commission* v. *Raladam*, 283 U.S. 643 (1931).

20. A manufacturer advertised that a medicated oil was beneficial in the treatment of certain skin diseases. The label on the bottle did not contain any statement of or directions for such use. He was enjoined from shipping the oil in interstate commerce on the ground that it violated the federal act. He claimed that it did not. Decide. *Colgrove* v. *United States*, 176 F.2d 614 (CCA 9th 1949).

21. Acting under the authority of the federal statute prohibiting the interstate shipment of deceptively or fraudently labeled goods, 95 barrels labeled "apple cider vinegar" were seized. It was admitted that the vinegar was not made from fresh apples, but it was claimed that the vinegar was in fact an apple cider vinegar since dried apples were soaked in water and then the vinegar was made from the apple cider produced from such apples. The government claimed that apple cider vinegar meant to the average person vinegar made from fresh apples and that because of this popular understanding the label, although technically truthful, was in fact deceptive. Was the shipper guilty of violating the federal statute? *United States* v. *Ninety-five Barrels of Alleged Apple Cider Vinegar*, 265 U.S. 438 (1924).

22. The Filled Milk Law of 1923 prohibits the shipment in interstate commerce of milk from which the natural butter fat has been removed and other fat or oil added. A shipper was prosecuted for sending filled milk through interstate commerce. His defense was that the article was not harmful. The government admitted that the article was not harmful, but it claimed that the filled milk was less nutritous than the natural milk. Was the shipper guilty of an unlawful practice? *United States* v. *Carolene Products Co.*, 304 U.S. 144 (1938).

23. A state law required that syrups containing more than 75% of glucose should be labeled on the retail package as "glucose." A federal statute provided a different form of label and permitted all syrups derived from corn to be labeled corn syrup. McDermott shipped across state lines corn

syrup containing 90% glucose. He was prosecuted under the state law for failing to label the retail packages in accordance with the state law. He claimed that the federal law gave him the right to label both wholesale and retail packages in the manner provided by the federal law and that the state law could not provide otherwise. Was he correct? *McDermott* v. *Wisconsin*, 228 U.S. 115 (1913).

24. The Winstead Hosiery Company labeled mixed wool articles as "natural wool," "Australian wool," and other similar labels that did not indicate the mixed nature of the article. The Federal Trade Commission ordered the company to stop the practice of using a "wool" label to describe a mixed article on the ground that it was an unfair trade practice. The company defended on the ground that all other manufacturers understood that the label was not to be taken as true and that the competitors of the company were not deceived. Is this a valid defense? *Federal Trade Commission* v. *Winstead Hosiery Company*, 258 U.S. 483 (1922).

25. A, a manufacturer, establishes a functional customer classification price list by which he sells at different rates to wholesalers, retailers, and consumers. A co-operative buying organization of retailers buys from A the same quantities as wholesalers and demands of him the lower wholesalers unit price. A refuses to sell at this price, and the co-operative complains to the Federal Trade Commission that A is guilty of an unfair trade practice. Decide. *George VanCamp & Sons, Co.* v. *American Can Co.*, 278 U.S. 245 (1929); *National Biscuit Co.* v. *F.T.C.*, 299 F.733 (1924).

26. The American Tobacco Company and the Puerto Rican Tobacco Company were independent companies, each competing for the cigarette trade of Puerto Ricans. The American Tobacco Company began a low-price selling campaign with the purpose of driving out the Puerto Rican Tobacco Company. The latter objected that such a sale was an unfair trade practice. Was the Puerto Rican Tobacco Company correct? *Puerto Rican Tobacco Co.* v. *American Tobacco Company*, 30 F.2d 234 (1929).

27. The local merchants in a small city are threatened by the competition of out-of-the-state mail order houses. In order to increase the operating expenses of the mail order houses, the local Chamber of Commerce entered into an agreement by which the local movies would accept mail-order catalogues in place of tickets of admission. Was this an unfair trade practice? *F.T.C.* v. *Chamber of Commerce of Missoula*, 5 F.T.C. 451 (1923).

28. The Delco Cleaners and Dyers did business in Delaware County. The name Delco was a contraction of the name of the county. A suit was brought to enjoin the use of the name "Delco" by another local concern calling itself the "Delco Valet Service." Decide *Berberian* v. *Ferm*, 166 Pa. Super. 108, 70 A.2d 394 (1950).

29. It has been proposed to create a separate Commerce Court dealing with the cases arising under the antitrust and trade practice laws. (a) May such a court be constitutionally created? (b) Can its decisions be made final?

30. List and describe five abuses relating to stocks and bonds that have been prohibited by state or federal laws.

31. What pattern has been followed by the laws regulating securities?

32. (a) What is the effect of a registration of securities with the SEC? (b) Should the SEC be given authority to approve securities as being safe investments?

33. How does the government restrict or prevent stock market speculation?

34. How can the federal government enforce its laws relating to security issuance and exchange?

35. During the period prior to national control of security holding companies, the National Electric Light Association spent twenty-five to thirty million dollars annually for the purpose of convincing the public of the soundness of the electric utility industry. These expenditures were paid for from funds donated by the electric companies that were members of the Association. In calculating the operating expenses of these member companies for the purpose of determining what rate they could charge for electricity, the amounts given to the Association for this purpose were listed. Was this proper? Does such an expense differ from an advertising expense?

36. X, a utility corporation, is affiliated with C, a holding company, and operates locally under a license from C. For this license, X makes an annual payment to C. A local state utility commission has jurisdiction over X but not over C outside the state. The state utility commission asks X questions with respect to the reasonableness of the payment it makes to C. X objects on the ground that this relates to C and the state utility commission cannot examine C's affairs. Is X correct? *Western Distributing Co.* v. *Public Service Commission,* 285 U.S. 119 (1932).

37. The Federal Investment Company and the Investment Advisors Act of 1940 require investment companies and advisors to register with the SEC in order to eliminate the various fraudulent practices that had developed in the investment business. What is the constitutional basis for bringing such companies and advisors under the control of a federal commission?

38. A legislature concludes that minority stockholders have abused the right to bring a suit against the officers and the directors, seeking to recover damages for mismanagement by them. To prevent the bringing of nuisance suits by minority stockholders, the legislature provides that the court may require a minority stockholder bringing such a suit to provide security to pay the defendant's expenses and attorney's fees in the event that the defendant has a valid defense. A stockholder who brings a derivative action against the officers and directors of the corporation refuses to give such security and claims that the act is unconstitutional. Is he correct? *Lapchak* v. *Baker,* 298 N.Y. 89, 80 N.E. 2d 751 (1948).

## Chapter 14

# REGULATION OF PRODUCTION



## § 14:1. Production and the Federal Commerce Power

The individual states, as incidental to their retained police power, may regulate production. Since the power to regulate production was not delegated to the national Congress, the conclusion required by a literal reading of the Constitution is that the federal government cannot regulate production. This was the view at first held by the Supreme Court of the United States, until, as noted in Chapter 9, the meaning of the commerce clause was expanded by the court. While the first four decisions in this chapter have been expressly or impliedly overruled by the later cases, a careful study of them is valuable in determining the scope of the doctrine of the later cases as well as in appreciating the judicial process.

### (a) *Manufacturing and commerce*

UNITED STATES v. E. C. KNIGHT CO.

156 U.S. 1 (1895)

OPINION BY FULLER, C.J.

By the purchase of the stock of the four Philadelphia refineries, with shares of its own stock, the American Sugar Refining Company acquired nearly complete control of the manufacture of refined sugar within the United States. . . .

The fundamental question is, whether . . . that monopoly can be directly suppressed under the [Sherman Antitrust Act]. . . .

"No distinction is more popular to the common mind, or more clearly expressed in economic and political literature, than that between manufacture and commerce. Manufacture is transformation—the fashioning of raw materials into a change of form for use. . . . If it be held that the term [commerce] includes the regulation of all such manufactures as are intended to be the subject of commercial transactions in the future, it is impossible to deny that it would also include all productive industries that contemplate the same thing. The result would be that Congress would be invested, to the exclusion of the States, with the power to regulate, not only manufactures, but also agriculture, horticulture, stock raising, domestic fisheries, mining—in short, every branch of human industry. For is there one of them that does not contemplate, more or less clearly, an interstate or foreign market? . . ."

Contracts, combinations, or conspiracies to control domestic enterprise in manufacture, agriculture, mining, production in all its forms, or to raise or lower prices or wages, might unquestionably tend to restrain external as well as domestic trade, but the restraint would be an indirect result, however inevitable and whatever its extent. . . .

There was nothing in the proofs to indicate any intention to put a restraint upon trade or commerce, and the fact, as we have seen, that trade or commerce might be indirectly affected was not enough to entitle complainants to a decree. . . .

## § 14:2. Extension of the Knight Doctrine

Upon this same theory that the commerce power permitted only the regulation of activities involving a change of place, the Court held invalid the attempt to prohibit the transportation of goods produced by employers employing child labor and the New Deal legislation attempting to regulate industry, agriculture, and mining.

### *(a) Embargo on child-labor-made goods*

HAMMER v. DAGENHART

247 U.S. 251 (1918)

Congress prohibited the interstate shipment of goods produced in plants that had employed children within thirty days prior to shipment.

OPINION BY DAY, J.

The power essential to the passage of this act, the Government contends, is found in the commerce clause of the Constitution. . . . The thing intended to be accomplished by this statute is the denial of the facilities of interstate commerce to those manufacturers in the states who employ children within the prohibited ages. The act in its effect does not regulate transportation among the states, but aims to standardize the ages at which children may be employed in mining and manufacturing within the states. The goods shipped are of themselves harmless. The act permits them to be freely shipped after thirty days from the time of their removal from the factory. When offered for shipment, and before transportation begins, the labor of their production is over, and the mere fact that they were intended for interstate commerce transportation does not make their production subject to federal control under the commerce power. . . . The making of goods and the mining of coal are not commerce, nor does the fact that these things are to be afterwards shipped, or used in interstate commerce, make their production a part thereof. . . . The production of articles intended for interstate commerce is a matter of local regulation. . . . This principle has been recognized often in this court. . . . If it were otherwise, all manufacture intended for interstate shipment would be brought under federal control to the practical exclusion of the authority of the States,—a result certainly not contemplated by the framers of the Constitution when they vested in Congress the authority to regulate commerce among the states. . . .

It is further contended that the authority of Congress may be exerted to control interstate commerce in the shipment of child-made goods because of the effect of the circulation of such goods in other states where the evil of this class of labor has been recognized by local legislation, and the right to thus employ child labor has been more rigorously restrained than in the state of production. In other words, that the unfair competition thus engendered may be controlled by closing the channels of interstate commerce to manufactures in those states where the local laws do not meet what Congress deems to be the more just standard of other states.

There is no power vested in Congress to require the states to exercise their police power so as to prevent possible unfair competition. Many causes may co-operate to give one state, by reason of local laws or conditions, an economic advantage over others. The commerce clause was not intended to give to Congress a general authority to equalize such conditions. In some of the states laws have been passed fixing minimum wages for women; in others the local law regulates the hours of labor of women in various employments. Business done in such states may be at an economic disadvantage when compared with states which have no such regulations; surely, this fact does not give Congress the power to deny transportation in interstate commerce to those who carry on business where the hours of labor and the rate of compensation for women have not been fixed by a standard in use in other states and approved by Congress. . . .

DISSENTING OPINION BY HOLMES, J.

. . . Congress is given power to regulate such commerce in unqualified terms. It would not be argued today that the power to regulate does not include the power to prohibit. . . .

The question, then, is narrowed to whether the exercise of its otherwise constitutional power by Congress can be pronounced unconstitutional because of its possible reaction upon the conduct of the States in a matter upon which I have admitted that they are free from direct control. . . . I should have thought that the most conspicuous decisions of this court had made it clear that the power to regulate commerce and other constitutional powers could not be cut down or qualified by the fact that it might interfere with the carrying out of the domestic policy of any State. . . . The States may regulate their internal affairs and their domestic commerce as they like. But when they seek to send their products across the state line they are no longer within their rights. If there were no Constitution and no Congress their power to cross the line would depend upon their neighbors. Under the Constitution such commerce belongs not to the States, but to Congress to regulate. It may carry out its views of public policy whatever indirect effect they may have upon the activities of the States. Instead of being encountered by a prohibitive tariff at her boundaries, the State encounters the public policy of the United States which it is for Congress to express. The public policy of the United States is shaped with a view to the benefit of the nation as a whole. . . . The national welfare as understood by Congress may require a different attitude within its sphere from that of some self-seeking State. It seems to me entirely constitutional for Congress to enforce its understanding by all the means at its command.

### *(b) Codes of competition for industry*

A.L.A. SCHECHTER POULTRY CORP. v. UNITED STATES

295 U.S. 495 (1935)

The National Industrial Recovery Act authorized representatives of the various industries in the United States to draw up individual codes of fair competition by which each industry was to be governed. It was hoped that by these codes unemployment would be relieved, the volume of business increased, working conditions improved, and child labor and unfair trade practices eliminated. United States officials co-operated in the preparation of these codes, which became effective when approved by the President of the United States. In the event that an industry could not agree to a code by which it was to be governed, the President was authorized to impose a code upon it. Once adopted, a code had the force of law and all members of the industry had to observe the code subject to civil and criminal liability for violation.

OPINION BY HUGHES, C.J.

The question of the application of the provisions of the Live Poultry Code to intrastate transactions . . . presents the question whether the particular provisions of the Live Poultry Code, which the defendants were convicted of violating and for having conspired to violate, were within the regulating power of Congress.

These provisions relate to the hours and wages of those employed by defendants in their slaughterhouses in Brooklyn and to the sales there made to retail dealers and butchers. . . . The interstate transactions in relation to that poultry then ended. . . .

The undisputed facts thus afford no warrant for the argument that the poultry handled by defendants at their slaughterhouse markets was in a "current" or "flow" of interstate commerce and was thus subject to congressional regulation. The mere fact that there may be a constant flow of commodities into a State does not mean that the flow continues after the property has arrived and has become commingled with the mass of property within the State and is there held solely for local disposition and use. So far as the poultry here in question is concerned, the flow in interstate commerce had ceased.

Did the defendants' transactions directly "affect" interstate commerce so as to be subject to federal regulation? The power of Congress extends not only to the regulation of transactions which are part of interstate commerce, but to the protection of that commerce from injury. . . .

In determining how far the federal government may go in controlling intrastate transactions upon the ground that they "affect" interstate commerce, there is a necessary and well-established distinction between direct and indirect effects. The precise line can be drawn only as individual cases arise, but the distinction is clear in principle. Direct effects are illustrated by the railroad cases . . . as e.g., the effect of failure to use prescribed safety appliances on railroads which are the highways of both interstate and intrastate commerce, injury to an employee engaged in interstate transportation by the negligence of an employee engaged in an intrastate movement, the fixing of rates for intrastate transportation which unjustly discriminate against interstate commerce. But where the effect of intrastate transactions upon interstate commerce is merely indirect, such transactions remain within the domain of state power. . . .

The question of chief importance relates to the provisions of the Code as to the hours and wages of those employed in defendants' slaughterhouse markets. It is plain that these requirements are imposed in order to govern the details of defendants' management of their local business. The persons employed in slaughtering and selling in local trade are not employed in interstate commerce. Their hours and wages have no direct relation to interstate commerce. The question of how many hours these employees should work and what they should be paid differs in no essential respect from similar questions in other local businesses which handle commodities brought into a State and there dealt in as a part of its internal commerce. . . . The argument of the Government proves too much. If the federal government may determine the wages and hours of employees in the internal commerce of a State, because of their relation to cost and prices and their indirect effect upon interstate commerce, it would seem that a similar control might be exercised over other elements of cost, also affecting prices, such as the number of employees, rents, advertising, methods of doing business, etc. All the processes of production and distribution that enter into cost could likewise be controlled. If the cost of doing an intrastate business is in itself the permitted object of federal control, the extent of the regulation of the cost would be a question of discretion and not of power.

The Government also makes the point that efforts to enact state legislation establishing high labor standards have been impeded by the belief that unless similar action is taken generally, commerce will be diverted from the States adopting such standards, and that this fear of diversion has led to demands for federal legislation on the subject of wages and hours. The apparent implication is that the federal authority under the commerce clause should be deemed to extend to the establishment of rules to govern wages and hours in intrastate trade and industry generally throughout the country, thus overriding the authority of the States to deal with domestic problems arising from labor conditions in their internal commerce.

It is not the province of the Court to consider the economic advantages or disadvantages of such a centralized system. It is sufficient to say that the Federal Constitution does not provide for it. . . . The authority of the federal government may not be pushed to such an extreme as to destroy the distinction, which the commerce clause itself establishes, between "commerce among the several States" and the internal concerns of a State. The same answer must be made to the contention that is based upon the serious economic situation which led to the passage of the Recovery Act,—the fall in prices, the decline in wages and employment, and the curtailment of the market for commodities. Stress is laid upon the great importance of maintaining wage distributions which would provide the necessary stimulus in starting "the cumulative forces making for expanding commercial activity." Without in any way disparaging this motive, it is enough to say that the recuperative efforts of the federal government must be made in a manner consistent with the authority granted by the Constitution. . . .

### *(c) Code of competition for bituminous coal industry*

CARTER v. CARTER COAL CO.

298 U.S. 238 (1936)

Congress adopted a law providing for a code for the bituminous coal industry similar to the NRA codes. The Court considered whether the Act was unconstitutional on the ground that working conditions, wages, and hours in mines could not be regulated by Congress under the commerce power.

OPINION BY SUTHERLAND, J.

We have seen that the word "commerce" is the equivalent of the phrase "intercourse for the purposes of trade." Plainly, the incidents leading up to and culminating in the mining of coal do not constitute such intercourse. The employment of men, the fixing of their wages, hours of labor and working conditions, the bargaining in respect of these things—whether carried on separately or collectively—each and all constitute intercourse for the purposes of production, not of trade. The latter is a thing apart from the relation of employer and employee, which in all producing occupations is purely local in character. Extraction of coal from the mine is the aim and the completed result of local activities. Commerce in the coal mined is not brought into being by force of these activities, but by negotiations, agreements and circumstances entirely apart from production. Mining brings the subject matter of commerce into existence. Commerce disposes of it. . . . Everything which moves in interstate commerce has had a local origin. Without local production somewhere, interstate commerce, as now carried on, would practically disappear. Nevertheless, the local character of mining, of manufacturing and of crop growing is a fact, and remains a fact, whatever may be done with the products. . . .

That the production of every commodity intended for interstate sale and transportation has some effect upon interstate commerce may be, if it has not already been, freely granted; and we are brought to the final and decisive inquiry, whether here that effect is direct, as the preamble [of the Act] recites, or indirect. The distinction is not formal, but substantial in the highest degree, as we pointed out in the *Schechter* case. . . .

Whether the effect of a given activity or condition is direct or indirect is not always easy to determine. . . . The distinction between a direct and an indirect effect turns, not upon the magnitude of either the cause or the effect, but entirely upon the manner in which the effect has been brought about. If the production by one man of a single ton of coal intended for interstate sale and shipment, and actually so sold and shipped, affects interstate commerce indirectly, the effect does not become direct by multiplying the tonnage, or increasing the number of men employed, or adding to the expense or complexities of the business, or by all combined. . . .

Much stress is put upon the evils which come from the struggle between employers and employees over the matter of wages, working conditions, the right of collective bargaining, etc., and the resulting strikes, curtailment and irregularity of production and effect on prices; and it is insisted that interstate commerce is greatly affected thereby. But, in addition to what has just been said, the conclusive answer is that the evils are all local evils over which the federal government has no legislative control. The relation of employer and employees is a local relation. At common law, it is one of the domestic relations. The wages are paid for the doing of local work. Working conditions are obviously local conditions. The employees are not engaged in or about commerce, but exclusively in producing a commodity. And the controversies and evils, which it is the object of the act to regulate and minimize, are local controversies and evils affecting local work undertaken to accomplish that local result. Such effect as they may have upon commerce, however extensive it may be, is secondary and indirect. An increase in the greatness of the effect adds to its importance. It does not alter its character. . . .

### § 14:3. The Stream-of-Commerce Doctrine

As opposed to the concept that local activity could not be regulated within the federal commerce power, the Supreme Court had recognized that local activity may be so vitally associated with interstate commerce that it could be regulated under the commerce power.

#### *(a) Stockyards and the stream of commerce*

STAFFORD v. WALLACE

258 U.S. 495 (1922)

OPINION BY TAFT, C.J.

The object to be secured by the [federal statute regulating the practices of brokers and commission men at stockyards] is the free and unburdened flow of live-stock from the ranges and farms of the West and the Southwest through the great stockyards and slaughtering centers on the borders of that region, and thence in the form of meat products to the consuming cities of the country in the Middle West and East, or, still as live-stock, to the feeding places and fattening farms in the Middle West or East for further preparation for the market.

The chief evil feared is the monopoly of the packers, enabling them unduly and arbitrarily to lower prices to the shipper who sells, and unduly and arbitrarily to increase the price to the consumer who buys. Congress thought that the power to maintain this monopoly was aided by control of the stockyards. Another evil which it sought to provide against by the act, was exorbitant charges, duplication of commissions, deceptive practices in respect of prices, in the passage of the livestock through the stockyards, all made possible by collusion between the stockyards management and the commission men, on the one hand, and the packers and dealers on the other. . . .

The stockyards are not a place of rest or final destination. . . . The stockyards are but a throat through which the current flows, and the transactions which occur therein are only incident to this current from the West to the East, and from one State to another. Such transactions cannot be separated from the movement to which they contribute and necessarily take on its character. . . . The sales are not in this aspect merely local transactions. They create a local change of title, it is true, but they do not stop the flow; they merely change the private interests in the subject of the current, not interfering with, but, on the contrary, being indispensable to its continuity. . . .

. . . The only question here is whether the business done in the stockyards between the receipt of the livestock in the yards and the shipment of them therefrom is a part of interstate commerce, or is so associated with it as to bring it within the power of national regulation. . . .

. . . Whatever amounts to more or less constant practice, and threatens to obstruct or unduly to burden the freedom of interstate commerce is within the regulatory power of Congress under the commerce clause, and it is primarily for Congress to consider and decide the fact of the danger and meet it. This court will certainly not substitute its judgment for that of Congress in such a matter unless the relation of the subject to interstate commerce and its effect upon it are clearly nonexistent. . . .

### § 14:4. The New Commerce Power and Production

From the decision in *Stafford* v. *Wallace* and the decision of the court sustaining a similar regulation of grain exchanges, it could have been argued that, whenever a local activity was such that disturbances or irregularities in the area of the local activity would interfere with the flow of goods in interstate commerce, the local activity came within the power of Congress to regulate commerce. It was argued by those who sought to extend the power of the federal government that, since the depression conditions in the various production and extractive industries were causing an interruption or slowing down of the flow of interstate goods, Congress was justified in regulating those industries. Why maintain a transportation system if nothing can be done to insure that there will be goods to transport? This was their argument, and this argument was rejected by the Supreme Court in the New Deal cases reported above until the Supreme Court reversed the basis for those New Deal cases and adopted the theory that, when an industry draws a substantial part of its raw materials or sends a substantial part of its finished products through channels of interstate commerce, any activity that interrupts production in that industry affects interstate commerce so directly that it may be regulated by Congress under the interstate commerce power.

The adoption of this broad construction was a repudiation of the classical view that manufacturing and other forms of production or extractive industry involved merely a change of form while commerce involved a change of place. The adoption of this view was, as many writers have observed, a constitutional revolution, and the vast area of local production activities has ceased to be reserved to the states alone by virtue of the Tenth Amendment and has become an area in which the national government as well as state governments may regulate. This change was made in the following case.

### *(a) National Labor Relations Act*

N.L.R.B. v. JONES & LAUGHLIN STEEL CORP.

301 U.S. 1 (1937)

OPINION BY HUGHES, C.J.

The scheme of the National Labor Relations Act . . . may be briefly stated. The first section sets forth findings with respect to the injury to commerce resulting from the denial by employers of the right of employees to organize and from the refusal of employers to accept the procedure of collective bargaining. There follows a declaration that it is the policy of the United States to eliminate these causes of obstruction to the free flow of commerce. The Act then defines the terms it uses, including the terms "commerce" and "affecting commerce." § 2. It creates the National Labor Relations Board and prescribes its organization. §§ 3-6. It sets forth the right of employees to self-organization and to bargain collectively through representatives of their own choosing. § 7. It defines "unfair labor practices." § 8. It lays down rules as to the representation of employees for the purpose of collective bargaining. § 9. The Board is empowered to prevent the described unfair labor practices affecting commerce and the Act prescribes the procedure to that end. . . .

. . . The respondent argues (1) that the Act is in reality a regulation of labor relations and not of interstate commerce; . . .

The facts as to the nature and scope of the business of the Jones & Laughlin Steel Corporation have been found by the Labor Board.

[The Court discussed in detail the interstate organization of the employer with various plants in different states.]

Summarizing these operations, the Labor Board concluded that the works in Pittsburgh and Aliquippa "might be likened to the heart of a self-contained, highly integrated body. They draw in the raw materials from Michigan, Minnesota, West Virginia, Pennsylvania in part through arteries and by means controlled by the respondent; they transform the materials and then pump them out to all parts of the nation through the vast mechanism which the respondent has elaborated."

To carry on the activities of the entire steel industry, 33,000 men mine ore, 44,000 men mine coal, 4,000 men quarry limestone, 16,000 men manufacture coke, 343,000 men manufacture steel, and 83,000 men transport its product. Respondent has about 10,000 employees in its Aliquippa plant, which is located in a community of about 30,000 persons. . . .

Practically all the factual evidence in the case, except that which dealt with the nature of respondent's business, concerned its relations with the employees in the Aliquippa plant whose discharge was the subject of the complaint. These employees were active leaders in the labor union. . . .

*First.* The Scope of the Act.—The Act is challenged in its entirety as an attempt to regulate all industry, thus invading the reserved powers of the States over their local concerns. . . .

. . . The grant of authority to the Board does not purport to extend to the relationship between all industrial employees and employers. Its terms do not impose collective bargaining upon all industry regardless of effects upon interstate or foreign commerce. It purports to reach only what may be deemed to burden or obstruct that commerce and, thus qualified, it must be construed as contemplating the exercise of control within constitutional bounds. It is a familiar principle that acts which directly burden or obstruct interstate or foreign commerce, or its free flow, are within the reach of the congressional power. Acts having that effect are not rendered immune because they grow out of labor disputes. . . . It is the effect upon commerce, not the source of the injury, which is the criterion. . . . Whether or not particular action does affect commerce in such a close and intimate fashion as to be subject to federal control, and hence to lie within the authority conferred upon the Board, is left by the statute to be determined as individual cases arise. . . .

We do not find it necessary to determine whether these features of defendant's business dispose of the asserted analogy to the "stream of commerce" cases. . . . The congressional authority to protect interstate commerce from burdens and obstructions is not limited to transactions which can be deemed to be an essential part of a "flow" of interstate or foreign commerce. Burdens and obstructions may be due to injurious action springing from other sources. The fundamental principle is that the power to regulate commerce is the power to enact "all appropriate legislation" for "its protection and advancement." . . . That power is plenary and may be exerted to protect interstate commerce "no matter what the source of the dangers which threaten it." . . . Although activities may be intrastate in character when separately considered, if they have such a close and substantial relation to interstate commerce that their control is essential or appropriate to protect that commerce from burdens and obstructions, Congress cannot be denied the power to exercise that control. *Schechter Corp.* v. *United States, supra.* . . .

It is thus apparent that the fact that the employees here concerned were engaged in production is not determinative. The question remains as to the effect upon interstate commerce of the labor practice involved. In the *Schechter* case, *supra,* we found that the effect there was so remote as to be beyond the federal power. To find "immediacy or directness" there was to find it "almost everywhere," a result inconsistent with the maintenance of our federal system. In the *Carter* case [298 U.S. 238], the Court was of the opinion that the provisions of the statute relating to production were invalid upon several grounds: that there was improper delegation of legislative power, and that the requirements not only went beyond any sustainable measure of protection of interstate commerce but were also inconsistent with due process. These cases are not controlling here.

. . . The stoppage of [respondent's] operations by industrial strife would have a most serious effect upon interstate commerce. In view of respondent's far-flung activities, it is idle to say that the effect would be indirect or remote. It is obvious that it would be immediate and might be catastrophic. We are asked to shut our eyes to the plainest facts of our national life and to deal with the question of direct and indirect effects in an intellectual vacuum. Because there may be but indirect and remote effects upon interstate commerce in connection with a host of local enterprises throughout the country, it does not follow that other industrial activities do not have such a close and intimate relation to interstate commerce as to make the presence of industrial strife a matter of the most urgent national concern. When industries organize themselves on a national scale, making their relation to interstate commerce the dominant factor in their activities, how can it be maintained that their industrial labor relations constitute a forbidden field into which Congress may not enter when it is necessary to protect interstate commerce from the paralyzing consequences of industrial war? We have often said that interstate commerce itself is a practical conception. It is equally true that interferences with that commerce must be appraised by a judgment that does not ignore actual experience.

Experience has abundantly demonstrated that the recognition of the right of employees to self-organization and to have representatives of their own choosing for the purpose of collective bargaining is often an essential condition of industrial peace. Refusal to confer and negotiate has been one of the most prolific causes of strife. This is such an outstanding fact in the history of labor disturbances that it is a proper subject of judicial notice and requires no citation of instances. The opinion in the case of *Virginia Railway Co.* v. *System Federation No. 40*, . . . points out that, in the case of carriers, experience has shown that before the amendment, of 1934, of the Railway Labor Act "when there was no dispute as to the organizations authorized to represent the employees and when there was a willingness of the employer to meet such representative for a discussion of their grievances, amicable adjustment of differences had generally followed and strikes had been avoided." That, on the other hand, "a prolific source of dispute had been the maintenance by the railroad of company unions and the denial by railway management of the authority of representatives chosen by their employees." The opinion in that case also points to the large measure of success of the labor policy embodied in the Railway Labor Act. But with respect to the appropriateness of the recognition of self-organization and representation in the promotion of peace, the question is not essentially different in the case of employees in industries of such a character that interstate commerce is put in jeopardy from the case of employees of transportation companies. And of what avail is it to protect the facility of transportation, if interstate commerce is throttled with respect to the commodities to be transported!

These questions have frequently engaged the attention of Congress and have been the subject of many inquiries. The steel industry is one of the great basic industries of the United States, with ramifying activities affecting interstate commerce at every point. The Government aptly refers to the steel strike of 1919-20 with its far-reaching consequences. The fact that there appears to have been no major disturbance in that industry in the more recent period did not dispose of the possibilities of future and like dangers to interstate commerce which Congress was entitled to foresee and to exercise its protective power to forestall. It is not necessary again to detail the facts as to respondent's enterprise. Instead of being beyond the pale, we think that it presents in a most striking way the close and intimate relation which a manufacturing industry may have to interstate commerce, and we have no doubt that Congress had constitutional authority to safeguard the right of respondent's employees to self-organization and freedom in the choice of representatives for collective bargaining.

### § 14:5. Present Federal Power Over Production

The new doctrine of the *Jones & Laughlin* case at the time of its adoption was regarded as a liberal or radical view, and the conservatives of that day had hopes that a later Court would repudiate this doctrine. This wish was disappointed, for the Court followed this view in other decisions, extended this view to agriculture and insurance, and held this view to warrant national price control in peacetime.

In the course of time, the view was accepted as an established fact by the conservatives, who then sought to use this doctrine to further their own objectives. The conservative group was thus found advocating the adoption of the Taft-Hartley Amendment, now known as the Federal Labor Management Relations Act of 1947, in order to restrict the activity of labor unions. The right to adopt such a restrictive statute is predicated upon the power of Congress under the commerce clause to regulate labor relations in industries manufacturing for interstate business. Both liberals and conservatives came to agree that the Congressional power extended to regulating labor relations in that production field. The ground of dispute had shifted from the existence of the power to regulate to the manner in which that power should be exercised.

The picture of the present federal power over production is not complete without adding to the new commerce power a reference to the broad powers that stem from the authority to wage war.

By virtue of the war power, Congress can impose any regulation on production. When the war power can be invoked, it is immaterial whether or not the production that is regulated would come within the scope of the commerce power. The war power is all-pervasive and reaches all economic activity if Congress deems it necessary for the proper prosecution of the war. The only limitation is that the regulation be reasonably related to preparation for, prosecution of, or recovery from war.

When the power to regulate production exists, it is immaterial what type of regulation is made. ". . . The state may regulate a business in any of its aspects, including the prices to be charged. . . ." *Nebbia* v. *New York,* 291 U.S. 502, 537. This breadth of the regulatory power is also enjoyed by the federal powers.

To date the forms of regulation have followed certain definite patterns. For the most part, regulations of production have been in terms of regulating working conditions, hours and wages of labor, and collective bargaining. Two newcomers in the field of regulation are the regulation of price and the regulation of quantity produced.

To date government has not attempted to specify what articles should be produced by manufacturers, although at different times in our history bounty or subsidy plans have been adopted to encourage production along certain lines. Some effort has been made along the line of standardizing production so that all manufacturers making the same article would follow the same pattern. This regulation has been mainly the securing of voluntary co-operation of producers rather than the establishment of standards to which manufacturers must adhere.

## Questions for Discussion

1. What was the difference between the *Knight* case and the *Mandeville Farms* case (page 132).

2. In the *Knight* case the Court stated that if the commerce power extended to production the duty would fall upon Congress to regulate many local details. How is the problem met today in view of the fact that the *Knight* case has been reversed?

3. What is the difference between the *Hammer* case and *United States* v. *Darby* (page 103)?

4. In the *Hammer* case the Court states: "The Act in a double sense is repugnant to the Constitution. It not only transcends the authority delegated to Congress over commerce, but also exerts a power as to a local matter to which the federal authority does not extend." Is this interpretation of the scope of the federal powers correct?

5. Did the Court in the *Schechter* case regard the payment of substandard wages as an unfair practice that was furthered by the use of the channels of interstate commerce? Compare with *United States* v. *Darby* page 103).

6. How would you define the Federal commerce power on the basis of the decisions in the:

(a) *Schechter* case.
(b) *Jones & Laughlin Steel Corp.* case.
(c) *American Light and Power* v. *S.E.C.* case.

7. In determining whether an activity may be regulated under the commerce power, does the Court consider whether the activity (a) is interstate commerce or (b) "directly affects" interstate commerce?

8. Name two cases in this chapter in which the Court was guided by:

(a) A belief that the spirit of the Constitution required that state control be preserved in "local" matters.
(b) A fear that, if federal power would be recognized in the case before it, it would be impossible to find any limitations upon the federal power in any other case.

9. What is the difference between the *Carter* case and *N.L.R.B.* v. *Jones & Laughlin Steel Corp.* and *United States* v. *Darby* (page 103)?

10. (a) Of what significance is the first section of the National Labor Relations Act, which sets forth findings by Congress that injury to commerce results from the refusal by employers to recognize labor unions and to bargain with them? (b) Would the statute be constitutional without such recitals? (c) Is the Court bound by the recitals or can it examine the facts to determine whether the recitals are true?

11. In the *Jones & Laughlin Steel Corporation* case the Court states that it is the effect upon commerce, not the source of the injury, that determines whether a matter may be regulated so as to prevent its harming interstate commerce. What is the test as to whether an activity has an effect upon interstate commerce?

12. Why did not the Court consider whether the activities of the Jones & Laughlin Steel Corporation amounted to a "stream of commerce" within the meaning of the decision in *Stafford* v. *Wallace* (page 203)?

13. Can this *Jones & Laughlin Steel Corporation* case be reconciled with the *Schechter* case and the *Carter Coal Company* case?

14. In the *Jones & Laughlin Steel Corporation* case the Court states: "and of what avail is it to protect the facilities of transportation, if interstate commerce is throttled with respect to the commodities to be transported!" What is the value of this statement as a legal argument?

15. Why is the *Jones & Laughlin Steel Corporation* case referred to as a constitutional revolution?

16. Does the *Jones & Laughlin Steel Corporation* case make the extension of the commerce power to a manufacturer dependent upon whether the bulk of his raw materials is brought in from another state and the bulk of his finished products is exported to other states?

17. Should it make any difference in the application of the *Jones & Laughlin Steel Corporation* decision whether the title to the goods is owned by the manufacturer or by a consignee or an agent of the manufacturer?

18. Is a manufacturer subject to the commerce power if he purchases all his raw materials locally within the state and sells all his finished products locally within the state?

19. The Consolidated Edison Company produced electricity and sold almost all of it for use within New York State. It sold power principally to interstate railroads, New York harbor lighting facilities, and interstate carriers. Proceedings were brought before the National Labor Relations Board on the claim that it violated the Wagner Labor Relations Act. The company claimed that it was not subject to the Act because it was not engaged in interstate commerce or production for interstate commerce. Decide. *N.L.R.B.* v. *Consolidated Edison Co.,* 305 U.S. 197 (1938).

20. The Jones Company made clothing from cloth that it purchased within the state and then resold within the state to distributors. It had no association or business transactions with anyone outside of the state. A complaint was filed before the National Labor Relations Board claiming that the Jones Company violated the national act. The company defended on the ground that it was not engaged in or producing for interstate commerce. If this defense is true, the Board did not have jurisdiction. Did the Board have jurisdiction over the complaint? *N.L.R.B.* v. *Fainblatt,* 306 U.S. 601 (1939).

# Chapter 15

# REGULATION OF LABOR



## § 15:1. Power to Regulate Labor

Regulation of labor by the national government is based primarily on the power to regulate interstate commerce. Prior to the decision of the *Jones & Laughlin Steel Corporation* case, this area was negligible since it was restricted to those employed by interstate carriers. With the decision in that case, however, the commerce power was broadened to permit the regulation of labor relations and labor practices within the large industries that formed part of a national economic activity. In addition, Congress may regulate labor under its war power.

The power of the states to regulate labor has been much broader in that it comes within their recognized police power to adopt laws for the benefit of the public health, safety, welfare, and morals.

In consequence of the extension of federal power into "local" areas of production, the bulk of the industries find themselves subject to regulation by both state and nation. As in the case of other areas of concurrent federal-state power, the federal law is supreme and sets aside any inconsistent state law.

In addition to these governmental powers, both the federal government and the state governments in making contracts for the construction of public buildings or in purchasing materials from private enterprisers can include in their contract any labor regulations that they may wish the private enterpriser to follow. This is not based on the power of government to regulate but merely on the economic pressure that the government as a customer or purchaser can bring to bear on the private enterpriser by threatening to refuse to purchase from him if he does not comply with those regulations.

Regulation of labor by political subdivisions, such as cities and towns, is also permitted if, under the law of the state, the political subdivision is permitted to exercise such powers.

In general, laws for the safety of the worker, laws for his protection in case of fire or disaster, or laws establishing sanitation standards were generally sustained although they constituted a restriction on the freedom of the enterpriser to run his own factory as he chose.

## § 15:2. Hours and Wages

The right of the lawmaker to regulate the hours of work and the wages received by the worker was not so readily recognized as the right to regulate the working conditions. Indirectly a change in the working conditions would reflect itself as a money loss to the employer, yet the courts treated working conditions as something separate from wage and hour regulation.

At first wage and hour laws were condemned as violating the freedom of both the employer and the employee to make any contract that they chose. Gradually this concept of due process of law was changed and the right to make a contract of employment was regarded as subject to the interest of the community, which could impose limitations on that freedom. Such regulations were first sustained within the field of hour regulation and within those areas of employment where the work was manifestly dangerous, as in the case of mining and smelting or where the workers concerned were women and children. Slowly these qualifications were removed until finally either a state government or the national government may now impose reasonable restrictions on the hours of employment of any person in any line of employment.

The vitality of laissez-faire freedom of contract was maintained much longer in the field of wage regulation. In 1923 the Supreme Court of the United States held that a minimum wage law for women violated the freedom of contract guaranteed by the due process clause. This view was reaffirmed in 1936, and it was not until the following year that minimum wage laws were held to be valid.

Laws regulating wages have thus far been principally minimum wage laws, with some provision made for payment of prevailing wages. The latter form of provision is most commonly found in contracts between the government and a private contractor or materialman by which the private enterpriser is bound by the contract to pay to his employees the prevailing rate of wages. The lawmaker has not yet attempted to fix a maximum wage rate or an exact wage rate.

Typical is the federal Fair Labor Standards Act of 1938, which established a minimum wage of 25 cents an hour and a 44-hour maximum week with time and a half for overtime, which by the terms of the statute gradually changed to 40 cents an hour and a 40-hour week with time and a half for overtime. By later amendments the minimum rate was increased to $1 an hour. The Act applies only to carriers and manufacturing plants operating in and producing for interstate commerce. Exceptions to the Act may be authorized by the Wage and Hour Administrator. It was under this statute that the famous portal-to-portal pay cases arose in which the Supreme Court held that compensation was to be allowed workers for the time spent in going from the entrance of the employer's premises to the worker's actual place of work, in preparing for work, in cleaning up after work, and in leaving the actual place of work and going to the exit of the employer's premises. By statute adopted in 1947, compensation for such periods is excluded unless agreed to by the parties by contract or established by custom.

The federal Walsh-Healey Act provides that anyone selling more than $10,000 worth of material to the federal government must conform to the federal employment standards of paying prevailing wages, maintaining an 8-hour day and a 40-hour week, maintaining safe and sanitary working conditions, and not employing convicts, males under sixteen years of age, or females under eighteen years of age. The Bituminous Coal Act and the Sugar Act also provide that the federal government will not purchase from any producer not conforming to federal labor standards.

Public works statutes commonly provide for the payment of wages at the rate prevailing in the locality and make it a criminal offense for the contractor to require a rebate or kickback to him of any part of the wages.

## § 15:3. Labor Supply

Laws restricting the labor supply have been inspired either by the desire to reduce competition for available jobs or by the desire to protect the persons excluded from working.

In the interest of reducing the number of persons available for employment, labor unions have been in favor of restricting immigration to the United States and of prohibiting convict labor and the labor of women and children. In general, such laws are valid provided they do not go to the extreme of preventing an able-bodied person from engaging in work that will not be harmful to him. For example, a statute restricting the right of aliens to work for private employers after they have been lawfully admitted into the United States is unconstitutional. Child labor laws and laws restricting or prohibiting labor by women do not come within this category, as the prohibition or restriction is based on the theory that it is for their protection to subject them to restraint and that, through benefiting them, society will also be benefited indirectly.

## § 15:4. Security

Within the last several decades, a group of labor laws have loomed into significance which have as their object the giving of security to a worker against the loss and the hardship caused by industrial accidents, unemployment, and old age.

At the common law, an employee who was injured while engaged in work could sue his employer if the employer was negligent and such negligence had been the cause of the employee's injury. If the employer was not negligent, then the employee could not recover from him. The plight of the worker was made more difficult by the fact that, even assuming that the employer had been at fault and that this fault had been the cause or a contributing cause of the worker's injury, the worker would still be barred from recovering any damages for his injury if it were shown that he had in any degree himself been negligent or had assumed the risk involved in the work, or that, with certain exceptions, the injury had been caused by a fellow servant.

In order to establish his right to damages, a worker was required to bring a suit at law for money damages. This action might take anywhere from one to three years to prosecute to a final conclusion. The worker might find it difficult to obtain witnesses to testify in his behalf. If his witnesses were still working for the employer, it is unlikely that they would testify for the worker to the detriment of the employer. The injured worker, or, if he had been killed, his family, would thus be put to the great burden of prosecuting a long law suit in which the chances of victory were comparatively small. These obstacles proved so great that many a worker or his family, faced with the need of money for immediate support, were willing to compromise the cause of action with the employer at a fraction of its face value.

In course of time, a rising wave of humanitarianism became conscious of this unsatisfactory treatment of the injured worker. The critics pointed to the fact that each year the employer would set aside a fund to repair and replace machines that had been broken, not because they were at fault or because the employer was at fault, but merely because the machines would, as machines do, wear out and break down in course of time. The critics contended that the men who were working for the employer should be given at least an equal treatment with the machines and that when they were injured or broke down in the course of employment they should be compensated. This gave rise to the philosophy of workmen's compensation under which the employee who is injured during the course of his employment is paid, not because his employer was at fault, but merely because he, the employee, was injured while engaged in work.

Under the workmen's compensation statutes the amount the worker receives is generally about one quarter to one half of what he would receive if he would be able to win a law suit against the employer. Since the odds are that he would lose a law suit against the employer, it is to the benefit of the worker to receive a smaller but certain amount rather than to take the chance of all or nothing.

The workmen's compensation statutes provide for payments according to a scheduled rate to employees to compensate them for injuries that they receive in the course of their employment. Under these statutes it is immaterial whether the employer or the worker is at fault, although the majority of the statutes bar the worker from recovering if the injury is due to the drunkenness or the willful misconduct of the worker himself.

Such workmen's compensation laws were at first held unconstitutional on the theory that the employer could not be required to pay money to an employee unless the employer were at fault and that he was being unconstitutionally deprived of property without due process of law if when not at fault he was made to pay money to the employee. To avoid this view a number of states adopted so-called optional plans, under which the employer and the employee were given the privilege at the time the contract of hiring was made, or within a short time thereafter, to reject the provisions of the workmen's compensation act. If no rejection was made, then the act was held to apply. Today this distinction is unimportant because the Supreme Court of the United States has sustained the constitutionality of compulsory workmen's compensation. This decision is binding as respects the interpretation of the federal constitution and, although not binding as respects state constitutions, is of course given great weight.

The problems relating to workmen's compensation today are details of administration and coverage. Originally the typical workmen's compensation law required a visible accident or happening and did not provide compensation for occupational diseases that developed slowly in the course of employment without having any visible time or accident of beginning. Today most workmen's compensation laws provide for such occupational diseases as well as the accidental injuries. An extension has also been made by many to provide compensation for a second injury received by a worker as well as for the first one received by him. Development has also been made of new forms of administering the workmen's compensation insurance funds.

Among newcomers to the field of worker's security are unemployment insurance and social security laws. These laws are designed to provide a payment to a worker while he is unemployed or after he is over a certain age for employment. The object of such laws is both to maintain morale and to support the worker during the period when he is not actually employed and also by maintaining his income to preserve the purchasing power of the community.

### § 15:5. Unions

For centuries, unions of working men were illegal regardless of the nature of their activity. It was not until the middle of the last century that the courts of this country adopted the view that it was lawful to form a labor union and that the question of liability for unlawfulness depended not upon the fact that there was a labor union but upon what the labor union was actually doing. The adoption of this new view was accelerated by the rise of the modern factory system. With a growing number of factory workers, it became increasingly impossible to continue to hold that workers by acting in concert were necessarily committing an unlawful act.

The era following the Civil War saw the rise of the Knights of Labor, a labor union that failed because of its attempt to include too many and to do too much. This union planned to operate as a national union, including within its membership all workers in the country regardless of their skill or lack of skill. As a program it advocated a general sweeping reform going beyond the limits of what might be termed a labor reform. It was not long before this vast organization collapsed of its own weight and dissensions within its ranks over differences in policy. It was gradually supplanted by the American Federation of Labor, which organized each craft or trade in a separate union and loosely linked these craft unions together by a central congress or federation. The policies of the Federation were restricted ordinarily to what might be called labor laws. During the same period the Brotherhoods of railway operating workers were formed. These Brotherhoods were, for practical purposes, the same as the types of unions found in the American Federation of Labor; but they remained outside the Federation and acted as a separate federation. Both the AFL and the Railway Brotherhoods were restricted to trained men who took pride in their skills. Because of these class distinctions, the unskilled and manual laborer found himself excluded from the significant labor unions. This exclusion encouraged the formation of the International Workers of the World. As its name implied, this was to be a world association of workers, primarily unskilled, who would be the proletariat in a coming socialist revolution. As a world organization the I. W. W. collapsed when World War I showed that the loyalty of some of its members to their respective countries was greater than their former alleged loyalty to a new international workers' world. At the same time, the organization was greatly weakened by treason and sedition prosecutions of others of its members who opposed the war on the ground that it was the work of capitalistic imperialism.

As a result of this historical development, the principal labor unions in the United States following World War I were those that belonged to the American Federation of Labor and the Railway Brotherhoods. These unions were unions of skilled men. But the

United States was embarking upon an era of industrial expansion in the mass-production industries in which skilled men were not involved. The long assembly line in which one worker did one simple mechanical job over and over and the plant in which operation was run by push-button presented a new worker whose skill was negligible compared to the trained craftsmen of the AFL and the Railway Brotherhoods. While these men did not fit into any union then existing, they were a continuing and growing threat to the safety of the existing unions. It was apparent that, in course of time, the mass-production worker would outnumber the skilled craft worker and, if all industry should be organized on a mass-production basis, the gains that the craft union men had slowly won would all be lost. This problem led to serious discussion within union ranks of the manner in which the new mass-production workers should be unionized. The AFL appointed a Committee on Industrial Organization, which reported in favor of the vertical or industrial unionization of each plant instead of the horizontal or craft organization on which the AFL was patterned. Sharp conflict within the AFL over these two policies led finally to the expulsion of John L. Lewis and the fellow-members of his committee. They in turn formed the Congress of Industrial Organizations. There then followed a period of rivalry between the CIO, advocating generally vertical unionization on the one hand, and the AFL advocating horizontal unionization on the other. In 1955, the AFL and the CIO merged.

### § 15:6. Labor Warfare

Over a long term, employer and employees are in a sense partners in a common enterprise. Each is essential to the other, and, if each does his task properly, each makes a material and essential contribution to the economic advance of all. Nevertheless, at a particular moment they are adverse parties with respect to the share that each shall take from the enterprise and also, in more modern times, with respect to whether the employee shall have any voice in the management of the enterprise.

Under a truly free enterprise system, the employer or entrepreneur is free to dictate all the terms of the employment contract. The only limitation on this freedom is the practical one that arises if workers cannot be found who are willing to work on those terms. The employer today is no longer able to contract with such freedom. Government, either national or state, tells him that he cannot make an employment contract which pays less than a stated number of cents an hour, or employ a person longer than a stated number of hours, or employ a person in a factory that does not conform to certain safety and sanitary requirements. The area in which the employer is thus free to exercise his choice has been narrowed by government regulation.

Within the permitted area of freedom of contract, what determines the terms of the contract? Over a long term, the factors of supply and demand and the productivity of labor will be the determining elements; but at any particular moment, the factor that controls is the bargaining power of the parties. For some, this bargaining power is based upon their possession of a natural talent so that the employer knows that, unless he pays their price, he will not be able to secure such services. For others, bargaining power exists in terms of political pressure that the party can bring to bear in securing favorable laws. For the greater part of those employed in the modern or factory industry, bargaining power exists in terms of union strength.

While not confined to unions, the picket, the boycott, and the strike have been the traditional weapons by which labor makes its bargaining power felt by the employer. These are met by the employer by the blacklist, the injunction, and the lockout.

It is difficult to make any simple statement respecting the legality of the weapons used by labor in its economic warfare. This is due to the fact that legality has not been established at one time for all practices but is a composite of decisions and statutes scattered over the years. The matter is further complicated by the fact that in recent years both courts and lawmakers have made many a right-about-face in determining the legality of such practices.

Certain general observations may be made that are most likely to remain true in the future. The first is that labor activity is more likely to be held legal where it relates to hours, wages, or working conditions. As the dispute in which the labor group is involved moves away from these primary subjects, the probability or possibility of illegality increases.

The second generalization is that labor activity is more likely to be held lawful when it is engaged in by employees against their own employer with whom they have a dispute. A tendency toward illegality is found where persons who are not employed by the employer who has the dispute try to bring pressure or where pressure is brought not upon the employer engaged in the dispute but upon persons with whom he deals or customers who patronize him. While some degree of stranger activity is permitted and while some degree of pressure on strangers is lawful, the danger increases that the labor activity will be held unlawful as it proceeds in the secondary area further and further away from the primary.

### § 15:7. Anti-Injunction Laws

One of the earliest evils from the standpoint of labor was the abusive use of the injunction. For centuries, courts of equity had granted injunctions or orders to stop or desist where it was shown to the chancellor that the person ordered to stop was about to engage in conduct that would cause irreparable harm to property that could not be adequately compensated for by the payment of money damages to the person injured. It was not until the closing decades of the last century that the courts made this remedy available to employers against labor. The practice soon developed by which an employer fearing any type of labor difficulty would obtain a sweeping injunction prohibiting the workers from engaging in any labor union activity. These injunctions would be issued upon no other proof than affidavits taken by the employer himself or by persons employed by him. The decree or injunction that the judge signed would be drawn by the attorney for the employer, and little effort was made to confine it to prohibiting only unlawful activity. Its sweeping terms would often prohibit lawful as well as unlawful activity.

While technically an injunction is not binding upon a person until he is served with it, little serious effort was given to apply this rule. Workers were arrested for contempt of the injunction before they knew that it had been granted. The problem was further complicated by the fact that in many areas the workers were foreign-born and did not understand English. Even when they did see the injunction, they did not know what it meant. Even those who did know English were not in a much better position, because the legal language of the day did not serve to clarify the scope of the injunction. The unfairness of the situation was further multiplied by the fact that those violating the injunction, although they could be fined or sent to jail for contempt, were not given a trial by jury but were tried by the very judge whose injunction they had violated. While this was established equity practice, it nevertheless ran counter to the Anglo-American concept that the maker of the law and the trier of the violator should not be one and the same person. In this case the judge who made the order also punished the violator. When there is finally added the observation that in many instances the judges shared the same social and economic beliefs as the employers, there is little cause to be surprised that labor considered the injunction one of its greatest enemies.

After years of political pressure, labor was able in 1932 to secure the passage of the Federal Anti-Injunction Act, commonly known as the Norris-LaGuardia Act. This law was paralleled by similar statutes in a number of states. The main object of such laws was to prohibit injunctions in "labor disputes" except under very strict limitations. "Labor disputes," as used in these statutes, was defined to include not merely employer-employee disputes but also controversies respecting employment in which outsiders were involved. This removed the injunction evil in labor disputes, but only by virtually destroying the injunction itself. It did not preserve the essential arm of equity of the injunction. In the course of subsequent years, the law-maker came to believe that this curtailment of the injunction went too far. As an illustration, the law-maker could show that the courts could not enjoin an outside union from picketing an employer for the purpose of forcing him to recognize the outside union, even though the employer was recognizing a union selected by the majority of his employees that he was required by the National Labor Relations Act to recognize. Thus employers could be caught in the dilemma that under the National Labor Relations Act they were required to recognize one union, but that, because of the Federal Anti-Injunction Act, they could not stop a second union from picketing them to make them recognize the second union.

Such cases as these led to the modification of the Norris-LaGuardia Act in 1947 by the Taft-Hartley amendment to the National Labor Relations Act. This injunction restoration movement was also imitated by a number of states. Under these more recent statutes, it was generally provided that certain acts by unions constituted unfair labor practices and that the labor relations board might obtain an injunction from the appropriate court to compel the labor unions to desist from such unfair labor practices. In addition, in the case of the federal law, an injunction might be obtained to delay for 80 days a strike in a national industry where national health or safety was threatened.

## § 15:8. Antitrust Laws and Labor

Little thought was at first given to the possibility that labor unions would come within the scope of the Sherman Antitrust Act of 1890. Great was the consternation of organized labor when the Supreme

Court in the *Danbury Hatters* case, 235 U.S. 522 (1908), held that a labor union could be prosecuted under the antitrust law. A concerted drive upon Congress was immediately begun by organized labor, which thought itself successful in securing exemption from the antitrust law when Congress in 1914 adopted the Clayton Act. This Act was either intentionally or accidentally vaguely drawn, and the Supreme Court shortly thereafter held that the Act did not change the pre-existing law. The Supreme Court later reversed itself to hold that labor unions when acting by themselves were not subject to the antitrust laws.

In the case of *United States* v. *Hutcheson* the Court concluded that, since certain conduct could no longer be enjoined because of the Norris-LaGuardia Act, it was illogical to hold that it could at the same time be illegal or subject the union to civil liability. The Supreme Court accordingly held that labor unions were no longer liable to either injunctive process or civil or criminal liability under the antitrust laws.

### *(a) Unions and the Sherman Act*

UNITED STATES v. HUTCHESON

312 U.S. 219 (1941)

OPINION BY FRANKFURTER, J.

Clearly, then, the facts here charged constitute lawful conduct under the Clayton Act unless the defendants cannot invoke that act because outsiders to the immediate dispute also shared in the conduct. But we need not determine whether the conduct is legal within the restrictions which *Duplex Co.* v. *Deering*, 254 U.S. 443, gave to the immunities of § 20 of the Clayton Act. Congress in the Norris-LaGuardia Act has expressed the public policy of the United States and defined its conception of a "labor dispute" in terms that no longer leave room for doubt.

. . .

To be sure, Congress expressed this national policy and determined the bounds of a labor dispute in an act explicitly dealing with the further withdrawal of injunctions in labor controversies. But to argue, as it was urged before us, that the *Duplex* case still governs for purposes of a criminal prosecution is to say that that which on the equity side of the court is allowable conduct may in a criminal proceeding become the road to prison. . . . That is not the way to read the will of Congress, particularly when expressed by a statute which, as we have already indicated, is practically and historically one of a series of enactments touching one of the most sensitive national problems. . . .

### § 15:9. National Labor Relations Act

Among the leaders of the New Deal regime, many thought that the strife then existing in the field of industrial relations was due largely to the refusal of the employers to recognize the right of workers to form their own unions and the refusal of the employers to bargain collectively with those unions selected by their workers. It was accordingly thought that, if the employers could be made to recognize and bargain with those unions, much of the industrial strife would be removed. It was therefore provided in the NRA that the codes of fair competition which were to be adopted for the various industries should specify that the workers would have the right to form their own unions and to bargain collectively. Although the NRA was held unconstitutional, this provision was extracted from the statute and was expanded into the Wagner or National Labor Relations Act of 1935.

The National Labor Relations Act declared that employees in interstate commerce or in industries producing goods for interstate commerce had the right to bargain collectively through representatives of their own choosing and that employers were guilty of unfair labor practices when they refused to bargain collectively with such unions, or maintained company unions, or discriminated in any way against employees because of their union membership or activity or because they testified before a National Labor Relations Board hearing. The Act created a National Labor Relations Board that was given the duty of determining the unit or the area for collective bargaining and of ascertaining by means of an election which union, if any, was selected by the majority of the workers to act as their collective bargaining agent. This Board was also authorized to hold hearings to determine when unfair labor practices had been committed and to order the employer to stop such practices, to reinstate workers improperly fired, and in certain cases to award them back pay for the period of their improper discharge. The statute was clearly a workers' law in that it did not impose any liability or duty on the worker and was aimed at conduct of employers alone.

A number of states adopted laws patterned after the federal law to apply to areas not within the reach of the federal commerce power. Among miscellaneous anti-employer practice laws that were adopted in this decade may be cited the Byrnes Act of 1936, which makes it a federal crime for a strikebreaker to move in interstate commerce or for any person to cause a strikebreaker to be so transported.

### § 15:10. National Labor Management Relations Act

Encouraged by the Wagner Act, certain labor practices appeared which gave rise to a move to change the law. In 1947 the Taft-Hartley Act was passed, amending the National Labor Relations Act and adding certain provisions not in that Act. It added a section of union practices that were condemned as unfair labor practices and repealed the Norris-LaGuardia Act to the extent that the National Labor Relations Board was authorized to obtain injunctions to stop such unfair labor practices. In the case of certain unfair labor practices, the party injured was given the right to sue the labor unions. In this connection, prior decisions were incorporated into statute law by providing that a union could sue or be sued in its collective name. The unions were also required to furnish detailed information as to their organization and financial condition, and their leaders were required to take affidavits that they were not Communists or members of other organizations advocating the forcible overthrow of the government. The Norris-LaGuardia Act was further restricted by permitting the issuance of an injunction upon the application of the United States Attorney General to enjoin for a period of 80 days a threatened strike or lockout in a major industry if the national health or safety would be harmed. Government employees were barred from striking by the provision that, if they did so, they would be discharged, could not be re-employed by the government for three years, and would lose their civil service status, if any. The Act further limited labor unions by restricting the use of money for political activities and regulated the creation and control of welfare funds established by unions.

The Taft-Hartley Act was paralled by a number of laws adopted in the states amending the state labor relation laws. Since that time a number of the state laws have been repealed.

Of the same nature as the Taft-Hartley Amendment was the Anti-Petrillo Act of 1946, amending the Communications Act of 1934, and making it a criminal offense to compel a radio station to hire musicians who were not needed, to pay for services that were not performed, or to refrain from broadcasting music of school children or music from foreign countries.

## § 15.11. Labor-Management Reporting and Disclosure Act

In order to insure the honest and democratic administration of unions, Congress adopted the Labor-Management Reporting and Disclosure Act of 1959 regulating unions operating in or affecting interstate commerce. Under it, such unions must adopt constitutions and bylaws, and file copies of them together with detailed reports on administrative and financial matters. Each officer and key employee is required to file a report that sets forth any interest he or a member of his family has which conflicts with his duties to the union. Reports are required of labor relations consultants, and employers must report payments to union officers. The grounds on which a national union may exercise control or trusteeship power over a local union or its funds are specified to prevent abuse of that power.

The Act protects rights of union members within their unions by guaranteeing equality, the right to vote on specified matters, and information on union matters and contract, and it protects members from interference with the enjoyment of these rights. The terms of office and the process of election are regulated to provide democratic elections by secret ballot by members in good standing. Communists and persons convicted of major crimes are barred as officers or employees of unions until a specified period of time has elapsed since termination of membership or conviction.

Union assets are protected from misappropriation by requiring those handling them to be bonded, imposing upon them a trustee's duty, making them criminally liable for theft or embezzlement, giving union members the right to sue them if the union fails to do so, and providing that the union cannot agree to release them from liability. Union assets are also protected by limiting loans to officers or employees and by prohibiting the union from paying fines imposed on officers or employees.

The Act prohibits and makes criminal picketing conducted to extort money and makes it an unfair labor practice to picket for recognition when a rival union is lawfully recognized and no representation issue can be raised. Agreements between unions and employers that the latter shall not use nonunion materials (hot cargo agreements) are made void and an unfair labor practice, except in the construction and garment industries. Secondary boycotts and the coercion of neutral employers thereby are made unfair labor practices, with exception to some extent of the garment industry. Neither the limitation of picketing nor the prohibition of secondary boycotts limits the union's right to publicize a labor dispute provided pressure is not exerted thereby on neutral employers nor their employees induced to refuse to work.

State authorities are authorized to act with respect to labor practices coming within the jurisdiction of the National Labor Relations Board when the latter refuses to exercise its jurisdiction, thus ending a "no man's land" in which no government acted.

### § 15.12. Settlement of Labor Disputes

Traditionally, disputes can be settled by mediation, conciliation, or voluntary or compulsory arbitration.

From the immediate point of view of the consuming public, compulsory arbitration seems to be the happy solution of labor problems. If there is compulsory arbitration, both employer and employee are required to keep at the job of production and to permit their dispute to be settled by the arbitrator. The use of compulsory arbitration faces a very serious constitutional limitation. The Supreme Court has held that except as to enterprises affected with a public interest, it is not constitutional to require a compulsory arbitration of labor disputes. The effect of this decision may be greatly impaired by the doctrine of the *Nebbia* case in which the court gives a very liberal if not self-destroying definition to the concept of "affected with a public interest." As a practical matter, both parties, both the employer and the employee group, generally fear compulsory arbitration because one or the other fears that the arbitrator or arbitrators will be prejudiced in favor of the other side. It is sometimes suggested that the union should select one arbitrator, the employer a second, and the government a third. This sounds like a happy solution except that there is the danger that the arbitrator selected by the government will respond to the tides of public and political sentiment. Because of that, one side of the controversy will always be fearful that the government man will be in favor of the adverse party.

The matter is further complicated by the realization that many of the labor disputes are not justiciable in nature; that is, the question to be decided does not call for the application of an established standard to facts resulting in a decision. If the dispute is over the wage rate, there is no standard of what a fair wage rate should be. It is more in the nature of a political issue; that is, what does good business or policy dictate in the particular instance. When this is appreciated, it can readily be understood why employers and employees generally agree to fight their battles out by themselves rather than submit them to arbitration.

### *(a) Compulsory arbitration*

WOLFF PACKING CO. v. COURT OF INDUSTRIAL RELATIONS
262 U.S. 522 (1923)

Kansas provided for the compulsory arbitration of labor disputes in key industries. The Wolff Packing Company was involved in a dispute with its employees and challenged the right of the state Industrial Court to arbitrate the dispute.

OPINION BY TAFT, C. J.

. . . [The Act] curtails the right of the employer on the one hand, and of the employee on the other, to contract about his affairs. This is part of the liberty of the individual protected by the guaranty of the due process clause of the Fourteenth Amendment. . . . While there is no such thing as absolute freedom of contract and it is subject to a variety of restraints, they must not be arbitrary or unreasonable. . . .

To say that a business is clothed with a public interest is not to determine what regulation may be permissible in view of the private rights of the owner. The extent to which an inn or a cab system may be regulated may differ widely from that allowable as to a railroad or other common carrier. It is not a matter of legislative discretion solely. It depends on the nature of the business, on the feature which touches the public, and on the abuses reasonably to be feared. To say that a business is clothed with a public interest is not to import that the public may take over its entire management and run it at the expense of the owner. The extent to which regulation may reasonably go varies with different kinds of business. The regulation of rates to avoid monopoly is one thing. The regulation of wages is another. A business may be of such character that only the first is permissible, while another may involve such a possible danger of monopoly on the one hand, and such disaster from stoppage on the other, that both come within the public concern and power of regulation. . . .

This brings us to the nature and purpose of the regulation under the Industrial Court Act. The avowed object is continuity of food, clothing and fuel supply. By Section 6 reasonable continuity and efficiency of the industries specified are declared to be necessary for the public peace, health and general welfare, and all are forbidden to hinder, limit or suspend them. Section 7 gives the industrial court power, in case of controversy between employers and workers which may endanger the continuity or efficiency of service, to bring the employer and employees before it and, after hearing and investigation, to fix the terms and conditions between them. The employer is bound by this act to pay the wages fixed. . . .

We think the Industrial Court Act, in so far as it permits the fixing of wages in plaintiff in error's packing house, is in conflict with the Fourteenth Amendment. . . .

### Questions for Discussion

1. What is the constitutional basis for a national law regulating labor? a state law? a city ordinance?

2. It has been estimated that during the five-year period from 1938 to 1942 the number of employees of the largest employers increased 22% while the number of employees of 95% of the employers declined by slightly more than that amount. The organization of labor on a nation-wide basis is necessary to combat and counterbalance this concentration of employment opportunities in the hands of a few great concerns. Discuss this statement. Do you agree with it?

3. A, B, and C are employed by D. They are dissatisfied with their wages. They discuss the problem and agree to demand more wages from D and to refuse to work for him if he does not give them a raise. They so inform D. D refuses to raise their wages, and they then stop work. D has A, B, and C arrested and prosecuted for criminal conspiracy. (a) Are they guilty of a crime? (b) Would it make any difference if the same case had arisen in 1750? in 1500?

4. How is the operation of the law of supply and demand affected by minimum wage statutes? by union collective bargaining?

5. Is there any relationship between the development of political democracy and the rise of unionization?

6. Why has the National Labor Relations Act of 1935 been called the Magna Charta of labor?

7. Could a state adopt a law making all labor unions illegal? Could Congress do so?

8. Is there any relationship between the trends in the government regulation of labor and the trends in the national economy? the existence of depressions? the occurrence of wars?

9. Congress adopts a law prohibiting all trusts and monopolies. A proviso in the law states that it shall not apply to labor unions or to combinations of working men. Is the law constitutional?

10. The Labor-Management Reporting and Disclosure Act of 1959 requires labor unions to file detailed information with respect to their organization and financial condition. Are employers required to file similar information?

11. Congress passes a law denying a labor union the right to bargain collectively if any of its members are also members of the Communist Party. Is this law constitutional? Would it make any difference if the law did not refer to the Communist Party but merely applied to labor unions any of whose members believed in communism?

12. When should an injunction be permitted in a labor dispute?

13. How far should a labor relations board be able to go in directing the reinstatement of workers improperly discharged? Should it be authorized to award back pay? Should it be authorized to order the employment of applicants who were improperly refused employment?

14. (a) Is a closed shop lawful? (b) What is the difference between a closed shop and a union shop?

15. What are the causes of industrial disputes?

16. (a) Define mediation, conciliation, and arbitration. (b) What is the difference between voluntary arbitration and compulsory arbitration?

17. Compulsory arbitration violates the guarantee of the Thirteenth Amendment that no one shall be required to work against his will. (a) Do you agree with this statement? (b) How is your conclusion affected by consideration of the compulsory draft law and state laws requiring citizens to work on the public highways for a stated number of days each year?

18. How does the settlement of a labor dispute by arbitration differ from the settlement of a law suit by a court?

# Chapter 16

# REGULATION OF AGRICULTURE



## § 16:1. Quantity of Production

Until recent times, the dominant character of government regulation of agriculture was that of encouragement of growth and expansion. Farmers were aided by grants of free land or lands at low cost. Extensive research and educational programs were conducted by national and state governments in order to make available to the farmer information about better ways of farming. Financial aid was given him directly in the form of subsidies or bounties or in the form of credit upon easier terms. Programs of electrification, flood control, and fertilizer production undertaken by the government contributed to the advancement of the farmer. His competitive position was further aided in recent years by a protective tariff on agricultural products and by the exemption of his co-operatives from the operation of antitrust laws.

In modern times, a "farm problem" has developed of such a nature that these past aids, most of which are still continued, are inadequate to meet the needs of the situation. The expansion of cultivation due to the greater demand of war years and the increased productivity of new methods and inventions, the creation of large surpluses of food products, the high debts of the farmer incurred during war years, the increasing trend toward commercial farming, and the rising incidence of farm tenancy have all brought the farmer an economic instability. The result has been the appearance of a group of curative regulations of agriculture.

Since, from many points of view, the heart of the farm problem is the existence of surpluses, modern regulation has aimed directly at eliminating such surpluses. Some effort was made to dissuade the farmer from producing the surplus part of his crop or to encourage the disposal of the surplus by the granting of export subsidies or the adoption of a food distribution plan, such as free lunches to school children or food stamps to the needy.

These methods proved inadequate and the direct regulation of acreage under cultivation was begun by the Federal government in the Agricultural Adjustment Act of 1933. In substance this act gave a bounty to farmers voluntarily reducing their acreage and obtained the money for the payment of this bounty by imposing a tax on the processors of the farm products. Thus a wheat farmer would be paid a bounty for reducing the acreage under cultivation, and this bounty would be obtained by placing a tax on the miller of the flour. This law was held unconstitutional, although today in view of the new interpretation of the commerce clause it would be valid. Congress amended the Act in 1938. This amendment sought to avoid the constitutional barrier raised against the Act of 1933 by basing the regulation upon the commerce power, which by that time had been liberally construed in the *Jones & Laughlin Steel Corporation* case. The declared purpose of the Act of 1938 as set forth in its statement of policy was "to regulate interstate and foreign commerce in cotton, wheat, corn, tobacco and rice to the extent necessary to provide an orderly, adequate, and balanced flow of such commodities in interstate and foreign commerce through storage of reserve supplies, loans, marketing, quotas, assisting farmers to obtain, in so far as practicable, parity prices for such commodities and parity of income, and assisting consumers to obtain an adequate and steady supply of such commodities at fair prices."

Under this Act the Secretary of Agriculture is authorized to determine the proper volume of production for the following year, that is, the amount which can be disposed of by sale in domestic and foreign markets. This amount or quota is then recommended to producers of the particular commodity who vote on whether that quota should be adopted. If those opposing the quota are less than one third of those voting, the quota is effective for the nation for that year. This national quota is then divided among the states according to their past production and is then subdivided within each state among the various producers. Production in excess of his quota subjects the farmer to a penalty even though the excess production is consumed by him at his home and is not sold in commerce. Farmers conforming to the quotas are permitted to receive subsidies for the maintenance of their prices and, if they store any excess production with the government, they are permitted to obtain loans on such excess as security.

### *(a) Agricultural Adjustment Act of 1938*

WICKARD v. FILBURN

317 U.S. 111 (1942)

OPINION BY JACKSON, J.

The appellee filed his complaint against the Secretary of Agriculture of the United States, three members of the County Agricultural Conservation Committee for Montgomery County, Ohio, and a member of the State Agricultural Conservation Committee for Ohio . . . to enjoin enforcement against himself of the marketing penalty imposed by the amendment of May 26, 1941, to the Agricultural Adjustment Act of 1938, upon that part of his 1941 wheat crop which was available for marketing in excess of the marketing quota established for his farm. He also sought a declaratory judgment that the wheat marketing quota provisions of the Act as amended and applicable to him were unconstitutional because not sustainable under the Commerce Clause or consistent with the Due Process Clause of the Fifth Amendment.

. . .

In July of 1940, pursuant to the Agricultural Adjustment Act of 1938, as then amended, there were established for the appellee's 1941 crop a wheat acreage allotment of 11.1 acres and a normal yield of 20.1 bushels of wheat an acre. . . . He sowed, however, 23 acres, and harvested from his 11.9 acres of excess acreage 239 bushels, which under the terms of the Act as amended on May 26, 1941, constituted farm marketing excess, subject to a penalty of 49 cents a bushel, or $117.11 in all. The appellee has not paid the penalty and he has not postponed or avoided it by storing the excess under regulations of the Secretary of Agriculture, or by delivering it up to the Secretary. The Committee, therefore, refused him a marketing card, which was, under the terms of Regulations promulgated by the Secretary, necessary to protect a buyer from liability to the penalty and upon its protecting lien.

The general scheme of the Agricultural Adjustment Act of 1938 as related to wheat is to control the volume moving in interstate and foreign commerce in order to avoid surpluses and shortages and the consequent abnormally low or high wheat prices and obstructions to commerce. Within prescribed limits and by prescribed standards the Secretary of Agriculture is directed to ascertain and proclaim each year a national acreage allotment for the next crop of wheat, which is then apportioned to the states and their counties, and is eventually broken up into allotments for individual farms. Loans and payments to wheat farmers are authorized in stated circumstances.

The Act provides further that whenever it appears that the total supply of wheat as of the beginning of any marketing year, beginning July 1, will exceed a normal year's domestic consumption and export by more than 35 per cent, the Secretary shall so proclaim not later than May 15 prior to the beginning of such marketing year; and that during the marketing year a compulsory national marketing quota shall be in effect with respect to the marketing of wheat. Between the issuance of the proclamation and June 10, the Secretary must, however, conduct a referendum of farmers who will be subject to the quota to determine whether they favor or oppose it; and if more than one-third of the farmers voting in the referendum do oppose, the Secretary must prior to the effective date of the quota by proclamation suspend its operation. . . .

It is urged that under the Commerce Clause . . . Congress does not possess the power it has in this instance sought to exercise. . . . The sum of this is that the Federal Government fixes a quota including all that the farmer may harvest for sale or for his own farm needs, and declares that wheat produced on excess acreage may neither be disposed of nor used except upon payment of the penalty or except it is stored as required by the Act or delivered to the Secretary of Agriculture.

Appellee says that this is a regulation of production and consumption of wheat. . . . In answer the Government argues that the statute regulates neither production nor consumption, but only marketing; . . .

In the Shreveport Rate Cases . . . the Court held that railroad rates of an admittedly intrastate character and fixed by authority of the state might, nevertheless, be revised by the Federal Government because of the economic effects which they had upon interstate commerce. The opinion of Mr. Justice Hughes found federal intervention constitutionally authorized because of "matters having such a close and substantial relation to interstate traffic that the control is essential or appropriate to the security of that traffic, to the efficiency of the interstate service, and to the maintenance of the conditions under which interstate commerce may be conducted upon fair terms and without molestation or hindrance." . . .

Questions of federal power cannot be decided simply by finding the activity in question to be "production" nor can consideration of its economic effects be foreclosed by calling them "indirect." . . . "The commerce power is not confined in its exercise to the regulation of commerce among the states. It extends to those activities intrastate which so affect interstate commerce, or the exertion of the power of Congress over it, as to make regulation of them appropriate means to the attainment of a legitimate end, the effective execution of the granted power to regulate interstate commerce. . . . The power of Congress over interstate commerce is plenary and complete in itself, may be exercised to its utmost extent, and acknowledges no limitations other than are prescribed in the Constitution. . . . It follows that no form of state activity can constitutionally thwart the regulatory power granted by the commerce clause to Congress. Hence the reach of that power extends to those intrastate activities which in a substantial way interfere with or obstruct the exercise of the granted power." . . .

Whether the subject of the regulation in question was "production," "consumption," or "marketing" is, therefore, not material for purposes of deciding the question of federal power before us. . . . Even if appellee's activity be local and though it may not be regarded as commerce, it may still, whatever its nature, be reached by Congress if it exerts a substantial economic effect on interstate commerce and this irrespective of whether such effect is what might at some earlier time have been defined as "direct" or "indirect."

[The Court summarized] the economics of the wheat industry.

In the absence of regulation the price of wheat in the United States would be much affected by world conditions. During 1941 producers who cooperated with the Agricultural Adjustment program received an average price on the farm of about $1.16 a bushel as compared with the world market price of 40 cents a bushel. . . .

The effect of consumption of homegrown wheat on interstate commerce is due to the fact that it constitutes the most variable factor in the disappearance of the wheat crop. Consumption on the farm where grown appears to vary in an amount greater than 20 per cent of average production. The total amount of wheat consumed as food varies but relatively little, and use as seed is relatively constant.

. . . The effect of the statute before us is to restrict the amount which may be produced for market and the extent as well to which one may forestall resort to the market by producing to meet his own needs. That appellee's own contribution to the demand for wheat may be trivial by itself is not enough to remove him from the scope of federal regulation where, as here, his contribution, taken together with that of many others similarly situated, is far from trivial. . . .

It is well established by decisions of this Court that the power to regulate commerce includes the power to regulate the prices at which commodities in that commerce are dealt in and practices affecting such prices. One of the primary purposes of the Act in question was to increase the market price of wheat and to that end to limit the volume thereof that could affect the market. It can hardly be denied that a factor of such volume and variability as home-consumed wheat would have a substantial influence on price and market conditions. This may arise because being in marketable condition such wheat overhangs the market and if induced by rising prices tends to flow into the market and check price increases. But if we assume that it is never marketed, it supplies a need of the man who grew it which would otherwise be reflected by purchases in the open market. Home-grown wheat in this sense competes with wheat in commerce. The stimulation of commerce is a use of the regulatory function quite as definitely as prohibitions or restrictions thereon. This record leaves us in no doubt that Congress may properly have considered that wheat consumed on the farm where grown if wholly outside the scheme of regulation would have a substantial effect in defeating and obstructing its purpose to stimulate trade therein at increased prices.

It is said, however, that this Act, forcing some farmers into the market to buy what they could provide for themselves, is an unfair promotion of the markets and prices of specializing wheat growers. It is of the essence of regulation that it lays a restraining hand on the self-interest of the regulated and that advantages from the regulation commonly fall to others. The conflicts of economic interest between the regulated and those who advantage by it are wisely left under our system to resolution by the Congress under its more flexible and responsible legislative process. Such conflicts rarely lend themselves to judicial determination. And with the wisdom, workability, or fairness, of the plan of regulation we have nothing to do. . . .

## § 16:2. Conservation and Reclamation

A secondary type of regulation of agriculture is found in the conservation and reclamation of farm lands. To the extent that a conservation measure restricts output, it can be regarded as an anti-surplus measure. At the same time, some conservation and most reclamation measures have as their result an increased productivity so that in effect the likelihood of a surplus is increased. This is particularly true where the reclamation calls back into cultivation land that was lying idle or where farmers are moved from marginal or submarginal lands and resettled on lands having greater productivity.

Here we have illustrated the curious conflict that may often arise between the individual and the group. In a given year there may be a national wheat surplus, yet at the same time there may be wheat farmers working poor lands who are barely able to make a living because of the low production of their lands. To move these farmers from the marginal or submarginal land to land producing a higher yield of wheat would to some extent solve their problem, but it would also increase the national surplus. This, at least in theory, should cause a further decrease in the national wheat price and thus harm the wheat farmers as a group.

The problem becomes one of great difficulty because of the problem of balancing competing interests: the interest of the individual farmer against farmers as a group, the interest of farmers as against society seeking food at low prices, the interest of society in maintaining the purchasing power of the farmer, and the interest of the community or the nation in having a sound agricultural economy and a well-fed and well-nourished people.

Under the new interpretation of the commerce power and the war power, there is little constitutional difficulty in sustaining any system of federal conservation. State conservation laws are also valid as long as they are not in conflict with federal laws or are not so written as to discriminate against interstate commerce or the citizens of other states in an unreasonable manner.

To the extent that conservation and reclamation preserve a steady water supply, prevent floods, and prevent the clogging of river channels with soil erosion, such measures may also be sustained under the federal power over navigable waterways.

### § 16:3. Standards, Marketing, and Price

Both state and national governments may impose regulations on agriculture for the purpose of maintaining standards. The object of these standards may be to protect the purchasing public from physical harm or financial loss through the purchase of agricultural products of inferior quality or grade, to maintain standard grade levels in order to facilitate merchandising, or to maintain trade reputation. Under the doctrine of the supremacy of the federal powers when exercised in an area in which a state has concurrent power, the federal standards become effective even as to locally produced and locally sold farm products, in order to avoid an unfair competition by them with the interstate products that are subjected to the federal regulation.

The marketing of farm products may be regulated by requiring their inspection prior to sale, by limiting their sale to designated regulated markets, or by requiring that the product be marketed through a central or governmental agency. Where farm products are sold at private markets or exchanges, the business practices and the charges of persons furnishing their services at such markets and exchanges may be regulated. Here again there is the concurrent power of national and state governments with the supremacy of the former when it acts.

While, for the greater part, price regulation of farm products has taken the form of subsidies to maintain the prices at a desired level, national and state government may regulate the prices of farm products.

To date, this power has not been extensively used and has been confined to the field of establishing minimum prices. Under the reported decisions, however, there is no reason why such control cannot be extended as far as the national congress or the state legislatures desire, nor is there any reason why the regulation cannot be the establishment of a maximum or an exact price rather than merely a minimum. Again the powers of the nation and the state are concurrent, with the supremacy of the national power being recognized not only as to sales in interstate commerce but also as to local sales that compete with the interstate sales.

### Questions for Discussion

1. What has been the pattern of governmental regulation of agriculture?

2. Is a law limiting the number of acres under cultivation the most effective way of preventing a crop surplus?

3. To what extent may the price of farm products be controlled by government?

4. Describe the operation of the antisurplus provisions of the Agricultural Adjustment Act.

5. (a) Is the statute before the Court in *Wickard* v. *Filburn* a regulation of production? (b) Was it so considered by the Court?

6. What test does the Court apply in the *Wickard* case to determine whether an activity comes within the regulatory scope of the commerce power?

7. Assuming the power to regulate wheat sold in interstate commerce, what is the justification for regulating wheat grown and used for home consumption of the farmer who raised it?

8. Did the Court consider the wisdom of the plan in determining the constitutionality of the statute in *Wickard* v. *Filburn*?

9. (a) Under what power can a state adopt a conservation of land reclamation law? (b) What is the basis for a federal law?

10. Compare the legality of:
   (a) An agreement between manufacturers to restrict output.
   (b) An agreement between members of a labor union to restrict output.
   (c) An agreement between farmers to restrict output.
   (d) A statute providing that the Secretary of Agriculture may direct farmers to restrict their output so that it will not exceed a quota fixed by him.

11. Assume that Congress passes a law regulating in detail the methods of farming, the crops to be grown, and the quantities of each crop to be produced. The first section of the statute recites that improper farming methods have impaired the agricultural potentiality of the country and are likely to make it vulnerable in time of war, and that to remedy this danger the Act in question is adopted. Discuss the constitutionality of this statute under (a) the commerce power, (b) the general welfare power, and (c) the war power.

12. Assume that Congress passes a law which recites that farm tenancy is rising and is a threat to American democratic institutions and that to correct this situation the law in question is adopted. The law then provides that anyone owning a farm in excess of 1,000 acres or owning a number of farms, the total acreage of which exceeds 1,000 must sell the surplus to the government at a fair value to be determined by legal proceedings. The Act further provides that the surplus lands thus acquired by the government will be divided into parcels of 100 acres each and be given free to tenant farmers provided they live on the land and properly farm it for five years. Discuss the constitutionality of this law.

13. What is the constitutional basis for the following statutes:
   (a) The Federal Meat Inspection Act of 1906 providing for the inspection of meat and slaughtering and processing methods.
   (b) The Packers and Stockyards Act of 1921 authorizing the Secretary of Agriculture to set rates and charges made by stockyard commissionmen and dealers.
   (c) The Commodity Exchange Act of 1936 regulating the sale and exchange transactions in major foods in order to eliminate improper market practices.

14. How many governments regulate the marketing of farm products?

# Chapter 17

## THE COMMERCE POWER AND THE STATES



### § 17:1. The Federal Power as Prohibiting State Regulation

By the Tenth Amendment, those powers not delegated to the federal government nor prohibited to the states are reserved to the states and the people thereof. This provision gave emphasis to the concept of a division of power between federal and state governments under which a power would be held either by the national government or the state governments but not concurrently by both. Under a literal interpretation of this Amendment, the granting of the power to regulate interstate commerce to the Congress would mean that no power exists in the states to regulate that commerce.

This interpretation fitted in well with the intent of the framers, who, seeing the evil effects of retaliatory state regulations of interstate commerce, wished to raise the field of commerce above the reach of the states. For the first part of our national life, the authority of the commerce power was invoked, not by the Congress as the basis for adopting a national law, but by the Supreme Court as the basis for declaring invalid a regulation of commerce made by a state, as was done in the following case.

### *(a) State monopoly of navigation*

GIBBONS v. OGDEN

9 Wheat. 1 (1824)

The state of New York, in order to encourage the development of the steamboat, gave to Livingston and Fulton the exclusive right to operate steam vessels on the waters of the state and prohibited the operation of such vessels by any person not licensed by them. Ogden obtained a license from them to operate a steam vessel on New York waters. Later he sought to enjoin Gibbons from operating on those waters without a license. The latter claimed that he was registered under the Act of Congress of 1793 to engage in the coastal trade and was therefore entitled to operate a steam vessel in the coastal waters of New York state by virtue of the protection of the federal commerce power.

OPINION BY MARSHALL, J.

. . . The words [of the Constitution] are: "Congress shall have power to regulate commerce with foreign nations, and among the several States, and with the Indian tribes." The subject to be regulated is commerce. . . . The counsel for the appellee would limit it to traffic, to buying and selling, or the interchange of commodities, and do not admit that it comprehends navigation. This would restrict a general term, applicable to many objects, to one of its significations. Commerce, undoubtedly, is traffic, but it is something more; it is intercourse. It describes the commercial intercourse between nations, and parts of nations, in all its branches, and is regulated by prescribing rules for carrying on that intercourse. The mind can scarcely conceive a system for regulating commerce between nations which shall exclude all laws concerning navigation, which shall be silent on the admission of the vessels of the one nation into the ports of the other, and be confined to prescribing rules for the conduct of individuals, in the actual employment of buying and selling, or of barter. . . .

. . . The sole question is, can a state regulate commerce with foreign nations and among the states while Congress is regulating it? . . .

. . . Steamboats may be enrolled and licensed, in common with vessels using sails. They are, of course, entitled to the same privileges and can no more be restrained from navigating waters and entering ports which are free to such vessels, than if they were wafted on their voyage by the winds, instead of being propelled by the agency of fire. The one element may be as legitimately used as the other, for every commercial purpose authorized by the laws of the Union; and the act of a state inhibiting the use of either to any vessel having a license under the act of Congress, comes, we think, in direct collision with that act. . . .

[The Court refused to enjoin Gibbons from operating without a license under the state law.]

### *(b) Supremacy of federal regulation*

LOCAL 24 v. OLIVER

358 U.S. 283 (1959)

Members of Local 24 owned their own trucks. They would hire out to drive their trucks as employees of various carriers. Through collective bargaining under the National Labor Management Relations Act, the union and the employing carriers had made an agreement, Article XXXII of which specified the "rental" to be paid by the employing carriers to each truck owner for his services in driving his truck for the carriers. Oliver, one of the truck-owning employees, sued in an Ohio state court to invalidate the rental provision of the agreement on the ground that the Ohio antitrust law made it illegal.

OPINION BY BRENNAN, J.

. . . The point of the Article is obviously not price fixing but wages. The regulations embody . . . a direct frontal attack upon a problem thought to threaten the maintenance of the basic wage structure established by the collective bargaining contract. The inadequacy of a rental which means that the owner makes up his excess costs from his driver's wages not only clearly bears a close relation to labor's efforts to improve working conditions but is in fact of vital concern to the carrier's employed drivers; an inadequate rental might mean the progressive curtailment of jobs through withdrawal of more and more carrier-owned vehicles from service. . . .

. . . We must decide whether Ohio's antitrust law may be applied to prevent the contracting parties from carrying out their agreement upon a subject matter as to which federal law directs them to bargain. Little extended discussion is necessary to show that Ohio law cannot be so applied. . . . The carriers as employers were under a duty to bargain collectively with the union as to the subject matter of the Article. . . .

The goal of federal labor policy, as expressed in the Wagner and Taft-Hartley Acts, is the promotion of collective bargaining; to encourage the employer and the representative of the employees to establish, through collective negotiation, their own charter for the ordering of industrial relations, and thereby to minimize industrial strife. . . . Within the area in which collective bargaining was required, Congress was not concerned with the substantive terms upon which the parties agreed. . . .

The purposes of the Acts are served by bringing the parties together and establishing conditions under which they are to work out their agreement themselves. To allow the application of the Ohio antitrust law here would wholly defeat the full realization of the congressional purpose. The application would frustrate the parties' solution of a problem which Congress has required them to negotiate in good faith toward solving, and in the solution of which it imposed no limitations relevant here. . . . We believe that there is no room in this scheme for the application here of this state policy limiting the solutions that the parties' agreement can provide to the problems of wages and working conditions. . . . Since the federal law operates here, in an area where its authority is paramount, to leave the parties free, the inconsistent application of state law is necessarily outside the power of the State. . . . Of course, the paramount force of the federal law remains even though it is expressed in the details of a contract federal law empowers the parties to make, rather than in terms in an enactment of Congress. . . . Clearly it is immaterial that the conflict is between federal labor law and the application of what the State characterizes as an antitrust law. ". . . Congress has sufficiently expressed its purpose to . . . exclude state prohibition, even though that with which the federal law is concerned as a matter of labor relations be related by the State to the more inclusive area of restraint of trade." . . .

We have not here a case of a collective bargaining agreement in conflict with a local health or safety regulation; the conflict here is between the federally sanctioned agreement and state policy which seeks specifically to adjust relationships in the world of commerce. If there is to be this sort of limitation on the arrangements that unions and employers may make with regard to these subjects, pursuant to the collective bargaining provisions of the Wagner and Taft-Hartley Acts, it is for Congress, not the States, to provide it.

### § 17:2. Silence of Congress

Admitting that a law passed by Congress regulating interstate commerce is supreme and prevails over a state law, what happens if Congress does not pass any law on the subject? Is the silence of Congress always to be regarded as permission to the states to regulate the commerce or may that silence be an indication that the subject should be unregulated?

The Court finally answered these questions by holding that if the subject matter of the state regulation were of such a nature that local regulation would not have any harmful effect on interstate commerce, the silence of Congress was to be deemed implied permission to the states to regulate in a nondiscriminatory way. Conversely, if the subject matter were such that any regulation should be uniform throughout the country, the silence of Congress was then an indication that it did not desire that there be any regulation.[1]

This doctrine sustains the right of states to make regulations, in the absence of federal legislation, of those local details of interstate commerce that do not require uniformity throughout the nation. A similar state power exists as to foreign commerce.

#### *(a) Conservation*

CITIES SERVICE GAS COMPANY v. PEERLESS OIL & GAS COMPANY
340 U.S. 179 (1950)

In order to prevent the wasteful exploitation of natural gas resources, Oklahoma adopted a statute authorizing the state corporation

---

[1] Cooley v. Board of Wardens of the Port of Philadelphia, 12 How. (U.S.) 299 (1852).

commission to fix the minimum price to be paid for gas at the wellhead. The Commission fixed the price with respect to gas produced at a field from which Cities Service Gas Company ran an interstate line. Cities Service claimed that the fixing of the price by the state commission burdened interstate commerce. This contention was rejected and Cities Service appealed.

OPINION BY CLARK, J.

. . . It is now well settled that a state may regulate matters of local concern over which federal authority has not been exercised, even though the regulation has some impact on interstate commerce. . . . The only requirements consistently recognized have been that the regulation not discriminate against or place an embargo on interstate commerce, that it safeguard an obvious state interest, and that the local interest at stake outweigh whatever national interest there might be in the prevention of state restrictions. Nor should we lightly translate the quiescence of federal power into an affirmation that the national interest lies in complete freedom from regulation. . . .

That a legitimate local interest is at stake in this case is clear. A state is justifiably concerned with preventing rapid and uneconomic dissipation of one of its chief natural resources. The contention urged by appellant that a group of private producers and royalty owners derive substantial gain from the regulations does not contradict the established connection between the orders and a state-wide interest in conservation. . . .

We recognize that there is also a strong national interest in natural gas problems. But it is far from clear that on balance such interest is harmed by the state regulations under attack here. . . . Moreover, the wellhead price of gas is but a fraction of the price paid by domestic consumers at the burner-tip, so that the field price as herein set may have little or no effect on the domestic delivered price. . . . Insofar as conservation is concerned, the national interest and the interest of producing states may well tend to coincide. In any event, in a field of this complexity with such diverse interests involved, we cannot say that there is a clear national interest so harmed that the state price-fixing orders here employed fall within the ban of the Commerce Clause. . . . Nor is it for us to consider whether Oklahoma's unilateral efforts to conserve gas will be fully effective. . . .

We hold that . . . the Oklahoma Corporation Commission issued valid orders, and . . . should be affirmed.

## § 17:3. State Regulation as a Burden

Within the area of regulation of local details allowed the states, the state regulation must not impose an unreasonable burden on interstate commerce. If it does, the state law is invalid, even though it imposes that same burden on intrastate as well as interstate commerce, without discrimination. A state statute that required all trains to slow down at grade crossings so that they could stop if necessary was held unconstitutional when applied to an interstate train where the result would have been to require it to slow down at 124 grade crossings in 123 miles with the result of doubling its running time through the state.

In recent years, less emphasis has been placed on the question of whether the power to regulate interstate commerce is concurrent. The Supreme Court has merely considered whether the state law, considered as a police power or tax law, was or was not an unreasonable burden when extended to interstate commerce. The statute is accordingly held valid if it does not discriminate against or single out interstate commerce alone and if its application to that commerce does not impose an unreasonable burden on it.

Under this doctrine a state law regulating the payment of wages may be applied to the wages paid to crews of trains moving in interstate commerce where it is a general nondiscriminatory regulation. A quarantine or inspection law may keep out of the state diseased or harmful products or may prohibit their sale within the state even though still in the original package.

The extent to which a state may seek to maintain producer prices by providing for collective marketing was considered in the following case.

### *(a) State marketing co-operative*

PARKER v. BROWN

317 U.S. 341 (1943)

A California statute requires each producer of raisins to deliver two thirds of his annual raisin crop to a state marketing committee to be sold collectively by it as the agency determines. It was claimed that this limitation on marketing was invalid because it was in conflict with the national commerce power.

Opinion by Stone, J. . . .

The court below found that approximately 95 per cent of the California raisin crop finds its way into interstate or foreign commerce. . . . The proration program . . . clothes the committee with power and imposes on it the duty to control marketing of the crop so as to enhance the price or at least to maintain prices by restraints on competition of producers in the sale of their crop. The program operates to eliminate competition of the producers in the terms of sale of the crop, including price. And since 95 per cent of the crop is marketed in interstate commerce, the program may be taken to have a substantial effect on the commerce, in placing restrictions on the sale and marketing of a product to buyers who eventually sell and ship it in interstate commerce.

The question is thus presented whether in the absence of Congressional legislation prohibiting or regulating the transactions affected by the state program, the restrictions which it imposes upon the sale within the state of a commodity by its producer to a processor who contemplates doing, and in fact does, work upon the commodity before packing and shipping it in interstate commerce, violate the Commerce Clause.

. . . No case has gone so far as to hold that a state could not license or otherwise regulate the sale of articles within the state because the buyer, after processing and packing them, will, in the normal course of business, sell and ship them in interstate commerce.

All of these cases proceed on the ground that the taxation or regulation involved, however drastically it may affect interstate commerce, is nevertheless not prohibited by the Commerce Clause where the regulation is imposed before any operation of interstate commerce occurs. Applying that test, the regulation here controls the disposition, including the sale and purchase, of raisins before they are processed and packed preparatory to interstate sale and shipment. The regulation is thus applied to transactions wholly intrastate before the raisins are ready for shipment in interstate commerce. . . .

Such regulations by the state are to be sustained, not because they are "indirect" rather than "direct" . . . not because they control interstate activities in such a manner as only to affect the commerce rather than to command its operations. But they are to be upheld because upon a consideration of all the relevant facts and circumstances it appears that the matter is one which may appropriately be regulated in the interest of the safety, health and wellbeing of local communities, and which, because of its local character, and the practical difficulties involved, may never be adequately dealt with by Congress. Because of its local character also there may be wide scope for local regulation without substantially impairing the national interest in the regulation of commerce by a single authority and without materially obstructing the free flow of commerce, which were the principal objects sought to be secured by the Commerce Clause. . . .

Examination of the evidence in this case and of available data of the raisin industry in California, of which we may take judicial notice, leaves no doubt that the evils attending the production and marketing of raisins in that state present a problem local in character and urgently demanding state action for the economic protection of those engaged in one of its important industries. . . .

The history of the industry, at least since 1929, is a record of a continuous search for expedients which would stabilize the marketing of the raisin crop and maintain a price standard which would bring fair return to the producers. . . .

This history shows clearly enough that the adoption of legislative measures to prevent the demoralization of the industry by stabilizing the marketing of the raisin crop is a matter of state as well as national concern and, in the absence of inconsistent Congressional action, is a problem whose solution is peculiarly within the province of the state. In the exercise of its power the state has adopted a measure appropriate to the end sought. The program was not aimed at nor did it discriminate against interstate commerce, although it undoubtedly affected the commerce by increasing the interstate price of raisins and curtailing interstate shipments to some undetermined extent. . . .

We conclude that the California proration program for the 1940 raisin crop is a regulation of state industry of local concern which, in all the circumstances of this case which we have detailed, does not impair national control over the commerce in a manner or to a degree forbidden by the Constitution.

## § 17:4. Federal Consent to State Regulation

In addition to the power which the states may exercise in the silence of Congress, it has also been held that Congress may consent to the operation of state laws upon what would otherwise be exempt as interstate commerce from state regulation. With respect to commodities, this principle of consent to state regulation has taken the form of waiving the immunity conferred by the original package doctrine. That doctrine found its origin in *Brown* v. *Maryland*, 12 Wheat. 419 (1827), in which Chief Justice Marshall held that goods imported from a foreign nation retained their character as imports and immunity from state taxation as long as they remained "the property of the importer, in his warehouse, in the original form of package in which it was imported." While this doctrine has been modified in the field of taxation and does not apply to goods brought into a state to fill a prior order, it has been applied to goods moving in interstate commerce in order to determine when they became subject to regulation by state law.

It has been held that liquor brought from one state into a prohibition state could be sold in the original package in spite of the state prohibition law on the theory that a prohibition of this first sale in the original package would burden interstate commerce by preventing the transaction that was the object of its importation. On the other hand, this protection when extended to such goods defeated the state policy of prohibition. In order to permit the state policy to operate, Congress waived the immunity conferred by the original package doctrine by expressly providing that the state law may operate upon the goods even though they are unsold and in the original package. Such waiver has now been made by Congress in the case of both intoxicating liquors and convict-made goods. Congress has even gone farther in these two cases and has made it a federal offense to carry goods through the channels of interstate commerce into a state where the possession or the sale of such goods is illegal under the state law. By this device it is possible for the state, with the permission of Congress, to make effective the state police power even as to goods that would ordinarily be protected by the immunity based on the federal commerce power. Such federal-state co-operation is a far cry from the federal-state rivalry of our early national life.

Federal consent to the operation of state law is also found in the McGuire Act sustaining the validity under federal law of resale price maintenance agreements when valid under the law of the state in which resale is made.

Federal consent to state legislation acting upon interstate commerce has not been confined to transactions relating to commodities. For example, by the McCarran-Ferguson Act, the federal government permits state regulations to apply to interstate insurance and insurance companies.

### *(a) Interstate insurance*

FEDERAL TRADE COMMISSION v. NATIONAL CASUALTY COMPANY

357 U.S. 560 (1958)

The Federal Trade Commission ordered two insurance companies to stop certain advertising practices on the ground that they were deceptive and violated the Federal Trade Commission Act. The insurance companies claimed that the Federal Trade Commission Act was not applicable because of the provisions of the McCarran-Ferguson Act. The Commission appealed to the Supreme Court.

OPINION BY THE COURT.

. . . Respondents, the National Casualty Company . . . and the American Hospital and Life Insurance Company . . . engage in the sale of health and accident insurance. National is licensed to sell policies in all States, as well as the District of Columbia and Hawaii, while American is licensed in fourteen States. Solicitation of business for National is carried on by independent agents who operate on commission. The company's advertising material is prepared by it and shipped in bulk to these agents, who distribute the material locally and assume the expense of such dissemination. Only an insubstantial amount of any advertising goes directly by mail from the company to the public, and there is no use of radio, television, or other means of mass communication by the company. American does not materially differ from National in method of operation.

The pertinent portions of the McCarran-Ferguson Act [provide] "That the Congress hereby declares that the continued regulation and taxation by the several States of the business of insurance is in the public interest, and that silence on the part of the Congress shall not be construed to impose any barrier to the regulation or taxation of such business by the several States.

"Sec. 2. (a) The business of insurance, and every person engaged therein, shall be subject to the laws of the several States which relate to the regulation or taxation of such business.

"(b) No Act of Congress shall be construed to invalidate, impair, or supercede any law enacted by any State for the purpose of regulating the business of insurance, or which imposes a fee or tax upon such business, unless such Act specifically relates to the business of insurance: *Provided,* That after June 30, 1948, . . . the Sherman Act, . . . the Clayton Act, and . . . the Federal Trade Commission Act . . . shall be applicable to the business of insurance to the extent that such business is not regulated by State law. . . ."

. . . An examination of that statute and its legislative history establishes that the Act withdrew from the Federal Trade Commission the authority to regulate respondents' advertising practices in those States which are regulating those practices under their own laws.

. . . Whatever may have been the intent of Congress with regard to interstate insurance practices which the States cannot for constitutional reasons regulate effectively, that intent is irrelevant in the cases before us. Respondents' advertising programs require distribution by their local agents, and there is no question but that the States possess ample means to regulate this advertising within their respective boundaries. . . .

Petitioner [Federal Trade Commission] also argues . . . that even if the McCarran-Ferguson Act bars federal regulation where state regulation has been effectively applied, the exercise of Commission authority in these cases should be upheld because the States have not "regulated" within the meaning of the section 2(b) proviso. This argument is not persuasive in the instant cases. Each State in question has enacted prohibitory legislation which proscribes unfair insurance advertising and authorizes enforcement through a scheme of administrative supervision. Petitioner does not argue that the statutory provisions here under review were mere pretense. Rather, it urges that a general prohibition designed to guarantee certain standards of conduct is too "inchoate" to be "regulation" until that prohibition has been crystallized into "administrative elaboration of these standards and application in individual cases." However, assuming there is some difference in the McCarran-Ferguson Act between "legislation" and "regulation," nothing in the language of that Act or its legislative history supports the distinctions drawn by petitioner. So far as we can determine from the records and arguments in these cases, the proviso in section 2(b) has been satisfied.

### § 17:5. State Taxation

Goods are not subject to state taxation when they are moving in interstate commerce, even though at the moment they may be stationary, as resting on a railroad platform awaiting reshipment. The protection conferred upon interstate commerce by the existence of the federal commerce power also precludes taxes in addition to property taxes when they impose a burden on interstate commerce. The mere fact, however, that there is an economic activity that utilizes the facilities of interstate commerce does not mean that in all its aspects such activity will be exempt from state taxation.

#### *(a) Occupation tax*

MICHIGAN-WISCONSIN PIPE LINE CO. v. CALVERT

347 U.S. 157 (1954)

The Michigan-Wisconsin Pipe Line Co. runs a gas line from the Phillips plant in Texas into other states. A Texas statute imposed a tax on all those engaged in the occupation of "gathering gas" and measured the tax by the total volume of gas taken. The Texas tax officer interpreted this occupation tax as applicable to the Michigan-Wisconsin Pipe Line Co. The latter then sued for an injunction to prevent the state official from enforcing the tax. From a decision in favor of the tax officer, the Pipe Line Company appealed.

OPINION BY CLARK, J.

The entire movement of the gas, from producing wells through the Phillips gasoline plant and into the Michigan-Wisconsin pipe line to consumers outside Texas, is a steady and continuous flow. All of Michigan-Wisconsin's gas is purchased from Phillips for transportation to points outside Texas, and is in fact so transported. . . .

. . . It is now well settled that a tax imposed on a local activity related to interstate commerce is valid if, and only if, the local activity is not such an integral part of the interstate process, the flow of commerce, that it cannot realistically be separated from it. . . . And if a genuine separation of the taxed local activity from the interstate process is impossible, it is more likely that other states through which the commerce passes or into which it flows can with equal right impose a similar levy on the goods, with the net effect of prejudicing or unduly burdening commerce.

The problem in this case is not whether the State could tax the actual gathering of all gas whether transmitted in interstate commerce or not . . . but whether here the State has delayed the incidence of the tax beyond the step where production and processing have ceased and transmission in interstate commerce has begun. . . . The incidence of the tax here at issue, as stated by the Texas appellate court, is appellants' "taking" of gas from Phillips' gasoline plant. This event, as stipulated, occurs after the gas has been produced, gathered and processed by others than appellants. The "taking" into appellants' pipelines is solely for interstate transmission and the gas at that time is not only actually committed to but is moving in interstate commerce. . . . But receipt of the gas in the pipeline is more than its "taking"; from a practical standpoint it is its "taking off" in appellants' carrier into commerce; in reality the tax is, therefore, on the exit of the gas from the State. This economic process is inherently unsusceptible of division into a distinct local activity capable of forming the basis for the tax here imposed, on the one hand, and a separate movement in commerce, on the other. It is difficult to conceive of a factual situation where the incidence of taking or loading for transmission is more closely related to the transmission itself. . . . We are therefore of the opinion that the taking of the gas here is essentially a part of interstate commerce itself.

Here it is perhaps sufficient that the privilege taxed, namely the taking of the gas, is not so separate and distinct from interstate transportation as to support the tax. But additional objection is present if the tax be upheld. It would "permit a multiple burden upon that commerce,". . . for if Texas may impose this "first taking" tax measured by the total volume of gas so taken, then Michigan and the other recipient states have at least equal right to tax the first taking or "unloading" from the pipeline of the same gas when it arrives for distribution. Oklahoma might then seek to tax the first taking of the gas as it crossed into that State. The net effect would be substantially to resurrect the customs barriers which the Commerce Clause was designed to eliminate. "The very purpose of the Commerce Clause was to create an area of free trade among the several States. That clause vested the power of taxing a transaction forming an unbroken process of interstate commerce in the Congress, not in the States. . . ."

### *(b) Income tax*

NORTHWESTERN STATES PORTLAND CEMENT CO. v. MINNESOTA
358 U.S. 450 (1959)

Northwestern States Portland Cement Company made interstate sales of cement, some of which were made in Minnesota. That state taxed the company on the income from the sales which it made in Minnesota by a general nondiscriminatory income tax. The corporation claimed that the tax was unconstitutional because it burdened interstate commerce since the income was produced in interstate commerce.

OPINION BY CLARK, J.

It has long been established doctrine that the Commerce Clause gives exclusive power to the Congress to regulate interstate commerce, and its failure to act on the subject in the area of taxation nevertheless requires that interstate commerce shall be free from any direct restrictions or impositions by the States. . . . It is beyond dispute that a State may not lay a tax on the "privilege" of engaging in interstate commerce. . . . Nor may a State impose a tax that discriminates against interstate commerce either by providing a direct commercial advantage to local business, . . . or by subjecting interstate commerce to the burden of "multiple taxation.". . . Such impositions have been stricken because the states, under the Commerce Clause, are not allowed "one single-tax worth of direct interference with the free flow of commerce." . . .

On the other hand, it has been established since 1918 that a net income tax on revenues derived from interstate commerce does not offend constitutional limitations upon state interference with such commerce. . . . The Court [then] held that though true it was that the Constitution provided "No Tax or Duty shall be laid on Articles exported from any State," Art. 1. § 9, still a net income tax on the profits derived from such commerce was not "laid on articles in course of exportation or on anything which inherently or by the usages of commerce is embraced in exportation or any of its processes. . . . At most, exportation is affected only indirectly and remotely.". . . [This doctrine was later extended to interstate commerce and] and the Court distinguished between an invalid direct levy which placed a burden on interstate commerce and a charge by way of net income derived from profits from interstate commerce.

. . . These cases stand for the doctrine that the entire net income of a corporation, generated by interstate as well as intrastate activities, may be fairly apportioned among the States for tax purposes by formulas utilizing in-state aspects of interstate affairs. . . .

While it is true that a State may not erect a wall around its borders preventing commerce an entry, it is axiomatic that the founders did not intend to immunize such commerce from carrying its fair share of the costs of the state government in return for the benefits it derives from within the State. . . .

### Dissenting Opinion by Frankfurter, J.

. . . I think that interstate commerce will be not merely argumentatively but actively burdened for two reasons:

*First.* It will not, I believe, be gainsaid that there are thousands of relatively small or moderate size corporations doing exclusively interstate business spread over several States. To subject these corporations to a separate income tax in each of these States means that they will have to keep books, make returns, store records, and engage legal counsel, all to meet the divers and variegated tax laws of forty-nine States, with their different times for filing returns, different tax structures, different modes for determining "net income," and, different, often conflicting, formulas of apportionment. This will involve large increases in bookkeeping, accounting, and legal paraphernalia to meet these new demands. The cost of such a far-flung scheme for complying with the taxing requirements of the different States may well exceed the burden of the taxes themselves, especially in the case of small companies doing a small volume of business in several States.

*Second.* The extensive litigation in this Court which has challenged formulas of apportionment in the case of railroads and express companies—challenges addressed to the natural temptation of the States to absorb more than their fair share of interstate revenue—will be multiplied many times when such formulas are applied to the infinitely larger number of other businesses which are engaged in exclusively interstate commerce. The division in this Court on these railroad apportionment cases is a good index of what might reasonably be expected when cases involving the more numerous non-transportation industries come before the Court. This is not a suggestion that the convenience of the Court should determine our construction of the Commerce Clause, although it is important in balancing the considerations relevant to the Commerce Clause against the claims of state power that this Court should be mindful of the kind of questions it will be called upon to adjudicate and its special competence for adjudicating them. Wholly apart from that, the necessity for litigation based on these elusive and essentially non-legal questions casts a burden on businesses, and consequently on interstate commerce itself, which should not be imposed.

. . . The question is not whether a fair share of the profits derived from the carrying on of exclusively interstate commerce should contribute to the cost of the state governments. The question is whether the answer to this problem rests with this Court or with Congress.

I am not unmindful of the extent to which federal taxes absorb the taxable resources of the Nation, while at the same time the fiscal demands of the States are on the increase. These conditions present far-reaching problems of accommodating federal-state fiscal policy. But a determination of who is to get how much out of the common fund can hardly be made wisely and smoothly through the adjudicatory process. In fact, relying on the courts to solve these problems only aggravates the difficulties and retards proper legislative solution. . . .

The problem calls for solution by devising a congressional policy. Congress alone can provide for a full and thorough canvassing of the multitudinous and intricate factors which compose the problem of the taxing freedom of the States and the needed limits on such state taxing power. . . . The solution to these problems ought not to rest on the self-serving determination of the States of what they are entitled to out of the Nation's resources. . . .[2]

## § 17:6. State Price Control

During periods of economic distress, it is natural for the states to seek to remedy their difficulties by statutes that place their local interest above that of the neighboring states. Such "beggar-my-neighbor" statutes had themselves been a reason for the adoption of the federal commerce clause. Statutes of this nature also followed in the wake of the depression of 1929. Again the commerce clause was invoked by the Supreme Court as authority for invalidating state laws that harmed interstate commerce although designed to afford local economic relief. A regulatory provision of this character was before the Supreme Court in the following case.

### *(a) Local price control of imported milk*

BALDWIN v. SEELIG

294 U.S. 511 (1935)

OPINION BY CARDOZO, J.

. . .

The New York Milk Control Act with the aid of regulations made thereunder has set up a system of minimum prices to be paid by dealers to producers. . . . From the farms of New York the inhabitants of the so-called Metropolitan Milk District, comprising the City of New York and certain neighboring communities, derive about 70% of the milk requisite for their use. To keep the system unimpaired by competition from afar, the Act has a provision whereby the protective prices are extended to that part of the supply (about 30%) which comes from other states. The substance of the provision is that, so far as such a prohibition is permitted by the Constitution, there shall be no sale within the state of milk bought outside unless the price paid to the producers was one that would be lawful upon a like transaction within the state. . . .

Seelig buys its milk from the Creamery in Vermont at prices lower than the minimum payable to producers in New York. The Commissioner of Farms and Markets refuses to license the trans-

---

2 The Court's decision was reversed by Congress by the Act of September 14, 1959, 73 Stat. 555, which prohibits state or local taxation on income derived in 1960 and thereafter by a nonresident or a foreign corporation on sales in interstate commerce when the only activity within the taxing unit is the solicitation of sales through agents, a local sales office, or an independent contractor.

action of its business unless it signs an agreement to conform to the New York statute and regulations in the sale of the imported product. This the applicant declines to do. . . . This suit has been brought to restrain the enforcement of the Act in its application to the complainant. . . .

New York has no power to project its legislation into Vermont by regulating the price to be paid in that state for milk acquired there. So much is not disputed. New York is equally without power to prohibit the introduction within her territory of milk of wholesome quality acquired in Vermont, whether at high prices or at low ones. This again is not disputed. Accepting those postulates, New York asserts her power to outlaw milk so introduced by prohibiting its sale thereafter if the price that has been paid for it to the farmers of Vermont is less than would be owing in like circumstances to farmers in New York. The importer in that view may keep his milk or drink it, but sell it he may not.

Such a power, if exerted, will set a barrier to traffic between one state and another as effective as if custom duties, equal to the price differential, had been laid upon the thing transported. . . . Imposts and duties upon interstate commerce are placed beyond the power of a state. . . . We are reminded in the opinion below that a chief occasion of the commerce clauses was "the mutual jealousies and aggressions of the States, taking form in customs barriers and other economic retaliation." . . . If New York, in order to promote the economic welfare of her farmers, may guard them against competition with the cheaper prices of Vermont, the door has been opened to rivalries and reprisals that were meant to be averted by subjecting commerce between the states to the power of the nation.

The argument is pressed upon us, however, that the end to be served by the Milk Control Act is something more than the economic welfare of the farmers or of any other class or classes. The end to be served is the maintenance of a regular and adequate supply of pure and wholesome milk, the supply being put in jeopardy when the farmers of the state are unable to earn a living income. . . . Price security, we are told, is only a special form of sanitary security; the economic motive is secondary and subordinate; the state intervenes to make its inhabitants healthy, and not to make them rich. On that assumption we are asked to say that intervention will be upheld as a valid exercise by the state of its internal police power, though there is an incidental obstruction to commerce between one state and another. This would be to eat up the rule under the guise of an exception. Economic welfare is always related to health, for there can be no health if men are starving. Let such an exception be admitted, and all that a state will have to do in times of stress and strain is to say that its farmers and merchants and workmen must be protected against competition from without, lest they go upon the poor relief lists or perish altogether. To give entrance to that excuse would be to invite a speedy end of our national solidarity. The Constitution was framed under the dominion of a political philosophy less parochial in range. It was framed upon the theory that the peoples of the several states must sink or swim together, and that in the long run prosperity and salvation are in union and not division.

We have dwelt up to this point upon the argument of the state that economic security for farmers in the milk-shed may be a means of assuring to consumers a steady supply of a food of prime necessity. There is, however, another argument which seeks to establish a relation between the well-being of the producer and the quality of the product. We are told that farmers who are underpaid will be tempted to save the expense of sanitary precautions. This temptation will affect the farmers outside New York as well as those within it. For that reason the exclusion of milk paid for in Vermont below the New York minimum will tend, it is said, to impose a higher standard of quality and thereby promote health. We think the argument will not avail to justify impediments to commerce between the states. There is neither evidence nor presumption that the same minimum prices established by order of the board for producers in New York are necessary also for producers in Vermont. But apart from such defects of proof, the evils springing from uncared for cattle must be remedied by measures of repression more direct and certain than the creation of a parity of prices between New York and other states. Appropriate certificates may be exacted from farmers in Vermont and elsewhere . . .; milk may be excluded if necessary safeguards have been omitted; but commerce between the states is burdened unduly when one state regulates by indirection the prices to be paid to producers in another, in the faith that augmentation of prices will lift up the level of economic welfare, and that this will stimulate the observance of sanitary requirements in the preparation of the product. The next step would be to condition importation upon proof of a satisfactory wage scale in factory or shop, or even upon proof of the profits of the business. Whatever relation there may be between earnings and sanitation is too remote and indirect to justify obstructions to the normal flow of commerce in its movement between states. . . . One state may not put pressure of that sort upon others to reform their economic standards. If farmers or manufacturers in Vermont are abandoning farms or factories, or are failing to maintain them properly, the legislature of Vermont and not that of New York must supply the fitting remedy.

. . . Subject to the paramount power of the Congress, a state may regulate the importation of unhealthy swine or cattle . . . or decayed or noxious food. . . . Things such as these are not proper subjects of commerce, and there is no unreasonable interference when they are inspected and excluded. So a state may protect its inhabitants against the fraudulent substitution, by deceptive coloring or otherwise, of one article for another. . . . None of these statutes . . . approaches in drastic quality the statute here in controversy which would neutralize the economic consequences of free trade among the states. . . .

. . . It is one thing for a state to exact adherence by an importer to fitting standards of sanitation before the products of the farm or factory may be sold in its markets. It is a very different thing to establish a wage scale or a scale of prices for use in other states, and to bar the sale of the products, whether in the original packages or in others, unless the scale has been observed. . . .

### § 17:7. Exclusion of the Indigent

If the states cannot shut their doors to goods coming in from other states in the absence of some dangerous condition of the goods themselves, can a state prohibit persons from other states or nations from coming into the state? During times of depression or regional disasters, the movement from one state to another of persons without any means of support is common. Can a state protect itself from the social and economic burden resulting from the entry of persons unable to support themselves by prohibiting their entry or making the act of bringing them into the state a crime?

A number of states made it a misdemeanor for anyone to bring a nonresident indigent person into the state. A statute of this nature was adopted in California. In the following case, the Supreme Court of the United States passed on the constitutionality of this law. Note, that, in addition to the opinion of the majority of the Court, a concurring opinion is given. This concurring opinion reached the same conclusion as that of the majority opinion but by a different process of reasoning.

### *(a) Penalty for bringing indigent into state*

EDWARDS v. CALIFORNIA
314 U.S. 160 (1941)

Edwards brought his indigent brother-in-law from Texas into California and was prosecuted under the California statute for the offense of bringing an indigent person into the state.

OPINION BY BYNRES, J.

. . . The issue presented in this case, therefore, is whether the prohibition embodied in § 2615 against the "bringing" or transportation of indigent persons into California is within the police power of that State. We think that it is not, and hold that it is an unconstitutional barrier to interstate commerce.

. . . [That] State asserts that the huge influx of migrants into California in recent years has resulted in problems of health, morals, and especially finance, the proportions of which are staggering. . . . We do not conceive it our function to pass upon "the wisdom, need, or appropriateness" of the legislative efforts . . . to solve such difficulties.

But this does not mean that there are no boundaries to the permissible area of State legislative activity. There are. And none is more certain than the prohibition against attempts on the part of any single State to isolate itself from difficulties common to all of them by restraining the transportation of persons and property across its borders. . . .

It is difficult to conceive of a statute more squarely in conflict with this theory than the section challenged here. Its express purpose and inevitable effect is to prohibit the transportation of indigent persons across the California border. The burden upon interstate commerce is intended and immediate; it is the plain and sole function of the statute. . . .

. . . The prohibition against transporting indigent non-residents into one State is an open invitation to retaliatory measures, and the burdens upon the transportation of such persons become cumulative. . . .

CONCURRING OPINION BY JACKSON, J.

. . . The migrations of a human being, of whom it is charged that he possesses nothing that can be sold and has no wherewithal to buy, do not fit easily into my notions as to what is commerce. . . .

. . . This Court has not been timorous about giving concrete meaning to such obscure and vagrant phrases as "due process," "general welfare," "equal protection," or even "commerce among the several States." But it has always hesitated to give any real meaning to the privileges and immunities clause lest it improvidently give too much.

This Court should, however, hold squarely that it is a privilege of citizenship of the United States, protected from state abridgment, to enter any state of the Union, either for temporary sojourn or for the establishment of permanent residence therein and for gaining resultant citizenship thereof. If national citizenship means less than this, it means nothing. . . .

It is here that we meet the real crux of this case. Does "indigence" as defined by the application of the California statute constitute a basis for restricting the freedom of a citizen, as crime or contagion warrants its restriction? We should say now, and in no uncertain terms, that a man's mere property status, without more, cannot be used by a state to test, qualify, or limit his rights as a citizen of the United States. "Indigence" in itself is neither a source of rights nor a basis for denying them. The mere state of being without funds is a neutral fact—constitutionally an irrelevance, like race, creed, or color. I agree with what I understand to be the holding of the Court that cases which may indicate the contrary are overruled.

Any measure which would divide our citizenry on the basis of property into one class free to move from state to state and another class that is poverty-bound to the place where it has suffered misfortune is not only at war with the habit and custom by which our country has expanded, but is also a short-sighted blow at the security of property itself. Property can have no more dangerous, even if unwitting, enemy than one who would make its possession a pretext for unequal or exclusive civil rights. . . .

If I doubted whether his federal citizenship alone were enough to open the gates of California to Duncan, my doubt would disappear on consideration of the obligations of such citizenship. Duncan owes a duty to render military service, and this Court has said that this duty is the result of his citizenship. Mr. Chief Justice White declared in the Selective Draft Law Cases . . . : "It may not be doubted that the very conception of a just government and its duty to the citizen includes the reciprocal obligation of the citizen to render military service in case of need and the right to compel it." A contention that a citizen's duty to render military service is suspended by "indigence" would meet with little favor. Rich or penniless, Duncan's citizenship under the Constitution pledges his strength to the defense of California as a part of the United States, and his right to migrate to any part of the land he must defend is something she must respect under the same instrument. Unless this Court is willing to say that citizenship of the United States means at least this much to the citizen, then our heritage of constitutional privileges and immunities is only a promise to the ear to be broken to the hope, a teasing illusion like a munificent bequest in a pauper's will.

## § 17:8. State Export Barriers

The converse of the problem of subjecting incoming goods or persons to restrictions or barriers is found in laws that seek to restrict the exportation of goods from a state or to preserve a local monopoly in natural resources. Except as respects wild game, a state law may not prohibit the export of property or of its natural resources or discriminate against foreign business in the regulation or preservation of its natural resources. The fact that a state law is restrictive does not in itself determine its invalidity. If the restriction is reasonably related to the furtherance of public health, safety, morals, or welfare, as distinguished from creating a mere economic preference or barrier, the law is valid until superseded by a federal law regulating the same subject.

### *(a) Crop standard maintenance*

SLIGH v. KIRKWOOD
237 U.S. 52 (1915)

OPINION BY DAY, J.

A statute of the state of Florida undertakes to make it unlawful for any one to sell, offer for sale, ship, or deliver for shipment, any citrus fruits which are immature or otherwise unfit for consumption.

. . . Was it within the authority of the state of Florida to make it a criminal offense to deliver for shipment in interstate commerce citrus fruits,—oranges in this case,—then and there immature and unfit for consumption?

It will be observed that the oranges must not only be immature, but they must be in such condition as renders them unfit for consumption; that is, giving the words their ordinary signification, unfit to be used for food. . . .

That Congress has the exclusive power to regulate interstate commerce is beyond question, and when that authority is exerted by the state, even in the just exercise of the police power, it may not interfere with the supreme authority of Congress over the subject; while this is true, this court from the beginning has recognized that there may be legitimate action by the state in the matter of local regulation, which the state may take until Congress exercises its authority upon the subject. . . .

While this proposition seems to be conceded, and the competency of the state to provide local measures in the interest of the safety and welfare of the people is not doubted, although such regulations incidentally and indirectly involve interstate commerce, the contention is that this statute is not a legitimate exercise of the police power, as it has the effect to protect the health of people in other states who may receive the fruits from Florida in a condition unfit for consumption; and however commendable it may be to protect the health of such foreign peoples, such purpose is not within the police power of the state.

The power of the state to prescribe regulations which shall prevent the production within its borders of impure foods, unfit for use, and such articles as would spread disease and pestilence, is well established. Such articles, it has been declared by this court, are not the legitimate subject of trade or commerce, nor within the protection of the commerce clause of the Constitution. "Such articles are not merchantable; they are not legitimate subjects of trade and commerce. They may be rightly outlawed as intrinsically and directly the immediate sources and causes of destruction to human health and life. The self-protecting power of each state, therefore, may be rightfully exerted against their introduction, and such exercises of power cannot be considered regulations of commerce prohibited by the Constitution." . . .

. . . Police power . . . may be none the less efficiently called into play because by doing so interstate commerce may be remotely and indirectly affected. . . .

So it may be taken as established that the mere fact that interstate commerce is indirectly affected will not prevent the state from exercising its police power, at least until Congress, in the exercise of its supreme authority, regulates the subject. Furthermore, this regulation cannot be declared invalid if within the range of the police power, unless it can be said that it has no reasonable relation to a legitimate purpose to be accomplished in its enactment; and whether such regulation is necessary in the public interest is primarily within the determination of the legislature, assuming the subject to be a proper matter of state regulation.

We may take judicial notice of the fact that the raising of citrus fruits is one of the great industries of the state of Florida. It was competent for the legislature to find that it was essential for the success of that industry that its reputation be preserved in other states wherein such fruits find their most extensive market. The shipment of fruits so immature as to be unfit for consumption, and consequently injurious to the health of the purchaser, would not be otherwise than a serious injury to the local trade, and would certainly affect the successful conduct of such business within the state. The protection of the state's reputation in foreign markets, with the consequent beneficial effect upon a great home industry, may have been within the legislative intent, and it certainly could not be said that this legislation has no reasonable relation to the accomplishment of that purpose. . . . No act of Congress has been called to our attention undertaking to regulate shipments of this character, which would be contravened by the act in question. . . . Therefore until Congress does legislate upon the subject, the state is free to enter the field.

## Questions for Discussion

1. Compare the definition of the commerce power in *Gibbons* v. *Ogden*, with the definitions in *N.L.R.B.* v. *Jones & Laughlin Steel Corporation* (page 205) and *Wickard* v. *Filburn* (page 234).

2. Has there been any change in the type of cases involving the commerce clause that have come before the Supreme Court?

3. What effect does the *Baldwin* decision have on the effectiveness of the New York state law?

4. (a) Could New York have excluded the milk purchased in other states if it found as a fact that the milk did not meet the New York standards of sanitation? (b) Would it make any difference if the New York standards were higher than those prevailing in other states?

5. By what standard was the movement of the indigent person in the *Edwards* case deemed interstate commerce?

6. To what extent was the Court's interpretation of the commerce power in the *Edwards* case influenced by the view that relief is no longer a local matter?

7. Compare the concurring opinion in the *Edwards* case with the majority opinion.

8. (a) What decision would have been made in the *Sligh* case if it was found as a fact that the citrus fruits were mature and fit for consumption? (b) Is the problem solved by stating that unfit foods are not "legitimate subjects of trade and commerce"?

9. Would the decision of the Court in the *Sligh* case have been different if the property involved had been wild game that had been caught within the state of Florida?

10. Could Florida adopt a law authorizing a state official to prohibit the extra-state shipment of any citrus fruits when, because of a reduction in the quantity produced, there is a shortage and the quantity that is produced is required by domestic users for the protection of their health and welfare?

11. In *Local 24* v. *Oliver* was there an express federal statutory provision declaring lawful the agreement that the state law condemned?

12. What elements are regarded as important in determining whether the silence of Congress should be deemed permission to the states to impose local regulations?

13. What standard did the Court use in the *Parker* case to determine whether a matter comes within the area that is free from regulation by the states?

14. Why was not the state statute in the *Parker* case regarded as conflicting with the federal antitrust law?

15. (a) Could Congress have passed a law similar to the state law considered in the *Parker* case? (b) Would the Court then call the program "a regulation of state industry of local concern"?

16. A Virginia law was adopted "to prevent the selling of unwholesome meat." To carry out this purpose, the law provided that any meat slaughtered more than 100 miles away from the place of sale must be inspected by a state or local official and an inspection fee of 1 cent a pound must be paid. This law was attacked as unconstitutional. Decide. *Brimmer* v. *Rebman,* 128 U.S. 78 (1891).

17. A Minnesota statute provided that no cattle, sheep, or swine could be sold for food within the state unless examined by state inspectors within twenty-four hours before they had been slaughtered. Barbour was prosecuted for selling cattle that had not been so inspected. He claimed that the law was unconstitutional because it discriminated against cattle slaughtered outside the state. He pointed out that it was physically impossible to have cattle brought into the state, inspected, and then slaughtered outside the state and returned for sale within the state within twenty-four hours. He claimed that the natural effect and purpose of the statute was to require live animals to be bought in the state and to have them slaughtered locally to the financial advantage of the local slaughter houses. He therefore claimed that the state law was unconstitutional. Was he correct? *Minnesota* v. *Barbour,* 136 U.S. 313 (1890).

18. A state constitution provides that no foreign corporation may do business within the state. The Interstate Commerce Commission authorizes a foreign corporation to acquire by purchase a railway lying within that

state. The railroad seeks an injunction to prevent officers of the state from preventing the railroad from conducting its operations. Is the railroad entitled to an injunction? Decide. *Seaboard Airline R.R.* v. *Daniel*, 333 U.S. 118 (1948).

19. D operated a steamboat sailing on an interstate river from one point to another within the same state. Much of the freight carried by the steamboat originated in other states and was then brought into the state by various means of transportation, transferred to the steamboat, and then reshipped at the end of the steamboat's run for transportation to points outside of the state. D refused to obtain a steamboat license for his boat in accordance with the provisions of the federal navigation law. He claimed that the law could not constitutionally apply to him as he did not engage in interstate commerce. Decide. *The Daniel Ball*, 10 Wallace (U.S.) 557 (1871).

20. The Federal Safety Appliance Act and regulations lawfully issued by the United States Post Office Department regulated the construction of the last car on all interstate trains. Pennsylvania adopted a law that provided different specifications. A railroad chartered in Pennsylvania complied with the Pennsylvania law but failed to comply with the federal law, which was inconsistent with the state law. The railroad was prosecuted for failing to follow the federal law. It defended on the ground that the Pennsylvania law controlled, since it was a Pennsylvania corporation. Decide. *Pennsylvania R.R.* v. *Pennsylvania*, 250 U.S. 566 (1919).

21. In 1907 Congress adopted a safety law providing that employees working on interstate railways could not be employed for more than 16 continuous hours in one day. The X Railroad employed a number of men for 20 consecutive hours each. When prosecuted for violating the law, the X Railroad claimed that the first 10 hours in the case of each man was spent on intrastate commerce and therefore the federal law had not been violated. Decide. *B. & O. R.R.* v. *I.C.C.*, 221 U.S. 612 (1911).

22. In 1903 Congress adopted a law requiring the use of automatic couplers and safety brakes on all trains operating in interstate commerce. The Z Railroad ran certain intrastate trains on the same tracks used by the interstate trains. The coupling devices on one of the intrastate trains did not conform to the federal standards. The railroad was sued for violating the federal law. It defended on the ground that the federal law could apply only to interstate trains. Decide. *Southern Railway* v. *United States*, 222 U.S. 20 (1911).

23. The Interstate Commerce Commission prescribed rates for interstate train shipments between points in Texas and Louisianna. In order to encourage domestic trade, the Texas Railway Commission established a rate for travel between points within Texas that was substantially lower than the rates for the same distances between points in Texas and Louisiana as established by the Interstate Commerce Commission. Because of this difference, trade was diverted from Louisiana to local points within Texas.

The Interstate Commerce Commission ordered the Texas Railroad Commission to raise the intrastate rates to eliminate this discrimination against the interstate traffic. The state commission objected on the ground that state rates were exclusively within the control of the state. Decide. *The Shreveport Case,* 234 U.S. 342 (1914).

24. The Interstate Commerce Commission granted increases in interstate railroad rates. Wisconsin maintained the former level of rates for intrastate commerce. The effect of this was to require a greater increase for the interstate rates or to cause the railroads to use the proceeds of interstate operations to meet deficits incurred in intrastate operations. The Interstate Commerce Commission requested the Wisconsin State Commission to raise the rates for intrastate transportation. The state commission refused to do so on the ground that the federal authority could not require a change in intrastate rates. Decide. *Wisconsin* v. *C. B. & Q. R. R.,* 257 U.S. 563 (1922).

25. The Pennsylvania State Board of Censors ordered that all motion picture films intended for television broadcast must be approved by the board. X objected to the regulation. Is the regulation valid? Decide. *Allen B. Du Mont Laboratories* v. *Carroll,* 86 F.Supp. 813 (DC Pa. 1949), affirmed 184 F.2d 153 (CA 3rd 1950) cert. den. 340 U.S. 929.

26. Is a state law merely prohibiting specified conduct a regulation of insurance within the meaning of the McCarran-Ferguson Act?

27. Would the decision in the *Michigan-Wisconsin Pipe Line Company* case have been different if the tax had been assessed against the Phillips company for gathering it?

28. May the act of removing natural gas from an interstate pipeline be taxed locally?

29. Is a tax on income earned locally from interstate commerce transactions a burden on interstate commerce?

30. What is the basis for the dissent in the *Northwestern States Portland Cement Company* case?

## Chapter 18

## REGULATION OF PRICE



### § 18:1. Nature of the Problem

In its broadest sense, a price is the amount that a seller receives and the amount that a buyer pays for services or property. The purpose of the regulation of price may be to prevent the seller from securing an exorbitant price or to guarantee to him the receipt of a reasonable price. The regulation of prices may be inspired by the premise that, under the existing circumstances, either generally or with respect to a particular price, the natural laws of supply and demand do not result in the establishment of a price that is socially desirable. It may also be inspired by the premise that, due to monopolistic or other restrictive practices, the natural laws of supply and demand are not able to operate and therefore government regulation must intervene to establish a fair price.

In addition to direct regulation of prices, there may be intentional or unintentional indirect regulation. The requirement that factories install fire escapes or safety devices, while not intended as a price regulation, may indirectly have that effect as the factory owners seek to place the greater cost of their plant upon the purchasers of their goods. Laws restricting the hours of work or excluding women and children from certain types of labor will also have the effect of raising the labor cost of a manufacturer, and this added cost may ultimately result in the purchasers paying a greater price. An illustration of an intentional indirect regulation of price is the case of the national government's devaluing of the dollar in 1933 and 1934 in order to cause a rise of the price level. A similar approach is found in the Agricultural Adjustment Act of 1938, which seeks to raise the price of various basic farm commodities by restricting the quantity produced.

### § 18:2. State Regulation

The right of the state by virtue of its police power to enact laws for the general welfare, safety, health, and morals was early recognized in the case of public utilities. In addition to regulation of public utilities proper, the Supreme Court also sustained the right to regulate those businesses that were affected with a public interest. In *Munn* v. *Illinois* the court sustained a maximum rate fixed by a state legislature for the charges of grain elevator operators. The court rejected the argument that the grain elevator was merely private property devoted to a private business and held that it was affected with a public interest. The difficulty of defining the scope of this phrase "affected with a public interest" is seen from the conflict between the majority and the dissenting opinions.

#### *(a) Business affected with a public interest*

MUNN v. ILLINOIS
94 U.S. 113 (1876)

OPINION BY WAITE, C. J.

The question . . . is whether Illinois can . . . fix . . . the maximum . . . charges for the storage of grain in warehouses at Chicago and other places in the State having not less than one hundred thousand inhabitants, "in which grain is stored in bulk, and in which the grain of different owners is mixed together. . . ."

When one becomes a member of society, he necessarily parts with some rights or privileges which, as an individual not affected by his relations to others, he might retain. . . . This is the very essence of government. . . . From this source come the police powers, which . . . "are nothing more or less than the powers of government inherent in every sovereignty, . . . that is to say, . . . the power to govern men and things." Under these powers the government regulates the conduct of its citizens one towards another, and the manner in which each shall use his own property, when such regulation becomes necessary for the public good. . . .

This brings us to inquire as to the principles upon which this power of regulation rests, in order that we may determine what is within and what without its operative effect. Looking, then, to the common law, from whence came the right which the Constitution protects, we find that when private property is "affected with a public interest, it ceases to be *juris privati* only." . . . Property does become clothed with a public interest when used in a manner to make it of public consequence, and affect the community at large. When, therefore, one devotes his property to a use in which the public has an interest, he, in effect, grants to the public an interest in that use, and must submit to be controlled by the public for the common good, to the extent of the interest he has thus created. He may withdraw his grant by discontinuing the use; but, so long as he maintains the use, he must submit to the control. . . .

. . . "The great producing region of the West and Northwest sends its grain by water and rail to Chicago, where the greater part of it is shipped by vessel for transportation to the seaboard by the Great Lakes, and some of it is forwarded by railway to the Eastern ports. . . . Vessels, to some extent, are loaded in the Chicago harbor, and sailed through the St. Lawrence directly to Europe. . . . This business has created a demand for means by which the immense quantity of grain can be handled or stored, and these have been found in grain warehouses, which are commonly called elevators. . . . The grain warehouses . . . are located with the river harbor on one side and the railway tracks on the other; and the grain is run through them from car to vessel, or boat to car, . . ."

. . . In 1874 there were in Chicago fourteen warehouses adapted to this particular business, . . . owned by about thirty persons, nine business firms controlled them, and . . . the prices charged and received for storage were such "as have been from year to year agreed upon and established by the different elevators or warehouses in the city of Chicago." . . . Thus it is apparent that all the elevating facilities through which these vast productions "of seven or eight great States of the West" must pass on the way "to four or five of the States on the seashore" may be a "virtual" monopoly.

Under such circumstances it is difficult to see why, if the common carrier, or the miller, or the ferryman, or the inn keeper, or the wharfinger, or the baker, or the cartman, or the hackney-coachman, pursues a public employment and exercises "a sort of public office," these plaintiffs in error do not. . . . Their business most certainly "tends to a common charge, and has become a thing of public interest and use." . . . Certainly, if any business can be clothed "with a public interest, and cease to be *juris privati* only," this has been. It may not be made so by the operation of the Constitution of Illinois or this statute, but it is by the facts. . . .

DISSENTING OPINION BY FIELD, J.

The question presented, therefore, is one of the greatest importance,—whether it is within the competency of a State to fix the compensation which an individual may receive for the use of his own property in his private business, and for his services in connection with it. . . .

. . . But it would seem from its opinion that the court holds that property loses something of its private character when employed in such a way as to be generally useful. The doctrine declared is that property "becomes clothed with a public interest when used in a manner to make it of public consequence, and affect the community at large;" and from such clothing the right of the legislature is deduced to control the use of the property, and to determine the compensation which the owner may receive for it. When Sir Matthew Hale, and the sages of the law in his day, spoke of property as affected by a public interest, and ceasing from that cause to be *juris privati* solely, that is, ceasing to be held merely in private right, they referred to property dedicated by the owner to public uses, or to property the use of which was granted by the government, or in connection with which special privileges were conferred. Unless the property was thus dedicated, or some right bestowed by the government was held with the property, . . . the property was not affected by any public interest so as to be taken out of the category of property held in private right. But it is not in any such sense that the terms "clothing property with a public interest" are used in this case. From the nature of the business under consideration—the storage of grain—which, in any sense in which the words can be used, is a private business . . . it is clear that the court intended to declare that, whenever one devotes his property to a business which is useful to the public,—"affects the community at large,"—the legislature can regulate the compensation which the owner may receive for its use, and for his own services in connection with it. . . .

If this be sound law, . . . all property and all business in the State are held at the mercy of a majority of its legislature. . . .

The power of the State over the property of the citizen under the constitutional guaranty is well defined. The State may take his property for public uses, upon just compensation being made therefor. It may take a portion of his property by way of taxation for the support of the government. It may control the use and possession of his property, so far as may be necessary for the protection of the rights of others, and to secure to them the equal use and enjoyment of their property. . . . Except in cases where property may be destroyed to arrest a conflagration or the ravages of pestilence, or be taken under the pressure of an immediate and overwhelming necessity to prevent a public calamity, the power of the State over the property of the citizen does not extend beyond such limits. . . .

## § 18:3. Expansion of State Power

The Supreme Court thereafter refused to extend this concept of businesses affected with a public interest to other businesses in which the public was in fact vitally interested. The Court invalidated state limitations upon the profit of theatre-ticket brokers, the rates charged by private employment agencies, the price of gasoline, and a statute that required that anyone entering the business of manufacturing and distributing ice must first obtain a certificate to do business.

At this point, regulation was confined to public utilities proper or to those businesses that the Court considered so like public utilities that they could be classified with them. Such price regulations as were permitted were designed to set a ceiling on the charges that could be made by the businesses regulated in order to protect the public from exorbitant rates. With the advent of the 1929 depression a new era in price regulation began. In the case of *Nebbia* v. *New York,* the Supreme Court held that a business could be affected with a public interest although it was neither a monopoly nor held a franchise and was not like a public utility and that the regulation of prices was not limited to setting maximum prices but also permitted the establishment of minimum prices below which distributors could not resell the products of the business. Here the regulation is not to protect the consumer from exorbitant prices but to insure the producer a fair return so that he may continue in business. Again the conflict between the majority and the dissenting opinion found in the *Munn* case is repeated.

### *(a) Nullification of public interest concept*

NEBBIA v. NEW YORK

291 U.S. 502 (1934)

OPINION BY ROBERTS, J.

The Legislature of New York established . . . a Milk Control Board with power . . . to "fix minimum and maximum . . . retail prices to be charged by . . . stores to consumers for consumption off the premises where sold." The Board fixed nine cents as the price to be charged by a store for a quart of milk. Nebbia, the proprietor of a grocery store . . . sold two quarts and a five cent loaf of bread for eighteen cents; and was convicted for violating the Board's order. . . .

The question for decision is whether the Federal Constitution prohibits a state from so fixing the selling price of milk. . . .

Under our form of government the use of property and the making of contracts are normally matters of private and not of public concern. The general rule is that both shall be free of governmental interference. But neither property rights nor contract rights are absolute; for government cannot exist if the citizen may at will use his property to the detriment of his fellows, or exercise his freedom of contract to work them harm. Equally fundamental with the private right is that of the public to regulate it in the common interest. . . .

The Fifth Amendment, in the field of federal activity, and the Fourteenth, as respects state action, do not prohibit governmental regulation for the public welfare. They merely condition the exertion of the admitted power, by securing that the end shall be accomplished by methods consistent with due process. And the guaranty of due process, as has often been held, demands only that the law shall not be unreasonable, arbitrary, or capricious, and that the means selected shall have a real and substantial relation to the object sought to be attained. It results that a regulation valid for one sort of business, or in given circumstances, may be invalid for another sort, or for the same business under other circumstances, because the reasonableness of each regulation depends upon the relevant facts.

The milk industry in New York has been the subject of longstanding and drastic regulation in the public interest. The legislative investigation of 1932 was persuasive of the fact that for this and other reasons unrestricted competition aggravated existing evils, and the normal law of supply and demand was insufficient to correct maladjustments detrimental to the community. The inquiry disclosed destructive and demoralizing competitive conditions and unfair trade practices which resulted in retail price-cutting and reduced the income of the farmer below the cost of production. We do not understand the appellant to deny that in these circumstances the legislature might reasonably consider further regulation and control desirable for protection of the industry and the consuming public. That body believed conditions could be improved by preventing destructive price-cutting by stores which, due to the flood of surplus milk, were able to buy at much lower prices than the larger distributors and to sell without incurring the delivery costs of the latter. In the order of which complaint is made the Milk Control Board fixed a price of ten cents per quart for sales by a distributor to a consumer, and nine cents by a store to a consumer, thus recognizing the lower costs of the store, and endeavoring to establish a differential which would be just to both. In the light of the facts the order appears not to be unreasonable or arbitrary, or without relation to the purpose to prevent ruthless competition from destroying the wholesale price structure on which the farmer depends for his livelihood, and the community for an assured supply of milk.

But we are told that because the law essays to control prices it denies due process. Notwithstanding the admitted power to correct existing economic ills by appropriate regulation of business, even though an indirect result may be a restriction of the freedom of contract or a modification of charges for services or the price of commodities, the appellant urges that direct fixation of prices is a type of regulation absolutely forbidden. . . . The argument runs that the public control of rates or prices is *per se* unreasonable and unconstitutional, save as applied to businesses affected with a public interest; that a business so affected is one in which property is devoted to an enterprise of a sort which the public itself might appropriately undertake, or one whose owner relies on a public grant or franchise for the right to conduct the business, or in which he is bound to serve all who apply; in short, such as is commonly called a public utility; or a business in its nature a monopoly. The milk industry, it is said, possesses none of these characteristics, and, therefore, not being affected with a public interest, its charges may not be controlled by the state. Upon the soundness of this contention the appellant's case against the statute depends.

We may as well say at once that the dairy industry is not, in the accepted sense of the phrase, a public utility. We think the appellant is also right in asserting that there is in this case no suggestion of any monopoly or monopolistic practice. It goes without saying that those engaged in the business are in no way dependent upon public grants or franchise for the privilege of conducting their activities. But if, as must be conceded, the industry is subject to regulation in the public interest, what constitutional principle bars the state from correcting existing maladjustments by legislation touching prices? We think there is no such principle. The due process clause makes no mention of sales or of prices any more than it speaks of business or contracts or buildings or other incidents of property. The thought seems nevertheless to have persisted that there is something peculiarly sacrosanct about the price one may charge for what he makes or sells, and that, however able to regulate other elements of manufacture or trade, with incidental effect upon price, the state is incapable of directly controlling the price itself. This view was negatived many years ago. *Munn* v. *Illinois,* 94 U.S. 113. . . .

Many other decisions show that the private character of a business does not necessarily remove it from the realm of regulation of charges or prices. The usury laws fix the price which may be exacted for the use of money, although no business more essentially private in character can be imagined than that of loaning one's personal funds. . . . Insurance agents' compensation may be regulated, though their contracts are private, because the business of insurance is considered one properly subject to public control. . . . Statutes prescribing in the public interest the amounts to be charged by attorneys for prosecuting certain claims, a matter ordinarily one of personal and private nature, are not a deprivation of due process. . . . A stockyards corporation, "while not a common carrier, nor engaged in any distinctively public employment, is doing a work in which the public has an interest," and its charges may be controlled. . . . Private contract carriers, who do not operate under a franchise, and have no monopoly of the carriage of goods or passengers, may, since they use the highways to compete with railroads, be compelled to charge rates not lower than those of public carriers for corresponding services, if the state, in pursuance of a public policy to protect the latter, so determines. . . .

It is clear that there is no closed class or category of businesses affected with a public interest, and the function of courts in the application of the Fifth and Fourteenth Amendments is to determine in each case whether circumstances vindicate the challenged regulation as a reasonable exertion of governmental authority or condemn it as arbitrary or discriminatory. . . . The phrase "affected with a public interest" can, in the nature of things, mean no more than that an industry, for adequate reason, is subject to control for the public good. . . .

So far as the requirement of due process is concerned, and in the absence of other constitutional restriction, a state is free to adopt whatever economic policy may reasonably be deemed to promote the public welfare, and to enforce that policy by legislation adapted to its purpose. The courts are without authority either to declare such policy, or, when it is declared by the legislature, to override it. . . . With the wisdom of the policy adopted, with the adequacy or practicability of the law enacted to forward it, the courts are both incompetent and unauthorized to deal. . . .

The law-making bodies have in the past endeavored to promote free competition by laws aimed at trusts and monopolies. The consequent interference with private property and freedom of contract has not availed with the courts to set these enactments aside as denying due process. Where the public interest was deemed to require the fixing of minimum prices, that expedient has been sustained. If the law-making body within its sphere of government concludes that the conditions or practices in an industry make unrestricted competition an inadequate safeguard of the consumer's interests, produce waste harmful to the public, threaten ultimately to cut off the supply of a commodity needed by the public, or portend the destruction of the industry itself, appropriate statutes passed in an honest effort to correct the threatened consequences may not be set aside because the regulation adopted fixes prices reasonably deemed by the legislature to be fair to those engaged in the industry and to the consuming public. And this is especially so where, as here, the economic maladjustment is one of price, which threatens harm to the producer at one end of the series and the consumer at the other. The Constitution does not secure to anyone liberty to conduct his business in such fashion as to inflict injury upon the public at large, or upon any substantial group of the people. Price control, like any other form of regulation, is unconstitutional only if arbitrary, discriminatory, or demonstrably irrelevant to the policy the legislature is free to adopt, and hence an unnecessary and unwarranted interference with individual liberty.

Tested by these considerations we find no basis in the due process clause of the Fourteenth Amendment for condemning the provisions of the Agriculture and Markets Law here drawn into question.

DISSENTING OPINION BY MCREYNOLDS, J.

Is the milk business so affected with public interest that the Legislature may prescribe prices for sales by stores? This Court has approved the contrary view; has emphatically declared that a State lacks power to fix prices in similar private businesses. . . .

Regulation to prevent recognized evils in business has long been upheld as permissible legislative action. But fixation of the price at which "A," engaged in an ordinary business, may sell, in order to enable "B," a producer, to improve his condition, has not been regarded as within legislative power. This is not regulation, but management, control, dictation—it amounts to the deprivation of the fundamental right which one has to conduct his own affairs honestly and along customary lines. The argument advanced here would support general prescription of prices for farm products, groceries, shoes, clothing, all the necessities of modern civilization, as well as labor, when some legislature finds and declares such action advisable and for the public good. This Court has declared that a State may not by legislative fiat convert a private business into a public utility. . . . And if it be now ruled that one dedicates his property to public use whenever he embarks on an enterprise which the Legislature may think is desirable to bring under control, this is but to declare that rights guaranteed by the Constitution exist only so long as supposed public interest does not require their extinction. To adopt such a view, of course, would put an end to liberty under the Constitution. . . .

Not only does the statute interfere arbitrarily with the rights of the little grocer to conduct his business according to standards long accepted—complete destruction may follow; but it takes away the liberty of twelve million consumers to buy a necessity of life in an open market. It imposes direct and arbitrary burdens upon those already seriously impoverished with the alleged immediate design of affording special benefits to others. To him with less than nine cents it says—You cannot procure a quart of milk from the grocer although he is anxious to accept what you can pay and the demands of your household are urgent! A superabundance; but no child can purchase from a willing storekeeper below the figure appointed by three men at headquarters! And this is true although the storekeeper himself may have bought from a willing producer at half that rate and must sell quickly or lose his stock through deterioration. The fanciful scheme is to protect the farmer against undue exactions by prescribing the price at which milk disposed of by him at will may be resold! . . .

### § 18:4. Appraisal of the Nebbia Doctrine

It should also be noted that the Supreme Court which decided the *Nebbia* case in 1934 was not the New Deal Court nor even the old Court subjected to the influence of the New Deal controversy. It was the same strict constructionist Court that, in *Hammer* v. *Dagenhart,* had limited the power of Congress over commerce and, in *Adkins* v. *Children's Hospital,* had exalted freedom of contract by invalidating a minimum wage law for women. It was the Court that, in the two years after the *Nebbia* case, was to declare unconstitutional many of the federal New Deal laws and was not to show the new "federalism" until three years later in the *Jones & Laughlin Steel Corporation* case.

This is particularly significant in indicating that the trend seen in the *Nebbia* case cannot be regarded as a swing of the pendulum to the "left" but as a new basic doctrine that is established in our constitutional law. The exact meaning of this doctrine cannot be determined because it is difficult to deny the argument of the dissent that the broad definition of "affected with a public interest" virtually brings within the regulatory power all modern business enterprise. It is difficult to see in what respect farming, steel production, mining, and the other great basic industries that supply our modern economic system are not to be deemed affected with a public interest. In truth, it would appear that the *Nebbia* case, in attempting to define "affected with a public interest" in a manner sufficiently broad to sustain price regulation, destroyed that concept. In *Olsen* v. *Nebraska,* 313 U.S. 236 (1941), the Court later refers to the concept of "affected with a public interest" as "discarded in *Nebbia* v. *New York.*" In *Cities Service Gas Co.* v. *Peerless Oil & Gas Co.,* 340 U.S. 179 (1950), the Court sustained the state fixing of minimum prices for natural gas at the wellhead without invoking expressly any concept of "affected with a public interest." The Court simply commented that "like any other regulation, a price fixing order is lawful if substantially related to a legitimate end sought to be attained" and cited the *Nebbia* case.

The doctrine of the *Nebbia* case has been in effect carried forward by the decisions sustaining the federal regulation of the selling price of interstate milk and coal.

While the *Nebbia* case sustained state price regulation, the rising federal power of price regulation may be exercised so as greatly to restrict the area of operation of state law. While a state may require a middleman to pay a local producer a minimum price, it cannot constitutionally regulate the price that the middleman pays to a producer in another state, even though the goods are resold locally. This confines state regulation of resale price to goods purchased by the seller within the state. If Congress desires, it can exclude the state from even this area of regulation in order to remove differentials between the price that the federal government has set on such commodities in interstate commerce and the price that the state has set as to local sales.

### § 18:5. Federal Regulation under the Commerce Power

Under the commerce power, the national Congress has created the Interstate Commerce Commission, which among other things regulates the rates that may be charged by interstate carriers. As such carriers have a natural monopoly because of the capital investment required and have a legal monopoly by virtue of their government franchise, the courts find little difficulty in sustaining the legality of regulating the rates charged by them. Here the object of the rate or price regulation is to prevent the customers or the public from being charged exorbitant prices. Government interference is justified on the ground that, because of the natural and legal monopoly factors, the natural forces of supply and demand do not adjust the rates to a proper level.

On a somewhat similar basis, a federal regulation of the charges made by commission brokers at the great cattle exchanges was sustained. At these exchanges, cattle brought from one state would be held over long enough to be sold, after which they were shipped to other states for ultimate slaughter, packing, and final sale to the public. It was found that at such an exchange, which in the words of the court was as a throat through which flowed interstate commerce, a number of evil practices had arisen, including exorbitant charges by brokers for their services in connection with the sale and temporary holdover of the cattle. In order to protect the flow of interstate commerce from this danger, Congress was held to have the authority under the commerce power to regulate such commissions. Similar federal control has been sustained over the grain exchanges.

The most significant extension of this power to regulate prices of services or labor under the commerce power is found in the establishment of minimum wages made by the Federal Fair Labor Standards Act. Under its present provisions, this Act provides that, in interstate commerce and in all factories producing for interstate commerce, $1 an hour shall be the minimum wage and 40 hours a week the maximum work week, with time and a half for overtime.

This ability of Congress to reach beyond the facilities of interstate transportation into the local areas of production is sustained under the new interpretation of the commerce clause.

Under the commerce power, Congress can regulate the price of commodities that are sold in interstate transactions or that move through interstate commerce channels. This power has been sustained with respect to the regulation of the price of milk and of coal. Congress has also authorized the Federal Power Commission to fix the rates for interstate transmission and transfer of electricity and natural gas.

The power to regulate the prices of interstate commodities is held to include the power to regulate the prices of local goods that compete with the goods which have moved through interstate commerce. Thus the power to regulate the price of interstate milk gives Congress the power to regulate the price of milk produced and sold in the state of its production where that local milk competes in the local markets with the interstate milk. Stated differently, if an article commonly moves in interstate commerce, Congress may regulate the sale price of that commodity throughout the country without regard to whether the particular unit of the commodity being sold has itself been in interstate commerce or not.

### *(a) Commerce power*

### UNITED STATES v. ROCK ROYAL COOPERATIVE, INC.

307 U.S. 533 (1939)

The Agricultural Marketing Agreement Act of 1937 authorizes the Secretary of Agriculture to designate milk marketing areas and to prescribe minimum prices to be paid to producers within that area.

OPINION BY REED, J.

These appeals involve the validity of Order No. 27 of the Secretary of Agriculture, issued under the Agricultural Marketing Agreement Act of 1937, . . . regulating the handling of milk in the New York metropolitan area. . . .

. . . The challenge is to the regulation "of the price to be paid upon the sale by a dairy farmer who delivers his milk to some country plant." It is urged that the sale, a local transaction, is fully completed before any interstate commerce begins and that the attempt to fix the price or other elements of that incident violates the Tenth Amendment. But where commodities are bought for use beyond state lines, the sale is a part of interstate commerce. We have likewise held that where sales for interstate transportation were commingled with intrastate transactions, the existence of the local activity did not interfere with the Federal power to regulate inspection of the whole. Activities conducted within state lines do not by this fact alone escape the sweep of the Commerce Clause. Interstate commerce may be dependent upon them. Power to establish quotas for interstate marketing gives power to name quotas for that which is to be left within the state of production. Where local and foreign milk alike are drawn into a general plan for protecting the interstate commerce in the commodity from the interferences, burdens and obstructions, arising from excessive surplus and the social and sanitary evils of low values, the power of the Congress extends also to the local sales.

This power over commerce when it exists is complete and perfect. It has been exercised to fix a wage scale for a limited period, railroad tariffs and fees and charges for live-stock exchanges. . . .

### *(b) Federal regulation applied to local goods*

UNITED STATES v. WRIGHTWOOD DAIRY CO.

315 U.S. 110 (1942)

Acting under the Agricultural Marketing Agreement Act of 1937, the Secretary of Agriculture defined a Chicago milk sale area and established a minimum price to be paid producers. Application of the price fixing regulations to milk produced, sold, and purchased within the state was challenged on the ground that only the sales price of commodities moving in interstate commerce could be regulated.

OPINION BY STONE, J.

. . .

Competitive practices which are wholly intrastate may be reached by the Sherman Act . . . because of their injurious effect on the interstate commerce. . . . So too the marketing of a local product in competition with that of a like commodity moving interstate may so interfere with interstate commerce or its regulation as to afford a basis for Congressional regulation of the intrastate activity. It is the effect upon the interstate commerce or its regulation, regardless of the particular form which the competition may take, which is the test of the federal power. . . .

. . . The marketing of intrastate milk which competes with that shipped interstate will tend seriously to break down price regulation of the latter. . . .

It is no answer to suggest . . . that the federal power to regulate intrastate transactions is limited to those who are engaged also in interstate commerce. . . . It is the effect upon interstate commerce or upon the exercise of the power to regulate it, not the source of the injury, which is the criterion of Congressional power. . . .

We conclude that the national power to regulate the price of milk moving interstate into the Chicago, Illinois, marketing area, extends to such control of intrastate transactions there as is necessary and appropriate to make regulation of the interstate commerce effective; and that it includes authority to make like regulations for the marketing of intrastate milk whose sale and competition with the interstate milk affects its price structure so as in turn to affect adversely the Congressional regulation.

## § 18:6. Federal Regulation under the War Power

The war power confers upon Congress the power to fix any and all prices, including wages and rents. This not only may be done during the actual period of hostilities but may be made effective during the prior preparatory period. The power to fix the prices does not end with the cessation of hostilities but continues thereafter for a reasonable period until the economic dislocation caused by the war has been corrected.

It must appear that either preparation for, prosecution of, or recovery from war underlies the regulation. In a truly normal time, this power could not be exercised. Here a difficult question arises in view of the fact that modern war is such a total war enlisting not only all manpower but also all commodities. It therefore becomes difficult to say that a regulation, which if effective would place an industry on a sound basis and enable the government to be sure of a source of supply, is not in a sense a proper preparation for war. In sustaining the TVA, the Supreme Court has already recognized that a law may be valid as a preparation for war even though at the time there is no reason to suspect that there will be a particular war. The right to prepare for war includes the right to be generally prepared in the event that a war does arise.

In regulating prices under the war power, greater latitude would probably be permitted the Congress than under the commerce power. While it would be necessary to establish some link between the regulation and war, it would not be necessary to show that the article or the service of which the price or the cost was regulated was in interstate commerce or competed with goods or services in interstate commerce. As under the commerce power, it would not be necessary to adopt a regulation applicable throughout the United States. As illustrating the latter point, the National Rent Control Act was held constitutional even though it applied only to restricted areas and not to the entire nation.

### § 18:7. Limitations upon Price Regulation

Assuming that the price of a particular commodity or service may be regulated by statute, are there any limitations that determine at what level prices can be set? To the extent that the price is either too low or too high, it is clear that either the property of the seller or the property of the buyer is being taken from him and given to the other party without his receiving equal property or a fair payment in exchange. The same principle that declares it a deprivation of property without due process to take property from one man and give it to another would also theoretically condemn the price that was too low or too high.

The fact that the price is being regulated by government instead of being a matter reserved for the decision or the agreement of the parties is no longer an objection. The long period of colonial and early state regulation of prices, during which even the charges to be made by barbers were regulated, was forgotten in the course of our westward expansion. During the era in which the Supreme Court regarded the due process clause as the guardian of the economic principle of laissez faire, the Supreme Court regarded any regulation of price as an unconstitutional violation of freedom of contract and therefore a denial of due process unless the service could come within the category of a public utility or a business affected with a public interest. This view has been abandoned, and today the regulation of a price does not in itself necessarily constitute a denial of due process.

Beginning with *Smyth* v. *Ames*,[1] the Supreme Court held that the property of a common carrier was unconstitutionally confiscated if its rates were set so low that it did not earn a fair return on its investment. After following this concept of a constitutionally protected right for half a century, the Supreme Court, in passing upon rates fixed by the Federal Power Commission under the Natural Gas Act, held that the Constitution does not specifically require a fair return on the fair value of the investment. That is, the constitutional rights of a utility are satisfied if the utility has had a fair hearing, and the regulating authority has given fair considera-

[1] 169 U.S. 466 (1898).

tion to the rights of the utility, the investors, and the consuming public.[2]

The problem of determining the fair price is complicated by the fact that it is not merely an abstract question to be decided by itself, but is a question that must be decided in relation to its effect upon the various parties involved. The *Nebbia* case illustrated how there may be a conflict of interests that are in themselves socially desirable. It was there socially desirable that the milk producers receive a sufficient return for their economic activity to permit them to continue. At the same time it was socially desirable that the price of milk be as low as possible so that the poorer sections of society could afford this very vital food product. Yet the more one interest was advanced, the more the other was sacrificed. The impossibility of reconciling such conflicting interests has led to the suggestion, where there is not a single price that is fair to both buyer and seller, that society, if it is so much concerned over the matter, should by subsidy or other payment make up the difference separating the buyer's fair price and the seller's fair price. Under this view, if fairness to the milk producer requires him to obtain 5 cents a quart of milk more than the purchaser can fairly afford to pay, society should through its government pay to the milk producer the differential of 5 cents so that the milk producer receives his fair price while the purchaser spends only what to him would be a fair price.

The problem of price regulation on an extended scale presents a picture of almost hopeless complexity. Intelligent regulation requires knowledge of all the conditions relating to or affecting the price, and this in turn requires uniform national methods of bookkeeping, accounting, and reporting to the government agencies. Furthermore, it will be necessary for national and state governments to reach some definite conclusion as to the social policy or purpose toward which they wish to strive by making the price regulation. In addition, extensive price regulation requires such increased government personnel to enforce the regulations and adds to government expenditures to such an extent that the economic disadvantage of operating a system of regulation may in ordinary times offset its merits.

Because of these factors, therefore, it is most probable that price regulation will not be generally embarked upon and that practical and political considerations will operate as a greater limitation than the provisions of the Constitution.

---

[2] Federal Power Commission v. Natural Gas Pipeline Company, 315 U.S. 575 (1942); Federal Power Commission v. Hope Natural Gas Company, 320 U.S. 591 (1944).

## Questions for Discussion

1. Would a statute of the type involved in *Munn* v. *Illinois* violate the equal protection clause by exempting areas having less than 100,000 population?

2. Can the decision in *Munn* v. *Illinois* be justified without invoking the social compact theory of government?

3. Would it have affected the decision in *Munn* v. *Illinois* if there had been 100 grain warehouses in Chicago instead of 14?

4. (a) When is property affected with a public interest under the principles of *Munn* v. *Illinois*? (b) Can you answer the objection of the dissenting opinion to the definition given by the majority to "business affected with a public interest"?

5. (a) What is the state police power? (b) How is this power defined by the court in *Munn* v. *Illinois*? (c) Is there any difference between this definition and your definition?

6. If the Sherman antitrust law had been in effect in 1876, could the problem faced in *Munn* v. *Illinois* have been met by compelling the grain elevator operators to cease their practice of fixing prices by agreement?

7. When was the *Nebbia* decision made with respect to the broadening interpretation of the commerce and the due process clauses of the Constitution?

8. How does this decision compare with *Munn* v. *Illinois*?

9. What conflicting interests are involved in the *Nebbia* type of statute? Is the same class benefited by the statute in the *Nebbia* case as in *Munn* v. *Illinois*?

10. Is the price control approved by the *Nebbia* case subject to any qualification that the price be sufficient to give the enterprise a fair return on its investment?

11. (a) What is the constitutional basis for regulating the milk industry in the *Nebbia* case? (b) Was it affected with a public interest in the same way as the warehouses in *Munn* v. *Illinois*?

12. (a) Compare the dissenting opinion in *Munn* v. *Illinois* with the majority opinion in *Nebbia* v. *New York*. (b) Compare the majority opinion in *Munn* v. *Illinois* with the dissenting opinion in *Nebbia* v. *New York*.

13. Did the court in the *Nebbia* case conclude that there was an economic peril and that the law adopted by the legislature was a sound way to meet that danger?

14. (a) Did the regulation in the *Nebbia* case violate the equal protection clause because it established a different price for a sale by a distributor than by a store? (b) How great was the difference between the

prices allowed each of these two types of sellers? (c) How would it affect your answer if the difference had been ten times as great as it was?

15. Does the *Rock Royal* case preserve a distinction between interstate and intrastate commerce so far as the power of regulation by the national government is concerned?

16. (a) What is the purpose of price regulation? (b) What forms may price regulation take?

17. Give three examples of an indirect regulation of price produced by a regulation of business that is not intended as a regulation of price.

18. What is the constitutional basis for a regulation of price by a state? by the national government?

19. Congress adopts a law fixing the price for the sale of potatoes throughout the United States. Is this law constitutional? Explain.

20. (a) Would it make any difference in your answer to Question 19 if Congress established a national potato administrator and gave him authority to divide the country into potato marketing zones and fix the price in each zone? (b) Would it make any difference if he established a different price for each zone?

21. (a) Can Congress prohibit the sale of milk? (b) Can it regulate the price for the sale of milk? Explain.

22. (a) How is the state regulation of price affected by the federal commerce power? (b) Can Congress regulate prices of sales in interstate commerce? in intrastate commerce?

23. To what extent does social policy or social planning enter the field of price and rent regulation?

24. (a) A proposal is made in Congress to fix all food prices at the 1914 level to enable the community to purchase necessary foods. Would this law be constitutional? (b) Assume that it is also proposed as part of this plan to give all food producers a government subsidy equal to the difference between the current price of food and the 1914 prices. Would this law be constitutional? If constitutional, what social or political effects might appear?

25. Congress adopts a law fixing the price of bread at a higher price than would otherwise be obtained in the open market. The sellers of poultry foods claim that the law is unconstitutional because it selects a particular commodity and does not regulate prices generally. Is the law constitutional?

26. In *Sunshine Anthracite Coal Co.* v. *Atkins,* 310 U.S. 381 (1940), the Supreme Court, in sustaining the Bituminous Coal Act of 1937, stated that great weight would be given to the judgment of Congress that price-fixing was an appropriate means of eliminating evils existing in the in-

dustry. (a) Under what circumstances would the Court refuse to accept the Congressional judgment? (b) Is the attitude of the Court an abandonment of the right to supervise or judicially review legislation aimed at correcting a social or economic evil?

27. (a) Can the national government regulate food prices in order to avoid a depression by maintaining price stability? (b) Can the separate states adopt such laws? (c) What happens if a state law and a federal law set a different price for the same product?

28. Congress passes a law fixing commodity prices at such a level that the producers will obtain a 20% profit. The statute recites in its preamble that Congress adopts such a law because it believes that the best insurance against future depression is to enable producers to set aside a surplus fund. A citizens committee brings a suit to have the law declared unconstitutional. They point out that the return allowed the producers is several times greater than the legal rate of interest and more than could be obtained by making investments in the security market. Is the law constitutional?

29. Congress decides that depressions are caused by inequality of purchasing power. To correct this defect Congress adopts a law providing that every person shall be paid an identical wage regardless of the nature of the work done by him. B, an employee, sues M, his employer, for twice the amount of the statutory wage, claiming that he is worth double what the law provides. M defends on the ground that he is bound to pay the statutory wage. B claims the law is unconstitutional. Is he correct?

30. A state legislature decides that excessive rates are being charged by insurance companies. It adopts a law prescribing a schedule of premiums that may be charged by insurance companies and making it a crime to charge greater amounts. The X Insurance Company charges higher premiums than allowed by the statute. The company is prosecuted under the statute and defends by claiming that the statute is unconstitutional. Is the company correct? *German Alliance Insurance Co.* v. *Lewis*, 233 U.S. 389 (1914).

31. Does the *Nebbia* case redefine the phrase "affected with a public interest" or does it hold that in determining the validity of price regulation it is no longer necessary to determine whether the business is "affected with a public interest"?

32. What is the relation of price regulation to due process?

33. How does the court define "due process" in the *Nebbia* case?

34. Assume that a law of Congress establishes a price for the sale of sugar. Is the law unconstitutional if it does not yield a fair return to the sugar producer or manufacturer? Is the law unconstitutional as to the purchasing public if the return to the producers or manufacturers is more than a fair return?

35. (a) If a government may regulate the prices in a particular business, does it make any difference if the manufacturer or producer of the particular commodity began business before the law regulating the price was established? (b) Does it make any difference if such manufacturer or producer will not be able to operate at a profit under the price regulation and that if he goes out of business he will be required to sell his plant at a loss?

36. The Transportation Act of 1920 directed the Interstate Commerce Commission to fix such rates for carriers as would permit them to earn "an aggregate annual net railway operating income equal, as nearly as may be, to a fair return upon the aggregate value of the property of such carriers held for and used in the service of transportation" and that in arriving at a fair value the Commission should consider "all the elements of value recognized by the law of the land for rate-making purposes."

The Transportation Act of 1933 provided that "in the exercise of its power to prescribe just and reasonable rates the Commission shall give due consideration, among other factors, to the effect of rates on the movement of traffic; to the need, in the public interest, of adequate and efficient railway transportation service at the lowest cost consistent with the furnishing of such service; and to the need of revenues sufficient to enable the carriers, under earnest, economic, and efficient management, to provide such service."

(a) What is the difference between these two provisions? (b) Why was the change made? (c) Which standard do you prefer?

37. The Pennsylvania legislature authorized the Utility Commission to issue temporary rate orders pending the final decision of fair value and reasonable rates. The statute further provided that if the final rate allowed was in excess of that permitted by the temporary order, the utility would be allowed an additional increase to make up the difference. Is the Act constitutional? *Driscoll* v. *Edison Light and Power Co.*, 307 U.S. 104 (1939).

# Chapter 19

# THE TAXING POWER



## § 19:1. Extent of the Taxing Power

Taxes may affect business in a number of ways. Regarded as items of economic cost, taxes reduce the margin of profit of the enterpriser. If taxes are too large, they may make continuation of the business at a profit impossible. Long before this point is reached, the existence of a high tax may make it impossible to set aside adequate reserve funds, although some taxes allow deductions for such purposes. The reduction of profits may dissuade investors from investing in the business. Looking at business as an overall picture, the prospect of lower profits may have the effect of reducing incentive and of giving rise to a business panic psychology. In addition, a continued high tax level may leave the economy in a condition where it is unable to cope with a sudden peace or wartime emergency.

Indirectly, business is affected not only by taxes on business but also by taxes on customers of the businesses and on the public. If the products of a particular business are taxed, it might cause some purchasers to change to a substitute or entirely different nontaxed article.

In any event, to the extent that taxes reduce the purchasing power of each customer, business ultimately feels the effect of taxes.

Generally, taxes will subject business to a money loss or a regulation to which it is opposed, although in the case of a high protective tariff we find a tax that is sought by business as a protecting wall against the influx of foreign goods that could be sold more cheaply than local products.

Taxes affecting business may be levied either for the sole purpose of obtaining revenue, or for the purpose of regulating or prohibiting an activity, or for both reasons.

The Federal Constitution provides that "Congress shall have the power to lay and collect taxes, duties, imposts and excises, to pay the debts and provide for the common defense and general welfare of the United States." (Art. I, Sec. 8, Cl. 1) Subject to the expressed and implied limitations arising from the Constitution, the states may impose such taxes as they desire and as their own individual constitutions permit. The extent to which political subdivisions may tax is determined by the constitution and the statutes of each state, subject to the limitations arising from the Federal Constitution. In addition to express constitutional limitations, both national and local taxes are subject to the unwritten limitation that they be imposed for a public purpose.

The federal government is subject to certain limitations on the form of the taxes imposed by it. Capitation or poll taxes and all direct taxes must be apportioned among the states according to the census-determined population. (Art. I, Sec. 9, Cl. 4) Today, direct taxes include taxes on real estate or personal property and taxes imposed on persons because of their ownership of property. Income taxes, to the extent that they tax the income from property, are direct, although by virtue of the Sixteenth Amendment their apportionment is no longer required.

All other taxes imposed by the federal government are regarded as indirect taxes. These include customs duties, taxes on consumption (such as gasoline and cigarette taxes), taxes on the exercise of a privilege (such as an amusement tax), taxes on the transmission of property upon death (such as estate or inheritance taxes), taxes upon the privilege of making a gift (such as gift taxes), or taxes upon the privilege of employing workers (such as the federal employer's social security tax). In the case of a federal tax upon the exercise of a privilege, it is immaterial whether the privilege arises by virtue or a state or a federal law.

The only restriction upon the form of indirect federal taxes is that they be uniform throughout the continental United States and the incorporated territories. This requirement of uniformity does not prohibit a progressively graduated tax by which the greater the money value of the tax base, the greater the rate of tax. The requirement of uniformity is also not violated by a provision allowing credits against the federal tax for taxes paid to a state, even though the amount of the federal tax paid will vary from state to state, depending upon the existence of a state tax for which credit is allowable.

Congress is also prohibited from imposing taxes on goods exported from any state for shipment to a foreign country or on the bills of lading, insurance policies, or charter parties executed for such shipment. Congress further may not give preference by any tax law to the ports of one state over those of another and may not require vessels bound to or from one state to enter, clear, or pay taxes in another. (Art. I, Sec. 9)

The taxing power of the states and the political subdivisions is generally subject to the limitations contained in state constitutions or statutes. In addition, each state is prohibited from levying "without the Consent of the Congress, . . . any Imposts or Duties on Imports or Exports, except what may be absolutely necessary for executing its inspection laws: and the net Produce of all Duties and Imposts, laid by any State on Imports or Exports, shall be for the Use of the Treasury of the United States; and all such Laws shall be subject to the Revision and the Control of the Congress." (Art. I, Sec. 10, Cl. 2)

### *(a) Federal Social Security Act*

STEWARD MACHINE CO. v. DAVIS

301 U.S. 548 (1937)

The Federal Social Security Act of 1935 provided for the payment of unemployment compensation from a fund created in part by the taxation of the employers. The tax was challenged as unconstitutional.

OPINION BY CARDOZO, J.

. . . The tax, which is described in the statute as an excise, is laid with uniformity throughout the United States as a duty, an impost or an excise upon the relation of employment.

1. We are told that the relation of employment is one so essential to the pursuit of happiness that it may not be burdened with a tax. Appeal is made to history. From the precedents of colonial days we are supplied with illustrations of excises common in the colonies. They are said to have been bound up with the enjoyment of particular commodities. Appeal is also made to principle or the analysis of concepts. An excise, we are told, imports a tax upon a privilege; employment, it is said, is a right, not a privilege, from which it follows that employment is not subject to an excise. Neither the one appeal nor the other leads to the desired goal.

As to the argument from history: Doubtless there were many excises in colonial days and later that were associated, more or less intimately, with the enjoyment or the use of property. . . . But in truth other excises *were* known, and known since early times. Thus in 1695 (6 & 7 Wm. III. c. 6), Parliament passed an act which granted "to His Majesty certain Rates and Duties upon Marriage, Births and Burials," all for the purpose of "carrying on the War against France with Vigour." . . . In 1777, before our Constitutional Convention, Parliament laid upon employers an annual "duty" of 21 shillings for "every male Servant" employed in stated forms of work. Revenue Act of 1777, 17 George III. c. 39. . . . A statute of Virginia passed in 1780 [imposed] . . . a tax of three pounds, six shillings and eight pence to be paid for every male tithable above the age of twenty-one years (with stated exceptions), and a like tax for "every white servant whatsoever, except apprentices under the age of twenty-one years." 10 Hening's Statutes of Virginia, p. 244. Our colonial forbears knew more about ways of taxing than some of their descendants seem to be willing to concede.

The historical prop failing, the prop or fancied prop of principle remains. We learn that employment for lawful gain is a "natural" or "inherent" or "inalienable" right, and not a "privilege" at all. But natural rights, so called, are as much subject to taxation as rights of less importance. An excise is not limited to vocations or activities that may be prohibited altogether. It is not limited to those that are the outcome of a franchise. It extends to vocations or activities pursued as of common right. What the individual does in the operation of a business is amenable to taxation just as much as what he owns, at all events if the classification is not tyrannical or arbitrary. . . . Indeed, ownership itself, as we had occasion to point out the other day, is only a bundle of rights and privileges invested with a single name. . . . "A state is at liberty, if it pleases, to tax them all collectively, or to separate the faggots and lay the charge distributively." . . . Employment is a business relation, if not itself a business. It is a relation without which business could seldom be carried on effectively. The power to tax the activities and relations that constitute a calling considered as a unit is the power to tax any of them. The whole includes the parts. . . .

### § 19:2. Intergovernmental Taxation

The federal government and the state governments may not directly tax each other. At first this immunity was given a very wide application, but of recent years it has been narrowed so that not much more than the actual governments and instruments of government are exempt. This exemption from taxation extends to the bonds issued by the other government unless it consents to such taxation.

#### *(a) State enterprises*

NEW YORK v. UNITED STATES

326 U.S. 572 (1946)

OPINION BY FRANKFURTER, J.

. . . The United States brought this suit to recover taxes assessed against the State of New York on the sale of mineral waters taken from Saratoga Springs, New York. The State claims immunity from this tax on the ground that "in the bottling and sale of the said waters the defendant State of New York was engaged in the exercise of a usual, traditional and essential governmental function." . . .

. . . The fear that one government may cripple or obstruct the operations of the other early led to the assumption that there was a reciprocal immunity of the instrumentalities of each from taxation by the other. It was assumed that there was an equivalence in the implications of taxation by a State of the governmental activities of the National Government and the taxation by the National Government of State instrumentalities. This assumed equivalence was nourished by the phrase of Chief Justice Marshall that "the power to tax involves the power to destroy." *McCulloch* v. *Maryland*, . . . To be sure, it was uttered in connection with a tax of Maryland which plainly discriminated against the use by the United States of the Bank of the United States as one of its instruments. What he said may not have been irrelevant in its setting. But Chief Justice Marshall spoke at a time when social complexities did not so clearly reveal as now the practical limitations of a rhetorical absolute. . . . The phrase was seized upon as the basis of a broad doctrine of intergovernmental immunity, while at the same time an expansive scope was given to what were deemed to be "instrumentalities of the government" for purposes of tax immunity. As a result, immunity was until recently accorded to all officers of one government from taxation by the other, and it was further assumed that the economic burden of a tax on any interest derived from a government imposes a burden on that government so as to involve an interference by the taxing government with the functioning of the other government. . . .

In the meantime, cases came here, as we have already noted, in which States claimed immunity from a federal tax imposed generally on enterprises in which the State itself was also engaged. This problem did not arise before the present century, partly because State trading did not actively emerge until relatively recently, and partly because of the narrow scope of federal taxation. . . . Immunity from a federal tax on a dispensary system, whereby South Carolina monopoplized the sale of intoxicating liquors, was denied by drawing a line between taxation of the historically recognized governmental functions of a State, and business engaged in by a State of a kind which theretofore had been pursued by private enterprise. . . . That there is a Constitutional line between the State as government and the State as trader, was still more recently made the basis of a decision sustaining a liquor tax against Ohio. "If a state chooses to go into the business of buying and selling commodities, its right to do so may be conceded so far as the Federal Constitution is concerned; but the exercise of the right is not the performance of a governmental function. . . . When a state enters the market place seeking customers it divests itself of its quasi sovereignty pro tanto, and takes on the character of a trader, so far, at least, as the taxing power of the federal government is concerned." . . .

When this Court came to sustain the federal taxing power upon a transportation system operated by a State, it . . . edged away from reliance on a sharp distinction between the "governmental" and the "trading" activities of a State, by denying immunity from federal taxation to a State when it "is undertaking a business enterprise of a sort that is normally within the reach of the federal taxing power and is distinct from the usual governmental functions that are immune from federal taxation in order to safeguard the necessary independence of the state." . . . But this likewise does not furnish a satisfactory guide for dealing with such a practical problem as the constitutional power of the United States over State activities. To rest the federal taxing power on what is "normally" conducted by private enterprise in contradiction to the "usual" governmental functions is too shifting a basis for determining constitutional power and too entangled in expediency to serve as a dependable legal criterion. The essential nature of the problem cannot be hidden by an attempt to separate manifestations of indivisible governmental powers. . . .

In the older cases, the emphasis was on immunity from taxation. The whole tendency of recent cases reveals a shift in emphasis to that of limitation upon immunity. They also indicate an awareness of the limited role of courts in assessing the relative weight of the factors upon which immunity is based. Any implied limitation upon the supremacy of the federal power to levy a tax like that now before us, in the absence of discrimination against State activities, brings fiscal and political factors into play. The problem cannot escape issues that do not lend themselves to judgment by criteria and methods of reasoning that are within the professional training and special competence of judges. Indeed the claim of implied immunity by States from federal taxation raises questions not wholly unlike provisions of the Constitution, such as that of Art. IV, § 4, guaranteeing States a republican form of government, . . . which this Court has deemed not within its duty to adjudicate.

We have already held that by engaging in the railroad business a State cannot withdraw the railroad from the power of the federal government to regulate commerce. . . . Surely the power of Congress to lay taxes has impliedly no less a reach than the power of Congress to regulate commerce. There are, of course, State activities and State-owned property that partake of uniqueness from the point of view of intergovernmental relations. These inherently constitute a class by themselves. Only a State can own a Statehouse; only a State can get income by taxing. These could not be included for purposes of federal taxation in any abstract category of taxpayers without taxing the State as a State. But so long as Congress generally taps a source of revenue by whomsoever earned and not uniquely capable of being earned only by a State, the Constitution of the United States does not forbid it merely because its incidence falls also on a State. If Congress desires, it may of course leave untaxed enterprises pursued by States for the public good while it taxes like enterprises organized for private ends. . . .

. . .

The process of Constitutional adjudication does not thrive on conjuring up horrible possibilities that never happen in the real world and devising doctrines sufficiently comprehensive in detail to cover the remotest contingency. . . . We reject limitations upon the taxing power of Congress derived from such untenable criteria as "proprietary" against "governmental" activities of the States, or historically sanctioned activities of government or activities conducted merely for profit, and find no restriction upon Congress to include the States in levying a tax exacted equally from private persons upon the same subject matter.

### § 19:3. Taxation of Persons Dealing with a Government

The question frequently arises whether the immunity of one government from taxation by the other is to be extended to exempt independent contractors dealing with one government from taxation by the other with respect to such dealings. It is generally held that a contractor purchasing materials or equipment is subject to state taxation on the purchase or ownership of such materials or equipment even though the materials and equipment are used in the performance of a contract with the United States. The fact that the economic burden of the tax on the contractor will be transferred to and be ultimately borne in whole or in part by the federal government is not regarded as giving rise to an immunity. Correspondingly, there is no immunity merely because the activity performed by the independent contractor is useful to the government.

In a given case, the question of liability to or immunity from state taxation may be affected by federal statute, for it is within the power of Congress to expressly waive an immunity that might otherwise exist or to confer an immunity by declaring that the activity in question shall be exempt from state taxation.

#### *(a) Lessees of government property*

UNITED STATES v. DETROIT
355 U.S. 466 (1958)

A Michigan statute provides that when tax-exempt real property is used by a private person in a business conducted for profit, the private person must pay a tax that would be the same as though he owned the exempt property. The United States owned an industrial plant in Detroit, which it leased to the Borg-Warner Corporation for use by the latter for private production. The City of Detroit assessed a tax under the Michigan statute against the corporation in the same amount as though the corporation owned the leased plant. The corporation and the United States claimed that this imposed a burden on the United States and that the tax law was therefore invalid.

OPINION BY BLACK, J.

. . . The Michigan statute challenged here imposes a tax on private lessees and users of tax-exempt property who use such property in a business conducted for profit. Any taxes due under the statute are the personal obligation of the private lessee or user. The owner is not liable for their payment nor is the property itself subject to any lien if they remain unpaid. So far as the United States is concerned as the owner of the exempt property used in this case it seems clear that there was no attempt to levy against its property or treasury.

Nevertheless the Government argues that since the tax is measured by the value of the property used it should be treated as nothing but a contrivance to lay a tax on that property. We do not find this argument persuasive. A tax for the beneficial use of property, as distinguished from a tax on the property itself, has long been a commonplace in this country. . . . In measuring such a use tax it seems neither irregular nor extravagant to resort to the value of the property used; indeed no more so than measuring a sales tax by the value of the property sold. [The state law] was apparently designed to equalize the annual tax burden carried by private businesses using exempt property with that of similar businesses using nonexempt property. Other things being the same, it seems obvious enough that use of exempt property is worth as much as use of comparable taxed property during the same interval. In our judgment it was not an impermissible subterfuge but a permissible exercise of its taxing power for Michigan to compute its tax by the value of the property used.

A number of decisions by this Court support this conclusion. For example in *Curry* v. *United States*, 314 U.S. 14, we upheld unanimously a state use tax on a contractor who was using government-owned materials although the tax was based on the full value of those materials. Similarly in *Esso Standard Oil Co.* v. *Evans*, 345 U.S. 495, the Court held valid a state tax on the privilege of storing gasoline even though that part of the tax which was challenged was measured by the number of gallons of government-owned gasoline stored with the taxpayer. While it is true that the tax here is measured by the value of government property instead of by its quantity as in *Esso* such technical difference has no meaningful significance in determining whether the Constitution prohibits this tax. Still other cases further confirm the proposition that it may be permissible for a state to measure a tax imposed on a valid subject of state taxation by taking into account government property, which is itself tax-exempt. . . .

It is undoubtedly true, as the Government points out, that it will not be able to secure as high rentals if lessees are taxed for using its property. But . . . the imposition of an increased financial burden on the Government does not, by itself, vitiate, a state tax. . . .

It still remains true, as it has from the beginning, that a tax may be invalid even though it does not fall directly on the United States if it operates so as to discriminate against the Government or those with whom it deals. . . . But here the tax applies to every private party who uses exempt property in Michigan in connection with a business conducted for private gain. Under Michigan law this means persons who use property owned by the Federal Government, the State, its political subdivisions, churches, charitable organizations and a great host of other entities. The class defined is not an arbitrary or invidiously discriminatory one. . . .

### § 19:4. Regulatory Taxation

Apart from constitutional provision, a tax may be adopted either for the purpose of raising revenue or as a method of regulating or prohibiting the sale of a particular article or the doing of certain acts, or a combination of both purposes. Will the court examine the tax law to determine whether it is a regulatory law? Will the constitutionality of the tax be affected if the court concludes that its purpose is regulation?

If the object of the tax is a regulation that could be imposed by the government directly as a regulation, it is immaterial whether the court would make such inquiry, for it will conclude that, since the power existed to regulate, a tax could be used as the means of enforcing the regulation. If the purpose of the tax statute is merely to enforce a regulation that cannot be made openly as such, the tax may be held unconstitutional. This limitation on the tax power is less significant today in view of the fact that, if a state law is concerned, the state through its police power has a wide ability to impose regulations and that, if a national law is concerned, the broadened interpretation of the commerce clause will probably give the national government power to make the regulation in question if it chooses to do so.

In a number of instances the Supreme Court has refused to consider the ulterior regulatory purpose of tax laws even though such purpose was readily apparent. Thus the Supreme Court sustained a 10 per cent tax on state bank notes for the purpose of driving them out of existence, a tax of 10 cents a pound on oleo colored to resemble butter,[1] and a $200 annual license fee on vendors of firearms, with an additional $200 tax on the sale of each machine gun, sawed-off shotgun, and silencer.[2] The federal tariff is held valid in spite of its prohibitive effect.

### *(a) Federal Narcotics Act*

The extreme application of this doctrine is seen in *United States v. Doremus,* where the Supreme Court was confronted with a federal law imposing a license tax on persons selling narcotics. The obvious purpose of the law was to obtain federal control of the illicit drug traffic. Such trade could not be directly prohibited by Congress, since the power to do so was reserved to the states. The annual tax or license fee of each vendor was, for many years, $1, although later this was increased to $25. The validity of the statute was brought before the Supreme Court when the tax was only $1 and the gross proceeds of the tax much less than the cost of its administration.

UNITED STATES v. DOREMUS

249 U.S. 86 (1919)

OPINION BY DAY, J.

. . . From an early day the court has held that the fact that other motives may impel the exercise of federal taxing power does not authorize the courts to inquire into that subject. If the legislation enacted has some reasonable relation to the exercise of the taxing authority conferred by the Constitution, it cannot be invalidated because of the supposed motives which induced it. . . .

Nor is it sufficient to invalidate the taxing authority given to the Congress by the Constitution that the same business may be regulated by the police power of the State. . . .

The act may not be declared unconstitutional because its effect may be to accomplish another purpose as well as the raising of revenue. If the legislation is within the taxing authority of Congress—that is sufficient to sustain it. . . .

---

[1] A. Magnano Co. v. Hamilton, 292 U.S. 40 (1934).
[2] Sonzinsky v. United States, 300 U.S. 506 (1937).

. . . Considering the full power of Congress over excise taxation the decisive question here is: Have the provisions in question any relation to the raising of revenue? That Congress might levy an excise tax upon such dealers . . . cannot be successfully disputed. The provisions of Sec. 2, to which we have referred, aim to confine sales to registered dealers and to those dispensing the drugs as physicians, and to those who come to dealers with legitimate prescriptions of physicians. Congress, with full power over the subject, short of arbitrary and unreasonable action which is not to be assumed, inserted these provisions in an act specifically providing for the raising of revenue. Considered of themselves, we think they tend to keep the traffic aboveboard and subject to inspection by those authorized to collect the revenue. They tend to diminish the opportunity of unauthorized persons to obtain the drugs and sell them clandestinely without paying the tax imposed by the federal law. . . .

We cannot agree with the contention that the provisions of Sec. 2, controlling the disposition of these drugs in the ways described, can have nothing to do with facilitating the collection of revenue, as we should be obliged to do if we were to declare this act beyond the power of Congress to impose excise taxes. . . .

## § 19:5. Regulatory Taxation Invalid because of Hidden Motive

These decisions would seem to warrant the belief that the Supreme Court would sustain any tax law, and that activity beyond the reach of Congress could be indirectly regulated by imposing a tax on those activities which Congress wished to prohibit. The Supreme Court has not adhered to this view and has held unconstitutional a federal law attempting to end child labor by imposing a tax on the profits of employers employing child labor,[3] a law imposing a $1,000 annual tax on persons selling liquor in violation of a state prohibition law, and a tax on the processors of farm products levied to raise a fund to pay farmers to reduce their production.

With the subsequent expansion of the commerce power,[4] the problem here considered of whether a hidden motive of regulation will invalidate a tax law has become academic. Today the Congress can directly impose regulations on local activities affecting the economic welfare of the nation, and it has the choice of imposing such regulation in the form of a direct limitation or in the indirect form of a tax or penalty upon those not conforming to the federal statute.

---

[3] Bailey v. Drexel Furniture Co., 259 U.S. 20 (1922).
[4] See Chapter 9.

### *(a) Federal Agricultural Adjustment Act of 1933*

UNITED STATES v. BUTLER

297 U.S. 1 (1936)

The Agricultural Adjustment Act of 1933 was designed to eliminate surpluses in agricultural products. Money payments were made to farmers who would reduce their acreage under cultivation. The funds to pay for such payments were raised by taxing the first industrial processors of the agricultural products, such as the millers grinding the farmers' wheat into flour. The law was attacked as unconstitutional.

OPINION BY ROBERTS, J.

. . . The tax can only be sustained by ignoring the avowed purpose and operation of the act, and holding it a measure merely laying an excise upon processors to raise revenue for the support of government. Beyond cavil the sole object of the legislation is to restore the purchasing power of agricultural products to a parity with that prevailing in an earlier day; to take money from the processor and bestow it upon farmers who will reduce their acreage for the accomplishment of the proposed end, and, meanwhile to aid these farmers during the period required to bring the prices of their crops to the desired level.

The tax plays an indispensable part in the plan of regulation. . . . A tax automatically goes into effect for a commodity when the Secretary of Agriculture determines that rental or benefit payments are to be made for reduction of production of that commodity. The tax is to cease when rental or benefit payments cease. The rate is fixed with the purpose of bringing about crop-reduction and price-raising. It is to equal the difference between the "current average farm price" and "fair exchange value." It may be altered to such amount as will prevent accumulation of surplus stocks. If the Secretary finds the policy of the act will not be promoted by the levy of the tax for a given commodity, he may exempt it. . . . The whole revenue from the levy is appropriated in aid of crop control; none of it is made available for general governmental use. The entire agricultural adjustment program . . . is to become inoperative when, in the judgment of the President, the national economic emergency ends. . . .

It is inaccurate and misleading to speak of the exaction from processors prescribed by the challenged act as a tax, or to say that as a tax it is subject to no infirmity. A tax, in the general understanding of the term, and as used in the Constitution, signifies an exaction for the support of the Government. The word has never been thought to connote the expropriation of money from one group for the benefit of another. We may concede that the latter sort of imposition is constitutional when imposed to effectuate regulation of a matter in which both groups are interested and in respect of which there is a power of legislation. But manifestly no justification for it can be found unless as an integral part of such regulation. The exaction cannot be wrested out of its setting, denominated an excise for raising revenue and legalized by ignoring its purpose as a mere instrumentality for bringing about a desired end. . . .

We conclude that the act is one regulating agricultural production; that the tax is a mere incident of such regulation and that the respondents have standing to challenge the legality of the exaction. . . .

. . . The Government concedes that the phrase "to provide for the general welfare" qualifies the power "to lay and collect taxes." The view that the clause grants power to provide for the general welfare, independently of the taxing power, has never been authoritatively accepted. . . . The true construction undoubtedly is that the only thing granted is the power to tax for the purpose of making funds for payment of the nation's debts and making provision for the general welfare. . . .

Since the foundation of the Nation sharp differences of opinion have persisted as to the true interpretation of the phrase. Madison asserted it amounted to no more than a reference to the other powers enumerated in the subsequent clauses of the same section; that, as the United States is a government of limited and enumerated powers, the grant of power to tax and spend for the general national welfare must be confined to the enumerated legislative fields committed to the Congress. In this view the phrase is mere tautology, for taxation and appropriation are or may be necessary incidents to the exercise of any of the enumerated legislative powers. Hamilton, on the other hand, maintained the clause confers a power separate and distinct from those later enumerated, is not restricted in meaning by the grant of them, and Congress consequently has a substantive power to tax and to appropriate, limited only by the requirement that it shall be exercised to provide for the general welfare of the United States. Each contention has had the support of those whose views are entitled to great weight. This court has noticed the question, but has never found it necessary to decide which is the true construction.

Mr. Justice Story, in his Commentaries, espouses the Hamiltonian position. We shall not review the writings of public men and commentators or discuss the legislative practice. Study of all these leads us to conclude that the reading advocated by Mr. Justice Story is the correct one. While, therefore, the power to tax is not unlimited, its confines are set in the clause which confers it, and not in those of Sec. 8 which bestow and define the legislative powers of the Congress. It results that the power of Congress to authorize expenditure of public moneys for public purposes is not limited by the direct grants of legislative power found in the Constitution. . . .

It is an established principle that the attainment of a prohibited end may not be accomplished under the pretext of the exertion of powers which are granted. . . .

The power of taxation, which is expressly granted, may, of course, be adopted as a means to carry into operation another power also expressly granted. But resort to the taxing power to effectuate an end which is not legitimate, not within the scope of the Constitution, is obviously inadmissible. . . .

If the act before us is a proper exercise of the federal taxing power, evidently the regulation of all industry throughout the United States may be accomplished by similar exercises of the same power. It would be possible to exact money from one branch of an industry and pay it to another branch in every field of activity which lies within the province of the states. . . .

## Questions for Discussion

1. (a) Can taxes be imposed by the United States? by the states? by counties? by cities? by school districts? (b) If so, what is the source of the power of each of these units to tax? (c) What is the source of limitations on the power of each of these units to tax?

2. (a) What is a direct tax? an indirect tax? (b) Why is this distinction made? (c) Does this distinction apply to national taxes, state taxes, or local taxes?

3. What is the nature of an income tax?

4. State whether the following taxes are direct or indirect:
   - (a) A tax of $10 levied on each immigrant arriving in the United States.
   - (b) A tax of 1 cent on each $100 worth of land owned.
   - (c) A tax of 1 cent on each acre of land owned.
   - (d) A tax on interest payments made on a mortgage of land.
   - (e) A tax on interest payments made on a promissory note.

(f) A tax of 5% on the cost of each theater ticket.
(g) A tax of 20% on the cost of each theater ticket.
(h) A tax of 25 cents on each person purchasing a theater ticket regardless of the cost of the ticket.

5. The federal government determines that in order to obtain stability in the gasoline industry the retail sale price of gasoline should be regulated to eliminate a two-cent differential between the East Coast and the West Coast. Instead of adopting a law directly regulating the price, Congress adopts a gasoline tax law and provides that the tax should be 3 cents a gallon in the area where the price is lower and 1 cent a gallon in the area where the price is higher. Would this tax be constitutional?

6. Does the *Doremus* case sustain the use of the federal taxing power as a police power?

7. Was the Court correct in the *Doremus* case in referring to the object of narcotic trade control as "the supposed motives which induced" the adoption of the law?

8. Would the decision in the *Doremus* case have been the same if the subject involved was not one recognized as socially harmful?

9. (a) What is meant by the statement, "The power to tax is the power to destroy"? (b) Has the meaning or the applicability of that statement changed? In what way? Why?

10. Does the due process clause protect a business from being destroyed by taxation?

11. A statute imposes a tax on oleomargarine but not on butter. Because of the tax oleo can only be sold at a price higher than butter to avoid loss. Does the statute violate the equal protection clause?

12. Can a state impose a tax on the sale of each loaf of bread equal to 1% of the sale price? equal to 10%? equal to 50%? equal to 100%?

13. State M adopts a general income tax law applicable to all persons residing or earning income within the state. One of the residents of the state is a judge of a federal court of a district that is within the state. The federal judge claims that he is not subject to the state income tax. Decide.

14. (a) In the *Steward Machine Company* case the objection was made that the tax was not uniform because the amount of the federal tax varied depending on whether or not a state tax had been paid. How would you dispose of that objection? (b) What is the constitutional basis for this objection?

15. In the *Steward Machine Company* case the objection was made that the tax did not apply to all employers and therefore was a denial of equal protection of the laws. How would you dispose of that objection?

16. Decide the constitutionality of a law that taxes:

(a) Electric typewriters and office equipment but exempts manually operated typewriters and equipment.
(b) The use of gas for fuel but not for cooking or lighting.
(c) The use of electricity for lighting at a greater rate than the use of electricity for heating.
(d) All uses of electricity by industrial plants but exempts the use of electricity in home.
(e) The use of electricity by steam or electrical railroads but exempts all other kinds of use.

17. A state passes a law imposing a tax on every ton of anthracite coal that is mined but exempting bituminous coal. The X Coal Distributing Company claims that this discrimination is unreasonable and unconstitutional. Decide. *Heisler* v. *Thomas Colliery Co.*, 260 U.S. 245 (1922).

18. Florida adopted a law taxing the supplies or stock of goods in the possession of stores. The chain stores were taxed at a rate nearly double that for independent stores. The X Chain Store claimed that this was an unconstitutional discrimination. Decide. *Liggett* v. *Lee,* 288 U.S. 517 (1933).

19. Louisiana adopted a law under which the tax on chain stores increased with the number of stores operated by the chain without regard to whether they were within Louisiana or within other states. The A. & P. Company refused to pay the tax on the ground that it was unconstitutional and also interfered with interstate commerce. Decide. *Great A. & P. Tea Co.* v. *Grosjean,* 301 U.S. 412 (1937).

20. Indiana adopted a tax law imposing a tax that increased in size as the number of stores in a chain of stores increased. Chain stores refused to pay the tax on the ground that it was unconstitutional since the tax they were required to pay was proportionately greater than the tax that smaller chain stores were required to pay or that independent single stores were required to pay. Is this claim correct? *Tax Commissioners of Indiana* v. *Jackson,* 283 U.S. 527 (1931).

21. (a) Is there any activity that cannot be subjected to an indirect tax? (b) Would a tax on printing a newspaper or attending church be valid?

22. A federal tax is imposed on the right to use an automobile. It is claimed that the law is unconstitutional because the right to use automobiles on the state highway is conferred by state law. Decide.

23. To what extent was the Court in the *Butler* case influenced by the feeling that the operation of the statute was to take property from A and give it to B in that it taxed the processors of industrial products and gave that tax money to the farmers?

24. Is a state tax an unconstitutional burden when it is assessed against a person dealing with the United States government who charges the United States a greater price because of the tax that he pays the state?

25. Does Article I, Section 8, Cl. 3, of the Constitution confer power on the federal government to adopt any law on behalf of the general welfare?

26. (a) Compare the decision in the *Butler* case with *Wickard* v. *Filburn* (page 234). (b) Would the Agricultural Adjustment Act of 1933 be constitutional if the case now came before the Supreme Court for the first time?

27. (a) Does the Court hold the tax unconstitutional in *United States* v. *Butler* because the power to impose the regulation on farming was not granted to Congress, because the imposition of such a regulation would interfere with the private concerns of the states, or because of both reasons? (b) What do you think of the opinion as a matter of legal reasoning?

28. State Z decides to eradicate evils connected with the business of selling liquor by creating a state monopoly of liquor stores. It refuses to pay federal taxes due from liquor stores throughout the country on the ground that it is running the enterprise as a government and is not subject to taxation. Decide. Does the fact that the state government maintains a monopoly of the business affect your answer? *South Carolina* v. *United States,* 199 U.S. 437 (1905).

29. What is the standard established in *New York* v. *United States* in determining whether an activity when conducted by a state is subject to a federal tax?

30. In 1921 Congress by the Future Trading Act sought to regulate trading in grain futures at grain exchanges. A tax of 20 cents a bushel was imposed on future delivery grain sales unless the Secretary of Agriculture had approved the exchange as a "contract market" after the exchange had satisfied certain standards set by the Secretary of Agriculture. This Act was held unconstitutional in *Hill* v. *Wallace,* 259 U.S. 44 (1922). (a) Why was it held unconstitutional? (b) What would the decision be if the case were decided today?

31. The United States passed a tariff law which imposed rates so high that its purpose was obviously protection. The act was attacked as unconstitutional in attempting to regulate manufacturing. Is the act unconstitutional? *Hampton* v. *United States,* 276 U.S. 394 (1928).

32. A state legislature decides to eliminate the fraud of renovated butters and milk. This occurs when the natural animal fats are removed and other fats are substituted. The state imposes a 25-cent tax on every pound or quart of any milk or butter product that has been renovated. A distributor of renovated butter claims that his product is not harmful in itself, which is admitted, and that he is not concealing the nature of the product, which is true, and that the law is unconstitutional because the

tax is so high that it makes it impossible to sell his product and he is being driven out of business. Is the law unconstitutional?

33. A person died in the County of Spokane, Washington, owing taxes to the county and to the United States. There was insufficient property left to pay both the national and the county taxes. The national government claimed the right to be paid first under the authority of Revised Statutes, section 3466, providing that "whenever any person indebted to the United States is insolvent or whenever the estate of any deceased debtor, in the hands of the executors or administrators, is insufficient to pay all the debts of the decedent, the debt due to the United States shall be first satisfied." The county claimed that as a branch of the state it had an equal right to share in what property there was. Decide. *County of Spokane* v. *United States*, 279 U.S. 80 (1929).

34. Heald was the executor of a deceased person who had lived in Washington, D. C. The executor refused to pay federal tax owed by the estate on the ground that the tax had been imposed by an act of Congress but that, as residents of the District of Columbia had no vote in Congress, the tax law was necessarily adopted without their representation. In addition to having no voice in the adoption of the tax laws, the proceeds from taxes collected in the District were paid into the general treasury of the United States and were not maintained as a separate District of Columbia fund. Heald objected that the tax law was void as contrary to the Constitution because it amounted to taxation without representation. Decide. *Heald* v. *District of Columbia*, 259 U.S. 114 (1922).

35. The State of New York imposed an income tax on all residents of the state. It collected the tax from O'Keefe, who was an attorney for the Federal Home Owners Loan Corporation, residing in New York. He claimed that his salary was not subject to a state income tax because his work was done to advance the interests of the national government. The state tax collector claimed that the law was constitutional because it did not discriminate between state and federal employees but taxed all equally. Was the state law constitutional? *Graves* v. *New York ex rel. O'Keefe*, 306 U.S. 466 (1939).

36. The University of Georgia built a stadium in which football games were held. It received a profit from the sale of admission tickets and used this profit to defray the expenses of its educational program. The Federal Tax Collector sought to collect the amusement tax from the admissions to the football games. The University claimed that the admissions were not subject to tax since the profits were not privately received but were used for education, which was a regular function of the state government. The University contended that to tax the admissions when so used interfered with the state's functions. Were the admissions taxable? *Allen* v. *Regents of the University of Georgia*, 304 U.S. 439 (1938).

# Chapter 20

# THE BORROWING POWER



## § 20:1. The Federal Borrowing Power

Congress is authorized "to borrow money on the credit of the United States." [Art. I, Sec. 8, Cl. 2]

No limitation is prescribed as to the purposes for which the United States can borrow. Since the power to borrow parallels the power to tax, both being needed to raise funds for the United States, it would seem logical that borrowed money may be spent for any purpose for which tax money may be spent. A contrary decision would also create the mechanical difficulty of earmarking borrowed money to distinguish it from tax money, since the latter may be spent for the general welfare.

Obligations of the United States issued to those lending money to the United States are binding, and the Congress cannot attempt to repudiate them or to make them repayable in a less valuable currency than called for by the obligations without violating the legal rights of the holders. Accordingly it is unconstitutional for Congress to provide that the holders of United States bonds that specify repayment in gold should be paid in dollars having a smaller gold content than the amount of gold specified in the bonds.

### *(a) Devaluation of federal gold bonds*

PERRY v. UNITED STATES

294 U.S. 330 (1935)

The holder of four $10,000 liberty bonds brought suit against the United States in the Court of Claims. The bonds provided that "the principal and interest hereof are payable in United States gold coin of the present standard of value." When the bonds were issued and purchased by the plaintiff, a dollar was valued in gold at 25.8

grains .9 fine. When the bonds were presented for redemption, the gold content of the dollar had been reduced to $15\frac{5}{21}$ grains of gold .9 fine. The United States refused to redeem the bonds in gold coin and offered to pay $10,000 in legal tender, which was paper currency based on the reduced gold content. The bondholder brought suit to be paid an amount of the devaluated paper currency that would have the same total gold content as $10,000 of paper currency having the former gold content.

OPINION BY HUGHES, C. J.

... The Joint Resolution of June 5, 1933 ... declared that provisions requiring "payment in gold or a particular kind of coin or currency" were "against public policy," and provided that "every obligation, heretofore or hereafter incurred ... shall be discharged "upon payment, dollar for dollar, in any coin or currency which at the time of payment is legal tender for public and private debts." This enactment was expressly extended to obligations of the United States, and provisions for payment in gold, "contained in any law authorizing obligations to be issued by or under authority of the United States," were repealed.

There is no question as to the power of Congress to regulate the value of money, that is, to establish a monetary system and thus to determine the currency of the country. The question is whether the Congress can use that power so as to invalidate the terms of the obligations which the Government has theretofore issued in the exercise of the power to borrow money on the credit of the United States. In attempted justification of the Joint Resolution in relation to the outstanding bonds of the United States, the Government argues that "earlier Congresses could not validly restrict the 73rd Congress from exercising its constitutional powers to regulate the value of money, borrow money, regulate foreign and interstate commerce"; and, from this premise, the Government seems to deduce the proposition that when, with adequate authority, the Government borrows money and pledges the credit of the United States, it is free to ignore that pledge and alter the terms of its obligations in case a later Congress finds their fulfillment inconvenient. The Government's contention thus raises a question of far greater importance than the particular claim of the plaintiff. On that reasoning, if the terms of the Government's bond as to the standard of payment can be repudiated, it inevitably follows that the obligation as to the amount to be paid may also be repudiated. The contention necessarily imports that the Congress can disregard the obligations of the Government at its discretion and that, when the Government borrows money, the credit of the United States is an illusory pledge.

We do not so read the Constitution. . . . To say that the Congress may withdraw or ignore that pledge, is to assume that the Constitution contemplates a vain promise, a pledge having no other sanction than the pleasure and convenience of the pledgor. This Court has given no sanction to such a conception of the obligations of our Government. . . .

The argument in favor of the Joint Resolution, as applied to government bonds, is in substance that the Government cannot by contract restrict the exercise of a sovereign power. But the right to make binding obligations is a competence attaching to sovereignty. In the United States, sovereignty resides in the people, who act through the organs established by the Constitution. . . . The Congress as the instrumentality of sovereignty is endowed with certain powers to be exerted on behalf of the people in the manner and with the effect the Constitution ordains. The Congress cannot invoke the sovereign power of the people to override their will as thus declared. The powers conferred upon the Congress are harmonious. The Constitution gives to the Congress the power to borrow money on the credit of the United States, an unqualified power, a power vital to the Government,—upon which in an extremity its very life may depend. The binding quality of the promise of the United States is of the essence of the credit which is so pledged. . . . The fact that the United States may not be sued without its consent is a matter of procedure which does not affect the legal and binding character of its contracts. While the Congress is under no duty to provide remedies through the courts, the contractual obligation still exists and, despite infirmities of procedure, remains binding upon the conscience of the sovereign. . . .

. . . The action is for breach of contract. As a remedy for breach, plaintiff can recover no more than the loss he has suffered and of which he may rightfully complain. He is not entitled to be enriched. . . .

. . . Plaintiff has not shown or attempted to show, that in relation to buying power he has sustained any loss whatever. . . .

[Recovery was denied for lack of proof of loss.]

## § 20:2. The State and Local Borrowing Powers

The states and the political subdivisions are not limited by the Federal Constitution in their borrowing. Limitations upon them are commonly found in state constitutions or statutes. The most common form of limitation is the placing of a maximum or ceiling on the amount of indebtedness that may be created by borrowing. In the case of political subdivisions, limitations in terms of the purpose for which the borrowing is made are also common.

Protection against repudiation by the states or their political subdivisions is found in the guarantee of Article I, Section 10, Cl. 1, of the Constitution that no state shall pass any "law impairing the obligation of contracts."

### Questions for Discussion

1. What is the basis for the decision in the *Perry* case that the obligation of the United States cannot be repudiated?

2. Would this decision in the *Perry* case be applicable to a case of complete repudiation of an obligation of the United States?

3. (a) In the event that the national debt rose to such a level that it could never be repaid, would the *Perry* case permit the calling of a constitutional convention or the adoption of a constitutional amendment that would expressly authorize the repudiation of all pre-existing debts of the United States? (b) Would it make any difference if a "corporate reorganization" of the United States was authorized by the convention or constitutional amendment, under which reorganization all debts were not repudiated in full but were modified as to term, interest rate, or medium of currency in which payable?

4. (a) Would your answer to Question 3 be affected if it were admitted at the time that the debts in fact could not be paid and were worthless? (b) If this would make a difference, would it be necessary to show that the debts were absolutely worthless? (c) Would the debts be treated as worthless if the creditors would only receive 5% of the amount due them? 10%? 20%?

5. City X borrows $5,000,000 for the purpose of constructing flood control projects outside the city limits to protect the city from the overflooding of the river that runs through the city. What constitutional questions are involved?

# Chapter 21

# THE SPENDING POWER



## § 21:1. General Welfare

The Federal Constitution confers upon Congress the power to "lay and collect taxes . . . to pay the debts and provide for the common defense and general welfare of the United States." [Art. I, Sec. 8, Cl. 1] From the earliest days of our national history, there was a sharp dispute as to whether this general welfare clause was in itself authorization to Congress to enact any law for the general welfare of the nation or whether it limited in some way the scope of the tax power. Among those claiming that the general welfare clause was restricted to the taxing power, there was also a division of thought between those like Madison, who contended that its effect was to prohibit the spending of tax-raised money for any purpose that could not be directly regulated or legislated upon by Congress, and those like Hamilton, who claimed that the money, once raised by the government, could be spent for any purpose beneficial to the public welfare as contrasted with private welfare, without regard to whether Congress could legislate directly upon the object for which the money was spent.

This controversy came to the fore when the federal government embarked upon a program of granting subsidies to the states. This plan was attacked as a method of bribing the states to do for the national government that which the national government could not legally under the Constitution do itself or require the states to do. At first the subsidy plan was sustained by the Supreme Court on the technical ground that no one could show any legal injury to himself and therefore had no standing to sue. The Court, in *United States* v. *Butler*, although then invalidating the law under consideration, approved the broader Hamiltonian view of the spending power that it finally adopted in the social security cases.

### *(a) Federal Social Security Act*

HELVERING v. DAVIS

301 U.S. 619 (1937)

The Federal Social Security Act of 1935 imposed a tax on both employer and employee to create a fund for the payment of old-age benefits to employees. The constitutionality of these provisions was challenged.

OPINION BY CARDOZO, J.

The Social Security Act . . . is challenged once again . . .

Congress may spend money in aid of the "general welfare" . . . The conception of the spending power advocated by Hamilton and strongly reinforced by Story has prevailed over that of Madison. . . . Yet difficulties are left when the power is conceded. The line must still be drawn between one welfare and another, between particuiar and general. Where it shall be placed cannot be known through a formula in advance of the event. There is a middle ground or certainly a penumbra in which discretion is at large. The discretion, however, is not confided to the courts. The discretion belongs to Congress, unless the choice is clearly wrong, a display of arbitrary power, not an exercise of judgment. This is now familiar law. "When such a contention comes here we naturally require a showing that by no reasonable possibility can the challenged legislation fall within the wide range of discretion permitted to Congress." . . . Nor is the concept of the general welfare static. Needs that were narrow or parochial a century ago may be interwoven in our day with the well-being of the nation. What is critical or urgent changes with the time.

The purge of nation-wide calamity that began in 1929 has taught us many lessons. Not the least is the solidarity of interests that may once have seemed to be divided. Unemployment spreads from state to state. . . . Spreading from state to state, unemployment is an ill not particular but general, which may be checked, if Congress so determines, by the resources of the nation. . . . The ill is all one, or at least not greatly different, whether men are thrown out of work because there is no longer work to do or because the disabilities of age make them incapable of doing it. . . .

Congress did not improvise a judgment when it found that the award of old age benefits would be conducive to the general welfare. . . . [The court then discussed the extensive committee hearings and reports that preceded the adoption of the Social Security Act and on which it was based. The court also emphasized the conclusion of both national and state investigations that the number of persons over 65 is increasing proportionately as well as absolutely and that in an increasingly industrialized economy such persons are increasingly less able to support themselves.]

The problem is plainly national in area and dimensions. Moreover, laws of the separate states cannot deal with it effectively. Congress, at least, had a basis for that belief. . . . Apart from the failure of resources, states and local governments are at times reluctant to increase so heavily the burden of taxation to be borne by their residents for fear of placing themselves in a position of economic disadvantage as compared with neighbors or competitors. . . . A system of old age pensions has special dangers of its own, if put in force in one state and rejected in another. The existence of such a system is a bait to the needy and dependent elsewhere, encouraging them to migrate and seek a haven of repose. Only a power that is national can serve the interests of all.

Whether wisdom or unwisdom resides in the scheme of benefits set forth in [the old age provisions] it is not for us to say. The answer to such inquiries must come from Congress, not the courts . . . [The objection was made that the Social Security Act would adopt a paternalistic philosophy that might be contrary to the political philosophy of individual states.] . . . One might ask with equal reason whether the system of protective tariff is to be set aside whenever local policy prefers the rule of laissez faire. The issue is a closed one. It was fought out long ago. When money is spent to promote the general welfare, the concept of welfare or the opposite is shaped by Congress, not the states. So the concept be not arbitrary, the locality must yield. Constitution, Art. VI, Par. 2. . . .

Justices McReynolds and Butler dissented on the ground that the "Provisions of the Act . . . are repugnant to the Tenth Amendment."

### *(b) Federal tax credit for state tax payment*

STEWARD MACHINE CO. v. DAVIS
301 U.S. 548 (1937)

The Federal Social Security Act of 1935 imposed a tax on employers to create a fund for the payment of unemployment compensation. It provided, however, that up to 90 per cent of tax payments made under a state social security law could be deducted from the amount due the federal government when the state statute conformed to specified federal standards. The constitutionality of these provisions was challenged.

OPINION BY CARDOZO, J.

. . . The excise is not void as involving the coercion of the states in contravention of the Tenth Amendment or of restrictions implicit in our federal form of government. . . .

. . . The assailants of the statute say that its dominant end and aim is to drive the state legislatures under the whip of economic pressure into the enactment of unemployment compensation laws at the bidding of the central government. . . .

The Social Security Act is an attempt to find a method by which . . . [national and state] agencies may work together to a common end. Every dollar of the new taxes will continue in all likelihood to be used and needed by the nation as long as states are unwilling, whether through timidity or for other motives, to do what can be done at home. At least the inference is permissible that Congress so believed, though retaining undiminished freedom to spend the money as it pleased. On the other hand fulfilment of the home duty will be lightened and encouraged by crediting the taxpayer upon his account with the Treasury of the nation to the extent that his contributions under the laws of the locality have simplified or diminished the problem of relief and the probable demand upon [national] resources. . . . Duplicated taxes, or burdens that approach them, are recognized hardships that government, state or national, may properly avoid. . . . If Congress believed that the general welfare would better be promoted by relief through local units than by the system then in vogue, the cooperating localities ought not in all fairness to pay a second time.

. . . The difficulty with the petitioner's contention is that it confuses motive with coercion. . . . Every rebate from a tax when conditioned upon conduct is in some measure a temptation. But to hold that motive or temptation is equivalent to coercion is to plunge the law in endless difficulties. The outcome of such a doctrine is the acceptance of philosophical determinism by which choice becomes impossible. . . .

[The State of Alabama had adopted a relief law entitling her taxpayers to a credit under the Federal law.] . . . We cannot say that [Alabama] was acting, not of her unfettered will, but under the strain of a persuasion equivalent to undue influence, when she chose to have relief administered under laws of her own making, by agents of her own selection, instead of under federal laws, administered by federal officers, with all the ensuing evils, at least to many minds, of federal patronage and power. There would be a strange irony, indeed, if her choice were now to be annulled on the basis of an assumed duress in the enactment of a statute which her courts have accepted as a true expression of her will. . . .

## § 21:2. Public Purpose

Since the states by virtue of their police power may spend money for the general welfare, the expenditure of public funds of both nation and state are now on the same basis. The requirement that the power be exercised to advance the general welfare is frequently paraphrased in the rule that the money must be spent for a public purpose.

### *(a) Purchase of private enterprises*

GREEN v. FRAZIER

253 U.S. 233 (1920)

OPINION BY DAY, J.

This is an action by taxpayers of the state of North Dakota . . . to enjoin the enforcement of certain state legislation. . . .

. . .

The legislation involved consists of . . . (1) An act creating an Industrial Commission of North Dakota, . . . which is authorized to conduct and manage on behalf of that state certain utilities, industries, enterprises, and business projects, to be established by law. . . . (2) The Bank of North Dakota Act . . . , which establishes a bank under the name of "The Bank of North Dakota," operated by the state. . . . (3) An act providing for the issuing of bonds of the state in the sum of $2,000,000, the proceeds of which are to constitute the capital of the Bank of North Dakota. . . . (4) An act providing for the issuing of bonds in the sum of not exceeding $10,000,000, to be known as "Bonds of North Dakota, Real Estate Series" . . . for the purpose of raising money to procure funds for the Bank of North Dakota. . . . (5) An act declaring the purpose of the state of North Dakota to engage in the business of manufacturing and marketing farm products, and to establish a warehouse, elevator, and flour mill system under the name of "North Dakota Mill & Elevator Association," to be operated by the state. . . . The purpose is declared that the state shall engage in the business of manufacturing farm products and for that purpose shall establish a system of warehouses, elevators, flour mills, factories, plants, machinery and equipment, owned, controlled, and operated by it under the name of the "North Dakota Mill & Elevator Association." The Industrial Commission is placed in control of the association, with full power, and it is authorized to acquire by purchase, lease, or right of eminent domain, all necessary property or properties, etc.; to buy, manufacture, store, mortgage, pledge, sell, and exchange all kinds of raw and manufactured farm food products, and by-products, and to operate exchanges, bureaus, markets and agencies within and without the state, and in foreign countries. . . . An appropriation is made out of state funds, together with the funds procured from the sale of state bonds, to be designated as the capital of the association. (6) An act providing for the issuing of bonds of the state of North Dakota in a sum not exceeding $5,000,000, to be known as "Bonds of North Dakota, Mill & Elevator Series," . . . to be issued and sold for the purpose of carrying on the business of the Mill & Elevator Association. . . . (7) The Home Building Act declares the purpose of the state to engage in the enterprise of providing homes for its residents and to that end to establish a business system operated by it under the name of "The Home Building Association of North Dakota." . . .

. . . This legislation was adopted under the broad power of the state to enact laws raising by taxation such sums as are deemed necessary to promote purposes essential to the general welfare of its people. Before the adoption of the Fourteenth Amendment this power of the state was unrestrained by any federal authority. That amendment introduced a new limitation upon state power into the federal Constitution. The states were forbidden to deprive persons of life, liberty or property without due process of law. . . .

The due process of law clause contains no specific limitation upon the right of taxation in the states, but it has come to be settled that the authority of the states to tax does not include the right to impose taxes for merely private purposes. . . .

. . . What is a public purpose has given rise to no little judicial consideration. Courts, as a rule, have attempted no judicial definition of a "public" as distinguished from a "private" purpose, but have left each case to be determined by its own peculiar circumstances. . . .

With the wisdom of such legislation, and the soundness of the economic policy involved we are not concerned. Whether it will result in ultimate good or harm it is not within our province to inquire.

We come now to examine the grounds upon which the Supreme Court of North Dakota held this legislation not to amount to a taking of property without due process of law. The questions involved were given elaborate consideration in that court, and it held, concerning what may in general terms be denominated the "banking legislation," that it was justified for the purpose of providing banking facilities, and to enable the state to carry out the purposes of the other acts, of which the Mill & Elevator Association Act is the principal one. It justified the Mill & Elevator Association Act by the peculiar situation in the state of North Dakota, and particularly by the great agricultural industry of the state. It estimated from facts of which it was authorized to take judicial notice, that 90 per cent. of the wealth produced by the state was from agriculture, and stated that upon the prosperity and welfare of that industry other business and pursuits carried on in the state were largely dependent; that the state produced 125,000,000 bushels of wheat each year. The manner in which the present system of transporting and marketing this great crop prevents the realization of what are deemed just prices was elaborately stated. It was affirmed that the annual loss from these sources (including the loss of fertility to the soil and the failure to feed the by-products of grain to stock within the state), amounted to fifty-five millions of dollars to the wheat raisers of North Dakota. It answered the contention that the industries involved were private in their nature, by stating that all of them belonged to the state of North Dakota, and therefore the activities authorized by the legislation were to be distinguished from business of a private nature having private gain for its objective.

As to the Home Building Act, that was sustained because of the promotion of the general welfare in providing homes for the people, a large proportion of whom were tenants moving from place to place. It was believed and affirmed by the Supreme Court of North Dakota that the opportunity to secure and maintain homes would promote the general welfare, and that the provisions of the statutes to enable this feature of the system to become effective would redound to the general benefit.

As we have said, the question for us to consider and determine is whether this system of legislation is violative of the federal Constitution because it amounts to a taking of property without due process of law. The precise question herein involved so far as we have been able to discover has never been presented to this court. The nearest approach to it is found in *Jones* v. *City of Portland,* 245 U.S. 217, . . . in which we held that an act of the state of Maine authorizing cities or towns to establish and maintain wood, coal and fuel yards for the purpose of selling these necessaries to the inhabitants of cities and towns, did not deprive taxpayers of due process of law within the meaning of the Fourteenth Amendment. In that case we reiterated the attitude of this court towards state legislation, and repeated what had been said before, that what was or was not a public use was a question concerning which local authority, legislative and judicial, had especial means of securing information to enable them to form a judgment; and particularly, that the judgment of the highest court of the state, declaring a given use to be public in its nature, would be accepted by this court unless clearly unfounded. In that case the previous decisions of this court, sustaining this proposition, were cited with approval, and a quotation was made from the opinion of the Supreme Court of Maine justifying the legislation under the conditions prevailing in that state. We think the principle of that decision is applicable here.

. . . In many instances states and municipalities have in late years seen fit to enter upon projects to promote the public welfare which in the past have been considered entirely within the domain of private enterprise.

Under the peculiar conditions existing in North Dakota, which are emphasized in the opinion of its highest court, if the state sees fit to enter upon such enterprises as are here involved, with the sanction of its constitution, its legislature and its people, we are not prepared to say that it is within the authority of this court, in enforcing the observance of the Fourteenth Amendment, to set aside such action by judicial decision.

### § 21:3. Special Fund Taxes

A variation of the requirement that there be a public purpose is found in the principle that, under the guise of a tax law, property cannot be taken from A and given to B. Is the purpose materially different if property is taken from a group consisting of A, B, and C and held for the benefit of a group consisting of L, M, and N? This problem arises in laws of the social security type under which employers are taxed to raise a fund that is held for the benefit of employees. It is customary for the employees and the government to make a contribution to this fund. This, however, does not alter the fact that each employer is paying money, not for the general expenses of operating the government, but for the benefit of a private class of employees. Whether such a law is socially and economically desirable is not being considered here. The fact remains that property is being taken from one person and given to another, although, of course, it is impossible to determine the source or destination of any particular dollar of social security tax money. The Supreme Court has held that this law is constitutional.

A similar application arose under workmen's compensation laws where employers are required to contribute to a state fund from which employees are compensated without regard to the identity of their employers. Such a law was held constitutional.

The fact that the law which imposes the tax also allocates the proceeds for a particular purpose does not make the law invalid, although the flight of the tax dollar from the taxpayer to the expenditure is more apparent. As stated in *Cincinnati Soap Co.* v. *United States*, 301 U.S. 308 (1937): "If the tax . . . be good, . . . and the purpose specified be one which would sustain a subsequent and separate appropriation made out of the general funds of the Treasury, neither is made invalid by being bound to the other in the same act of legislation."

### § 21:4. Minor Limitations

Another limitation prohibits the expenditure of public money for the furtherance of religion or religious education on the theory that a complete separation of church and state was intended by the framers of the Constitution.

The federal spending power is also subject to the limitation that "No money shall be drawn from the Treasury but in Consequence of Appropriations made by law." [Art. I, Sec. 9, Ch. 7] State constitutions commonly establish similar restrictions.

During recent years, additional mechanical limitations in the form of a budget system have been placed upon the exercise of the spending power. The purpose of such a system is to forecast the expenses and the revenues for the approaching year or other fiscal period and to specify just what sum is to be spent for each purpose. If the expenses can be kept within the expendable revenues, the budget is said to balance and is regarded as a good budget. The balancing of the budget is not a true criterion of its merit. It may be that some of the expenditures of government are for unnecessary items or could be reduced by greater efficiency. For political reasons, these items may be left unreduced in a budget while false economies are effected by curtailing or omitting items of absolutely essential expenditure. In such a case, while the budget is good to the extent that it balances, it is bad in that the money is not properly spent. A good budget should therefore make the wisest and most economical use of revenue and should keep the expenditures within the expectable revenue.

This latter standard cannot always be observed. Emergency conditions, such as war, disaster, or depression, or necessary innovations or improvements may make it impossible to finance the government on a pay-as-you-go basis. In such cases the government, whether national, state, or local, will necessarily resort to borrowing.

After a budget is adopted, the administrative problem arises of keeping within the budget. The items of expenditure and receipt may not behave during the fiscal period in the manner expected of them. It may therefore be necessary to depart from the budget. This again is a difficult problem, for if departures from a budgetary plan are too frequent or too extensive, there soon ceases to be any budgetary control.

A further mechanical limitation upon the spending of money is found in various statutes that prescribe the manner in which contracts shall be made by the government for the purchase of supplies, materials, services, or the construction of public works. The customary pattern of regulation is to require: (1) that in all such cases written contracts be made between the government and the supplier or contractor; and (2) that the letting of the contract be advertised in advance and the contract awarded to the lowest responsible bidder, who is then required to furnish the government with a performance bond by which he and his sureties agree to indemnify the government in the event that the contractor fails to perform his contract properly.

## Questions for Discussion

1. What are the limitations on the spending of tax money?

2. To what extent was the Court in the *Helvering* case influenced by the statistical data presented to Congress before it adopted the Social Security Act?

3. (a) To what extent was the Court in *Helvering* v. *Davis* influenced by the economic effect of the depression? (b) Does this mean that a depression or an emergency creates a power that did not exist before?

4. (a) Is the Court influenced in *Helvering* v. *Davis* by consideration of what might happen if a few states adopted a more liberal old-age security law than the other states? (b) Compare this approach with *Hammer* v. *Dagenhart*, page 197. (c) How do you explain the difference?

5. Does the Court in *Helvering* v. *Davis* determine that the social security law is based on sound economic principles?

6. Can a state prevent the operation within its boundaries of a federal law on the ground that it is based on an economic theory with which the state does not agree?

7. (a) What is the attitude of the Court to a provision in a federal tax statute allowing a credit for taxes paid to the taxpayer's state government under a state law modeled after the federal statute? (b) Does the Court hold that the states are coerced into conforming to a pattern of regulation that the federal government could not directly impose?

8. To what extent is the court in the *Steward Machine Company* case influenced by the depression of 1929-36?

9. In the *Steward Machine Company* case the Court states: "To hold that motive or temptation is equivalent to coercion is to plunge the law in endless difficulties. The outcome of such a doctrine is the acceptance of philosophic determinism by which choice becomes impossible." Discuss.

10. In the *Steward Machine Company* case the Court stated: "We do not say that a tax is valid when imposed by an Act of Congress if it is laid upon the condition that a state may escape its operation through an adoption of a statute unrelated in subject matter to activities fairly within the scope of national policy and power. . . ." (a) Give an illustration of a statute that would be condemned under this standard. (b) Appraise the value of this statement by the Court.

11. Are there any limitations on the purposes for which the states may impose taxes or expend tax money? Does the Fourteenth Amendment impose any limitation?

12. By whom are the limitations on the state taxing power enforced?

13. Does the Supreme Court pass upon the economic wisdom of a state or federal tax law? What is the reason for this policy?

14. What rule does the Court establish in the *Frazier* case for determining whether the purpose of a tax law is public or private?

15. How would the Court have decided the *Frazier* case if a federal instead of a state law had been involved?

16. Is it constitutional for a state to spend tax money for the ownership and operation of:

(a) A library.
(b) A baseball park.
(c) A motion picture house.
(d) A radio station.
(e) A school.
(f) A first-aid clinic.
(g) A slum-clearance and low-cost housing project.

17. Would it make any difference in your answer to Question 16 if no charge or only a nominal charge is made by this state for its services or facilities? If a charge is made sufficient to defray expenses? If a charge is made sufficient to yield a profit?

18. Would it make any difference in your answer to Question 16 if the public institution competes with a private enterprise and diverts the public from the private enterprise?

## Chapter 22

## THE CURRENCY POWER



### § 22:1. The Nature of the Power

The Constitution authorizes Congress "to coin Money, regulate the Value thereof" and "provide for the Punishment of counterfeiting the Securities and . . . Coin of the United States." [Art. 1, Sec. 8, Cls. 5, 6] This federal power is made exclusive by prohibiting the states from coining money, emitting bills of credit, or making anything but gold and silver coins legal tender in payment of debts. [Art. 1, Sec. 10]

The national government can determine what shall be legal tender and is not restricted to the use of metallic money. Congress can establish such base as it desires for the issue of paper currency and may change the base of existing currency, even though this interferes with or makes impossible the performance of private contracts calling for a different type of money.

#### *(a) Paper currency*

JUILLIARD v. GREENMAN
110 U.S. 421 (1884)

United States paper notes issued during the Civil War, the famous "greenbacks," were, under the authority of a federal statute, redeemed by the government and then reissued or put back into circulation and declared by the statute to be legal tender. A debtor offered to pay his creditor with this paper currency. The creditor refused to accept this payment and sued the debtor for the amount of the debt. The question before the court was whether such paper currency could be made legal tender.

OPINION BY GRAY, J. . . .

That clause of the Constitution which declares that "the Congress shall have the power to lay and collect taxes, duties, imposts and excises, to pay the debts and provide for the common defence and general welfare of the United States," either embodies a grant of power to pay the debts of the United States, or presupposes and assumes that power as inherent in the United States as a sovereign government. . . . The government is to pay the debt of the Union, and must be authorized to use the means which appear to itself the most eligible to effect that object. . . .

The power "to borrow money on the credit of the United States" is the power to raise money for the public use on a pledge of the public credit, and may be exercised to meet either present or anticipated expenses and liabilities of the government. It includes the power to issue in return for the money borrowed, the obligations of the United States in any appropriate form, of stock, bonds, bills or notes; . . . Congress has authority to issue these obligations in a form adapted to circulation from hand to hand in the ordinary transactions of commerce and business. In order to promote and facilitate such circulation, to adapt them to use as currency, and to make them more current in the market, it may provide for their redemption in coin or bonds, and may make them receivable in payment of debts to the government. . . .

. . . Congress has the power to issue the obligations of the United States in such form, and to impress upon them such qualities as currency for the purchase of merchandise and the payment of debts, as accord with the usage of sovereign governments. The power . . . was a power universally understood to belong to sovereignty, in Europe and America, at the time of the framing and adoption of the Constitution of the United States. . . . The exercise of this power not being prohibited to Congress by the Constitution, it is included in the power expressly granted to borrow money on the credit of the United States. . . .

The power of making the notes of the United States a legal tender in payment of private debts, being included in the power to borrow money and to provide a national currency, is not defeated or restricted by the fact that its exercise may affect the value of private contracts. . . .

So, under the power to coin money and to regulate its value, Congress may (as it did with regard to gold by the act of June 28th, 1834, ch. 95, and with regard to silver by the act of February 28th, 1878, ch. 20) issue coins of the same denomination as those already current by law, but of less intrinsic value than those, by reason of containing a less weight of the precious metals, and thereby enabled debtors to discharge their debts by the payment of coins of the less real value. A contract to pay a certain sum in money, without any stipulation as to the kind of money in which it shall be paid, may always be satisfied by payment of that sum in any currency which is lawful money at the place and time at which payment is to be made. . . .

Congress, as the legislature of a sovereign nation, being expressly empowered by the Constitution "to lay and collect taxes, to pay the debts and provide for the common defence and general welfare of the United States," and "to borrow money on the credit of the United States," and "to coin money and regulate the value thereof and of foreign coin;" and being clearly authorized, as incidental to the exercise of those great powers, to emit bills of credit, to charter national banks, and to provide a national currency for the whole people, in the form of coin, treasury notes, and national bank bills; and the power to make the notes of the government a legal tender in payment of private debts being one of the powers belonging to sovereignty in other civilized nations, and not expressly withheld from Congress by the Constitution; we are irresistibly impelled to the conclusion that the impressing upon the treasury notes of the United States the quality of being legal tender in payment of private debts is an appropriate means, conducive and plainly adapted to the execution of the undoubted powers of Congress, consistent with the letter and spirit of the Constitution, and therefore, within the meaning of that instrument, "necessary and proper for carrying into execution the powers vested by this Constitution in the government of the United States."

Such being our conclusion in matter of law, the question whether at any particular time, in war or in peace, the exigency is such, by reason of unusual and pressing demands on the resources of the government, or of the inadequacy of the supply of gold and silver coin to furnish the currency needed for the uses of the government and of the people, that it is, as matter of fact, wise and expedient to resort to this means, is a political question, to be determined by Congress when the question of exigency arises, and not a judicial question, to be afterwards passed upon by the courts. . . .

### *(b) Devaluation of private gold bonds*

NORMAN v. B. & O. R. R. CO.

294 U.S. 240 (1935)

OPINION BY HUGHES, C. J.

These cases present the question of the validity of the Joint Resolution of the Congress of June 5, 1933, with respect to the "gold clauses" of private contracts for the payment of money. . . .

This resolution . . . declares that "every provision contained in or made with respect to any obligation which purports to give the obligee a right to require payment in gold or a particular kind of coin or currency, or in an amount in money of the United States measured thereby" is "against public policy." Such provisions in obligations thereafter incurred are prohibited. The Resolution provides that "Every obligation, heretofore or hereafter incurred, whether or not any such provision is contained therein or made with respect thereto, shall be discharged upon payment, dollar for dollar, in any coin or currency which at the time of payment is legal tender for public and private debts."

. . . The suit was brought upon a coupon of a bond made by the Baltimore and Ohio Railroad Company. . . . The bond provided that the payment of principal and interest "will be made . . . in gold coin of the United States of America of or equal to the standard of weight and fineness existing on February 1, 1930." The coupon in suit, for $22.50, was payable on February 1, 1934. The complaint alleged that on February 1, 1930, the standard weight and fineness of a gold dollar of the United States as a unit of value "was fixed to consist of twenty-five and eight-tenths grains of gold, nine-tenths fine," . . . and by the order of the President . . . , the standard unit of value of a gold dollar of the United States "was fixed to consist of fifteen and five-twenty-firsts grains of gold, nine-tenths fine," from and after January 31, 1934. On presentation of the coupon, defendant refused to pay the amount in gold or the equivalent of gold in legal tender of the United States which was alleged to be, on February 1, 1934, according to the standard of weight and fineness existing on February 1, 1930, the sum of $38.10, and plaintiff demanded judgment for that amount. . . .

We are of the opinion that the gold clauses now before us were not contracts for payment in gold coins as a commodity, or in bullion, but were contracts for the payment of money. The bonds were severally for the payment of one thousand dollars. We also think that, fairly construed, these clauses were intended to afford a definite standard or measure of value, and thus to protect against a depreciation of the currency and against the discharge of the obligation by a payment of lesser value than that prescribed. When these contracts were made they were not repugnant to any action of the Congress. . . . Congress may make treasury notes legal tender in payment of debts previously contracted, as well as of those subsequently contracted, whether that authority be exercised in course of war or in time of peace. . . .

. . . Contracts, however express, cannot fetter the constitutional authority of the Congress. Contracts may create rights of property, but when contracts deal with a subject matter which lies within the control of the Congress, they have a congenital infirmity. Parties cannot remove their transactions from the reach of dominant constitutional power by making contracts about them. . . .

This principle has familiar illustration in the exercise of the power to regulate commerce. If shippers and carriers stipulate for specified rates, although the rates may be lawful when the contracts are made, if Congress through the Interstate Commerce Commission exercises its authority and prescribes different rates, the latter control and override inconsistent stipulations in contracts previously made. . . .

The same reasoning applies to the constitutional authority of the Congress to regulate the currency and to establish the monetary system of the country. If the gold clauses now before us interfere with the policy of the Congress in the exercise of that authority they cannot stand.

. . . Whether they may be deemed to be such an interference depends upon an appraisement of economic conditions and upon determinations of questions of fact. With respect to those conditions and determinations, the Congress is entitled to its own judgment. We may inquire whether its action is arbitrary or capricious, that is, whether it has reasonable relation to a legitimate end. If it is an appropriate means to such an end, the decision of the Congress as to the degree of the necessity for the adoption of that means, is final. . . .

We are not concerned with consequences, in the sense that consequences, however serious, may excuse an invasion of constitutional right. We are concerned with the constitutional power of the Congress over the monetary system of the country and its attempted frustration. Exercising that power, the Congress has undertaken to establish a uniform currency, and parity between kinds of currency, and to make that currency, dollar for dollar, legal tender for the payment of debts. In the light of abundant experience, the Congress was entitled to choose such a uniform monetary system, and to reject a dual system, with respect to all obligations within the range of the exercise of its constitutional authority. The contention that these gold clauses are valid contracts and cannot be struck down proceeds upon the assumption that private parties, and states and municipalities, may make and enforce contracts which may limit that authority. Dismissing that untenable assumption, the facts must be faced. We think that it is clearly shown that these clauses interfere with the exertion of the power granted to the Congress and certainly it is not established that the Congress arbitrarily or capriciously decided that such an interference existed.

### § 22:2. Regulation of Currency

During the Colonial and Revolutionary days many forms and nationalities of currency were in use, among which the Spanish dollar was regarded as the standard. Local American money was subject to increasing depreciation the further away from the place of issuance it circulated. During the Revolutionary War, the attempt to finance the war with the issue of paper money led to such depreciation that the phrase "not worth a continental" became a byword.

It was against this background that the Fathers of the Constitution gave the new Congress the power to regulate the currency of the United States.

In his famous report to the First Congress, Hamilton urged the adoption of a national currency. In 1792, Congress established bimetallic currency of silver and gold at a mint ratio of 15½ to 1 and adopted the decimal system of monetary notation. In 1834, the mint ratio of silver and gold was changed to 16 to 1. This undervalued silver dollars, as the result of which, obeying Gresham's Law, they disappeared from circulation. In 1873, Congress recognized the fact that silver was no longer in circulation as coin and declared that no further minting of silver should be made. This demonetization of silver, made famous by the silverites as the "Crime of 1873," gave birth to a new political movement. New silver mines were opened in the 70's and the silver mine interests desired that silver should again be made coin so that a steady customer could be found in the United States Mint. At the same time farmers who had suffered by the falling prices of the then current depression saw in the increased volume of coin that would result from the minting of silver a means of making the price level rise and by such inflation enable them to discharge their debts in money of the same purchasing power as that for which they incurred those debts. These forces joined and were successful in securing the adoption of Silver Purchasing Acts of 1878 and 1890. These Acts, however, caused gold to flow steadily from the Treasury as the government was making silver purchases. The result of this was a panic, which in 1893 caused Congress to repeal the Silver Purchase Act.

Finally in 1900 Congress definitely placed the country on the gold standard by the adoption of the Gold Standard Act, which defined the dollar as equivalent in value to 25.8 grains of gold .9 fine.

While the struggle between gold and silver was continuing, another struggle was taking place between hard and paper money.

Although the Constitution prohibited the states from coining money, emitting bills of credit, or making other than gold and silver coin legal tender in the payment of debts, the Supreme Court had interpreted this prohibition as merely preventing a state from issuing paper money on the strength of its own promise as a state. It was held that, when a state owned a bank that issued paper money, this issuance of paper money did not violate the Constitution in cases where only the assets of the bank were pledged or stood as security for the payment of the paper money or bills of credit. As long as the property of the state itself was not security for the paper money, the Constitution was not violated. This interpretation made it possible for the country to become flooded with paper currencies issued by innumerable state banks that sprang up all over the country in an effort to share in the Western expansion and the eras of prosperity that the growing country was experiencing.

The federal government did not attempt to issue paper money until the necessities of the Civil War drove it to issue nonredeemable paper money which from its color was given the name of "greenback." Within two years after issuance, the greenbacks had depreciated to 35 cents on the dollar, and it was not until after the war when provision was made for their redemption that their value was restored.

Meanwhile another form of paper currency was authorized by the Congress. Under the Act of 1863, which created the national banking system, the national banks were permitted to issue national bank notes up to 90 per cent of the face value of bonds held by them.

These national bank notes remained the main body of the American monetary system until the Federal Reserve currency appeared in 1913.

The national paper currency of the Civil War faced the competition of the bank notes issued by state banks. This competition was eliminated by a federal tax of 10 per cent placed on the state bank notes, which drove them out of circulation.

In 1913 the Federal Reserve banking system was established, authorizing the issuance of Federal Reserve bank notes, since then retired, and of Federal Reserve notes backed by gold, gold certificates, and commercial paper upon which loans had been made by the member banks and which had been rediscounted with the Federal Reserve banks.

The depression of 1929 and the years following saw a progressively decreasing price level. This was a serious threat to debtors who had incurred their debt at a time when the price level was high. In the effort to remedy this, one of the main features of the Roosevelt New Deal Program was the suspension of the gold standard and the devaluation of the dollar. The first step in this program was to remove gold from circulation and to place the title to gold in the national government. The use of gold as money was prohibited. Persons having gold coin or gold certificates were required with small exception to surrender them to the national treasury. The payment of debts in gold even when called for by contract was prohibited, and the creditor was required to accept payment in legal tender. Gold could be obtained for industrial use or for export upon obtaining a license from the government. The nation was thus in effect on a domestic inconvertible paper standard and an international gold bullion standard.

The next step was the devaluation of the dollar from a gold content of 25.8 grains .9 pure to $15\frac{5}{21}$ grains .9 pure or to .5906 of its former value. As stated by the President, "the administration has the definite objective of raising commodity prices to such an extent that those who have borrowed money will, on the average, be able to repay that money in the same kind of dollars they borrowed."

This measure was predicated in part upon the theory that it would permit the government to issue more money by allowing the government to hold a smaller amount of gold in reserve for each dollar outstanding, which, by increasing the volume of money in circulation, would tend to create higher prices. There was some difficulty with this traditional volume theory of money and prices in view of the fact that the stock of money on March, 1933, was in fact 59 per cent greater than in 1926, which was the high price level year that was sought to be regained.

As the result of this devaluation of the dollar, the United States Treasury made a profit of approximately 2 billion dollars, which was set aside as a stabilization fund to make the dollar stable by purchasing United States securities and foreign exchange in the open market. The long-echoed arguments in favor of silver as an inflationary form of currency were again given heed, and in 1933 and 1934 the purchase of silver by the United States government from the domestic market and from foreign governments was authorized until the government silver stock should be one fourth that of its gold or until the price of silver exceeded $1.29 an ounce. The results of the purchases made by the government under this legislation do not appear significant.

Today the Federal Reserve notes constitute the most important form of our national money. The second most important form of paper money is the silver certificate. These are in effect warehouse receipts, as each is backed by a dollar's worth of silver on deposit with the treasury.

Gold certificates are still in existence but not in general circulation. At present they are held by the Federal Reserve banks as reserves for outstanding reserve notes.

In the area of metallic money the silver dollar, the subsidiary coins consisting of dimes, quarters, and half-dollars, and the minor coins consisting of nickels and pennies, round out the picture of current forms of money. These coins are all token money in that the bullion or metallic value of the coins is less than the face value of the coins themselves.

### Questions for Discussion

1. Does the Constitution authorize Congress to issue paper currency? What is the historical explanation for the form of the constitutional provision governing currency?

2. What effect did the existence of war have on the federal power with respect to the issuance of paper currency?

3. To what extent is the power to issue paper currency based on the inherent right of a sovereign nation?

4. (a) Is the *Julliard* case an illustration of strict or liberal construction? (b) How does it compare with *McCulloch* v. *Maryland*, page 5?

5. What does the Court mean in the *Julliard* case when it states that the question whether paper currency is to be issued "is a political question, to be determined by Congress when the question of exigency arises, and not a judicial question, to be afterwards passed upon by the courts"?

6. A, B and C are private individuals. They apply to the state in which they live for a charter to operate a banking corporation. The charter authorizes the bank to issue bank notes. It is claimed that the charter violates the Constitution of the United States. Decide.

7. (a) Does Congress impair the obligation of contracts when it authorizes the use of a new currency in the payment of private debts that were created before the new currency was authorized? (b) Does it make any difference if the new currency has a greater or a lower purchasing value than the former legal tender?

8. (a) Is there any way in which the parties to a contract can assure themselves that payment will be made in currency of the same value as the currency that was legal tender at the time their debt was contracted? (b) Is there any way that they can provide that the same gold content shall be paid irrespective of devaluation of the dollar?

9. What is the meaning of the provision of Article I, Section 10, Cl. 1, of the Constitution that "no state shall . . . emit bills of credit; [or] make anything but gold and silver coin a tender in payment of debts . . ."?

10. Was not the federal 10% tax on state bank notes a penalty to drive them out of circulation? How did the Supreme Court sustain the tax as constitutional?

11. Does the Constitution require the adoption of a bimetallic base for currency?

12. When the Supreme Court handed down the decision in *Norman* v. *Baltimore & Ohio R. R. Co.*, one of the dissenting judges orally announced from the bench that the decision amounted to "a repudiation of national obligations" and "a breaking of solemn pledges" and that "as for the Constitution, it does not seem too much to say that it is gone." (a) Do you agree with these statements? (b) Do they mean that this case goes farther than any other case? (c) How does this case compare with decisions under the commerce clause? with the decision in *Nebbia* v. *New York*, page 274.

13. The dollar was devalued in order to aid domestic debtors and to increase foreign trade. The plan was that, by lowering the value of the dollar, prices would be maintained at a higher level, thus enabling the debtors to pay off their debts in dollars of the same purchasing power as those that they had borrowed. Foreign trade was to be aided, since the foreign currencies would have a greater purchasing power relative to the cheaper American dollar and this would induce foreign countries to purchase more heavily within the United States. Does Congress have the

power to undertake such economic planning? Can it do so under the guise of regulating currency?

14. *De minimis non curat lex* is a maxim of the law that means that the law does not bother with trifles. Why did not the Court refuse to decide the *Norman* case because the amount involved was so small?

15. The Court stated in the *Norman* case: "We are of the opinion that the gold clauses now before us were not contracts for payment in gold coins as a commodity, or in bullion, but were contracts for the payment of money." (a) What does this mean? (b) Would the decision have been different if the Court held that it was a contract for the delivery of a commodity, such as gold in bar or bullion form?

16. (a) Were the gold clauses valid when made? (b) Why does not the Court apply the prohibition against *ex post facto* laws? (c) What effect does the concept of freedom of contract have on this decision?

17. Would it have affected the decision in the *Norman* case if a city had issued the bond on which suit was brought?

18. Does the *Norman* case represent a liberal or a strict construction of the Constitution? Explain.

19. Define the extent of judicial review in the light of the *Norman* case.

## Chapter 23

## REGULATION OF BANKING



### § 23:1. Regulation before 1913

The federal government is not expressly authorized to conduct a banking business or to authorize the organization and operation of banks. The power to do so has been implied, however, from the power to lay and collect taxes and the practical necessity of safeguarding and providing for the disposition of government money in some manner. The power of the states to create banks is an incident of the general police power of the state.

At the time of the adoption of the United States Constitution, there were only three banks in existence in the United States, incorporated under state law: the Bank of North America, Philadelphia, organized in 1781; the Bank of Massachusetts, Boston, organized in 1784; and the Bank of New York, New York City, organized in 1784. Upon the proposal of Hamilton and over the vigorous protest of the farmer and debtor class who feared a money domination by the commercial and urban classes, the First Congress of the United States chartered the first Bank of the United States. This charter ran from 1791 until 1811. Opposition to the bank was so great that, when its charter expired in 1811, it was not renewed. This removal of the competition of the Bank of the United States was an added impetus to the incorporation of state banks. While a second bank of the United States was incorporated in 1816 and its charter continued until 1836, the trend of incorporating state banks continued.

These state banks were incorporated under general corporation laws or by special acts incorporating them in the same manner as ordinary corporations. Generally no special provision was made by the law creating state banks with respect to reserves, the making of loans, or supervision of the banking operations by a state official. Many of the state banks were run by persons who were merely seeking the profit to be obtained during the various boom eras but who had no particular knowledge or skill in the management of banks. As the result of such an unsound basis for the banking structure, the panic of 1837 caused many state banks to suspend specie payment or to fail completely.

Following the expiration of the charter of the second Bank of the United States, as a result of Jackson's personal political and economic dislike for the Bank and those associated with its administration, the United States government continued until 1863 without any national banks. In 1840, the absence of national banks was to some degree remedied by the adoption of the subtreasury plan under which funds of the United States were kept in a small number of designated state banks in addition to the Treasury of the United States.

The demands of the Civil War made the creation of new banks highly desirable. More money was needed to be put into circulation in order to pay the obligations of the government in financing the war, and new purchasers were needed to buy the bonds issued by the government in order to raise funds for the prosecution of the war. The Banking Act of 1863 was then adopted. Under its provisions, any five persons satisfying the requirements could form a national bank. These national banks were required to purchase stated amounts of government bonds and were then permitted to issue notes against them. For purposes of security, the bonds themselves were deposited with the federal government. In this manner the federal government created for itself a market for its bonds and also made possible the issuance of additional paper currency.

The creation of these national banks did not destroy the right of the states to continue the creation of state banks. Congress, however, did tax out of existence bank notes issued by the state banks so that, while the state and national banks existed concurrently, the former ceased to issue paper money or bank notes and confined themselves to other banking activities.

While the national banking system established by the Act of 1863 as superimposed upon the state banking systems went far in supplying the banking needs of the day, it was not long before various defects became apparent. The volume of paper money that could be issued by the national banks was inelastic, that is, the maximum amount that could be issued was fixed and remained constant in terms of the amount of reserve that was held by the bank. It was impossible to expand the volume of outstanding paper currency in good times when a larger amount of currency was needed because of the greater number of financial transactions. Conversely, it was not possible to contract the volume of outstanding currency during less prosperous times when a smaller volume of currency would be desirable. Another difficulty with the system was that reserves held by the various banks were scattered or isolated throughout the country and it was difficult if not impossible for one bank with an adequate reserve to come to the aid of another bank to withstand a temporary run on the other bank. The result was that each bank stood or fell upon the basis of its own strength rather than the combined strength of all national banks.

This isolation of the individual national banks also gave rise to a difficulty in connection with the collection or clearance of commercial paper. Since each bank acted separately, it was necessary for each bank to make a shipment of gold or other suitable coin or metal in order to discharge an obligation. A check drawn by a California debtor on a California bank and sent to his creditor in Pennsylvania would finally be paid off by the California bank's sending a shipment of gold to the Pennsylvania bank. The high cost of transportation and insurance for such a gold shipment and the difficulties, both mechanical and for a number of years human in the form of highwaymen or Indians, made such collection expensive and hazardous.

The isolated method of operating each national bank also made it impossible for the banks to follow any common pattern in regard to banking policies or methods.

### § 23:2. The Federal Reserve System

In 1913 the Congress remedied these defects by the creation of the Federal Reserve System. Under this system the country is divided into twelve districts, each of which has a Federal Reserve bank. All national banks must, and state banks upon compliance with statutory regulations may, join the Federal Reserve bank of their district by purchasing a specified amount of stock in that bank.

Each Federal Reserve bank is a banker's bank and has the functions of (1) rediscounting commercial paper on which the member banks have made loans, (2) issuing notes or paper currency (the Federal Reserve notes and the Federal Reserve bank notes), (3) acting as a clearing house or collecting agency, (4) acting as a depository of reserve funds of the member banks, and (5) acting as fiscal agent and depository for the government.

Unity of operations of the twelve Federal Reserve banks is obtained by overall boards and committees that establish the general policy for the Federal Reserve banks. The national control fixes the rediscount rate to be charged by Federal Reserve banks, fixes the reserve ratios that the member banks are required to maintain between the amount of their deposits and the reserves to meet those deposits, and engages in open market operations.

This system is designed to correct the defects of the former banking system. In place of the inelastic currency of the former system, the national banks may expand their currency or note issue when they are receiving more commercial paper because they are making more loans to businessmen and other persons. Conversely, as the loans are paid off, the volume of the paper currency that can be outstanding is reduced. This expansion and contraction is not directly proportional to the amount of the increase or the decrease of the commercial paper held by the banks, for the reason that the banks are not permitted to issue paper currency dollar for dollar as against the commercial paper; nevertheless there is a large degree of elasticity imparted to the currency structure. Fluidity is given to the reserves, since these are held to a large degree by the Federal Reserve bank in the district rather than by each individual member bank. Accordingly it is merely a matter of bookkeeping for a Federal Reserve bank to make available to any of its members the reserves that are held by it. Each Federal Reserve bank is in turn required to maintain a certain portion of its reserves on deposit in the gold reserve fund at Washington. This makes possible the extension of reserve funds from one Federal Reserve district to another in the same manner.

The fact that the Federal Reserve bank holds on deposit money belonging to each of its member banks and that the gold fund in Washington holds on deposit money belonging to each of the Federal Reserve banks makes it unnecessary to send gold when an item is collected. Instead of the California bank sending a gold shipment to the Pennsylvania bank in the previous illustration, it is only necessary to make a series of bookkeeping entries by which the Federal Reserve bank of which the California bank is a member is debited by the amount of the check and the Federal Reserve bank of which the Pennsylvania bank is a member is credited in like amount. This bookkeeping is then carried a step further within each of the Federal Reserve districts in question. The Federal Reserve bank of which the California bank is a member then debits the California bank with the amount of the check. The Federal Reserve bank of which the Pennsylvania bank is a member credits the Pennsylvania bank with the amount of the check. Payment has thus been made across the country without the movement of any money. Where both banks involved are within the same Federal Reserve district, the collecting of an item is made by a bookkeeping entry in the Federal Reserve bank of which both banks are members, the Federal Reserve bank debiting the account of one and crediting the account of the other.

In addition to advancing sound banking practices and insuring the maintenance of adequate reserves against deposits, the Federal Reserve System permits some degree of control or direction of the economy, although here it is controversial whether the means given the Federal Reserve System are adequate and whether they have had any substantial success in achieving their purpose. The power to alter the rediscount rate was designed to give the Federal Reserve banks the power to encourage or discourage lending by member banks. Since a bank loans money in order to earn the discount or interest paid on the loan, it is obvious that the greater the rediscount rate it must pay when it resells the commercial paper taken to secure the loan, the less it is likely to make such loans. Conversely, the lower the rediscount rate, the more likely the bank is to make loans, since the loans will prove more profitable to it. Furthermore, the higher the rediscount rate, the higher will probably be the discount rate that the member banks will charge their customers on the loans. The successful operation of this control device has been greatly handicapped by the psychological factor that in good times the optimism of borrowers makes them willing to pay greater rates, while in bad times or approaching bad times a lower interest rate is not sufficient to induce business to borrow money and to make new investments.

The power of the Federal Reserve System to set the minimum reserve ratios to be maintained against deposits is not only a valuable aid in maintaining the solvency of the banks and their strength against runs, but it is also a means of restricting the loans that the member banks can make. In the latter capacity it thus serves as a check against boom expansion. The reserve ratio that each member bank is required to maintain is determined by adding the cash held by the bank and that due it from other banks and dividing this total by the deposits. As bank loans are ordinarily made in the form of giving the borrower a deposit credit with the bank, it is apparent that the larger the volume of loans that a bank makes, the greater is the volume of its deposits and therefore the smaller is its reserve because the total of cash held by the bank and due from other banks is then divided by a larger number. By increasing the reserve ratio it is therefore possible to place a limit on the amount of the loans that the member bank can make. While this is a valuable means of checking boom loan expansion, the exercise of the power in the opposite direction by lowering the reserve ratio and thus permitting the bank to make a larger amount of loans is not effective. The mere fact that the bank is permitted to make a greater volume of loans does not cause more borrowers to come to the bank and borrow the money if, because of bad times or approaching bad times, business is fearful of making such loans.

By virtue of open market operations, the Federal Reserve System can increase or decrease the volume of currency in circulation and, following the volume theory of money and prices, thus exercise a control on prices and the business cycle. If it is believed that the volume of circulating money is too large, securities held by the Federal Reserve System can be sold in the open market, thus absorbing this extra volume of money. Conversely, if the volume of circulating money is deemed too small, the Federal Reserve System can use its money to purchase in the open market securities held by others and thus place in the hands of others a larger volume of money. The efficacy of this operation is limited in terms of the extent to which it may be carried on and in terms of validity or accuracy of the volume theory of money and prices.

During the era of the 30's, a number of changes were made in the Federal Reserve System to make it more efficient as a banking system and more effective as a control on the economy. These changes did not alter the basic pattern of the system.

The depression era of the 30's is also of interest in indicating the extent to which the federal banking power may go. At the time of Roosevelt's inauguration, depositors across the country were making runs on the banks by demanding from them the full amount of their deposits. Since a bank does not maintain dollar for dollar reserves against deposits, many banks that were financially sound were broken because they could not supply sufficient money at the moment to pay off all of their depositors, although if they had had time they could have done so. In order to prevent the wrecking of the national banking structure by such runs, President Roosevelt declared a national bank moratorium that lasted for several days, during which no bank was permitted to conduct any banking business nor to pay money to any depositors. This gave a breathing space in which reserves could be gathered. The banks were then reopened one by one as each was made adequate to meet demands. With the adoption of deposit insurance, public confidence in the banks returned. The spirit of panic that caused the runs on the banks was broken and the banks were able to return to substantially a normal degree of operation.

### § 23:3. Other Federal Financial Institutions

In addition to the Federal Reserve System, the national government established a large number of banking and lending institutions.

The Postal Saving System which began operations in 1911, offers a savings bank service to all members of the public. A low interest rate is paid and deposits may not exceed $2,500.

As the result of the great depression in real estate values following 1929, the federal government extended financial aid to the home owner through the Federal Home Loan banks, the Federal Home Owners' Loan Corporation, the Federal Savings and Loan associations, and the Federal Savings and Loan Insurance Corporation, which protects the investments in the Federal Savings and Loan associations. Bank depositors are protected by the Federal Deposit Insurance Corporation plan, under which the deposit of each depositor in a bank that is a member of that corporation is insured up to a maximum amount, originally $5,000, but since increased by amendment of the statute to $10,000. All banks that are members of the Federal Reserve System must join this corporation, and others may do so. The corporation is financed partly by the national government and partly by the banks that have joined it. These banks are assessed a small percentage of the total of their deposits.

Business is aided by the Reconstruction Finance Corporation, which was organized first under President Hoover and then expanded under the New Deal to permit loans to practically all forms of economic activity. The Export-Import Bank was organized in 1934 to encourage foreign trade. It may make loans to individuals and governments, and its scope of operations has so broadened that it has become a very valuable arm in the conduct of dollar diplomacy. As an illustration of the latter, it was used in 1940 to make a large loan to China. Special provision has been made for the aid of small businesses. In addition, there are a number of other minor lending agencies that are linked in with the Reconstruction Finance Corporation in one way or another.

Special banking institutions have been set up for the farmer. The Federal Land banks, the Joint Stock Land banks, the Federal Farm Mortgage Corporation, the Federal Intermediate Credit banks, the National Agricultural Credit Corporation, and the Co-operative Aid banks, as their names imply, have been created to perform the specialized services of making loans to farmers on the security of farm mortgages, of making them loans for intermediate and short terms, and for aiding farmer co-operatives. A number of these agencies have been brought under the control of the Department of Agriculture.

The problem of co-ordinating the various banking institutions is obviously difficult. There have been a number of assignments and re-assignments of different institutions either to special agencies or to one department or another of the government.

There is every likelihood that, apart from mechanical rearrangement or reorganization of these federal banking and credit institutions, the number, extent, and importance of their operations will increase. In many areas, the national banking institutions, particularly farm credit facilities, have operated at a loss that could not be sustained by private enterprise. In a sense, the extending of loans where it is not economically feasible in itself to do so is a subsidy to the borrower. The continuation or the expansion of such a system raises a difficult question of policy and the extent to which government should seek to affect the operation of the so-called natural laws of economics.

## Questions for Discussion

1. (a) Describe the National Bank System of 1863. (b) What were its defects?

2. (a) Describe the Federal Reserve System of 1913. (b) How did it remedy the defects of the system of 1863? (c) Does it have any defects of its own? (d) How can they be remedied?

3. Illustrate the operation of the deposit reserve ratio. Why is the reserve ratio affected by bank loans?

4. What is the authority for the creation of the National Bank System of 1863? the Federal Reserve System of 1913?

5. What functions are performed by the Federal Reserve System?

6. Is the Federal Reserve System an effective agency in offsetting depressions? Are its powers adequate for that purpose?

7. While Congress may create a bank to act as a fiscal agent, as was contemplated in *McCulloch* v. *Maryland*, it cannot create a bank or banking system with authority to seek to control the economy by regulating the volume of loans, currency in circulation, and interest rates. Do you agree? Discuss.

8. What is the volume theory of currency? Is it correct to say that, since it is agreed by everyone that the volume theory of money is correct, it is constitutional for Congress to give a national banking institution power to regulate the volume of currency?

9. (a) What has been the trend in the growth of national financial aid institutions? (b) Do these institutions operate at a profit? (c) What is the future trend of their development? (d) Does this trend have any relation to free enterprise?

10. Is there any parallel between the contest over the ratification of the Constitution, the contest over the adoption of the first national bank, and Jackson's controversy with the second national bank?

11. The early history of state banking proves the desirability of permitting banks to operate without government supervision. Do you agree? Discuss.

12. (a) What banking systems could be adopted by the United States apart from a bank owned outright by the United States? (b) What would be the constitutional basis for each plan? Would it be the same in each case?

13. (a) What was the constitutional basis for the Roosevelt national bank moratorium? (b) What is the constitutional basis for a state bank moratorium? (c) Does a bank moratorium impair the obligation of contracts by denying a depositor the right to withdraw his money?

14. A national bank is created. To encourage savings, it is provided that 6% interest shall be paid on deposits. It is admitted that even with the most efficient operation it would not be possible to pay more than 3% interest. The law provides for the payment of any deficit of interest from the national treasury. The law is attacked as unconstitutional on the ground that it would take money from the public funds and use it for a private purpose. Decide.

15. Would it make any difference in your answer to Question 14 if the statute provided that, instead of taking the deficit from the public funds, a special tax should be imposed on the sale of all property and the deficit paid from that fund?

16. Name and state the purpose of five federal financial aid institutions. What is the constitutional basis for each of them?

# Chapter 24

# REGULATION OF BANKRUPTCY



## § 24:1. The Federal Power

Congress is authorized to establish "uniform Laws on the subject of Bankruptcies throughout the United States." [Art. I, Sec. 8, Cl. 4] This power is authorization for laws providing for the voluntary or involuntary adjudication of a debtor and the distribution of his property among his creditors, for the readjustment of debts by a plan of composition, or for the reorganization of the security and debt structure of a corporate debtor and the modification of its liabilities through the adoption of a reorganization plan.

Bankruptcy laws must be uniform throughout the United States, which means that the law must be the same everywhere in the United States. The requirement of uniformity, however, does not prohibit the recognition by the federal bankruptcy law of such exemptions as are allowed by the local state law, although this in effect introduces some element of nonuniformity. Actually, the lack of uniformity caused by these variations in accordance with local state law is not substantial for the reason that there is a general tendency for the state exemption laws to follow a common pattern.

The states may adopt insolvency or bankruptcy laws in the absence of a federal bankruptcy law. The scope of insolvency laws is somewhat narrower than that of federal bankruptcy laws, as the states cannot discharge liability incurred prior to the adoption of a state insolvency law nor the claims of nonresident creditors not parties to the action. The subject is unimportant today because the adoption of federal bankruptcy laws has superseded or displaced the bulk of state insolvency laws.

## § 24:2. Bankruptcy

The present federal bankruptcy law provides that an individual debtor may be adjudged bankrupt on his own petition or, with the exception of wage earners earning under $1,500 a year or farmers, upon the petition of three or more creditors with unsecured claims of $500 or more.[1] The petition for bankruptcy sets forth that the debtor owes $1,000 or more and is insolvent in that the fair valuation of his assets is less than his liabilities. The petition also avers that the debtor has committed an act of bankruptcy and requests that the debtor be declared a bankrupt.

A business corporation may be declared bankrupt on its own or its creditors' petition where the corporation owes $1,000 or more, with the exception of banks, political subdivisions, insurance companies, railroads, and building and loan associations.

In bankruptcy proceedings, in addition to the insolvency of the debtor, it must be shown that he, whether an individual or a corporation, has committed an act of bankruptcy within the preceding four months. The Bankruptcy Act specifies certain types of conduct as being "acts of bankruptcy." These include certain frauds upon creditors, giving a preference to a creditor either directly or through legal proceedings, making a general assignment for benefit of creditors, appointing a receiver for the debtor, or the admission in writing by the debtor of "his inability to pay his debts and his willingness to be adjudged a bankrupt."

After a hearing on this petition, if the bankruptcy court determines that the debtor is a bankrupt, he is so adjudged and the case is referred to a referee. The bankrupt is then required to file a schedule or list of all his creditors. The referee calls a meeting of these creditors at which they present their claims against the bankrupt, question him as to his assets, and elect a trustee to administer the bankrupt's estate or assets. It is then the trustee's duty to collect all the assets of the debtor; if necessary, to set aside improper transfers of property that the debtor has made; and to distribute the debtor's assets to the creditors according to the statutory priority given to their claims.

After this administration has been completed, the bankrupt may be discharged if he has not been guilty of any improper practice as specified in the statute. His discharge may be opposed by any credi-

[1] If the debtor has less than twelve creditors the petition may be filed by one of them.

tor or the trustee on the ground that he has been guilty of such improper conduct. If the discharge is granted, the debtor is thereby relieved of further liability for all claims against him, whether or not they have been paid in full by the distribution of his assets by the trustee, with the exception of certain claims that are listed in the Bankruptcy Act as not being discharged.

The fact that the claim of a creditor against the debtor is destroyed by the discharge in bankruptcy, even though the creditor has not been paid in full, is not regarded as depriving the creditor of his property without due process of law. Such a conclusion is inevitable, since by definition a bankruptcy power could not operate unless it were permitted to discharge the debtor of his debts regardless of whether his creditors were paid in full. If it did not do this, a bankruptcy statute would merely be a plan for the distribution of the debtor's property or a judicially supervised execution.

If, however, the creditor has security for his claim, as in the case of a mortgagee, the bankruptcy proceeding can not destroy that security and deny that creditor the right to liquidate his security by foreclosing the mortgage. A bankruptcy law directed at the economic rehabilitation of the debtor may postpone the foreclosure of the mortgage or security for a reasonable period, provided reasonable compensation is given the creditor for the postponement of his right; but the law cannot be allowed to deprive him of the value of the security by either destroying or indefinitely postponing the right to foreclose.

### § 24:3. Reorganization

One of the main objections to bankruptcy proceedings is that it terminates or kills the business operated by the bankrupt. As a going concern the business might have a value greatly in excess of the value of the tangible assets of the business. The effect of bankruptcy proceedings is to sell or otherwise dispose of the assets of the company, thus failing to realize on the going-concern or goodwill value. A less extreme remedy thus suggested itself by which a debtor could be placed under court supervision with the object of restoration rather than liquidation.

It was with this thought in mind that the equity courts developed the device of corporate receivership. Under this plan, a business under certain conditions could be placed in the hands of a receiver who would act as its manager until the business could be returned to the hands of its former owners or, if the business had failed so far that it could not be restored, until the receiver court would authorize the sale of the assets. While this had the desirable objective of curing rather than killing the business, the equity receivership was subject to numerous delays and was limited in the extent to which the court could revise the debtor's affairs.

With the background of the equity receivership and the powers under bankruptcy in mind, Congress amended the Bankruptcy Act to provide for corporate reorganization. For simplicity, this might be called a modernized receivership in which an effort has been made to eliminate the causes for delay and abuse and to give the court greater power in bringing about necessary financial reconstruction.

Either upon the petition of the corporation or the petition of three creditors or more with claims of $5,000 or more, or the trustee of corporate securities under certain circumstances, the court may appoint a reorganization trustee for a corporation. If the corporate debts exceed $250,000, the trustee is placed in charge of the business. If the debts are less than that amount, the court may place the trustee in charge or may permit the original owners to remain in charge. The trustee in any case has the responsibility of preparing a plan of reorganization in which he may suggest the scaling down or even the wiping out of the various claims of creditors, bondholders, and stockholders. If the debt of the corporation exceeds $3,000,000, the opinion of the Securities and Exchange Commission must be obtained as to the merits of the plan. If the court is of the opinion that the plan is fair and equitable, it approves the plan, which is then submitted to the various classes that are affected by the plan. After the consent of two thirds of each class affected by the plan has been obtained, the plan becomes effective. By this is meant that, from then on, the debts, the bond issues, and the stock of the corporation are only such as are set forth in the plan, and any interest not recognized or provided for in the plan is deemed destroyed or discharged.

As an illustration of this power, it may be decided by the trustee and the court that a certain bond issue of the corporation carries a rate of interest which is too high for the continued operation of the corporation. Let us assume that it is decided that the interest rate on these bonds should be scaled from 5 per cent to 3 per cent. If the court approves this scaling down and if two thirds of the holders of these bonds approve, then from that time on these bonds pay only 3 per cent interest and a claim for 5 per cent cannot be made by any of the bondholders, whether or not they were included in the majority or the minority that voted on the issue of scaling down. In this manner the corporation can come out of reorganization with a new capitalization and debt structure. If the difficulty that the corporation had experienced before was due to the fact that it had a capitalization and debt structure which subjected it to excessive fixed charges, it may be that such a scaling down of liabilities is all that the corporation needs to restore it financially. The fact that a creditor or a security holder of a corporation finds the value of his claim or security reduced or even totally destroyed by a plan of corporate reorganization does not deprive him of property without due process of law.

If the corporate reorganization fails because no plan can be devised or agreed upon, the court may either dismiss the petition for reorganization or may adjudge the debtor a bankrupt and then proceed according to the ordinary bankruptcy procedure.

A system of railroad reorganization comparable to corporate reorganization is provided under the bankruptcy law. A significant point of difference is that approval by the Interstate Commerce Commission must also be obtained.

### *(a) Scope of bankruptcy law*

CONTINENTAL & ILLINOIS NATIONAL BANK & TRUST CO. v. CHICAGO, R. I. & P. RY.

294 U.S. 648 (1935)

By an amendment to the Federal Bankruptcy Law, Section 77 was added providing for the corporate reorganization of railroads. The validity of this law was challenged on the ground that it was not a bankruptcy law.

OPINION BY SUTHERLAND, J.

. . .

The English law of bankruptcy, as it existed at the time of the adoption of the Constitution, was conceived wholly in the interest of the creditor and proceeded upon the assumption that the debtor was necessarily to be dealt with as an offender. Anything in the nature of voluntary bankruptcy was unknown to that system. The persons who were permitted to fall within the term "bankrupt" were limited to traders. But the notion that the framers of the Constitution, by the bankruptcy clause, intended to limit the power of Congress to the then existing English law and practice upon the subject long since has been dispelled.

. . . It was definitely decided that the extent of the power of Congress was not limited to the principle upon which the English bankruptcy system was founded. . . .

But, while it is true that the power of Congress under the bankruptcy clause is not to be limited by the English or Colonial law in force when the Constitution was adopted, it does not follow that the power has no limitations. Those limitations have never been explicitly defined. . . . Probably the most satisfactory approach to the problem of interpretation here involved is to examine it in the light of the acts, and the history of the acts, of Congress which have from time to time been passed on the subject. . . .

The first act, that of 1800 so far ignored the English law, which was confined to traders, as to include bankers, brokers, and underwriters as well. The act of 1841 added merchants; and other additions have been made by later acts until now practically all classes of persons and corporations are included. . . . The act of 1800 was one exclusively in the interest of the creditor. But the act of 1841 took what then must have been regarded as a radical step forward by conferring upon the debtor the right by voluntary petition to surrender his property, with some exceptions, and relieve himself of all future liability in respect of past debts. The act of 1800, like the English law, was conceived in the view that the bankrupt was dishonest; while the act of 1841 and the later acts proceeded upon the assumption that he might be honest but unfortunate. One of the primary purposes of these acts was to "relieve the honest debtor from the weight of oppressive indebtedness, and permit him to start afresh free from the obligations and responsibilities consequent upon business misfortunes," and to give him "a new opportunity in life and a clear field for future effort, unhampered by the pressure and discouragement of pre-existing debt." . . .

By the Act of March 2, 1867, as amended by the Act of 1874, . . . the debtor for the first time was permitted, either before or after an adjudication in bankruptcy, to propose terms of composition to his creditors to become binding upon their acceptance by a designated majority and confirmation by the judge.

The fundamental and radically progressive nature of these extensions becomes apparent upon their mere statement; but all have been judicially approved or accepted as falling within the power conferred by the bankruptcy clause of the Constitution. Taken altogether, they demonstrate in a very striking way the capacity of the bankruptcy clause to meet new conditions as they have been disclosed as a result of the tremendous growth of business and development of human activities from 1800 to the present day. And these acts, far-reaching though they be, have not gone beyond the limit of congressional power; but rather have constituted extensions into a field whose boundaries may not yet be fully revealed.

Section 77 advances another step in the direction of liberalizing the law on the subject of bankruptcies. Railway corporations had been definitely excluded from the operation of the law in 1910 . . . , probably because such corporations could not be liquidated in the ordinary way or by a distribution of assets. A railway is a unit; it can not be divided up and disposed of piecemeal like a stock of goods. It must be sold, if sold at all, as a unit and as a going concern. Its activities can not be halted because its continuous, uninterrupted operation is necessary in the public interest; and, for the preservation of that interest, as well as for the protection of the various private interests involved, reorganization was evidently regarded as the most feasible solution whenever the corporation had become "insolvent or unable to meet its debts as they mature."

Equity receiverships, resorted to for that purpose, have never been satisfactory for many reasons. Partly, no doubt, in recognition of that situation, Congress, by § 77, added railroad corporations to the category of those who might have relief by legislation passed in virtue of the bankruptcy clause of the Constitution; and determined, after consideration, that such relief to be effectual should take the form of a reorganization, and should extend to cases where the corporation is "unable to meet its debts as they mature." The last phrase, since it is used as an alternative for the word "insolvent," obviously means something less than a condition of "bankruptcy" or "insolvency" as those words are employed in the law. See Bankruptcy Act, § 1(15), which defines an "insolvent" as one whose assets, at a fair valuation, are not sufficient to pay his debts. It may be construed to include a debtor who, although unable to pay promptly, may be able to pay if time to do so be sufficiently extended. Obviously, § 77 does no more than follow the line of historical and progressive development projected by previous acts.

As outlined by that section, a plan of reorganization, when confirmed, cannot be distinguished in principle from the composition with creditors authorized by the act of 1867, as amended by the act of 1874. It is not necessary to the validity of either that the proceeding should result in an adjudication of bankruptcy. The constitutionality of the old provision for a composition is not open to doubt. . . . That provision was . . . sustained upon the broad ground that the "subject of bankruptcies" was nothing less than "the subject of the relations between an insolvent or non-paying or fraudulent debtor, and his creditors, extending to his and their relief." That it was not necessary for the proceedings to be carried through in bankruptcy was held not to warrant the objection that the provision did not constitute a law on the subject of bankruptcies. The same view sustains the validity of § 77. Both contemplate an adjustment of a failing debtor's obligations; and although actual bankruptcy may not supervene in either, they are none the less laws on the subject of bankruptcies. With due regard for consistency, the constitutional validity of the one cannot well be sustained and that of the other denied. . . .

### § 24:4. Compositions

In addition to these forms of corporate reorganization, the bankruptcy laws also establish the machinery by which an agreement for the extension or the composition of claims can be obtained with the requisite agreement of the parties. The effect of these arrangement systems is to provide a modified sort of reorganization in the hope that such additional aid is all that the debtor requires. The composition or arrangement plans are available to individual debtors, whereas reorganization proper is restricted to corporations.

### Questions for Discussion

1. Define *receivership, bankruptcy, corporate reorganization,* and *composition of debts.*

2. May a federal bankruptcy law impair the obligation of a private contract?

3. What is the source of federal power for a law relating to the following:

   (a) Equity receiverships.
   (b) Individual bankruptcy.
   (c) Corporate bankruptcy.
   (d) Corporate reorganization.
   (e) Composition of creditors' claims.

4. For whose protection or benefit are bankruptcy laws designed?

5. Has there been any noticeable trend in the history of bankruptcy laws? Discuss.

6. The bankruptcy power is clearly limited by the Constitution. Is this correct? Discuss.

7. The national bankruptcy law permits the debtor to keep the same amount of property in bankruptcy proceedings as would be exempt if a creditor had obtained a judgment in a state court against him and were selling his property to pay the judgment. Assume that in most of the states the debtor has such a state exemption of $200 but that in a few states he has an exemption of $600. In consequence of this, a debtor going into bankruptcy in the former states may retain only $200 worth of property, while a debtor in one of the latter states may retain $600. A debtor in the former state attacks the law as unconstitutional. (a) Decide. (b) Would it make any difference if a creditor in the second state claimed the law unconstitutional because he would not be paid in full if the debtor is permitted to keep the $600 worth of property rather than $200 worth?

8. Assume that, to correct the condition existing in Question 7, Congress provides that the exemption in bankruptcy proceedings should be $400 irrespective of the law of the state in which the debtor lives. Is such a law constitutional? Discuss.

9. Does the present bankruptcy law apply to all corporations? If not, is the bankruptcy law unconstitutional or does it violate the requirement of uniformity specified by the Constitution?

10. A bankruptcy law is adopted providing that all property of the debtor shall be distributed equally among his creditors and that there shall be included in this distribution of property any land of the debtor, whether subject to a mortgage or not, and that any mortgagee shall be required to share in the distribution of the debtor's total assets equally with other creditors. B, a bankrupt, had mortgaged his house to A. B owes A $10,000 on the mortgage and owes all his other creditors another $10,000. The only property B owns other than the house mortgaged to A has the value of $200. The debtor's exemption is $200. A forecloses on B's house and at the sale receives $10,000. The trustee in bankruptcy claims that under the statute A must pay this $10,000 to the trustee to be distributed equally among A and the other creditors so that everyone would receive 50% of his claim. A contends that the law is unconstitutional and that he is entitled to keep the full amount of the proceeds even though the other creditors will then receive nothing. Is the law constitutional? Is A entitled to keep the full proceeds of the sale? Decide.

11. What is an act of bankruptcy? Why is it important to prove an act of bankruptcy?

12. Describe the general plan of procedure in bankruptcy.

13. What is the significance of a discharge in bankruptcy?

14. A petition is filed to declare B a bankrupt. It is shown that the total assets of B are reasonably appraised at $100,000 and his total liabilities at $50,000 but that, because of the specialized nature of B's property,

only $25,000 could be realized if his property were sold. B claims that he is not insolvent since he has every prospect of continuing in business and would not be selling the property. Decide.

15. Corporation K undergoes a reorganization under the federal law. J is a creditor whose claim is wiped out by the adoption of the reorganization plan. J claims that the law under which the reorganization was held was unconstitutional because the Congress can only adopt bankruptcy laws which require a procedure ending in a determination of bankruptcy and the distribution of the debtor's assets, while the law in question permits the proceedings to end with a reorganization without an adjudication in bankruptcy and without a distribution of the corporate property. Is he correct? Decide.

16. Corporation C undergoes corporate reorganization. As part of the plan of reorganization, two thirds of the holders of participating preferred stock agree to accept shares of cumulative preferred stock in lieu of their participating preferred stock. The plan is approved by the trustee and the court. M owns five shares of the participating preferred stock and had voted against the plan of stock substitution. He now claims that the operation of the plan takes his property from him without due process of law and claims that it is fundamental that one's neighbors cannot vote one's property away and that if the government takes property for a public purpose it must pay for it. Is he correct? Discuss.

17. Does a railroad present any problem in bankruptcy or reorganization that an ordinary business corporation does not?

# Chapter 25

# WAR POWERS AND FOREIGN AFFAIRS



## § 25:1. The War Power

The Constitution confers the national war power upon the Congress (Art. I, Sec. 8, Cl. 10 to 16). Except to the extent necessary to repel invasion or in the event of imminent danger that will not admit of delay (Art. I, Sec. 10, Cl. 3), the states are denied any war power. The federal war power includes the power to do everything reasonably necessary to the prosecution of the war, and the courts have shown very little desire to interfere with the congressional or presidential determination of what is reasonably necessary. The power to wage war is a "power to wage war successfully and thus it permits the harnessing of the entire energies of the people in a supreme cooperative effort to preserve the nation." Chief Justice Hughes in *Home B. & L. Assn* v. *Blaisdell,* 290 U.S. 398 (1934). The absence of any real constitutional limitation upon the war power was recognized by Hamilton in the *Federalist*: "The circumstances that endanger the safety of nations are infinite, and for this reason no constitutional channels can safely be imposed on the power to which the care of it is committed." [1]

The Congress may not only draft men, but it may subject private industry to any regulation it deems appropriate or it may seize private plants and transportational facilities. If Congress chooses to obtain war materials through contracts let to private plants, it may provide

[1] Quoted with approval in Lichter v. United States, 334 U.S. 742 (1948).

for any type of contract and may authorize the renegotiation of the contracts in order to recapture excess profits realized by the contractor. If the government desires, it may construct and operate its own production plants and transportational facilities. Congress may establish price, rationing, and prohibition controls of everything that is related to the war effort or to the maintaining of the national economy or security.

The war power is not restricted to the time of actual war but may be used in advance to prepare for war, even though there is no immediate threat of danger. It may be exercised after hostilities have ceased in order to bind up the wounds of economic dislocation caused by the war, even though such effects may last for years. It must be recognized that, in an era of total war, it is difficult to claim that a bona fide element of war preparation is not present in any regulation of business. There is no significant industry or business the strengthening of which cannot plausibly be claimed as legitimate preparation for war. Also, because of the increasing complexity of our economic system, the repercussions of war are felt many years after the conclusion of hostilities. The question of the duration of war power confronted the Supreme Court in the following case in determining the validity of a rent control law passed after the termination of hostilities.

### *(a) Federal Rent Control Act*

WOODS v. CLOYD W. MILLER CO.

333 U.S. 138 (1948)

The United States Rent Control Act of 1947 was claimed unconstitutional because it was adopted after the President had proclaimed the termination of hostilities of World War II.

OPINION BY DOUGLAS, J.

. . .

We conclude that the war power sustains this legislation. . . . The war power includes the power "to remedy the evils which have arisen from its rise and progress" and continues for the duration of that emergency. Whatever may be the consequences when war is officially terminated, the war power does not necessarily end with the cessation of hostilities. . . . Prohibition laws which were enacted after the Armistice in World War I were sustained as exercises of the war power because they conserved manpower and increased efficiency of production in the critical days during the period of demobilization, and helped to husband the supply of grains and cereals depleted by the war effort. . . .

The legislative history of the present Act makes abundantly clear that there has not yet been eliminated the deficit in housing which in considerable measure was caused by the heavy demobilization of veterans and by the cessation or reduction in residential construction during the period of hostilities due to the allocation of building materials to military projects. Since the war effort contributed heavily to that deficit, Congress has the power even after the cessation of hostilities to act to control the forces that a short supply of the needed articles created. If that were not true . . . the result would be paralyzing. It would render Congress powerless to remedy conditions the creation of which necessarily followed from the mobilization of men and materials for successful prosecution of the war. So to read the Constitution would be to make it self-defeating.

We recognize the force of the argument that the effects of war under modern conditions may be felt in the economy for years and years, and that if the war power can be used in days of peace to treat all the wounds which war inflicts on our society, it may not only swallow up all other powers of Congress but largely obliterate the Ninth and Tenth Amendments as well. There are no such implications in today's decision. We deal here with the consequences of a housing deficit greatly intensified during the period of hostilities by the war effort. Any power, of course, can be abused. But we cannot assume that Congress is not alert to its constitutional responsibilities. And the question whether the war power has been properly employed in cases such as this is open to judicial inquiry. . . .

. . . Here it is plain from the legislative history that Congress was invoking its war power to cope with a current condition of which the war was a direct and immediate cause. . . .

## § 25:2. The Foreign Affairs Power

Within the area of the forty-eight states, the national government shares the power of governing with the states. Domestically, it is a dual or federal governmental system. Internationally, the forty-eight states have no legal existence and it is the national government alone that exists. As such, the national government has the full power of a sovereign government to make treaties and to enter into foreign relations. (Art. II, Sec. 2, Cl. 2; Art. I, Sec. 10, Cls. 1, 3)

### *(a) Supremacy of federal power*

## UNITED STATES v. BELMONT

301 U.S. 324 (1937)

A Russian corporation deposited money with Belmont, a private banker, in New York. Following the Russian Revolution of 1917, the assets of the corporation were confiscated by the Soviet Government. In 1933, the Soviet Government made an agreement with the President of the United States with respect to the settlement of claims, and as part of the settlement the Soviet Government assigned to the United States the money on deposit with Belmont. The United States sued Belmont for the money. The defense was raised that according to the New York law the decree of confiscation by the Russian Government was not recognized and therefore the Soviet Government could not assign the right to the deposit to the United States.

OPINION BY SUTHERLAND, J.

. . . We are of [the] opinion that no state policy can prevail against the international compact here involved.

. . . We take judicial notice of the fact that coincident with the assignment set forth in the complaint, the President recognized the Soviet Government, and normal diplomatic relations were established between that government and the Government of the United States, followed by an exchange of ambassadors. The effect of this was to validate, so far as this country was concerned, all acts of the Soviet Government here involved from the commencement of its existence. The recognition, establishment of diplomatic relations, the assignment, and agreements with respect thereto, were all parts of one transaction, resulting in an international compact between the two governments. That the negotiations, acceptance of the assignment and agreements and understandings in respect thereof were within the competence of the President may not be doubted. Governmental power over internal affairs is distributed between the national government and the several states. Governmental power over external affairs is not distributed, but is vested exclusively in the national government. And in respect of what was done here, the Executive had authority to speak as the sole organ of that government. The assignment and the agreements in connection therewith did not, as in the case of treaties, as that term is used in the treaty making clause of the Constitution (Art. II, § 2), require the advice and consent of the Senate.

A treaty signifies "a compact made between two or more independent nations with a view to the public welfare." . . . But an international compact, as this was, is not always a treaty which requires the participation of the Senate. There are many such compacts, of which a protocol, a modus vivendi, a postal convention, and agreements like that now under consideration are illustrations. . . .

. . . Although this might not be a treaty requiring ratification by the Senate, it was a compact negotiated and proclaimed under the authority of the President, and as such was a "treaty" within the meaning of the Circuit Court of Appeals Act, the construction of which might be reviewed upon direct appeal to this court.

Plainly, the external powers of the United States are to be exercised without regard to state laws or policies. The supremacy of a treaty in this respect has been recognized from the beginning. Mr. Madison, in the Virginia Convention, said that if a treaty does not supersede existing state laws, as far as they contravene its operation, the treaty would be ineffective. . . . And while this rule in respect of treaties is established by the express language of cl. 2, Art VI, of the Constitution, the same rule would result in the case of all international compacts and agreements from the very fact that complete power over international affairs is in the national government and is not and cannot be subject to any curtailment or interference on the part of the several states. . . . In respect of all international negotiations and compacts, and in respect of our foreign relations generally, state lines disappear. As to such purposes the State of New York does not exist. Within the field of its powers, whatever the United States rightfully undertakes, it necessarily has warrant to consummate, And when judicial authority is invoked in aid of such consummation, state constitutions, state laws, and state policies are irrelevant to the inquiry and decision. It is inconceivable that any of them can be interposed as an obstacle to the effective operation of a federal constitutional power. . . .

. . . The public policy of the United States relied upon as a bar to the action is that declared by the Constitution, namely, that private property shall not be taken without just compensation. But the answer is that our Constitution, laws and policies have no extraterritorial operation, unless in respect of our own citizens. . . . What another country has done in the way of taking over property of its nationals, and especially of its corporations, is not a matter for judicial consideration here. Such nationals must look to their own government for any redress to which they may be entitled. . . .

## § 25:3. Effect of Treaty Power on Legislative Power

Some treaties are self-executing and are fully effective from the time of agreement. Other treaties are executory and require adoption of laws by the participating nations to carry out and give effect to the terms of the treaty. No provision is found in the Federal Constitution as to the scope of the legislative power of Congress when it is adopting laws to carry out treaties.

### *(a) Protection of migratory birds*

MISSOURI v. HOLLAND
252 U.S. 416 (1920)

Congress had enacted a game law for migratory birds, which several lower federal courts had held unconstitutional as beyond the federal regulatory power. A treaty was then executed between the United States and Great Britain by which it was provided that each should adopt a game law for migratory birds. In order to carry out its obligation under the treaty, Congress enacted a law similar to that which had already been held unconstitutional by the lower courts. The constitutionality of this second law was then challenged.

OPINION BY HOLMES, J.

. . . The question raised is the general one whether the treaty and statute are void as an interference with the rights reserved to the States.

To answer this question it is not enough to refer to the Tenth Amendment, reserving the powers not delegated to the United States, because by Article II, § 2, the power to make treaties is delegated expressly, and by Article VI treaties made under the authority of the United States, along with the Constitution and laws of the United States made in pursuance thereof, are declared the supreme law of the land. If the treaty is valid there can be no dispute about the validity of the statute under Article I, § 8, as a necessary and proper means to execute the powers of the Government. . . .

It is said that a treaty cannot be valid if it infringes the Constitution, that there are limits, therefore, to the treaty-making power, and that one such limit is that what an act of Congress could not do unaided, in derogation of the powers reserved to the States, a treaty cannot do. An earlier act of Congress that attempted by itself and not in pursuance of a treaty to regulate the killing of migratory birds within the States had been held bad in the District Court. . . .

Whether the . . . cases . . . were decided rightly or not they cannot be accepted as a test of the treaty power. Acts of Congress are the supreme law of the land only when made in pursuance of the Constitution, while treaties are declared to be so when made under the authority of the United States. It is open to question whether the authority of the United States means more than the formal acts prescribed to make the convention. We do not mean to imply that there are no qualifications to the treaty-making power; but they must be ascertained in a different way. It is obvious that there may be matters of the sharpest exigency for the national well being that an act of Congress could not deal with but that a treaty followed by such an act could, and it is not lightly to be assumed that, in matters requiring national action, 'a power which must belong to and somewhere reside in every civilized government' is not to be found. . . . What [has been said] with regard to the powers of the States applies with equal force to the powers of the nation in cases where the States individually are incompetent to act. We are not yet discussing the particular case before us but only are considering the validity of the test proposed. With regard to that we may add that when we are dealing with words that also are a constituent act, like the Constitution of the United States, we must realize that they have called into life a being the development of which could not have been foreseen completely by the most gifted of its begetters. It was enough for them to realize or to hope that they had created an organism; it has taken a century and has cost their successors much sweat and blood to prove that they created a nation. The case before us must be considered in the light of our whole experience and not merely in that of what was said a hundred years ago. The treaty in question does not contravene any prohibitory words to be found in the Constitution. The only question is whether it is forbidden by some invisible radiation from the general terms of the Tenth Amendment. We must consider what this country has become in deciding what that amendment has reserved.

. . . No doubt the great body of private relations usually fall within the control of the State, but a treaty may override its power. . . .

Here a national interest of very nearly the first magnitude is involved. It can be protected only by national action in concert with that of another power. The subject matter is only transitorily within the State and has no permanent habitat therein. But for the treaty and the statute there soon might be no birds for any powers to deal with. We see nothing in the Constitution that compels the Government to sit by while a food supply is cut off and the protectors of our forests and our crops are destroyed. It is not sufficient to rely upon the States. The reliance is vain, and were it otherwise, the question is whether the United States is forbidden to act. We are of opinion that the treaty and statute must be upheld. . .

### § 25:4. Social Reform by Treaty

The implications of the doctrine of *Missouri* v. *Holland*,[2] are far-reaching. Extended to its logical conclusion, it would permit the execution of treaties with foreign nations designed to further international welfare and then sustain the validity of federal laws adopted to carry out such provisions, without regard to whether the laws without the treaties would be constitutional. Prior to the modern extension of the commerce power, this treaty and statute combination offered a possible means of outlawing child labor and of making the various other social reforms that Congress could not make directly. It was suggested that the President and the Senate should make a treaty prohibiting child labor and then Congress should adopt a federal law prohibiting child labor within the United States upon the authority of the above case. The extension of the commerce power, however, has made it unnecessary to resort to this device, as Congress is now able to regulate the most substantial part of the economic and the social area and to achieve by direct regulation reforms that were formerly prohibited.

The problem of *Missouri* v. *Holland* may be revived, however, in the field of human or personal rights to the extent that the United Nations should adopt a declaration or agreement binding on the United States and all its members, requiring the members to observe and maintain specified standards with respect to human and personal rights with their respective territories.

### Questions for Discussion

1. (a) What is the extent of the national war power? (b) What is the extent of the state war power?

2. Are there any limitations to the regulations that may be imposed on business during wartime?

3. Does the war power give Congress the authority to provide for a complete socialization or nationalization of all industries in time of war?

---

[2] See § 25:3(a).

4. A federal law may be sustained as preparation for war.
 (a) Is there any time limitation on this preparatory power?
 (b) Is the Supreme Court bound by the Congressional determination that a law is required in order to prepare for war?

5. A federal law may be sustained under the war power although it relates to postwar recovery. How long after a war has ended can this power be exercised?

6. Is the question of what is needed for war a judicial question that the courts will pass upon or a political question that they will not decide?

7. In the *Woods* case, the Court stated: "Since the war effort contributed heavily to [the deficit of housing facilities], Congress has the power even after the cessation of hostilities to act to control the forces that a short supply of the needed articles created. If that were not true . . . the result would be paralyzing. . . . So to read the Constitution would make it self-defeating. . . ." (a) What do you think of this as a constitutional argument? (b) How does it compare with the approach of the Court in *Schechter* v. *United States*, page 199, and *N. L. R. B.* v. *Jones & Laughlin Steel Corp.*, page 205.

8. (a) Are there any limitations on a wartime supply or price rationing system? (b) Can such a system be adopted by the national government in peacetime?

9. (a) Would it have made any difference in *Missouri* v. *Holland* if the subject regulated by the treaty and statute was a business enterprise in which private citizens had money invested, such as factories, mines, or farms? (b) Can the case be distinguished on the ground that the benefits to be attained would be great compared to the comparative insignificance of the restraint imposed?

10. Is the scope of the treaty-making power defined by the Constitution?

11. What limitations are there on the treaty power? on statutes adopted to carry out treaties?

12. Compare the national-state relations with respect to domestic matters within the United States and foreign matters with other countries.

13. How do you classify the decision of *Missouri* v. *Holland* according to the following classifications: (a) liberal construction; (b) strict construction; (c) emergency power; (d) necessity power.

14. How does the executive compact in the *Belmont* case differ from a formal treaty (a) as to procedure, (b) as to effect?

## Chapter 26

# THE POWER OF EMINENT DOMAIN



## § 26:1. Taking for a Public Purpose

Both the United States and the individual states possess the power to take private property as an implied power of government traditionally held by the sovereign.

In the case of the federal government, the power must be exercised to accomplish or to aid the furthering of an object within the scope of the expressed federal powers. Such a purpose is necessarily for a public use. The federal eminent domain power may be exercised within a state without regard to whether the state consents to the federal government's exercising that power. It is not necessary that the federal government directly exercise the power of eminent domain. It may confer it upon a corporation that has been created to carry out the governmental purpose.

A state exercising the power of eminent domain must do so for a public purpose or a public use. If it fails to do so and takes property for a private or a nonpublic use, the taking will be held unconstitutional as depriving the former owner of his property without due process of law.

The concept of what is a public use is not clearly defined. Property is clearly taken for a public use when it is taken by the government and used for essential government buildings. The power may, however, be conferred upon a political subdivision or a private corporation. A railroad authorized to acquire its right of way by eminent domain is regarded as taking property for a public use even though the corporation is a private corporation that hopes to make profit through the operations of the road over the right of way and even though the public will have no right to use that property unless it pays the railroad a fare or a freight charge. The courts have endeavored to define public use in terms of governmental function; that is, if the purpose is regarded as one which a government may properly undertake itself, then the taking of land for that purpose, whether by the government itself or by a private corporation or a semipublic corporation, is also regarded as a public use. This, however, is not a clear definition because the scope of governmental functions is itself a changing concept as society moves from a negative police state to a positive paternalistic state. Irrigation and drainage works and gas, electric, and water supply works are regarded as being sufficiently within the public use area that government may use the power of eminent domain to acquire property for that purpose or may grant private enterprisers the right of taking property for such use.

As an illustration of the limitation upon the public use concept, it is generally held that excess land, that is, more land than is needed for an improvement, cannot be taken by eminent domain with the object of thereafter reselling the unnecessary surplus; but this does not preclude the condemnation of an entire blighted area for redevelopment purposes with the intention of selling any surplus areas that should not be required for the project as completed.

The requirement that a taking be for a public purpose is to a large extent nullified in practice by the principle that the determination of Congress as to whether a purpose is public is virtually final. While the courts have the power to review the Congressional determination, the rule is followed that "when Congress has spoken . . .

'its decision is entitled to deference until it is shown to involve an impossibility.' "[1]

### *(a) Redevelopment project*

**BERMAN v. PARKER**

**348 U.S. 26 (1954)**

The District of Columbia Redevelopment Act authorizes the taking of land by eminent domain in order to clear blighted or slum areas and the use of such land for redevelopment projects. The agency under the Act declared a certain area to be blighted and proceeded to acquire the land. Berman and others owned a department store within the area. They claimed that the Act was unconstitutional as to them because the building was not used as a dwelling and did not contribute to the blighted character of the surrounding neighborhood. They brought an action to prevent the condemnation of their store.

OPINION BY DOUGLAS, J.

. . . Appellants . . . claim that their property may not be taken constitutionally for this project. It is commercial, not residential property; it is not slum housing. . . . To take for the purpose of ridding the area of slums is one thing; it is quite another, the argument goes, to take a man's property merely to develop a better balanced, more attractive community. . . .

We do not sit to determine whether a particular housing project is or is not desirable. . . . In the present case, the Congress and its authorized agencies have made determinations that take into account a wide variety of values. It is not for us to reappraise them. If those who govern the District of Columbia decide that the Nation's Capital should be beautiful as well as sanitary, there is nothing in the Fifth Amendment that stands in the way. . . .

In the present case, Congress and its authorized agencies attack the problem of the blighted parts of the community on an area rather than on a structure-by-structure basis. That, too, is opposed by appellants. They maintain that since their building does not imperil health or safety nor contribute to the making of a slum or a blighted area, it cannot be swept into a redevelopment plan by the mere dictum of the Planning Commission or the Commissioners. The particular uses to be made of the land in the project were determined with regard to the needs of the particular community. The experts concluded that

[1] United States v. Welch, 327 U.S. 546 (1946).

if the community were to be healthy, if it were not to revert again to a blighted or slum area, as though possessed of a congenital disease, the area must be planned as a whole. It was not enough, they believed, to remove existing buildings that were insanitary or unsightly. It was important to redesign the whole area so as to eliminate the conditions that cause slums—the overcrowding of dwellings, the lack of parks, the lack of adequate streets and alleys, the absence of recreational areas, the lack of light and air, the presence of outmoded street patterns. It was believed that the piecemeal approach, the removal of individual structures that were offensive, would be only a palliative. The entire area needed redesigning so that a balanced, integrated plan could be developed for the region, including not only new homes but also schools, churches, parks, streets, and shopping centers. In this way it was hoped that the cycle of decay of the area could be controlled and the birth of future slums prevented. . . .

. . . It is the need of the area as a whole which Congress and its agencies are evaluating. . . .

. . . It is not for the courts to oversee the choice of the boundary line nor to sit in review on the size of a particular project area. Once the question of the public purpose has been decided, the amount and character of land to be taken for the project and the need for a particular tract to complete the integrated plan rests in the discretion of the legislative branch. . . .

The District Court indicated grave doubts concerning the Agency's right to take full title to the land as distinguished from the objectionable buildings located on it. . . . We do not share those doubts. If the Agency considers it necessary in carrying out the redevelopment project to take full title to the real property involved, it may do so. It is not for the courts to determine whether it is necessary for successful consummation of the project that unsafe, unsightly, or unsanitary buildings alone be taken or whether title to the land be included, any more than it is the function of the courts to sort and choose among the various parcels selected for condemnation.

The rights of these property owners are satisfied when they receive that just compensation which the Fifth Amendment exacts as the price of the taking.

## § 26:2. Property Subject to Eminent Domain

Lands and buildings, regardless of how the title to them is held, are all subject to the power of eminent domain. The right of government to take property for eminent domain is not affected by the existence of contracts between the owner of the property and third parties.

### *(a) Municipal trust*

UNITED STATES v. CARMACK

329 U.S. 230 (1946)

OPINION BY BURTON, J.

. . . Was the Federal Works Administrator authorized . . . to acquire by condemnation land held in trust and used by the City for such public purposes as those of a local park, courthouse, city hall and public library?

. . . The United States petitioned to condemn as a site for a United States Post Office and Custom House about one and one-half acres, near the center of the City . . . together with the improvements thereon except a public library building. . . .

The power of eminent domain is essential to a sovereign government. If the United States has determined its need for certain land for public use that is within its federal sovereign powers, it must have the right to appropriate that land. . . .

. . . ". . . Such an authority is essential to its independent existence and perpetuity. These cannot be preserved if the obstinacy of a private person, or of any other authority, can prevent the acquisition of the means or instruments by which alone governmental functions can be performed. . . . If the right to acquire property . . . may be made a barren right by the unwillingness of property-holders to sell, or by the action of a state prohibiting a sale to the federal government, the constitutional grants of power may be rendered nugatory, and the government is dependent for its practical existence upon the will of a state, or even upon that of a private citizen. This cannot be. . . ." . . .

It makes little difference that the site here to be condemned is held by the city in trust. . . .

### *(b) Franchised water works*

LONG ISLAND WATER-SUPPLY CO. v. BROOKLYN

166 U.S. 685 (1897)

It was claimed that certain water works could not be taken by eminent domain because it held a contract for supplying water to a political subdivision.

OPINION BY BREWER, J.

. . . All private property is held subject to the demands of a public use. The constitutional guaranty of just compensation is not a limitation of the power to take, but only a condition of its exercise. Whenever public uses require, the government may appropriate any private property on the payment of just compensation. That the supply of water to a city is a public purpose cannot be doubted, and hence the condemnation of a water-supply system must be recognized as within the unquestioned limits of the power of eminent domain. It matters not to whom the water-supply system belongs, individual or corporation, or what franchises are connected with it—all may be taken for public uses upon payment of just compensation. It is not disputed by counsel that, were there no contract between the company and the town, the waterworks might be taken by condemnation. And so the contention is practically that the existence of the contract withdraws the property, during the life of the contract, from the scope of the power of eminent domain, because taking the tangible property will prevent the company from supplying water, and, therefore, operate to relieve the town from the payment of hydrant rentals. In other words, the prohibition against a law impairing the obligation of contracts stays the power of eminent domain in respect to property which otherwise could be taken by it. Such a decision would be far-reaching in its effects. There is probably no water company in the land which has not some subsisting contract with a municipality which it supplies, and within which its works are located, and a ruling that all those properties are beyond the reach of the power of eminent domain during the existence of those contracts is one which, to say the least, would require careful consideration before receiving judicial sanction. The fact that this particular contract is for the payment of money for hydrant rental is not vital. Every contract is equally within the protecting reach of the prohibitory clause of the Constitution. The charter of a corporation is a contract, and its obligations cannot be impaired. So it would seem to follow, if plaintiff in error's contention is sound, that the franchise of a corporation could not be taken by condemnation, because thereby the contract created by the charter is impaired. The privileges granted to the corporation are taken away, and the obligation of the corporation to perform is also destroyed.

. . . Eminent domain . . . is, as its name imports, paramount to all private rights vested under the government, and these last are, by necessary implication, held in subordination to this power, and must yield in every instance to its proper exercise. . . .

. . . A distinction has been attempted, in argument, between the power of a government to appropriate for public uses property which is corporeal, or may be said to be in being, and the like power in the government to resume or extinguish a franchise. The distinction . . . has no foundation. . . . We are aware of nothing peculiar to a franchise which can class it higher, or render it more sacred, than other property. A franchise is property, and nothing more. . . .

### § 26:3. What Amounts to a Taking

By the express provision of the Fifth Amendment and the interpretation of the due process clause of the Fourteenth Amendment, just compensation must be made whenever property is taken by eminent domain, that is, taken for a public use.

Where the government takes exclusive physical possession of property, no question arises but that it has been "taken." The government, without actually taking possession of the property, may carry on activities of such a nature in its vicinity as to interfere with the use of the property by its owner and to reduce its value. Under such circumstance a question arises as to whether there has been a "taking" for which compensation must be made. It is held that there is a "taking" if the activity of the government or the body having power of eminent domain so materially impairs the use or so damages the property of the private owner that it in effect has taken away from him or destroyed a substantial part or all of its value. The fact that he technically holds the title to the now worthless or greatly depreciated land does not deprive him of the right to compensation.

#### *(a) Loss of value*

UNITED STATES v. CAUSBY
328 U.S. 256 (1946)

OPINION BY DOUGLAS, J.

. . . The problem presented is whether respondents' property was taken within the meaning of the Fifth Amendment, by frequent and regular flights of army and navy aircraft over respondents' land at low altitudes. . . .

Respondents own 2.8 acres near an airport outside of Greensboro, North Carolina. . . . The 30 to 1 safe glide angle approved by the

Civil Aeronautics Authority passes over this property at 83 feet, which is 67 feet above the house, 63 feet above the barn and 18 feet above the highest tree. . . .

. . . Since the United States began operations in May, 1942, its four-motored heavy bombers, other planes of the heavier type, and its fighter planes have frequently passed over respondents' land and buildings in considerable number and rather close together. They come close enough at times to appear barely to miss the tops of the trees and at times so close to the tops of the trees as to blow the old leaves off. The noise is startling. And at night the glare from the planes brightly lights up the place. As a result of the noise, respondents had to give up their chicken business. . . . The result was the destruction of the use of the property as a commercial chicken farm. Respondents are frequently deprived of their sleep and the family has become nervous and frightened. Although there have been no airplane accidents on respondents' property, there have been several accidents near the airport and close to respondents' place. These are the essential facts found by the Court of Claims. On the basis of these facts, it found that respondents' property had depreciated in value. It held that the United States had taken an easement over the property on June 1, 1942, . . .

It is ancient doctrine that a common law ownership of the land extended to the periphery of the universe—*Cujus est solum ejus est usque ad coelum.* But that doctrine has no place in the modern world. The air is a public highway, as Congress has declared. Were that not true, every transcontinental flight would subject the operator to countless trespass suits. Common sense revolts at the idea. To recognize such private claims to the airspace would clog these highways, seriously interfere with their control and development in the public interest, and transfer into private ownership that to which only the public has a just claim.

. . . If, by reason of the frequency and altitude of the flights, respondents could not use this land for any purpose, their loss would be complete. It would be as complete as if the United States had entered upon the surface of the land and taken exclusive possession of it.

We agree that in those circumstances there would be a taking. Though it would be only an easement of flight which was taken, that easement, if permanent and not merely temporary, normally would be the equivalent of a fee interest. It would be a definite exercise of complete dominion and control over the surface of the land. . . . The owner's right to possess and exploit the land—that is to say, his beneficial ownership of it—would be destroyed. . . .

. . . The path of glide for airplanes might reduce a valuable factory site to grazing land, an orchard to a vegetable patch, a residential section to a wheat field. Some value would remain. But the use of airspace immediately above the land would limit the utility of the land and cause a diminution in its value. . . .

We have said that the airspace is a public highway. Yet it is obvious that if the landowner is to have full enjoyment of the land, he must have exclusive control of the immediate reaches of the enveloping atmosphere. Otherwise buildings could not be erected, trees could not be planted, and even fences could not be run. The principle is recognized when the law gives a remedy in case overhanging structures are erected on adjoining land. The landowner owns at least as much of the space above the ground as he can occupy or use in connection with the land. . . . The fact that he does not occupy it in a physical sense—by the erection of buildings and the like—is not material. As we have said, the flight of airplanes, which skim the surface but do not touch it, is as much an appropriation of the use of the land as a more conventional entry upon it. We would not doubt that if the United States erected an elevated railway over respondents' land at the precise altitude where its planes now fly, there would be a partial taking, even though none of the supports of the structure rested on the land. The reason is that there would be an intrusion so immediate and direct as to subtract from the owner's full enjoyment of the property and to limit his exploitation of it. While the owner does not in any physical manner occupy the stratum of airspace or make use of it in the conventional sense, he does use it in somewhat the same sense that space left between buildings for the purpose of light and air is used. The superadjacent airspace at this low altitude is so close to the land that continuous invasions of it affect the use of the surface of the land itself. We think that the landowner, as an incident to his ownership, has a claim to it and that invasions of it are in the same category as invasions of the surface.

### *(b) Seizure in labor dispute*

UNITED STATES v. PEWEE COAL COMPANY

341 U.S. 114 (1951)

During World War II, the President ordered the seizure of coal mines to avert a national strike. The government held and operated the mine of the Pewee Coal Co. from May 1 to October 12, 1943. After the mine was restored to the Pewee company, it brought suit in the Court of Claims to recover compensation on the theory that its property had been taken and that the measure of damages was its total operating loss for the period of the government seizure. The Court of Claims held that there was a taking but allowed damages for only $2,241.26 on the basis that that amount was the portion of the operating loss which was attributable to government operation of the mine through compliance with a wage increase order of the War Labor Board. The United States appealed.

OPINION BY BLACK, J.

. . . To convince the operators, miners and public that the United States was taking possession for the bona fide purpose of operating the mines, the Government formally and ceremoniously proclaimed that such was its intention. It required mine officials to agree to conduct operations as agents for the Government; required the American flag to be flown at every mine; required placards reading "United States Property!" to be posted on the premises; and appealed to the miners to dig coal for the United States as a public duty. Under these circumstances and in view of the other facts which were found, it should not and will not be assumed that the seizure of the mines was a mere sham or pretense to accomplish some unexpressed governmental purpose instead of being the proclaimed actual taking of possession and control. In *United States* v. *United Mine Workers,* 330 U.S. 258, there had been a government seizure of the mines under presidential and secretarial orders, which, insofar as here material, were substantially the same as those issued in the present case. We rejected the contention of the mine workers that "the Government's role in administering the bituminous coal mines [was] for the most part fictional and for the remainder nominal only." We treated that seizure as making the mines government facilities "in as complete a sense as if the Government held full title and ownership." . . . It follows almost as a matter of course from our holding in *United Mine Workers* that the Government here "took" Pewee's property and became engaged in the mining business.

. . . Having taken Pewee's property, the United States became liable under the Constitution to pay just compensation. Ordinarily, fair compensation for a temporary possession of a business enterprise is the reasonable value of the property's use. . . . But in the present case, there is no need to consider the difficult problems inherent in fixing the value of the use of a going concern because Pewee neither claimed such compensation nor proved the amount. It proceeded on the ground that the Fifth Amendment requires the United States to bear operating losses incurred during the period the Government operates private property in the name of the public without the owner's consent. We believe that this contention expresses a correct general principle which . . . supports the judgment for $2,241.26.

Like any private person or corporation, the United States normally is entitled to the profits from, and must bear the losses of, business operations which it conducts. When a private business is possessed and operated for public use, no reason appears to justify imposition of losses sustained on the person from whom the property was seized. This is conceptually distinct from the Government's obligation to pay fair compensation for property taken, although in cases raising the issue, the Government's profit and loss experience may well be one factor involved in computing reasonable compensation for a temporary taking. Of course, there might be an express or implied agreement between the parties that the Government should not receive operating profits nor bear the losses, in which event the general principle would be inapplicable. . . .

Where losses resulting from operation of property taken must be borne by the Government, it makes no difference that the losses are caused in whole or in part by compliance with administrative regulations requiring additional wages to be paid. With or without a War Labor Board order, when the Government increased the wages of the miners whom it employed, it thereby incurred the expense. Moreover, it is immaterial that governmental operation resulted in a smaller loss than Pewee would have sustained if there had been no seizure of the mines. Whatever might have been Pewee's losses had it been left free to exercise its own business judgment, the crucial fact is that the Government chose to intervene by taking possession and operating control. By doing so, it became the proprietor and, in the absence of contrary arrangements, was entitled to the benefits and subject to the liabilities which that status involves. . . .

CONCURRING OPINION BY REED, J.

I agree that in this case there was a "taking" by eminent domain that requires the Government to pay just compensation to the owner of the property for its use. However, it is impossible for me to accept the view that the "taking" in this case requires the United States to bear all operating losses during the period it controls the property without the owner's consent or agreement. Such a view would lead to disastrous consequences where properties necessarily taken for the benefit of the Nation have a long record of operating losses, *e. g.*, certain railroads, coal mines, or television broadcasting stations. The question of who bears such losses is not, I think, "conceptually distinct" from the question of just compensation. Losses or profits on the temporary operation after the declaration or judgment of taking are factors to be taken into consideration in determining what is just compensation to the owner.

This is a temporary taking. The relatively new technique of temporary taking by eminent domain is a most useful administrative device: many properties, such as laundries, or coal mines, or railroads, may be subjected to public operation only for a short time to meet war or emergency needs, and can then be returned to their owners. However, the use of the temporary taking has spawned a host of difficult problems, . . . especially in the fixing of the just compensation. Market value, despite its difficulties, provides a fairly acceptable test for just compensation when the property is taken absolutely.

. . . But in the temporary taking of operating properties, . . . market value is too uncertain a measure to have any practical significance. The rental value for a fully functioning railroad for an uncertain period is an unknowable quantity. . . . The most reasonable solution is to award compensation to the owner as determined by a court under all the circumstances of the particular case.

Temporary takings can assume various forms. There may be a taking in which the owners are ousted from operation, their business suspended, and the property devoted to new uses. . . . A second kind of taking is where, as here, the Government, for public safety or the protection of the public welfare, "takes" the property in the sense of assuming the responsibility of its direction and employment for national purposes, leaving the actual operations in the hands of its owners as government officials appointed to conduct its affairs with the assets and equipment of the controlled company. Examples are the operation of railroads, motor carriers, or coal mines. . . .

When in a temporary taking, no agreement is reached with the owners, the courts must determine what payments the Government must make. Whatever the nature of the "taking," the test should be the constitutional requirement of "just compensation." However, there is no inflexible requirement that the same incidents must be used in each application of the test.

So far as the second kind of temporary "taking" is concerned, the Government's supervision of a losing business for a temporary emergency ought not to place upon the Government the burden of the losses incurred during that supervision unless the losses were incurred by governmental acts, *e. g.*, if the business would not have been conducted at all but for the Government, or if extra losses over what would have been otherwise sustained were occasioned by Government operations. Where the owner's losses are what they would have been without the "taking," the owner has suffered no loss or damage for which compensation is due. . . . The measure of just compensation has always been the loss to the owner, not the loss or gain to the Government. . . .

### *(c) Restriction on use*

UNITED STATES v. CENTRAL EUREKA MINING COMPANY

357 U.S. 155 (1958)

In order to divert miners and mining equipment from gold mining to other more essential forms of mining, the War Production Board issued an order L-208 in 1942, classifying gold mining as nonessential and ordering all gold mines to shut down. After World War II, Central Eureka Mining Company, which was one of the gold mines closed down by the government order, brought suit in the Court of Claims against the United States to recover compensation for the loss sustained by the closing of the mine.

OPINION BY BURTON, J.

. . . It is clear from the record that the Government did not occupy, use, or in any manner, take physical possession of the gold mines or of the equipment connected with them. Cf. *United States* v. *Pewee Coal Co.*, 341 U.S. 114, 95 L.Ed. 809, 71 S.Ct. 670. All that the Government sought was the cessation of the consumption of mining equipment and manpower in the gold mines and the conservation of such equipment and manpower for more essential war uses. The Government had no need for the gold or the gold mines.

. . . Traditionally, we have treated the issue as to whether a particular governmental restriction amounted to a constitutional taking as being a question properly turning upon the particular circumstances of each case. . . . The mere fact that the regulation deprives the property owner of the most profitable use of his property is not necessarily enough to establish the owners right to compensation. . . . In the context of war, we have been reluctant to find that degree of regulation which, without saying so, requires compensation to be paid for resulting losses of income. . . . The reasons are plain. War, particularly in modern times, demands the strict regulation of nearly all resources. It makes demands which otherwise would be insufferable. But wartime economic restrictions, temporary in character, are insignificant when compared to the widespread uncompensated loss of life and freedom of action which war traditionally demands.

We do not find in the temporary restrictions here placed on the operation of gold mines a taking of private property that would justify a departure from the trend of the above decisions. The WPB here sought, by reasonable regulation, to conserve the limited supply of equipment used by the mines and it hoped that its order would divert available miners to more essential work. Both purposes were proper objectives; both matters were subject to regulation to the extent of the order. L-208 did not order any disposal of property or transfer of men. . . . The damage to the mine owners was incidental to the Government's lawful regulation of matters reasonably deemed essential to the war effort. . . .

DISSENTING OPINION BY HARLAN, J.

I dissent because I believe that the Fifth Amendment to the Constitution requires the Government to pay just compensation to the respondents for the temporary "taking" of their property accomplished by WPB Order L-208. . . .

L-208 was the only order promulgated during World War II which by its terms required a lawful and productive industry to shut down at a severe economic cost. . . . As a result of the Order the respondents were totally deprived of the beneficial use of their property. Any suggestion that the mines could have been used in such a way (that is, other than to mine gold) so as to remove them from the scope of the Order would be chimerical. Not only were the respondents completely prevented from making profitable use of their property, but the Government acquired all that it wanted from the mines—their complete immobilization and the resulting discharge of the hardrock miners. It is plain that as a practical matter the Order led to consequences no different from those that would have followed the temporary acquisition of physical possession of these mines by the United States.

In these circumstances making the respondents' right to compensation turn on whether the Government took the ceremonial step of planting the American Flag on the mining premises, cf. *United States*

v. *Pewee Coal Co.*, 341 U.S. 114, 116, 95 L.Ed. 809, 813, 71 S.Ct. 670, is surely to permit technicalities of form to dictate consequences of substance. In my judgment the present case should be viewed precisely as if the United States, in order to accomplish its purpose of freeing gold miners for essential work, had taken possession of the gold mines and allowed them to lie fallow for the duration of the war. Had the Government adopted the latter course it is hardly debatable that respondents woud have been entitled to compensation. See *United States* v. *Pewee Coal Co.*, (U.S.) supra. . . .

### *(d) Wartime destruction*

### UNITED STATES v. CALTEX

### 344 U.S. 149 (1952)

Caltex and other oil companies had terminal facilities in Manila harbor in the Philippine Islands at the outbreak of World War II. In order to prevent these facilities from falling into the control of the advancing enemy, the United States Army notified the oil companies that the facilities were requisitioned by the army and then demolished them. After the war, Caltex and the other companies sued the United States in the Court of Claims for compensation for the taking of their properties. From a decision in their favor, the United States appealed.

OPINION BY VINSON, C.J.

. . . *United States* v. *Pacific R. Co.*, 120 U.S. 227 (1887), . . . involved bridges which had been destroyed during the War Between the States by a retreating Northern Army to impede the advance of the Confederate Army. Though the point was not directly involved, the Court raised the question of whether this act constituted a compensable taking by the United States and answered it in the negative:

> "The destruction or injury of private property in battle, or in the bombardment of cities and towns, and in many other ways in the war, had to be borne by the sufferers alone as one of its consequences. Whatever would embarrass or impede the advance of the enemy, as the breaking up of roads, or the burning of bridges, or would cripple and defeat him, as destroying his means of subsistence, were lawfully ordered by the commanding general. Indeed, it was his imperative duty to direct their destruction. The necessities of the war called for and justified this. The safety of the state in such cases overrides all considerations of private loss."

. . . The common law had long recognized that in times of imminent peril—such as when fire threatened a whole community—the sovereign could, with immunity, destroy the property of a few that the property of many and the lives of many more could be saved. And what was said in the *Pacific Railroad* case was later made the basis for the holding in *Juraqua Iron Co.* v. *United States,* 212 U.S. 297 (1909), where recovery was denied to the owners of a factory which had been destroyed by American soldiers in the field in Cuba because it was thought that the structure housed the germs of a contagious disease.

Had the army hesitated, had the facilities only been destroyed after retreat, respondents would certainly have no claims to compensation. The Army did not hesitate. It is doubtful that any concern over the legal niceties of the situation entered into the decision to destroy the plants promptly while there was yet time to destroy them thoroughly. Nor do we think it legally significant that the destruction was effected prior to withdrawal. The short of the matter is that this property, due to the fortunes of war, had become a potential weapon of great significance to the invader. It was destroyed, not appropriated for subsequent use. It was destroyed that the United States might better and sooner destroy the enemy.

The terse language of the Fifth Amendment is no comprehensive promise that the United States will make whole all who suffer from every ravage and burden of war. This Court has long recognized that in wartime many losses must be attributed solely to the fortunes of war, and not to the sovereign. No rigid rules can be laid down to distinguish compensable losses from noncompensable losses. Each case must be judged on its own facts. But the general principles laid down in the *Pacific Railroad* case seem especially applicable here. Viewed realistically, then, the destruction of respondents' terminals by a trained team of engineers in the face of their impending seizure by the enemy was no different than the destruction of the bridges in the *Pacific Railroad* case. Adhering to the principles of that case, we conclude that the court below erred in holding that respondents have a constitutional right to compensation on the claims presented to this Court.

DISSENTING OPINION BY DOUGLAS, J., in which BLACK, J., concurs.

I have no doubt that the military had authority to select this particular property for destruction. But whatever the weight of authority may be, I believe that the Fifth Amendment requires compensation for the taking. The property was destroyed, not because it was in the nature of a public nuisance, but because its destruction was deemed necessary to help win the war. It was as clearly appropriated to that end as animals, food, and supplies requisitioned for the defense effort. As the Court says, the destruction of this property deprived the enemy of a valuable logistic weapon.

It seems to me that the guiding principle should be this: Whenever the Government determines that one person's property—whatever it may be—is essential to the war effort and appropriates it for the common good, the public purse, rather than the individual, should bear the loss. . . .

### § 26:4. Measurement of Damages

The property owner is not entitled to compensation for every depreciation caused to his property. No compensation need be made for what are termed indirect or consequential damages from the exercise of otherwise proper governmental powers.

When compensation is made, the body taking the land must pay the fair value of the property taken or of the amount of the depreciation determined as of the date that the taking occurred.

#### *(a) Market value*

UNITED STATES v. MILLER
317 U.S. 369 (1943)

OPINION BY ROBERTS, J.

. . .

The Fifth Amendment of the Constitution provides that private property shall not be taken for public use without just compensation. Such compensation means the full and perfect equivalent in money of the property taken. The owner is to be put in as good position pecuniarily as he would have occupied if his property had not been taken.

It is conceivable that an owner's indemnity should be measured in various ways depending upon the circumstances of each case and that no general formula should be used for the purpose. In an effort, however, to find some practical standard, the courts early adopted, and have retained, the concept of market value. The owner has been said to be entitled to the "value", the "market value", and the "fair market value" of what is taken. The term "fair" hardly adds anything to the phrase "market value", which denotes what "it fairly may be believed that a purchaser in fair market conditions would have given", or, more concisely, "market value fairly determined". . . . Where, for any reason, property has no market, resort must be had to other data to ascertain its value; and, even in the ordinary case, assessment of market value involves the use of assumptions, which make it unlikely that the appraisal will reflect true value with nicety. It is usually said that market value is what a willing buyer would pay in cash to a willing seller. Where the property taken, and that in its vicinity, has not in fact been sold within recent times, or in significant amounts, the application of this concept involves, at best, a guess by informed persons.

Again, strict adherence to the criterion of market value may involve inclusion of elements which, though they affect such value, must in fairness be eliminated in a condemnation case, as where the formula is attempted to be applied as between an owner who may not want to part with his land because of its special adaptability to his own use, and a taker who needs the land because of its peculiar fitness for the taker's purposes. These elements must be disregarded by the fact finding body in arriving at "fair" market value.

Since the owner is to receive no more than indemnity for his loss, his award cannot be enhanced by any gain to the taker. Thus although the market value of the property is to be fixed with due consideration of all its available uses, its special value to the condemnor as distinguished from others who may or may not possess the power to condemn, must be excluded as an element of market value. . . .

There is, however, another possible element of market value, which is the bone of contention here. Should the owner have the benefit of any increment of value added to the property taken by the action of the public authority in previously condemning adjacent lands? If so, were the lands in question so situate as to entitle respondents to the benefit of this increment?

Courts have had to adopt working rules in order to do substantial justice in eminent domain proceedings. One of these is that a parcel of land which has been used and treated as an entity shall be so considered in assessing compensation for the taking of part or all of it.

This has begotten subsidiary rules. If only a portion of a single tract is taken the owner's compensation for that taking includes any element of value arising out of the relation of the part taken to the entire tract. Such damage is often, though somewhat loosely, spoken of as severance damage. On the other hand, if the taking has in fact benefited the remainder the benefit may be set off against the value of the land taken.

As respects other property of the owner consisting of separate tracts adjoining that affected by the taking, the Constitution has never been construed as requiring payment of consequential damages; and unless the legislature so provides, as it may, benefits are not assessed against such neighboring tracts for increase in their value.

If a distinct tract is condemned, in whole or in part, other lands in the neighborhood may increase in market value due to the proximity of the public improvement erected on the land taken. Should the Government, at a later date, determine to take these other lands, it must pay their market value as enhanced by this factor of proximity. If, however, the public project from the beginning included the taking of certain tracts but only one of them is taken in the first instance, the owner of the other tracts should not be allowed an increased value for his lands which are ultimately to be taken any more than the owner of the tract first condemned is entitled to be allowed an increased market value because adjacent lands not immediately taken increased in value due to the projected improvement.

The question then is whether the respondents' lands were probably within the scope of the project from the time the Government was committed to it. If they were not, but were merely adjacent lands, the subsequent enlargement of the project to include them ought not to deprive the respondents of the value added in the meantime by the proximity of the improvement. If, on the other hand, they were, the Government ought not to pay any increase in value arising from the known fact that the lands probably would be condemned. The owners ought not to gain by speculating on probable increase in value due to the Government's activities.

## Questions for Discussion

1. What is the importance of "public purpose" or "public use" in connection with eminent domain?

2. When a law is adopted prohibiting the manufacture of intoxicating liquor, is the owner of the brewery entitled to compensation on the grounds that the government has taken his property from him when as a practical matter he cannot use the building for any other purpose?

3. Is the brewery case to be classified the same as the gold mine in the *Eureka* case?

4. Give six illustrations of purposes for which land may be taken by eminent domain.

5. Compare the concept of "public purpose" in eminent domain, "public purpose" in government spending, and "business affected with a public interest" in the regulation of business. Do these three concepts have the same meaning? Have they changed meaning during the past century?

6. Can the national power of eminent domain be exercised to further any purpose for which money can be spent?

7. The Congress of the United States grants a charter to a new transcontinental railroad corporation and gives it authority to take private property by eminent domain for the purpose of building its roadbed and operating facilities. The corporation proceeds to take property of X by eminent domain. X seeks an injunction on the ground that the statute is unconstitutional because:

(a) Congress does not have the authority to charter a corporation.
(b) Congress does not have authority to charter a railroad corporation.
(c) Congress cannot authorize a private corporation to exercise the powers of eminent domain.
(d) The condemning of land for a privately owned railroad is not the taking of land for a public purpose.

Decide and discuss the merits of each of these contentions.

8. What are the arguments for and against compensation in the *Caltex* case?

9. X owns land in Utah. There is no water supply on his land. The nearest water supply is a river one-half mile away. To reach the river it is necessary to cross the land belonging to Z. A statute of Utah provides that a land-locked property owner may construct an irrigation ditch across neighboring land and that this may be done by exercising the power of eminent domain. When X proceeds to construct a ditch on Z's land, Z objects, refuses to accept compensation for such interference with his land, and claims that the statute is unconstitutional since the ditch would benefit X alone and is therefore not a public purpose for which eminent domain may be exercised. Decide. *Himonas* v. *Denver & R. G. W. R.*, 179 F.2d 171 (CCA 10th 1949).

10. What kind of property is subject to eminent domain? Can the owner of property block the exercise of eminent domain by placing his property in trust or by making a contract to sell it to another person?

11. The state of N erects a public electric power plant. The dam of the plant causes water to back up and flood neighboring farm land. The owners demand compensation for their land. The state refuses to pay the owners of the land on the ground that they still own their land and that the state has not taken it from them and does not receive any benefit from it. Decide.

12. (a) How is compensation in eminent domain determined? (b) What difference does it make if the government of the United States in exercising the power of eminent domain: (1) takes the earth beneath the surface of the ground without affecting the surface or the use of the surface; (2) takes the surface of the land; (3) interferes with the air space immediately above the land? Discuss.

13. (a) Why is market value selected as the measure of damages for property taken by eminent domain? (b) How is market value ordinarily determined? (c) How is market value determined for property that has no market?

14. What is the difference between true value and market value?

15. What is the measure of damages when only part of the land is taken?

16. A state highway commission exercised its power to take land by eminent domain. It took land owned by M. There were buildings on the land that could be removed and placed on other land owned by M which was not affected by the taking by eminent domain. The commission made an award of eminent domain compensation to M in an amount equal to the value of the land without buildings plus the cost to M of moving the existing buildings to the other land. M objects to this standard of damages. Decide. *Proctor* v. *State Highway & Public Works Commission,* 230 N.C. 687, 55 S.E.2d 479 (1949).

17. With respect to condemnation for redevelopment, (a) can an entire area be taken on the basis that it is a blighted area? (b) can a property owner within an area which is predominantly blighted object to the condemnation of his property on the ground that it is in excellent condition?

18. When land is taken for redevelopment, will the court review (a) the necessity for taking the particular area that has been taken? (b) the nature of the interest taken by the condemning body?

19. Is there a taking within the eminent domain concept when the government takes a steel mill (a) to keep it permanently and use it as a steel mill? (b) to keep it for the duration of a war and use it as a steel mill? (c) to keep it temporarily until a labor dispute is settled and to continue it in operation as a steel mill during that period?

20. In the *Pewee* case the court stressed that the government actually took possession of the mine and was operating it. Does this mean that everyone in management, in the office, and in the mines were government employees or soldiers who displaced the former private workers?

21. What do you think of the statement in the *Pewee* case that the government is entitled to the profits of a plant seized during a labor dispute?

22. Appraise the dissenting opinion of J. Harlan, in the *Pewee* case.

# Chapter 27

## GOVERNMENT OWNERSHIP OF BUSINESS



### § 27:1. The Background

In a sense, government ownership of what would ordinarily be deemed a private business represents the ultimate in the regulation of private business. Government ownership may affect private business in one of three different ways. The operation of business by the government may remove a potential customer from other private enterprises. For example, the United States Government maintains its own printing office, which deprives private printing houses of a very large customer. Government ownership may go a step further and sell goods or services to the public in competition with private enterprises that furnish the same goods or services to the public. This can be illustrated by the Tennessee Valley Authority by which the United States Government sells electrical power to public and private consumers in competition with private electrical power plants. The final stage of government ownership is where the government maintains a monopoly of a particular type of enterprise so that the private enterpriser cannot enter that field even if he is willing to face the competition of the government-operated business. This type of total absorption by the government of a field of enterprise is more characteristic of nationalization or socialization programs than it has been of government ownership of business in the United States to date.

It is significant to note that, in the instances in which government in the United States has embarked upon government ownership, the move has rarely been influenced by a doctrine of state socialization. Three other factors have loomed more important in bringing government into the operation of business.

The first factor that has always been significant is that government is able to operate a business which private industry could not operate at a profit. This does not mean that governmental operation is more efficient than private enterprise, but only that private enterprise in the last analysis cannot exist unless it makes a profit, whereas government activity does not have to meet this standard. If the people of the nation or a state wish their government to offer a particular service, that service can be rendered at a loss and the deficit can be made up from public funds. The United States Postal System illustrates this situation, for the mail traffic in certain areas is so small that a private enterprise would not wish to furnish service to those areas.

The second significant factor in government ownership is that reform movements, convinced rightly or wrongly that certain evils in private management cannot be eliminated, have taken the business away from private hands and placed it under the government. This has been typical of many of the state moves to acquire and run industry.

The third factor in government operation of business has been the inability of government to transfer to private ownership enterprises entered into during times of war or emergency. The federal government owns and operates the Inland Waterways Corporation [1] today because it has been unable to find a private purchaser for the system. Rather than permit the large investment of the federal government to be sacrificed, the government continues in the inland waterways transportation business. The same is true of the TVA, which began in 1917 as a plant for the generation of electricity for use in the production of nitrates for explosives. The actual working facilities were not completed until 1926. Partly because there was no feasible way of disposing of this large investment, the federal government began active development and operation of the TVA as a hydro-electric plant. In this connection it should be noted, however, that the advent of the New Deal was responsible to a large degree for expanding the TVA as a desirable asset rather than regarding it as a liability to be scrapped as soon as possible.

---

[1] See § 10:7.

Every proposal for government ownership naturally brings forth the protests of those who will be adversely affected by the activity or the competition of the government in addition to those who object as a sincere matter of principle. A government caring for the welfare of all its peoples cannot lightly make a change that will have the effect of depriving a substantial segment of society of its existing means of obtaining a livelihood or that will substantially depreciate the value of its investment. The economic misfortune of any segment of society soon is shared by other segments as the result of the reduced purchasing power of the group first adversely affected. A government therefore must proceed carefully so that the sum of government ownership is a benefit to the public.

On behalf of public ownership of industry, it is claimed that it eliminates the need for regulation of private industry by government agencies. The difficulties found in regulation of business, particularly in the field of rate-making for utilities, are certainly such that it is desirable to avoid them if possible. It is answered, however, that the happy solution of avoiding them by government ownership of the business is not as happy as it first seems, for the net result, it is claimed, is a lowered efficiency and a lowered productivity because of a lower caliber of leadership, divided responsibility, and "red tape."

It is claimed that government ownership would make it safe to permit extensive integration of industry with resultant large-scale economies that would benefit the public. Waste in advertising and in duplication of plant facilities and railroads are pointed out as cost items of a system of free enterprise that would be eliminated by government ownership. This is answered by the contention that service to the public would in fact deteriorate if there were no longer the incentive between competing, although duplicating, enterprisers.

It is claimed that government-owned plants could be financed at a lower interest rate because of the lower risk that results from the backing of the government. This, however, might have the dangerous effect of encouraging unhealthy overexpansion of government-owned enterprise.

It is urged that government ownership of industry would eliminate much of the present labor-management conflict. It is doubtful whether labor is desirous of this possible solution for the conflict. The right of government employees to strike has been generally denied and in recent years has been expressly prohibited. The Taft-

Hartley Amendment of 1947 to the Wagner Labor Relations Act provides that a striking federal employee shall be discharged, shall lose his civil service status, if any, and may not be rehired by the government for a period of three years. It is likely that organized labor would prefer to retain its right to wage economic war.

It is urged that government ownership would make the goal of industry the greatest service for the greatest number rather than profit. This would be offset by the danger that operation of business at a loss in order to give greater services would merely mean the imposing of a greater tax burden on the rest of the community and on the remaining private businesses. In addition there is the great danger that the government industries would have their policies affected by the whims and accidents of political fortune.

### § 27:2. The Tennessee Valley Authority

Government ownership has been carried further by the states than by the national government, although the activities of the latter have served to draw more attention and comment. Different states or political subdivisions have at various times maintained public-owned fuel yards, utilities, coal mines, grain elevators, banks, and housing projects. Examples of United States Government ownership of business are the United States Government Printing Office, the United States Post Office, the Inland Waterways Corporation, the Panama Canal Railroad, and the Tennessee Valley Authority.

The TVA is of particular interest in connection with these problems because of the extent and the breadth of its operation. As previously stated, it began its career as a nitrate production plant to aid in World War I and it was not until the New Deal came into power that the project was broadened into a plan for the development of the Tennessee Valley watershed. To carry out this plan, a corporation was created of which the United States Government is the sole stockholder. This corporation, the Tennessee Valley Authority, is managed by three directors who are appointed by the President of the United States. The project has as its purposes the control of floods along the Tennessee Valley with the accompanying conservation and elimination of soil erosion; the improvement of water transportation by increasing the area of navigability of the Tennessee river; the manufacture and sale of fixed nitrogen for fertilizer use; and the production of electrical power in surplus quantities for sale to political subdivisions, corporations, and individuals.

The express plan as set forth in the statute creating the TVA was to further the domestic and agricultural use of electricity by furnishing power to such consumers at the lowest possible rates. In order to insure that TVA-produced electricity would find its way to the consumers at a low rate, TVA was given authority to require that any business or enterprise purchasing electrical power from it should not charge more than stated maximum prices upon making a resale of that power to ultimate consumers.

It was also an objective of President Roosevelt, although not expressly stated in the statute, that the operations at TVA would show reasonable costs for producing electricity and that TVA operations could therefore serve as a yardstick in determining what rates should be allowed by utilities commissions for private electrical energy producers.

As a result of TVA operation, material advance has been made in the control of floods in the Tennessee Valley and a real service has been done to the farms and thus indirectly to the nation. The bulk of goods transported by water and the length of navigable waterways in the valley have also increased. The consumption of electrical power in the area has greatly increased, and the expansion in the number and bulk of users for the Tennessee Valley has been almost double the expansion for the rest of the country. Comparatively little development has been made along the lines of selling fixed nitrates for fertilizer.

It is difficult to assess the net benefit to the area and the nation of the TVA. Water transportation has been increased, but this may perhaps mean that to that extent transportation by other means has been injured. This would be true unless it could be shown that the area has produced such an additional bulk of goods that the increase in transportation was not at the expense of other existing means. It is claimed that private electrical power companies have been injured by the government competition. This would certainly appear to be a reasonable claim, as the government electrical output has been sold at a substantially lower figure than that of private enterprise. The difficulty with the contention of private industry in this respect is that it assumes that, had it not been for the government's offering the electricity at a lower price, the government's customers would have bought the electricity from the private enterprise at the higher price. The fact that the new government users had not been purchasing electricity from the private enterprisers before TVA began its operation, or if they had, had been purchasing at much lower consumption levels, suggests that the government consumers would not have patronized private enterprise to any greater extent. If this is true, government industry does not necessarily compete with private industry because, though the same service or commodity is being sold, it is being sold at different economic levels that would not mix if left to themselves. Of course this is merely a generalization and it is undoubtedly true that many of the persons now using TVA electricity would in time have come to use the electricity furnished by private enterprise, although it seems clear that the rate at which they would have turned over to privately produced electricity would have been much slower because of its greater cost.

The value of TVA as a yardstick in determining reasonable production costs has merely led to another debate. This has been due to the fact that TVA is not limited merely to the production of electrical energy but, as indicated above, has a number of different activities. In order to determine its cost of producing electrical energy, it is necessary to place a valuation on the property that it has devoted to that purpose. At this point two unknown factors enter the equation because it is difficult if not impossible to determine just how much of the TVA plant should be allocated to electrical energy production and what part should be regarded as devoted to flood control, conservation, improvement of navigation, and other activities engaged in by TVA. Any figure would be more or less an arbitrary decision or reasonable guess; yet a difference of 5 or 10 per cent in the guess or the allocation could make a very substantial difference in determining what the reasonable rate or cost would be. In addition to this question of allocation, there is also the question of placing a value on what has been allocated, and here again we are faced with the difficulty of valuing property for rate-making purposes.

Because of these uncertainties in the calculation, there is ample ground on which critics of TVA can base the claim that it is not producing electrical energy at a lower-than-private cost and still making a profit. They can claim as they have done that, if a different allocation and a different valuation were placed upon the property used for the purpose of making electrical energy, it would really be shown that the production of electricity was costing the government a greater amount and that, unless the rates were raised so that they were comparable to those charged by private enterprise, TVA would operate at a loss. If this contention is correct, it means that the rates charged by private enterprises are reasonable and also means that the government in furnishing electricity at a lower rate is not obtaining an economic benefit but is merely furnishing services at a loss that is made up by the general body of taxpayers.

In view of the fact that so many uncertainties and so many points of expert opinion are involved, it is impossible for the private citizen to determine where lies the truth.

### § 27:3. Constitutionality of Government Ownership

Speaking generally, there is no constitutional barrier against government ownership and operation of business. If the government is building a new plant or buying an existing plant, the question of constitutionality is merely one of the spending power. As long as the purpose of the expenditure is for a public purpose or for the general welfare, the expenditure will be held valid. While it has always been readily assumed that there were certain purposes that were not public or not for the general welfare which were clearly distinguished from those that were public or for the general welfare, it would seem that it is increasingly difficult to prohibit a government from entering into any particular business on the ground that to do so is not in furtherance of a public purpose or does not advance the general welfare. Manifestly this represents a change in our philosophy of government and economics, but as Justice Holmes repeatedly complained, the Constitution does not incorporate and preserve any particular theory of economics.

As stated by the Supreme Court in *Puget Sound Power & Light Company* v. *Seattle*, 291 U.S. 619 (1934), "the decisions of this Court leave no doubt that a state may, in the public interest, constitutionally engage in a business commonly carried on by private enterprise, levy a tax to support it . . . and compete with private interests engaged in a like activity." The private enterprise that is faced with government competition cannot claim exemption from such taxation. As stated by the Court, it cannot be claimed that the public body "upon entering the business forfeited its power to tax any competitor."

In a world periodically the subject of wars and war scares, it could be urged that the government should own and operate the essential industries which produce for war in order to insure that the government will have a large supply of needed war materials at a low cost. The extension made to the war power repels any argument that such a program could not be followed in what would be considered normal peace time. While technically the war power is possessed only by the national government, it is likely that the police power of the states to advance the general welfare would be regarded as authorizing action by states designed to further defense.

If the question is not one of government beginning a new factory or a new plant but of acquiring the ownership of an existing plant or industry, the power of eminent domain will come into play if the property is not voluntarily sold to the government. If the enterprise is deemed a purpose sufficiently public to warrant the expenditure of tax money for its operation, then it will also be held to be sufficiently public to justify its being taken from the private ownership by use of the power of eminent domain. When this is done, however, the government, whether state or national, must make reasonable compensation to the owners for the value of the property taken. Because of this constitutional restriction, it is impossible in the United States for government to expropriate private enterprise. The government cannot take private industry away from its owners without making compensation for such taking.

In the case of the United States, it must also be remembered that, as a sovereign nation, it may acquire land or any other property by any means. It may do so by war, purchase, treaty, discovery and occupation, or eminent domain. Congress is authorized to "dispose of and make all needful rules and regulations respecting the territory or other property belonging to the United States."

This "property" power embraces the product of industrial activity. The power to dispose of it permits Congress to compete with private enterprise and to dispose of its product at any price it chooses, without regard to whether the price is below cost or not. No constitutional privilege of the private enterpriser is violated by the fact that he is underbid by the government.

### *(a) Tennessee Valley Authority*

ASHWANDER v. TVA

297 U.S. 288 (1936)

OPINION BY HUGHES, C. J.

. . . The Tennessee Valley Authority, . . . entered into a contract with the Alabama Power Company, providing (1) for the purchase by the Authority from the Power Company of certain transmission lines, substations, and auxiliary properties for $1,000,000; (2) for the purchase by the Authority from the Power Company of certain real property for $150,000; (3) for an interchange of hydroelectric energy, and, in addition, for the sale by the Authority to the Power Company of its "surplus power," on stated terms; and (4) for mutual restrictions as to the areas to be served in the sale of power. . . .

The Alabama Power Company is a corporation organized under the laws of Alabama, and is engaged in the generation of electric energy and its distribution generally throughout that state, its lines reaching 66 counties. The transmission lines to be purchased by the Authority extend from Wilson Dam, at the Muscle Shoals plant owned by the United States on the Tennessee river in northern Alabama, into seven counties in that state, within a radius of about 50 miles. These lines serve a population of approximately 190,000, including about 10,000 individual customers, or about one-tenth of the total number served directly by the Power Company. The real property to be acquired by the Authority (apart from the transmission lines above mentioned and related properties) is adjacent to the area known as the "Joe Wheeler dam site," upon which the Authority is constructing the Wheeler Dam.

The contract . . . also provided for co-operation between the Alabama Power Company and the Electric Home & Farm Authority, Inc., a subsidiary of the Tennessee Valley Authority, to promote the sale of electrical appliances. . . . The Congress may not, "under the pretext of executing its powers, pass laws for the accomplishment of objects not intrusted to the government." . . . The government's argument recognizes this essential limitation. The government's contention is that the Wilson Dam was constructed, and the power plant connected with it was installed, in the exercise by the Congress of its war and commerce powers; that is, for the purposes of national defense and the improvement of navigation.

Wilson Dam . . . was begun in 1917 and completed in 1926. Authority for its construction is found in § 124 of the National Defense Act of June 3, 1916. . . . It authorized the President . . . "to construct, maintain, and operate" on any such site "dams, locks, improvements to navigation, power houses, and other plants and equipment or other means than water power as in his judgment is the best and cheapest, necessary or convenient for the generation of electrical or other power and for the production of nitrates or other products needed for munitions of war and useful in the manufacture of fertilizers and other useful products." The President was authorized to lease or acquire by condemnation or otherwise such lands as might be necessary and there was further provision that "the products of such plants shall be used by the President for military and naval purposes to the extent that he may deem necessary, and any surplus which he shall determine is not required shall be sold and disposed of by him under such regulations as he may prescribe." . . .

We may take judicial notice of the international situation at the time the act of 1916 was passed, and it cannot be successfully disputed that the Wilson Dam and its auxiliary plants, including the hydroelectric power plant, are, and were intended to be, adapted to the purposes of national defense. While the District Court found that there is no intention to use the nitrate plants or the hydroelectric units installed at Wilson Dam for the production of war materials in time of peace, "the maintenance of said properties in operating condition and the assurance of an abundant supply of electric energy in the event of war, constitute national defense assets." This finding has ample support.

The act of 1916 also had in view "improvements to navigation." Commerce includes navigation. "All America understands, and has uniformly understood," said Chief Justice Marshall in *Gibbons* v. *Ogden*, . . ."the word 'commerce,' to comprehend navigation." The power to regulate interstate commerce embraces the power to keep the navigable rivers of the United States free from obstructions to navigation and to remove such obstructions when they exist. "For these purposes," said the Court in *Gilman* v. *Philadelphia*, . . . "Congress possesses all the powers which existed in the States before the adoption of the national Constitution, and which have always existed in the Parliament in England." . . .

The Tennessee river is a navigable stream, although there are obstructions at various points because of shoals, reefs, and rapids. The improvement of navigation on this river has been a matter of national concern for over a century. Recommendation that provision be made for navigation around Muscle Shoals was made by the Secretary of War, John C. Calhoun, in his report transmitted to the Congress by President Monroe in 1824, and, from 1852, the Congress has repeatedly authorized projects to develop navigation on that and other portions of the river, both by open channel improvements and by canalization. The Wilson Dam project, adopted in 1918, gave a nine-foot slack water development, for fifteen miles above Florence, over the Muscle Shoals rapids, and, as the District Court found, "flooded out the then existing canal and locks which were inadequate." The District Court also found that a "high dam of this type was the only feasible means of eliminating this most serious obstruction to navigation." By the act of 1930, after a protracted study by the Corps of Engineers of the United States Army, the Congress adopted a project for a permanent improvement of the main stream "for a navigable depth of nine feet."

While, in its present condition, the Tennessee river is not adequately improved for commercial navigation, and traffic is small, we are not at liberty to conclude either that the river is not susceptible of development as an important waterway, or that Congress has not undertaken that development, or that the construction of the Wilson Dam was not an appropriate means to accomplish a legitimate end.

The Wilson Dam and its power plant must be taken to have been constructed in the exercise of the constitutional functions of the federal government.

. . . The government acquired full title to the dam site, with all riparian rights. The power of falling water was an inevitable incident of the construction of the dam. That water power came into the exclusive control of the federal government. The mechanical energy was convertible into electric energy, and the water power, the right to convert it into electric energy, and the electric energy thus produced constitute property belonging to the United States. . . .

Authority to dispose of property constitutionally acquired by the United States is expressly granted to the Congress by § 3 of article IV of the Constitution. This section provides:

"The Congress shall have Power to dispose of and make all needful Rules and Regulations respecting the Territory or other Property belonging to the United States; and nothing in this Constitution shall be so construed as to Prejudice any Claims of the United States, or of any particular State."

To the extent that the power of disposition is thus expressly conferred, it is manifest that the Tenth Amendment is not applicable. And the Ninth Amendment . . . in insuring the maintenance of the rights retained by the people does not withdraw the rights which are expressly granted to the Federal Government. The question is as to the scope of the grant and whether there are inherent limitations which render invalid the disposition of property with which we are now concerned.

. . . The argument is stressed that, assuming that electrical energy generated at the dam belongs to the United States, the Congress has authority to dispose of this energy only to the extent that it is a surplus necessarily created in the course of making munitions of war or operating the works for navigation purposes; that is, that the remainder of the available energy must be lost or go to waste. We find nothing in the Constitution which imposes such a limitation. It is not to be deduced from the mere fact that the electrical energy is only potentially available until the generators are operated. The government has no less right to the energy thus available by letting the water course over its turbines than it has to use the appropriate process to reduce to possession other property within its control, as, for example, oil which it may recover from a pool beneath its land, and which is reduced to possession by boring oil wells and otherwise might escape its grasp. . . . And it would hardly be contended that, when the government reserves coal on its lands, it can mine and dispose of it only for the purpose of heating public buildings or for other governmental operations. . . . Or that when the government extracts the oil it has reserved, it has no constitutional power to sell it. Our decisions recognize no such restriction . . . the United States owns the coal, or the silver, or the lead, or the oil, it obtains from its lands, and it lies in the discretion of Congress, acting in the public interest, to determine of how much of the property it shall dispose.

We think the same principle is applicable to electrical energy. . . . Suppose for example, that in the erection of a dam for the improvement of navigation, it became necessary to destroy a dam and power plant which had previously been erected by a private corporation engaged in the generation and distribution of energy . . . . Would anyone say that, because the United States had built its own dam and plant in the exercise of its constitutional functions . . . no power could be supplied to communities and enterprises dependent on it . . . because . . . the supply to the communities and enterprises . . . must be limited to the slender amount of surplus unavoidably involved in the operation of the navigation works? . . .

. . . The constitutional provision is silent as to the method of disposing of property belonging to the United States. That method, of course, must be an appropriate means of disposition according to the nature of the property, it must be one adopted in the public interest as distinguished from private or personal ends, and we may assume that it must be consistent with the foundation principles of our dual system of government and must not be contrived to govern the concerns reserved to the states. . . .

The transmission lines which the Authority undertakes to purchase from the Power company lead from the Wilson dam to a large area within about 50 miles of the dam. . . . They furnish a method of reaching a market. The alternative method is to sell the surplus energy at the dam, and the market there appears to be limited to one purchaser. . . . We know of no constitutional ground upon which the federal government can be denied the right to seek a wider market. . . .

. . . The argument is earnestly presented that the government by virtue of its ownership of the dam and power plant could not establish a steel mill and make and sell steel products, or a factory to manufacture clothing or shoes for the public, and thus attempt to make its ownership of energy, generated at its dam, a means of carrying on competitive commercial enterprises, and thus drawing to the federal government the conduct and management of business having no relation to the purposes for which the federal government was established. . . . The government is not using . . . the energy generated at the dam to manufacture commodities of any sort for the public. The government is disposing of the energy itself which simply is the mechanical energy, incidental to falling water at the dam, converted into the electrical energy which is susceptible of transmission. The question here is simply as to the acquisition of the transmission lines as a facility for the disposal of that energy. . . .

### § 27:4. Scope of the TVA Doctrine

There would seem to be no effective limitation on the power of the government to dispose of its property on any terms it sees fit. It may sell at any price it desires without regard to the production cost or to the cost or sale price of like property by private enterprise. It may lease its property or give it away.

While two limitations were recognized in the *TVA* case, these limitations appear ineffective. The case stated that the disposition must be made to further public interest rather than private interest. This limitation is not any clearer in connection with the disposition of property of the government than it is in the case of the disposition of money by means of the spending power. It appears so broad as to be no limitation at all.

The Court also stated that the disposition must be "consistent" with the basic principles of "our dual system of government." This is one of the last times for this doctrine of "dual federalism" to make its appearance. By this is meant the peculiar interpretation found in several of the Supreme Court decisions that, not only must a particular power be delegated to Congress, but in addition the exercise of that power must not be in derogation of rights reserved to the states by the Tenth Amendment. This double barrier concept of the Tenth Amendment has been abandoned, and it is now recognized that the Tenth Amendment merely affirms what necessarily follows from the fact that Congress can only exercise those powers which have been delegated to it—of necessity all others remain with the states from which the national government derived its powers. That the Tenth Amendment has been violated follows automatically from the conclusion that a power has not been given Congress. The latter question is not affected by the consideration that the power is reserved to the states if not granted to Congress. This second limitation is accordingly meaningless today.

A third limitation may be implied from the *TVA* opinion; namely, that the government cannot acquire the property solely for the purpose of disposing of it. It is unlikely that the government would at any time set itself up as a middleman to purchase goods from private sources with the object of resale to the public, although even this could no doubt be sustained under the commerce power if evils in marketing and distribution existed that could be eliminated by government acting as the middleman. Sales of property will in all likelihood result, with the exception of such incidental matters as the sale of war surplus, either from the government's purchasing surplus goods, such as farm goods, as a means of maintaining prices, or from the government's establishing publicly owned essential industries and then selling the surplus products, as in the TVA. Neither of these most likely forms of competition with private enterprise would be condemned by the third limitation above stated.

In view of the later interpretations of the commerce power, there would be seem to be little significance today in the statement by the Court in the *TVA* case that "the government is not using the water power at the Wilson Dam to establish any industry or business. It is not using the energy generated at the dam to manufacture commodities of any sort for the public. . . ." Economically there is little merit to a distinction between the sale of electricity or the sale of loaves of bread at a cheaper rate than supplied by private enterprise. From the standpoint of private enterprise the nature and effect of the competition is the same. If it should be held that the production of bread was a matter vital to the national health and security or a desirable way of disposing of a surplus wheat crop, the suggested limitation is not likely to be controlling.

While there is a distinction between the *TVA* case and those just posed, the limitation is one that may be readily avoided. There would be few enterprises of which the government could not take some part of the output and then have on its hands a surplus that it could sell under the authority of the *TVA* decision. This has added significance when it is realized that many modern industrial plants must be run at a certain production level in order to achieve efficiency of operation. It may very well be that in slack periods the government consumption would not consume the entire output when production is maintained at the level of greatest efficiency. It would not necessarily follow that the government would be required to curtail and thus decrease the efficiency of production. There is apparently no limitation that would prevent it from making the most efficient use of the taxpayer's money by maintaining the higher level of production and then selling the surplus under the authority of the *TVA* case.

The *TVA* decision attains added significance when considered in the light of the Atomic Energy Control Act of 1946. Under this law, the federal government has nationalized all fissionable materials and has the monopoly of their use for peace-time productive purposes as well as military purposes. If the full economic potential of atomic energy can be realized, it would be possible for all the industries and all the homes in the United States to pipe in all their heat, power, and light from one gigantic government atomic energy plant. Private enterprise in the traditional types of heat, power, and light could not compete with such an enterprise.

### § 27:5. Intergovernmental Relations

To what extent is a government-owned enterprise to be treated by other governments as being a government activity or a private enterprise? Where the enterprise is one that is ordinarily conducted by private enterprise and as such is subject to a federal tax, it is clear that the enterprise will remain subject to that tax without regard to the fact of its public ownership. The converse should also be true, that a federal enterprise is subject to a local tax that would be imposed if the federal activity were privately operated.

As regards governmental regulations, an enterprise owned by a state or a political subdivision must conform to the same federal regulations as though it were privately owned where it is a type of enterprise that is ordinarily privately owned. It would seem that the converse is also true for federal-owned enterprise, although if the local regulation interferes with the federal program, the doctrine of federal supremacy will prevail over the local regulation.

The experience with the TVA has not given a definitive answer to the questions of tax liability and governmental regulation. The question of tax liability has been avoided by the practice of the TVA of voluntarily paying such local taxes as it would be required to pay if it were privately owned. In addition to avoiding the question of constitutionality of a state tax on a federally owned enterprise, this policy also avoids the objection that TVA operations cannot be used as a yardstick because of a favored tax status.

Local utility commissions have already asserted jurisdiction over contracts made by the TVA. Just how far this jurisdiction will extend and to what extent state regulation will be permitted by the Court to conflict with the federal objectives of the TVA project remain for future determination.

### *(a) Applicability of federal statute*

CALIFORNIA v. TAYLOR

353 U.S. 553 (1957)

California owns the Belt Railroad that serves San Francisco Harbor and, through connections with other lines, handles interstate traffic. It is a common carrier and files tariffs with the Interstate Commerce Commission. A collective bargaining agreement was entered into between the state and the employees of the Belt Railroad. A number of employees later presented claims arising under the agreement to the National Railroad Adjustment Board. The Board refused to take jurisdiction of the matter on the theory that the Railway Labor Act did not apply to a state-owned railroad. The employees then brought an action against the Board to compel it to exercise jurisdiction.

OPINION BY BURTON, J.

. . . If the Railway Labor Act applies to the Belt Railroad, then the carrier's employees can invoke its machinery established for adjustment of labor controversies, and the National Railway Adjustment Board has jurisdiction over respondents' claims. . . .

Under the Railway Labor Act, not only would the employees of the Belt Railroad have a federally protected right to bargain collectively with their employer, but the terms of the collective-bargaining agreement that they have negotiated with the Belt Railroad would take precedence over conflicting provisions of . . . state . . . laws. . . .

We turn now to the applicability of the Railway Labor Act to the Belt Railroad. Section 1, First, of that Act defines generally the carriers to which it applies as "*any* carrier by railroad, subject to the Interstate Commerce Act. . . ." . . . The Interstate Commerce Act, 24 Stat. 379, as amended, 49 U. S. C. § 1(1), applies to all common carriers by railroad engaged in interstate transportation. The Belt Railroad concededly is a common carrier engaged in interstate transportation. It files its tariffs with the Interstate Commerce Commission, and the Commission has treated it and other state-owned interstate rail carriers as subject to its jurisdiction. . . . The fact that Congress chose to phrase the coverage of the Act in all-embracing terms indicates that state railroads were included within it. In fact, the consistent congressional pattern in railway legislation which preceded the Railway Labor Act was to employ all-inclusive language of coverage with no suggestion that state-owned railroads were not included. . . .

The fact that the Act's application will supersede state civil service laws which conflict with its policy of promoting collective bargaining does not detract from the conclusion that Congress intended it to apply to any common carrier by railroad engaged in interstate transportation, whether or not owned or operated by a State. The principal unions in the railroad industry are national in scope, and their officials are intimately acquainted with the problems, traditions and conditions of the railroad industry. Bargaining collectively with these officials has often taken on a national flavor, and agreements are uniformly negotiated for an entire railroad system. "[B]reakdowns in collective bargaining will typically affect a region or the entire nation." . . . It is by no means unreasonable to assume that Congress, aware of these characteristics of labor relations in the interconnected system which comprises our national railroad industry, intended that collective bargaining, as fostered and protected by the Railway Labor Act, should apply to all railroads. Congress no doubt concluded that a uniform method of dealing with the labor problems of the railroad industry would tend to eliminate inequities, and would promote a desirable mobility within the railroad labor force.

Finally, the State suggests that Congress has no constitutional power to interfere with the "sovereign right" of a State to control its employment relationships on a state-owned railroad engaged in interstate commerce. In *United States* v. *California* [297 U.S. 175], this Court said that the State, although acting in its sovereign capacity in operating this Belt Railroad, necessarily so acted "in subordination to the power to regulate interstate commerce, which has been granted specifically to the national government. . . . California, by engaging in interstate commerce by rail, has subjected itself to the commerce power, and is liable for a violation of the Safety Appliance Act, as are other carriers. . . ." That principle is no less applicable here. If California, by engaging in interstate commerce by rail, subjects itself to the commerce power so that Congress can make it conform to federal safety requirements, it also has subjected itself to that power so that Congress can regulate its employment relationships. . . .

### Questions for Discussion

1. (a) What is the constitutional basis for ownership of a private industry by the United States? by a state? (b) Does it make any difference to your answer if it is wartime? depression? peacetime?

2. How does government ownership affect private enterprise?

3. What factors have influenced government ownership of business in the United States?

4. What are (a) the advantages and (b) the disadvantages of government ownership?

5. (a) Is it desirable to maintain private ownership even though government ownership may be more efficient? (b) Does this problem bear any relation to the question of whether small enterprise should be maintained even though big enterprise may be more efficient?

6. What is the basis for the decision in the TVA case?

7. Would the TVA be constitutional if it had been constructed in peacetime and operated in peacetime?

8. What is the organization of the TVA? By whom is it owned? By whom is it controlled?

9. (a) What are the objectives of the TVA? (b) What is the constitutional basis for seeking to achieve each of these objectives?

10. Discuss the value of the TVA as a yardstick for measuring electrical energy production costs.

11. City A operates a series of auto service stations that compete with private auto service stations. The city stations sell gasoline, oil, and services at a lower price than the private stations. The private stations seek an injunction to stop the operation of the public stations on the ground that the law authorizing their operation is unconstitutional because:

(a) The city has no authority to enter such a business, as it is not affected with a public interest.
(b) The city cannot spend public money for the purpose of running such a business.
(c) The private stations are deprived of their property without due process of law as the city is able to undersell them.
(d) The city is guilty of unfair methods of competition by underselling the private concerns, as it can make up any deficit from the tax money.
(e) The city cannot operate public service stations if it taxes the private stations.

Decide and discuss each of the objections.

12. What is the constitutional basis for the action of the United States in (a) owning property, (b) manufacturing goods, (c) selling goods, and (d) selling goods below cost?

13. In most of the countries of the world the major railroad networks, and to a lesser degree the national or central banks, are owned by the national government. (a) Could such a plan be followed in the United States? (b) What limitations or conditions must be observed in order to make such ownership lawful? (c) To what extent does government ownership in these fields exist today?

14. In *Ashwander* v. *TVA* the Court stated: "While, in its present condition, the Tennessee River is not adequately improved for commercial navigation, and traffic is small, we are not at liberty to conclude either that the river is not susceptible of development as an important waterway, or that Congress has not undertaken that development, or that the construction of the Wilson Dam was not an appropriate means to accomplish a legitimate end." Compare this with the approach of the Court in *McCulloch* v. *Maryland*, page 5.

15. Does *Ashwander* v. *TVA* authorize the United States to enter the farming business? the coal business? the mining business generally?

16. Is the doctrine of *Ashwander* v. *TVA* limited to extractive industries that involve the removal of a substance contained in land owned by the United States?

17. (a) Can Congress constitutionally adopt a law providing that whenever any war surplus materials are sold by the United States to private citizens, the purchasers cannot make a resale of the materials at a price greater than the price of purchase from the government plus 10%?

(b) Would the statute be constitutional if it prohibited resale by the purchaser under any condition?

18. Is there any limitation on the power recognized in *Ashwander* v. *TVA?* Discuss.

19. A coalyard is owned and operated by City X. Can the United States tax this property and make it subject to regulations imposed on all privately owned coalyards?

20. A series of coalyards are owned and operated throughout the United States by the United States government. (a) Can a state tax the property of such coalyards located within its boundaries? (b) Can a state make its trade regulations apply to the national coalyards?

# PART IV. ADMINISTRATION

## Chapter 28

## ADMINISTRATIVE RULE-MAKING

§ 28:1. Necessity for Delegation of Rule-making Authority
- (a) Details of administration
- (b) Flexibility of administration
- (c) Expert administration
- (d) Localized administration

§ 28:2. Legislative Nature of Rule-making
- (a) Rule-making and the Federal Administrative Procedure Act
- (b) Rule as "law of the state"—
  United States v. Howard

§ 28:3. Constitutionality of Delegation of Rule-making Authority
- (a) Prescribing the policy for price control—
  Yakus v. United States
- (b) Prescribing the policy for milk price control—
  United States v. Rock Royal Cooperative, Inc.
- (c) Prescribing the policy for dissolution of holding companies—
  American Power & Light Co. v. Securities and Exchange Commission
- (d) Prescribing the policy for war contract renegotiation—
  Lichter v. United States
- (e) Creating banking administrator without prescribing policy—
  Fahey v. Mallonee
- (f) Creating transportation administrator without prescribing policy—
  American Trucking Associations v. United States

§ 28:4. Delegation to Nongovernmental Bodies or Persons
- (a) Cooperation between administrator and producers—
  United States v. Rock Royal Cooperative, Inc.

§ 28:5. Public Participation in Matters Preliminary to Rule-making

§ 28:6. Public Knowledge of Rule
- (a) Effect of publication—
  Federal Crop Insurance Corp. v. Merrill

## § 28:1. Necessity for Delegation of Rule-making Authority

In a relatively simple or primitive community, society can content itself with the adoption of rules or law decrees prohibiting certain lines of conduct and specifying the penalty to be imposed for the violation of those standards. In such a state, the conduct that is permitted and the conduct that is prohibited are relatively clearly divided. It is not necessary to correlate the economic conditions or other circumstances to determine whether a practice is condemned. The classification or division between that which is lawful and that which is unlawful is both universal and static.

To illustrate, larceny has for centuries been set apart as being unlawful conduct. While technicalities arise as to the precise definition of larceny, for practical purposes it is a course of conduct that may be readily separated or isolated from other forms of conduct. A prohibition against larceny is likewise a universal concept within the particular community or state; that is, the conduct is condemned to the same extent regardless of the geographic place of its commission. Larceny is also larceny independently of the conduct of any other party or of the community in which it is committed. Moreover, there is virtually no need to change the standard of larceny at any particular moment. It is true that the course of law has been to widen the definition of larceny beyond that of the common law so as to include takings that were not condemned at the common law. This has been done by expanding the category of the places from which a taking of property is larceny, the nature of property that may be the subject of larceny, and the persons who may commit it. This growth has been the work of several centuries and from the standpoint of any one year presents a static rather than a dynamic picture.

### *(a) Details of administration*

As we move into the more modern era of regulation, particularly the regulation of business, the picture changes. The lawmaker widens his horizon, not merely to attempt prohibition of specific types of conduct, but to regulate enterprises or activities generally in the interest of achieving a social betterment. It is no longer possible or desirable for the lawmaker to prescribe every detail. When he passes a statute based on the policy that prices should be "reasonable" or that licenses should be granted where required by the "public interest," it becomes impossible for the lawmaker to give a precise definition of "reasonable" or "public interest." The practice has therefore developed of appointing or selecting an administrator who is charged with the duty of making regulations to carry out the legislative purpose of maintaining reasonable prices or of granting licenses in the public interest.

Had the lawmaker not been willing to entrust this authority to the administrator, it would have been necessary for the statute to specify in detail every fact situation in which the price would be reasonable or the issuance of a license would be in the public interest. The inability of the lawmaker, however far-sighted, to foresee every possible contingency is obvious. Even assuming such an ability, the statute would be so long and detailed that few persons would be able to know its full meaning. By delegating authority to the administrator, the legislative body is free to confine its attention to the basic or underlying principles of policy, leaving to the administrator the task of filling out the details.

### *(b) Flexibility of administration*

This entrusting or delegation of authority to the administrator is further necessitated by the fact that what is "reasonable" or in the "public interest" depends upon a correlation of facts to arise in the future. A sudden shortage or an unexpected surplus may throw out of line any prior rigid fixing of a "reasonable price." The regulation must therefore be dynamic rather than static, and it would be unsatisfactory and productive of great injustice for the lawmaker to fix a rigid price. The necessity for correlation of the regulation to other factors that are subject to change demands a flexibility of regulation that cannot be possessed by a lawmaking body meeting only at intervals.

The flexibility of administration made possible by regulation by an administrator is also desirable from the standpoint of the mechanics of regulation. The period of the regulation of modern business has been comparatively short. While we have obtained considerable experience in certain lines of regulation, there are many fields recently embarked on in which regulation of necessity has been made on the basis of trial and error. In the absence of prior experience, no other course is available than to adopt the regulation that appears the best and then to modify or change it from time to time as experience dictates. To do this requires both a day-to-day surveillance of the workings of the regulation and the ability to change the regulation quickly as wisdom dictates. A statute cannot provide this flexibility.

All lawmaking bodies in the United States meet at intervals. In many of the states, the legislature meets only every other year. Under such a system, regulation by the lawmaker necessarily assumes a spasmodic, intermittent character and cannot be currently adjusted to change with the times.

### *(c) Expert administration*

In addition to the necessity of the situation, which requires the delegation of regulation or rule-making authority to the administrator, there is also the advantage to be gained of administration by an expert. If the administrator is properly qualified for his position, he will have a far greater knowledge of his subject than could be expected of the lawmaker. The regulation by the administrator should therefore be better than the amateur regulation by the lawmaker. This is not intended to belittle the lawmaker, but is merely a recognition of the fact that each member of a lawmaking body cannot have the experience and the knowledge of a specialist in every field of business that the government may wish to regulate. It is also a recognition of the fact that, if a business is to be regulated, the person making the regulation cannot know too much about that business.

Of course, if the administrator is not competent, these benefits will not be obtained by delegating to him the authority to regulate. If he is not expert in the field, if he is not alert to change, if he is not quick to realize the good or the bad effects of a particular regulation, there may result confusion, hardship, and partisanship as great as though the matter was not in the hands of an administrator. This obviously is not an argument against delegating legislative authority, but is merely an argument to exert all the power of a democracy to make certain that those authorized to administer are competent to do so.

### *(d) Localized administration*

The administrative regulation may also lack the universality of a traditional statute. It may be necessary to divide the country into areas or zones to regulate price within the separate units. A "reasonable" price for one area of supply or competition may be unreasonable for another. It would be extremely difficult if not impossible for a lawmaking body to devise a law with such variations.

### § 28:2. Legislative Nature of Rule-making

Before considering the validity of a statute that authorizes an administrator to adopt rules, it is necessary to determine the nature of the function of rule-making. Since the regulation or rule of the administrator will govern the community in the same manner as an Act of Congress or other appropriate legislature, authorization to an administrator to adopt rules in effect gives him power to make laws. In adopting a regulation or rule, he exercises a legislative rather than an executive or judicial function. It is true that the administrator is not given the power to make laws generally and that he must keep his regulation within the area prescribed by him by the lawmaker; nevertheless, within the area of permitted action he is making law. This at first does violence to constitutional provisions and traditional concepts that governmental powers are divided into three branches—executive, legislative, and judiciary—and that of these the legislative is exclusively the domain of the publicly elected lawmaker. In contrast, in the field of regulation we find an administrator, generally not elected and generally unknown to the public, making the laws. Because of this conflict between the necessity of administration and constitutional and traditional policies, the courts for a long time have been reluctant to admit the legislative nature of the administrative function when the administrator prescribes general rules for future conduct that will apply to all persons coming within their field of operation.

The rule or regulation may be either a rule of conduct, as that term is generally used, or it may be a rule of conduct as to a specific thing, such as a rule fixing rents, prices, or production quotas. Conduct is regulated by specifying the price at which an article is to be sold just as much as when the sale itself is prohibited. In either case, the rule or regulation is a "law."

The legislative nature of the rule-making function was recognized in *Prentis* v. *Atlantic Coastline Co.*, 211 U.S. 210 (1908), where in speaking of the Interstate Commerce Commission, Justice Holmes stated:

". . . we think it equally plain that the proceedings drawn in question here are legislative in their nature, and none the less so that they have taken place with a body which at another moment, or in its principal or dominant aspect, is a court such as is meant by § 720. A judicial inquiry investigates, declares, and enforces liabilities as they stand on present or past facts and under laws supposed already to exist. That is its purpose and end. Legislation, on the other hand, looks to the future and changes existing conditions by making a new rule to be applied thereafter to all or some part of those subject to its power. The establishment of a rate is the making of a rule for the future, and therefore is an act legislative, not judicial, in kind. . . ."

### *(a) Rule-making and the Federal Administrative Procedure Act*

The legislative nature of the rule-making function is also recognized by the Federal Administrative Procedure Act,[1] which, in a general way, provides that the administrator in adopting his regulations shall follow a procedure of notice, hearing, and inquiry similar to that followed by a legislative body. The Act provides:

> Sec. 4. Except to the extent that there is involved (1) any military, naval, or foreign affairs function of the United States or (2) any matter relating to agency management or personnel or to public property, loans, grants, benefits, or contracts—
>
> (a) NOTICE.—General notice of proposed rule making shall be published in the Federal Register (unless all persons subject thereto are named and either personally served or otherwise have actual notice thereof in accordance with law) and shall include (1) a statement of the time, place, and nature of public rule making proceedings; (2) reference to the authority under which the rule is proposed; and (3) either the terms or substance of the proposed rule or a description of the subjects and issues involved. Except where notice or hearing is required by statute, this subsection shall not apply to interpretative rules, general statements of policy, rules of agency organization, procedure, or practice, or in any situation in which the agency for good cause finds (and incorporates the finding and a brief statement of the reasons therefor in the rules issued) that notice and public procedure thereon are impracticable, unnecessary, or contrary to the public interest.
>
> (b) PROCEDURES.—After notice required by this section, the agency shall afford interested persons an opportunity to participate in the rule making through submission of written data, views, or arguments with or without opportunity to present the same orally in any manner; and, after consideration of all relevant matter presented, the agency shall incorporate in any rules adopted a concise general statement of their basis and purpose. Where rules are required by statute to be made on the record after opportunity for an agency hearing, the requirements of sections 7 and 8 shall apply in place of the provisions of this subsection.

[1] This Act establishes uniform procedure for all federal administrators not otherwise regulated.

(c) EFFECTIVE DATES.—The required publication or service of any substantive rule (other than one granting or recognizing exemption or relieving restriction or interpretative rules and statements of policy) shall be made not less than thirty days prior to the effective date thereof except as otherwise provided by the agency upon good cause found and published with the rule.

(d) PETITIONS.—Every agency shall accord any interested person the right to petition for the issuance, amendment, or repeal of a rule.

### *(b) Rule as "law of the state"*

UNITED STATES v. HOWARD

352 U.S. 212 (1957)

The Congress made it a federal crime to transport fish in interstate commerce from a state if such transportation was "contrary to the law of the state." Howard transported fish from Florida. No Florida statute made it unlawful, but such transportation violated a rule of the Florida Game and Fresh Water Fish Commission. Howard was prosecuted for violating the federal statute. She claimed that she had not violated the statute because no Florida "law" prohibited such transportation.

OPINION BY REED, J.

. . . The sole question presented is whether Rule 14.01 of the Commission's regulations, . . . is a "law" of the State of Florida as that term is used in the Federal Act.

This Court has repeatedly ruled, in other circumstances, that orders of state administrative agencies are the law of the State. . . . In *Grand Trunk R. Co.* v. *Indiana R. Comm'n,* 221 U.S. 400, 403, the Court stated, citing *Prentis* v. *Atlantic Coast Line Co.,* 211 U.S. 210, 226: "the order [of the Indiana Railroad Commission] . . . is a law of the State within the meaning of the contract clause of the Constitution. . . ." And, in *Lake Erie & W. R. Co.* v. *Public Utilities Comm'n,* 249 U.S. 422, 424, it was said that an order of the state public utilities commission "being legislative in its nature . . . is a state law within the meaning of the Constitution of the United States and the laws of Congress regulating our jurisdiction." A similar statement may be found in *Arkadelphia Co.* v. *St. Louis S. W. R. Co.,* 249 U.S. 134, 141. . . .

Appellee argues that the rules of the Florida Commission are so subject to change that they lack sufficient substance and permanence to be the "law" of Florida. We need not decide now whether a state agency could make a rule of such a temporary nature and so unaccompanied by the procedural niceties of rule making that the declaration should not be considered the law of the State for purposes of a statute such as the Black Bass Act. . . .

Accordingly we hold that the phrase "law of the State," as used in this Act, is sufficiently broad to encompass the type of regulation used in Florida. . . .

### § 28:3. Constitutionality of Delegation of Rule-making Authority

Apart from the question of desirability of delegating authority to the administrator in a particular case, the question arises, under both national and state constitutions, whether a particular delegation by the lawmaker to the administrator is constitutional. In the case of the Federal Constitution there is the express limitation of Article I that "all legislative powers herein granted shall be vested in a Congress of the United States."

The delegation of legislative powers also runs counter to the traditional American principle of a tripartite government consisting of executive, legislative, and judicial branches. This division of powers was inspired by the desire to prevent rule by a tyrant. If governmental powers are all concentrated in one man or one group of men, it then depends merely upon the goodness of his nature or their natures whether government is or is not tyrannical. If, on the other hand, no one man or group had more than a segment of the governing powers, it would be clear that each segment would serve as a check to block potential tyranny on the part of the other.

This theory of tripartite division of governmental powers is defeated in part by a statute that delegates the power of one segment to another.

On this basis laws by which the Congress authorized the President to do certain acts when he had made certain determinations have been attacked as unconstitutional on the ground that they destroyed the division of powers between the Congress and the President by entrusting to the latter those which belong to the former. Where the delegation is made to a separate or independent administrator, this problem of destroying the fundamental division of power is not presented in such an acute form. If the Congress chooses to give part of its power to a separate agency, this does not increase the power of either the executive or the judicial branch. In such case the argument against delegation is fundamentally that the body entrusted with the original duty cannot shirk that duty or permit it to be performed by anyone else.

In the earlier years, when the administrators performed relatively simple tasks, the law maker generally instructed the administrator exactly what he should do when certain facts existed. In this period, it was therefore necessary to find in the statute a standard to govern the administrator. Today the field of administative regulation is too complex for the establishment of a statutory standard, and the law maker must content himself with stating an objective or policy to the administrator and then allowing the administrator to do whatever he deems proper and whenever he deems it proper in order to achieve that objective or carry out the policy. Today the courts generally hold that there is no improper delegation if the law maker has established the policy for the administrator to follow, although many cases will find that the statutes in question declare both a standard and a policy. That is, such cases give recognition to both the earlier test of a statutory standard and the modern test of a statutory policy.

There is even authority that the law is moving into a third stage in which neither a standard nor a policy need be declared, and it is sufficient to create an administrator to regulate a given area of the economy and then allow him to decide for himself what rules should be adopted and what policies should be followed.

Although the constitutionality of delegation has been much litigated, there have only been three instances in which the United States Supreme Court has invalidated an Act of Congress for that reason.[2] The significance of these cases may be readily discounted on the ground that the condemnation of the statutes in question on the ground of improper delegation was merely part of a general condemnation of those statutes because they exceeded the bounds of the Federal commerce power. With the changing concept of that power,[3] it appears unlikely that the statutes in question would be invalidated on the sole ground of delegation.

With respect to state legislation, the doctrine of nondelegation has greater vitality and a number of state laws have been declared void on that ground. Many state courts continue to require a standard to be specified although a few have recognized the impracticality of so doing as the complexity of regulation and of the economy increases.[4]

---

[2] A.L.A. Schechter Poultry Corp. v. United States, § 14:2(b). Carter v. Carter Coal Co., § 14:2(c). Panama Refining Co. v. Ryan, 293 U.S. 388 (1935).

[3] See Chapter 9.

[4] Pressman v. Barnes, 209 Md. 544, 121 A. 2d 816 (1956).

### *(a) Prescribing the policy for price control*

YAKUS v. UNITED STATES

321 U.S. 414 (1944)

Acting under the Emergency Price Control Act of 1942, as amended by the Inflation Control Act of 1942, the Price Control Administrator fixed maximum prices for specified commodities. Certain dealers were convicted for selling these commodities at prices above the set levels. The dealers claimed that the law was unconstitutional in delegating the legislative power of Congress to the Price Administrator.

OPINION BY STONE, C. J.

. . .

The Emergency Price Control Act provides for the establishment of the Office of Price Administration under the direction of a Price Administrator appointed by the President, and sets up a comprehensive scheme for the promulgation by the Administrator of regulations or orders fixing such maximum prices of commodities and rents as will effectuate the purpose of the Act and conform to the standards which it prescribes. The Act was adopted as a temporary wartime measure, and provides in § 1 (b) for its termination on June 30, 1943, unless sooner terminated by Presidential proclamation or concurrent resolution of Congress. By the amendatory act of October 2, 1942, it was extended to June 30, 1944.

Section 1 (a) declares that the Act is "in the interest of the national defense and security and necessary to the effective prosecution of the present war," and that its purposes are:

"to stabilize prices and to prevent speculative, unwarranted, and abnormal increases in prices and rents; to eliminate and prevent profiteering, hoarding, manipulation, speculation, and other disruptive practices resulting from abnormal market conditions or scarcities caused by or contributing to the national emergency; to assure that defense appropriations are not dissipated by excessive prices; to protect persons with relatively fixed and limited incomes, consumers, wage earners, investors, and persons dependent on life insurance, annuities, and pensions, from undue impairment of their standard of living; to prevent hardships to persons engaged in business, . . . and to the Federal, State, and local governments, which would result from abnormal increases in prices; to assist in securing adequate production of commodities and facilities; to prevent a post emergency collapse of values; . . ."

The standards which are to guide the Administrator's exercise of his authority to fix prices, so far as now relevant, are prescribed by § 2(a) and by § 1 of the amendatory Act of October 2, 1942, and Executive Order 9250. . . . By § 2(a) the Administrator is authorized, after consultation with representative members of the industry so far as practicable, to promulgate regulations fixing prices of commodities which "in his judgment will be generally fair and equitable and will effectuate the purposes of this Act" when, in his judgment, their prices "have risen or threaten to rise to an extent or in a manner inconsistent with the purposes of this Act."

The section also directs that

"So far as practicable, in establishing any maximum price, the Administrator shall ascertain and give due consideration to the prices prevailing between October 1 and October 15, 1941 (or if, in the case of any commodity, there are no prevailing prices between such dates, or the prevailing prices between such dates are not generally representative because of abnormal or seasonal market conditions or other cause, then to the prices prevailing during the nearest two-week period in which, in the judgment of the Administrator, the prices for such commodity are generally representative) . . . and shall make adjustments for such relevant factors as he may determine and deem to be of general applicability, including. . . . Speculative fluctuations, general increases or decreases in costs of production, distribution, and transportation, and general increases or decreases in profits earned by sellers of the commodity or commodities, during and subsequent to the year ended October 1, 1941."

By the Act of October 2, 1942, the President is directed to stabilize prices, wages and salaries "so far as practicable" on the basis of the levels which existed on September 15, 1942, except as otherwise provided in the Act. By Title I, § 4 of Executive Order No. 9250, he has directed "all departments and agencies of the Government" "to stabilize the cost of living in accordance with the Act of October 2, 1942."

Revised Maximum Price Regulation No. 169 was issued December 10, 1942, under authority of the Emergency Price Control Act as amended and Executive Order No. 9250. The Regulation established specific maximum prices for the sale at wholesale of specified cuts of beef and veal. As is required by § 2(a) of the Act, it was accompanied by a "statement of the considerations involved" in prescribing it. From the preamble to the Regulation and from the Statement of Considerations accompanying it, it appears that the prices fixed for sales at wholesale were slightly in excess of those prevailing between March 16 and March 28, 1942, and approximated those prevailing on September 15, 1942. Findings that the Regulation was necessary, that the prices which it fixed were fair and equitable, and that it otherwise conformed to the standards prescribed by the Act, appear in the Statement of Considerations.

. . .

Congress enacted the Emergency Price Control Act in pursuance of a defined policy and required that the prices fixed by the Administrator should further that policy and conform to standards prescribed by the Act. The boundaries of the field of the Administrator's permissible action are marked by the statute. It directs that the prices fixed shall effectuate the declared policy of the Act to stabilize commodity prices so as to prevent war-time inflation and its enumerated disruptive causes and effects. In addition the prices established must be fair and equitable, and in fixing them the Administrator is directed to give due consideration, so far as practicable, to prevailing prices during the designated base period, with prescribed administrative adjustments to compensate for enumerated disturbing factors affecting prices. In short the purposes of the Act specified in § 1 denote the objective to be sought by the Administrator in fixing prices—the prevention of inflation and its enumerated consequences. The standards set out in § 2 define the boundaries within which prices having that purpose must be fixed. It is enough to satisfy the statutory requirements that the Administrator finds that the prices fixed will tend to achieve that objective and will conform to those standards, and that the courts in an appropriate proceeding can see that substantial basis for those findings is not wanting.

The Act is thus an exercise by Congress of its legislative power. In it Congress has stated the legislative objective, has prescribed the method of achieving that objective—maximum price fixing—and has laid down standards to guide the administrative determination of both the occasions for the exercise of the price-fixing power, and the particular prices to be established. . . .

The Constitution as a continuously operative charter of government does not demand the impossible or the impracticable. It does not require that Congress find for itself every fact upon which it desires to base legislative action or that it make for itself detailed determinations which it has declared to be prerequisite to the application of the legislative policy to particular facts and circumstances impossible for Congress itself properly to investigate. The essentials of the legislative function are the determination of the legislative policy and its formulation and promulgation as a defined and binding rule of conduct—here the rule, with penal sanctions, that prices shall not be greater than those fixed by maximum price regulations which conform to standards and will tend to further the policy which Congress has established. These essentials are preserved when Congress has specified the basic conditions of fact upon whose existence or occurrence, ascertained from relevant data by a designated administrative agency, it directs that its statutory command shall be effective. It is no objection that the determination of facts and the inferences to be drawn from them in the light of the statutory standards and declaration of policy call for the exercise of judgment, and for the formulation of subsidiary administrative policy within the prescribed statutory framework. . . .

Nor does the doctrine of separation of powers deny to Congress power to direct that an administrative officer properly designated for that purpose have ample latitude within which he is to ascertain the conditions which Congress has made prerequisite to the operation of its legislative command. Acting within its constitutional power to fix prices it is for Congress to say whether the data on the basis of which prices are to be fixed are to be confined within a narrow or a broad range. In either case the only concern of courts is to ascertain whether the will of Congress has been obeyed. This depends not upon the breadth of the definition of the facts or conditions which the administrative officer is to find but upon the determination whether the definition sufficiently marks the field within which the Administrator is to act so that it may be known whether he has kept within it in compliance with the legislative will.

. . . Congress is not confined to that method of executing its policy which involves the least possible delegation of discretion to administrative officers. . . . It is free to avoid the rigidity of such a system, which might well result in serious hardship, and to choose instead the flexibility attainable by the use of less restrictive standards. . . . Only if we could say that there is an absence of standards for the guidance of the Administrator's action, so that it would be impossible in a proper proceeding to ascertain whether the will of

Congress has been obeyed, would we be justified in overriding its choice of means for effecting its declared purpose of preventing inflation.

The standards prescribed by the present Act, with the aid of the "statement of the considerations" required to be made by the Administrator, are sufficiently definite and precise to enable Congress, the courts and the public to ascertain whether the Administrator, in fixing the designated prices, has conformed to those standards. . . . Hence we are unable to find in them an unauthorized delegation of legislative power. The authority to fix prices only when prices have risen or threaten to rise to an extent or in a manner inconsistent with the purpose of the Act to prevent inflation is no broader than the authority to fix maximum prices when deemed necessary to protect consumers against unreasonably high prices . . . or the authority to take possession of and operate telegraph lines whenever deemed necessary for the national security or defense . . . or the authority to suspend tariff provisions upon findings that the duties imposed by a foreign state are "reciprocally unequal and unreasonable" . . . [These had been sustained by the Court.]

The directions that the prices fixed shall be fair and equitable, that in addition they shall tend to promote the purposes of the Act, and that in promulgating them consideration shall be given to prices prevailing in a stated base period, confer no greater reach for administrative determination than the power to fix just and reasonable rates . . . or the power to approve consolidations in the "public interest" . . . or the power to regulate radio stations engaged in chain broadcasting "as public interest, convenience or necessity requires" . . . or the power to prohibit "unfair methods of competition" not defined or forbidden by the common law . . . or the direction that in allotting marketing quotas among states and producers due consideration be given to a variety of economic factors . . . or the similar direction that in adjusting tariffs to meet differences in costs of production the President "take into consideration" "in so far as he finds practicable" a variety of economic matters . . . or the similar authority, in making classifications within an industry, to consider various named and unnamed "relevant factors" and determine the respective weights attributable to each. . . . [These had been sustained by the Court in earlier decisions.]

Justice Roberts dissented on the ground that the "purpose, or 'standard,' [of the Act] seems to permit adoption by the Administrator of any conceivable policy."

### *(b) Prescribing the policy for milk price control*

UNITED STATES v. ROCK ROYAL COOPERATIVE, INC.
307 U.S. 533 (1939)

The Agricultural Marketing Agreement Act of 1937 authorized the Secretary of Agriculture to designate marketing areas in which he could set minimum prices for certain basic farm products. Under certain circumstances, an order of the Secretary was to be submitted to the producers of the area affected and would become binding when approved by two thirds of the producers. The law was challenged as a delegation of authority to the Secretary.

OPINION BY REED, J.

. . .

From the earliest days the Congress has been compelled to leave to the administrative officers of the government authority to determine facts which were to put legislation into effect and the details of regulations which would implement the more general enactments. It is well settled, therefore, that it is no argument against the constitutionality of an act to say that it delegates broad powers to executives to determine the details of any legislative scheme. This necessary authority has never been denied. In dealing with legislation involving questions of economic adjustment, each enactment must be considered to determine whether it states the purpose which the Congress seeks to accomplish and the standards by which that purpose is to be worked out with sufficient exactness to enable those affected to understand these limits. Within these tests the Congress needs specify only so far as is reasonably practicable. The present Act, we believe, satisfies these tests.

1. *Delegation to the Secretary of Agriculture.* The purpose of the Act is "to establish and maintain such orderly marketing conditions for agricultural commodities in interstate commerce as will establish prices to farmers at a level that will give agricultural commodities a purchasing power with respect to articles that farmers buy, equivalent to the purchasing power of agricultural commodities in the base period." To accomplish this, the Secretary of Agriculture is directed to issue orders, whenever he has reason to believe the issuance of an order will tend to effectuate the declared policy of the act. Unlike the language of the National Industrial Recovery Act condemned in the *Schechter* case . . . the tests here to determine the purpose and the powers dependent upon that conclusion are defined. In the Re-

covery Act the Declaration of Policy was couched in most general terms. In this Act it is to restore parity prices, Section 2. Under the Recovery Act, general welfare might be sought through codes of any industry, formulated to express standards of fair competition for the businesses covered. Here the terms of orders are limited to the specific provisions, minutely set out in Sections 8c(5) and (7). While considerable flexibility is provided by Section 8c(7) (D), it gives opportunity only to include provisions auxiliary to those definitely specified.

The Secretary is not permitted freedom of choice as to the commodities which he may attempt to aid by an order. The Act, Section 8c(2), limits him to milk, fresh fruits except apples, tobacco, fresh vegetables, soybeans and naval stores. The Act authorizes a marketing agreement and order to be issued for such production or marketing regions or areas as are practicable. A city milkshed seems homogeneous. This standard of practicality is a limit on the power to issue orders. It determines when an order may be promulgated.

. . . The Secretary must have first determined the prices in accordance with Section 2 and Section 8e, that is, the prices that will give the commodity a purchasing power equivalent to that of the base period, considering the price and supply of feed and other pertinent economic conditions affecting the milk market in the area. If he finds the price so determined unreasonable, it is to be fixed at a level which will reflect such factors, provide adequate quantities of wholesome milk and be in the public interest. This price cannot be determined by mathematical formula but the standards give ample indications of the various factors to be considered by the Secretary.

### *(c) Prescribing the policy for dissolution of holding companies*

AMERICAN POWER & LIGHT CO. v. SECURITIES AND EXCHANGE COMMISSION

329 U.S. 90 (1946)

The Securities and Exchange Commission Act authorized the Securities and Exchange Commission to order the dissolution of holding companies that served no useful economic purpose. The validity of the Act was challenged on the ground that it did not establish an adequate standard for the guidance of the Commission in exercising this power.

OPINION BY MURPHY, J.

. . . We . . . reject the claim that [the Securities and Exchange Commission Act] . . . constitutes an unconstitutional delegation of legislative power to the Securities and Exchange Commission because of an alleged absence of any standards for guidance in carrying out its functions.

[The Act] . . . itself provides that the Commission shall act so as to insure that the corporate structure or continued existence of any company in a particular holding company system does not "unduly or necessarily complicate the structure" or "unfairly or inequitably distribute voting power among security holders." It is argued that these phrases are undefined by the act, are legally meaningless in themselves and carry with them no historically defined concepts. As a result, it is said, the Commission is forced to use its unlimited whim to determine compliance or noncompliance with [the Act] . . . ; and in framing its orders, the Commission has unfettered discretion to decide whose property shall be taken or destroyed and to what extent. Objection is also made on the score that no standards have been developed or announced by the Commission which justify its action in this case.

These contentions are without merit. Even standing alone, standards in terms of unduly complicated corporate structures and inequitable distributions of voting power cannot be said to be utterly without meaning, especially to those familiar with corporate realities. But these standards need not be tested in isolation. They derive much meaningful content from the purpose of the act, its factual background and the statutory context in which they appear. . . . These standards are certainly no less definite in nature than those speaking in other contexts in terms of "public interest," "just and reasonable rates," "unfair methods of competition" or "relevant factors." . . .

The judicial approval accorded these "broad" standards for administrative action is a reflection of the necessities of modern legislation dealing with complex economic and social problems. . . . The legislative process would frequently bog down if Congress were constitutionally required to appraise beforehand the myriad situations to which it wishes a particular policy to be applied and to formulate specific rules for each situation. Necessity therefore fixes a point beyond which it is unreasonable and impracticable to compel Congress to prescribe detailed rules; it then becomes constitutionally sufficient if Congress clearly delineates the general policy, the public agency which is to apply it, and the boundaries of this delegated authority. . . .

Nor is there any constitutional requirement that the legislative standards be translated by the Commission into formal and detailed rules of thumb prior to their application to a particular case. If that agency wishes to proceed by the more flexible case-by-case method, the Constitution offers no obstacle. All that can be required is that the Commission's actions conform to the statutory language and policy.

### *(d) Prescribing the policy for war contract renegotiation*

LICHTER v. UNITED STATES

334 U.S. 742 (1948)

Congress authorized the Secretary of War to renegotiate war contracts with private manufacturers when, in his opinion, "excessive profits" had been realized. The constitutionality of the Act was challenged on the ground that it did not establish an adequate standard for the guidance of the Secretary.

OPINION BY BURTON, J. . . .

The degree to which Congress must specify its policies and standards in order that the administrative authority granted may not be an unconstitutional delegation of its own legislative power is not capable of precise definition. . . .

It is not necessary that Congress supply administrative officers with a specific formula for their guidance in a field where flexibility and adaptation of the congressional policy to infinitely variable conditions constitute the essence of the program. "If Congress shall lay down by legislative act an intelligible principle . . . such legislative action is not a forbidden delegation of legislative power." . . . Standards prescribed by Congress are to be read in the light of the conditions to which they are to be applied. . . .

### *(e) Creating banking administrator without prescribing policy*

FAHEY v. MALLONEE

332 U.S. 245 (1947)

The Federal Home Loan Bank, acting under regulations adopted by its Board under the Federal Home Owners' Loan Act, appointed a conservator to take possession of and manage the Long Beach Federal

Savings and Loan Association. The Association brought an action to remove the conservator on the ground that the Home Owners' Loan Act was unconstitutional.

OPINION BY JACKSON, J.

. . . [The] defect [of the statute] is said to consist of delegation of legislative functions to the supervising authority without adequate standards of action or guides to policy. Section 5(d) of the Act gives to the Board "full power to provide in the rules and regulations herein authorized for the reorganization, consolidation, merger, or liquidation of such associations, including the power to appoint a conservator or a receiver to take charge of the affairs of any such association, and to require an equitable readjustment of the capital structure of the same; and to release any such association from such control and permit its further operation." . . . This, the District Court held, was unconstitutional delegation of the congressional function. It relied on *Panama Refining Co.* v. *Ryan*, 293 U.S. 388, and *Schechter Corp.* v. *United States*, 295 U.S. 495.

Both cited cases dealt with delegation of a power to make federal crimes of acts that never had been such before and to devise novel rules of law in a field in which there had been no settled law or custom.

The savings and loan associations with which § 5(d) deals, on the other hand, are created, insured and aided by the Federal Government. It may be that explicit standards in the Home Owners' Loan Act would have been a desirable assurance of responsible administration. But the provisions of the statute under attack are not penal provisions. . . . The provisions are regulatory. They do not deal with unprecedented economic problems of varied industries. They deal with a single type of enterprise and with the problems of insecurity and mismanagement which are as old as banking enterprise. The remedies which are authorized are not new ones unknown to existing law to be invented by the Board in exercise of a lawless range of power. Banking is one of the longest regulated and most closely supervised of public callings. It is one in which accumulated experience of supervisors, acting for many states under various statutes, has established well-defined practices for the appointment of conservators, receivers and liquidators. Corporate management is a field, too, in which courts have experience and many precedents have crystallized into well-known and generally acceptable standards. A discretion to make regulations to guide supervisory action in such matters may be constitutionally permissible while it might not be allowable to authorize creation of new crimes in uncharted fields.

The Board adopted rules and regulations governing appointment of conservators. They provided the grounds upon which a conservator might be named, and they are the usual and conventional grounds found in most state and federal banking statutes. They are sufficiently explicit, against the background of custom, to be adequate for proper administration and for judicial review if there should be a proper occasion for it. . . .

### *(f) Creating transportation administrator without prescribing policy*

AMERICAN TRUCKING ASSOCIATIONS v. UNITED STATES
344 U.S. 298 (1953)

The practice developed for owners of trucks who drive their loaded trucks from one point to another to hire themselves and their trucks out to a common carrier so that the return trip would not be made with empty trucks. The Interstate Commerce Commission concluded that these one-trip rentals made it possible for the carriers to operate in part without satisfying the requirements otherwise applicable to them. In order to stop this, the Commission adopted a set of rules which provided that trucks could not be rented by a carrier for less than thirty days. A number of suits were brought to prevent the enforcement of these rules on the ground that they were not authorized by the Interstate Commerce Act.

OPINION BY REED, J.

. . . All agree that the rules . . . abolish trip-leasing. Unfortunate consequences are predicted for the public interest because the exempt owner-operator will no longer be able to hire himself out at will—in sum, that the industry's ability to serve a fluctuating demand will suffer and transportation costs accordingly go up. It is the Commission's position that the industry and the public will benefit directly because of the stabilization of conditions of competition and rate schedules, and that in fact the continued effectiveness of the Commission's functions under the Motor Carrier Act is dependent on regulation of leasing and interchange. Needless to say, we are ill equipped to weigh such predictions of the economic future. Nor is it our function to act as a super-commission. So we turn to the legal considerations so strongly urged on us.

Here, appellants have framed their position as a broadside attack on the Commission's asserted power. All urge upon us the fact that nowhere in the Act is there an express delegation of power to control, regulate or affect leasing practices, and it is further insisted that in each separate provision of the Act granting regulatory authority there is no direct implication of such power. Our function, however, does not stop with a section-by-section search for the phrase "regulation of leasing practices" among the literal words of the statutory provisions. As a matter of principle, we might agree with appellants' contentions if we thought it a reasonable canon of interpretation that the draftsmen of acts delegating agency powers, as a practical and realistic matter, can or do include specific consideration of every evil sought to be corrected. But no great acquaintance with practical affairs is required to know that such prescience, either in fact or in the minds of Congress, does not exist. . . . Its very absence, moreover, is precisely one of the reasons why regulatory agencies such as the Commission are created, for it is the fond hope of their authors that they bring to their work the expert's familiarity with industry conditions which members of the delegating legislatures cannot be expected to possess. . . .

Moreover, we must reject at the outset any conclusion that the rules as a whole represent an attempt by the Commission to expand its power arbitrarily; there is clear and adequate evidence of evils attendant on trip-leasing. The purpose of the rules is to protect the industry from practices detrimental to the maintenance of sound transportation services consistent with the regulatory system. Sections 216 (b) and 218 (a) of the Act, for instance, require the filing of a just and reasonable rate schedule by each common carrier, and the violation of these rates and the demoralization of rate structures generally are a probable concomitant of current leasing practices. Section 204 (a) (2) requires the Commission to impose rules relating to safety of operation for vehicles and drivers. These are likewise threatened by the unrestricted use of nonowned equipment by the common carriers. And the requirements of continuous service . . . of observance of authorized routes and termini . . . and the prohibitions of rebates . . . also may be ignored through the very practices here proscribed.

So the rules in question are aimed at conditions which may directly frustrate the success of the regulation undertaken by Congress. Included in the Act as a duty of the Commission is that "[t]o administer, execute, and enforce all provisions of this part, to make all necessary orders in connection therewith, and to prescribe rules, regulations, and procedure for such administration." § 204 (a)(6). And this necessary rule-making power, coterminous with the scope of agency regulation itself, must extend to the "transportation of passengers or property by motor carriers engaged in interstate or foreign commerce and to the procurement of and the provision of facilities for such transportation," regulation of which is vested in the Commission. . . .

We hold then that the promulgation of these rules for authorized carriers falls within the Commission's power, despite the absence of specific reference to leasing practices in the Act. . . . This result . . . is foreshadowed . . . by *United States* v. *Pennsylvania R. Co.,* 323 U.S. 612. That case validated an order requiring railroads to lease cars to a competing carrier by sea, in spite of the inability of the Commission to ground its action on some specific provision of the Act. . . . This Court pointed to the fact that the "unquestioned power of the Commission to require establishment of [through] routes would be wholly fruitless, without the correlative power to abrogate the Association's rule which prohibits the interchange." . . . There is evidence here that convinces us that that regulation of leasing practices is likewise a necessary power; in fact, we think its exercise more crucial than in *United States* v. *Pennsylvania R. Co.* The enforcement of only one phase of the Act was there endangered; here, practically the entire regulatory scheme is affected by trip-leasing.

### § 28:4. Delegation to Nongovernmental Bodies or Persons

In some instances, the lawmaker will not merely establish an administrator with power to make regulations but will provide that an administrative regulation cannot go into effect until a certain percentage of persons affected by the regulation agree thereto. Thus a production quota regulation of the administrator may require the approval of two thirds of the producers before it becomes effective. Such a requirement is imposed for a variety of reasons. It may be done to make the administrative program more acceptable to, or popular with, the persons regulated by giving them a part in the promulgation of the program. It may be designed as a check upon the administrator. Again it may be intended as an indirect way of pooling the experience or judgment of a wide number of persons in the formulation of the program.

As against such delegation, it may be argued that rules which have the effect of laws are being made by persons who are neither the duly elected lawmakers nor even administrators created by statutes adopted by such lawmakers. Moreover objection may be made that the procedure has an element of class discrimination when the nongovernmental group whose consent is required does not represent a cross section of all society, as when merely the wheat producers, but not the millers, distributors, bakers, or consumers, are permitted to vote on the quantity of wheat to be produced. Under the present federal theory such objections are without merit, and it is constitutional to provide for the adoption of an administrative rule with the consent of a specified percentage of a specified class of persons. There is a conflict as to the validity of state laws making such provision.

### *(a) Cooperation between administrators and producers*

UNITED STATES v. ROCK ROYAL COOPERATIVE, INC.
307 U.S. 533 (1939)

The Agricultural Marketing Agreement Act of 1937 described in the portion of this opinion set forth under § 28:3(b) was further challenged as making an unconstitutional delegation of legislative power by requiring two thirds of the producers to approve a quota proposed by the Secretary of Agriculture.

OPINION BY REED, J.

. . . Under Section 8c(9) (B) of the Act it is provided that any order shall become effective notwithstanding the failure of 50 per cent of the handlers to approve a similar agreement, if the Secretary of Agriculture with the approval of the President determines, among other things, that the issuance of the order is approved by two-thirds of the producers interested or by interested producers of two-thirds of the volume produced for the market of the specified production area. By subsection (19) it is provided that for the purpose of ascertaining whether the issuance of such order is approved "the Secretary may conduct a referendum among producers." The objection is made that this is an unlawful delegation to producers of the legislative power to put an order into effect in a market. In considering this question, we must assume that the Congress had the power to put this Order into effect without the approval of anyone. Whether producer approval by election is necessary or not, a question we reserve, a requirement of such approval would not be an invalid delegation.

### § 28:5. Public Participation in Matters Preliminary to Rule-making

In some instances, nongovernmental bodies or persons play a part in furnishing information or opinions that may ultimately affect the adoption or nature of the rule adopted by the administrator. When the information furnished or the recommendations made by the nongovernmental body or persons are not binding on the administrator but are for his information only, no question arises of delegation of the rule making power.

This pattern of cooperation with the administrator may be illustrated by the Federal Trade Commission practice, begun in 1919, of calling together members of each significant industry so that the members could discuss which practices were fair trade practices and which were not. The conclusions of these conferences were not automatically binding on the Federal Trade Commission, but they served as a valuable means of bringing to the Commission detailed information respecting the conduct of the particular industry or business in question. Under the Federal Trade Commission practice, the rules of fair practice agreed to at the trade conferences may be approved or disapproved by the Commission. When the rules are approved, a further distinction is made between those rules that are "affirmatively approved" by the Commission and those that are merely "accepted as expressions of the trade." In the case of the former, the Commission will enforce compliance by the members of the industry. In the case of the latter, the Commission will accept the practices as fair trade practices but will not enforce compliance by persons not willing to comply.

### § 28:6. Public Knowledge of Rule

The adoption of a rule or a regulation by an administrator gives rise to an important practical problem. How can the rule or regulation be brought to the attention of the persons who are to obey it? And how can this be done quickly in order to avoid a substantial delay between the time when the regulation is adopted and the time when the public learns of its existence? An effort is made to solve this problem, in the case of the national government, by printing in the Government Printing Office a daily magazine or newspaper called the *Federal Register* in which are printed all presidential proclamations and executive orders and such other documents and classes of documents as the President or an Act of Congress may from time to time direct. The Federal Administrative Procedure Act provides:

> Sec. 3. Except to the extent that there is involved (1) any function of the United States requiring secrecy in the public interest or (2) any matter relating solely to the internal management of an agency—
>
> (a) RULES.—Every agency shall separately state and currently publish in the *Federal Register* (1) descriptions of its central and field organization including delegations by the agency of final authority and the established places at which, and methods whereby, the public may secure information or make submittals or requests; (2) statements of the general course and method by which its functions are channeled and determined, including the nature and requirements of all formal or informal procedures available as well as forms and instructions as to the scope and contents of all papers, reports, or examinations; and (3) substantive rules adopted as authorized by law and statements of general policy or interpretations formulated and adopted by the agency for the guidance of the public, but not rules addressed to and served upon named persons in accordance with law. No person shall in any manner be required to resort to organization or procedure not so published.

Under the terms of the Federal Register Act, filing such documents with the administrator in charge of the *Federal Register* is made "sufficient to give notice of the contents of such documents to any person subject thereto or affected thereby." If this is not done, the rule is binding only on persons having actual knowledge of its existence. The Federal Register Act also provides that publication of the document in the *Federal Register* "shall create a rebuttable presumption that (a) it was duly issued, prescribed, or promulgated; . . . (c) that the copy contained in the *Federal Register* is a true copy of the original. . . ."

Every five years, beginning with July 1, 1948, each agency of the national government is required to file "a complete codification of all documents which, in the opinion of the agency, have general applicability and legal effect" and which are then in force.

This is a reasonably satisfactory solution to the problem in the case of a big business that has an attorney or a legal staff to examine the *Register*. In the case of a smaller business that cannot afford an attorney or does not have a legal staff, the *Federal Register* is not a satisfactory solution, although it is difficult to determine what further step, if any, could be taken by the government.

A number of states have statutes similar to the Federal Register Act.

### (a) Effect of publication

## FEDERAL CROP INSURANCE CORP. v. MERRILL

332 U.S. 380 (1947)

Administrative regulations adopted under the Federal Wheat Crop Insurance Act were published in the *Federal Register* but were in fact unknown to the applicant for insurance. He claimed that he was not bound by them.

OPINION BY FRANKFURTER, J.

. . . Just as everyone is charged with knowledge of the United States Statutes at Large, Congress has provided that the appearance of rules and regulations in the *Federal Register* gives legal notice of their contents. . . . Accordingly, the Wheat Crop Insurance Regulations were binding on all who sought to come within the Federal Crop Insurance Act, regardless of actual knowledge of what is in the Regulations or of the hardship resulting from innocent ignorance.

### Questions for Discussion

1. Why is it desirable to delegate rule-making authority to the administrator?

2. What are the legal and the practical objections to delegation?

3. To what extent may legislative power be delegated? Are there any limitations on the power?

4. (a) When an administrator adopts a rule or a regulation, is he exercising an executive, judicial, or legislative function? (b) Does it affect your answer if the rule or regulation is adopted after a hearing is held at which evidence is presented to the administrator with respect to what type of rule or regulation should be adopted?

5. State and compare the opposing arguments that can be made as to whether a state administrative rule is the law of the state.

6. Appraise the merits of the argument that an administrator's decision should not be regarded as the law of the state, because it may be so readily changed.

7. Appraise the concept of the court in the *Fahey* case that because banking regulation had long existed and a pattern of law and practice had developed, it was not necessary to state specifically the grounds for the appointment of a conservator.

8. On the basis of the *American Trucking Association* case, would the Interstate Commerce Commission have authority to stop riots in a given

city on the ground that the rioting was interfering with the movement of interstate trains?

9. (a) Is a statute constitutional that sets forth the policy to be followed by the administrator? (b) Has the requirement that the administrator conform to a "standard" been replaced by the broader view that it is sufficient for Congress to define the general policy? See *American Power & Light Co.* v. *Securities Exchange Commission.*

10. Can the administrator apply rules that he has adopted after a particular case has been begun? Is he restricted to the rules that existed before the action was taken?

11. Would the statute considered in *United States* v. *Rock Royal Cooperative* have been unconstitutional if the Secretary were given freedom in selecting any agricultural product as to which he deemed action necessary?

12. Is the Court correct in stating in *United States* v. *Rock Royal Cooperative* that the standards there considered give ample assurance that the various factors will be considered by the Secretary?

13. (a) How does the administrator inform the public of his regulations? (b) Is the problem the same in the case of a health officer as in the case of a public utility commission?

14. (a) What does the Federal Register Act provide with regard to the publication of regulations? (b) What are the disadvantages of this method? (c) Can you suggest a better method?

15. (a) Why does the Administrative Procedure Act provide for a hearing when the administrator proposes to make rules? (b) Is the hearing a legislative or a judicial function?

16. In *United States* v. *Morton Salt Co.*, 338 U.S. 632 (1950), the Court stated: "The Administrative Procedure Act was framed against a background of rapid expansion of the administrative process as a check upon administrators whose zeal might otherwise have carried them to excesses not contemplated in legislation creating their offices. It created safeguards even narrower than the constitutional ones, against arbitrary official encroachment upon private rights. . . ." To what extent can this policy be seen in the provisions of the Administrative Procedure Act that are quoted on page 410?

17. A federal statute applicable to the District of Columbia created a board for the condemnation of unsanitary buildings and conferred upon the board "jurisdiction and authority to examine into the sanitary conditions of all buildings in said District, to condemn those buildings which are in such insanitary condition as to endanger the health or lives of the occupants thereof or of persons living in the vicinity, and to cause all buildings to be put into sanitary conditions or to be vacated, demolished, and removed. . . ." Acting under this authority the Board condemned a

building. The owner claimed that the law was unconstitutional in failing to establish standards for the guidance of the Board. Decide. *Keys* v. *Madesen,* 179 F.2d 40 (App. D.C. 1949).

18. (a) In the *Yakus* case does the Court indicate whether it is necessary that the Court agree with the price administrator as to the amount of the price to be established? (b) If the administrator sets a price of 7 cents a unit, would the court reverse him if it believed that the fair price should be 8 cents or 6 cents instead?

19. How does the court define the legislative process or function in the *Yakus* case?

20. Why is it constitutional to provide that a statute shall not go into effect until approved by a certain percentage of those affected?

21. What type of administrator is the Federal Trade Commission? Is it legislative, executive, or judicial? Discuss.

22. Is there any difference between the scope of judicial inquiry and of administrative inquiry?

## Chapter 29

## ADMINISTRATIVE DETERMINATION OF ISSUES



### § 29:1. Pattern of Administrative Procedure

At the beginning of the era of modern regulation of business, the administrator was, to a large extent, a minor executive or police officer charged with the responsibility of enforcing the laws applicable to limited fact situations. The health officer empowered to condemn and destroy diseased cattle was typical. In view of the need for prompt action and because of the relative simplicity of the fact determination to be made, it was customary for him to exercise summary powers; that is, upon finding cattle which he believed diseased, he could have them killed immediately without delaying to find their true owner or without holding a formal hearing to determine whether they were in fact diseased.

As we come down to the present day, the exercise of summary powers becomes the exceptional case. Today it is permitted mainly in connection with the fraudulent use of the mails or the sending of improper matter such as lottery tickets or obscene matter through the mails, the enforcement of navigation regulations and tax laws, and the exercise of the police power in order to protect the public health and safety. As the regulation of business assumes the aspect of economic rather than health or safety regulation, the need for immediate action by the administrator diminishes, if not disappears, when the administrator acts to determine whether particular conduct comes within the scope of a regulation or whether there has been a violation thereof, and accordingly, concepts of due process generally require that some notice be given those who will be adversely affected and that some form of hearing be held at which they may present their case. As a practical matter, also, the more complicated the nature of the determinations to be made, the longer the period of investigation and deliberation required.

In the more modern type of regulation, the proceedings before the administrator tend to follow the general pattern of an action in the law court. It is commonly provided that either a private individual aggrieved by the conduct of another or the administrator on his own motion may present a complaint. This complaint is served on the alleged wrongdoer, and he is given opportunity to file an answer. There may be other phases of pleading between the parties and the administrator, but eventually the matter comes before the administrator to be heard. After a hearing, the administrator makes a decision and enters an order either dismissing the complaint or directing the adverse party to do or not to do certain acts. This order is generally not self-executing and, in order to enforce it, provision is generally made for an application by the administrator to a court. Sometimes the converse is provided so that the order of the administrator becomes binding upon the adverse party unless he appeals to a court within a stated period for a review of the order.

The complaint filing and pre-hearing stage of the procedure may be more detailed than just stated. In many of the modern administrative statutes, provision is made for an examination of the informal complaint by some branch of the administrator to determine whether it presents a case coming within the scope of the administrator's authority. It is also commonly provided that an investigation be made by the administrator to determine whether the facts are such as warrant a hearing of the complaint. If it is decided that the complaint is within the jurisdiction of the administrator and that the facts appear to justify it, a formal complaint is issued and served on the adverse party, and an answer is filed by him as above stated.

With the rising complexity of the subjects regulated by administrative procedure, the trend is increasingly in the direction of greater preliminary examination upon the basis of an informal complaint.

Cutting across these procedures are the practical devices of informal settlement and consent decrees. In many instances, the alleged wrongdoer will be willing to change his practices or his conduct upon being informally notified that a complaint has been made against him. It is therefore sound public relations as well as expeditious handling of the matter for the administrator to inform the alleged wrongdoer of the charge made against him prior to the filing of any formal complaint in order to give him the opportunity to settle the matter voluntarily. A matter that has already gone into the formal hearing stage may also be terminated by agreement, and a stipulation or consent decree may be entered or filed setting forth the terms of the agreement.

A further modification of this general pattern is made in the case of the Interstate Commerce Commission. Complaints received by the Commission are referred to the Bureau of Informal Cases, which endeavors to secure an amicable adjustment with the carrier. If this cannot be done, the complainant is notified that it will be necessary to file a formal complaint. At this stage of the proceedings, the parties can expedite the matter by agreeing that the case may be heard on the pleadings alone. If this is done, the complainant files a pleading or memorandum to which the defendant files an answering memorandum, the plaintiff then filing a reply or rebuttal memorandum. If the parties do not agree to this procedure, a hearing is held after the pleadings have been filed.

### § 29:2. Delegation of Judicial Power

Paralleling the unsuccessful argument that the power to make rules cannot be delegated to the administrator [1] is the assertion that the administrator cannot be given the power to make judicial determinations, on the theory that only a body with judicial power can make determinations affecting matters of private right. In the federal area this argument has never been sustained.[2] In the state courts, it has sometimes been held that there was an improper delegation of judicial power when the power is given to an administrator to determine matters involving common-law rights and liabilities but not when questions relating to new administrative rights are determined. One court has held that even in such latter case the power to make a judicial determination cannot be conferred.[3] Generally, however, the state decisions follow the federal rule.

### § 29:3. Necessity of Notice and Hearing

In order to satisfy the requirements of due process, it may be necessary for the administrator to give notice and to hold a hearing. This raises two questions, whether notice and hearing are necessary and, if they are, whether satisfactory notice and hearing has been given and allowed. The attempt has been made by the courts to define the necessity for notice and hearing in terms of whether the administrator exercises a legislative or a judicial function. In the case of the legislative function, the administrator makes a determination of or adopts a rule to govern future cases. In the case of a judicial function, the administrator applies the existing law to the facts of a particular case to determine the liability of the parties. If the function exercised by the administrator is judicial or quasi-judicial, notice and hearing are required. Although rate-making is classified as a legislative function, notice and hearing are also required as in the case of a judicial function.

If due process requires a notice and hearing, this does not necessarily take place at the administrative level. In some instances, it is held that a notice given the party affected after the administrator makes his decision and a hearing held before a court on appeal from the decision of the administrator are sufficient notice and hearing. The same is true where the administrative determination cannot be

[1] See § 28:1.

[2] Sunshine Anthracite Coal Co. v. Adkins, 310 U.S. 381 (1940).

[3] State ex rel. Hovey Concrete Products Co. v. Mechem, 63 N.M. 250, 316 P. 2d 1069 (1957).

enforced by the administrator but only by an action at law against the party affected. Here it is held that the notice to the person that he is being sued and the opportunity for a hearing in that suit satisfy the requirements of due process.

### *(a) Abolition of railroad grade crossings*

### SOUTHERN RAILWAY v. VIRGINIA

### 290 U.S. 190 (1933)

A state statute authorized an administrator to order railroads to eliminate grade crossings whenever in his opinion this was necessary for the public safety and convenience. No express provision was made for a notice or a hearing on the question of the necessity of eliminating grade crossings, and no provision was made for a review of the officer's decision other than that which was afforded by resort to the injunction power of a court.

OPINION BY MCREYNOLDS, J.

. . . The Highway Commissioner, without prior notice, advised [the railroad] that in his opinion public safety and convenience required elimination of the grade crossing. . . .

As authoritatively interpreted the challenged Act permits the Highway Commissioner—an executive officer—without notice or hearing to command a railroad company to abolish any designated grade crossing and construct an overhead when, in his opinion, necessary for public safety and convenience. His opinion is final upon the fundamental question whether public convenience and necessity require the elimination, unless what the Supreme Court denominates "arbitrary" exercise of the granted power can be shown. Upon petition, filed within sixty days, the Corporation Commission may consider the proposed plans and approve or modify them, but nothing more. The statute makes no provision for review by any court. But the Supreme Court [of the state] has declared that a court of equity may give relief under an original bill where "arbitrary" action can be established.

As construed and applied, we think the statute conflicts with the Fourteenth Amendment.

Certainly, to require abolition of an established grade crossing and the outlay of money necessary to construct an overhead would take the railway's property in a very real sense. This seems plain enough. . . .

If we assume that by proper legislation a State may impose upon the railways the duty of eliminating grade crossings, when deemed necessary for public safety and convenience, the question here is whether the challenged statute meets the requirements of due process of law. Undoubtedly, it attempts to give an administrative officer power to make final determination in respect of facts—the character of a crossing and what is necessary for the public safety and convenience—without notice, without hearing, without evidence; and upon this ex parte finding, not subject to general review, to ordain that expenditures shall be made for erecting a new structure. The thing so authorized is no mere police regulation. . . .

Counsel submit that the legislature, without giving notice or opportunity to be heard, by direct order might have required elimination of the crossing. Consequently, they conclude the same may be accomplished in any manner which it deems advisable without violating the Federal Constitution. But if we assume that a state legislature may determine what public welfare demands and by direct command require a railway to act accordingly, it by no means follows that an administrative officer may be empowered, without notice or hearing, to act upon his own opinion and ordain the taking of private property. There is an obvious difference between legislative determination and the finding of an administrative official not supported by evidence. In theory at least, the legislature acts upon adequate knowledge after full consideration and through members who represent the entire public.

. . . It is clear that no such authority as that claimed for the Commissioner could be entrusted to an administrative officer or body under the power to tax, to impose assessments for benefits, to regulate common carriers, to establish drainage districts or to regulate business. . . .

This court has often recognized the power of a state, acting through an executive officer or body, to order the removal of grade crossings; but in all these cases there was the right to a hearing and review by some court. . . .

. . . The court below said: "The railroad is not without remedy. Should the power vested in the Highway Commissioner be arbitrarily exercised, equity's long arm will stay his hand." But, by sanctioning the order directing the Railway to proceed, it, in effect, approved action without hearing, without evidence, without opportunity to know the basis therefor. This was to rule that such action was not necessarily "arbitrary." There is nothing to indicate what that court would deem arbitrary action or how this could be established in the absence of evidence or hearing. In circumstances like those here disclosed no contestant could have full opportunity for relief in a court of equity. There would be nothing to show the grounds upon which the Commissioner based his conclusion. He alone would be cognizant of the mental processes which begot his urgent opinion.

The infirmities of the enactment are not relieved by an indefinite right of review in respect of some action spoken of as arbitrary. Before its property can be taken under the edict of an administrative officer the appellant is entitled to a fair hearing upon the fundamental facts. This has not been accorded. . . .

### *(b) Rate determination*

CHICAGO, MILWAUKEE & ST. PAUL RAILWAY CO. v. MINNESOTA
134 U.S. 418 (1890)

A state commission was authorized to fix the rates to be charged by common carriers whenever it found that unreasonable rates were charged. If a carrier failed to comply with the order of the commission, the latter was authorized to obtain a writ of mandamus or court order to compel compliance. If the carrier then failed to comply with the court order it could be punished for contempt. No provision was made for a hearing before the commission at which a carrier could offer evidence as to the reasonable character of the rate it charged.

OPINION BY BLATCHFORD, J.

. . . The supreme court of Minnesota . . . declares . . . that the rates recommended and published by the commission, if it proceeds in the manner pointed out by the act, are not simply advisory, nor merely *prima facie* equal and reasonable, but final and conclusive as to what are equal and reasonable charges; that the law neither contemplates nor allows any issue to be made or inquiry to be had as to their equality or reasonableness in fact; that, under the statute, the rates published by the commission are the only ones that are lawful, and therefore, in contemplation of law, the only ones that are equal and reasonable; and that, in a proceeding for a *mandamus* under the statute, there is no fact to traverse except the violation of law in not complying with the recommendations of the commission. In other words, although the railroad company is forbidden to establish rates that are not equal and reasonable, there is no power in the courts to stay the hands of the commission, if it chooses to establish rates that are unequal and unreasonable. This being the construction of the statute . . . it conflicts with the constitution of the United States. . . . It deprives the company of its right to a judicial investigation, by due process of law, under the forms and with the machinery provided by the wisdom of successive ages for the investigation judicially of the truth of a matter in controversy, and substitutes therefor, as an absolute finality, the action of a railroad commission which, in view of the powers conceded to it by the state court, cannot be regarded as clothed with judicial functions, or possessing the machinery of a court of justice. Under section 8 of the statute, which the supreme court of Minnesota says is the only one which relates to the matter of the fixing by the commission of general schedules of rates, and which section, it says, fully and exclusively provides for that subject, and is complete in itself, all that the commission is required to do is on the filing with it by a railroad company of copies of schedules of charges, to "find" that any part thereof is in any respect unequal or unreasonable, and then it is authorized and directed to compel the company to change the same, and adopt such charge as the commission "shall declare to be equal and reasonable;" and to that end it is required to inform the company in writing in what respect its charges are unequal and unreasonable. No hearing is provided for; no summons or notice to the company before the commission has found what it is to find, and declared what it is to declare; no opportunity provided for the company to introduce witnesses before the commission,—in fact, nothing which has the semblance of due process of law; and although, in the present case, it appears that, prior to the decision of the commission, the company appeared before it by its agent, and the commission investigated the rates charged by the company for transporting milk, yet it does not appear what the character of the investigation was, or how the result was arrived at. By the second section of the statute in question, it is provided that all charges made by a common carrier for the transportation of passengers or property shall be equal and reasonable. Under this provision, the carrier has a right to make equal and reasonable charges for such transportation. In the present case, the return alleged that the rate of charge fixed by the commission was not equal or reasonable, and the supreme court held that the statute deprived the company of the right to show that judicially. The question of the reasonableness of a rate of charge for transportation by a railroad company, involving, as it does, the element of reasonableness both as regards the company and as regards the public, is eminently a question for judicial investigation, requiring due process of law for its determination. If the company is deprived of the power of charging reasonable rates for the use of its property, and such deprivation takes place in the absence of an investigation by judicial machinery, it is deprived of the lawful use of its property, and thus, in substance and effect, of the property itself, without due process of law, and in violation of the constitution of the United States; . . .

DISSENTING OPINION BY BRADLEY, J.

. . . The legislature might have fixed the rates in question. If it had done so, it would have done it through the aid of committees appointed to investigate the subject, to acquire information, to cite parties, to get all the facts before them, and finally to decide and report. No one could have said that this was not due process of law. And if the legislature itself could do this, acting by its committees, and proceeding according to the usual forms adopted by such bodies, I can see no good reason why it might not delegate the duty to a board of commissioners, charged, as the board in this case was, to regulate and fix the charges so as to be equal and reasonable. Such a board would have at its command all the means of getting at the truth, and ascertaining the reasonableness of fares and freights, which a legislative committee has. It might or it might not swear witnesses and examine parties. Its duties being of an administrative character, it would have the widest scope for examination and inquiry. All means of knowledge and information would be at its command; just as they would be at the command of the legislature which created it. Such a body, though not a court, is a proper tribunal for the duties imposed upon it. . . .

It is complained that the decisions of the board are final and without appeal. So are the decisions of the courts in matters within their jurisdiction. There must be a final tribunal somewhere for deciding every question in the world. Injustice may take place in all tribunals. All human institutions are imperfect,—courts as well as commissions and legislatures. Whatever tribunal has jurisdiction, its decisions are final and conclusive, unless an appeal is given therefrom. The important question always is, what is the lawful tribunal for the particular case? In my judgment, in the present case, the proper tribunal was the legislature, or the board of commissioners which it created for the purpose. . . .

### § 29:4. Time for Hearing

While a hearing must be granted the carrier, it is not necessary that this hearing be had before the commission makes a determination of the rates. It is sufficient if an opportunity is given for a full hearing before the order fixing the rates becomes operative. It is thus constitutional to authorize a commission to fix the rate first and then grant a hearing on this proposed rate if the carrier applies for a hearing. If the carrier does not apply for the hearing, the procedure is not objectionable because in the particular case there was in fact no hearing. It is likewise constitutional to provide that at such a hearing the burden of proof shall be on the carrier to show that the rates proposed by the commission are unreasonable, rather than placing the burden on the commission to justify its rates as reasonable.

#### *(a) Rent control*

BOWLES v. WILLINGHAM

321 U.S. 503 (1944)

The Emergency Price Control Act of 1942 authorized the Price Control Administrator to fix maximum rentals for areas in which such control was, in his opinion, needed. A property owner sought to enjoin the enforcement of a rent order issued under the Act. It was claimed that the Act was unconstitutional because there was no hearing provided prior to the entry of a rent order.

OPINION BY DOUGLAS, J.

. . .

In June 1943, the Rent Director gave written notice to Mrs. Willingham that he proposed to decrease the maximum rents for three apartments owned by her, and which had not been rented on April 1, 1941, but were first rented in the summer of 1941, on the ground that the first rents for these apartments received after April 1, 1941 were in excess of those generally prevailing in the area for comparable accommodations on April 1, 1941. Mrs. Willingham filed objections to that proposed action together with supporting affidavits. The Rent Director thereupon advised her that he would proceed to issue an order reducing the rents. . . .

. . . It is finally [argued] that the Act violates the Fifth Amendment because it makes no provision for a hearing to landlords before the order or regulation fixing rents becomes effective. Obviously, Congress would have been under no necessity to give notice and provide a hearing before it acted, had it decided to fix rents on a national basis the same as it did for the District of Columbia. See 55 Stat. 788. We agree with the Emergency Court of Appeals . . . that Congress need not make that requirement when it delegates the task to an administrative agency. In *Bi-Metallic Investment Co.* v. *State Board,* 239 U.S. 441, a suit was brought by a taxpayer and landowner to enjoin a Colorado Board from putting in effect an order which increased the valuation of all taxable property in Denver 40 per cent. Such action, it was alleged, violated the Fourteenth Amendment as the plaintiff was given no opportunity to be heard. Mr. Justice Holmes, speaking for the court, stated . . . "Where a rule of conduct applies to more than a few people it is impracticable that every one should have a direct voice in its adoption. The Constitution does not require all public acts to be done in town meeting or an assembly of the whole. General statutes within the state power are passed that affect the person or property of individuals, sometimes to the point of ruin, without giving them a chance to be heard. Their rights are protected in the only way that they can be in a complex society, by their power, immediate or remote, over those who make the rule." We need not go so far in the present case. Here Congress has provided for judicial review of the Administrator's action. To be sure, that review comes after the order has been promulgated; and no provision for a stay is made. . . ."Where only property rights are involved, mere postponement of the judicial enquiry is not a denial of due process, if the opportunity given for the ultimate judicial determination of the liability is adequate. . . . Delay in the judicial determination of property rights is not uncommon where it is essential that government needs be immediately satisfied."

Language in the cases that due process requires a hearing before the administrative order becomes effective . . . is to be explained on two grounds. In the first place the statutes there involved required that procedure.

Secondly, as we have held in *Yakus* v. *United States,* Congress was dealing here with the exigencies of war time conditions and the insistent demands of inflation control. . . . Congress chose not to fix rents in specified areas or on a national scale by legislative fiat. It chose a method designed to meet the needs for rent control as they might arise and to accord some leeway for adjustment within the formula which it prescribed. At the same time, the procedure which Congress adopted was selected with the view of eliminating the necessity for "lengthy and costly trials with concomitant dissipation of the time and energies of all concerned in litigation rather than in common war effort." . . . To require hearings for thousands of landlords before any rent control order could be made effective might have defeated the program of price control. Or Congress might well have thought so. National security might not be able to afford the luxuries of litigation and the long delays which preliminary hearings traditionally have entailed.

We fully recognize . . . that "even the war power does not remove constitutional limitations safeguarding essential liberties." . . . But where Congress has provided for judicial review after the regulations or orders have been made effective it has done all that due process under the war emergency requires. . . .

### § 29:5. Nature of Hearing

When a hearing is required, to what extent must it conform to the standards observed in a court trial?

Certain requirements of a court trial should be observed at the administrative hearing if the testimony of witnesses is presented. Experience and common sense have shown that certain devices or procedures of a court trial are aids in the determination of the truth. At the hearing before the administrator, witnesses should be sworn or affirmed in the same manner as in a jury trial. Persons against whom testimony is given should have the privilege of confronting or facing those who have testified against them. The right to cross-examine the opposing witnesses and to offer evidence in rebuttal of their testimony should be preserved. Similarily, the right to make objections to the proceedings and the introduction of evidence and to obtain rulings either in the course of the hearing or in the opinion or report filed by the administrator should also be observed.

The various privileges against testifying must also be honored before the administrator. Communications between husband and wife, physician and patient, attorney and client, which are deemed "privileged" in an action in a law court, must also be regarded as privileged before an administrator. The consequence is that a witness may refuse to testify on what was said to him because that statement was a privileged communication because of the relationship of the speaker to the witness. Similarly the guarantee against self-incrimination applies to a witness testifying before the administrator.

When it is provided that the administrator is not bound by the rules of evidence or by procedure applicable to a proceeding before a law court, the question arises whether any procedure is valid or whether some limitation is imposed in place of those that would bind a court. That there must be some limitations was recognized in *Interstate Commerce Commission* v. *Louisville & Nashville Railroad,* 227 U.S. 88 (1913), in which the court stated: ". . . the more liberal the practice in admitting testimony, the more imperative the obligation to preserve the essential rules of evidence by which rights are asserted or defended. In such cases the Commissioners cannot act upon their own information, as could jurors in primitive days. All parties must be fully apprised of the evidence submitted or to be considered, and must be given opportunity to cross-examine witnesses, to inspect documents, and to offer evidence in explanation or rebuttal. In no other way can a party maintain its rights or make its defense. In no other way can it test the sufficiency of the facts to support the findings; for otherwise, even though it appeared that the order was without evidence, the manifest deficiency could always be explained on the theory that the Commission had before it extraneous, unknown but presumptively sufficient information to support the finding."

### *(a) Basis of decision*

UNITED STATES AND INTERSTATE COMMERCE COMMISSION v. ABILENE & SOUTHERN RAILWAY CO.

265 U.S. 274 (1924)

The examiner of the Interstate Commerce Commission informed the carrier that it might be necessary to refer to the annual reports of the carriers at a hearing that was to be held before the Commission. The reports were not offered in evidence at the hearing, but the order of the Commission on the division of rates was in part based upon the information contained in them. The order of the Commission was attacked on this ground.

OPINION BY BRANDEIS, J.

. . . The plaintiffs contend that the order is void because it rests upon evidence not legally before the Commission. It is conceded that the finding rests, in part, upon data taken from the annual reports filed with the Commission by the plaintiff carriers pursuant to law; that these reports were not formally put in evidence; that the parts containing the data relied upon were not put in evidence through excerpts; that attention was not otherwise specifically called to them; and that objection to the use of the reports, under these circumstances was seasonably made by the carriers and was insisted upon. The parts of the annual reports in question were used as evidence of facts which it was deemed necessary to prove, not as a means of verifying facts of which the Commission, like a court, takes judicial notice. The contention of the Commission is that, because its able examiner gave notice that "no doubt it will be necessary to refer to the annual reports of all these carriers," its Rules of Practice permitted matter in the reports to be used as freely as if the data had been formally introduced in evidence.

The mere admission by an administrative tribunal of matter which under the rules of evidence applicable to judicial proceedings would be deemed incompetent does not invalidate its order. . . . But a finding without evidence is beyond the power of the Commission. Papers in the Commission's files are not always evidence in a case. . . . Nothing can be treated as evidence which is not introduced as such. . . . If the proceeding had been, in form, an adversary one commenced by the Orient system, that carrier could not, under rule XIII, have introduced the annual reports as a whole. For they contain much that is not relevant to the matter in issue. By the terms of the rule, it would have been obliged to submit copies of such portions as it deemed material; or to make specific reference to the exact portion to be used. The fact that the proceeding was technically an investigation instituted by the Commission would not relieve the Orient, if a party to it, from this requirement. Every proceeding is adversary, in substance, if it may result in an order in favor of one carrier as against another. Nor was the proceeding under review any the less an adversary one, because the primary purpose of the Commission was to protect the public interest through making possible the continued operation of the Orient system. The fact that it was on the Commission's motion that use was made of the data in the annual reports is not of legal significance.

. . . The objection to the use of the data contained in the annual reports is not lack of authenticity or untrustworthiness. It is that the carriers were left without notice of the evidence with which they were, in fact, confronted, as later disclosed by the finding made. The requirement that in an adversary proceeding specific reference be made, is essential to the preservation of the substantial rights of the parties.

. . . The general notice that the Commission would rely upon the voluminous annual reports is tantamount to giving no notice whatsoever. The matter improperly treated as evidence may have been an important factor in the conclusions reached by the Commission. The order must, therefore, be held void. . . .

### *(b) Adjournment of hearing*

CONSOLIDATED EDISON CO. v. NATIONAL LABOR RELATIONS BOARD

305 U.S. 197 (1938)

The National Labor Relations Act of 1935 made it unlawful for an employer to engage in specified "unfair labor practices." The Consolidated Edison Company was found guilty of certain of these practices by the National Labor Relations Board and was ordered to desist from such practices and to reinstate employees discharged because of their union activities.

OPINION BY HUGHES, C. J.

. . . Between May 28, 1937, and June 16, 1937, the [Consolidated Edison and its affiliated] companies had entered into agreements with the International Brotherhood of Electrical Workers and its local unions. . . . The Board found that these contracts were . . . invalid and required the companies to desist from giving them effect. . . .

The companies petitioned the Circuit Court of Appeals to set aside the order and a petition for the same purpose was presented by the Brotherhood and its locals. . . .

A . . . serious question grows out of the refusal to receive the testimony of certain witnesses. The taking of evidence began on June 3, 1937, and was continued from time to time until June 23d when the attorney for the Board unexpectedly announced that its case would probably be closed on the following day. At that time the Board completed its proof, with the reservation of one matter, and at the request of the companies' counsel the hearing was adjourned until July 6th in order that Mr. Carlisle, the chairman of the board of trustees of the Consolidated Edison Company, and Mr. Dean, the vice president of one of its affiliates, who were then unavailable, could testify. In response to the examiner's inquiry, the companies' counsel stated that the direct examination of all witnesses on their behalf would not occupy more than a day. On July 6th the testimony of Mr. Carlisle and Mr. Dean was taken and the companies also offered the testimony of two other witnesses (then present in the hearing room) in relation to the discharge of the employee with respect to whom the complaint had been amended as above stated. The examiner refused to receive testimony following a ruling of the Board (made in the course of correspondence with the companies' counsel during the adjournment) to the effect that no other testimony than that of Mr. Carlisle and Mr. Dean would be received on the adjourned day. An offer of proof was made which showed the testimony to be highly important with respect to the reasons for the discharge. It was brief and could have been received at once without any undue delay in the closing of the hearing.

We agree with the Circuit Court of Appeals that the refusal to receive the testimony was unreasonable and arbitrary. Assuming, as the Board contends, that it had a discretionary control over the conduct of the proceeding, we cannot but regard this action as an abuse of discretion. But the statute did not leave the petitioners without remedy. The court below pointed to that remedy, that is, to apply to the Circuit Court of Appeals for leave to adduce the additional evidence; on such an application and a showing of reasonable grounds the court could have ordered it to be taken. § 10(e) (f). Petitioners did not avail themselves of this appropriate procedure. . . .

### *(c) Cross-examination*

NORWEGIAN NITROGEN PRODUCTS CO. v. UNITED STATES
288 U.S. 294 (1933)

The Tariff Commission refused to disclose to an importer who had objected to an increase in tariff rates the details relating to costs that had been given to the Commission by an American producer with the understanding that such information would be kept secret. The importer contended that the refusal to disclose this information and the refusal to permit him to cross-examine the experts of the Commission deprived him of the "hearing" to which he was entitled.

OPINION BY CARDOZO, J.

The Tariff Act of 1922 . . . gives authority to the President to increase or decrease the rates of duty specified in the act if he finds upon investigation that increase or decrease is necessary in order to equalize the differences in the cost of production in the United States and elsewhere. This provision is followed by others designed to give protection against hasty or ill-considered changes. There shall be no proclamation under the authority of the statute until an investigation to assist the President has been made by the United States Tariff Commission, which is "authorized to adopt such reasonable procedure, rules, and regulations as it may deem necessary." Coupled with these general directions is a mandate more particular which is the petitioner's chief reliance. "The commission shall give reasonable public notice of its hearings, and shall give reasonable opportunity to parties interested to be present, to produce evidence, and to be heard." § 315(c).

The decision of this case hinges upon our answer to the question whether the petitioner has been "heard" in accordance with the statute. Does the requirement of a hearing mean that every producer or importer affected by a tariff may explore at will the data collected by the Commission as to the capital, the wages, the cost of material and manufacture, in the business of any other person similarly affected, and may cross-examine investigators and competitors upon the data thus laid bare? If something less than this is exacted, is there still a minimum of disclosure without which the purpose of the hearing will be thwarted altogether, and was this minimum attained by what was done by the Commission here?

. . .

The process of tariff making by Congress and congressional committees is not different in essentials from that for legislation generally. If the bill has gone to a committee, the practice has been general to give the privilege of a hearing to business men and others affected by its provisions. The hearing is not one that may be demanded as of right. A change of the tariff laws like a change of any other statute is not subject to impeachment on the score of invalidity though notice to those affected has been omitted altogether. . . . Even so, the privilege is now so fortified by practice that it may fairly be taken for granted. But the hearing when given is not similar to a trial as conducted in a court. The proponents of a bill and the contestants make their statements for and against, bringing forward such confirmatory documents, trade journals, letters, governmental reports, and what not, as they believe to be important. The kind of information thus supplied can be gathered from the proceedings of the committees that reported the Tariff Act in question, the act of 1922, as well as from those leading up to the tariff acts of other years. In none of these congressional hearings has the practice ever prevailed of permitting the advocates of a measure to cross-examine the opponents, or the opponents the advocates, or of compelling the committee itself to submit to an inquisition as to data collected by its members through independent investigation. The committee determines for itself whether its sessions shall be public or private. "Investigations [in Congress] often proceed behind closed doors, for the manifest reason that otherwise some witnesses would not be frank, perhaps would not attend, putting themselves if possible beyond the reach of the committee." . . . It is all a matter of discretion. What is done by the Tariff Commission and the President in changing the tariff rates to conform to new conditions is in substance a delegation, though a permissible one, of the legislative process. . . . The inference is, therefore, a strong one that the kind of hearing assured by the statute to those affected by the change is a hearing of the same order as had been given by congressional committees when the legislative process was in the hands of Congress and no one else. . . .

We are not unmindful of cases in which the word "hearing" as applied to administrative proceedings has been thought to have a broader meaning. All depends upon the context. There is no denial of the power of Congress to lay bare to the business rivals of a producer and indeed to the public generally every document in the office of this Commission and all the information collected by its agents. The question for us here is whether there was the will to go so far. The answer will not be found in definitions of a hearing lifted from their setting and then applied to new conditions. The answer will be found in a consideration of the ends to be achieved in the particular conditions that were expected or foreseen. To know what they are, there must be recourse to all the aids available in the process of construction, to history and analogy, and practice as well as to the dictionary. Much is made by the petitioner of the procedure of the Interstate Commerce Commission when regulating the conduct or the charges of interstate carriers, and that of the Public Service Commissions of the states when regulating the conduct or the charges of public service corporations. The Tariff Commission advises; these others ordain. There is indeed this common bond that all alike are instruments in a governmental process which according to the accepted classification is legislative, not judicial. . . . Whatever the appropriate label, the kind of order that emerges from a hearing before a body with power to ordain is one that impinges upon legal rights in a very different way from the report of a commission which merely investigates and advises. The traditionary forms of hearing appropriate to the one body are unknown to the other. What issues from the Tariff Commission as a report and recommendation to the President, may be accepted, modified, or rejected. If it happens to be accepted, it does not bear fruit in anything that trenches upon legal rights. No one has a legal right to the maintenance of an existing rate or duty. Neither the action of Congress in fixing a new tariff nor that of the President in exercising his delegated power is subject to impeachment if the prescribed forms of legislation have been regularly observed. It is very different, however, when orders are directed against public service corporations limiting their powers in the transaction of their business. They may be challenged in the courts if the effect is to reduce the charges to the point of confiscation. . . . They may be challenged for other reasons when they are without evidence supporting them, and are merely arbitrary edicts. . . . The "hearing" that such commissions are to give must be adapted to the consequences that are to follow, to the attack and the review to which their orders will be subject. . . . The Commerce Act, as it stands today, and kindred statutes in the states, are instinct with the recognition of a duty to give a hearing of such a kind that the courts will understand why a Commission has acted as it has if their supervisory powers are afterwards invoked for enforcement or revision. No such inference is to be drawn from the act before us now. . . .

### *(d) Hearing for rate-making*

MORGAN v. UNITED STATES

298 U.S. 468 (1936)

Under the Packers and Stockyards Act of 1921, the Secretary of Agriculture is authorized to fix maximum rates to be charged by marketing agencies buying and selling livestock. In April, 1930, he began an inquiry into the reasonableness of existing rates in the Kansas City stockyards. Litigation testing the propriety of the procedure under this Act and of the conduct of the Secretary of Agriculture in connection with this particular inquiry came before the Supreme Court in 1936, 1938, 1939, and 1941.

OPINION BY HUGHES, C. J.

. . .

The proceeding is not one of ordinary administration, conformable to the standards governing duties of a purely executive character. It is a proceeding looking to legislative action in the fixing of rates of market agencies. And, while the order is legislative and gives to the proceeding its distinctive character . . . it is a proceeding which by virtue of the authority conferred has special attributes. The Secretary, as the agent of Congress in making the rates, must make them in accordance with the standards and under the limitations which Congress has prescribed. Congress has required the Secretary to determine, as a condition of his action, that the existing rates are or will be "unjust, unreasonable, or discriminatory." If and when he so finds, he may "determine and prescribe" what shall be the just and reasonable rate, or the maximum or minimum rate, thereafter to be charged. That duty is widely different from ordinary executive action. It is a duty which carries with it fundamental procedural requirements. There must be a full hearing. There must be evidence adequate to support pertinent and necessary findings of fact. Nothing can be treated as evidence which is not introduced as such. . . . Facts and circumstances which ought to be considered must not be excluded. Facts and circumstances must not be considered which should not legally influence the conclusion. Findings based on the evidence must embrace the basic facts which are needed to sustain the order. . . .

A proceeding of this sort requiring the taking and weighing of evidence, determinations of fact based upon the consideration of the evidence, and the making of an order supported by such findings, has a quality resembling that of a judicial proceeding. Hence it is frequently described as a proceeding of a *quasi-judicial* character. The requirement of a "full hearing" has obvious reference to the tradition of judicial proceedings in which evidence is received and weighed by the trier of the facts. The "hearing" is designed to afford the safeguard that the one who decides shall be bound in good conscience to consider the evidence, to be guided by that alone, and to reach his conclusion uninfluenced by extraneous considerations which in other fields might have play in determining purely executive action. The "hearing" is the hearing of evidence and argument. If the one who determines the facts which underlie the order has not considered evidence or argument, it is manifest that the hearing has not been given.

. . .

### *(e) Federal Administrative Procedure Act*

The substance of these decisions is restated in the Federal Administrative Procedure Act, which provides that:

> . . . no sanction shall be imposed or rule or order be issued except upon consideration of the whole record or such portions thereof as may be cited by any party and as supported by and in accordance with the reliable, probative and substantial evidence. Every party shall have the right to present his case or defense by oral or documentary evidence, to submit rebuttal evidence, and to conduct such cross-examination as may be required for a full and true disclosure of the facts. In rule making or determining claims for money or benefits or applications for initial licenses any agency may, where the interest of any party will not be prejudiced thereby, adopt procedures for the submission of all or part of the evidence in written form.
>
> . . . The transcript of testimony and exhibits, together with all papers and requests filed in the proceeding, shall constitute the exclusive record for decision in accordance with section 8 and, upon payment of lawfully prescribed costs, shall be made available to the parties. Where any agency decision rests on official notice of a material fact not appearing in the evidence in the record, any party shall on timely request be afforded an opportunity to show the contrary.

## § 29:6. Administrative Evidence

The rules of evidence may properly be relaxed in a hearing before an administrative officer. The general trend of statutory provision is expressly to provide that the rules of evidence are not binding upon the administrator. At first glance, this distinction between the courts of law and the administrative agencies on the rules of evidence is anomalous. It finds its explanation in the fact that the rules of evidence had developed certain exclusionary principles in order to protect the jury from being misled by statements or evidence.

Thus under the "hearsay" evidence rule, a witness in a trial before a jury is ordinarily not permitted to testify that he was told by another person that a certain fact had occurred. The weakness in such testimony lies in the fact that the other person referred to by the witness is not in court, is not under oath, and cannot be cross-examined as to the basis for his statement nor confronted by the opposing party or witnesses. There is accordingly no way of determining what, if any, basis the other person had for his statement. The jury, however, which ordinarily is untrained in the law and the sifting of evidence, is likely to regard as true the statement made by the other person to the witness.

Such testimony, however, may be offered without harm before a trained administrator. The fact that it is admitted does not mean that he is bound to give it to any particular weight and that he cannot ignore it completely if he does not find that it is worthy of belief. Since the administrator is engaged in searching out the truth, he may be aided by the fact that the hearsay statements, although only hearsay, may give him a clue to a line of inquiry or the names of other witnesses from whom he can obtain more direct evidence. Of course, if the administrator is not trained, he may be confused and misled by the second-hand statements made by the witnesses and it would be most unjust to rest a decision solely on the ground of what was said to the witness by an absent person.

Other exclusionary rules of evidence, such as the rule of *res inter alios acta,* may also be relaxed in proceedings before an administrator. This principle prohibits offering proof of the commission of other similar acts in order to establish the commission of a particular act. Thus when a defendant is sued for carelessly driving his automobile into the plaintiff's car, this principle bars evidence that he did the same thing on a number of other occasions. There are certain exceptions to this rule, as where the proof of the commission of the other acts shows a common plan of which the act in controversy is part or where the commission of the other acts shows the ability of the person charged to have committed the act in question, as where a person is shown to be able to forge a signature by proof that he had committed other forgeries. The admission of such evidence is highly prejudicial in a trial by jury, for the jury is likely to conclude that the person charged did commit the particular act since he committed the others; or the jury may take a rough-and-ready-justice attitude in the matter and decide that the person charged has done enough to warrant his being punished, whether or not he has done the particular act in controversy. Such evidence should be admissible before an administrator, whether or not it is established that it comes within the exceptions to the rule as recognized in actions at law.

The public records evidence rule should also be relaxed before the administrator. In its strict form, the rule prohibits the introduction in evidence in a law suit of a record or writing made by a public official unless it was made by him in the performance of his duty and for the purpose of providing a record for public examination. Under this rule, reports or data that are not expressly for public use, made or collected by governmental agencies, even though the public is permitted to obtain copies of them or to examine them, are not admissible. This is an unfortunate limitation since in many instances there is no way of duplicating the evidence contained in such reports, as where lack of time or money or the death of the persons concerned makes it impossible to obtain again the information that had been collected by the public official. The administrative agency should be permitted to avail itself of such public records, which, being made before the controversy arose, should be free of any partisan bias and therefore impartial. Again it is to be noted that the mere fact that evidence is admitted does not mean that it is controlling. The administrator still has freedom of decision to conclude that the report is not a fair report or that its conclusions are unsound or that the data have been sifted in such a way as to distort the true facts. The only effect of relaxing the evidence rule is to permit the administrator to consider the otherwise excluded evidence; it does not to require him to decide the case on the basis of such evidence.

### *(a) Federal administrators*

The general federal rule is that administrators are not bound by the rules of evidence for "the technical rules for the exclusion of evidence applicable in jury trials do not apply to proceedings before federal administrative agencies in the absence of a statutory requirement that such rules are to be observed." [4] This concept has been restated by the Federal Administrative Procedure Act which provides that "any oral or documentary evidence may be received, but every agency shall as a matter of policy provide for the exclusion of irrelevant, immaterial, or unduly repetitious evidence. . . ." [5] This section omits the qualification of "competent" or any other term indicating that the administrative evidence is to be governed by the ordinary law court rules of evidence.

The outstanding exception to the rule of admissibility of administrative evidence is the provision of the National Labor Management Relations Act that hearings before the Board "shall, so far as practicable, be conducted in accordance with the rules of evidence applicable in the district courts of the United States under the rules of civil procedure for such courts, adopted by the Supreme

[4] Opp Cotton Mills v. Administrator, 312 U.S. 126, 155 (1941).
[5] A.P.A. § 7(c).

Court. . . ." [6] In actual application this provision may not be as restrictive as it first appears because of the qualification of "so far as practicable."

## § 29:7. Weight of Administrative Evidence

If the administrator is not bound by the rules of evidence, questions arise as to the effect to be given evidence that would otherwise be inadmissible. Is it to be given the same weight as evidence that would be admissible at a jury trial? May a determination before the administrator be made solely upon the basis of such evidence that would otherwise be inadmissible? To date no clear answer has been given by the courts.

### *(a) Weight of hearsay statements*

CARROLL v. KNICKERBOCKER ICE CO.

218 N.Y. 435, 113 N.E. 507 (1916)

The decedent was employed delivering ice. The Workmen's Compensation Commission found that he had been fatally injured in the course of his employment and awarded workmen's compensation to his widow. The Commission found that he had been fatally injured when an ice tong slipped and a large cake of ice struck him in the stomach causing internal hemorrhage. The decedent was admitted to a hospital where, after developing delirium tremens, he died six days later. The award of compensation by the Commission was challenged on the ground that there was not adequate evidence to establish that the decedent had been fatally injured in the course of his employment.

OPINION BY CUDDEBACK, J.

. . .

Section 21 of the Workmen's Compensation Law . . . provides that in any proceeding upon a claim for compensation . . . "it shall be presumed in the absence of substantial evidence to the contrary (1) that the claim comes within the provisions [of the law]. . . ." There was in this case substantial evidence to overcome the statutory presumption. A helper on the ice wagon and two cooks employed in the saloon where the ice was delivered testified before the commission that they were present at the time and place when

[6] N.L.M.R.A. § 10(b).

it was alleged the plaintiff was injured, and that they did not see any accident whatsoever happen to him, and that they did not see any cake of ice fall. The physicians who subsequently examined the decedent testified that there were no bruises, discolorations, or abrasions on the surface of his body.

The finding of the commission is based solely on the testimony of witnesses who related what [the decedent] told them as to how he was injured. [His] wife testified that when he came home from his work he told her that he was putting a 300 pound cake of ice in Daly's cellar and the tong slipped and the ice came back on him. The physician who was called to treat the injured man at his home, a neighbor who dropped in, and the physicians at the hospital, where he was taken later in the day, testified that he made like statements to them.

The question is presented whether this hearsay testimony is sufficient under the circumstances of the case to sustain the finding of the commission. . . .

We have only to consider whether the law of this state excluding such testimony has been changed in cases coming within the Workmen's Compensation Law by Section 68 of that law. That section is as follows:

"Section 68. Technical rules of evidence or procedure not required. The commission or a commissioner or deputy commissioner in making an investigation or inquiry or conducting a hearing shall not be bound by common law or statutory rules of evidence or by technical or formal rules of procedure, except as provided in this chapter; but may make such investigation or inquiry or conduct such hearing in such manner as to ascertain the substantial rights of the parties."

This section has plainly changed the rules of evidence in all cases affected by the act. It gives the workmen's compensation commission free rein in making its investigations and in conducting its hearings and authorizes it to receive not only hearsay testimony, but any kind of evidence that may throw light on a claim pending before it. The award of the commission cannot be overturned on account of an alleged error in receiving evidence.

This is all true, but . . . Section 68 . . . does not make the hearsay testimony offered by the claimant sufficient ground to uphold the award which the commission made. That section does not declare the probative force of any evidence, but it does declare that the aim and end of the investigation by the commission shall be "to ascertain the substantial rights of the parties." No matter what latitude the commission may give to its inquiry, it must result in a determination of the substantial rights of the parties. Otherwise the statute becomes grossly unjust and a means of oppression.

The act may be taken to mean that while the commission's inquiry is not limited by the common law or statutory rules of evidence or by technical or formal rules of procedure, and it may in its discretion accept any evidence that is offered; still in the end there must be a residuum of legal evidence to support the claim before an award can be made. . . .

"There must be in the record some evidence of a sound, competent, and recognizedly probative character to sustain the findings and award made, else the findings and award must in fairness be set aside by [the] court."

It is not necessary to consider in this case the constitutional limitations upon the power of the legislature to change the rules of evidence. It is sufficient to say that the intention of the legislature as revealed in the Workmen's Compensation Law was not so revolutionary in character as to declare that an award can be sustained which is dependent altogether on hearsay testimony where the presumption created by Section 21 of the statute is overcome by substantial evidence.

The only substantial evidence before the Workmen's Compensation Commission was to the effect that no cake of ice slipped and struck the decedent, and there were no bruises or marks upon his body which indicated that he had been so injured. The findings to the contrary rest solely on the decedent's statement made at a time when he was confessedly in a high nervous state, which ended in his death from delirium tremens. Such hearsay testimony is no evidence. . . .

DISSENTING OPINION BY SEABURY, J.

. . . I think the decision which is now the subject of review is correct. To sustain this award does not mean that the commission are obliged to act upon all hearsay evidence that is presented, but only that it may act upon it where the circumstances are such that the evidence offered is deemed by the commission to be trustworthy. . . .

. . . The Workmen's Compensation Law is a new step in the field of social legislation. We should interpret it in accordance with the spirit which called it into existence. Our reverence for the traditional rules of our common law system should not lead us to restrict it by subjecting it to the operation of these rules. This court is under no obligation to see to it that laws enacted to remedy abuses arising from new industrial and social conditions shall be made to square with ancient conceptions of the principles of the common law. . . . The difficulty in proving the cause of death in cases where the person injured dies as a result of the injury has long been recognized, and even in ordinary actions based on negligence the rules requiring proof of freedom from contributory negligence on the part of the deceased are relaxed to some extent. In the case now under consideration the injured man was taken from the place where he was working to his home, and into the presence of his wife and physician. The wife and physician naturally inquired as to how the accident happened, and the injured man told them. The evidence of these persons is now the only evidence available which can explain the cause of death. The commission examined and cross-examined these witnesses, and was satisfied that they correctly reported what the injured man had related shortly before his death and believed that the narrative which the injured man gave was correct. I think that the commission were justified in basing an award upon this testimony, and that the language of Section 68 . . . expressly authorized them so to do.

. . . We should frankly recognize that the commission are not limited by the common law methods of proof, and that if they were satisfied that the so-called hearsay evidence that was offered was creditable they were justified in basing their award upon that evidence.

It is said in the prevailing opinion that: "this section does plainly permit the introduction of hearsay testimony . . . but still it does not . . . make hearsay testimony, unsupported by other evidence, sufficient ground to sustain such a finding of fact as the commission made in this case." The distinction sought to be made between admitting such evidence and basing an award upon it seems to me to be unreasonable and not to find support in anything contained in Section 68. In conceding that Section 68 sanctions the introduction of hearsay evidence the argument of the appellant is left without any foundation upon which to rest. If the legislature sanctioned the admission of this evidence it follows by necessary implication that it intended to authorize the commission to act upon it. In resting the judgment about to be rendered upon this ground the court concedes that evidence upon which the commission acted was legal evidence, but holds that it was insufficient to sustain an award. . . .

DISSENTING OPINION BY POUND, J.

I think that this case should not be disposed of by deciding that all evidence held to be objectionable as hearsay in the courts of this state is without probative force. . . .

Hearsay is said by old writers to be "of no value in the court of justice" . . . and "no evidence" . . . yet the rule against hearsay, even at common law, is subject to many exceptions, and is not inelastic either in statement or application. . . .

The rule and its exceptions are not always and everywhere the same. The decisions are not in harmony. What is admissible in one jurisdiction is sometimes excluded in another. In the same jurisdiction the exception at first formulated is sometimes limited or extended by later cases. In *Insurance Co.* v. *Mosley* (8 Wall 397) the question was whether the assured died from the effects of an accidental fall downstairs in the night or from natural causes. Assured had left his bed between 12 and 1 o'clock at night and it was held that his declaration to his wife when he came back that he had fallen down the back stairs and hurt himself badly were competent and sufficient proof of the fall because they were made so soon thereafter as to be in the nature of *res gestae*—declarations contemporaneous with the main fact and part thereof. The evidence was, nevertheless, the narrative by a person since deceased of a past, although a recent, event. This court . . . very properly characterized the *Mosley* case as "an extreme case" and . . . said "the distinction to be made [in such cases] is in the character of the declaration whether it is so spontaneous, or natural, an utterance as to exclude the idea of fabrication; or whether it be in the nature of narrative of what had occurred." . . . Can we say that evidence which the Supreme Court of the United States held competent and sufficient, i.e., the declarations of a deceased person made soon after the alleged accidental injury and under circumstances entitling them to credit, is not competent and sufficient proof before the industrial commission under the rule of Section 68 . . . which says that the commission shall not be bound by the common law rules of evidence? May not the commission, under this statute, adopt the rule of the Supreme Court of the United States and in its discretion give it an extremely liberal application and reject the stricter rule laid down by this court without being open to the charge of making an award on no evidence whatever? Could not "the substantial rights of the parties" be thereby ascertained? If it may go so far, we need only hold that where the common law rule against hearsay is not uniformly stated or applied, the commission may base an award upon evidence received under the exceptions to a rule most favorable to the claimant, without being bound by the decisions of this court thereon. I think that the evidence of Carroll's declarations to his wife when he came home from work and to the physician called to treat him might, without too violent a wrench to our established ideas, be held competent under the exception to the rule against hearsay applied to the *Mosley* case. In any event as pointed out by my brother Seabury in his opinion the evidence was legal and admissible. If it had any probative force, its weight was for the commission as triers of fact, and their decision thereon was final. . . . I think that we cannot say as a matter of law that it had no probative force under Section 68 of the act, but I do not thereby conclude that all hearsay has probative force, or that awards in contested cases may be allowed or disallowed on rumor or report to which the circumstances give no weight. It is not to be anticipated that the commission will become confused, waste time, lose sight of the main issue, and base awards or refuse them on haphazard hearsay, as our convention is that a jury might if it were permitted to hear everything relevant. . . .

## Questions for Discussion

1. What type of administrator would you suggest for control or regulation of the following:
   - (a) Agricultural parasite control.
   - (b) Narcotics trade.
   - (c) Regulation of interest on bank loans.
   - (d) Unfair labor practices.
   - (e) River pilot licensing.
   - (f) Removal of public nuisances from highways.

2. (a) Describe the typical pattern of procedure before an administrator having authority to regulate business. (b) What trends have there been in such procedure during recent years?

3. (a) Could a statute prohibit all railroads from maintaining grade crossings? (b) In what respect does such a statute differ from the plan of the statute under consideration in the *Southern Railway* case? (c) Would it make any difference if the subject matter condemned were diseased food or other articles that in themselves were harmful to the public?

4. In the *Southern Railway* case the Court makes a distinction between a regulation requiring the abolition of grade crossings when the regulation is made by an administrator and when it is made by a legislature. Is this a valid distinction?

5. Would the Court have decided the *Southern Railway* case differently if the administrator had conducted an investigation and filed a public report setting forth his observations and conclusions before he ordered the condemnation of the grade crossing?

6. Is the majority or the minority opinion in *C. M. & St. P. Ry. Co.* v. *Minnesota* correct?

7. Does the majority opinion in the *C. M. & St. P. Ry. Co.* case require the holding of a hearing before there can be any price regulation?

8. Is a statute setting a minimum wage unconstitutional if the legislature does not order a "judicial" hearing to determine the proper wage rate? Why not?

9. Where a hearing is required, must there be a jury?

10. Is a public utility denied due process by the fact that the administrator who makes the regulation is also the one to hear and decide the case?

11. Compare the decision in the *C. M. & St. P. Ry. Co.* case with the *Southern Railway* case. What is the attitude of the Court in these cases to administrative action?

12. In the *Willingham* case the Court approved of a hearing that came after the entry of an administrative order. Was this based upon the fact that the administrator derived its authority from the war power or was it because the inherent nature of the problem made any other procedure impractical?

13. What decision would have been made in the *Willingham* case in peacetime?

14. What practical difference is there between placing the administrative hearing before or after the administrator makes his determination?

15. What is the practical effect of placing on the person affected by the order the burden of proof to disprove the reasonableness of the rates set by the administrator?

16. When must the administrator give notice to the parties to be affected and hold a hearing before he acts?

17. What are the fundamentals of procedure that should be followed in an administrative hearing?

18. Can any safeguard be adopted to prevent the administrator from being prejudiced by evidence that would have been excluded if the strict rules of evidence were applicable at a hearing before the administrator?

19. A state law provides that a tax commission shall assess taxes and that any taxpayer aggrieved by the assessment must appeal to the commission instead of to a court. Is this constitutional? *Opinion of the Justices,* 96 N.H. 513, 68 A. 2d 859 (1949).

20. (a) What is the hearsay evidence rule? (b) What is the reason for its existence?

21. Which of the three opinions in *Carroll* v. *Knickerbocker* is most persuasive?

22. Does the majority opinion in the *Carroll* case give any weight to evidence that would not be admissible in a law court?

23. (a) In the *Carroll* case, to what extent was the majority of the court affected by the fact that the "legally admissible" testimony was in conflict with the hearsay statements? (b) What decision would have been made if there was no testimony by other witnesses as to whether the cake of ice had slipped or as to the condition of the decedent's body after the alleged injury?

24. Ordinarily the testimony of a witness at a trial in one case is not admissible as evidence in the trial of a different case involving different parties. W, a workman, was injured and filed a workmen's compensation claim. He testified before the compensation board with respect to his injuries. He thereafter died and his widow began a new proceeding before the board to recover damages for his death under the workmen's compensation statute. At the trial of this second case, brought by the widow, the testimony of the deceased husband in the first case was offered in evidence. Should it have been admitted? *Welch* v. *Essex County,* 6 N.J.S. 422, 68 A. 2d 787 (1949).

25. (a) Why did the Court in the *Abilene* case consider it important that the records be offered in evidence? (b) Why cannot an administrator examine any records that he pleases just as he may look at a book in the library to determine what the law is?

26. Why did the Court in the *Abilene* case hold that it was not enough to inform the parties that use would be made by the Commission of the information contained in the annual reports?

27. The National Labor Management Relations Act provides that unfair labor practice proceedings before the National Labor Relations Board "shall, so far as practicable, be conducted in accordance with the rules of evidence applicable in the district courts of the United States. . . ." (a) Is this characteristic of modern administrative statutes? (b) Why was this provision adopted?

28. Is the hearing under the Tariff Act in the *Norwegian Nitrogen* case a judicial or a legislative hearing?

29. Is the decision in the *Norwegian Nitrogen* case affected by the nature of the hearing?

30. Is it material whether the Tariff Commission orders or advises, once it is determined that the administrator exercises a legislative function?

31. (a) To what extent does the decision in the *Norwegian Nitrogen* case turn upon the fact that the law to be adopted was a tariff law? (b) Could Congress provide that a new interstate commerce commission could, without any hearing, make recommendations of railroad rates to the President, which rates could be rejected, modified, or accepted by him?

32. What is the basis for the Court's decision in the *Consolidated Edison* case?

33. Would it have made any difference in the *Consolidated Edison* case if the additional testimony offered was not brief and could not have been presented at the closing of the hearing?

34. Why does the hearing sought in the *Morgan* case differ in nature from the trial of a case on an ordinary contract made by the United States?

35. The owner of land applied to the zoning board for permission to erect a type of building not permitted by the zoning restrictions. The owner was not permitted to cross-examine the witness who testified against allowing such variation from the zoning regulations. The zoning board based its refusal on the ground that it had been its experience that, when cross-examination was permitted, it would frequently result in personal and irrelevant quarrels between the examiner and the witness. The commission stated, however, that any questions which the owner might wish to ask the witness could be presented to the commission, which would in turn question the witness. The owner attacked the proceedings on the ground that he was improperly denied the right of cross-examination. Decide. *Wadell* v. *Board of Zoning Appeals,* 136 Conn. 1, 68 A. 2d 152 (1949).

36. A commission holds a hearing to determine whether an employee is physically fit to perform the duties of his job. The employee is present and takes part in the hearing. Thereafter, a later hearing, unknown to the employee, is held by the commission, which considers additional evidence on the basis of which it finds that the employee is not physically fit. The employee seeks a review of the decision on the ground that the commission acted improperly. Decide. *English* v. *City of Long Beach,* 35 Cal. 2d 155, 217 P. 2d 22 (1950).

## Chapter 30

# ADMINISTRATIVE INVESTIGATION



### § 30:1. Extent of Power to Investigate

The administrator who is given authority to determine the existence of facts, to decide issues, or to adopt rules is generally given power to make such investigation as is necessary to carry out such purposes. In some instances, the purpose for which examinations may be conducted are expressly defined by statute. Subject to the limitations considered in this chapter, the administrator charged with regulating some phase of business will generally have the power to compel witnesses to testify and to produce papers and documents when they are not willing to do so. The subpoena power has broadened greatly so that such orders may be issued as incidental to an administrative investigation whether or not the determination of the right of particular parties is involved and without regard to whether it is probable that the person subpoenaed has been violating an administrative regulation.

In order to protect the individual from the improper use of information secured by administrative investigations, it is often made a criminal offense for an administrator to disclose or make improper publication of any information obtained by him from his investigation.

### *(a) Subpoena power*

ENDICOTT JOHNSON CORP. v. PERKINS

317 U.S. 501 (1943)

The Walsh-Healey Act requires that contracts to supply the United States materials at a cost greater than $10,000 specify that the contractor shall pay his employees in the manufacture of the materials not less than the minimum wages set by the Secretary of Labor nor employ them for more than 40 hours a week except with the permission of the Secretary, in which case wages of not less than 1½ times the basic hourly rate must be paid. Endicott Johnson Corporation had several contracts in excess of $10,000 to supply shoes to the United States. The contracts conformed to the Act and specified the plants in which the shoes were to be made. The Secretary of Labor made an investigation which showed minor wage violations in the plants named in the contract. The Secretary of Labor then ordered the Corporation to produce records as to wages and hours in other plants that were physically separate from the plants in which the contracts were being performed because the Secretary "had reason to believe" that the employees in those plants were also covered by the contracts. The Corporation refused to produce the records on the ground that the subpoena power extended only to the plants specified in the contracts.

OPINION BY JACKSON, J.

. . . The Secretary is directed "to administer the provisions of this Act" and empowered to "make investigations and findings as herein provided, and prosecute any inquiry necessary to his functions." . . . And that he may the better and the more fairly discharge his functions, he is authorized to hold hearings "on complaint of a breach or violation of any representation or stipulation" and "to issue orders requiring the attendance and testimony of witnesses and the production of evidence under oath. . . . In case of contumacy, failure, or refusal of any person to obey such an order," the District Court of the United States "shall have jurisdiction to issue to such person an order requiring such person to appear before him or representative designated by him, to produce evidence if, as, and when so ordered, and to give testimony relating to the matter under investigation or in question; and any failure to obey such order of the court may be punished by said court as a contempt thereof." . . .

The Act directs the Secretary to administer its provisions. It is not an Act of general applicability to industry. It applies only to contractors who voluntarily enter into competition to obtain government business on terms of which they are fairly forewarned by inclusion in the contract. . . .

The matter which the Secretary was investigating and was authorized to investigate was an alleged violation of this Act and these contracts. Her scope would include determining what employees these contracts and the Act covered. . . . But because she sought evidence of underpayment before she made a decision on the question of coverage and alleged that she "had reason to believe" the employees in question were covered, the District Court refused to order its production, tried the issue of coverage itself, and decided it against the Secretary. This ruling would require the Secretary, in order to get evidence of violation, either to allege she had decided the issue of coverage before the hearing or to sever the issues for separate hearing and decision. The former would be of dubious propriety, and the latter of doubtful practicality. The Secretary is given no power to investigate mere coverage, as such, or to make findings thereon except as incident to trial of the issue of violation. No doubt she would have discretion to take up the issues of coverage for separate and earlier trial if she saw fit. Or, in a case such as the one revealed by the pleadings in this one, she might find it advisable to begin by examining the payroll, for if there were no underpayments found, the issue of coverage would be academic. On the admitted facts of the case, the District Court had no authority to control her procedure or to condition enforcement of her subpoenas upon her first reaching and announcing a decision on some of the issues in her administrative proceeding.

DISSENTING OPINION BY MURPHY, J., in which ROBERTS, J., concurs.

Because of the varied and important responsibilities of a quasi-judicial nature that have been entrusted to administrative agencies in the regulation of our political and economic life, their activities should not be subjected to unwarranted and ill-advised intrusions by the judicial branch of the government. Yet, if they are freed of all restraint upon inquisitorial activities and are allowed uncontrolled discretion in the exercise of the sovereign power of government to invade private affairs through the use of the subpoena, to the extent required or sought in situations like the one before us and other inquiries of much broader scope, under the direction of well-meaning but over-zealous officials they may at times become instruments of intolerable oppression and injustice. This is not to say that the power to enforce their subpoenas should never be entrusted to administrative agencies, but thus far Congress, for unstated reasons, has not seen fit to confer such authority upon any agency which it has created. So here, while the Secretary of Labor is empowered to administer the Walsh-Healey Act, to "prosecute any inquiry necessary to his functions," and "to issue orders requiring the attendance and the testimony of witnesses and the production of evidence under oath," he alone cannot compel obedience of those orders. "Jurisdiction" so to do is conferred upon the district courts of the United States and it is our immediate task to delineate the proper function of those courts in the exercise of this jurisdiction. Specifically the question is: What is the duty of the courts when the witness or party claims the proceeding is without authority of law?

This Court, in recognition of the drastic nature of the subpoena power and the possibilities of severe mischief inherent in its use, has insisted that it be kept within well-defined channels. . . . In conditioning enforcement of the Secretary's administrative subpoenas upon application therefor to a district court, Congress evidently intended to keep the instant subpoena power within limits, and clearly must have meant for the courts to perform more than a routine ministerial function in passing upon such applications. If this were not the case, it would have been much simpler to lodge the power of enforcement directly with the Secretary, or else to make disregard of his subpoenas a misdemeanor. . . .

The Government concedes that the district courts are more than mere rubber stamps of the agencies in enforcing administrative subpoenas and lists as examples of appropriate defenses, claims that a privilege of the witness, like that against self-incrimintion, would be violated; or that the subpoena is unduly vague or unreasonably oppressive; or that the hearing is not of the kind authorized; or that the subpoena was not issued by the person vested with the power; or that it is plain on the pleadings that the evidence sought is not germane to any lawful subject of inquiry. But the Government insists that the issue of "coverage," i. e., whether the Act extends to plants of petitioner's establishment which manufactured materials used in making complete shoes but not named in the contracts, is not a proper ground for attack in this case. I think it is.

If petitioner is not subject to the Act as to the plants in question, the Secretary has no right to start proceedings or to require the production of records with regard to those plants. In other words, there would be no lawful subject of inquiry, and under present statutes giving the courts jurisdiction to enforce administrative subpoenas, petitioner is entitled to a judicial determination of this issue before its privacy is invaded. . . .

It is within the competence and authority of the court to inquire and satisfy itself whether there is probable legal justification for the proceeding, before it exercises its judicial authority to require a witness or a party to reveal his private affairs or be held in contempt.

Just how much of a showing of statutory coverage should be required to satisfy the district court, and just how far it should explore the question, are difficult problems, to be solved best by a careful balancing of interests and the exercise of a sound and informed discretion. If the proposed examination under the subpoena or the proceeding itself would be relatively brief and of a limited scope, any doubt should ordinarily be resolved in favor of the agency's power. If it promises to be protracted and burdensome to the party, a more searching inquiry is indicated. A formal finding of coverage by the agency, which the Secretary did not make here, should be accorded some weight in the court's deliberation, unless wholly wanting in either legal or factual support, but it should not be conclusive. In short, the responsibility resting upon the court in this situation is not unlike that of a committing magistrate on preliminary examination to determine whether an accused should be held for trial.

With these considerations in mind, let us turn to the facts of this case. Petitioner has willingly complied with all demands of the Secretary relating to the plants of its establishment, named in the contracts, in which the shoes were manufactured. It resists the application for enforcement of the subpoenas directing the production of records of other plants, not named in the contracts, in which some component parts for the shoes were manufactured, on the ground that the Walsh-Healey Act does not extend to those plants. It is true that petitioner voluntarily entered into the contracts with the Government, but those referred only to the specific plants where the finished product was made. And, it was not until 1939, after all the contracts were completed, that the Secretary issued rulings specifically dealing with "integrated establishments." The mere fact that petitioner voluntarily contracted with reference to some plants does not necessarily mean that the Secretary is free to investigate petitioner's entire business without let or hindrance. That depends upon whether or not the Act extends to those other plants. Petitioner was entitled to have this question determined by the district court before the subpoena was enforced over its objection. . . . Under the facts of this case the district court should not be compelled mechanically to enforce the Secretary's subpoena, in the exercise of its statutory jurisdiction. It should first satisfy itself that probable cause exists for the Secretary's contention that the Act covers the plants in question.

### § 30:2. Investigation for Rule-making

When the administrator is seeking information to guide him in the formulation of a rule, the problem is the same as that of a legislative body conducting an examination or holding a hearing to determine the facts to enlighten it in drafting a statute. In the case of a legislative body, it is recognized that the power to legislate carries with it by necessary implication the right to obtain information appropriate to a determination of matters within the scope of the authority to legislate. Under some statutes, a duty is placed upon the administrator to make certain types of investigations or to hold certain types of hearings before he may adopt specified classes of rules.

### § 30:3. Investigation for Proposed Legislation

#### *(a) Absence of authority*

HARRIMAN v. INTERSTATE COMMERCE COMMISSION

211 U.S. 407 (1908)

The Interstate Commerce Act formerly authorized the Interstate Commerce Commission to investigate complaints made to it and to "institute any inquiry on its own motion in the same manner and to the same effect as though complaint had been made." The Commission, acting upon its own motion and not upon complaint, began an investigation of consolidations and combinations of carriers.

In the course of its inquiry, the Commission asked Harriman, who was a director and president and chairman of the executive committee of the Union Pacific Railroad, questions relating to the manipulation of stock of that and other railroads. He refused to answer these questions.

OPINION BY HOLMES, J.

. . . The contention of the Commission is that it may make any investigation that it deems proper, not merely to discover any facts tending to defeat the purposes of the act of February 4, 1887, but to aid it in recommending any additional legislation relating to the regulation of commerce that it may conceive to be within the power of Congress to enact; and that in such an investigation it has power, with the aid of the courts, to require any witness to answer any question that may have a bearing upon any part of what it has in mind. . . .

Whatever may be the power of Congress, it did not attempt, in the act of February 4, 1887, . . . to do more than to regulate the interstate business of common carriers, and the primary purpose for which the Commission was established was to enforce the regulations which Congress had imposed. . . .

The Commission, it will be seen, is given power to require the testimony of witnesses "for the purposes of this Act." The argument for the Commission is that the purposes of the act embrace all the duties that the act imposes and the powers that it gives the Commission; that one of the purposes is that the Commission shall keep itself informed as to the manner and method in which the business of the carriers is conducted, as required by § 12; that another is that it shall recommend additional legislation under § 21, to which we shall refer again, and that for either of these general objects it may call on the courts to require anyone whom it may point out to attend and testify if he would avoid the penalties for contempt.

We are of opinion, on the contrary, that the purposes of the act for which the Commission may exact evidence embrace only complaints for violation of the act, and investigations by the Commission upon matters that might have been made the object of the complaint. As we already have implied the main purpose of the act was to regulate the interstate business of carriers, and the secondary purpose, that for which the Commission was established, was to enforce the regulations enacted. These, in our opinion, are the purposes referred to; in other words the power to require testimony is limited, as it usually is in English-speaking countries, at least, to the only cases where the sacrifice of privacy is necessary,—those where the investigations concern a specific breach of the law.

. . .

### (b) Grant of authority

SMITH v. INTERSTATE COMMERCE COMMISSION
245 U.S. 33 (1917)

Section 13 of the Interstate Commerce Act, which had been the basis for decision in the *Harriman* case, was amended by Congress following that decision to give the Interstate Commerce Commission "full authority and power at any time to institute an inquiry, on its own motion, in any case and as to any matter or thing concerning which a complaint is authorized to be made, to or before said Commission by any provision of this act, or concerning which any question may arise under any of the provisions of this Act, or relating to the enforcement of any provisions of this Act."

The Interstate Commerce Commission sought to compel the appellant, the president of the Louisville & Nashville Railroad, to answer questions as to efforts to maintain a monopoly and the expenditure of money of the railroad for political purposes and the method followed in charging such expenditures in the company's books.

OPINION BY MCKENNA, J.

The fundamental contention of appellant is that the Interstate Commerce Commission has no power to ask the questions in controversy and in emphasis of this he asserts "the inquiry was confined exclusively to supposed political activities and efforts to suppress competition." And these, it is further asserted, "are not matters which the Commission 'is legally entitled to investigate.'" . . .

The Interstate Commerce Act confers upon the Commission powers of investigation in very broad language and this court has refused by construction to limit it so far as the business of the carriers is concerned and their relation to the public. And it would seem to be a necessary deduction from the cases that the investigating and supervising powers of the Commission extend to all of the activities of carriers and to all sums expended by them which could affect in any way their benefit or burden as agents of the public. If it be grasped thoroughly and kept in attention that they are public agents, we have at least the principle which should determine judgment in particular instances of regulation or investigation; and it is not far from true—it may be it is entirely true, as said by the Commission—that "there can be nothing private or confidential in the activities and expenditures of a carrier engaged in interstate commerce."

Turning to the specialties of the Interstate Commerce Act we find there that all charges and treatment of all passengers and property shall be just and reasonable, and there is a specific prohibition of preferences and discriminations in all the ways that they can be executed, with corresponding regulatory power in the Commission. And authority and means are given to enable it to perform its duty. By section 12 it is authorized to inquire into the management of the business of carriers and keep itself informed as to the manner and method in which the same is conducted, and has the right to obtain from the carriers full and complete information. It may . . . institute an inquiry of its own motion, and may . . . require detailed accounts of all the expenditures and revenues of carriers and a complete exhibit of their financial operations and prescribe the forms of accounts, records and memoranda to be kept. And it is required to report to Congress all data collected by it.

It would seem to be an idle work to point out the complete comprehensiveness of the language of these sections and we are not disposed to spend any time to argue that it necessarily includes the power to inquire into expenditures and their proper assignment in the accounts, and the questions under review, we have seen, go no further. They are incidental to an investigation as to the "manner and method" . . . in which the business of the carriers is conducted; they are in requisition of a detailed account of their expenditures and revenues and an exhibit of their financial operations . . . and the answers to them may be valuable as information to Congress. . . .

A limitation, however, is deduced from section 13. It is said to be confined to cases where an inquiry is instituted "as to any matter or thing concerning which a complaint is authorized to be made, . . . or concerning which any question may arise under any of the provisions" of the act "or relating to the enforcement of any of the provisions" of the act. In other words, that the inquiry is determined by the manner of procedure. The objection overlooks the practical and vigilant function of the Commission. . . .

The expenditures of the carriers essentially concern their business. Section 20 declares it and gives the Commission power to require a detail of them, and necessarily not only of their amount but purpose and how charged. And the Commission must have power to prevent evasion of its orders and detect in any formal compliance or in the assignment of expenses a "possible concealment of forbidden practices."

It may be said that our comments are not applicable to questions . . . which relate to the expenditure of money in Alabama "in a campaign against rate reduction." That is, those questions are not directed to "political activities" strictly so called, nor to the suppression of competition. They are directed, however, to the use of funds in a campaign against state legislative action. But this, appellant asserts, is at the farthest an attempt to "influence legislation or to mold public opinion" and that there is nothing in the Interstate Commerce Act "which forbids it or gives to the Commission any power to investigate the subject." . . .

Abstractly speaking, we are not disposed to say that a carrier may not attempt to mold or enlighten public opinion, but we are quite clear that its conduct and the expenditures of its funds are open to inquiry. If it may not rest inactive and suffer injustice, it may not on the other hand use its funds and its power in opposition to the policies of government. Beyond this generality it is not necessary to go. The questions in the case are not of broad extent. They are quite special, and we regard them, as the learned judge of the court below regarded them, as but incident to the amount of expenditures and to the manner of their charge upon the books of the companies. This, we repeat, is within the power of the Commission. The purpose of an investigation is the penetration of disguises or to form a definite estimate of any conduct of the carriers that may in any way affect their relation to the public. We cannot assume that an investigation will be instituted or conducted for any other purpose or in mere wanton meddling.

### § 30:4. Investigation for Enforcement

In the case of the more complex forms of business regulation, the action of the administrator is a continuing action and investigation becomes a continuing process to determine the effectiveness of the administrator's regulation and whether the parties have complied with his decision. Investigation for the purpose of determining compliance will, as a practical matter, assume a narrower scope than investigation for rule-making, but the extent to which the investigation may go within the proper area can be regarded as the same in each case.

### *(a) Compliance with court order*

UNITED STATES v. MORTON SALT CO.

338 U.S. 632 (1950)

As the result of proceedings originating before the Federal Trade Commission, the Morton Salt Company and others were ordered by the Supreme Court to cease certain practices with respect to the pricing, producing, and marketing of salt and to file with the Commission a report showing compliance with this order. The Federal Trade Commission thereafter ordered the Morton Salt Company to furnish additional reports on its method of operation in order to determine whether the company was continuing to comply with the order. The company challenged the authority of the Federal Trade Commission to require the additional reports.

OPINION BY JACKSON, J.

. . . [Subsequent to the filing of an initial report directed by the original decree] the Commission ordered additional and highly particularized reports to show continuing compliance with the decree. This was done without application to the court, was not authorized by any provision of its decree, and is not provided for in § 5 of the statute under which the Commission's original cease and desist order had issued. . . .

The Trade Commission Act is one of several in which Congress, to make its policy effective, has relied upon the initiative of administrative officials and the flexibility of the administrative process. Its agencies are provided with staffs to institute proceedings and to follow up decrees and police their obedience. While that process at times is adversary, it also at times is inquisitorial. These agencies are expected to ascertain when and against whom proceedings should be set in motion and to take the lead in following through to effective results. It is expected that this combination of duty and power always will result in earnest and eager action but it is feared that it may sometimes result in harsh and overzealous action.

To protect against mistaken or arbitrary orders, judicial review is provided. Its function is dispassionate and disinterested adjudication, unmixed with any concern as to the success of either prosecution or defense. Courts are not expected to start wheels moving or to follow up judgments. Courts neither have, nor need, sleuths to dig up evidence, staffs to analyze reports, or personnel to prepare prosecutions for contempts. . . .

This case illustrates the difference between the judicial function and the function the Commission is attempting to perform. The respondents argue that since the Commission made no charge of violation either of the decree or the statute, it is engaged in a mere "fishing expedition" to see if it can turn up evidence of guilt. We will assume for the argument that this is so. Courts have often disapproved the employment of the judicial process in such an enterprise. Federal judicial power itself extends only to adjudication of cases and controversies and it is natural that its investigative powers should be jealously confined to these ends. The judicial subpoena power not only is subject to specific constitutional limitations, which also apply to administrative orders, such as those against self-incrimination, unreasonable search and seizure, and due process of law, but also is subject to those limitations inherent in the body that issues them because of the provisions of the Judiciary Article of the Constitution.

We must not disguise the fact that sometimes, especially early in the history of the federal administrative tribunal, the courts were persuaded to engraft judicial limitations upon the administrative process. The courts could not go fishing, and so it followed neither could anyone else. . . . It must not be forgotten that the administrative process and its agencies are relative newcomers in the field of law and that it has taken and will continue to take experience and trial and error to fit this process into our system of judicature. More recent views have been more tolerant of it than those which underlay many older decisions. . . .

The only power that is involved here is the power to get information from those who best can give it and who are most interested in not doing so. Because judicial power is reluctant if not unable to summon evidence until it is shown to be relevant to issues in litigation, it does not follow that an administrative agency charged with seeing that the laws are enforced may not have and exercise powers of original inquiry. It has a power of inquisition, if one chooses to call it that, which is not derived from the judicial function. It is more analogous to the Grand Jury, which does not depend on a case or controversy for power to get evidence but can investigate merely on suspicion that the law is being violated, or even just because it wants assurance that it is not. When investigative and accusatory duties are delegated by statute to an administrative body, it, too, may take steps to inform itself as to whether there is probable violation of the law.

... Even if one were to regard the request for information in this case as caused by nothing more than official curiosity, nevertheless law-enforcing agencies have a legitimate right to satisfy themselves that corporate behavior is consistent with the law and the public interest.

Of course a governmental investigation into corporate matters may be of such a sweeping nature and so unrelated to the matter properly under inquiry as to exceed the investigatory power. . . . But it is sufficient if the inquiry is within the authority of the agency, the demand is not too indefinite and the information sought is reasonably relevant. "The gist of the protection is in the requirement, expressed in terms, that the disclosure sought shall not be unreasonable." . . . Nothing on the face of the Commission's order transgressed these bounds. . . . In upholding this order upon this record, we are not to be understood as holding such orders exempt from judicial examination or as extending a license to exact as reports what would not reasonably be comprehended within that term as used by Congress in the context of this Act. . . .

## § 30:5. Constitutional Limitations on Investigation

For the most part, the constitutional guarantee against unreasonable search and seizure does not afford much protection against the investigation of an administrator, since in the absence of an actual seizure that guarantee does not apply. That is, a subpoena to testify or to produce records cannot be opposed on the ground that it is a search and seizure as the constitutional protection is limited to cases of actual search and seizure rather than the obtaining of information by compulsion.

The protection afforded by the guarantee against self-incrimination is likewise narrow, for it cannot be invoked (1) as to records which by law must be kept by the person subject to investigation; (2) as to corporate records even though the officer or employee of the corporation in producing them may be producing evidence that would incriminate him; and (3) the protection of the amendment may be denied when a sufficient immunity from future prosecution is given to the person who is compelled to present evidence that incriminates him.

### *(a) Representation by counsel*

IN RE GROBAN

352 U.S. 330 (1957)

By statute the Ohio State Fire Marshal may investigate the cause of fires, may hold investigations privately and exclude any persons whose presence is not required, may compel witnesses to be sworn and to testify, and may summarily commit for contempt any witness refusing to be sworn or to testify. Groban and another witness refused to be sworn and to testify unless they had the assistance of counsel. The Marshal refused them permission to be represented by counsel and summarily committed them to the county jail for refusing to be sworn and to testify. The witnesses applied for a writ of habeas corpus to obtain their release. The writ was denied and they appealed.

OPINION BY REED, J.

. . . It is clear that a defendant in a state criminal trial has an unqualified right, under the Due Process Clause, to be heard through his own counsel. . . . Prosecution of an individual differs widely from administrative investigation of incidents damaging to the economy or dangerous to the public. The proceeding before the Fire Marshal was not a criminal trial, nor was it an administrative proceeding that would in any way adjudicate appellants' responsibilities for the fire. It was a proceeding solely to elicit facts relating to the causes and circumstances of the fire. The Fire Marshal's duty was to "determine whether the fire was the result of carelessness or design," and to arrest any person against whom there was sufficient evidence on which to base a charge of arson.

The fact that appellants were under a legal duty to speak and that their testimony might provide a basis for criminal charges against them does not mean that they had a constitutional right to the assistance of their counsel. Appellants here are witnesses from whom information was sought as to the cause of the fire. A witness before a grand jury cannot insist, as a matter of constitutional right, on being represented by his counsel, nor can a witness before other investigatory bodies. There is no more reason to allow the presence of counsel before a Fire Marshal trying in the public interest to determine the cause of a fire. Obviously in these situations evidence obtained may possibly lay a witness open to criminal charges. When such charges are made in a criminal proceeding, he then may demand the presence of his counsel for his defense. Until then his protection is the privilege against self-incrimination. . . . See *Adamson* v. *California,* 332 U.S. 46, 52. This is a privilege available in investigations as well as in prosecutions. . . .

Ohio, like many other States, maintains a division of the state government directed by the Fire Marshal for the prevention of fires and reduction of fire losses. Section 3737.13, which has been in effect since 1900, represents a determination by the Ohio Legislature that investigations conducted in private may be the most effective method of bringing to light facts concerning the origins of fires, and, in the long run, of reducing injuries and losses from fires caused by negligence or by design. We cannot say that this determination is unreasonable. The presence of advisors to witnesses might easily so far encumber an investigatory proceeding as to make it unworkable or unwieldy. And with so weighty a public interest as fire prevention to protect, we cannot hold that the balance has been set in such a way as to be contrary to "fundamental principles of liberty and justice." . . . That is the test to measure the validity of a state statute under Due Process Clause.

. . . We hold that appellants had no constitutional right to be assisted by their counsel in giving testimony at the investigatory proceeding conducted by the Fire Marshal, and that § 3737.13, insofar as it authorizes the exclusion of counsel while a witness testifies, is not repugnant to the Due Process Clause of the Fourteenth Amendment.

### *(b) Production of records required by law*

SHAPIRO v. UNITED STATES

335 U.S. 1 (1948)

Shapiro was a wholesaler of fruit and produce. The Price Administrator acting under the federal Emergency Price Control Act subpoenaed him to produce his business records. Under protest of constitutional privilege he furnished the records. He was later prosecuted for making illegal tie-in sales contrary to the Emergency Price Control Regulations. The evidence on which the prosecution was based was obtained from information found in the records that he had been required to produce before the administrator. He claimed that he was entitled to immunity from prosecution for any matter arising out of those records. His claim of privilege was overruled and he was convicted. He appealed from the conviction.

OPINION BY VINSON, C. J.

. . . The Circuit Court of Appeals ruled that the records which petitioner was compelled to produce were records required to be kept by a valid regulation under the Price Control Act; that thereby they became public documents, as to which no constitutional privilege against self-incrimination attaches. . . .

. . . The language of the statute and its legislative history, viewed against the background of settled judicial construction of the immunity provision, indicate that Congress required records to be kept as a means of enforcing the statute and did not intend to frustrate the use of those records for enforcement action by granting an immunity bonus to individuals compelled to disclose their required records to the Administrator.

. . . A corporate officer has no such constitutional privilege as to corporate records in his possession, even though they contain entries made by himself which disclose his crime. . . .

> "The physical custody of incriminating documents does not of itself protect the custodian against their compulsory production. The question still remains with respect to the nature of the documents and the capacity in which they are held. It may yet appear that they are of a character which subjects them to the scrutiny demanded and that the custodian has voluntarily assumed a duty which overrides his claim of privilege. . . . The principle applies not only to public documents in public offices, but also to *records required by law to be kept in order that there may be suitable information of transactions which are the appropriate subjects of governmental regulation and the enforcement of restrictions validly established. There the privilege, which exists as to private papers, cannot be maintained.*"

As illustrations of documents meeting this "required records" test, the Court cited with approval state supreme court decisions that business records kept under requirements of law by private individuals in *unincorporated* enterprises were " 'public documents, which the defendant was required to keep, not for his private uses, but for the benefit of the public, and for public inspection.' " . . .

It may be assumed at the outset that there are limits which the Government cannot constitutionally exceed in requiring the keeping of records which may be inspected by an administrative agency and may be used in prosecuting statutory violations committed by the record-keeper himself. But no serious misgiving that those bounds have been overstepped would appear to be evoked when there is a sufficient relation between the activity sought to be regulated and the public concern so that the Government can constitutionally regulate or forbid the basic activity concerned, and can constitutionally require the keeping of particular records, subject to inspection by the Administrator. . . .

## Questions for Discussion

1. Discuss the *Endicott* case with reference to the advantages and disadvantages of its holding.

2. Would it have been possible for the Court in the *Harriman* case to reach a contrary decision under the statute?

3. Do you think it desirable that an administrator have the power of investigation approved in the *Smith* case?

4. What limitation on the investigatory power is recognized in the *Smith* case?

5. What is the function or scope of inquiry of a court when an administrator applies to it for a subpoena?

6. What is the controlling factor in the *Groban* case?

7. What danger to the individual is to be feared from the *Groban* doctrine?

8. Does it make any difference with respect to the administrator's power of investigation whether the person to be investigated is a natural person or a corporation?

9. Were the records in the *Shapiro* case public documents?

10. In the *Shapiro* case, the Court indicates that there is a limit upon the power of the government to require the keeping of records that the government may examine. Appraise the validity of such a limitation.

## Chapter 31

# ENFORCEMENT OF ADMINISTRATIVE ACTION

§ 31:1. Enforcement by Public Opinion
  (a) Constitutionality of publication of violator—Holcombe v. Creamer
  (b) Federal legislation

§ 31:2. Enforcement by Court Action

§ 31:3. Who may bring Court Action
  (a) National Labor Relations Act—Amalgamated Utility Workers v. Consolidated Edison Co.

§ 31:4. Action for Damages

§ 31:5. Injunction Action
  (a) Federal Price Control Act—The Hecht Co. v. Bowles

§ 31:6. Criminal Prosecution
  (a) Requirement of definiteness—M. Kraus & Bros. v. United States

§ 31:7. Defense of Invalid Regulation
  (a) Restriction on right to challenge validity of regulation—Yakus v. United States

## § 31:1. Enforcement by Public Opinion

In the early days of regulation, an attempt was sometimes made to enforce the prohibition of a condemned practice by invoking public opinion. Instead of imposing a fine or a penalty for engaging in the condemned practice, publicity would be given to the fact that a particular person or business was engaged in such unlawful practice. Hope was placed on the social consciousness of the community, which, aware that a particular enterpriser was an offender, would stop doing business with him. The purpose of the law was to induce the community to boycott the wrongdoer until by this economic pressure he would be coerced into obeying the regulation.

### *(a) Constitutionality of publication of violator*

HOLCOMBE v. CREAMER

231 Mass. 99, 120 N.E. 154 (1918)

A Massachusetts law authorized a commission to fix minimum wages. The commission was not given power to enforce its standards but was authorized to publish the names of employers who failed to comply.

OPINION BY RUGG, C. J. . . .

The act is not mandatory as to rates of wages. It contains no words of compulsion upon either the employer or employee. It does not restrain freedom of action by either employer or employee as to the wages to be paid or received. . . . The chief purpose of the act . . . is that there shall be an investigation as to the facts, a statement of the conclusions drawn from those facts and a making public of those conclusions, all by or under the supervision of an administrative board. The utmost authority of the commission is to make recommendations. It cannot issue any order. . . .

Doubtless one aim of the act is to bring to bear the force of public opinion in support of the acceptance of the recommendations of the commission. This may be a kind of coercion. But it can go no further than ascertained and published facts induce members of the public as individuals to the action of giving or withholding custom or patronage. . . .

Since the statute is not compulsory either in form or effect, there is no ground for holding that it is invalid. . . .

### *(b) Federal legislation*

In 1903, the Bureau of Corporations was created as a subdivision of the Department of Commerce and Labor. It was authorized to investigate corporate practices of business engaged in interstate commerce and to report this information to the President. The threat of publicity by such investigation was effective in preventing the development of many improper corporate plans at the beginning of this century. The use of publicity to prevent improper corporate practices has been carried over into the Securities and Exchange Act of 1934.

A more recent example of resort to public opinion is found in the provisions of the National Labor Management Relations Act of 1947. This Act provides that, whenever a strike or a lockout occurs or is threatening in an industry that is in interstate commerce or that produces goods for interstate commerce and would endanger or harm the national health or safety, the President may appoint a fact-finding board to make a report. This report is made public. After it is filed, the President may direct the Attorney General to petition the proper federal court for an injunction. The court issues the injunction against the strike or the lockout if it finds that the strike or the lockout affects an industry engaged in interstate commerce or in the production of goods for interstate commerce and that the strike or the lockout if permitted to occur or continue would imperil the national health or safety. After the injunction has been issued, it is the duty of the parties to attempt to reach a solution by agreement. If none has been reached by the end of sixty days, the original board of inquiry makes a report to the President of the then current position of the parties and the efforts that they have made to effect a settlement. This report includes a statement by each party of its position and a statement of the employer's last offer of settlement. This report also is made available to the public. The National Labor Relations Board is then required within the following fifteen days to take a secret ballot of the employees on the question of whether they wish to accept the final offer of settlement made by the employer. The result of this election is then certified to the Attorney General within five days. If the dispute has not been settled, the Attorney General is required to move the court to dissolve the injunction upon receiving the certification of the election results. The President then submits to Congress a complete report of the proceedings, including the findings of the board of inquiry and the results of the election held by the National Labor Relations Board, together with any recommendation that he deems appropriate.

Under the statute, the matters in dispute thus come before the public upon three occasions: the first two upon the filing of the reports of the board of inquiry and the third upon the filing by the President of his report to Congress. The object of this informing of the public is to pave the way for congressional action and to bring pressure to bear upon the disputants who might fear either a boycott by the public or legislative action by Congress backed by an angered public.

Provisions relying upon public opinion for their enforcement are of doubtful value. In a world of complicated and interrelated economics, public opinion does not readily come to bear directly upon a wrongdoer. The purchasing public may be scattered throughout the country or the world, thus making it impossible to marshal any substantial public opinion against a particular business. Even if this can be done, there is still the practical question of whether the public is in a position where it can express its sentiments by boycotting the particular business. It may well be that many persons have not been in sympathy with various coal miners' strikes; yet those who have coal furnaces are not in a position to refrain from purchasing coal merely to show the way they feel about the matter. Moreover, a boycott might hurt everyone and not merely the side that has angered the public. A coal boycott would not only hurt the miners but also the mine operators.

Enforcement by public opinion also has the disadvantage that many persons who are willing to be wrongdoers in the first instance are not likely to change their ways merely because the public has an unfavorable opinion of them. If the condemned practice in which they are engaging yields them a sufficient profit, they are more than likely to continue their practices and ignore or take the risk of a hostile public opinion. The problem is further complicated by the fact that, where there is not a clear issue of right and wrong or where the determination of the truth requires the examination of complicated facts and records, the wrongdoer may easily cloud the issue in the mind of the public by engaging in a publicity campaign to prove that he is right and that those opposed to him are wrong. The field of labor disputes has seen many illustrations of this practice in which both employer and employee have carried their dispute to the public by means of statements in newspapers and radio advertising, with the result of confusing rather than clarifying the issue.

## § 31:2. Enforcement by Court Action

Under our legal system, anyone violating a principle or a standard of law may find himself subject to court action. The precise form of the action varies. It may be a civil action to recover damages, as for a breach of contract or for a personal injury inflicted upon the person bringing the action. It may be an action in what historically was called equity to compel the wrongdoer to stop his misconduct or in some instances to do an act. It may be a criminal prosecution by the government against the wrongdoer for violating its laws.

With this background of resort to the courts to remedy a breach of duty, it was natural that the enforcement of early administrative regulations was left to court action. Under this plan a law would be adopted by the legislative body prohibiting a particular practice, such as the giving of illegal rebates by carriers or the formation of a conspiracy to restrain interstate trade. It was then provided that, if the condemned practice was engaged in, the person injured might sue the wrongdoer to recover money to compensate him for the damages he had sustained. The law may instead provide that the wrongdoer shall be subject to criminal prosecution. It may also combine several procedures, as in the case of the Federal Antitrust Law, which authorizes a suit for damages by the person injured, a suit for an injunction to stop the illegal practice, and a criminal prosecution of the wrongdoer.

As the story of the development of business regulation continues, we find the appearance of rules made by an administrator which have the same effect as a law passed by the lawmaker. In many instances these rules are enforced in the same manner as statutes, although the more modern period of regulation introduces variations in the form of court enforcement.

As a properly adopted rule has the effect of a statute, the word "statute" or "act" will be used in this chapter, unless otherwise indicated by the context, to include both statutes or laws adopted by the lawmaker and rules adopted by the administrator.

## § 31:3. Who may bring Court Action

Whenever the aid of a court is sought, the person seeking such aid must show that he is a person who is entitled to bring the action. Under some statutes the administrator is given the exclusive right to seek enforcement in the courts. The fact that a person is injured by a violation of the statute or that he would have been benefited by its observance does not in itself give him standing to bring an action to compel obedience to the order or to impose a penalty for its violation.

Under some statutes, resort to the courts is not limited to the administrator. Some statutes provide that any person aggrieved or any "party in interest" may bring an action. Where this is authorized, a question arises whether a particular plaintiff comes within the statutory class entitled to sue.

In a given case the determination may be merely the result of historical accident or precedent or it may be the conscious weighing of the practical consequences of permitting or prohibiting the bringing of the action by a given person or class of persons.

### *(a) National Labor Relations Act*

AMALGAMATED UTILITY WORKERS v. CONSOLIDATED EDISON CO.

309 U.S. 261 (1940)

The National Labor Relations Board ordered the Consolidated Edison Company and its affiliates to desist from certain unfair labor practices. The Board obtained an order from the court directing that the Company observe the Board's order. The Company and its affiliates refused to do so. The Amalgamated Utilities Workers then began an action to punish the Company and its affiliates for contempt in failing to comply with the order.

OPINION BY HUGHES, C. J. . . .

Petitioner contends that the National Labor Relations Act "creates private rights"; that the Act recognizes the rights of labor organizations; and that it gives the parties upon whom these rights are conferred status in the courts for their vindication. . . .

Congress declared that certain labor practices should be unfair, but it prescribed a particular method by which such practices should be ascertained and prevented. By the express terms of the Act, the Board was made the exclusive agency for that purpose. Section 10(a) provides:

"The Board is empowered, as hereinafter provided, to prevent any person from engaging in any unfair labor practice (listed in section 8) affecting commerce. This power shall be exclusive, and shall not be affected by any other means of adjustment or prevention that has been or may be established by agreement, code, law, or otherwise."

The Act then sets forth a definite and restricted course of procedure. . . . It is apparent that Congress has entrusted to the Board exclusively the prosecution of the proceeding by its own complaint, the conduct of the hearing, the adjudication and the granting of appropriate relief. The Board as a public agency acting in the public interest, not any private person or group, not any employee or group of employees, is chosen as the instrument to assure protection from the described unfair conduct in order to remove obstructions to interstate commerce.

When the Board has made its order, the Board alone is authorized to take proceedings to enforce it. For that purpose the Board is empowered to petition the Circuit Court of Appeals for a decree of enforcement. The court is to proceed upon notice to those against whom the order runs and with appropriate hearing. If the court, upon application by either party, is satisfied that additional evidence should be taken, it may order the Board, its member or agent, to take it. The Board may then modify its findings of fact and make new findings. The jurisdiction conferred upon the court is exclusive and its decree is final save as it may be reviewed in the customary manner. § 10(e). Again, the Act gives no authority for any proceeding by a private person or group, or by any employee or group of employees, to secure enforcement of the Board's order. The vindication of the desired freedom of employees is thus confided by the Act, by reason of the recognized public interest, to the public agency the Act creates. Petitioner emphasizes the opportunity afforded to private persons by § 10(f). But that opportunity is given to a person aggrieved by a final order of the Board which has granted or denied in whole or in part the relief sought. That is, it is an opportunity afforded to *contest* a final order of the Board, not to *enforce* it. The procedure on such a contest before the Circuit Court of Appeals is assimilated to that provided in § 10(e) when the Board seeks an enforcement of its order. But the assimilation does not change the nature of the proceeding under § 10(f), which seeks not to require compliance with the Board's order but to overturn it.

What Congress said at the outset, that the power of the Board to prevent any unfair practice as defined in the Act is exclusive, is thus fully carried out at every stage of the proceeding. . . .

In both Houses of Congress, the Committees were careful to say that the procedure provided by the bill was analogous to that set up by the Federal Trade Commission Act, § 5, which was deemed to be "familiar to all students of administrative law." That procedure, which was found to be prescribed in the public interest as distinguished from provisions intended to afford remedies to private persons, was fully discussed by this Court in *Federal Trade Commission* v. *Klesner*, 280 U.S. 19, 25, where it was said:

"Section 5 of the Federal Trade Commission Act does not provide private persons with an administrative remedy for private wrongs. The formal complaint is brought in the Commission's name; the prosecution is wholly that of the government; and it bears the entire expense of the prosecution. A person who deems himself aggrieved by the use of an unfair method of competition is not given the right to institute before the Commission a complaint against the alleged wrongdoer. Nor may the Commission authorize him to do so. He may of course bring the matter to the Commission's attention and request it to file a complaint. But a denial of his request is final. And if the request is granted and a proceeding is instituted, he does not become a party to it or have any control over it."

That sort of procedure concerning unfair competition was contrasted with that provided by the Interstate Commerce Act in relation to unjust discrimination. We said that "in their bearing upon private rights" they are "wholly dissimilar." The Interstate Commerce Act, imposes upon the carrier many duties and creates in the individual corresponding rights. For the violation of the private right it affords "a private administrative remedy." The interested person can file as of right a complaint before the Interstate Commerce Commission and the carrier is required to make answer. . . . The present Act, drawn in analogy to the Federal Trade Commission Act, contains no such features. . . .

. . . Congress has . . . created a public agency entrusted . . . with the exclusive authority for the enforcement of the provisions of the Act. . . .

We think that the provision of the National Labor Relations Act conferring exclusive power upon the Board to prevent any unfair labor practice, as defined,—a power not affected by any other means of "prevention that has been or may be established by agreement, code, law, or otherwise," necessarily embraces exclusive authority to institute proceedings for the violation of the court's decree directing enforcement. The decree in no way alters, but confirms, the position of the Board as the enforcing authority. It is the Board's order on behalf of the public that the court enforces. It is the Board's right to make that order that the court sustains. The Board seeks enforcement as a public agent, not to give effect to a "private administrative remedy." Both the order and the decree are aimed at the prevention of the unfair labor practice. If the decree of enforcement is disobeyed, the unfair labor practice is still not prevented. The Board still remains as the sole authority to secure that prevention. The appropriate procedure to that end is to ask the court to punish the violation of its decree as a contempt. As the court has no jurisdiction to enforce the order at the suit of any private person or group of persons, we think it is clear that the court cannot entertain a petition for violation of its decree of enforcement save as the Board presents it. As the Conference Report upon the bill stated, in case the unfair labor practice is resumed, "there will be immediately available to the Board an existing court decree to serve as a basis for contempt proceedings."

## § 31:4. Action for Damages

Enforcement of regulations is frequently sought by authorizing the person injured by the violation of the statute to bring an action against the wrongdoer to recover damages. These damages may be merely remedial, or they may be punitive or exemplary. In the case of remedial damages, the object of the law is to give the plaintiff or injured person a sum of money that will compensate him for the damages that he has suffered. In the case of punitive or exemplary damages, which give the plaintiff more than is needed to compensate him for the damage done, the object of the law is to punish the defendant or to make an example of him by having him pay an amount in excess of that needed to compensate for the actual damages sustained. An illustration of this second class of damages is found in the provision of the Federal Antitrust Law under which the person injured may recover from the wrongdoer three times the amount of the damages that he has sustained. If the plaintiff owned a business valued at $100,000 and is able to prove that the defendant's illegal trust activities totally destroyed this business, the plaintiff is allowed to recover $300,000 rather than the actual amount of his loss.

At first glance, it would seem that the authorization of an action for damages, particularly punitive damages, is a certain way of obtaining observance of a particular regulation. Such actions are subject to certain disadvantages, however, that seriously impair their usefulness as an enforcement method.

First, an action for damages can only be brought where the defendant can be found or served or arrested or his property located, depending upon the nature of the proceeding and whether the defendant is a natural person or a corporation or other enterprise. In some cases, this may require the plaintiff to go halfway or more across the country to a jurisdiction in which suit can be brought against the defendant. The expense of a trial in a distant state may be prohibitive and may have the practical effect of denying the plaintiff his right to sue.

Assuming that the action has been properly brought against the defendant, there are still many more delays and costs that confront the plaintiff. While there is great variety among the practices in the various state and federal courts, there is a certain common pattern of procedure. The plaintiff at some point at or shortly after the beginning of the action will file a pleading setting forth his claim against the defendant. To this, the defendant will be permitted to file an answer. It may be that the pleadings will continue further, with the plaintiff filing a reply and, in some states, the defendant filing a counter-reply in certain circumstances. In addition to these pleadings on the merits of the case, each party is permitted to raise various questions as to the form or technicalities of the proceedings. The assertion and disposition of all these objections may take a substantial amount of time. If the court has a crowded docket or does not have frequent argument lists, it may be several months before an objection raised by one party or another comes before the court for decision. If the defendant is bent on delaying the action, he may prolong the litigation over a substantial period of time by raising every possible objection that might be raised, whether or not there is any merit to it.

In addition to the delay caused by the filing of the pleadings, a modern development in procedure has made the discovery process available. In its broadest form, this procedure permits a party to take the testimony of witnesses or to examine documents or records or property at any time or any place. While there are certain restrictions and limitations, depending upon the jurisdiction in which the action was brought, this new procedure of discovery makes it possible for the dilatory defendant further to delay the plaintiff's suit. Unless otherwise controlled, the defendant may take the testimony of witnesses in Chicago and then, when that is completed, take the testimony of witnesses in California, and in this manner pursue witnesses all over the countryside. While this procedure is highly desirable where the testimony of such witnesses is essential to a just disposition of the cause, it is possible in many jurisdictions to pursue such a course without regard to the merit of the testimony to be obtained. While most jurisdictions have some procedure for curtailing improper use of discovery procedure, the very application to the court to restrict the discovery produces further delay.

The fact that an ill-meaning defendant can abuse the procedure of the court to delay the plaintiff does not necessarily condemn such procedure as improper. While in many states and in the federal courts, reform in court procedure has reduced the time required by actions for damages, there is a certain irreducible minimum of delay that cannot be avoided. The defendant in all cases must be permitted to raise certain basic objections. He must be permitted to attack the right of the plaintiff to bring the action in the particular court, to object to the pleading of the adverse party as not sufficiently specific to inform him of the main facts of dispute, to object to the pleading of the adverse party on the ground that it does not conform to the applicable procedural requirements with respect to the manner in which the action is to be brought, and finally to claim that the complaint filed against him, even if true, does not amount to a cause of action and does not entitle the plaintiff to sue him. The right to take these procedural steps cannot be foreclosed. While some states provide for the above defenses being raised at the same time, thus reducing the overall period of time consumed, the basic distinction between the nature of these objections cannot be eliminated.

The fact that the dilatory defendant may use these procedures to delay an action does not justify denying them to one who is unjustly or improperly sued. In view of the fact that it cannot be determined beforehand whether the plaintiff or the defendant or both are at fault, it is not possible to frame a rule in such a way that the defenses would be available to the meritorious defendant but denied to the dilatory one. The same observation is applicable to the use of discovery by the defendant.

At some point the pleadings have been completed and the discovery before trial is ended. The case then goes to trial. This in itself may take a considerable period of time. Apart from delay that may be caused by waiting for a place on the trial list, the actual trial of the case itself may be long and expensive. The delay and the expense may then be further increased by taking an appeal from the decision of the lower court. Quite frequently there is an intermediate stage before the appeal is taken in which the lower court or all the judges of the lower court are asked to set aside or to reverse in some manner the conclusion made by the judge who tried the case or by the jury. Again these procedural steps may be abused by a defendant who is endeavoring to wear out the plaintiff.

Apart from the obvious expenses of an appeal, it must be borne in mind that the record in the court below must be printed on appeal. While provision is frequently made for deleting or omitting part of the record to take an appeal, this may not be feasible in many of the business regulation suits. This means that all the testimony and the evidence that was admitted by the lower court must be printed and then handed to the appellate court so that it can determine what took place in the trial court. The printing of this record is a very expensive item when there is a large record, as is generally the case where complicated business transactions are involved.

All in all, a plaintiff bringing a suit may not be willing to risk the money and to tolerate the delay necessary to enforce his claim. In some instances the total delay may be considerable. An important antitrust case, for example, ordinarily requires four to five years to prosecute, and some have taken ten years or more. The injured party may conclude that it is better to write off his loss and to forget the matter rather than to send good money after bad in what may be a vain chance to obtain redress.

To this general picture must be added the factor that the increasing complexity of the subjects regulated means that the action brought by the plaintiff is more time-consuming and more costly.

This complexity of the problem involved introduces another element that, in a sense, disqualifies or eliminates the court as a desirable method of enforcing a regulation. The matters to be considered become so complicated that a judge who occasionally hears such a type of case and a jury that probably has never even sat as a jury before is not trained or equipped to hear and to decide the case correctly.

The plaintiff bringing the action must further recognize that, even though he is in the right, he may not be able to establish that fact to the satisfaction of the jury and the court. In many matters the issues are not clear-cut or the solution depends on believing one group of witnesses and disbelieving another group. There is as yet no judicially recognized way of determining who is telling the truth. Accordingly every plaintiff takes the chance that he may be disbelieved by the trier of fact.

## § 31:5. Injunction Action

The courts of equity have traditionally granted relief against threatened irreparable harm to property by issuing an injunction against the about-to-be wrongdoer ordering him to refrain from causing harm. If a person threatens to destroy another's property and that property is unique so that, if unlawfully destroyed, money damages paid by the wrongdoer will not compensate the plaintiff for its loss, equity will issue such a stop order or injunction. Unlike the action at law in which a judgment may only be obtained after trial, the injunction may be obtained in equity at the beginning of the action to order the defendant to stop his threatened conduct and to keep things as they are or maintain the status quo until the court is able to decide which party is in the wrong.

In addition, the injunction may be employed under certain circumstances to compel the wrongdoer to undo what he has done rather than to pay money damages for having done it.

Translated to the field of government regulation of business, the injunction, when available, gives to the person in danger of being injured by violation of a regulation a surer remedy against the wrongdoer by compelling him in advance of violation of the law to conform to the law or by compelling him to stop his improper practice or to right the wrong that he has committed. The fact that the injunction may be obtained at the beginning of a proceeding to determine whether the defendant's threatened conduct is unlawful makes it possible to abuse this remedy and safeguards have been developed for the protection of the defendant.

Under many statutes the administrator or the government is also given the right to obtain an injunction.

Although the equity injunction has a comparative advantage over the action for damages, the injunction proceeding is itself an action in the courts. Many of the defects or the causes for delay or expense discussed in connection with the action for damages are found also in equity. At one time there was a marked advantage of equity procedure over the procedure in the action for damages. To a large extent this difference has been today eliminated as the result of procedural reforms that have either combined law and equity into one action or have molded them after the same pattern.

Under the ordinary practice in equity, the issuance of an injunction rests within the discretion of the court. This means that the court may refuse to grant the injunction where, under all the circumstances, it deems that refusal is the fairest result. This discretionary power does not give the court the power to refuse an injunction because of arbitrary whim or caprice not founded on good reason. The policy of treating the injunction as a discretionary remedy continues into the field of administration of regulations, and an injunction may be refused under the same circumstances as under the general equity practice.

### *(a) Federal Price Control Act*

#### THE HECHT CO. v. BOWLES

321 U.S. 321 (1944)

The Emergency Price Control Act of 1942 provided that "whenever in the judgment of the Administrator any person has engaged or is about to engage in any acts or practices which constitute or will constitute a violation of any provision of Section 4 of this Act, he may make application to the appropriate court for an order enjoining such acts or practices, or for an order enforcing compliance with such provision, and upon a showing by the Administrator that such person has engaged or is about to engage in any such acts or practices a permanent or temporary injunction . . . shall be granted without bond."

The issue presented in this case was whether the phrase "shall be granted" made it mandatory in every case to issue the injunction or whether the court had the discretion to refuse it where it found that the violator had stopped the unlawful practices and had taken measures to prevent further violation.

OPINION BY DOUGLAS, J.

[The Administrator] insists that the mandatory character of § 205 (a) is clear from its language, history and purpose. He argues that "shall be granted" is not permissive, that since the same section provides that the Administrator "may" apply for an injunction and that, if so, the injunction "shall" be granted, "may" and "shall" are each used in the ordinary sense. It is pointed out that when the bill (for which the Act in its final form was substituted) passed the House, § 205 (a) provided that "upon a proper showing" an injunction or other order "shall be granted without bond." The words "upon a proper showing" were stricken in the Senate and were replaced by the words "upon a showing by the Administrator that such person has engaged or is about to engage in any such acts or practices." And the Senate Report in its analysis of § 205 (a) stated that "upon a showing by the Administrator that such person has engaged or is about to engage in any such acts or practices, a temporary or permanent injunction, restraining order or other order is to be granted without bond." . . . Further support for the view that the issuance of an injunction is mandatory once violations are shown is sought in the pattern of federal legislation which provides relief by injunction in aid of law enforcement. Some of those statutes contain provisions quite close to the language of § 205 (a). Others provide that an injunction or restraining order shall be granted "upon a proper showing" or that federal district courts shall have jurisdiction to restrain violations "for cause shown." The argument is that when Congress desired to give the district courts discretion to grant or withhold relief by injunction it chose apt words to make its desire plain.

We agree that the cessation of violations, whether before or after the institution of a suit by the Administrator, is no bar to the issuance of an injunction under § 205 (a). But we do not think that under all circumstances the court must issue the injunction or other order which the Administrator seeks.

It seems apparent on the face of § 205 (a) that there is some room for the exercise of discretion on the part of the court. For the requirement is that a "permanent or temporary injunction, restraining order, or other order" be granted. Though the Administrator asks for an injunction, some "other order" might be more appropriate, or at least so appear to the court. Thus in the present case one judge in the Court of Appeals felt that the District Court should not have dismissed the complaint but should have entered an order retaining the case on the docket with the right of the Administrator, on notice, to renew his application for injunctive relief if violations recurred. It is indeed not difficult to imagine that in some situations that might be the fairest course to follow and one which would be as practically effective as the issuance of an injunction. Such an order, moreover, would seem to be a type of "other order" which a faithful reading of § 205 (a) would permit a court to issue in a compliance proceeding. However that may be, it would seem clear that the court might deem some "other order" more appropriate for the evil at hand than the one which was sought. We cannot say that it lacks the power to make that choice. Thus it seems that § 205 (a) falls short of making mandatory the issuance of an injunction merely because the Administrator asks it.

There is, moreover, support in the legislative history of § 205 (a) for the view that "shall be granted" is less mandatory than a literal reading might suggest. We have already referred to a portion of the Senate Report which lends some support to the position of the Administrator. But in another portion of that Report there is the following reference to suits to enjoin violations of the Act: "In common with substantially all regulatory statutes, the bill authorizes the official charged with the duty of administering the act to apply to any appropriate court, State or Federal, for an order enjoining any person who has engaged or is about to engage in any acts or practices which constitute or will constitute a violation of any provision of the bill. Such courts are given jurisdiction to issue whatever order to enforce compliance is proper in the circumstances of each particular case." . . . A grant of jurisdiction to issue compliance orders hardly suggests an absolute duty to do so under any and all circumstances. We cannot but think that if Congress had intended to make such a drastic departure from the traditions of equity practice, an unequivocal statement of its purpose would have been made. . . .

### § 31:6. Criminal Prosecution

In a general way, a criminal prosecution brought against a person for violating a regulation is subject to all the defects of an action for damages brought against him by the injured person. There is the delay incident to legal proceedings generally. The procedure in a criminal case varies from both the action for damages and the injunction action with respect to the pleadings, which are simpler than in either of the other forms of action. For this reason an ordinary criminal prosecution moves more quickly through the pretrial phases than do the other actions. This time-saving feature tends to disappear when the criminal prosecution is not for a traditional crime such as larceny or murder but is the violation of a business regulation that cannot be proven without long and elaborate proof.

The criminal prosecution also presents a question of costs, although this is borne by the government rather than the injured individual. The burden of the criminal prosecution thus falls on the taxpayers or on society generally. This distinction is based on the rationale that the criminal action is brought to punish the wrong done to society or the state by the commission of the crime. It is not brought for the benefit of the injured person, who therefore does not bear the expense of the prosecution. Consistent with this approach to the criminal action, the injured person is denied any direct benefit from it. If the defendant is fined, the fine is not paid to the plaintiff to indemnify him but is paid to the state. The criminal prosecution is therefore subject to the criticism that, like the action for damages, it comes after the harm has been done, but unlike that action, does nothing to help the injured person.

The merit of criminal prosecutions generally is under attack in the 20th Century. It is difficult to state whether the criminal prosecution for violation of regulations has any value as a deterrent on either the wrongdoer himself or on others or whether it is nothing more than punishing the wrongdoer for what he has done. As a form of punishment, the criminal prosecution is not particularly efficient. Assuming that a conviction can be obtained and is sustained, the penalty imposed is often too small to be significant. In some instances only a fine has been imposed which was in an amount so small as to be nearly a fraction of what the defendant had obtained through his improper practices.

The defendant criminally prosecuted for the violation of a business regulation is entitled to the same constitutional guaranties as the defendant prosecuted for the commission of a traditional crime of like magnitude or grade. Criminal liability for the violation of a business regulation must be determined and punishment, either by fine or imprisonment, must be imposed by a court. Although the administrator may be given authority to establish the standard the violation of which is a crime, he cannot be made the trier of the violation as well. If violation of the regulation of the administrator is punishable as a crime, the regulation must be as explicit as a criminal statute and will be strictly construed.

### *(a) Requirement of definiteness*

M. KRAUS & BROS. v. UNITED STATES

327 U.S. 614 (1946)

OPINION BY MURPHY, J.

. . .

This delegation to the Price Administrator of the power to provide in detail against circumvention and evasion, as to which Congress has imposed criminal sanctions, creates a grave responsibility. In a very literal sense the liberties and fortunes of others may depend upon his definitions and specifications regarding evasion. Hence to these provisions must be applied the same strict rule of construction that is applied to statutes defining criminal action. In other words, the Administrator's provisions must be explicit and unambiguous in order to sustain a criminal prosecution; they must adequately inform those who are subject to their terms what conduct will be considered evasive so as to bring the criminal penalties of the Act into operation. . . . The dividing line between unlawful evasion and lawful action cannot be left to conjecture. The elements of evasive conduct should be so clearly expressed by the Administrator that the ordinary person can know in advance how to avoid an unlawful course of action.

In applying this strict rule of construction to the provisions adopted by the Administrator, courts must take care not to construe so strictly as to defeat the obvious intention of the Administrator. Words used by him to describe evasive action are to be given their natural and plain meaning, supplemented by contemporaneous or longstanding interpretations publicly made by the Administrator. But patent omissions and uncertainties cannot be disregarded when dealing with a criminal prosecution. A prosecutor in framing an indictment, a court in interpreting the Administrator's regulations or a jury in judging guilt cannot supply that which the Administrator failed to do by express word or fair implication. Not even the Administrator's interpretations of his own regulations can cure an omission or add certainty and definiteness to otherwise vague language. The prohibited conduct must, for criminal purposes, be set forth with clarity in the regulations and orders which he is authorized by Congress to promulgate under the Act. Congress has warned the public to look to that source alone to discover what conduct is evasive and hence likely to create criminal liability. . . .

## § 31:7. Defense of Invalid Regulation

In a criminal prosecution, the defendant may defend himself in the same general manner as a defendant in an ordinary action. This usually includes the right to claim that the prosecution is invalid because the law or the regulation that is enforced is unconstitutional or invalid. It is constitutional, however, to provide that the validity of an administrative regulation of business cannot be tested in an action brought for its violation nor to enjoin its enforcement but must be raised in a separate proceeding in another court.

### *(a) Restriction on right to challenge validity of regulation*

YAKUS v. UNITED STATES

321 U.S. 414 (1944)

The Emergency Price Control Act established a special Emergency Court of Appeals and provided that any person objecting to the validity of the Price Control Regulation must make protest to this Emergency Court. The defendant was prosecuted in a criminal action for violating a price control regulation applicable to him. As a defense in the criminal action he attempted to attack the validity of this regulation. The Supreme Court considered the provisions of the Act under which he was denied this right and was limited to raising the question of the validity of the regulation in the Emergency Court of Appeals.

OPINION BY STONE, C. J. ANNOUNCED BY ROBERTS, J. . . .

[The Court first held that the federal statute did not unconstitutionally delegate legislative power to the Price Administrator.]

We consider next the question whether the procedure which Congress has established for determining the validity of the Administrator's regulations is exclusive so as to preclude the defense of invalidity of the Regulation in this criminal prosecution for its violation under §§ 4(a) and 205(b). Section 203(a) sets up a procedure by which "any person subject to any provision of a regulation or order" may within sixty days after it is issued "file a protest specifically setting forth objections to any such provision and affidavits or other written evidence in support of such objections." He may similarly protest later, on grounds arising after the expiration of the original sixty days. The subsection directs that within a reasonable time and in no event more than thirty days after the filing of a protest or ninety days after the issue of the regulation protested, whichever is later, "the Administrator shall either grant or deny such protest in whole or in part, notice such protest for hearing, or provide an opportunity to present further evidence in connection therewith. In the event that the Administrator denies any such protest in whole or in part, he shall inform the protestant of the grounds upon which such decision is based, and of any economic data and other facts of which the Administrator has taken official notice."

Section 204(c) creates a court to be known as the Emergency Court of Appeals consisting of United States district or circuit judges designated by the Chief Justice of the United States. Section 204(a) authorizes any person aggrieved by the denial or partial denial of his protest to file a complaint with the Emergency Court of Appeals within thirty days after the denial, praying that the regulation, order or price schedule protested be enjoined or set aside in whole or in part. The court may issue an injunction only if it finds that the regulation, order or price schedule "is not in accordance with law, or is arbitrary or capricious." [Subsection (b).] It is denied power to issue a temporary restraining order or interlocutory decree. [Subsection (c).] The effectiveness of any permanent injunction it may issue is postponed for thirty days, and if review by this Court is sought upon writ of certiorari, as authorized by subsection (d), its effectiveness is further postponed until final disposition of the case by this Court by denial of certiorari or decision upon the merits. [Subsection (b).]

Section 204(d) declares:

"The Emergency Court of Appeals, and the Supreme Court upon review of judgments and orders of the Emergency Court of Appeals, shall have exclusive jurisdiction to determine the validity of any regulation or order issued under section 2, of any price schedule effective in accordance with the provisions of section 206, and of any provision of any such regulation, order, or price schedule. Except as provided in this section, no court, Federal, State, or Territorial, shall have jurisdiction or power to consider the validity of any such regulation, order, or price schedule, or to stay, restrain, enjoin, or set aside, in whole or in part, any provision of this Act authorizing the issuance of such regulations or orders, or making effective any such price schedule, or any provision of any such regulation, order, or price schedule, or to restrain or enjoin the enforcement of any such provision."

. . . The provisions of § 204(d), conferring upon the Emergency Court of Appeals and this Court "exclusive jurisdiction to determine the validity of any regulation or order," coupled with the provision that "no court, Federal, State, or Territorial, shall have jurisdiction or power to consider the validity of any such regulation," are broad enough in terms to deprive the district court of power to consider the validity of the Administrator's regulation or order as a defense to a criminal prosecution for its violation. . . .

Congress . . . gave clear indication that the validity of the Administrator's regulations or orders should not be subject to attack in criminal prosecutions for their violation, at least before their invalidity had been adjudicated by recourse to the protest procedure prescribed by the statute. . . .

We come to the question whether the provisions of the Act, so construed as to deprive petitioners of opportunity to attack the Regulation in a prosecution for its violation, deprive them of the due process of law guaranteed by the Fifth Amendment. . . .

. . . It is appropriate to take into account the purposes of the Act and the circumstances attending its enactment and application as a war-time emergency measure. [The Court then discussed the war-time background of the Act and the necessity for immediate and universal regulation to prevent inflation.]

Congress sought to avoid or minimize [delay in putting the regulations into operation caused by litigation in courts throughout the country] by the establishment of a single procedure for review of the Administrator's regulations, beginning with an appeal to the Administrator's specialized knowledge and experience gained in the administration of the Act, and affording to him an opportunity to modify the regulations and orders complained of before resort to judicial determination of their validity. . . . It was though desirable to preface all judicial action by resort to expert administrative knowledge and experience, and thus minimize the confusion that would result from inconsistent decisions of district and circuit courts rendered without the aid of an administrative interpretation. In addition the present Act seeks further to avoid that confusion by restricting judicial review of the administrative determination to a single court. Such a procedure, so long as it affords to those affected a reasonable opportunity to be heard and present evidence, does not offend against due process. . . .[1]

## Questions for Discussion

1. To what extent can public opinion be constitutionally employed in enforcing regulations?

2. Discuss the advantages and the disadvantages of public opinion as an enforcement method.

3. Could public opinion be made a more effective sanction than it is? What change would you suggest?

4. Should government take any step in giving publicity to the relative merits of labor disputes? Would its interest in securing a settlement disqualify it for this role?

5. Would public opinion be more effective if an initiative and referendum were available?

6. To what extent is public opinion employed under present federal laws as a means of enforcement?

7. (a) What is meant by summary administrative action? (b) Name four situations in which it may be employed.

---

[1] The strictness of the result in the *Yakus* case was relieved by amending the statute involved to afford a defendant a second opportunity to raise the question of regulation validity in the Emergency Court of Appeals. The amendment provided that within sixty days after arraignment in any criminal proceeding or within sixty days after the commencement of any civil proceeding based upon regulation violation, the defendant may apply to the court in which the prosecution or action is pending for leave to file in the Emergency Court a complaint against the regulation. The court is required to grant such leave if it finds that the applicant is acting in good faith and there is a reasonable and substantial excuse for his failure to have raised the question before in the Emergency Court. After granting of such leave, the Emergency Court has jurisdiction to determine the validity of the regulation. 50 U.S.C. App. § 924(e)(1).

8. (a) To what extent can the administrative decision be enforced by court action? (b) What kinds of court action are available?

9. Who may bring court action to enforce the administrative decision?

10. Why do some statutes limit the right of bringing court action to the administrator?

11. (a) In the *Amalgamated Utility Workers* case, why did the Court hold that only the N.L.R.B. could bring an action to compel obedience to the decision of the Board? (b) Why could not a rival union that was benefited by the Board's decision bring such an action?

12. (a) Should any taxpayer be entitled to bring an action in order that the laws may be enforced? (b) Why is a contrary rule applied?

13. Can a citizen bring an action to compel obedience to an order of the Federal Trade Commission? of the Interstate Commerce Commission?

14. (a) What is meant by "a party in interest"? (b) If the law provides that "any party in interest" may sue to recover excessive freight charges imposed by a carrier, does the "party in interest" include:

- (a) The shipper who was charged the excess freight.
- (b) A chamber of commerce to which the shipper belongs that is concerned over business in the area being hurt by such improper practices.
- (c) Employees of the shipper who claim that they would receive higher wages if lower freight rates were charged the shipper.
- (d) Stockholders of the shipper who claim that they would receive larger dividends if lower freight rates were charged.
- (e) The police department of the city, which desires to see that the law is enforced.
- (f) A private citizen who wishes to see that the law is enforced.

15. In defining "party in interest" does it make any difference if the court action is one to make the defendant pay money damages? pay a fine? go to jail? be ordered to stop?

16. (a) Was the administrator acting within the scope of the statute in the *Hecht* case? (b) Was the decision of the Court in accordance with the provisions of the statute? (c) Do you prefer the interpretation of the administrator or the Court?

17. In the *Hecht* case did the Court apply the statute or general principles of equity law existing independently of the statute?

18. Compare a criminal prosecution to enforce an administrative regulation with other methods of court enforcement. Comment with respect to delay, expense to the parties, expense to the community, court procedure, effectiveness, and redress to the injured person.

19. (a) What are damages? (b) What are punitive damages? (c) What are exemplary damages?

20. How is a suit for damages employed as a means of enforcing a regulation of business?

21. Appraise the action for damages as an enforcement method. What are its advantages and disadvantages?

22. How can a civil action for damages be delayed by filing pleadings?

23. (a) What is discovery? (b) How can it be used to delay an action for damages? (c) Can the defects of procedure be eliminated so as to improve the civil action for damages as an enforcement method?

24. Do you believe that trial by jury should be limited to ordinary law suits and should not be used in the enforcement of technical regulation of business? Discuss.

25. (a) What is an equity action? (b) How does it differ from a law action for damages?

26. (a) What is a proceeding or action for an injunction? (b) How does it differ from an action for damages?

27. (a) How is the injunction action employed in the enforcement of regulations? (b) What are its advantages and disadvantages?

28. What is the basis for sustaining a law that a person accused of violating a business regulation cannot attack the validity of the regulation in the court in which he is prosecuted but must bring a separate action in a different court to review the action of the administrator?

29. (a) Appraise the procedure considered in the *Yakus* case as a method for attacking an administrative regulation. (b) Does the procedure favor the administrator or the persons regulated? (c) Does it operate differently with respect to big business and little business?

30. What was the constitutional basis in the *Yakus* case for limiting to one court the right to question the validity of a federal administrative regulation?

31. To what extent is the procedure considered in the *Yakus* case sustained because of the war power?

32. Why did not the Court in the *Yakus* case hold that the statute made an illegal delegation of legislative power when it conferred upon the administrator power to suspend the operation of a regulation pending appeal?

33. (a) Is it desirable to provide that attacks on the validity of a regulation must be brought in a special court, as distinguished from being made in any action in which a person is sued or prosecuted for violation of the regulation? (b) Does this place any burden on the person desiring to attack the regulation?

34. Would the procedure provided by the Emergency Rent Control Act, which was considered in the *Yakus* case, have been valid if not in a war measure relating to inflation control?

## Chapter 32

## REVIEW OF ADMINISTRATOR'S ACTION



### § 32:1. In General

To what extent should a determination or a regulation of an administrator be final? May it be set aside or ignored by the courts, or should they be bound by his action? This has been one of the most difficult problems facing the courts.

In most instances the administrator is not elected but is appointed by a particular officer. In some instances the appointment may be made by one person with the approval of others, as in the case of certain appointments made by the President of the United States with the advice and the consent of the Senate. Assume that finality is accorded the action of the administrator, and his action cannot be called into question in any manner. The result would soon be condemned as government by bureaucracy that had not been elected by the people and was not responsible to them at the polls. Such finality would also run counter to our traditional Anglo-American concept that it is an inherent element of justice that one's property rights cannot be affected without a trial by jury, although it should be recognized that for centuries equity has done just this, acting without making use of the common law jury. As a practical matter, there would be no means of correcting an error of the administrator, or an abuse by him of his authority, or an action of his in excess of his authority. It is also likely that in many instances an administrator, knowing that he could not be reviewed or checked in any way would tend to become arbitrary and capricious.

Turning now to the converse situation under which the determination or the regulation of the administrator can be fully reviewed, we would find waste of time and money through the court's duplication of the work of the administrator. This would be not only a waste of the court's time and the taxpayer's money, but also of the time and the money of the parties or businessmen affected who would be required to produce again before the court the testimony and the evidence that they had already presented before the administrator. The ability of the court to go over every point decided by the administrator would also have the unhealthy effect of lowering the administrator in the eyes of the persons subject to his jurisdiction. They would know that whatever he did was unimportant, since the court would go through the entire case again and make its own decision. In instances in which a full review has been permitted, this psychological reaction has been apparent. The practice developed that the persons subject to the administrator's jurisdiction would withhold information or testimony from him with the intention of appealing the matter and then presenting the new testimony or evidence if the administrator decided against them.

A complete review of the matter by the court would place the making of the ultimate administrative decision in the court. This is in conflict with the basic principle justifying the existence of the administrator, namely, that a specialized or technical field was involved in which the courts were not competent and that the problems should therefore be given to a full-time expert in the field. If the court is sufficiently expert to review fully the determination or the regulation of the administrator, then there was no need for the administrator in the first instance. In addition, the exercise by the court of this broad function of review would place upon it a burden of work in addition to its ordinary judicial duties that would be too great for the court to handle.

Between these extremes the law has sought to find a suitable median: one that will make the administrator sufficiently strong to command respect and make full use of his expert training, yet at the same time avoid raising him above the law. In the more modern statute, the extent to which review is permitted may be expressly stated. In some instances the act creating the office of the administrator is silent as to the right to appeal, while in others there may be an express provision that the action of the administrator shall be final. As a general rule, where no appeal is authorized or where it is expressly provided that the administrator's findings shall be conclusive, a restricted review is still permitted by means of a writ of certiorari, at least in state practice.

The review of an administrator is not limited to an appeal from his action; his decisions may be questioned to some extent in collateral procedures. Illustrative of the latter, his decisions may be challenged and called into question in an action brought by him to compel obedience to his order,[1] in an injunction action brought by the person adversely affected by his decision to prevent its enforcement; in a hearing upon an application by the administrator made to a court for an enforcement order against the administrator; or in an action brought against him to impose personal liability for his official actions.[2]

The fact that in the absence of statutory provision or prohibition, it is the courts that by case law determine the extent to which the administrator is subject to review, has influenced the solution of the

[1] See generally Chapter 31.

[2] In discussing the forms of collateral review in this chapter, the classical names of the proceedings have been retained. In many states and under the federal practice, the names of some of these actions have been changed or the action has in name been abolished. The relief obtained under these actions, although changed in name or technically abolished, may still be obtained under other forms of procedure.

problem. In the early days of regulation, the administrator was not always warmly received by the courts, and they tended to expand the right of review in order to make the administrator clearly subordinate to the courts. In recent years this spirit of rivalry has materially weakened and the courts have recognized that the administrator is in effect a new branch of the government and must be accepted as such. This new attitude has naturally had the result of according greater finality to the decisions of the administrator.

Thus the Supreme Court has declared that it must be guided by the "cardinal principle . . . that in construing a statute setting up an administrative agency and providing for judicial review of its action, court and agency are not to be regarded as wholly independent and unrelated instrumentalities of justice, each acting in the performance of its prescribed statutory duty without regard to the appropriate function of the other in securing the plainly indicated objects of the statute. Court and agency are the means adopted to attain the prescribed end, and so far as their duties are defined by the words of the statute, those words should be construed so as to obtain that end through coördinated action. Neither body should repeat in this day the mistake made by the courts of law when equity was struggling for recognition as an ameliorating system of justice; neither can rightly be regarded by the other as an alien intruder, to be tolerated if must be, but never to be encouraged or aided by the other in the attainment of the common aim. . . ."[3]

## § 32:2. Injunction Action

This is the same form of action discussed as a method of compelling obedience to the administrator's decision. Subject to certain exceptions, it may also be brought by the person subject to the decision to enjoin or stop the administrator from enforcing the decision on the ground that the statute creating the administrator's office is unconstitutional or that the action of the administrator is improper.

United States Code, 26 § 3653(a) prohibits federal courts from enjoining the collection of federal taxes. The Supreme Court has, however, held that a tax may be enjoined in case of "special and extraordinary facts and circumstances" or when what is named a tax is in reality a penalty for doing what Congress may not directly

[3] United States v. Morgan, 307 U.S. 183 (1939). "In construing the enforcement provisions of legislation like the [Agricultural Marketing Agreement] Act, it is important to remember that courts and administrative agencies are collaborative 'instrumentalities of justice,' and not business rivals. . . ." United States v. Ruzicka, 329 U.S. 287 (1946).

forbid the party to do. Apart from these exceptions, the statute has been further circumvented by the device of testing the validity of federal taxing statutes as applied to corporations by the use of a stockholders' bill to enjoin the corporation from paying the tax on the ground that such tax is unlawful.

As an exception to the availability of the injunction, it is held under certain statutes that the jurisdiction of the administrator is exclusive and that his action cannot be reviewed by enjoining him from acting.

### *(a) Prevention of exercise of jurisdiction*

**MYERS v. BETHLEHEM STEEL CORP.**
**303 U.S. 41 (1938)**

The Bethlehem Shipbuilding Corporation brought an injunction action in a District Court against the Director of the First Region of the National Labor Relations Board to prevent the holding of a hearing by him under that Act to determine whether the employer had committed an unfair labor practice.

OPINION BY BRANDEIS, J.

. . . We are of opinion that the District Court was without power to enjoin the Board from holding the hearings.

*First.* There is no claim by the Corporation that the statutory provisions and the rules of procedure prescribed for such hearings are illegal; or that the Corporation was not accorded ample opportunity to answer the complaint of the Board; or that opportunity to introduce evidence on the allegations made will be denied. The claim is that the provisions of the Act are not applicable to the Corporation's business at the Fore River Plant, because the operations conducted there are not carried on, and the products manufactured are not sold, in interstate or foreign commerce; that, therefore, the Corporation's relations with its employees at the plant cannot burden or interfere with such commerce; that hearings would, at best, be futile; and that the holding of them would result in irreparable damage to the Corporation, not only by reason of their direct cost and the loss of time of its officials and employees, but also because the hearings would cause serious impairment of the good will and harmonious relations existing between the Corporation and its employees, and thus seriously impair the efficiency of its operations.

*Second.* The District Court is without jurisdiction to enjoin hearings because the power "to prevent any person from engaging in any unfair practice affecting commerce" has been vested by Congress in the Board and the Circuit Court of Appeals, and Congress has declared: "This power shall be exclusive, and shall not be affected by any other means of adjustment or prevention that has been or may be established by agreement, code, law, or otherwise." The grant of that exclusive power is constitutional, because the Act provided for appropriate procedure before the Board and in the review by the Circuit Court of Appeals an adequate opportunity to secure judicial protection against possible illegal action on the part of the Board. No power to enforce an order is conferred upon the Board. To secure enforcement, the Board must apply to a Circuit Court of Appeals for its affirmance. And, until the Board's order has been affirmed by the appropriate Circuit Court of Appeals, no penalty accrues for disobeying it. The independent right to apply to a Circuit Court of Appeals to have an order set aside is conferred upon any party aggrieved by the proceeding before the Board. The Board is even without power to enforce obedience to its subpoena to testify or to produce written evidence. To enforce obedience it must apply to a District Court; and to such an application appropriate defense may be made.

As was said in National Labor Relations Board v. Jones & Laughlin Steel Corp., 301 U.S. 1, 46, 47, the procedural provisions "do not offend against the constitutional requirements governing the creation and action of administrative bodies. . . . The act establishes standards to which the Board must conform. There must be complaint, notice and hearing. The Board must receive evidence and make findings. The findings as to the facts are to be conclusive, but only if supported by evidence. The order of the Board is subject to review by the designated court, and only when sustained by the court may the order be enforced. Upon that review all questions of the jurisdiction of the Board and the regularity of its proceedings, all questions of constitutional right or statutory authority are open to examination by the court. We construe the procedural provisions as affording adequate opportunity to secure judicial protection against arbitrary action in accordance with the well-settled rules applicable to administrative agencies set up by Congress and aid in the enforcement of valid legislation."

It is true that the Board has jurisdiction only if the complaint concerns interstate or foreign commerce. Unless the Board finds that it does, the complaint must be dismissed. And if it finds that interstate or foreign commerce is involved, but the Circuit Court of Appeals concludes that such finding was without adequate evidence to support it, or otherwise contrary to law, the Board's petition to enforce it will be dismissed, or the employer's petition to have it set aside will be granted. Since the procedure before the Board is appropriate and the judicial review so provided is adequate, Congress had power to vest exclusive jurisdiction in the Board and the Circuit Court of Appeals. . . .

### § 32:3. Mandamus Action

The effect of this action is to send a mandate to a public officer to compel him to perform a ministerial act or function. Such an act is one that is performed mechanically by the public officer or that does not call for the exercise by him of any judgment or discretion. As an illustration, a ministerial function would be imposed on an officer if a statute provided that he should issue a license to anyone paying him a certain sum of money as a license fee. In such case he does not exercise any judgment or discretion beyond that of determining that he is being paid the amount of money specified by the statute. If he refuses to perform such a mechanical act, an action of mandamus may be brought to compel him to do so.

If, on the other hand, the officer has any judgment or discretion in the matter, the action of mandamus cannot be employed to make him reach a particular decision. Thus in the license case, if the officer could refuse to issue the license if he believes that the applicant is not a proper or a duly qualified person or that the issuance of additional licenses would have a harmful effect on the public, the action then cannot be brought. If the officer should refuse to exercise his discretion or to make any decision whatever, the action could be brought to compel him to reach some decision; but, since the particular decision lies within his discretion, the action of mandamus cannot compel him to reach any particular result. There is a further qualification to this rule under which a writ of mandamus can be issued to compel an official to decide a matter over again where his decision has been so manifestly arbitrary or capricious that it cannot be sustained as being an exercise of his discretion.

Apart from this qualification, the action of mandamus cannot be used as a means of reviewing or appealing from the decision of an administrative officer if discretion is involved.

The action of mandamus may be brought either by the government or by an individual. In the case of the former, it is most commonly brought in the name of the attorney general against the officer or in some cases in the name of a district or local prosecuting attorney against the defendant administrator. If it is brought by a private individual, it is necessary for him to show not only a breach of public duty by the defendant administrator but also that he has a special interest or suffers damages peculiar to himself over and above the general damage that he would sustain as a member of the public as the result of the defendant's failure to perform or improper performance.

The exact procedure in the action of mandamus varies greatly from jurisdiction to jurisdiction. Originally it was a writ issued directly by the King to the defendant and as such was known as a prerogative writ. Its use appears as early as the reigns of Edward II and Edward III. It was not until the reign of Queen Anne, however, that mandamus assumed its more typical form. The action of mandamus by that name has been abolished in some jurisdictions, although the substance of the remedy continues. Under the Federal Rules of Civil Procedure the action is nominally abolished and the relief formerly obtained in that action is now sought by a petition addressed to the court. In some states, as in Pennsylvania, the action has been assimilated to the ordinary action for breach of contract.

In those jurisdictions in which mandamus has been retained in substantially its common law form, the rule is followed that the issuance of a writ of mandamus lies within the discretion of the court and it is an extraordinary remedy that will only be granted as a last resort. The granting is further qualified by the rule that the plaintiff must clearly be entitled to relief and that if there is any doubt the writ cannot issue. In jurisdictions retaining these limitations, the existence of another adequate remedy at law bars the issuance of the writ of mandamus. In jurisdictions that have abandoned this concept of the action of mandamus, the plaintiff is not required to obtain permission of the court to bring the action. Instead, the plaintiff brings suit just as though he were suing on a contract and is then granted the special form of relief sought if he establishes facts showing the duty of the officer and either a public interest in its performance or a private interest peculiar to the plaintiff.

### *(a) Exercise of jurisdiction*

INTERSTATE COMMERCE COMMISSION v. HUMBOLDT STEAMSHIP CO.

224 U.S. 474 (1912)

The Interstate Commerce Commission, interpreting the jurisdiction conferred upon it by the Interstate Commerce Act, held that violations of the Act committed within Alaska were not within its jurisdiction. The Supreme Court considered whether this decision was erroneous and whether the Interstate Commerce Commission should be compelled by mandamus to take jurisdiction of such violations.

OPINION BY MCKENNA, J.

The ultimate question in the case is whether Alaska is a territory of the United States within the meaning of the Interstate Commerce Act as amended.

The Interstate Commerce Commission resolved the question in the negative and dismissed the petition of the Humbolt Steamship Company . . . which alleged violations of the act by the White Pass & Yukon Railway Company operating in Alaska. . . .

The steamship company instituted an action . . . praying for a mandamus against the Commission to require it to take jurisdiction and to proceed as required by the act. . . .

It is . . . contended by the Commission that "mandamus is not a proper proceeding to correct an error of law like that alleged in the petition."

The general principle which controls the issue of a writ of mandamus is familiar. It can be issued to direct the performance of a ministerial act, but not to control discretion. It may be directed against a tribunal or one who acts in a judicial capacity to require it or him to proceed, the manner of doing so being left to its or his discretion. It is true there may be a jurisdiction to determine the possession of jurisdiction. . . . But the full doctrine . . . cannot be extended to administrative officers. The Interstate Commerce Commission is purely an administrative body. It is true it may exercise and must exercise quasi judicial duties, but its functions are defined, and in the main, explicitly directed by the act creating it. It may act of its own motion in certain instances—it may be petitioned to move by those having rights under the act. It may exercise judgment and discretion, and, it may be, cannot be controlled in either. But if it absolutely refuse to act, deny its power, from a misunderstanding of the law, it cannot be said to exercise discretion. Give it that latitude and yet give it the power to nullify its most essential duties, and how would its non-action be reviewed? The answer of the Commission is, by "a reversal by the tribunal of appeal." And such a tribunal, it is intimated, is the United States Commerce Court.

But the proposition is plainly without merit, even although it may be conceded, for the sake of argument, that the Commerce Court is by law vested with the exclusive power to review any and every act of the Commission taken in the exertion of the authority conferred upon it by statute; that is, to exclusively review, not only affirmative orders of the Commission granting relief, but also the action of that body in refusing to award relief on the ground that an applicant was not entitled to relief. This is so because the action of the Commission refusing to entertain a petition on the ground that its subject matter was not within the scope of the powers conferred upon it would not be embraced within the hypothetical concessions thus made. A like view disposes of the cases relied upon in which it was decided that certain departmental orders were not susceptible of being reviewed by mandamus. . . .

In the case at bar the Commission refused to proceed at all, though the law required it to do so; and to do so as required—that is, to take jurisdiction, not in what manner to exercise it—is the effect of the decree of the Court of Appeals, the order of the court being that a preemptory writ of mandamus be issued directing the Commission to "take jurisdiction of said cause and proceed therein as by law required." In other words, to proceed to the merits of the controversy, at which point the Commission stopped because [it had wrongly believed that it was] without jurisdiction to make the order sought by the complainant, the steamship company.

### *(b) Procedure before administrator*

FEDERAL COMMUNICATIONS COMMISSION v. POTTSVILLE BROADCASTING CO.

309 U.S. 134 (1940)

The Broadcasting Company applied for a license under the Federal Communications Act of 1934. This was refused by the Federal Communications Commission and the applicant appealed to the Federal Court of Appeals, which held that the basis of the decision of the Commission was wrong and sent the case back to the Commission for reconsideration. Instead of considering this application alone, the Commission scheduled it for a hearing with the applications of two rival companies for the same facilities in order to determine which of the three applicants would best serve the public interest. The Broadcasting Company then sought a writ of mandamus to compel the Commission to consider its application alone without considering the two rival applications.

OPINION BY FRANKFURTER, J.

. . . In its essentials the Communications Act of 1934 derives from the Federal Radio Act of 1927. . . . By this Act Congress, in order to protect the national interest involved in the new and far-reaching science of broadcasting, formulated a unified and comprehensive regulatory system for the industry. . . .

. . . In granting or withholding permits for the construction of stations, and in granting, denying, modifying or revoking licenses for the operation of stations, "public convenience, interest, or necessity" was the touchstone for the exercise of the Commission's authority. . . . Necessarily, . . . the subordinate questions of procedure in ascertaining the public interest, when the Commission's licensing authority is invoked—the scope of the inquiry, whether applications should be heard contemporaneously or successively, whether parties should be allowed to intervene in one another's proceedings, and similar questions—were explicitly and by implication left to the Commission's own devising, so long, of course, as it observes the basic requirements designed for the protection of private as well as public interest. . . . Underlying the whole law is recognition of the rapidly fluctuating factors characteristic of the evolution of broadcasting and of the corresponding requirement that the administrative process possess sufficient flexibility to adjust itself to these factors. Thus, it is highly significant that although investment in broadcasting stations may be large, a license may not be issued for more than three years; and in deciding whether to renew the license, just as in deciding whether to issue it in the first place, the Commission must judge by the standard of "public convenience, interest, or necessity." The Communications Act is not designed primarily as a new code for the adjustment of conflicting private rights through adjudication. Rather it expresses a desire on the part of Congress to maintain, through appropriate administrative control, a grip on the dynamic aspects of radio transmission. . . .

Courts, like other organisms, represent an interplay of form and function. The history of Anglo-American courts and the more or less narrowly defined range of their staple business have determined the basic characteristics of trial procedure, the rules of evidence, and the general principles of appellate review. Modern administrative tribunals are the outgrowth of conditions far different from those. To a large degree they have been a response to the felt need of governmental supervision over economic enterprise—a supervision which could effectively be exercised neither directly through self-executing legislation nor by the judicial process. That this movement was natural and its extension inevitable, was a quarter century ago the opinion of eminent spokesmen of the law. Perhaps the most striking characteristic of this movement has been the investiture of administrative agencies with power far exceeding and different from the conventional judicial modes for adjusting conflicting claims—modes whereby interested litigants define the scope of the inquiry and determine the data on which the judicial judgment is ultimately based. Administrative agencies have power themselves to initiate inquiry, or, when their authority is invoked, to control the range of investigation in ascertaining what is to satisfy the requirements of the public interest in relation to the needs of vast regions and sometimes the whole nation in the enjoyment of facilities for transportation, communication and other essential public services. These differences in origin and function preclude wholesale transplantation of the rules of procedure, trial and review which have evolved from the history and experience of courts. Thus, this Court has recognized that bodies like the Interstate Commerce Commission, into whose mould Congress has cast more recent administrative agencies, "should not be too narrowly constrained by technical rules as to the admissibility of proof," . . . should be free to fashion their own rules of procedure and to pursue methods of inquiry capable of permitting them to discharge their multitudinous duties. . . . To be sure, the laws under which these agencies operate prescribe the fundamentals of fair play. They require that interested parties be afforded an opportunity for hearing and that judgment must express a reasoned conclusion. But to assimilate the relation of these administrative bodies and the courts to the relationship between lower and upper courts is to disregard the origin and purposes of the movement for administrative regulation and at the same time to disregard the traditional scope, however far-reaching, of the judicial process. Unless these vital differentiations between the functions of judicial and administrative tribunals are observed, courts will stray outside their province and read the laws of Congress through the distorting lenses of inapplicable legal doctrine. . . .

On review the court may . . . correct errors of law and on remand the Commission is bound to act upon the correction. . . . But an administrative determination in which is imbedded a legal question open to judicial review does not impliedly foreclose the administrative agency, after its error has been corrected, from enforcing the legislative policy committed to its charge.

. . . Congress which creates and sustains these agencies must be trusted to correct whatever defects experience may reveal. Interference by the courts is not conducive to the development of habits of responsibility in administrative agencies. Anglo-American courts as we know them are themselves in no small measure the product of a historic process. . . .

### § 32:4. Minor Forms of Collateral Review

#### *(a) Quo warranto action*

The effect of this action is to call upon the defendant administrator to show by what warrant or authority he holds his office or exercises a particular power or privilege. In the state courts, this remedy may be used to challenge the constitutionality of the statute under which the administrator acts or the existence of a power asserted by him. This remedy is rarely used in federal practice, although it is fairly common in the state courts.

#### *(b) Review on certiorari*

In common law jurisdictions, a writ of certiorari may be issued by a court to an administrative body exercising judicial or quasi-judicial functions. In its common law scope, it may be employed only to question whether a defect of jurisdiction is apparent on the face of the record of the proceedings before the officer. Thus limited, it does not serve as a review of whether his decision was correct or not. In some states, such as New York, this limitation has been abandoned and the writ of certiorari has been made to serve the purpose of a writ of error by which the merits of the case are thrown open for reexamination by the court to determine whether the decision of the administration was correct. Very little use is made of the writ in federal administrative practice.

### (c) *Habeas corpus proceeding*

The writ of habeas corpus is also available to bring into review the action of an administrator where, as the result of his action, a person is placed under arrest or in custody. The effect of the writ is to direct the administrator or officer detaining the aggrieved person to produce him in court and then to follow whatever course the court shall direct. Habeas corpus is comparatively little used in the field of government regulation of business. Although formerly used in tax cases, its use has gradually been abandoned and is now primarily found in cases involving quarantine, detention in institutions or under martial law, extradition, and deportation.

### (d) *Prohibition proceeding*

The writ of prohibition is occasionally available to review the action of an administrative officer. Traditionally the writ is directed against an inferior court to prevent it from exercising a jurisdiction that it does not possess. Its object is limited to this negative purpose of preventing the lower court from hearing the case. Its use in administrative practice has been very scant because the courts have not regarded many administrators as being tribunals or courts for the purpose of the issuance of the writ. A further reason for its disuse even if otherwise available is its purely negative effect of preventing the administrator from taking any action.

### (e) *Declaratory judgment action*

The declaratory judgment procedure is generally restricted to controversies between private litigants, and there is great reluctance on the part of the courts to make this procedure available in the field of administrative law.

## § 32:5. Action for Damages Against Administrator

The decision of the administrator may also be called into question in a suit brought against him to recover damages for his official conduct, assuming that such an action may be brought.

The general rule is that an administrator exercising discretionary powers is not liable to the person injured by an error in judgment so long as he acted in good faith. An exception is made to this rule in some jurisdictions where, if private property has been destroyed or taken by the administrator, he is liable for damages to its owner if in a subsequent action for damages brought against the administrator it is determined that he had acted wrongly. This view is undesirable, for it has a paralyzing effect upon the administrator because he necessarily is made afraid to take any action unless the case is so clear that no jury could disagree with him at a later date. In many instances the right or wrong of the case may not be so manifest; yet the danger of peril to the public may be so great as to warrant the administrator's acting as though it were a clear case. This situation arises most frequently in connection with the abatement of nuisances or the enforcement of health and quarantine laws. The interest of society in the immediate abatement of a nuisance or the taking of every step possible for the protection of the public health or safety may be such as to justify the administrator's acting in the doubtful case.

### *(a) Literal interpretation of authority*

MILLER v. HORTON

152 Mass. 540, 26 N.E. 100 (1891)

OPINION BY HOLMES, J.

This is an action of tort for killing the plaintiff's horse. The defendants admit the killing, but justify as members of the Board of Health . . . under an order addressed to the board and signed by two of the three commissioners on contagious diseases among domestic animals appointed under [the authority of statute]. . . . This order declared that it was adjudged that the horse had the glanders, and that it was condemned, and directed the defendants to cause it to be killed. The judge before whom the case was tried found that the horse had not glanders, but declined to rule that the defendants had failed to make out their justification and found for the defendants. . . .

The language of the material part of . . . the act . . . is: "In all cases of farcy or glanders, the commissioners, having condemned the animal infected therewith, shall cause such animal to be killed without an appraisal, but may pay the owner or any other person an equitable sum for killing and burial thereof." Taken literally, these words only give the commissioners jurisdiction and power to condemn a horse that really has the glanders. The question is whether they go further by implication, so that, if a horse which has not the disease is condemned by the commissioners, their order will protect the man who kills it in a subsequent suit by the owner for compensation.

The main ground for reading into the statute an intent to make the commissioners' order an absolute protection is, that there is no provision for compensation to the owner in this class of cases, and therefore, unless the order is a protection, those who carry it out will do so at their peril. Such a construction when once known would be apt to destroy the efficiency of the clause, as few people could be found to carry out orders on these terms.

On the other hand, this same absence of any provision for compensation to the owner, even if not plainly founded on the assumption that only a worthless thing and a nuisance is in question, still would be an equally strong argument for keeping to the literal and narrower interpretation. If the Legislature had had in mind the possible destruction of healthy horses, there was no reason in the world why it should not have provided for paying the owners. Section 12 does not provide for paying them in all cases where they are not in fault, unless this is an exception. When, as here, the horse not only is not paid for, but may be condemned without appeal and killed without giving the owner a hearing or even notice, the grounds are very strong for believing that the statute means no more than it says, and is intended to authorize the killing of actual infected horses only. If the commissioners had felt any doubt, they could have had the horse appraised under Section 12. . . .

The reasons for this construction seem decisive to a majority of the court, when they consider the grave questions which would arise as to the constitutionality of the clause if . . . construed the other way. . . . The act . . . by implication, declares horses with the glanders to be nuisances, and we assume in favor of the defendant that it may do so constitutionally, and may authorize them to be killed without compensation to the owners. But the statute does not declare all horses to be nuisances, and the question is, whether, if the owner of the horse denies that his horse falls within the class declared to be so, the Legislation can make the ex parte decision of a board like this conclusive upon him. That question is answered by the decision in *Fisher* v. *McGirr*, 1 Grey 1. It is decided that there the owner has a right to be heard, and, further, that only a trial by jury satisfies the provision of [the constitution] that no subject shall be deprived of his property but by the judgment of his peers, or the law of the land. . . . Of course there cannot be a trial by jury before killing an animal supposed to have a contagious disease, and we assume that the Legislature may authorize its destruction in such emergencies without a hearing beforehand. But it does not follow that it can throw the loss on the owner without a hearing. If he cannot be heard beforehand, he may be heard afterward. The statute may provide for paying him in case it should appear that his property was not what the Legislature has declared to be a nuisance, and give him his hearing in that way. If it does not do so, the statute may leave those who act under it to proceed at their peril, and the owner gets his hearing in an action against them. . . .

But we are led . . . to consider another possible suggestion. It may be said, suppose that the decision of the board is not conclusive, that the plaintiff's horse had the glanders, still the Legislature may consider that self-protection requires the immediate killing of all horses which a competent board deem infected, whether they are so or not, and, if so, the innocent horses that are killed are a sacrifice to necessary self-protection, and need not be paid for.

In *Train* v. *Boston Disinfecting Co.*, 144 Mass. 523, it was held that all imported rags might be required to be put through a disinfecting process at the expense of the owner. Of course, the order did not mean that the Legislature or board of health declared all imported rags to be infected, but simply that the danger was too great to risk an attempt at discrimination. If the Legislature could throw the burden on owners of innocent rags in that case, why could it not throw the burden on the owners of innocent horses in this? If it could order all rags to be disinfected, why might it not have ordered such rags to be disinfected as a board of three determine, summarily, and without notice or appeal? The latter provision would have been more favorable to the owners, as they would have had a chance at least of escaping the burden, and it would stand on the same ground as the severer law.

The answer, or part of it, is this. Whether the motive of the Legislature is the same or not in the two cases supposed, it declares different things to be dangerous and nuisances unless disinfected. In the one it declares all imported rags to be so, in the other, only all infected rags. Within limits it may thus enlarge or diminish the number of things to be deemed nuisances by the law, and courts cannot inquire why it includes certain property, and whether the motive was to avoid an investigation. But wherever it draws the line, an owner has a right to a hearing on the question whether his property falls within it, and this right is not destroyed by the fact that the line might have been drawn so differently as unquestionably to include that property. Thus, in the first case, the owner has a right to try the question whether his rags were imported; in the second whether they were infected. . . .

Still it may be asked if self-protection require the act, why should not the owner bear the loss? It may be answered, that self-protection does not require all that is believed to be necessary to that end, nor even all that reasonably is believed to be necessary to that end. If only requires what is actually necessary. It would seem doubtful, at least, whether actual necessity ought not to be the limit when the question arises under the Constitution between the public and an individual. . . . It is enough to say, that in this case actual necessity required the destruction only of infected horses, and that was all that the Legislature purported to authorize.

. . . The literal, and as we think the true construction of [the statute] seems to us the only safe one to adopt, and accordingly we are of opinion that the authority and jurisdiction of the commissioners to condemn the plaintiff's horse . . . was conditional upon its actually having the glanders. If this be so, their order would not protect the defendants in a case where the commissioners acted outside their jurisdiction. . . . The fact as to the horse having the disease was open to investigation in the present action, and on the finding that the horse did not have it, the plaintiff was entitled to a ruling that the defendants had failed to make out their justification. . . .

### *(b) Errors of judgment*

A contrary view was taken in *Raymond* v. *Fish*, 51 Conn. 80 (1883) in which the court stated, "The statute does not mean to destroy property which is not in fact a nuisance, but who shall decide whether it is so? All legal investigations require time, and cannot be thought of. If the board of health are to decide at their peril, they will not decide at all."

This latter view is also expressed in *Crayton* v. *Larrabee*, 220 N.Y. 493, 116 NE 355 (1917), in which a health officer was held not liable for damages to a person improperly quarantined. The health officer had acted under an ordinance authorizing the establishment of a quarantine whenever he deemed such action necessary. The court held that "As a preliminary to his action, the health officer must deem the action necessary. He must adjudge his conclusion, that is, his conclusion must rest upon his knowledge of the facts and of the correct rules for their interpretation and application acquired through a reasonable and fair investigation and consideration at such sources as a person of ordinary intelligence and perception, charged with the responsibilities of the office, would regard as authentic and trustworthy. The conclusion thus reached must be that the action he orders is essential to public health. Conditions must exist which render, within reason and fair apprehension, his action essential for the preservation of the health of the public. For a mere error of judgment the officer cannot be held liable. Unreasonable or arbitrary action or malicious or partial action, or action in excess of his authority, causing injuries, supports his liability."

The conflict between the view set forth in this and in the preceding subsection (a) has not been resolved by statute or decision. The result is that whether an administrator is liable for damages depends upon the law of the particular government under which he acts. There is, however, a definite trend in favor of exempting the administrator from liability in the modern decisions and in the cases applicable to administrators regulating a segment of the economic activity generally rather than acting with respect to the property of individual persons.

A superior officer or administrator is ordinarily not liable for the wrong committed by his subordinate. Exceptions to this rule exist when the superior officer has been negligent in selecting the subordinate or in retaining him or when the superior knows or should know of his incompetence. The superior officer is also liable when he has directed or co-operated in the perpetration of the wrong.

## § 32:6. Who May Obtain Review

As a general rule, only a party having a legally recognized interest in the proceedings has standing to obtain a review of the administrator's action. The mere fact that a person is interested or curious about the action of the administrator does not give him standing to obtain a review. Even the fact that a person is affected or harmed by the administrative action does not give him standing to obtain a review unless his interest in the matter is recognized as a legal interest. A number of statutes and the Federal Administrative Procedure Act avoid the distinction between being harmed in fact and being harmed in the eyes of the law by conferring the right of review upon "any person suffering legal wrong because of any agency action, or adversely affected or aggrieved by such action within the meaning of any relevant statute. . . ." [4]

---

[4] A.P.A., § 10(a).

Under such statutes, there is relatively little difficulty in determining whether a person has a right to review. In the absence of such a statutory provision, it is necessary to find, as stated above, that the complaining party has a legal interest. By analogy to general principles of law when a party to a contract claims that it has been broken by the other contracting party or where a person claims that he has been injured by the automobile of another, it is clear that the complaining party has, if his complaint is true, sustained a legal wrong and has a legal interest that he may assert in an action at law. In the field of administrative law it is not always as simple as this to determine whether a person has a legal interest that entitles him to do so, as distinguished from being merely solicitous or personally curious rather than legally interested in the proceedings, or even sustaining economic harm, as through being improperly exposed to competition.

### *(a) Loss caused by reducing payments to complainant*

STARK v. WICKARD

321 U.S. 288 (1944)

Under the Agricultural Marketing Agreements Act of 1937, the Secretary of Agriculture has the authority to fix the minimum price to be paid by handlers of milk to the producer. In establishing the price, the Secretary of Agriculture is authorized to make certain administrative cost deductions from the uniform price so that the balance or "blended" price is the payment that is actually received. Under the authority of this Act, such a milk price control system was established for the greater Boston area. Among the deductions directed to be made from the uniform price, was the deduction of a sum that was to be paid to co-operatives. A group of milk producers brought a class action against the Secretary of Agriculture, claiming that this deduction made for the co-operatives diverted money that belonged to the producers. The objection was made that the producers had no legal standing to seek a review of the action of the Secretary in authorizing such deductions.

OPINION BY REED, J. . . .

Were no administrative deductions necessary, the blended price per hundredweight of milk could readily be determined by dividing the total value of the milk used in the marketing area at the minimum prices for each classification by the number of hundredweight of raw milk used in the area. However, the Order requires several adjustments for purposes admittedly authorized by statute, so that the determination of the blended price as actually made is drawn from the total use value less a sum which the administrator is directed to retain to meet various incidental adjustments. In practice, each handler discharges his obligation to the producers of whom he bought milk by making two payments: one payment, the blended price, is apportioned from the values at the minimum price for the respective classes less administrative deductions and is made to the producer himself; the other payment is equal to these deductions and is made, in the language of the Order, "to the producer, through the market administrator," in order to enable the administrator to cover the differentials and deductions in question. It is the contention of the petitioners that [by] the Order the Secretary has directed the administrator to deduct a sum for the purpose of meeting payments to cooperatives . . . and that the Act does not authorize the Secretary to include in his order provision for payments of that kind or for deductions to meet them. Apparently, this deduction for payments to cooperatives is the only deduction that is an unrecoverable charge against the producers. The other items deducted . . . are for a revolving fund or to meet differentials in price because of location, seasonal delivery, *et cetera.*

It is this deduction which the producers challenge as beyond the Secretary's statutory power. The respondents answer that the petitioners have not such a legal interest in this expenditure or in the administrator's settlement fund as entitles them to challenge the action of the Secretary in directing the disbursement. The Government says that as the producers pay nothing into the settlement fund and receive nothing from it, they have no legally protected right which gives them standing to sue. There is, of course, no question but that the challenged deduction reduces pro tanto the amount actually received by the producers for their milk.

. . . In substance petitioners' allegation is that in effect the Order directed without statutory authority a deduction of a sum to pay the United States a sales tax on milk sold. The statute and Order create a right in the producer to avail himself of the production of a minimum price afforded by Governmental action. Such a right created by statute is mandatory in character and obviously capable of judicial enforcement. For example the Order could not bar any qualified producers in the milk shed from selling to area handlers. . . . It cannot be fairly said that because producers may choose not to sell in the area, those who do choose to sell there necessarily must sell, without a right of challenge, in accordance with unlawful requirements of administrators. Upon purchase of his milk by a handler, the statute endows the producer with other rights, e. g., the right to be paid a minimum price. . . .

The mere fact that Governmental action under legislation creates an opportunity to receive a minimum price does not settle the problem of whether or not the particular claim made here is enforceable by the District Court. The deduction for cooperatives may have detrimental effect on the price to producers and that detriment be *damnum absque injuria.* It is only when a complainant possesses something more than a general interest in the proper execution of the laws that he is in a position to secure judicial intervention. His interest must rise to the dignity of an interest personal to him and not possessed by the people generally. Such a claim is of that character which constitutionally permits adjudication by courts under their general powers.

We deem it clear that on the allegations of the complaint these producers have such a personal claim as justifies judicial consideration. . . . The Order directs the handler to pay that minimum as follows:

A. . . . The handler is to make a preliminary part payment of the blended price and later . . . the handler makes the final payment to the producer of the blended price computed as the Order directs. . . . The blended price is reached by subtracting among other items the cooperative payment, here in question, from the minimum price. . . .

B. The balance of the minimum price, which the handler owes to the producer, he must pay "to the producer, through the market administrator" by payment into the settlement or equalization fund two days ahead of the final date for payment of the blended price. . . . This balance of the minimum purchase price is then partly used by the administrator to pay the cooperatives. . . . The handler is simply a conduit from the administrator who receives and distributes the minimum prices. The situation would be substantially the same if an administrator received as trustee for the producers the purchase price of their milk, paid expenses incurred in the operation, and paid the balance to the producers. Under such circumstances we think the producers have legal standing to object to illegal provisions of the Order.

However, even where a complainant possesses a claim to executive action beneficial to him, created by federal statute, it does not necessarily follow that actions of administrative officials, deemed by the owner of the right to place unlawful restrictions upon his claim, are cognizable in appropriate federal courts of first instance. When the claims created are against the United States, no remedy through the courts need be provided. . . . To reach the dignity of a legal right in the strict sense, it must appear from the nature and character of the legislation that Congress intended to create a statutory privilege protected by judicial remedies. Under the unusual circumstances of the historical development of the Railway Labor Act, . . . this Court has recently held that an administrative agency's determination of a controversy between unions of employees as to which is the proper bargaining representative of certain employees is not justiciable in federal courts. . . . Under the same Act it was held on the same date that the determination by the National Mediation Board of the participants in an election for representatives for collective bargaining likewise was not subject to judicial review. . . . This result was reached because of this Court's view that jurisdictional disputes between unions were left by Congress to mediation rather than adjudication. . . . That is to say, no personal right of employees, enforcible in the courts, was created in the particular instances under consideration. . . . But where rights of collective bargaining, created by the same Railway Labor Act, contained definite prohibitions of conduct or were mandatory in form, this Court enforced the rights judicially. . . .

"If the absence of jurisdiction of the federal courts meant a sacrifice or obliteration of a right which Congress had created, the inference would be strong that Congress intended the statutory provisions governing the general jurisdiction of those courts to control." . . . The only opportunity these petitioners had to complain of the contested deduction was to appear at hearings and to vote for or against the proposed order. . . . So long as the provisions of the Order are within the statutory authority of the Secretary such hearings and balloting furnish adequate opportunity for protest. . . . But where as here the issue is statutory power to make the deduction required by Order, . . . under the authority . . . of the Act, a mere hearing or opportunity to vote cannot protect minority producers against unlawful exactions which might be voted upon them by majorities. It can hardly be said that opportunity to be heard on matters within the Secretary's discretion would foreclose an attack on the inclusion in the Order of provisions entirely outside of the Secretary's delegated powers.

Without considering whether or not Congress could create such a definite personal statutory right in an individual against a fund handled by a Federal agency, as we have here, and yet limit its enforceability to administrative determination, despite the existence of federal courts of general jurisdiction established under Article III of the Constitution, the Congressional grant of jurisdiction of this proceeding appears plain. There is no direct judicial review granted by this statute for these proceedings. The authority for a judicial examination of the validity of the Secretary's action is found in the existence of courts and the intent of Congress as deduced from the statutes and precedents as hereinafter considered.

The Act bears on its face the intent to submit many questions arising under its administration to judicial review. . . . It specifically states that the remedies specifically provided . . . are to be in addition to any remedies now existing at law or equity. . . . This Court has heretofore construed the Act to grant handlers judicial relief in addition to the statutory review [therein] specifically provided. . . . On complaint by the United States, the handler was permitted by way of defense to raise issues of a want of statutory authority to impose provisions on handlers which directly affect such handlers. *United States* v. *Rock Royal Co-op*. . . . In the *Rock Royal* case the Government had contended that the handlers had no legal standing in the suit for enforcement to attack provisions of the order relating to handlers. While we upheld the contention of the Government as to the lack of standing of handlers to object to the operation of the producer settlement fund on the ground that the handlers had no "financial interest" in that fund, we recognized the standing of a proprietary handler to question the alleged discrimination shown in favor of the co-operative handlers. The producer settlement fund is created to meet allowable deductions by the payment of a part of the minimum price to producers through the market administrator. . . . *Rock Royal* pointed out that handlers were without standing to question the use of the fund, because handlers had no financial interest in the fund or its use. It is because every dollar of deduction comes from the producer that he may challenge the use of the fund. The petitioners' complaint is not that their blended price is too low, but that the blended price has been reduced by a misapplication of money deducted from the producers' minimum price.

With this recognition by Congress of the applicability of judicial review in this field, it is not to be lightly assumed that the silence of the statute bars from the courts an otherwise justiciable issue. . . . Here, there is no forum, other than the ordinary courts, to hear this complaint. When, as we have previously concluded in this opinion, definite personal rights are created by federal statute, similar in kind to those customarily treated in courts of law, the silence of Congress as to judicial review is, at any rate in the absence of an administrative remedy, not to be construed as a denial of authority to the aggrieved person to seek appropriate relief in the federal courts in the exercise of their general jurisdiction. When Congress passes an Act empowering administrative agencies to carry on governmental activities, the power of those agencies is circumscribed by the authority granted. This permits the courts to participate in law enforcement entrusted to administrative bodies only to the extent necessary to protect justiciable individual rights against administrative action fairly beyond the granted powers. The responsibility of determining the limits of statutory grants of authority in such instances is a judicial function entrusted to the courts by Congress by the statutes establishing courts and marking their jurisdiction. . . . This is very far from assuming that the courts are charged more than administrators or legislators with the protection of the rights of the people. Congress and the Executive supervise the acts of administrative agents. The powers of departments, boards and administrative agencies are subject to expansion, contraction or abolition at the will of the legislative and executive branches of the government. These branches have the resources and personnel to examine into the working of the various establishments to determine the necessary changes of function or management. But under Article III, Congress established courts to adjudicate cases and controversies as to claims of infringement of individual rights whether by unlawful action of private persons or by the exertion of unauthorized administrative power.

It is suggested that such a ruling puts the agency at the mercy of objectors, since any provisions of the Order may be attacked as unauthorized by each producer. To this objection there are adequate answers. The terms of the Order are largely matters of administrative discretion as to which there is no justiciable right or are clearly authorized by a valid act. . . . Technical details of the milk business are left to the Secretary and his aides. The expenses of litigation deter frivolous contentions. If numerous parallel cases are filed, the courts have ample authority to stay useless litigation until the determination of a test case. . . . Should some provisions of an order be held to exceed the statutory power of the Secretary, it is well within the power of a court of equity to so mold a decree as to preserve in the public interest the operation of the portion of the order which is not attacked pending amendment.

It hardly need be added that we have not considered the soundness of the allegations made by the petitioners in their complaint. The trial court is free to consider whether the statutory authority given the Secretary is a valid answer to the petitioners' contention. We merely determine the petitioners have shown a right to a judicial examination of their complaint.

DISSENTING OPINION BY FRANKFURTER, J.

The immediate issue before us is whether these plaintiffs, milk producers, can in the circumstances of this case go to court to complain of an order by the Secretary of Agriculture fixing rates for the distribution of milk within the Greater Boston marketing area. The solution of that question depends, however, upon a proper approach toward such a scheme of legislation as that formulated by Congress in the Agricultural Marketing Agreement Act of 1937.

Apart from legislation touching the revenue, the public domain, national banks and patents, not until the Interstate Commerce Act of 1887 did Congress begin to place economic enterprise under systems of administrative control. These regulatory schemes have varied in the range of control exercised by government; they have varied no less in the procedures by which the control was exercised. More particularly, these regimes of national authority over private enterprise reveal great diversity in the allotment of power by Congress as between courts and administrative agencies. Congress has not made uniform provisions in defining who may go to court, for what grievance, and under what circumstances, in seeking relief from administrative determinations. Quite the contrary. In the successive enactments by which Congress has established administrative agencies as major instruments of regulation, there is the greatest contrariety in the extent to which, and the procedures by which, different measures of control afford judicial review of administrative action.

Except in those rare instances, as in a claim of citizenship in deportation proceedings, when a judicial trial becomes a constitutional requirement . . . whether judicial review is available at all and, if so, who may invoke it, under what circumstances, in what manner, and to what end, are questions that depend for their answer upon the particular enactment under which judicial review is claimed. Recognition of the claim turns on the provisions dealing with judicial review in a particular statute and on the setting of such provisions in that statute as part of a scheme for accomplishing the purposes expressed by that statute. Apart from the text and texture of a particular law in relation to which judicial review is sought "judicial review" is a mischievous abstraction. There is no such thing as a common law of judicial review in the federal courts. The procedural provisions in more than a score of these regulatory measures prove that the manner in which Congress has distributed responsibility for the enforcement of its laws between courts and administrative agencies runs a gamut all the way from authorizing a judicial trial de novo of a claim determined by the administrative agency to denying all judicial review and making administrative action definitive.

Congress has not only devised different schemes of enforcement for different Acts. It has from time to time modified and restricted the scope of review under the same Act. . . . Moreover the same statute, as is true of the Interstate Commerce Act, may make some orders not judicially reviewable for any purpose . . . or reviewable by some who are adversely affected and not by others. . . . The oldest scheme of administrative control—our customs revenue legislation—shows in its evolution all sorts of permutations and combinations in using available administrative and judicial remedies. . . . Were this list of illustrations extended and the various regulatory schemes thrown into a hotchpot, the result would be hopeless discord. And to do so would be to treat these legislative schemes as though they were part of a single body of law instead of each being a self-contained scheme.

The divers roles played by judicial review in the administration of regulatory measures other than the Agricultural Marketing Act cannot tell us when and for whom judicial review of administrative action can be had under that Act. . . .

An elaborate enactment like this, devised by those who know the needs of the industry and drafted by legislative specialists, is to be treated as an organism. Every part must be related to the scheme as a whole. The legislation is a self-contained code, and within it must be found whatever remedies Congress saw fit to afford. For the Act did not give new remedies for old rights. It created new rights and new duties, and precisely defined the remedies for the enforcement of duties and the vindication of rights. Of course the statute concerns the interests of producers, handlers and consumers. But it does not define or create any legal interest for the consumer, and it specifically provides that "No order issued under this title shall be applicable to any producer in his capacity as a producer." . . .

The statute as an entirety makes it clear that obligations are imposed on handlers alone. . . .

To create a judicial remedy for producers when the statute gave none is to dislocate the Congressional scheme of enforcement. . . .

By denying them access to the courts Congress has not left producers to the mercy of the Secretary of Agriculture. Congress merely has devised means other than judicial for the effective expression of producers' interests in the terms of an order. Before the Secretary may issue an order he is required to "give due notice of and an opportunity for a hearing upon a proposed order." . . . At such a hearing all interested persons may submit relevant evidence, and the procedure makes adequate provision for notice to those who may be affected by an order. . . . Nor are these the only or the most effective means for safeguarding the producer's interest. While an order may be issued despite the objection of handlers of more than 50% of the volume of the commodity covered by the order, no order may issue when not approved by at least two-thirds—either numerically or according to volume of production—of the producers. . . .

The fact that Congress made specific provision for submission of some defined questions to judicial review would hardly appear to be an argument for inferring that judicial review even of broader scope is also open as to other questions for which Congress did not provide judicial review. . . .

The Court is thus adding to what Congress has written a provision for judicial relief of producers. And it sanctions such relief in a case in which petitioners have no standing to sue on any theory. The only effect of the deduction which is challenged by the producers is to fix a minimum price to which they are entitled perhaps lower than that which might otherwise have been determined. But the Act does not prevent their bargaining for a price higher than the minimum, and we are advised by the Government of what is not denied by petitioners, that such arrangements are by no means unusual. This Court has held that a consumer has no standing to challenge a minimum price order like the one before us. . . . Surely a producer who may bargain for prices above the minimum is in no better legal position than a consumer who urges that too high a minimum has been improperly fixed. The Commonwealth of Massachusetts which purchased milk for its public institutions valued at $105,232.97 in 1940, and $117,-584.50 in 1941, has hardly a less substantial interest in the minimum price than that of the petitioners. And yet Massachusetts has no standing to object to the minimum fixed by an order. . . .

. . . If handlers may not attack payments to cooperatives, as this Court held in *United States* v. *Rock Royal Co-op.* . . . I am unable to see how producers can be in a better position to attack such payments.

### *(b) Review by "person aggrieved" by loss through competition*

FEDERAL COMMUNICATIONS COMMISSION v. SANDERS RADIO STATION
309 U.S. 470 (1940)

A license was granted to construct a broadcasting station in a particular city. The respondent held a broadcasting station license and had operated a station in the city for several years. It opposed the granting of the new license on the ground that it would be harmed by such competition, and appealed from the grant of the license. From a decision in the respondent's favor, the Commission appealed by petition.

OPINION BY ROBERTS, J.

. . . The petitioner's contentions are that under the Communications Act economic injury to a competitor is not a ground for refusing a broadcasting license and that, since this is so, the respondent was not a person aggrieved or whose interests were adversely affected, by the Commission's action, within the meaning of Section 402(b) of the Act . . . which authorizes appeals from the Commission's orders. . . .

*First.* We hold that resulting economic injury to a rival station is not, in and of itself, and apart from considerations of public convenience, interest, or necessity, an element the petitioner must weigh, and as to which it must make findings, in passing on an application for a broadcasting license. . . .

*Second.* It does not follow that, because the licensee of a station cannot resist the grant of a license to another, on the ground that the resulting competition may work economic injury to him, he has no standing to appeal from an order of the Commission granting the application.

Section 402(b) of the Act provides for an appeal to the Court of Appeals of the District of Columbia (1) by an applicant for a license or permit, or (2) "by any other person aggrieved or whose interests are adversely affected by any decision of the Commission granting or refusing any such application."

The petitioner insists that as economic injury to the respondent was not a proper issue before the Commission it is impossible that § 402(b) was intended to give the respondent standing to appeal, since absence of right implies absence of remedy. This view would deprive subsection (2) of any substantial effect.

Congress had some purpose in enacting section 402(b)(2). It may have been of opinion that one likely to be financially injured by the issue of a license would be the only person having a sufficient interest to bring to the attention of the appellate court errors of law in the action of the Commission in granting the license. It is within the power of Congress to confer such standing to prosecute an appeal.

We hold, therefore, that the respondent has the requisite standing to appeal and to raise, in the court below, any relevant question of law in respect of the order of the Commission. . . .

### *(c) Review by "party in interest" as to loss through competition*

L. SINGER & SONS v. UNION PACIFIC RAILWAY CO.

311 U.S. 295 (1940)

The Transportation Act of 1920 authorizes "any party in interest" to bring an action to enjoin an illegal extension of a carrier line. An action to enjoin an extension by the Union Pacific was brought by: (1) Kansas City, claiming that the unlawful extension would cause a property loss to the public and a loss to the city through depreciation of market facilities that were being constructed by the city and through a reduction of taxes received by the city because of reduced property values; and (2) owners of business property in the existing market area, claiming that their property would be reduced in value through the diversion of trade to a rival market based along the proposed extension. The railroad opposed the action on the ground that the city and the property owners did not have standing to bring the action.

OPINION BY MCREYNOLDS, J. . . .

The Circuit Court made the following summation of the bill—"The complaint of the plaintiffs shows that they are commission merchants doing business on the Kansas City, Missouri, produce market, an old and well-established market which adequately serves the consuming public in its vicinity and receives produce from, and ships produce to, other states; that Kansas City, Missouri, is now engaged in constructing new market buildings for this market at a cost of about $500,000; that the market has suitable and adequate transportation facilities of all kinds; that the adjoining city of Kansas City, Kansas, proposes to build and is building a 'Food Terminal' or produce market on a tract of land which it owns, at a cost of about $4,000,000, of which $1,710,000 is a grant from the Public Works Administration of the United States, and that the balance of the necessary funds will be procured by a sale of the City's bonds to the defendant railroad company; that the defendant proposes, at an expense of some $500,000, to furnish trackage to serve this Kansas City, Kansas, market; that this trackage constitutes an extension of the defendant's lines of railroad, for the construction of which it has procured no certificate of convenience and necessity from the Interstate Commerce Commission as required by law; that the construction and operation of the proposed extension in Kansas City, Kansas, will adversely affect and will destroy the business and properties of the plaintiffs and the large investments which they have made in and adjacent to the Kansas City, Missouri, produce market; that it will create an unnecessary and uncalled for rival market at an inconvenient place without creating any more produce to be handled or any more customers to be served; that it will result in the unnecessary duplication of railroad facilities at a cost of $500,000 without increasing the amount of freight to be handled; that it will divert traffic from other railroads which are now adequately handling the traffic to the Kansas City, Missouri, produce market, and will cause destructive competition between the defendant and other railroads and will cause a wasteful and needless expenditure of money by the defendant; that 'for each and all of the reasons aforesaid, the construction and operation, or the construction, or the operation of the said extension or extensions of railroad by the defendant to said proposed produce market in Kansas City, Kansas, will directly and adversely affect the property interests of the plaintiffs and the public generally by bringing about a material change in the transportation situation, and will constitute an unnecessary burden upon interstate commerce, directly and adversely affecting the welfare of plaintiffs and the public interest.' " . . .

It is not alleged that the respondent has ever served the produce market in Kansas City, Missouri, or that petitioners make or receive shipments over its lines or that the proposed extension will deprive them of any shipping facilities. Evidently the real purpose was to obstruct construction of a competitor and the theory upon which the proceeding rests would permit petitioners to sue if any railroad should extend its lines to any market competing with the market at Kansas City, Missouri.

Concerning the purport of the allegations of the bill, the Circuit Court of Appeals rightly said: "It is obvious that the only basis for the plaintiffs' claim that the alleged extension of the lines of the defendant to the Kansas City, Kansas, market will particularly injure them is that they do business upon the Kansas City, Missouri, market, and that if the proposed rival market in Kansas City, Kansas, functions, it will divert business from the market upon which they operate and will thus hurt them, their business, and their investments in Kansas City, Missouri, and that, since the proposed extension of its tracks by the defendant is necessary to enable the rival market to function, such extension will therefore injure the plaintiffs. It seems equally obvious that, except for the fact that the proposed extension is essential to the operation of the rival market in Kansas, it could not possibly have any direct or immediate effect upon the plaintiffs, their property or their business in Missouri, other than the effect which a wasteful expenditure by the defendant of its money would have upon the public generally. The proximate cause of the injury to the plaintiffs will be the competition created by the construction and operation of the rival market, and not the construction or operation of the transportation facilities furnished to it by the defendant or by others engaged in the transportation business."

It declared . . . "The plaintiffs have no definite legal right which is threatened. They are, however, persons whose welfare may be adversely affected by the bringing about of a material change in the transportation situation, in the sense that the extension proposed by the defendant, if built and operated, will enable a competitive market to function to their detriment. In that sense, we think it may safely be said that the proposed extension of defendant's lines may adversely affect the plaintiffs' welfare. We are of the opinion, however, that their complaint discloses that their welfare cannot be directly, but only indirectly and consequentially affected by the proposed extension. They are not in competition with the defendant. They are not engaged in the transportation business. Their only peculiar interest in that business is in the effect which changes in it may have upon the market where they do business and upon rival markets now or hereafter established in the territory which the plaintiffs serve. . . . We conclude that the statute is not to be so liberally construed as to enable those who fear adverse effects upon their business from the establishment of competitive enterprises requiring transportation facilities, to maintain suits to enjoin railroads from constructing what are claimed to be unauthorized extensions. . . ."

The Transportation Act, 1920 was designed to protect the public against action which might endanger its interest. In order to aid that general purpose, Paragraph 20, § 402, provides that suit for an injunction may be instituted by the United States, the Commission (I.C.C.), any Commission or Regulative Body of the state or states affected, or any "party in interest." Such a suit cannot be instituted by an individual unless he "possesses something more than a common concern for obedience to law." The general or common interest finds protection in the permission to sue granted to public authorities. An individual may have some special and peculiar interest which may be directly and materially affected by alleged unlawful action. . . . If such circumstances are shown he may sue; he is then a "party in interest" within the meaning of the statute. In the absence of these circumstances he is not such a party.

We cannot think Congress supposed that the development and maintenance of an adequate railway system would be aided by permitting any person engaged in business within or adjacent to a public market to demand an injunction against a carrier seeking only to serve a competing market by means of an extension not authorized by the Interstate Commerce Commission. . . .

The Circuit Court of Appeals after reviewing all the facts reached the conclusion that the welfare of petitioners could only be indirectly and consequentially affected by the proposed extension; that their interest in the transportation situation "is in the effect which changes in it may have upon the market where they do business and upon rival markets now or hereafter established in the territory which the plaintiffs serve." It held this was not enough. We agree. A mere extension to the plant of a competitor which in no other way affects the complaining parties in no proper sense brings about a material change in the transportation system directly affecting their peculiar interest which they have the right to prevent by suit. . . .

DISSENTING OPINION BY STONE, J.

I think that [the property owners] are proper parties to maintain this suit. . . .

The interest of petitioners in maintaining the suit as shown by the pleadings is derived from the injury to the public which, it is specifically alleged, will result from the proposed extension through the injury to the community in Kansas City, Missouri, and vicinity, of which community petitioners are a part and in which they are property owners, and the consequent injury alleged to affect them individually. The public injury, it is alleged will be caused by (a) the loss or serious impairment in utility of the Kansas City public produce market and the destruction or serious diminution of values of property and business and of financial investments in and about the market, which will be brought about by the extension, through the creation of a rival market and the diversion of traffic to it at a point in Kansas City, Kansas, far removed from the center of population of Kansas City, Missouri, and to the inconvenience of the great majority of the citizens of both cities who are served by the existing market, which is adequate to the needs of the community; (b) by the unnecessary duplication of railroad facilities in the Kansas City district at large cost, with wasteful and needless expenditures by respondent and no increase in freight to be handled; and (c) by the diversion of traffic to respondent railroad from other railroads and destructive competition between the railroads operating in the vicinity.

Special injury is shown to complainants . . . by the allegations that they are owners of business property and investments in the existing market area and vicinity, and that their property will be reduced in value in consequence of the diversion of traffic to the rival market. The petitioner, Kansas City, Missouri, . . . alleges the like injury to the public which it represents and sets up specifically the threatened loss in value and utility of a large public market structure which it is now building at great cost, and the threatened loss to it of taxes through diminution in property values in the city.

The statute does not define the "parties in interest" whom it permits to sue to restrain an unauthorized extension. It cannot be assumed that the phrase is meaningless or that the statute should be read as though the words were omitted. Obviously the parties intended must have, as do petitioners, an interest in the outcome of the litigation other than the "common concern for obedience to law." . . . And as the language of the statute plainly indicates, and as we have held, they may be, as are petitioners, others than the public bodies named in the statute as appropriate plaintiffs. . . . And they may maintain the suit although the injury which they allege is not strictly an actionable wrong independently of the paragraphs in question. . . .

The statute draws no distinction between direct and indirect injury as the test of plaintiff's interest. Nor is any reason advanced for saying that his interest is more significant because the injury which he suffers is labeled "direct" rather than "indirect." In any case, that suffered by petitioners does not seem to be any the less direct than that which an extension may inflict upon a competing railroad which admittedly may sue to enjoin it. . . . If the statute imposes any requirements other than those indicated by the phrase "party in interest," they must be implied from the purposes of the statute, its context, and from the reasons for permitting others than the public bodies named in it to bring the suit. . . . On the other hand if maintenance of the present suit by petitioners is consistent with those purposes and aids them and is in harmony with the reasons for allowing any party in interest to sue, the conclusion would seem inescapable that petitioners are proper plaintiffs.

It is not denied that the statutory language and the legislative history of the paragraphs in question require consideration by the Commission of the interests of cities, towns and communities which are adversely affected by a proposed extension of a line of railroad, in order to determine whether "public convenience and necessity" require the extension. The phrase "public convenience and necessity" has long been used to signify the final result of the balancing of the consequences which flow from the proposed action to all those matters of public concern which are affected by it. . . . And we have held that in the administration of the cognate provision relating to abandonment of railroad lines the Commission must consider as a part of the public convenience and necessity the interests of local communities affected by the proposed abandonment. . . . A community may suffer injury through the loss of railroad service and diversion of traffic resulting from the construction and operation of a railroad extension without any compensating public advantage which is comparable in kind and amount with injury sustained by the abandonment of a line of railroad. One as well as the other should receive the consideration of the Commission in determining whether it should grant or withhold a certificate. Such appears to be its settled practice on applications for a certificate authorizing extension. . . .

But it has never held, unless it has done so now, that the public concern in protecting large communities from destruction of their business and financial interests by diversion of traffic to rival communities by railroad extensions, is not included in that public convenience and necessity which the Commission must consider in granting or withholding a certificate; or that one not a railroad who is a member of a community adversely affected and whose own business or property interests are so adversely affected is not a "party in interest" within the meaning of the statute. . . .

Maintenance of the suit by complainants is thus within the fair meaning of the words of the statute. It aids rather than obstructs the administration of the Act; it effectuates the public policy of the Act and is within the reason for permitting others than public agencies to bring the suit. They are "parties in interest" to which the statute refers.

## Questions for Discussion

1. Describe the following procedures:
   (a) Injunction.
   (b) Mandamus.
   (c) Quo warranto.
   (d) Habeas corpus.
   (e) Prohibition.
   (f) Declaratory judgment.
   (g) Damage suit.

2. How are these procedures in Question 1 employed as a means of obtaining judicial review of administrative action? Discuss their value for that purpose.

3. Is there a well-defined body of uniform law prescribing when judicial review may be had of an administrator's action? Explain.

4. In the *Wickard* case the court stated: "The expenses of litigation deter frivolous contentions." Does it also deter the assertion of meritorious objections?

5. Is the silence of a federal statute with respect to the right to review to be regarded as prohibiting the courts from permitting a review of the administrator's action?

6. What was the nature of the act the performance of which the plaintiff sought to compel in *I. C. C.* v. *Humboldt Steamship Co.*?

7. Does the *Humboldt* case sustain the right to review any determination by the Commission whenever the Court disagrees with the Commission's interpretation as to the law applicable?

8. What was the nature of the act the performance of which the plaintiff sought to compel in *F. C. C.* v. *Pottsville Radio Broadcasting Co.*?

9. Why did the Court refuse to grant relief to the plaintiff in the *Pottsville Radio Broadcasting Co.* case?

10. What procedure was invoked in the *Pottsville Radio Broadcasting Company* case to review the action of the administrator? Why?

11. Are there any limitations imposed on the procedure that the Federal Communications Commission may follow?

12. Appraise the decision of the Supreme Court in the *Sanders Brothers Radio Station* case upholding the right of a rival radio station to appeal from the granting of a license to another station.

13. Are there any circumstances under which the Court can enjoin the holding of a hearing by the National Labor Relations Board?

14. What was the basis for refusing the injunction in *Myers* v. *Bethlehem Steel*?

15. Did the administrator in *Miller* v. *Horton* have any discretion?

16. Is there any way that the property owner can be protected against improper administrative action without impeding the administrative action or without making the administrator reluctant to act?

17. (a) Should an administrator be liable in damages whenever he makes a wrong decision? (b) Is it a satisfactory rule to impose such liability but to permit the administrator to defend by showing that he acted in good faith? (c) How can good faith be shown?

18. (a) Did the defendants in the *Miller* case make the decision to kill the plaintiff's horse or were they following the decision of someone else? (b) Should the rule as to an administrator's liability depend on whether the administrator makes the decision himself or whether he follows orders given by another?

19. What is the basis for the decision of the court in the *Miller* case?

20. Was the error in the *Miller* case an error of fact? an error of law? a jurisdictional fact?

21. (a) Is the administrator liable for damages whenever he does an act on the basis of a wrong belief that a particular fact or condition exists? (b) Compare *Raymond* v. *Fish* with the *Miller* case.

22. Who may obtain a judicial review of an administrative action?

23. Can a law court be given power to review a case on the application or appeal of a member of the public at large?

24. Why is there not a uniform definition of the persons entitled to obtain a review of administrative action?

25. What interest did the producers have in the *Wickard* case that gave them legal standing to seek a review of the administrative order?

26. Would the producers in Question 25 have been entitled to a review if the price had been fixed by the legislature rather than by administrative action?

27. (a) Does a person have legal standing to complain of an order when he is prevented by the order from receiving money that he would otherwise receive or must he show that he has lost money that he had? (b) What view is adopted by the Court in the *Wickard* case?

28. (a) May a consumer attack a minimum price set by the Secretary of Agriculture? (b) Should he be given the same right as a producer?

29. What factors required the Court to make its decision in the *Wickard* case?

30. Compare the majority and the minority opinions in the *Wickard* case. Which do you prefer? Explain.

31. Compare the decision in the *Wickard* case with that in *United States* v. *Butler,* 297 U.S. 1 (1936), in which the court held unconstitutional a crop reduction program that provided for the payment of money to farmers who reduced their production and then imposed a tax on industrial processors of farm products, such as millers, to create the fund from which the payments to the farmers were to be made.

32. What is the basis on which the majority opinion in the *Singer* case denied the plaintiffs the right to bring suit?

33. Compare the majority and the minority opinions in the *Singer* case. Is either influenced by any particular economic philosophy?

34. (a) Do you agree with the Court in the *Singer* case? (b) To what extent was the Court in the *Singer* case influenced by the view that the plaintiffs had no legal objection, since their objection was basically that they opposed the appearance of a competitor and the effect of competition? (c) Would it have made any difference if the complainant's contention was that their area would not be adequately served with transportation if the proposed extension was made rather than that another area would compete with them?

## Chapter 33

# LIMITATIONS ON REVIEW OF ADMINISTRATOR'S ACTION

## § 33:1. Jurisdiction of Court to Review

A further refinement on the reviewability of an administrator's order is found in the principle that the Supreme Court of the United States will not entertain an appeal from the decision of another court reviewing an administrator's action if the administrator acted "legislatively" or "administratively" and the lower court is authorized to enter such judgment as would have properly been entered by the administrator, as distinguished from merely affirming or reversing the action of the administrator or remanding the case to him. The entry of such judgment as would have been properly entered by the administrator makes the reviewing court sit as an administrator and not as a court performing a judicial function.

This doctrine is not applicable when the administrator is deemed to have acted "judicially" in the entering of the order sought to be reviewed. This distinction in turn raises difficulties in determining whether in a given instance the administrator was acting "legislatively" or "administratively" on the one hand, or, "judicially" on the other. There is a conflict in the state courts as to the extent to which this limitation on review is applicable.

### *(a) Administrative review*

FEDERAL RADIO COMMISSION v. GENERAL ELECTRIC CO.

281 U.S. 464 (1930)

The Federal Radio Act of 1927 authorized an appeal from a licensing order of the Federal Radio Commission to the Court of Appeals and provided that the court could alter or revise the Commission's decision and enter such judgment as would be just. The Supreme Court refused to entertain an appeal from the decision of the Court of Appeals.

OPINION BY VAN DEVANTER, J. . . .

We think it plain . . . that the powers confided to the commission respecting the granting and renewal of station licenses are purely administrative and that the provision for appeals to the Court of Appeals does no more than make that court a superior and revising agency in the same field. The court's province under that provision is essentially the same as the province under the legislation which up to a recent date permitted appeals to it from administrative decisions of the Commissioner of Patents. Indeed, the provision in the Act of 1927 is patterned largely after that legislation. . . .

Referring to the provisions for patent appeals this Court said . . . that the function of the court thereunder was not that of exercising ordinary jurisdiction at law or in equity, but of taking a step in the statutory proceeding under the patent laws in aid of the patent office. . . . [In] . . . a like appeal in a trade-mark proceeding, this court held: "The decision of the Court of Appeals under Section 9 of the Act of 1905 is not a judicial judgment. It is a mere administrative decision. It is merely an instruction to the Commissioner of Patents by a court which is made a part of the machinery of the Patent Office for the administrative purposes." . . . [In] . . . a statutory proceeding in the courts of the District of Columbia to revise an order of a commission fixing the valuation of the property of a public utility for future rate-making purposes . . . this Court held that the function assigned to the courts of the District in the statutory proceeding was not judicial in the sense of the Constitution, but was legislative and advisory, because it was that of instructing and aiding the commission in the exertion of power which was essentially legislative. . . .

But this Court cannot be invested with jurisdiction of that character, whether for purposes of review or otherwise. It was brought into being by the judiciary article of the Constitution, is invested with judicial power only and can have no jurisdiction other than of cases and controversies falling within the classes enumerated in that article. It cannot give decisions which are merely advisory; nor can it exercise or participate in the exercise of functions which are essentially legislative or administrative. . . .

Our conclusion is that the proceeding in [the Court of Appeals] was not a case or controversy in the sense of the judiciary article, but was an administrative proceeding, and therefore that the decision therein is not reviewable by this Court.

### *(b) Judicial review*

FEDERAL RADIO COMMISSION v. NELSON BROS. BOND & MORTGAGE CO.

289 U.S. 266 (1933)

Following the decision in the *General Electric* case, the Radio Act of 1927 was amended to limit the review by the Court of Appeals to "questions of law" and it was expressly provided that "findings of fact by the commission, if supported by substantial evidence, shall be conclusive unless it shall clearly appear that the findings of the commission are arbitrary or capricious." As thus restricted, the function of the Court of Appeals was no longer administrative but solely judicial, and the Supreme Court thereafter held that an appeal could then be taken from the Court of Appeals to the Supreme Court.

OPINION BY HUGHES, C. J.

. . . In the light of the decision in the *General Electric* case . . . the Congress . . . amended . . . the Radio Act of 1927 so as to limit the review by the Court of Appeals. . . . That review is now expressly limited to "questions of law" and it is provided that "findings of fact by the commission, if supported by substantial evidence, shall be conclusive unless it shall clearly appear that the findings of the commission are arbitrary or capricious." This limitation is in sharp contrast with the previous grant of authority. No longer is the Court entitled to revise the Commission's decision and to enter such judgment as the Court may think just. The limitation manifestly demands judicial, as distinguished from administrative, review. Questions of law form the appropriate subject of judicial determinations. Dealing with activities admittedly within its regulatory power, the Congress established the Commission as its instrumentality to provide continuous and expert supervision and to exercise the administrative judgment essential in applying legislative standards to a host of instances. These standards the Congress prescribed. The powers of the Commission were defined, and definition is limitation. Whether the Commission applies the legislative standards validly set up, whether it acts within the authority conferred or goes beyond it, whether its proceedings satisfy the pertinent demands of due process, whether, in short, there is compliance with the legal requirements which fix the province of the Commission and govern its action, are appropriate questions for judicial decision. These are questions of law upon which the Court is to pass. The provision that the Commission's findings of fact, if supported by substantial evidence, shall be conclusive unless it clearly appears that the findings are arbitrary or capricious, cannot be regarded as an attempt to vest in the Court an authority to revise the action of the Commission from an administrative standpoint and to make an administrative judgment. A finding without substantial evidence to support it—an arbitrary or capricious finding—does violence to the law. It is without the sanction of the authority conferred. And an inquiry into the facts before the Commission, in order to ascertain whether its findings are thus vitiated, belongs to the judicial province, and does not trench upon, or involve the exercise of, administrative authority. Such an examination is not concerned with the weight of evidence or with the wisdom or expediency of the administrative action. . . .

### § 33:2. Exhaustion of Administrative Remedy

As a general rule the courts refuse to review an administrative determination unless it is final. If, under the statute creating the office of the administrator, there is provision for a further appeal or review before the administrator or before another adminstrative body, this administrative remedy must first be exhausted before the court will review the matter. This rule has developed in part as a matter of common sense and orderly procedure. If the matter has not been finally concluded before the administrator, it is obviously too early to complain to the courts. The courts have also based their view upon a principle of comity: a respect by the courts for another branch of the government, in this case the administrator, should compel the court to refrain from taking any action while the matter is still uncompleted before the administrator. For the court to step into the picture before the administrative phase had been completed would be regarded as impolite intermeddling.

Another reason for the refusal of the courts to take action prior to the conclusion of the administrative phase is that, to a large extent, judicial review of administrative action has been by injunction issued by the court of equity. Traditionally an injunction issues only when there is no other adequate remedy. By definition there is another adequate remedy if the complainant has a right to appeal or to obtain a review within the administrative area. Until he has exhausted this other remedy, he is not in a position to ask the court of equity to grant him relief.

In certain instances the doctrine of exhaustion of administrative remedy has not been observed. If it can be shown to the court that the administrative action would produce irreparable injury before the complainant could complete the appeal or other procedure before the administrative body or that resort to administrative remedy would produce a multiplicity of suits, an injunction may be issued. The same conclusion is reached where the complainant is able to show that resort to the administrative remedy would be futile because it is manifestly inadequate or because the administrator or administrative body refuses to act.

The exact limits of the exhaustion of the administrative remedies rule are not clearly defined. The result of an evolutionary process, it has at different times been stated in slightly different ways and has been limited at different points so that its exact boundaries are not now precise.

### *(a) Order to produce records*

NATURAL GAS PIPELINE CO. v. SLATTERY

302 U.S. 300 (1937)

The Illinois Commission ordered the appellant to permit the inspection of its records and to furnish the Commission with certain statistical data. The appellant objected to furnishing the data because of the cost of preparing it.

OPINION BY STONE, J.

. . . Appellant urges that, in requiring statistical reports, the expense of whose preparation is said to be great, the order transcends statutory authority, or exercises it so arbitrarily as to place an unconstitutional burden on commerce and infringe the Fourteenth Amendment. It is said that equity alone can afford adequate relief because of the cumulative penalties for failure to comply with the order. . . .

. . . The statute itself provides an adequate administrative remedy which appellant has not sought. By §§ 64 and 65 of the Act the commission was authorized on its own motion or on application of appellant to order a hearing to ascertain whether present order was "improper, unreasonable or contrary to law." Section 67 authorizes the commission at any time, upon proper notice and hearing to "rescind, alter or amend any . . . order or decision made by it." We see no reason, and appellant suggests none, for rejecting the trial court's ruling that the commission, if asked, could have modified its order, or for concluding that the commission was without authority to suspend or postpone the date of the effective operation of the order so as to avoid the running of penalties, pending application for its modification. . . .

As the Act imposes penalties of from $500 to $2,000 a day for failure to comply with the order, any application of the statute subjecting appellant to the risk of the cumulative penalties pending an attempt to test the validity of the order in the courts and for a reasonable time after decision, would be a denial of due process . . . but no reason appears why appellant could not have asked the commission to postpone the date of operation of the order pending application to the commission for modification. Refusal of postponement would have been the occasion for recourse to the courts. . . . But appellant did not ask postponement.

A temporary injunction was not necessary to protect appellant from penalties pending final determination of the suit. The commission agreed not to enforce the order before the decision of the lower court on the application for interlocutory injunction. In order to give appellant opportunity to appear here, the district court stayed, for thirty days, its order denying an injunction, and by an order of a Justice of this Court the operation of the commission's order and the running of penalties were enjoined pending the disposition of the cause here.

The rule that a suitor must exhaust his administrative remedies before seeking the extraordinary relief of a court of equity . . . is of especial force when resort is had to the federal courts to restrain the action of state officers . . . and the objection has been taken by the trial court. . . .

The extent to which a federal court may rightly relax the rule where the order of the administrative body is assailed in its entirety, rests in the sound discretion which guides exercise of equity jurisdiction. . . . But there are cogent reasons for requiring resort in the first instance to the administrative tribunal when the particular method by which it has chosen to exercise authority, a matter peculiarly within its competence, is also under attack, for there is the possibility of removal of these issues from the case by modification of its order. Here the commission had authority to pass upon every question raised by the appellant and was able to modify the order. In such circumstances the trial court is free to withhold its aid entirely until administrative remedies have been exhausted.

### *(b) Tax assessment*

FIRST NATIONAL BANK v. WELD COUNTY

264 U.S. 450 (1924)

OPINION BY SUTHERLAND, J.

. . . Under the Colorado statute . . . a bank is required to make a list of its shares, stating their market value, and of its shareholders for the information of the county assessor, who is thereupon directed to assess such shares for taxation in all respect the same as similar property belonging to other corporations and individuals. . . . If any taxpayer is of the opinion that his property has been assessed too high, or otherwise illegally assessed, he may appear before the assessor and have the same corrected. . . . The county commissioners of each county are constituted a Board of Equalization, with power to adjust and equalize the assessment among the several taxpayers. . . .

. . . Plaintiff made and delivered to the County Assessor of Weld County the statement required by law. The Assessor thereupon fixed the value of its shares, as well as that of the shares of other banks within the county, at their full cash and market value; but fixed the assessed value of the property of the remaining taxpayers in the county at 61% for 1913 and 80% for 1914, of such cash and market value. . . . The Tax Commission determined that the property of the county as a whole had been underassessed and recommended a horizontal increase of 63% in 1913 and 25% in 1914, as necessary to bring it to the full cash value. This determination was approved by the State Board of Equalization, and the County Assessor was directed to make the increase with the result, as alleged, that plaintiff's assets, and those of all other banks in the county, were in fact assessed at an amount 63% in excess of their value for the year 1913 and 25% in excess thereof for the year 1914. In other counties of the State, either no increase of valuation was made, or the increase was comparatively small. The result was that the banks of Weld County were assessed and compelled to pay upon a valuation grossly in excess of that put upon other property in the same county, and likewise in excess of that put upon other banks in other counties of the state. It does not appear from the complaint that the plaintiff applied to any of the taxing authorities to reduce the assessment of its property or correct the alleged inequalities, prior to the final levy of the tax, but sometime after such levy had been completed, it made application for abatement and rebate, which application was approved by the County Board but disallowed by the State Tax Commission.

We are met at the threshold of our consideration of the case with the contention that the plaintiff did not exhaust its remedies before the administrative boards and consequently cannot be heard by a judicial tribunal to assert the validity of the tax. We are of the opinion that this contention must be upheld. . . .

It is further urged that it would have been futile to seek a hearing before the State Tax Commission because, first, no appeal to a judicial tribunal was provided in the event of a rejection of a taxpayer's complaint; and, second, because the time at the disposal of the Commission for hearing individual complaints was inadequate. But, aside from the fact that such an appeal is not a matter of right but wholly dependent upon the statute . . . we cannot assume that if application had been made to the Commission proper relief would not have been accorded by that body, in view of the statutory authority to receive complaints and examine into all cases where it is alleged that property has been fraudulently, improperly, or unfairly assessed. . . . Nor will plaintiff be heard to say that there was not adequate time for a hearing, in the absence of any effort on its part to obtain one. In any event the decision of the State Supreme Court . . . that such remedies were, in fact, available, is controlling here. . . .

Plaintiff not having availed itself of the administrative remedies afforded by the statutes as construed by the state court, it results that the question whether the tax is vulnerable to the challenge in respect of its validity upon any or all of the grounds set forth, is one which we are not called upon to consider. . . .

### *(c) Primary jurisdiction rule distinguished*

To be distinguished from the requirement of the exhaustion of remedy is the rule of primary judisdiction under which a court will not act with respect to a particular matter over which it would be otherwise competent to act until the administrator has made a decision on the matter. " 'Exhaustion' applies where a claim is cognizable in the first instance by an administrative agency alone; judicial interference is withheld until the administrative process has run its course. 'Primary jurisdiction,' on the other hand, applies where a claim is originally cognizable in the courts, and comes into play whenever enforcement of the claim requires the resolution of issues which, under a regulatory scheme, have been placed within the special competence of an administrative body. In such a case, the judicial process is suspended pending referral of such issues to the administrative body for its views." [1]

As an illustration of the doctrine of primary jurisdiction, a law court has original common-law jurisdiction to entertain a suit by a shipper against a common carrier to recover charges paid by him in

---

[1] United States v. Western Pac. R. Co., 352 U.S. 59 (1956).

excess of reasonable rates. That is, the court has the power to act initially without first requiring that the shipper assert and exhaust a remedy before an administrative body. If, however, the determination of the reasonableness of the rate depends upon disputed facts or calls for the exercise of discretion by an administrator, such as the Interstate Commerce Commission, the court, although it has the power to proceed, will defer action until the shipper has brought his claim before the administrator to establish that the rate in fact is unreasonable. Thereafter, if the administrator finds that the rate is unreasonable, the shipper may sue on that basis in the law court. If the administrator finds that the rate is reasonable, the shipper cannot sue in the law court, since it has been determined that the rate in question was reasonable.

In a given case, the net result of the application of the two doctrines of exhaustion and of primary jurisdiction may be the same, namely, that the court refuses to decide the matter before the administrator has acted. In the former, however, the court has no power to act, while in the latter it refuses to exercise the power that it possesses. The doctrine of primary jurisdiction is sometimes confused with the doctrine of exhaustion because of the similarity of results; because it is not applied when the question involved is a question of law, such as the interpretation of a tariff or rate; and because it is ignored or rejected in some cases.

### § 33:3. Orders Subject to Review

Apart from the question of the standing of a particular person seeking the review of an action of an administrator, it is also necessary that the particular order of which the review is sought be one that is reviewable. Some actions taken by administrators are not regarded, under the particular statutes creating the office of those administrators, as giving rise to a justiciable question or a question that is subject to review by the courts. The result is that the questions which are classified as nonreviewable are left to the final determination of the administrator. The trend, however, is in the direction of increased reviewability.

For some time the Supreme Court endeavored to work out the right of review in terms of whether an order by an administrator was negative or affirmative. That is, a review, if otherwise proper, could be obtained of an order that granted relief, granted a license, or took some other affirmative action; but when the administrator refused to act or make the order sought, no review could be obtained of such refusal. This doctrine was ultimately abandoned as unsound.[2]

### *(a) Implied right of review*

UNITED STATES v. INTERSTATE COMMERCE COMMISSION
337 U.S. 426 (1949)

The United States filed a complaint with the Interstate Commerce Commission requesting the Commission to find that certain railroads had improperly charged the government for unperformed services and to award to the government damages or reparations for such unlawful charges. The Commission denied the government's claim, from which action an appeal was taken. The appeal was opposed on the ground that no provision was made by statute for the review of the Commission's denial of a reparation claim.

OPINION BY BLACK, J.

. . . The Commission and the railroads contend, . . . that § 9 of the Interstate Commerce Act, . . . bars the United States or any other shipper from judicial review of an order denying damages in reparation proceedings initiated before the Commission. Section 9 provides in part:

> "Any person or persons claiming to be damaged by any common carrier . . . may either make complaint to the commission . . . or may bring suit . . . for the recovery of the damages . . . in any district court of the United States of competent jurisdiction; but such person or persons shall not have the right to pursue both of said remedies, and must in each case elect which one of the two methods of procedure herein provided for he or they will adopt."

The contention of the Commission and the railroads as to § 9 is this. A shipper has an alternative. He may bring his action before the Commission or before the courts. But he must make an election. If he elects to "bring suit" in a court and is unsuccessful, he retains the customary right of appellate review. If he elects to "make complaint to" the Commission, as the Government did, and relief is denied, he is said to be barred by the statutory language of § 9 from seeking any judicial review of the Commission order. Under the contention the order is final and not reviewable by any court even though

[2] Rochester Telephone Corporation v. United States, 307 U.S. 125 (1939).

entered arbitrarily, without substantial supporting evidence, and in defiance of law.

Such a sweeping contention for administrative finality is out of harmony with the general legislative pattern of administrative and judicial relationships. . . . And this Court has consistently held Commission orders reviewable upon charges that the Commission had exceeded its lawful powers. . . . The language of § 9 does not suggest an abandonment of these consistent holdings. It does suggest that a shipper who elects either to "make complaint to" the Commission or to "bring suit" in a court is thereafter precluded from initiating a § 9 proceeding in the other. It may therefore be assumed that after a shipper has elected to initiate a Commission proceeding for damages he could not later initiate an original district court action for the same damages. But forfeiture of the right to *initiate* his claim in the court under § 9 is one thing; forfeiture of his right . . . to obtain judicial review of an unlawful Commission order is another. Section 9's language controls the forum in which reparation claims may be begun and tried to judgment or order; it does not purport to give complete finality to a court judgment or to a Commission order merely because a shipper elected to proceed in one forum rather than the other. So we can find nothing in the language of § 9 that bars a court from reviewing a reparation order upon allegations by a shipper that the order was entered in defiance of standards established by Congress to determine when reparations are due.

Furthermore, the section's careful provision for judicial protection of railroads against improper Commission awards argues against interpretation of the same section to deny to shippers any judicial review whatever. Under the suggested interpretation a shipper could recover nothing if the Commission decided against him. But a Commission award favorable to a shipper is not final or binding upon the railroad. . . . It hardly seems possible to find from the language of § 9 a congressional intent to guarantee railroads complete judicial review of adverse reparation orders while denying shippers any judicial review at all. . . .

### *(b) Order which court may not make*

FEDERAL POWER COMMISSION v. PACIFIC POWER & LIGHT CO.
307 U.S. 156 (1939)

Section 203 (a) of the Federal Power Act provides that "no public utility shall sell, lease, or otherwise dispose of the whole of its facilities subject to the jurisdiction of the Commission, or any part thereof of a value in excess of $50,000, or by any means whatsoever, directly or indirectly, merge or consolidate such facilities or any part thereof with those of any other person, or purchase, acquire, or take any security of any public utility, without first having secured an order of the Commission authorizing it to do so. . . . After notice and opportunity for hearing, if the Commission finds that the proposed disposition, consolidation, acquisition, or control will be consistent with the public interest, it shall approve the same."

In this case the question was whether an order of the Federal Power Commission denying an application under Section 203(a) of the Federal Power Act was reviewable under Section 313(b) of the Act.

OPINION BY FRANKFURTER, J. . . .

The Inland Power & Light Company, an Oregon corporation, owns three hydro-electric projects in Oregon and Washington, two of which are operated under license of the Federal Power Commission, and the third, under a permit issued by the Secretary of the Interior. The Pacific Power & Light Company, a Maine corporation, is engaged in generating and distributing electric energy in Washington and Oregon, and owns and operates facilities for interstate transmission of electricity. The Inland and Pacific Companies filed a joint application with the Power Commission for approval . . . of a proposed transfer of all the assets, including licenses, of Inland to Pacific, and of the termination of Inland's existence. Having found after due hearing and consideration that "applicants have failed to establish that said transfer will be consistent with the public interest within the contemplation of Section 203(a) of the Federal Power Act," the Commission ordered that "the application be and the same is hereby denied."

Invoking Section 313(b) of the Federal Power Act, the applicants initiated the present proceedings in the Circuit Court of Appeals for the Ninth Circuit to review the order of the Commission as unwarranted in law and unsupported in its findings. The exact scope of the prayer is postponed for later consideration. The Power Commission challenged the jurisdiction of the Circuit Court of Appeals by a motion to dismiss the petition on the ground that the court was without jurisdiction under Section 313(b), since the order sought to be set aside was negative in character. The denial of that motion brought the case here.

. . . The Power Act contains a distinctive formulation of the conditions under which resort to the courts may be made and Congress determines the scope of jurisdiction of the lower federal courts. Section 313(b) provides that "Any party to a proceeding under this chapter aggrieved by an order issued by the Commission in such proceeding may obtain a review of such order in the Circuit Court of Appeals of the United States." The denial by the Commission of approval of the application by petitioners of the transfer of Inland to Pacific as not "consistent with the public interest" was an "order," and the petitioners were "aggrieved" by it since without such approval the transfer was forbidden. Section 203(a). . . .

But it is urged that review of the Power Commission's order does not present a "Case" or "Controversy," because the court itself cannot lift the prohibition of the statute by granting permission for the transfer, nor order the Commission to grant such permission. And so it is claimed that any action of a court in setting aside the order of the Commission would be an empty gesture, since without permission a transfer would be unlawful. But this proves too much. In none of the situations in which an action of the Interstate Commerce Commission or of a similar federal regulatory body comes for scrutiny before a federal court can judicial action supplant the discretionary authority of a commission. A federal court cannot fix rates nor make divisions of joint rates nor relieve from the long-short haul clause nor formulate car practices. So here it is immaterial that the court itself cannot approve or disapprove the transfer. The court has power to pass judgment upon challenged principles of law insofar as they are relevant to the disposition made by the Commission. ". . . A judgment rendered will be a final and indisputable basis of action as between the Commission and the defendant." . . . In making such a judgment the court does not intrude upon the province of the Commission, while the constitutional requirements of "Case" or "Controversy" are satisfied. For purposes of judicial finality there is no more reason for assuming that a Commission will disregard the direction of a reviewing court than that a lower court will do so.

### *(c) Federal Administrative Procedure Act*

The Federal Administrative Procedure Act defines the extent to which the administrator's actions are reviewable in the following terms:

Sec. 10. Except so far as (1) statutes preclude judicial review or (2) agency action is by law committed to agency discretion—

. . .

(c) REVIEWABLE ACTS.—Every agency action made reviewable by statute and every final agency action for which there is no other adequate remedy in any court shall be subject to judicial review. Any preliminary, procedural, or intermediate agency action or ruling not directly reviewable shall be subject to review upon the review of the final agency action. Except as otherwise expressly required by statute, agency action otherwise final shall be final for the purposes of this subsection whether or not there has been presented or determined any application for a declaratory order, for any form of reconsideration, or (unless the agency otherwise requires by rule and provides that the action meanwhile shall be inoperative) for an appeal to superior agency authority.

## § 33:4. Discretion of Administrator

Review of the administrator's action will be denied where the decision is one the making of which is vested in his discretion. In such case, the fact that the court may reach a conclusion contrary to the administrator's is not a basis for granting a review. There is a qualification to this rule, however, which permits the court to review an administrator's action, even though within the area of his discretionary power, where the action of the administrator is manifestly arbitrary or capricious so that it is apparent that the administrator has not exercised his discretion but has abused it. This in substance is a question of degree. If the administrator is clothed with discretion and his conclusion is one that a reasonable man could make, the court will not review his action. If the conclusion of the administrator is such that no reasonable man would agree with him, he is deemed guilty of having abused his discretion and his action becomes subject to review.

Thus the Supreme Court has said ". . . The very breadth of the statutory language precludes a reversal of the Commission's judgment save where it has plainly abused its discretion in these matters . . . such an abuse is not present in this case.

. . . The Commission's conclusion here rests squarely in that area where administrative judgments are entitled to the greatest amount of weight by appellate courts. It is the product of administrative experience, appreciation of the complexities of the problem, realization of the statutory policy, and responsible treatment of the uncontested facts. It is the type of judgment which administrative agencies are best equipped to make and which justifies the use of the administrative process. . . . Whether we agree or disagree with the result reached, it is an allowable judgment which we cannot disturb."[3]

The Federal Administrative Procedure Act expressly excepts from the definition of reviewable acts "agency action [that] is by law committed to agency discretion."

### *(a) Unfair competition*

MOOG INDUSTRIES v. FEDERAL TRADE COMMISSION
355 U.S. 411 (1958)

Moog Industries was ordered to stop certain pricing practices by the Federal Trade Commission. It raised the objection that its competitors were also guilty of the same practices and that Moog would be ruined if it were required to stop the practices without also requiring its competitors to stop such practices. The Commission rejected this argument. Moog appealed.

OPINION BY THE COURT.

The general question presented . . . is whether it is within the scope of the reviewing authority of a Court of Appeals to postpone the operation of a valid cease and desist order of the Federal Trade Commission against a single firm until similar orders have been entered against that firm's competitors. . . .

In view of the scope of administrative discretion that Congress has given the Federal Trade Commission, it is ordinarily not for courts to modify ancillary features of a valid Commission order. This is but recognition of the fact that in the shaping of its remedies within the framework of regulatory legislation, an agency is called upon to exercise its specialized, experienced judgment. Thus, the decision as to whether or not an order against one firm to cease and desist from engaging in illegal price discrimination should go into effect before others are similarly prohibited depends on a variety of factors peculiarly within the expert understanding of the Commission. Only the Commission, for example, is competent to make an initial determination as to whether and to what extent there is a

---

[3] Securities and Exchange Commission v. Chenery Corporation, 332 U.S. 194 (1947).

". . . But it is the Commission, not the courts, which must be satisfied that the public interest will be served by renewing the license. And the fact that we might not have made the same determination on the same facts does not warrant a substitution of judicial for administrative discretion since Congress has confided the problem to the latter. . . ." Federal Communications Commission v. WOKO, 329 U.S. 223 (1946).

relevant "industry" within which the particular respondent competes and whether or not the nature of that competition is such as to indicate identical treatment of the entire industry by an enforcement agency. Moreover, although an allegedly illegal practice may appear to be operative throughout an industry, whether such appearances reflect fact and whether all firms in the industry should be dealt with in a single proceeding or should receive individualized treatment are questions that call for discretionary determination by the administrative agency. It is clearly within the special competence of the Commission to appraise the adverse effect on competition that might result from postponing a particular order prohibiting continued violations of the law. Furthermore, the Commission alone is empowered to develop that enforcement policy best calculated to achieve the ends contemplated by Congress and to allocate its available funds and personnel in such a way as to execute its policy efficiently and economically.

The question, then, of whether orders such as those before us should be held in abeyance until the respondents' competitors are proceeded against is for the Commission to decide. . . . If the Commission has decided the question, its discretionary determination should not be overturned in the absence of a patent abuse of discretion. . . .

### *(b) Production quota*

SECRETARY OF AGRICULTURE v. CENTRAL ROIG REFINING CO.
338 U.S. 604 (1950)

Acting under the Sugar Act of 1948, the Secretary of Agriculture made quota allowances to sugar refiners in the Puerto Rico area. Appeals were taken from his action on the ground that the Act was unconstitutional and that if constitutional the Secretary had acted improperly in establishing the quota.

OPINION BY FRANKFURTER, J. . . .

In the course of this opinion all expressions of an economic character are to be attributed to those who have authority to make such economic judgments—the Congress and the Secretary of Agriculture—and are not to be deemed the independent judgments of the Court. It is not our right to pronounce economic views; we are confined to passing on the right of the Congress and the Secretary to act on the basis of entertainable economic judgments.

. . . By a series of enactments Congress addressed itself to what it found to be serious evils resulting from an uncontrolled sugar market. The central aim of this legislation was to rationalize the mischievous fluctuations of a free sugar market by the familiar device of a quota system. . . .

The volume of sugar moving to the continental United States market was controlled to secure a harmonious relation between supply and demand. To adapt means to the purpose of the sugar legislation, the Act of 1918 defines five domestic sugar-producing areas: two in the continental United States, Hawaii, Puerto Rico and the Virgin Islands. To each area is allotted an annual quota of sugar, specifying the maximum number of tons which may be marketed on the mainland from that area. § 202(a). A quota is likewise assigned to the Philippines. § 202(b). The balance of the needs of consumers in the continental United States, to be determined each year by the Secretary, § 201, is met by importation from foreign countries, predominantly from Cuba, of the requisite amount of sugar. § 202(c).

The quotas thus established apply to sugar in any form, raw or refined. In addition, § 207 of the Act establishes fixed limits on the tonnage of "direct consumption" or refined sugar which may be marketed annually on the mainland from the offshore areas as part of their total sugar quotas. But mainland refiners are not subject to quota limitations upon the marketing of refined sugar.

The Puerto Rican quota for "direct consumption" sugar is 126,033 tons. This figure had its genesis in the Jones-Costigan Act of 1934, which provided that the quota for each offshore area was to be the largest amount shipped to the mainland in any one of the three preceding years. . . . In the case of Puerto Rico this was computed by the Secretary at 126,033 tons. . . . By the Sugar Acts of 1937 and 1948, Congress embedded this amount in legislation. All the details for the control of a commodity like sugar could not, of course, be legislatively predetermined. Administrative powers are an essential part of such a regulatory scheme. The powers conferred by § 205(a) upon the Secretary of Agriculture raise some of the serious issues in this litigation. By that section Congress authorized the Secretary to allot the refined sugar quota as well as the inclusive allowance of a particular area among those marketing the sugar on the mainland from that area. The section provides that "Allotments shall be made in such manner and in such amounts as to provide a fair, efficient, and equitable distribution of such quota or proration thereof, by taking into consideration" three factors: (1) "processings of sugar . . . to which proportionate shares . . . pertained"; (2) past marketings; and (3) ability to market the amount allotted.

To help effectuate the marketing controls § 301 of the Act provides that certain payments will be made to farmers only if they limit the marketing of sugar cane or beets grown on their farms to a "proportionate share" of the quantity necessary to fill the area's quota, plus a normal carry-over. The relevance of this provision here is that processings of sugar grown within the "proportionate share" restriction are one of the three factors to be considered by the Secretary in the making of allotments under § 205(a).

On January 21, 1948, the Secretary issued Puerto Rico Sugar Order No. 18, 13 Fed.Reg. 310, allotting the 1948 Puerto Rican refined sugar quota among the various refineries of the island. Having satisfied himself of the need for an allotment the Secretary, in conformity with the procedural requirements of § 205(a), apportioned the quota among the individual refiners, setting forth in appropriate findings the manner in which he applied the three statutory standards for allotment.

As to "past marketings" he found that the proper measure was the average of the highest five years of marketings during the seven-year period of 1935-1941. While recognizing that ordinarily the most recent period of marketings furnished the appropriate data, he concluded that the period 1942-1947 was unrepresentative in that the war needs made those years abnormal and not a fair basis for purposes of the economic stabilization which was the aim of the 1948 Act. Shortages as to transportation, storage and materials, caused by the war, led to special government control. These circumstances resulted in hardships or advantages in varying degrees to different refiners, quite unrelated to a fair system of quotas for the post-war period.

Likewise as to "the ability . . . to market," the Secretary recognized that marketings during a recent period ordinarily furnished the best measure. But again he found that the derangements of the war years served to make that measure abnormal. He therefore concluded that a fairer guide to his judgment came from the highest marketings of any year during the 1935-1947 period, using, however, present plant capacity as a corrective.

The Secretary duly considered "the processings of sugar" to which proportionate shares pertained, but concluded that this factor could not fairly be applied. This was so because it referred to processings of raw sugar from sugar cane, whereas the three largest Puerto Rican refining concerns restricted themselves to refining raw sugar after it had already been processed. He felt bound, therefore, to give no weight to this factor in the sum he finally struck, and gave equal weight to past marketings and ability to market.

Availing themselves of § 205 (b), respondents, Central Roig Refining Company and Western Sugar Refining Company . . . appealed from the Secretary's order. . . .

In making quota allotments the Secretary of Agriculture must of course keep scrupulously within the limits set by the Sugar Act of 1948. In devising the framework of control Congress fixed the flat quotas for the sugar-producing areas. Congress could not itself, as a practical matter, allot the area quotas among individual marketers. The details on which fair judgment must be based are too shifting and judgment upon them calls for too specialized understanding to make direct congressional determination feasible. Almost inescapably the function of allotting the area quotas among individual marketers becomes an administrative function entrusted to the member of the Cabinet charged with oversight of the agricultural economy of the nation. He could not be left at large and yet he could not be rigidly bounded. Either extreme would defeat the control system. They could be avoided only by laying down standards of such breadth as inevitably to give the Secretary leeway for his expert judgment. Its exercise presumes a judgment at once comprehensive and conscientious. Accordingly, Congress instructed the Secretary to make allotments "in such manner and in such amounts as to provide a fair, efficient, and equitable distribution" of the quota.

In short, Congress gave the Secretary discretion commensurate with the legislative goal. Allocation of quotas to individual marketers was deemed an essential part of the regulatory scheme. The complexity of problems affecting raw and refined sugar in widely separated and economically disparate areas, accentuated by the instability of the differentiating factors, must have persuaded Congress of the need for continuous detailed administrative supervision. In any event, such is the plain purport of the legislation.

With respect to the Secretary's comparable function of fixing proportionate shares for farms under § 302 of the Act, the House Committee on Agriculture stated: "In view of the differences in conditions of production obtaining in the various sugar-producing areas, the committee has not attempted to specify the exact manner in which the Secretary shall use production history. It is the judgment of the committee that considerable discretion should be left to the Secretary to deal with the varied and changing conditions in the various producing areas, in order to establish fair and equitable proportionate shares for farms in such areas." . . .

By way of guiding the Secretary in formulating a fair distribution of individual allotments, Congress directed him to exercise his discretion "by taking into consideration" three factors: past marketings, ability to market, and processings to which proportionate shares pertained. Plainly these are not mechanical or self-defining standards. They in turn imply wide areas of judgment and therefore of discretion. The fact that the Secretary's judgment is finally expressed arithmetically gives an illusory definiteness to the process of reaching it. Moreover, he is under a duty merely to take "into consideration" the particularized factors. The Secretary cannot be heedless of these factors in the sense, for instance, of refusing to hear relevant evidence bearing on them. But Congress did not think it was feasible to bind the Secretary as to the part his "consideration" of these three factors should play in his final judgment—what weight each should be given, or whether in a particular situation all three factors must play a quantitative share in his computation.

It was evidently deemed fair that in a controlled market each producer should be permitted to retain more or less the share of the market which he had acquired in the past. Accordingly, past marketings were to be taken into consideration in the Secretary's allotments. But the past is relevant only if it furnishes a representative index of the relative positions of different marketers. And there is no calculus available for determining whether a base period for measurement is fairly representative. Whether conditions have been so unusual as to make a period unrepresentative is not a matter of counting figures but of weighing imponderables. If he is to exercise the function of allotting a limited supply among avid contenders for it, the Secretary cannot escape the necessity of passing judgment on their relative competitive positions. For Congress announced that one of the main purposes justifying the making of allotments is "to afford all interested persons an equitable opportunity to market sugar." § 205 (a).

In directing the Secretary to take into consideration ability to market, Congress in effect charged the Secretary with making a forecast of the marketers' capacity to perform in the immediate future. Such a forecast no doubt draws heavily on experience, but history never quite repeats itself even in the vicissitudes of industry. Whether ability to market is most rationally measured by plant capacity or by past performance, whether, if the latter, the base period should be a year and what year or a group of years and what group—these are not questions to be dealt with as statistical problems. They require a disinterested, informed judgment based on circumstances themselves difficult of prophetic interpretation.

The proper mode of ascertaining "processings of sugar . . . to which proportionate shares . . . pertained" is not here in controversy. Perhaps this factor too implies choice. But the question common to all three standards is whether the Secretary may conclude, after due consideration, that in the particular situation before him it is not essential that each of the three factors be quantitatively reflected in the final allotment formula. Concededly, § 205 (a) empowers the Secretary to attribute influences to the three factors. Obviously one factor may be more influential than another in the sense of furnishing a better means of achieving a "fair, efficient, and equitable distribution." But it is not consonant with reason to authorize the Secretary to find in the context of the situation before him that a criterion has little value and is entitled to no more than nominal weight, but to find it unreasonable for him to conclude that this factor has no significance and therefore should not be at all reflected quantitatively.

Congress did not predetermine the periods of time to which the standards should be related or the respective weights to be accorded them. In this respect the sugar-quota scheme differs from the quotas designed by Congress for tobacco, wheat, cotton and rice respectively. . . . Nor do the bare words of § 205 (a) confine the Secretary in the responsible exercise of discretion beyond the limitation inherent upon such delegated authority. He is not free to be capricious, to act without reason, that is, in relation to the attainment of the objects declared by § 205 (a). The very standards for his conduct, the attainment of "fair, efficient, and equitable distribution" preclude abstract or doctrinaire categories. A variety of plans of allotment may well conform to the statutory standards. But the choice among permissive plans is necessarily the Secretary's; he is the agency entrusted by Congress to make the choice.

These considerations dispose of this phase of the case. We would have to replace the Secretary's judgment with our own to hold that on the record before us he acted arbitrarily in reaching the conviction that the years 1935-1941 furnished a fairer measure of past marketings than the war years 1942-1947. Nor can we hold that it was baseless for him to decide that increased marketings during the war years may be taken to mean improved ability to market but decreased marketings do not justify the opposite conclusion. And it was within his province to exclude from his determination the processings of sugar to which proportionate shares pertained. It is not for us to reject the balance he struck on consideration of all the factors unless we can say that his judgment is not one that a fair-minded tribunal with specialized knowledge could have reached. This we cannot say. We conclude, therefore, that in issuing Order No. 18 the Secretary did not exceed the authority given him by Congress. . . .

The sugar problem of the country is an old and obstinate one. For fourteen years Congress grappled with it through the mechanism of quotas. Three enactments, culminating in the Sugar Act of 1948, represented an effort to deal with what were deemed to be the harmful effects on interstate and foreign commerce of progressively depressed sugar prices of earlier years by world surpluses, or, if one prefers it, by the conditions that reflected the imbalance between production and consumption. The legislation presupposes a finding by Congress that producers and marketers of sugar could not adequately respond to market changes merely through the mechanism of a free market and that the public interest, insofar as the Commerce Clause may be drawn upon to meet it, needed controls to supplement and replace the haggling of the market.

Congress might of course have limited its intervention to the raw sugar market, trusting that thereby stability in the refined-sugar market would be produced. Congress thought otherwise; it evidently felt that competition among refiners for a legally limited supply of raw sugar, in a period of overexpanded refining capacity, ought not to be left at large. In any event, Congress had the constitutional right to think otherwise and to bring the refining of sugar within its regulatory scheme. . . .

It is a commonplace that reforms may bring in their train new difficulties. In any scheme of reform, their prevention or mitigation becomes a proper legislative concern. While ameliorating the effect of disorderly competition, market controls generate problems of their own, not encountered under a competitive system. Such new problems are not outside the comprehensive scope of the great Commerce Clause. Nor does the Commerce Clause impose requirements of geographic uniformity. . . . Congress may devise, as it has done in the Sugar Act of 1948, a national policy with due regard for the varying and fluctuating interests of different regions. . . .

[The Court then concluded that the Act of 1948 did not violate Article I, Sec. 9, Clauses 5 and 6 of the Constitution which limit the power of Congress under the commerce clause.]

However, not even resort to the Commerce Clause can defy the standards of due process. We assume that these standards extend to regulations of commerce that enmesh Puerto Rico. . . . The Sugar Act of 1948 is claimed to offend the Due Process Clause of the Fifth Amendment because of the alleged discriminatory character and the oppressive effects of the refined sugar quota established by the Act. If ever claims of this sort carried plausibility, they seem to us singularly belated in view of the unfolding of the Commerce Clause.

The use of quotas on refined sugar, legislatively apportioned to different geographic areas and administratively allocated to individual beneficiaries, is a device based on the Agricultural Adjustment Act of 1938, . . . and sanctioned by this Court in *Mulford* v. *Smith.* The problem which confronted Congress was not the setting of quotas abstractly considered but so to fix their amount as to achieve approximate justice in the shares allotted to each area and the persons within it. To recognize the problem is to acknowledge its perplexities.

Congress was thus confronted with the formulation of policy peculiarly within its wide swath of discretion. It would be a singular intrusion of the judiciary into the legislative process to extrapolate restrictions upon the formulation of such an economic policy from those deeply rooted notions of justice which the Due Process Clause expresses. To fix quotas on a strict historical basis is hard on latecomers into the industry or on those in it who desire to expand. On the other hand, to the extent that newcomers are allowed to enter or old-timers to expand there must either be an increase in supply or a reduction in the quotas of others. Many other factors must plague those charged with the formulation of policy—the extent to which projected expansion is a function of efficiency or becomes a depressant of wage standards; the wise direction of capital into investments and the economic waste incident to what may be on the short or the long pull overexpansion of industrial facilities; the availability of a more suitable basis for the fixing of quotas, etc., etc. The final judgment is too apt to be a hodge-podge of considerations, including considerations that may well weigh with legislators but which this Court can hardly disentangle.

Suffice it to say that since Congress fixed the quotas on a historical basis it is not for this Court to reweigh the relevant factors and, perchance, substitute its notion of expediency and fairness for that of Congress. This is so even though the quotas thus fixed may demonstrably be disadvantageous to certain areas or persons. This Court is not a tribunal for relief from the crudities and inequities of complicated experimental economic legislation. . . .

Congress, it is insisted, has not established refined sugar quotas for the mainland refiners as it has for the offshore areas. Whatever inequalities may thereby be created this is not the forum for their correction for the all-sufficient reason that the extent and nature of inequalities are themselves controversial matters hardly meet for judicial solution. Thus, while the mainland refiners are legally free to purchase and refine all sugar within the raw sugar quota and Puerto Rico refiners are limited to their shares of the refined sugar quota, Congress apparently thought that Puerto Rico refiners operated at costs sufficiently low to insulate them from mainland competition. In addition, it is claimed that since the total supply of raw sugar permitted to enter the mainland market is limited the mainland refiners are in effect also subject to the refined sugar quota, although in contrast to the unchanging quotas of the territories the mainland quota will vary with changes in the total consumer demand. Because this demand tends to be stable, however, the mainland refiners' share of the refined sugar has not, it is urged, greatly expanded during the years when quotas were in effect. Congress might well have thought that relatively minor contractions and expansions in supply from year to year should thus be absorbed.

Plainly it is not the business of judges to sit in judgment on the validity or the significance of such views. The Act may impose hardships here and there; the incidence of hardship may shift in location and intensity. It is not for us to have views on the merits of this legislation. It suffices that we cannot say, as we cannot, that there is "discrimination of such an injurious character as to bring into operation the due process clause." . . . Expressions of dissatisfaction by the Executive and in some quarters of Congress that the refined sugar quotas were "arbitrary," "discriminatory," and "unfair" may reflect greater wisdom or greater fairness than the collective wisdom of Congress which put this Act on the statute books. But the issue was thrashed out in Congress; Congress is the place for its reconsideration. . . .

### (c) Food adulteration

HOUSTON v. ST. LOUIS INDEPENDENT PACKING CO.

249 U.S. 479 (1919)

The Federal Meat Inspection Act provides that "no . . . meat or meat food products shall be sold or offered for sale by any person, firm, or corporation in interstate or foreign commerce under any false or deceptive name; but established trade name or names which are usual to such products and which are not false and deceptive and which shall be approved by the Secretary of Agriculture are permitted, and that said Secretary of Agriculture shall, from time to time make such rules and regulations as are necessary for the efficient execution of the provisions of this act, and all inspections and examinations made under this act shall be such and made in such manner as described in the rules and regulations prescribed by the Secretary of Agriculture not inconsistent with the provisions of this Act."

Acting under the authority of this provision, the Secretary of Agriculture prohibited the use of the term "sausage" to describe or label any compound, chopped or minced meat product containing cereal in excess of 2% or water or ice in excess of 3%. A sausage manufacturer brought an action to enjoin the enforcement of this regulation on the ground that the Secretary of Agriculture was not authorized under the statute to condemn as fraudulent the use of the word "sausage" to describe a sausage product containing more than the specified percentages of cereal, water or ice.

OPINION BY CLARKE, J. . . .

The contention of the government is that the product of the appellee being a meat food product, put up in containers—casings or canvas coverings—it falls within the prohibition of the act that such product shall not be sold or offered for sale by any corporation in interstate commerce "under any false or deceptive name," and that the regulation being for the purpose of preventing its sale under the false or deceptive name of "sausage," it is plainly within the authority given to the Secretary of Agriculture to make rules and regulations for the efficient execution of the act.

On the other hand, the contention of the appellee is that the product being wholesome and containing no dyes or chemicals, which render it unfit for human food, an earlier provision of the act applies, which it is asserted deprives the Secretary of all discretion in such a case and requires that he shall cause the product to be marked "Inspected and passed," and also, it is claimed, that the word "sausage," when qualified as was required by prior regulations by including in the label such expressions as "Cereal added," or "Sausage and cereal," was not a false or deceptive name. . . .

Whether or not the term "sausage," when applied to the product of the appellee, in which more than the permitted amount of cereal and water is used, is false and deceptive is a question of fact, the determination of which is committed to the decision of the Secretary of Agriculture by the authority given him to make rules and regulations for giving effect to the act, and the law is that the conclusion of the head of an executive department on such a question will not be reviewed by the courts, where it is fairly arrived at with substantial evidence to support it. . . .

That the case before us is one for the application of this rule is shown by the record, which contains an interesting history of what large manufacturers have come, in a more or less gradual progress, to regard as the proper ingredients of the product which they have sold as sausage, and which also shows, without conflict, that the ultimate purchaser and consumer of the product is not informed and in general does not know of the presence of cereal and added water in it. The evidence shows that the poorer classes of beef and pork are used in making sausage, such as trimmings, hearts, ears, cheeks, liver, snouts and tripe, "and all that kind of things," but the preferred material is bull meat; that such meat, other than bull meat, is dry and has not the cohesive properties which will unite it when ground or minced into the mass popularly known as "sausage" and that, for this reason, corn meal, potato flour and other like substances have come to be used by the trade as "binders" to give it the desired cohesiveness and appearance.

The president of the appellee testified that when he first began making sausage 25 years ago he used anywhere from 5 per cent. to 12 per cent. of cereal and that when the regulation was promulgated he was using 2 or 3 per cent. to 10 per cent., when he used any at all, but that in a part of his product he did not use any, notably in that which was sent into Pennsylvania, where the use of cereal was prohibited by statute; that when he used 10 per cent. of cereal he added from 15 to 20 per cent. of water, and that in general water was added in double the percentage of cereal used; and that the cereal, usually corn meal or corn flour, was resorted to to cheapen the product and cost about 2 cents a pound, while the meat used cost from 6 to 15 cents a pound.

Before the regulation assailed was promulgated cereal and water were generally used by large manufacturers of sausage, but all of the representatives of manufacturers, other than those of the appellee, who were called as witnesses, testified that they were obeying the regulation, and the agreement of such witnesses was general that retail purchasers and consumers did not know of the presence of cereal in what they were buying as sausage. . . .

The result, thus stated, of the examination of the record before us shows beyond controversy, that the Secretary of Agriculture in promulgating the regulation complained of acted on substantial evidence and with sufficient reason in concluding that persons purchasing or using as "sausage" the appellee's compound of various meats, cereal and water would be deceived as to its composition and as to its value as a food product, and we cannot say that it was an abuse of discretion to prohibit the use of the word "sausage" as applied to it, rather than to prescribe qualifying terms explanatory of it. Few purchasers read long labels, many cannot read them at all, and the act of Congress having committed to the head of the department, constantly dealing with such matters, the discretion to determine as to whether the use of the word "sausage" in a label would be false and deceptive or not, under such circumstances as we have here this court will not review, and the Circuit Court of Appeals should not have reviewed and reversed the decision of the Secretary of Agriculture. . . .

### § 33:5. Legislative Function of Administrator

A distinction must be made in the scope of review permitted when the administrator is merely applying regulations and when he is in effect legislating or establishing the regulation. In the case of the former, his action is subject to review to determine whether he properly applied the law or the regulation. In the latter case, there can be no review of the wisdom of his decision in concluding that the rule adopted by him was desirable.

A rule or a regulation adopted by an administrator cannot be challenged on the ground that it is predicated upon a condition which does not exist throughout. As stated in *The Assigned Car Cases*, 274 U.S. 564 (1927): "In the case at bar, the function exercised by the Commission is wholly legislative. Its authority to legislate is limited to establishing a reasonable rule. But in establishing a rule of general application, it is not a condition of its validity that there be adduced evidence of its appropriateness in respect to every railroad to which it would be applicable. In this connection, the Commission, like other legislators, may reason from the particular to the general."

### *(a) Tariff regulations*

UNITED STATES v. GEORGE S. BUSH & CO., INC.
310 U.S. 371 (1940)

A taxpayer sought to review the action of the President in following the advice of the Tariff Commission in establishing a particular tariff rate.

The tariff law provided that the President "shall by proclamation approve the rates of duties and changes in classification and in basis of value specified in any report of the Commission under this section, if in his judgment such rates of duty and changes are shown by such investigation of the Commission to be necessary to equalize such differences in cost of production."

The Commission after investigation concluded that the existing tariff on canned clams imported from Japan did not equalize the difference between the cost of production of the domestic and the Japanese article and recommended an increase of the tariff, which was then put into effect by the President. It was objected that the Commission improperly determined the Japanese cost of production. Under the statute the Commission was authorized, when the cost of production of a foreign article could not be readily ascertained, to accept as evidence of such cost the "weighted average of the invoice prices or values for a representative period." The Commission took the weighted average of such prices for the period from December 1, 1930, to September 30, 1932. As those prices were expressed in Japanese yen, the Commission converted them into dollars based on the average rate of exchange for 1932. That period was selected because Japan abandoned the gold standard in December, 1931, and the value of the yen in terms of United States dollars declined steadily from that date to November, 1932.

OPINION BY DOUGLAS, J. . . .

The Court of Customs and Patent Appeals held that it was error to convert invoice prices for one period into United States dollars at the average rate of exchange for another period. In its view the phrase "weighted average of the invoice prices or values for a representative period" contained in § 336(e) (2) must be construed as though it read, "weighted average of the invoice prices or values in United States currency for a representative period." The government, however, urges that if the Commission were forced to take the conversion rate for the earlier period, to which it had to resort in order to obtain the invoice prices, it would use a rate which had merely an historical interest and which did not reflect the conditions which made desirable an increase in duties, viz. the depreciation in the value of the yen.

The determination of foreign exchange value was prescribed, in the procedure outlined by Congress, neither for the action of the Commission nor for that of the President. There is no express provision in the Act that the rate of exchange must be taken for the same period as the invoice prices. To imply it would be to add what Congress has omitted and doubtless omitted in view of the very nature of the problem. The matter was left at large. The President's method of solving the problem was open to scrutiny neither by the Court of Customs and Patent Appeals nor by us. Whatever may be the scope of appellate jurisdiction conferred by § 501 of the Tariff Act of 1930, it certainly does not permit judicial examination of the judgment of the President that the rates of duty recommended by the Commission are necessary to equalize the differences in the domestic and foreign costs of production.

The powers which Congress has entrusted to the President under the Act . . . do not essentially differ in kind from those which have been granted him under the tariff acts for well over a century. . . . Since its creation in 1916 the Commission has acted as an adviser to the Congress or to the President. Under § 336 of the Act of 1930 the Commission serves the President in that role. It does not increase or decrease the rates of duty; it is but the expert body which investigates and submits the facts and its recommendations to the President. It is the judgment of the President on those facts which is determinative of whether or not the recommended rates will be promulgated. In substance and to a great extent in form . . . the action of the Commission and the President is but one stage of the legislative process. . . . "No one has a legal right to the maintenance of an existing rate or duty." . . . And the judgment of the President that on the facts, adduced in pursuance of the procedure prescribed by Congress, a change of rate is necessary is no more subject to judicial review under this statutory scheme than if Congress itself had exercised that judgment. It has long been held that where Congress has authorized a public officer to take some specified legislative action when in his judgment that action is necessary or appropriate to carry out the policy of Congress, the judgment of the officer as to the existence of the facts calling for that action is not subject to review. . . . "Whenever a statute gives a discretionary power to any person, to be exercised by him upon his own opinion of certain facts, it is a sound rule of construction, that the statute constitutes him the sole and exclusive judge of the existence of those facts."

For the judiciary to probe the reasoning which underlies this Proclamation would amount to a clear invasion of the legislative and executive domains. Under the Constitution it is exclusively for Congress or those to whom it delegates authority, to determine what tariffs shall be imposed. Here the President acted in full conformity with the statute. No question of law is raised when the exercise of his discretion is challenged.

### *(b) Broadcasting regulations*

NATIONAL BROADCASTING CO. v. UNITED STATES
319 U.S. 190 (1943)

The Federal Communications Commission made a detailed investigation to determine whether special regulations applicable to chain broadcasting were required in the "public interest, convenience or necessity." Notice was given to the networks, which participated in the hearings held by the investigating committee. Of the 96 witnesses testifying before the committee, 45 were called by the networks. Twenty-seven volumes of testimony were offered before the committee. Tentative regulations were prepared and made public, and briefs respecting them were submitted by the networks to the Commission. The Commission adopted a set of chain broadcasting regulations. These regulations were challenged as invalid.

OPINION BY FRANKFURTER, J.

. . . We turn now to the Regulations themselves. . . . The Regulations, which the Commission characterized in its Report as "the expression of the general policy we will follow in exercising our licensing power," are addressed in terms to station licensees and applicants for station licenses. They provide, in general, that no licenses shall be granted to stations or applicants having specified relationships with networks. Each Regulation is directed at a particular practice found by the Commission to be detrimental to the "public interest," and we shall consider them seriatim. In doing so, however, we do not overlook the admonition of the Commission that the Regulations as well as the network practices at which they are aimed are interrelated: "In considering above the network practices which necessitate the regulations we are adopting, we have taken each practice singly, and have shown that even in isolation each warrants the regulation addressed to it. But the various practices we have considered do not operate in isolation; they form a compact bundle or pattern, and the effect of their joint impact upon licensees necessitates the regulations even more urgently than the effect of each taken singly.". . .

The Commission found that at the end of 1938 there were 660 commercial stations in the United States, and that 341 of these were affiliated with national networks. 135 stations were affiliated exclusively with the National Broadcasting Company, Inc., known in the industry as NBC, which operated two national networks, the "Red" and the "Blue." NBC was also the licensee of 10 stations, including 7 which operated on so-called clear channels with the maximum power available, 50 kilowatts; in addition, NBC operated 5 other stations, 4 of which had power of 50 kilowatts, under management contracts with their licensees. 102 stations were affiliated exclusively with the Columbia Broadcasting System, Inc., which was also the licensee of 8 stations, 7 of which were clear-channel stations operating with power of 50 kilowatts. 74 stations were under exclusive affiliation with the Mutual Broadcasting System, Inc. In addition, 25 stations were affiliated with both NBC and Mutual, and 5 with both CBS and Mutual. These figures, the Commission noted, did not accurately reflect the relative prominence of the three companies, since the stations affiliated with Mutual were, generally speaking, less desirable in frequency, power, and coverage. It pointed out that the stations affiliated with the national networks utilized more than 97% of the total night-time broadcasting power of all the stations in the country. NBC and CBS together controlled more than 85% of the total night-time wattage, and the broadcast business of the three national network companies amounted to almost half of the total business of all stations in the United States.

The Commission recognized that network broadcasting had played and was continuing to play an important part in the development of radio. "The growth and development of chain broadcasting," it stated, "found its impetus in the desire to give widespread coverage to programs which otherwise would not be heard beyond the reception area of a single station. Chain broadcasting makes possible a wider reception for expensive entertainment and cultural programs and also for programs of national or regional significance which would otherwise have coverage only in the locality of origin. Furthermore, the access to greatly enlarged audiences made possible by chain broadcasting has been a strong incentive to advertisers to finance the production of expensive programs. . . . But the fact that the chain broadcasting method brings benefits and advantages to both the listening public and to broadcast station licensees does not mean that the prevailing practices and policies of the networks and their outlets are sound in all respects, or that they should not be altered. The Commission's duty under the Communications Act of 1934, is not only to see that the public receives the advantages and benefits of chain broadcasting, but also, so far as its powers enable it, to see that practices which adversely affect the ability of licensees to operate in the public interest are eliminated." (Report, p. 4.)

The Commission found that eight network abuses were amenable to correction within the powers granted it by Congress:

*Regulation 3.101—Exclusive affiliation of station.* The Commission found that the network affiliation agreements of NBC and CBS customarily contained a provision which prevented the station from broadcasting the programs of any other network. . . .

*Regulation 3.102—Territorial exclusivity.* The Commission found another type of "exclusivity" provision in network affiliation agreements whereby the network bound itself not to sell programs to any other station in the same area. . . .

*Regulation 3.103—Term of affiliation.* The standard NBC and CBS affiliation contracts bound the station for a period of five years, with the network having the exclusive right to terminate the contracts upon one year's notice. The Commission, relying upon § 307(d) of the Communications Act of 1934, under which no license to operate a broadcasting station can be granted for a longer term than three years, found the five-year affiliation term to be contrary to the policy of the Act. . . .

*Regulation 3.104—Option time.* The Commission found that network affiliation contracts usually contained so-called network optional time clause. Under these provisions the network could upon 28 days' notice call upon its affiliates to carry a commercial program during any of the hours specified in the agreement as "network optional time.". . .

Regulation 3.104 called for the modification of the option-time provision in three respects: the minimum notice period for exercise of the option could not be less than 56 days; the number of hours which could be optioned was limited; and specific restrictions were placed upon exercise of the option to the disadvantage of other networks. . . .

*Regulation 3.105—Right to reject programs.* The Commission found that most network affiliation contracts contained a clause defining the right of the station to reject network commercial programs. . . .

The Commission undertook in Regulation 3.105 to formulate the obligations of licensees with respect to supervision over programs: "No license shall be granted to a standard broadcast station having any contract, arrangement, or understanding, express or implied, with a network organization which (a), with respect to programs offered pursuant to an affiliation contract, prevents or hinders the station from rejecting or refusing network programs which the station reasonably believes to be unsatisfactory or unsuitable; or which (b), with respect to network programs so offered or already contracted for, prevents the station from rejecting or refusing any program which, in its opinion, is contrary to the public interest, or from substituting a program of outstanding local or national importance."

*Regulation 3.106—Network ownership of stations.* The Commission found out NBC, in addition to its network operations, was the licensee of 10 stations, 2 each in New York, Chicago, Washington, and San Francisco, 1 in Denver, and 1 in Cleveland. CBS was the licensee of 8 stations 1 in each of these cities: New York, Chicago, Washington, Boston, Minneapolis, St. Louis, Charlotte, and Los Angeles. These 18 stations owned by NBC and CBS, the Commission observed, were among the most powerful and desirable in the country, and were permanently inaccessible to competing networks. . . .

Regulation 3.106 reads as follows: "No license shall be granted to a network organization, or to any person directly or indirectly controlled by or under common control with a network organization, for more than one standard broadcast station where one of the stations covers substantially the service area of the other station, or for any standard broadcast station in any locality where the existing standard broadcast stations are so few or of such unequal desirability (in terms of coverage, power, frequency, or other related matters) that competition would be substantially restrained by such licensing.". . .

*Regulation 3.108—Control by networks of station rates.* The Commission found that NBC's affiliation contracts contained a provision empowering the network to reduce the station's network rate, and thereby to reduce the compensation received by the station, if the station set a lower rate for non-network national advertising than the rate established by the contract for the network programs. Under this provision the station could not sell time to a national advertiser for less than it would cost the advertiser if he bought the time from NBC. . . .

. . . The Commission adopted Regulation 3.108, which provides as follows: "No license shall be granted to a standard broadcast station having any contract, arrangement, or understanding, express or implied, with a network organization under which the station is prevented or hindered from, or penalized for, fixing or altering its rates for the sale of broadcast time for other than the network's programs."

. . .

Section 1 of the Communications Act states its "purpose of regulating interstate and foreign commerce in communication by wire and radio so as to make available, so far as possible, to all the people of the United States a rapid, efficient, Nation-wide, and world-wide wire and radio communication service with adequate facilities at reasonable charges." . . .

Section 303 provides:

"Except as otherwise provided in this Act, the Commission from time to time, as public convenience, interest, or necessity requires, shall—

. . .

"(b) Prescribe the nature of the service to be rendered by each class of licensed stations and each station within any class;

. . .

"(i) Have authority to make special regulations applicable to radio stations engaged in chain broadcasting; . . ."

The criterion governing the exercise of the Commission's licensing power is the "public interest, convenience, or necessity.". . . In addition, § 307(b) directs the Commission that "In considering applications for licenses, and modifications and renewals thereof, when and insofar as there is demand for the same, the Commission shall make such distribution of licenses, frequencies, hours of operation, and of power among the several States and communities as to provide a fair, efficient, and equitable distribution of radio service to each of the same."

The Act itself establishes that the Commission's powers are not limited to the engineering and technical aspects of regulation of radio communication. Yet we are asked to regard the Commission as a kind of traffic officer, policing the wave lengths to prevent stations from interfering with each other. But the Act does not restrict the Commission merely to supervision of the traffic. It puts upon the Commission the burden of determining the composition of that traffic. The facilities of radio are not large enough to accommodate all who wish to use them. Methods must be devised for choosing from among the many who apply. And since Congress itself could not do this, it committed the task to the Commission.

The Commission was, however, not left at large in performing this duty. The touchstone provided by Congress was the "public interest, convenience, or necessity," a criterion which "is as concrete as the complicated factors for judgment in such a field of delegated authority permit.". . . "This criterion is not to be interpreted as setting up a standard so indefinite as to confer an unlimited power. . . . The requirement is to be interpreted by its context, by the nature of radio transmission and reception, by the scope, character, and quality of services.". . .

The "public interest" to be served under the Communications Act is thus the interest of the listening public in "the larger and more effective use of radio." § 303 (g). The facilities of radio are limited and therefore precious; they cannot be left to wasteful use without detriment to the public interest. "An important element of public interest and convenience affecting the issue of a license is the ability of the licensee to render the best practicable service to the community reached by his broadcasts." *Federal Communications Comm. v. Sanders Bros. Radio Station,* 309 U.S. 470. The Commission's licensing function cannot be discharged, therefore, merely by finding that there are no technological objections to the granting of a license. If the criterion of "public interest" were limited to such matters, how could the Commission choose between two applicants for the same facilities, each of whom is financially and technically qualified to operate a station? Since the very inception of federal regulation by radio, comparative considerations as to the services to be rendered have governed the application of the standard of "public interest, convenience, or necessity.". . .

The avowed aim of the Communications Act of 1934 was to secure the maximum benefits of radio to all the people of the United States. To that end Congress endowed the Communications Commission with comprehensive powers to promote and realize the vast potentialities of radio. Section 303(g) provides that the Commission shall "generally encourage the larger and more effective use of radio in the public interest"; subsection (i) gives the Commission specific "authority to make special regulations applicable to radio stations engaged in chain broadcasting"; and subsection (r) empowers it to adopt "such rules and regulations and prescribe such restrictions and conditions, not inconsistent with law, as may be necessary to carry out the provisions of this Act."

These provisions, individually and in the aggregate, preclude the notion that the Commission is empowered to deal only with technical and engineering impediments to the "larger and more effective use of radio in the public interest." We cannot find in the Act any such restriction of the Commission's authority. Suppose, for example, that a community can, because of physical limitations, be assigned only two stations. That community might be deprived of effective service in any one of several ways. More powerful stations in nearby cities might blanket out the signals of the local stations so that they could not be heard at all. The stations might interfere with each other so that neither could be clearly heard. One station might dominate the other with the power of its signal. But the community could be deprived of good radio service in ways less crude. One man, financially and technically qualified, might apply for and obtain the licenses of both stations and present a single service over the two stations, thus wasting a frequency otherwise available to the area. The language of the Act does not withdraw such a situation from the licensing and regulatory powers of the Commission, and there is no evidence that Congress did not mean its broad language to carry the authority it expresses.

In essence, the Chain Broadcasting Regulations represent a particularization of the Commission's conception of the "public interest" sought to be safeguarded by Congress in enacting the Communications Act of 1934. The basic consideration of policy underlying the Regulations is succinctly stated in its Report: "With the number of radio channels limited by natural factors, the public interest demands that those who are entrusted with the available channels shall make the fullest and most effective use of them. If a licensee enters into a contract with a network organization which limits his ability to make the best use of the radio facility assigned him, he is not serving the public interest. . . . The net effect . . . has been that broadcasting service has been maintained at a level below that possible under a system of free competition. Having so found, we would be remiss in our statutory duty of encouraging 'the larger and more effective use of radio in the public interest' if we were to grant licenses to persons who persist in these practices." (Report, pp. 81, 82.)

We would be asserting our personal views regarding the effective utilization of radio were we to deny that the Commission was entitled to find that the large public aims of the Communications Act of 1934 comprehend the considerations which moved the Commission in promulgating the Chain Broadcasting Regulations. True enough, the Act does not explicitly say that the Commission shall have power to deal with network practices found inimical to the public interest. But Congress was acting in a field of regulation which was both new and dynamic. "Congress moved under the spur of a widespread fear that in the absence of governmental control the public interest might be subordinated to monopolistic domination in the broadcasting field." . . . In the context of the developing problems to which it was directed, the Act gave the Commission not niggardly but expansive powers. It was given a comprehensive mandate to "encourage the larger and more effective use of radio in the public interest," if need be, by making "special regulations applicable to radio stations engaged in chain broadcasting." Section 303(g) (i).

Generalities unrelated to the living problems of radio communication of course cannot justify exercises of power by the Commission. Equally so, generalities empty of all concrete considerations of the actual bearing of regulations promulgated by the Commission to the subject-matter entrusted to it, cannot strike down exercise of power by the Commission. While Congress did not give the Commission unfettered discretion to regulate all phases of the radio industry, it did not frustrate the purposes for which the Communications Act of 1934 was brought into being by attempting an itemized catalogue of the specific manifestations of the general problems for the solution of which it was establishing a regulatory agency. That would have stereotyped the powers of the Commission to specific details in regulating a field of enterprise the dominant characteristic of which was the rapid pace of its unfolding. And so Congress did what experience had taught it in similar attempts at regulation, even in fields where the subject-matter of regulation was far less fluid and dynamic than radio. The essence of that experience was to define broad areas for regulation and to establish standards for judgment adequately related in their application to the problems to be solved.

For the cramping construction of the Act pressed upon us, support cannot be found in its legislative history. . . .

A totally different source of attack upon the Regulations is found in § 311 of the Act, which authorizes the Commission to withhold licenses from persons convicted of having violated the anti-trust laws. Two contentions are made—first, that this provision puts considerations relating to competition outside the Commission's concern before an applicant has been convicted of monopoly or other restraints of trade, and second, that in any event, the Commission misconceived the scope of its powers under § 311 in issuing the Regulations. Both of these contentions are unfounded. Section 311 derives from § 13 of the Radio Act of 1927, which expressly commanded, rather than merely authorized, the Commission to refuse a license to any person judicially found guilty of having violated the anti-trust laws. The change in the 1934 Act was made, in the words of Senator Dill, the manager of the legislation in the Senate, because "it seemed fair to the committee to do that.". . . The Commission was thus permitted to exercise its judgment as to whether violation of the anti-trust laws disqualified an applicant from operating a station in the "public interest." We agree with the District Court that "The necessary implication from this [amendment in 1934] was that the Commission might infer from the fact that the applicant had in the past tried to monopolize radio, or had engaged in unfair methods of competition, that the disposition so manifested would continue and that if it did it would make him an unfit licensee.". . .

That the Commission may refuse to grant a license to persons adjudged guilty in a court of law of conduct in violation of the anti-trust laws certainly does not render irrelevant consideration by the Commission of the effect of such conduct upon the "public interest, convenience, or necessity." A licensee charged with practices in contravention of this standard cannot continue to hold his license merely because his conduct is also in violation of the anti-trust laws and he has not yet been proceeded against and convicted. By clarifying in § 311 the scope of the Commission's authority in dealing with persons convicted of violating the anti-trust laws, Congress can hardly be deemed to have limited the concept of "public interest" so as to exclude all considerations relating to monopoly and unreasonable restraints upon commerce. Nothing in the provisions or history of the Act lends support to the inference that the Commission was denied the power to refuse a license to a station not operating in the "public interest," merely because its misconduct happened to be an unconvicted violation of the anti-trust laws.

Alternatively, it is urged that the Regulations constitute an ultra vires attempt by the Commission to enforce the anti-trust laws, and that the enforcement of the anti-trust laws is the province not of the Commission but of the Attorney General and the courts. This contention misconceives the basis of the Commission's action. The Commission's Report indicates plainly enough that the Commission was not attempting to administer the anti-trust laws:

"The prohibitions of the Sherman Act apply to broadcasting. This Commission, although not charged with the duty of enforcing that law, should administer its regulatory powers with respect to broadcasting in the light of the purposes which the Sherman Act was designed to achieve. . . . While many of the network practices raise serious questions under the antitrust laws, our jurisdiction does not depend on a showing that they do in fact constitute a violation of the antitrust laws. It is not our function to apply the antitrust laws as such. It is our duty, however, to refuse licenses or renewals to any person who engages or proposes to engage in practices which will prevent either himself or other licensees or both from making the fullest use of radio facilities. This is the standard of public interest, convenience or necessity which we must apply to all applications for licenses and renewals. . . . We do not predicate our jurisdiction to issue the regulations on the ground that the network practices violate the antitrust laws. We are issuing these regulations because we have found that the network practices prevent the maximum utilization of radio facilities in the public interest." (Report, pp. 46, 83, 83 n. 3.)

We conclude, therefore, that the Communications Act of 1934 authorized the Commission to promulgate regulations designed to correct the abuses disclosed by its investigation of chain broadcasting. There remains for consideration the claim that the Commission's exercise of such authority was unlawful.

The Regulations are assailed as "arbitrary and capricious." If this contention means that the Regulations are unwise, that they are not likely to succeed in accomplishing what the Commission intended, we can say only that the appellants have selected the wrong forum for such a plea. . . . "We certainly have neither technical competence nor legal authority to pronounce upon the wisdom of the course taken by the Commission." Our duty is at an end when we find that the action of the Commission was based upon findings supported by evidence, and was made pursuant to authority granted by Congress. It is not for us to say that the "public interest" will be furthered or retarded by the Chain Broadcasting Regulations. The responsibility belongs to the Congress for the grant of valid legislative authority and to the Commission for its exercise.

It would be sheer dogmatism to say that the Commission made out no case for its allowable discretion in formulating these Regulations. Its long investigation disclosed the existences of practices which it regarded as contrary to the "public interest." The Commission knew that the wisdom of any action it took would have to be tested by experience: "We are under no illusion that the regulations we are adopting will solve all questions of public interest with respect to the network system of program distribution. . . . The problems in the network field are interdependent, and the steps now taken may perhaps operate as a partial solution of problems not directly dealt with at this time. Such problems may be examined again at some future time after the regulations here adopted have been given a fair trial.". . . The problems with which the Commission attempted to deal could not be solved at once and for all time by rigid rules-of-thumb. The Commission therefore did not bind itself inflexibly to the licensing policies expressed in the Regulations. In each case that comes before it the Commission must still exercise an ultimate judgment whether the grant of a license would serve the "public interest, convenience, or necessity." If time and changing circumstances reveal that the "public interest" is not served by application of the Regulations, it must be assumed that the Commission will act in accordance with its statutory obligations. . . .

We come, finally to an appeal to the First Amendment. The Regulations, even if valid in all other respects, must fall because they abridge, say the appellants, their right of free speech. If that be so, it would follow that every person whose application for a license to operate a station is denied by the Commission is thereby denied his constitutional right of free speech. Freedom of utterance is abridged to many who wish to use the limited facilities of radio. Unlike other modes of expression, radio inherently is not available to all. That is its unique characteristic, and that is why, unlike other modes of expression, it is subject to governmental regulation. Because it cannot be used by all, some who wish to use it must be denied. But Congress did not authorize the Commission to choose among applicants upon the basis of their political, economic or social views, or upon any other capricious basis. If it did, or if the Commission by these Reglations proposed a choice among applicants upon some such basis, the issue before us would be wholly different. The question here is simply whether the Commission, by announcing that it will refuse licenses to persons who engage in specified network practices (a basis for choice which we hold is comprehended within the statutory criterion of "public interest"), is thereby denying such persons the constitutional right of free speech. The right of free speech does not include, however, the right to use the facilities of radio without a license. The licensing system established by Congress in the Communications Act of 1934 was a proper exercise of its power over commerce. The standard it provided for the licensing of stations was the "public interest, convenience, or necessity." Denial of a station license on that ground, if valid under the Act, is not a denial of free speech. . . .

## § 33:6. Government Privileges

Where the determination of the administrator relates to a privilege or a franchise granted or given by the government, the review is narrow. As an abstract matter, one would expect the scope of review to be the same as in any other case. The fact that the objecting party has no right but merely exercises a privilege or a franchise granted by the government, has, however, influenced the courts to modify or narrow his right to challenge the action taken by the administrator of the government that created the privilege or the franchise claimed.

### *(a) Classification of mail*

BATES & GUILD CO. v. PAYNE

194 U.S. 106 (1904)

The Postmaster General of the United States denied an application to classify as second-class mail certain printed matter purporting to be magazines. The applicant appealed from his decision.

OPINION BY BROWN, J.

The first number of Masters in Music was issued in January, 1903, and an application was immediately made to the Postmaster General for its admission to the mails as second-class matter. The application was denied, and plaintiff . . . filed this bill. The publication purports to be a "monthly magazine." . . . The first number is devoted to the works of Mozart and contains a portrait, a biography of four pages, an essay of ten pages upon his art, and thirty-two pages of music. The preliminary page contained a notice to the effect that "Masters in Music will be unlike any other magazine. Each monthly issue, complete in itself, will be devoted to one of the world's greatest musicians. . . ."

The Postmaster General placed his refusal to allow this magazine to be transmitted as second-class matter upon the grounds that each number was complete in itself; had no connection with other numbers save in the circumstances that they all treated of masters in music, and that these issues were in fact sheet music disguised as a periodical, and should be classified as third-class mail matter.

. . . We think that, although the question is largely one of law, . . . there is some discretion left in the Postmaster General with respect to the classification of such publications as mail matter, and that the exercise of such discretion ought not to be interfered with unless the court be clearly of opinion that it was wrong. The Postmaster General is charged with the duty of examining these publications and of determining to which class of mail they properly belong; and we think his decision should not be made the subject of judicial investigation in every case where one of the parties thereto is dissatisfied. The consequence of a different rule would be that the court might be flooded with appeals of this kind to review the decision of the Postmaster General in every individual instance. . . .

It has long been the settled practice of this court in land cases to treat the findings of the Land Department upon questions of fact as conclusive, although such proceedings involve, to a certain extent, the exercise of judicial power. . . . "Whether, for instance, a certain tract is swamp land or not, saline land or not, mineral land or not, presents a question of fact not resting on record, depending on oral testimony; and it cannot be doubted that the decision of the Land Department, one way or the other, in reference to these questions is conclusive and not open to relitigation in the courts, except in those cases of fraud, etc. which permit any determination to be re-examined." . . .

But there is another class of cases in which the rule is somewhat differently, and perhaps more broadly, stated, and that is, that where Congress has committed to the head of a department certain duties requiring the exercise of judgment and discretion, his action thereon, whether it involved questions of law or fact, will not be reviewed by the courts, unless he has exceeded his authority or this court should be of opinion that his action was clearly wrong. . . . The official duties of the head of a department, whether imposed by act of Congress or resolution, are not ministerial duties; and, . . . "Whether he decided right or wrong is not the question. Having jurisdiction to decide at all, he had necessarily jurisdiction, and it was his duty to decide as he thought the law was, and the courts have no power whatever, under those circumstances, to review his determination by mandamus or injunction." . . . The courts will not interfere . . . with the executive officers . . . in the exercise of their ordinary official duties, even where [they] require an interpretation of law. . . .

The rule upon this subject may be summarized as follows: That where the decision of questions of fact is committed by Congress to the judgment and discretion of the head of a department, his decision thereon is conclusive; and that even upon mixed questions of law and fact, or of law alone, his action will carry with it a strong presumption of its correctness, and the courts will not ordinarily review it, although they may have the power, and will occasionally exercise the right of so doing.

Upon this principle, and because we thought the question involved one of law rather than of fact, and one of great general importance, we have reviewed the action of the Postmaster General in holding serial novels to be books rather than periodicals; but it is not intended to intimate that in every case hereafter arising the question whether a certain publication shall be considered a book or a periodical shall be reviewed by this court. In such case the decision of the Post Office Department, rendered in the exercise of a reasonable discretion, will be treated as conclusive.

In the case of Masters in Music the question is really whether a pamphlet, complete in itself, treating of the works of a single master, with a greater part of the pamphlet devoted to specimens of his genius, shall be controlled by the cover, which declared that these numbers will be issued monthly, at a certain subscription price per year. Although a comparison of the exhibit with the statute may raise only a question of law, the action of the Postmaster General may have been, to a certain extent, guided by extraneous information obtained by him, so that the question involved would be found not merely a question of law, but a mixed question of law and fact. While . . . the question is one of doubt, we think the decision of the Postmaster General, who is vested by Congress with the power to exercise his judgment and discretion . . . should be accepted as final. . . .

## § 33:7. Foreign Affairs

When the subject matter relates to foreign affairs, the courts have been willing to recognize a greater degree of discretion on the part of the administrator.

### *(a) International air route certificate*

CHICAGO & SOUTHERN AIRLINES v. WATERMAN STEAMSHIP CORP.

333 U.S. 103 (1948)

The Civil Aeronautics Board, with the approval of the President, issued an order denying the Waterman Steamship Corporation a certificate of convenience and necessity to maintain a specified foreign international air route and granted the route to the Chicago & Southern Airlines, a rival applicant. The former company appealed.

OPINION BY JACKSON, J.

. . . The Waterman Steamship Corporation urges that review of the problems involved in establishing foreign air routes are of no more international delicacy or strategic importance than those involved in routes for water carriage. It says, "It is submitted that there is no basic difference between the conduct of the foreign commerce of the United States by air or by sea." From this premise it reasons that we should interpret this statute to follow the pattern of judicial review adopted in relation to orders affecting foreign commerce by rail. . . .

We find no indication that the Congress either entertained or fostered the narrow concept that air-borne commerce is a mere outgrowth or overgrowth of surface-bound transport. Of course, air transportation, water transportation, rail transportation, and motor transportation all have a kinship in that all are forms of transportation and their common features of public carriage for hire may be amenable to kindred regulations. But these resemblances must not blind us to the fact that legally, as well as literally, air commerce, whether at home or abroad, soared into a different realm than any that had gone before. . . . We see no reason why the efforts of the Congress to foster and regulate development of a revolutionary commerce that operates in three dimensions should be judicially circumscribed with analogies taken over from two-dimensional transit.

The "public interest" that enters into awards of routes for aerial carriers, who in effect obtain also a sponsorship by our government in foreign ventures, is not confined to adequacy of transportation service, as we have held when that term is applied to railroads. . . . That aerial navigation routes and bases should be prudently correlated with facilities and plans for our own national defenses and raise new problems in conduct of foreign relations, is a fact of common knowledge. Congressional hearings and debates extending over several sessions and departmental studies of many years show that the legislative and administrative processes have proceeded in full recognition of these facts.

. . . But when a foreign carrier seeks to engage in public carriage over the territory or waters of this country, or any carrier seeks the sponsorship of the Government to engage in overseas or foreign air transportation, Congress has completely inverted the usual administrative process. Instead of acting independently of executive control, the agency is then subordinated to it. Instead of its order serving as a final disposition of the application, its force is exhausted when it serves as a recommendation to the President. Instead of being handed down to the parties as the conclusion of the administrative process, it must be submitted to the President, before publication even can take place. Nor is the President's control of the ultimate decision a mere right of veto. It is not alone issuance of such authorizations that are subject to his approval, but denial, transfer, amendment, cancellation or suspension, as well. And likewise subject to his approval are the terms, conditions and limitations of the order. Thus, Presidential control is not limited to a negative but is a positive and detailed control over the Board's decisions, unparalleled in the history of American administrative bodies.

Congress may of course delegate very large grants of its power over foreign commerce to the President. . . . The President also possesses in his own right certain powers conferred by the Constitution on him as Commander-in-Chief and as the Nation's organ in foreign affairs. For present purposes, the order draws vitality from either or both sources. Legislative and Executive powers are pooled obviously to the end that commercial strategic and diplomatic interests of the country may be coordinated and advanced without collision or deadlock between agencies.

These considerations seem controlling on the question whether the Board's action on overseas and foreign air transportation applications by citizens are subject to revision or overthrow by the courts.

. . . The court below considered, and we think quite rightly, that it could not review such provisions of the order as resulted from Presidential direction. The President, both as Commander-in-Chief and as the Nation's organ for foreign affairs, has available intelligence services whose reports are not and ought not to be published to the world. It would be intolerable that courts, without the relevant information, should review and perhaps nullify actions of the Executive taken on information properly held secret. Nor can courts sit in camera in order to be taken into executive confidences. But even if courts could require full disclosure, the very nature of executive decisions as to foreign policy is political, not judicial. Such decisions are wholly confided by our Constitution to the political departments of the government, Executive and Legislative. They are delicate, complex, and involve large elements of prophecy. They are and should be undertaken only by those directly responsible to the people whose welfare they advance or imperil. They are decisions of a kind for which the Judiciary has neither aptitude, facilities nor responsibility and which has long been held to belong in the domain of political power not subject to judicial intrusion or inquiry. . . . We therefore agree that whatever of this order emanates from the President is not susceptible of review by the Judicial Department.

The court below thought that this disability could be overcome by regarding the Board as a regulatory agent of Congress to pass on such matters as the fitness, willingness and ability of the applicant, and that the Board's own determination of these matters is subject to review. . . . The legal incongruity of interposing judicial review between the action by the Board and that by the President are as great as the practical disadvantages. The latter arise chiefly from the inevitable delay and obstruction in the midst of the administrative proceedings. The former arises from the fact that until the President acts there is no final administrative determination to review. The statute would hardly have forbidden publication before submission if it had contemplated interposition of the courts at this intermediate stage. Nor could it have expected the courts to stay the President's hand after submission while they deliberate on the inchoate determination. The difficulty is manifest in this case. Review could not be sought until the order was made available, and at that time it had ceased to be merely the Board's tentative decision and had become one finalized by Presidential discretion.

**Until the decision of the Board has Presidential approval, it grants no privilege and denies no right. It can give nothing and can**

take nothing away from the applicant or a competitor. It may be a step, which if erroneous will mature into a prejudicial result, as an order fixing valuations in a rate proceeding may foreshow and compel a prejudicial rate order. But administrative orders are not reviewable unless and until they impose an obligation, deny a right or fix some legal relationship as a consummation of the administrative process. . . . The dilemma faced by those who demand judicial review of the Board's order is that before Presidential approval it is not a final determination even of the Board's ultimate action, and after Presidential approval the whole order, both in what is approved without change as well as in amendments which he directs, derives its vitality from the exercies of unreviewable Presidential discretion.

. . . We conclude that orders of the Board as to certificates for overseas or foreign air transportation are not mature and are therefore not susceptible of judicial review at any time before they are finalized by Presidential approval. After such approval has been given, the final orders embody Presidential discretion as to political matters beyond the competence of the courts to adjudicate.

## Questions for Discussion

1. Is the review of administrative action affected by the conclusion that the matter before the administrator did not involve a "case" or a "controversy?"

2. (a) What difference does it make if the action of the Court is "administrative" or "judicial"? (b) Could an act of Congress eliminate this difference with respect to the United States Supreme Court? (c) What effect would such a law have on the volume of the work of the Court?

3. (a) What is the maximum extent to which judicial review of administrative action may go and still retain its judicial character? (b) How was this scope defined in the *Nelson Brothers* case?

4. Is a question of law or fact presented when an administrator's finding of fact is challenged as being made without regard to the evidence?

5. When a court reviews the action of an administrator, does it, if it disagrees with him, enter such order as it believes the administrator should have entered?

6. What is meant by the negative order doctrine in the field of judicial review of administrative action? Appraise its value.

7. Why does the statute considered in *United States* v. *Interstate Commerce Commission* provide the alternative procedures discussed in that case?

8. What is the attitude of the Supreme Court to the allowance of a review when there is no express statutory provision either allowing or prohibiting review?

9. Did the Court in the *Moog* case consider possible economic harm that would be caused the regulated corporation by the order entered by the administrator?

10. Does the extent of judicial review vary directly or inversely with the amount of discretion given the administrator?

11. Is there any correlation between the extent of an administrator's rule-making authority and the extent of his discretion?

12. In *Houston* v. *St. Louis Independent Packing Company,* was the Court confronted with an administrative determination of a question of law or a question of fact?

13. In *Houston* v. *St. Louis Independent Packing Company,* did the Court base its decision on the existence of administrative discretion to make the decision involved or on the basis that the evidence before the administrator supported his action without regard to the existence of discretion?

14. What is the constitutional basis for the regulation involved in the *Central Roig Refining Company* case?

15. (a) To what extent does the Court examine the facts in the *Central Roig Refining Company* case? (b) Did the Court require the administrator to convince the Court of the wisdom of his regulation?

16. Is it constitutional for an administrator to provide that his regulations shall operate only in certain areas or zones?

17. (a) How does the Court classify the question of determining whether particular printed matter is a "magazine" within the law relating to postal rates? (b) Does it present a question of law, a question of fact, or a mixed question?

18. Is the scope of review influenced by considering the effect of the decision upon the administrator? upon the Court?

19. What is the basis of the Court's decision in the *Payne* case?

20. Does the decision in the *Payne* case ignore the distinction between questions of law, questions of fact, and mixed questions of law and fact?

21. To what extent is the decision in the *Chicago & Southern Airlines* case based on the following:

(a) The grant of discretion to the President.
(b) The President's knowledge of the subject superior to the Court's knowledge.
(c) The necessity for giving the executive a free hand in foreign affairs.
(d) Administrative necessity or convenience.

22. By the decision in the *Chicago & Southern Airline* case, to what extent is review of the administrator's action possible?

23. Discuss the basis for the decision in *United States* v. *George S. Bush & Co.* To what extent is it based upon:
   (a) The fact that the regulation was made by the President.
   (b) The view that a tariff law is not a regulation of existing individual property right.
   (c) The view that the Court will not inquire whether the facts existed which justified the President in exercising the power delegated to him.

24. Were the Commission and the President in the *Bush* case exercising a legislative or a judicial function in determining whether a tariff increase was desirable?

25. What was the question of statutory interpretation involved in *National Broadcasting Co.* v. *United States*?

26. May the Court consider the history of the business regulated in interpreting the statute giving the administrator authority to regulate the business?

27. Is an administrator limited to the adoption of rules regulating matters that are expressly authorized by the statute giving him authority?

28. Can a party raise in the courts the question of the wisdom of the regulations or rules adopted by an administrator?

29. Does the fact that the order of the administrator causes economic loss to the party regulated by the order show that there has been arbitrary action or an abuse of discretion by the administrator so as to justify a reversal of his action by a court?

30. In *National Broadcasting Company* v. *United States,* the Court in stating the scope of review of rules promulgated by the Federal Communications Commission stated: "Our duty is at an end when we find that the action of the Commission was based upon findings supported by evidence, and was made pursuant to authority granted by Congress." Is this in accord with the attitude of the Court in *United States* v. *George S. Bush & Co.*? Explain.

31. In *National Broadcasting Company* v. *United States,* how does the Court dispose of the argument that the regulations imposed by the Commission deprived the applicants for radio station licenses of freedom of speech?

32. (a) Describe the five evils that the Federal Communications Commission sought to eliminate by the chain broadcasting regulations considered in *National Broadcasting Company* v. *United States.* (b) Did the Communications Act of 1934 expressly authorize the Commission to make regulations with respect to such practices? (c) On what basis did the Court find that such regulations were justified?

33. Why does the Court require a party to exhaust his administrative remedy before granting him judicial relief?

34. Must a party exhaust his administrative remedy in every case before the Court will consider his claim?

35. In connection with the doctrine of the exhaustion of the administrative remedy, (a) does it make any difference whether the administrator is created by the same government that created the court in which the review of the administrator's action is sought? (b) is the rule applied more or less strictly when review of a state administrator is sought in a federal court?

36. To what extent is the applicability of the exhaustion of remedies rule affected by the adequacy of the hearing in the administrative stage?

37. Will the reviewing court pass upon the adequacy of an administrative remedy if the party has not availed himself of it?

38. (a) May an administrator be authorized to refuse an application for a license where the applicant has been guilty of a crime? (b) Is it necessary that the crime have some relation to the subject matter of the license? (c) Does it make any difference if the applicant has not been tried for the crime of which he is accused? (d) Does it make any difference if he has been tried but acquitted?

39. The courts have changed their point of view from one of extreme suspicion of the decisions of all administrative bodies to the point of view that they will not intervene and disturb the action of an administrative body unless it is manifest that there has been an abuse of power or a manifestly wrong decision. (a) Discuss this statement and give illustrations for or against its truth. (b) Is such a trend desirable? (c) What effect does such a trend have on society, democratic government, business, and the administrative commission?

## Chapter 34

# SCOPE OF REVIEW OF ADMINISTRATOR'S ACTION

## § 34:1. Review of Findings of Fact

If the administrator holds a judicial, as distinguished from a legislative, hearing, the customary statutory practice is to put down on paper all evidence offered at the hearing. Today, this is generally done by a stenographer who typewrites or has printed a transcript of the notes taken at the hearing. If a review of the action of the administrator is permitted, this transcript or copy of the testimony or evidence is then available for examination by the reviewing court. This places before the court not only the findings or conclusions made by the administrator, but also the basis on which he reached them.

The modern trend is for the reviewing court to examine the record to see if there is evidence that it believes would warrant the finding made by the administrator. If the findings of fact of the administrator are supported by evidence, the conclusions of the administrator will not be disturbed. As an illustration, in a case under the National Labor Relations Act in which the issue is whether an employee was unlawfully discharged, there may be some witnesses who testified that the discharge was based on the employee's carelessness, while others testified that it was because of the employer's discrimination against the employee's union activities. Faced with this conflict of testimony, the administrator must make a decision. Whichever way he decides in the case just stated, his findings of fact will not be set aside by a reviewing court. The court ordinarily will not examine the record to determine whether it would have agreed with the conclusion of fact of the administrator. In the instant case, should the administrator decide that the employee was discharged because of union membership, the reviewing court would sustain his decision since there was testimony in the record that if believed would justify this conclusion. The reviewing court would also sustain the decision if the administrator decided that the employee was discharged because of his own fault, since there is testimony in the record that would also support that conclusion.

By way of comparison, if all the testimony was that the worker was discharged because of his carelessness but the administrator found that he was discharged because of his union activities, the reviewing court would set this finding aside, since there is no evidence in the record to support it.

Under the general rule as above stated, the reviewing court only goes as far as determining whether the findings of fact of the administrator are supported by evidence or testimony. The reviewing court will not examine conflicting testimony to determine whether it would have agreed with the administrator, nor will it substitute its own opinion for his.

As a matter of linguistics or terminology, the issue is partly clouded by the fact that the courts speak of the issue of whether findings of fact are supported by evidence as being a question of law.

### *(a) Credibility of witnesses*

NATIONAL LABOR RELATIONS BOARD v. PITTSBURGH STEAMSHIP CO.
337 U.S. 656 (1949)

The National Labor Relations Board ordered an employer to cease and desist from specified unfair labor practices. The Court of Appeals refused to enforce this order on the ground that it was invalidated by the prejudice of the board's trial examiner as shown by the fact that he believed the witnesses of the board and disbelieved the employer's witnesses.

OPINION BY RUTLEDGE, J.

. . . We are constrained to reject the court's conclusion that an objective finder of fact would not resolve all factual conflicts arising in a legal proceeding in favor of one litigant. The ordinary law suit . . . normally depends for its resolution on which version of the facts in dispute is accepted by the trier of fact. . . . In the determination of litigated facts, the testimony of one who has been found unreliable as to one issue may properly be accorded little weight as to the next. Accordingly, total rejection of an opposed view cannot of itself impugn the integrity or competence of a trier of fact. . . . "The fact . . . that Examiner and Board uniformally credited the Board's witnesses and as uniformally discredited those of the respondent, though the Board's witnesses were few and the respondent's witnesses were many, would not furnish a basis for a finding by us that such a bias or partiality existed and therefore the hearings were unfair. . . ."

. . . Indeed, careful scrutiny of the record belies the view that the trial examiner did in fact believe all union testimony or that he even believed the union version of every disputed factual issue. Rather, the printed transcript suggests thoughtful and evaluating discrimination of the facts.

### *(b) Substantiation of findings of fact*

UNIVERSAL CAMERA CORPORATION v. NATIONAL LABOR RELATIONS BOARD

340 U.S. 474 (1951)

The National Labor Relations Board found that the Universal Camera Corporation had committed an unfair labor practice in dismissing an employee for having testified against it in proceedings before the Board. The Corporation appealed to the Court of Appeals, claiming that there was not "substantial evidence" in the record to support the finding of the Board.

OPINION BY FRANKFURTER, J.

The Wagner Act provided: "The findings of the Board as to the facts, if supported by evidence, shall be conclusive." . . . This Court read "evidence" to mean "substantial evidence," . . . and we said that "[s]ubstantial evidence . . . means such relevant evidence as a reasonable mind might accept as adequate to support a conclusion." . . . Accordingly, it "must do more than create a suspicion of the existence of the fact to be established, . . . it must be enough to justify, if the trial were to a jury, a refusal to direct a verdict when the conclusion sought to be drawn from it is one of fact for the jury." . . .

. . . The phrasing of this Court's process of review readily lent itself to the notion that it was enough that the evidence supporting the Board's result was "substantial" when considered by itself. . . . By imperceptible steps regard for the fact-finding function of the Board led to the assumption that the requirements of the Wagner Act were met when the reviewing court could find in the record evidence which, when viewed in isolation, substantiated the Board's findings. . . . This is not to say that every member of this Court was consciously guided by this view or that the Court ever explicitly avowed this practice as doctrine. What matters is that the belief justifiably arose that the Court had so constructed the obligation to review.

Criticism of so contracted a reviewing power reinforced dissatisfaction felt in various quarters with the Board's administration of the Wagner Act in the years preceding the war. . . . [In 1947 the Wagner Act was amended by the Taft-Hartley Act.] . . . We hold that the standard of proof specifically required of the Labor Board by the Taft-Hartley Act is the same as that to be exacted by courts reviewing every administrative action subject to the Administrative Procedure Act.

Whether or not it was ever permissible for courts to determine the substantiality of evidence supporting a Labor Board decision merely on the basis of evidence which in and of itself justified it, without taking into account contradictory evidence or evidence from which conflicting inferences could be drawn, the new legislation definitively precludes such a theory of review and bars its practice. The substantiality of evidence must take into account whatever in the record fairly detracts from its weight. . . .

To be sure, the requirement for canvassing "the whole record" in order to ascertain substantiality does not furnish a calculus of value by which a reviewing court can assess the evidence. Nor was it intended to negative the function of the Labor Board as one of those agencies presumably equipped or informed by experience to deal with a specialized field of knowledge, whose findings within that field carry the authority of an expertness which courts do not possess and therefore must respect. Nor does it mean that even as to matters not requiring expertise a court may displace the Board's choice between two fairly conflicting views, even though the court would justifiably have made a different choice had the matter been before it *de novo.* Congress has merely made it clear that a reviewing court is not barred from setting aside a Board decision when it cannot conscientiously find that the evidence supporting that decision is substantial, when viewed in the light that the record in its entirety furnishes, including the body of evidence opposed to the Board's view.

We conclude, therefore, that the Administrative Procedure Act and the Taft-Hartley Act direct that courts must now assume more responsibility for the reasonableness and fairness of Labor Board decisions than some courts have shown in the past. Reviewing courts must be influenced by a feeling that they are not to abdicate the conventional judicial function. Congress has imposed on them responsibility for assuring that the Board keeps within reasonable grounds. That responsibility is not less real because it is limited to enforcing the requirement that evidence appear substantial when viewed, on the record as a whole, by courts invested with the authority and enjoying the prestige of the Courts of Appeals. The Board's findings are entitled to respect; but they must nonetheless be set aside when the record before a Court of Appeals clearly precludes the Board's decision from being justified by a fair estimate of the worth of the testimony of witnesses or its informed judgment on matters within its special competence or both. . . .

Our power to review the correctness of application of the present standard ought seldom to be called into action. Whether on the record as a whole there is substantial evidence to support agency findings is a question which Congress has placed in the keeping of the Courts of Appeals. This Court will intervene only in what ought to be the rare instance when the standard appears to have been misapprehended or grossly misapplied. . . .

The decision of the Court of Appeals is assailed on [the] ground . . . that the court erred in holding that it was barred from taking into account the report of the examiner on questions of fact insofar as that report was rejected by the Board. . . .

The Court of Appeals deemed itself bound by the Board's rejection of the examiner's findings because the court considered these findings not "as unassailable as a master's." . . . They are not. Section 10 (c) of the Labor Management Relations Act provides that "If upon the preponderance of the testimony taken the Board shall be of the opinion that any person named in the complaint has engaged in or is engaging in any such unfair labor practice, then the Board shall state its findings of fact. . . ." . . . The responsibility for decision thus placed on the Board is wholly inconsistent with the notion that it has power to reverse an examiner's findings only when they are "clearly erroneous." . . .

We are aware that to give the examiner's findings less finality than a master's and yet entitle them to consideration in striking the account, is to introduce another and an unruly factor into the judgmatical process of review. But we ought not to fashion an exclusionary rule merely to reduce the number of imponderables to be considered by reviewing courts.

The Taft-Hartley Act provides that "The findings of the Board with respect to questions of fact if supported by substantial evidence on the record considered as a whole shall be conclusive." . . . Surely an examiner's report is as much a part of the record as the complaint or the testimony. According to the Administrative Procedure Act, "All decisions (including initial, recommended, or tentative decisions) shall become a part of the record. . . ." We found that this Act's provision for judicial review has the same meaning as that in the Taft-Hartley Act. The similarity of the two statutes in language and purpose also requires that the definition of "record" found in the Administrative Procedure Act be construed to be applicable as well to the term "record" as used in the Taft-Hartley Act.

It is therefore difficult to escape the conclusion that the plain language of the statutes directs a reviewing court to determine the substantiality of evidence on the record including the examiner's report. . . . Nothing suggests that reviewing courts should not give to the examiner's report such probative force as it intrinsically commands. To the contrary, § 11 of the Administrative Procedure Act contains detailed provisions designed to maintain high standards of independence and competence in examiners. Section 10(c) of the Labor Management Relations Act requires that examiners "shall issue . . . a proposed report, together with a recommended order." Both statutes thus evince a purpose to increase the importance of the role of examiners in the administrative process. High standards of public administration counsel that we attribute to the Labor Board's examiners both due regard for the responsibility which Congress imposes on them and the competence to discharge it. . . .

We do not require that the examiner's findings be given more weight than in reason and in the light of judicial experience they deserve. The "substantial evidence" standard is not modified in any way when the Board and its examiner disagree. We intend only to recognize that evidence supporting a conclusion may be less substantial when an impartial, experienced examiner who has observed the witnesses and lived with the case has drawn conclusions different from the Board's than when he has reached the same conclusion. The findings of the examiner are to be considered along with the consistency and inherent probability of testimony. The significance of his report, of course, depends largely on the importance of credibility in the particular case. To give it this significance does not seem to us materially more difficult than to heed the other factors which in sum determine whether evidence is "substantial." . . .

We therefore remand the cause to the Court of Appeals. On reconsideration of the record it should accord the findings of the trial examiner the relevance that they reasonably command in answering the comprehensive question whether the evidence supporting the Board's order is substantial. But the court need not limit its reexamination of the case to the effect of that report on its decision. We leave it free to grant or deny enforcement as it thinks the principles expressed in this opinion dictate.

## § 34:2. Review of Jurisdictional Facts

In every action or proceeding, there is some procedural step that must be taken or some preliminary fact that must exist in order to permit the court or the administrator to hear and to determine the particular case. The existence of this basic or jurisdictional fact is essential to the power of the court or the administrator to act. If the fact does not exist, the proceeding is a nullity and may be ignored or attacked in any other proceeding.

### *(a) Jurisdictional and quasi-jurisdictional facts*

NOBLE v. UNION RIVER LOGGING CO.
147 U.S. 165 (1893)

OPINION BY BROWN, J.

. . . It is true that in every proceeding of a judicial nature, there are one or more facts which are strictly jurisdictional, the existence of which is necessary to the validity of the proceedings, and without which the act of the court is a mere nullity; such, for example, as the service of process within the state upon the defendant in a common law action . . . ; the seizure and possession of the res within the bailiwick in a proceeding in rem . . . ; a publication in strict accordance with the statute, where the property of an absent defendent is sought to be charged. . . . So, if the court . . . condemns as lawful prize a vessel that was never captured . . . ; or the Land Department issues a patent for land which has already been reserved or granted to another person, the act is not voidable merely but void. In these and similar cases the action of the court or officer fails for want of jurisdiction over the person or subject matter. The proceeding is a nullity, and its invalidity may be shown in a collateral proceeding.

There is, however, another class of facts which are termed quasi jurisdictional, which are necessary to be alleged and proved in order to set the machinery of the law in motion, but which, when properly alleged and established to the satisfaction of the court, cannot be attacked collaterally. With respect to these facts, the finding of the court is as conclusively presumed to be correct as is its finding with respect to any other issue before the parties. Examples of these are the allegations and proof of the requisite diversity of citizenship, or the amount in controversy in a Federal court, which, when found by such court, cannot be questioned collaterally . . . ; the existence and amount of the debt of a petitioning debtor in an involuntary bankruptcy . . . ; the fact that there is insufficient personal property to pay the debts of a decedent, when application is made to sell his real estate . . . ; the fact that one of the heirs of an estate had reached his majority, when the act provided that the estate should not be sold if all the heirs were minors . . .; and others of a kindred nature, where the want of jurisdiction does not go to the subject matter or the parties, but a preliminary fact necessary to be proven to authorize the court to act. . . . In this class of cases . . . even if the court be imposed upon by false testimony, its finding can only be impeached in a proceeding instituted directly for that purpose. . . .

This distinction has been taken by a large number of cases in this court, in which the validity of land patents has been attacked collaterally, and it has always been held that the existence of lands subject to be patented was the only necessary pre-requisite to a valid patent. . . .

Upon the other hand, if the patent be for lands which the Land Department had authority to convey, but it was imposed upon, or was induced by false representations to issue a patent, the finding of the department upon such facts cannot be collaterally impeached, and the patent can only be avoided by proceedings taken for that purpose. . . . The action of the Secretary of the Interior identifying swamp lands, making lists thereof and issuing patents therefor, could not be impeached in an action at law by showing that the lands which the patent conveyed were not in fact swamp and overflowed lands, although his jurisdiction extended only to lands of that class. . . .

### § 34:3. Expansion of the Review of Jurisdictional Facts

For a brief period it seemed that the concept of "jurisdictional fact" would be expanded to permit a broader review of questions of fact. The Supreme Court indicated that, wherever the authority of a federal administrator to grant the relief sought depended on a question of fact, a broader review of the finding of that fact was required. Specifically it was held that the reviewing court was not bound by the record of evidence presented before the administrator but must hold an independent hearing of its own and hear all the evidence again insofar as it related to the jurisdictional facts.

This doctrine of granting a hearing *de novo* has been severely criticised and has not been further applied by the Supreme Court. It is doubtful whether it is still the law even on the very facts of the case, although a few lower Federal courts have followed the case or applied its doctrine. The case is of importance, however, as setting forth the principles affecting the determination of the problem of the extent to which facts found by the administrator should be subject to judicial review.

### *(a) Review de novo*

CROWELL v. BENSON
285 U.S. 22 (1932)

An injunction action was brought in the federal district court to enjoin carrying out an award of compensation made under the Federal Longshoremen's and Harbor Workers' Compensation Act. The objection to the award was based on the claim that the person to whom the compensation was awarded was not at the time of his injury acting as employee of the employer ordered to pay the compensation, and was not employed upon navigable waters of the United States, and was therefore not within the jurisdiction of the federal compensation statute.

OPINION BY HUGHES, C. J.

. . . The act has two limitations that are fundamental. It deals exclusively with compensation in respect of disability or death resulting "from an injury occurring upon the navigable waters of the United States" if recovery "through workmen's compensation proceedings may not validly be provided by State law," and it applies only when the relation of master and servant exists. . . .

. . . The contention under the due process clause of the Fifth Amendment relates to the determination of questions of fact. Rulings of the deputy commissioner upon questions of law are without finality. So far as the latter are concerned, full opportunity is afforded for their determination by the federal courts through proceedings to suspend or to set aside a compensation order . . . by the requirement that judgment is to be entered on a supplementary order declaring default only in case the order follows the law . . . and by the provision that the issue of injunction or other process in a proceeding by a beneficiary to compel obedience to a compensation order is dependent upon a determination by the court that the order was lawfully made and served. . . . Moreover, the statute contains no express limitation attempting to preclude the court, in proceedings to set aside an order as not in accordance with law, from making its own examination and determination of facts whenever that is deemed to be necessary to enforce a constitutional right properly asserted. . . .

Apart from cases involving constitutional rights to be appropriately enforced by proceedings in court, there can be no doubt that the Act contemplates that, as to questions of fact arising with respect to injuries to employees within the purview of the Act, the findings of the deputy commissioner, supported by evidence and within the scope of his authority, shall be final. To hold otherwise would be to defeat the obvious purpose of the legislation to furnish a prompt, continuous, expert, and inexpensive method for dealing with a class of questions of fact which are peculiarly suited to examination and determination by an administrative agency specially assigned to that task. The object is to secure within the prescribed limits of the employer's liability an immediate investigation and a sound practical judgment, and the efficacy of the plan depends upon the finality of the determinations of fact with respect to the circumstances, nature, extent, and consequences of the employee's injuries and the amount of compensation that should be awarded. And this finality may also be regarded as extending to the determination of the question of fact whether the injury "was occasioned solely by the intoxication of the employee or by the willful intention of the employee to injure or kill himself or another." While the exclusion of compensation in such case is found in what are called "coverage" provisions of the Act, the question of fact still belongs to the contemplated routine of administration, for the case is one of employment within the scope of the Act and the cause of the injury sustained by the employee as well as its character and effect must be ascertained by applying the provisions for compensation. The use of the administrative method for these purposes, assuming due notice, proper opportunity to be heard, and that findings are based upon evidence, falls easily within the principle of the decisions sustaining similar procedure against objections under the due process clauses of the Fifth and Fourteenth Amendments.

. . . What has been said thus far relates to the determination of claims of employees within the purview of the Act. A different question is presented where the determinations of fact are fundamental or "jurisdictional," in the sense that their existence is a condition precedent to the operation of the statutory scheme. These fundamental requirements are that the injury occurs upon the navigable waters of the United States, and that the relation of master and servant exists. These conditions are indispensable to the application of the statute, not only because the Congress has so provided explicitly . . . but also because the power of the Congress to enact the legislation turns upon the existence of these conditions.

In amending and revising the maritime law, the Congress cannot reach beyond the constitutional limits which are inherent in the admiralty and maritime jurisdiction. Unless the injuries to which the Act relates occur upon the navigable waters of the United States, they fall outside that jurisdiction. . . . If the person injured was not an employee of the person sought to be held, or if the injury did not occur upon the navigable waters of the United States, there is no ground for an assertion that the person against whom the proceeding was directed could constitutionally be subjected, in the absence of fault upon his part, to the liability which the statute creates.

In relation to these basic facts, the question is not the ordinary one as to the propriety of provision for administrative determinations. Nor have we simply the question of due process in relation to notice and hearing. It is rather a question of the appropriate maintenance of the Federal judicial power in requiring the observance of constitutional restrictions. It is the question whether the Congress may substitute for constitutional courts, in which the judicial power of the United States is vested, an administrative agency—in this instance a single deputy commissioner—for the final determination of the existence of the facts upon which the enforcement of the constitutional rights of the citizen depend. The recognition of the utility and convenience of administrative agencies for the investigation and finding of facts within their proper province, and the support of their authorized action, does not require the conclusion that there is no limitation of their use, and that the Congress could completely oust the courts of all determinations of fact by vesting the authority to make them with finality in its own instrumentalities or in the

Executive department. That would be to sap the judicial power as it exists under the Federal Constitution, and to establish a government of a bureaucratic character alien to our system, wherever fundamental rights depend, as not infrequently they do depend, upon the facts, and finality as to facts becomes in effect finality in law.

. . . The Congress has not expressly provided that the determinations by the deputy commissioner of the fundamental or jurisdictional facts as to the locality of the injury and the existence of the relation of master and servant shall be final. The finality of such determinations of the deputy commissioner is predicated primarily upon the provision . . . that he "shall have full power and authority to hear and determine all questions in respect of such claim." But "such claim" is the claim for compensation under the Act and by its explicit provisions is that of an "employee," as defined in the Act, against his "employer." The fact of employment is an essential condition precedent to the right to make the claim. The other provision upon which the argument rests is that which authorizes the federal court to set aside a compensation order if it is "not in accordance with law." . . . In the absence of any provision as to the finality of the determination by the deputy commissioner of the jurisdictional fact of employment, the statute is open to the construction that the court in determining whether a compensation order is in accordance with law may determine the fact of employment which underlies the operation of the statute. And, to remove the question as to validity, we think that the statute should be so construed. . . .

Assuming that the federal court may determine for itself the existence of these fundamental or jurisdictional facts, we come to the question,—Upon what record is the determination to be made? There is no provision of the statute which seeks to confine the court in such a case to the record before the deputy commissioner or to the evidence which he has taken. The remedy which the statute makes available is not by an appeal or by a writ of certiorari for a review of his determination upon the record before him. The remedy is "through injunction proceedings mandatory or otherwise." . . . The question in the instant case is not whether the deputy commissioner has acted improperly or arbitrarily as shown by the record of his proceedings in the course of administration in cases contemplated by the statute, but whether he has acted in a case to which the statute is inapplicable. By providing for injunction proceedings, the Congress evidently contemplated a suit as in equity, and in such a suit the complaint would have full opportunity to plead and prove either that the injury did not occur upon the navigable waters of the United States or that the relation of master and servant did not exist, and hence that the case lay outside the purview of the statute. As the question is one of the constitutional authority of the deputy commissioner as an administrative agency, the court is under no obligation to give weight to his proceedings pending the determination of that question. If the court finds that the facts existed which gave the deputy commissioner jurisdiction to pass upon the claim for compensation, the injunction will be denied in so far as these fundamental questions are concerned; if, on the contrary, the court is satisfied that the deputy commissioner had no jurisdiction of the proceedings before him, that determination will deprive them of their effectiveness for any purpose. We think that the essential independence of the exercise of the judicial power of the United States, in the enforcement of constitutional rights requires that the Federal court should determine such an issue upon its own record and the facts elicited before it. . . .

It cannot be regarded as an impairment of the intended efficiency of an administrative agency that it is confined to its proper sphere, but it may be observed that the instances which permit of a challenge to the application of the statute, upon the grounds we have stated, appear to be few. Out of the many thousands of cases which have been brought before the deputy commissioners throughout the country, a review by the courts has been sought in only a small number, and an inconsiderable proportion of these appear to have involved the question whether the injury occurred within the maritime jurisdiction or whether the relation of employment existed.

We are of the opinion that the District Court did not err in permitting a trial de novo on the issue of employment. Upon that issue the witnesses who had testified before the deputy commissioner and other witnesses were heard by the District Court. The writ of certiorari was not granted to review the particular facts but to pass upon the question of principle. With respect to the facts, the two courts below are in accord, and we find no reason to disturb their decision.

. . .

Dissenting Opinion by Brandeis, J.

Knudsen filed a claim against Benson under . . . the Longshoremen's and Harbor Workers' Compensation Act. . . . Benson's answer denied, among other things, that the relation of employer and employee existed between him and the claimant. The evidence introduced before the deputy commissioner, which occupies 78 pages of the printed record, was directed largely to that issue and was conflicting. The deputy commissioner found that the claimant was in Benson's employ at the time of the injury, and filed an order for compensation. . . . Benson brought this proceeding . . . to set aside the order. The district judge transferred the suit to the admiralty side of the court and held a trial de novo, refusing to consider upon any aspect of the case the record before the deputy commissioner. On the evidence introduced in court, he found that the relation of employer and employee did not exist, and entered a decree setting aside the compensation order. . . . The Circuit Court of Appeals affirmed the decree. . . . This Court granted certiorari. . . . In my opinion, the decree should be reversed, because Congress did not authorize a trial de novo.

. . . The courts below held that the respondent was entitled to a trial de novo; that all the evidence introduced before the deputy commissioner should go for naught; and that respondent should have the privilege of presenting new, and even entirely different, evidence in the District Court. . . .

*First.* The initial question is one of construction of the Longshoremen's Act. The act does not in terms declare whether there may be a trial de novo either as to the issue whether the relation of employer and employee existed at the time of the injury, or as to any other issue, tried or triable, before the deputy commissioner. It provides . . . that "the deputy commissioner shall have full power and authority to hear and determine all questions in respect of" a claim; . . . that the compensation order made by the deputy commissioner "shall become effective" when filed in his office, and, "unless proceedings for the suspension or setting aside of such order are instituted as provided in [a] subdivision (b) of this section, shall become final . . . "; and . . . that, "If not in accordance with law, a compensation order may be suspended or set aside, in whole or in part, through injunction proceedings . . . instituted in the Federal district court. . . ."

The phrase . . . providing that the order may be set aside "if not in accordance with law" was adopted from the statutory provision, enacted by the same Congress, for review by the Circuit Courts of Appeals of decisions of the Board of Tax Appeals. This Court has settled that the phrase as used in the tax statute means a review upon the record made before the Board. . . . The Compensation Commission has consistently construed the Longshoremen's Act as providing for finality of the deputy commissioner's findings on all questions of fact; and care has been taken to provide for formal hearings appropriate to that intention. . . . The lower federal courts, except in the case at bar, have uniformly construed the act as denying a trial de novo of any issue determined by the deputy commissioner; have held that, in respect to those issues, the review afforded must be held upon the record made before the deputy commissioner; and that the deputy commissioner's findings of fact must be accepted as conclusive if supported by evidence, unless there was some irregularity in the proceeding before him. Nearly all the state courts have construed the state workmen's compensation laws, as limiting the judicial review to matters of law. Provisions in other federal statutes, similar to those here in question, creating various administrative tribunals, have likewise been treated as not conferring the right to a judicial trial de novo.

The safeguards with which Congress has surrounded the proceedings before the deputy commissioner would be without meaning if those proceedings were to serve merely as an inquiry preliminary to a contest in the courts. Specific provisions of the Longshoremen's Act make clear that it was the aim of Congress to expedite the relief afforded. . . . Procedure of this character, instead of expediting relief, would entail useless expense and delay if the proceedings before the deputy commissioner were to be repeated in court, and the case tried from the beginning, at the option of either party. The conclusion that Congress did not so intend is confirmed by reference to the legislative history of the Act. . . .

*Second.* Nothing in the statute warrants the construction that the right to a trial de novo which Congress has concededly denied as to most issues of fact determined by the deputy commissioner has been granted in respect to the issue of the existence of the employer-employee relation. The language which is held sufficient to forclose the right to such a trial on some issues forecloses it as to all. . . . Congress expressly declared its intention to put, for purposes of review, all the issues of fact on the same basis, by conferring upon the deputy commissioner "full power to hear and determine all questions in respect of such claim," subject only to the power of the court to set aside his order "if not in accordance with law."

The suggestion that "such claim" may be construed to mean only a claim within the purview of the Act seems to me without substance. Logically applied, the suggestion would leave the deputy commissioner powerless to hear or determine any issue of asserted non-liability under the Act. For non-existence of the employer-employee relation is only one of many grounds of non-liability. Thus, there is no liability if the injury was occasioned solely by the intoxication of the employee; or if the injury was due to the willful intention of the employee to injure or kill himself or another; or if it did not arise "out of or in the course of employment"; or if the employer was not engaged in maritime employment in whole or in part; or if the injured person was the employee of a subcontractor who has secured payment of compensation; or if the proceeding is brought against the wrong person as employer; or if the disability or death is that of a master or a member of the crew of any vessel; or if it is that of a person engaged by the master to load or unload or repair any small vessel under eighteen tons net; or if it is that of an officer or employee of the United States or any agency thereof; or if it is that of an officer or employee of any state, or foreign government, or any political subdivision thereof; or if recovery for the disability or death through workmen's compensation proceedings may be validly provided by state law. And obviously there is no liability if there was in fact neither disability nor death. It is not reasonable to suppose that Congress intended to set up a fact-finding tribunal of first instance, shorn of power to find a portion of the facts required for any decision of the case; or that, in enacting legislation designed to withdraw from litigation the great bulk of maritime accidents, it contemplated a procedure whereby the same facts must be twice litigated before a longshoreman could be assured the benefits of compensation. . . .

. . . On bills in equity to set aside orders of a federal administrative board there is no trial de novo of issues of fact. . . .

*Fourth.* Trial de novo of the issue of the existence of the employer-employee relation is not required by the due process clause. That clause ordinarily does not even require that parties shall be permitted to have a judicial tribunal pass upon the weight of the evidence introduced before the administrative body. . . . The findings of fact of the deputy commissioner, the Court now decides, are conclusive as to most issues, if supported by evidence. Yet as to the issue of employment the Court holds, not only that such findings may not be declared final, but that it would create a serious constitutional doubt to construe the Act as committing to the deputy commissioner the simple function of collecting the evidence upon which the court will ultimately decide the issue.

It is suggested that this exception is required as to issues of fact involving claims of constitutional right. For reasons which I shall later discuss, I cannot believe that the issue of employment is one of constitutional right. But even assuming it to be so, the conclusion does not follow that trial of the issue must therefore be upon a record made in the district court. That the function of collecting evidence may be committed to an administrative tribunal is settled by a host of cases, and supported by persuasive analogies, none of which justify a distinction between issues of constitutional right and any others. . . . The holding that the difference between the procedure prescribed by the Longshoremen's Act and these historic methods of hearing evidence transcends the limits of congressional power when applied to the issue of the existence of a relation of employment, as distinguished from that of the circumstances of an injury or the existence of a relation of dependency, seems to me without foundation in reality. Certainly there is no difference to the litigant. . . .

*Fifth.* Trial de novo of the existence of the employer-employee relation is not required by the Judiciary Article of the Constitution. The mere fact that the act deals only with injuries arising on navigable waters, and that independently of legislation such injuries can be redressed only in courts of admiralty, obviously does not preclude Congress from denying a trial de novo. For the Court holds that it is compatible with the grant of power under Article III to deny a trial de novo as to most of the facts upon which rest the allowance of a claim and the amount of compensation. Its holding that the Constitution requires a trial de novo of the issue of the employer-employee relation is based on the relation which that fact bears to the statutory scheme propounded by Congress, and to the constitutional authority under which the Act was passed. The argument is that existence of the relation of employer and employee is, as a matter of substantive law, indispensable to the application of the statute, because the power of Congress to enact the legislation turns upon its existence; and that whenever the question of constitutional power depends upon an issue of fact that issue must, as a matter of procedure, be determinable independently upon evidence freshly introduced in a court. Neither proposition seems to me well founded. . . .

*Sixth.* Even if the constitutional power of Congress to provide compensation is limited to cases in which the employer-employee relation exists, I see no basis for a contention that the denial of the right to a trial de novo upon the issue of employment is in any manner subversive of the independence of the federal judicial power. Nothing in the Constitution, or in any prior decision of this Court to which attention has been called, lends support to the doctrine that a judicial finding of any fact involved in any civil proceeding to enforce a pecuniary liability may not be made upon evidence introduced before a properly constituted administrative tribunal, or that a determination so made may not be deemed an independent judicial determination. Congress has repeatedly exercised authority to confer upon the tribunals which it creates, be they administrative bodies or courts of limited jurisdiction, the power to receive evidence concerning the facts upon which the exercise of federal power must be predicated, and to determine whether those facts exist. The power of Congress to provide by legislation for liability under certain circumstances subsumes the power to provide for the determination of the existence of those circumstances. It does not depend upon the absolute existence in reality of any fact.

It is true that, so far as Knudsen is concerned, proof of the existence of the employer-employee relation is essential to recovery under the act. But under the definition laid down in *Noble* v. *Union River Logging R. Co.*, . . . that fact is not jurisdictional. It is quasi-jurisdictional. The existence of a relation of employment is a question going to the applicability of the substantive law, not to the jurisdiction of the tribunal. Jurisdiction is the power to adjudicate between the parties concerning the subject-matter. . . . Obviously, the deputy commissioner had not only the power but the duty to determine whether the employer-employee relation existed. When a duly constituted tribunal has jurisdiction of the parties and of the subject-matter, that jurisdiction is not impaired by errors, however grave, in applying the substantive law. . . . This is true of tribunals of special as well as of general jurisdiction. It is true of administrative, as well as of judicial, tribunals. If errors in the application of law may not be made the basis of collateral attack upon the decision of an administrative tribunal, once that decision has become final, no "jurisdictional" defect can compel the independent re-examination in court, upon direct review, of the facts affecting such applicability. . . .

*Eighth.* No good reason is suggested why all the evidence which Benson presented to the district court in this case could not have been presented before the deputy commissioner; nor why he should have been permitted to try his case provisionally before the administrative tribunal, and then to retry it in the district court upon additional evidence theretofore withheld. To permit him to do so violates the salutary principle that administrative remedies must first be exhausted before resorting to the court, imposes unnecessary and burdensome expense upon the other party and cripples the effective administration of the Act. Under the prevailing practice, by which the judicial review has been confined to questions of law, the proceedings before the deputy commissioners have proved for the most part noncontroversial; and relatively few cases have reached the courts. To permit a contest de novo in the district court of an issue tried, or triable, before the deputy commissioner will, I fear, gravely hamper the effective administration of the Act. The prestige of the deputy commissioner will necessarily be lessened by the opportunity of relitigating facts in the courts. The number of controverted cases may be largely increased. Persistence in controversy will be encouraged. And since the advantage of prolonged litigation lies with the party able to bear heavy expenses, the purpose of the act will be in part defeated.

### § 34:4. Review of Constitutional Facts

For a time, the scope of review of findings of fact was broadened with respect to the issue of confiscation. When the rates of a railroad or other utility were set at a figure that did not permit the business to earn a fair return on its capital, the objection could be raised by the utility that the fixing of the rate at that level amounted to a taking of its property or a confiscation to the extent that it prevented it from earning a fair return on that property.

Whether such confiscation existed was deemed a question of fact; but unlike other determinations of fact, it was not sufficient that the record contained evidence from which the administrator could have found that the rate fixed by him was reasonable and proper. In such a case, the utility was entitled to have the court examine the record of the proceedings before the administrator and reach its own independent conclusion on the basis of that record if it disagreed with the conclusion of the administrator. This broader review was justified by the Supreme Court on the theory that not an ordinary fact but a constitutional fact was involved.

The court could not consider evidence not in the record, nor could it hear additional witnesses; instead it was required to examine the record or the transcript of the evidence before the administrator and redecide the case if it did not agree with his conclusions.

While the court would thus interpose its own conclusion, the complainant was required to prove clearly to the satisfaction of the court that the administrative finding should be set aside.

Since in a broad sense one has a constitutional right to be free from any erroneous administrative or judicial determination, it is illogical to single out one particular factual determination and accord to it a greater review. Moreover, the burden imposed upon the courts defeats to some extent the object of creating an administrator to relieve the other branches of the government of the burden of being an expert in the field involved. The doctrine of the Ben Avon Borough case was gradually abandoned until finally the court adopted the "substantial evidence" standard of review on the issue of confiscation.[1] The basis for the Ben Avon Borough case was further undermined when the Supreme Court later held that ratemaking was merely "one species of price fixing," and therefore gave no ground for complaint because like other applications of the police power the value of the property was reduced.[2] The Ben Avon Borough case has not, however, been expressly overruled by the Supreme Court and is still followed in some states.

### *(a) Independent judgment of court on the record*

OHIO VALLEY WATER CO. v. BEN AVON BOROUGH
253 U.S. 287 (1920)

The Public Service Commission of Pennsylvania found that the value of the company's property was $924,744 and ordered the reduction of the company's rates to 7% of that sum over and above operating expenses and depreciation. The company claimed that the valuation was too low and that the use of this undervalued figure in determining the rates deprived it of its property without due process of law.

On appeal, the Superior Court of Pennsylvania, on examining the record, re-appraised the property at $1,324,621.80 and directed the Commission to authorize rates that would yield 7% of that sum.

---

1 Federal Power Commission v. Natural Gas Pipeline Co., 315 U.S. 575 (1942).

2 Federal Power Commission v. Hope Natural Gas Co., 320 U.S. 591 (1944). This rejects the concept of Smyth v. Ames, 169 U.S. 466 (1898), in which it had been held that the property of a carrier was confiscated contrary to due process of law if it were not permitted to earn a fair return on its investment. Since the Ben Avon Borough case was designed to protect the right created by the Smyth case, the rejection of the Smyth case eliminated the need for the Ben Avon Borough doctrine.

The Supreme Court of Pennsylvania reversed the Superior Court and reinstated the decree of the Commission on the ground that there was competent evidence tending to sustain the Commission's conclusions and that, as there was no abuse of discretion, the Superior Court should not have interfered with the order of the Commission for the purpose of substituting its own judgment as to the valuation to be placed on the property of the company.

OPINION BY MCREYNOLDS, J. . . .

Looking at the entire opinion we are compelled to conclude that the [state] Supreme Court interpreted the statute as withholding from the courts power to determine the question of confiscation according to their own independent judgment when the action of the Commission comes to be considered on appeal.

The order here involved prescribed a complete schedule of maximum future rates and was legislative in character. . . . In all such cases, if the owner claims confiscation of his property will result, the state must provide a fair opportunity for submitting that issue to a judicial tribunal for determination upon its own independent judgment as to both law and facts; otherwise the order is void because in conflict with the due process clause, Fourteenth Amendment. . . .

Here the insistence is that the Public Service Company Law as construed and applied by the Supreme Court has deprived plaintiff in error of the right to be so heard; and this is true if the appeal therein specifically provided is the only clearly authorized proceeding where the Commission's order may be challenged because confiscatory. Thus far plaintiff in error has not succeeded in obtaining the review for which the Fourteenth Amendment requires the state to provide.

Article VI, Public Service Company Law of Pennsylvania . . . :

"Section 31. No injunction shall issue modifying, suspending, staying or annulling any order of the commission, or of a commissioner, except upon notice to the commission and after cause shown upon a hearing. The court of common pleas of Dauphin county is hereby clothed with exclusive jurisdiction throughout the commonwealth of all proceedings for such injunctions, subject to an appeal to the Supreme Court as aforesaid. Whenever the commission shall make any rule, regulation, finding, determination, or order under the provisions of this act the same shall be and remain conclusive upon all parties affected thereby, unless set aside, annulled, or modified in an appeal or proceeding taken as provided in this act."

It is argued that this section makes adequate provision for testing judicially any order by the Commission when alleged to be confiscatory, and that plaintiff in error has failed to take advantage of the opportunity so provided.

. . . We are unable to say that § 31 offered an opportunity to test the order so clear and definite that plaintiff in error was obliged to proceed thereunder or suffer loss of rights guaranteed by the Federal Constitution. On the contrary, after specifying that within 30 days an appeal may be taken to the Superior Court (§ 17), the act provides (§ 22): "At the hearing of the appeal the court shall, upon the record certified to it by the commission, determine whether or not the order appealed from is reasonable and in conformity with law." But for the opinion of the Supreme Court in the present cause, this would seem to empower the Superior Court judicially to hear and determine all objections to an order on appeal and to make its jurisdiction in respect thereto exclusive. Of this the latter court apparently entertained no doubt; and certainly counsel did not fatally err by adopting that view, whatever meaning finally may be attributed to § 31.

Without doubt the duties of the courts upon appeals under the act are judicial in character—not legislative. . . . This is not disputed; but their jurisdiction, as ruled by the Supreme Court, stopped short of what must be plainly intrusted to some court in order that there may be due process of law.

Plaintiff in error has not had proper opportunity for an adequate judicial hearing as to confiscation; and unless such an opportunity is now available, and can be definitely indicated by the court below in the exercise of its power finally to construe laws of the state (including of course § 31), the challenged order is invalid.

. . .

## § 34:5. Review of Conclusions of Law

Unlike the narrow review of findings of fact permitted in most cases, the administrator's findings or conclusions of law are subject to a full review. If the reviewing court disagrees with him on the law, his action is reversed without regard to whether there is any authority that could be urged in support of his conclusion.

No distinction is made as to whether the question of law affects the jurisdiction of the administrator or the constitutional rights of the parties. All questions of law are given the same broad review.

### *(a) Employees subject to statute*

UNITED STATES v. AMERICAN TRUCKING ASSOCIATIONS
310 U.S. 534 (1940)

The Motor Carrier Act of 1935 authorized the Interstate Commerce Commission to fix the "qualifications and maximum hours of service of employees." The Fair Labor Standards Act established maximum hours for employees in interstate commerce or in industries producing goods for interstate commerce. The Interstate Commerce Commission concluded that the authorization of the Motor Carrier Act should be limited to those employees engaged in activities affecting the safety of operations. It was claimed that the Commission had jurisdiction as to all employees whether they were engaged in actual transport operations or not. The Court relies on the legislative history and administrative interpretation in reaching its conclusion.

OPINION BY REED, J.

. . . The difficulty and wide scope of the problems raised by the growth of the motor carrier industry were obvious. Congress sought to set out its purpose and the range of its action in a declaration of policy which covered the preservation and fostering of motor transportation in the public interest, tariffs, the coordination of motor carriage with other forms of transportation and cooperation with the several states in their efforts to systematize the industry.

While efficient and economical movement in interstate commerce is obviously a major objective of the Act, there are numerous provisions which make it clear that Congress intended to exercise its powers in the non-transportation phases of motor carrier activity. Safety of operation was constantly before the committees and Congress in their study of the situation.

The pertinent portions of the section of the Act immediately under discussion read as follows:

"Sec. 204(a). It shall be the duty of the Commission—

"(1) To regulate common carriers by motor vehicle as provided in this part, and to that end the Commission may establish reasonable requirements with respect to continuous and adequate service, transportation of baggage and express, uniform systems of accounts, records, and reports, preservation of records, qualifications and maximum hours of service of employees, and safety of operation and equipment.

"(2) To regulate contract carriers by motor vehicle as provided in this part, and to that end the Commission may establish reasonable requirements with respect to uniform systems of accounts, records, and reports, preservation of records, qualifications and maximum hours of service of employees, and safety of operation and equipment.

"(3) To establish for private carriers of property by motor vehicle, if need therefor is found, reasonable requirements to promote safety of operation, and to that end prescribe qualifications and maximum hours of service of employees, and standards of equipment. . . ."

Shortly after the approval of the Act, the Commission on its own motion undertook to and did fix maximum hours of service for "employees whose functions in the operation of motor vehicles make such regulations desirable because of safety considerations." A few months after this determination, the Fair Labor Standards Act was enacted. Section 7 of this act limits the work week at the normal rate of pay of all employees subject to its terms and Section 18 makes the maximum hours of the Fair Labor Standards Act subject to further reduction by applicable federal or state law or municipal ordinances. There were certain employees excepted, however, from these regulations by Section 13(b). It reads as follows:

"Sec. 13 . . . (b) The provisions of section 7 shall not apply with respect to (1) any employee with respect to whom the Interstate Commerce Commission has power to establish qualifications and maximum hours of service pursuant to the provisions of section 204 of the Motor Carrier Act, 1935; . . ."

This exemption brought sharply into focus the coverage of employees by Motor Carrier Act, Section 204(a). Clerical, storage and other non-transportation workers are under this or the Fair Labor Standards Act, dependent upon the sweep of the word employee in this act. The Commission again examined the question of its jurisdiction and in Ex parte No. Mc-28 again reached the conclusion that its power under "section 204(a) (1) and (2) is limited to prescribing qualifications and maximum hours of service for those employees . . . whose activities affect the safety of operation." It added: "The provisions of section 202 evince a clear intent of Congress to limit our jurisdiction to regulating the motor-carrier industry as a part of the transportation system of the nation. To extend that regulation to features which are not characteristic of transportation nor inherent in that industry strikes us as an enlargement of our jurisdiction unwarranted by any express or implied provision in the act, which vests in us all the powers we have." The Wage and Hour Division of the Department of Labor arrived at the same result in an interpretation.

Shortly thereafter appellees, an association of truckmen and various common carriers by motor, filed a petition with the Commission in the present case seeking an exercise of the Commission's jurisdiction under Section 204(a) to fix reasonable requirements "with respect to qualifications and maximum hours of service of all employees of common and contract carriers, except employees whose duties are related to safety of operations; . . . to disregard its report and order in Ex parte MC-28." The Commission reaffirmed its position and denied the petition. . . .

In the broad domain of social legislation few problems are enmeshed with the difficulties that surround a determination of what qualifications an employee shall have and how long his hours of work may be. Upon the proper adjustment of these factors within an industry and in relation to competitive activities may well depend the economic success of the enterprises affected as well as the employment and efficiency of the workers. The Motor Carrier Act lays little emphasis upon the clause we are called upon now to construe, "qualifications and maximum hours of service of employees." None of the words are defined by the Section, 203, devoted to the explanation of the meaning of the words used in the Act. They are a part of an elaborate enactment drawn and passed in an attempt to adjust a new and growing transportation service to the needs of the public. To find their content, they must be viewed in their setting.

In the interpretation of statutes, the function of the courts is easily stated. It is to construe the language so as to give effect to the intent of Congress. There is no invariable rule for the discovery of that intention. To take a few words from their context and with them thus isolated to attempt to determine their meaning, certainly would not contribute greatly to the discovery of the purpose of the draftsmen of a statute, particularly in a law drawn to meet many needs of a major occupation.

There is, of course, no more persuasive evidence of the purpose of a statute than the words by which the legislature undertook to give expression to its wishes. Often these words are sufficient in and of themselves to determine the purpose of the legislation. In such cases we have followed their plain meaning. When that meaning has led to absurd or futile results, however, this Court has looked beyond the words to the purpose of the act. Frequently, however, even when the plain meaning did not produce absurd results but merely an unreasonable one "plainly at variance with the policy of the legislation as a whole" this Court has followed that purpose, rather than the literal words. When aid to construction of the meaning of words, as used in the statute, is available, there certainly can be no "rule of law" which forbids its use, however clear the words may appear on "superficial examination." The interpretation of the meaning of statutes, as applied to justiciable controversies, is exclusively a judicial function. This duty requires one body of public servants, the judges, to construe the meaning of what another body, the legislators, has said. Obviously there is danger that the courts' conclusion as to legislative purpose will be unconsciously influenced by the judges' own views or by factors not considered by the enacting body. A lively appreciation of the danger is the best assurance of escape from its threat but hardly justifies an acceptance of a literal interpretation dogma which withholds from the courts available information for reaching a correct conclusion. Emphasis should be laid, too, upon the necessity for appraisal of the purposes as a whole of Congress in analyzing the meaning of clauses or sections of general acts. A few words of general connotation appearing in the text of statutes should not be given a wide meaning, contrary to a settled policy, "excepting as a different purpose is plainly shown."

The language here under consideration, if construed as appellees contend, gives to the Commission a power of regulation as to qualifications and hours of employees quite distinct from the settled practice of Congress. That policy has been consistent in legislating for such regulation of transportation employees in matters of movement and safety only. The Hours of Service Act imposes restrictions on the hours of labor of employees "actually engaged in or connected with the movement of any train." The Seamen's Act limits employee regulations under it to members of ships' crews. The Civil Aeronautics Authority has authority over hours of service of employees "in the interest of safety." It is stated by appellants in their brief with detailed citations, and the statement is uncontradicted, that at the time of the passage of the Motor Vehicle Act "forty states had regulatory measures relating to the hours of service of employees" and every one "applied exclusively to drivers or helpers on the vehicles." In the face of this course of legislation, coupled with the supporting interpretation of the two administrative agencies concerned with its interpretation, the Interstate Commerce Commission and the Wage and Hour Division, it cannot be said that the word "employee" as used in Section 204(a) is so clear as to the workmen it embraces that we would accept its broadest meaning. The word . . . frequently is carefully defined by the statute where it appears.

We are especially hesitant to conclude that Congress intended to grant the Commission other than the customary power to secure safety in view of the absence in the legislative history of the Act of any discussion of the desirability of giving the Commission broad and unusual powers over all employees. The clause in question was not contained in the bill as introduced. Nor was it in the Coordinator's draft. It was presented on the Senate Floor as a committee amendment following a suggestion of the Chairman of the Legislative Committee of the Commission, Mr. McManamy. The committee reports and the debates contain no indication that a regulation of the qualifications and hours of service of all employees was contemplated; in fact the evidence points the other way. The Senate Committee's report explained the provisions . . . as giving the Commission authority over common and contract carriers similar to that given over private carriers. . . . The Chairman of the Senate Committee expressed the same thought while explaining the provisions on the floor of the Senate. When suggesting the addition of the clause, the Chairman of the Commission's Legislative Committee said: ". . . it relates to safety." In the House the member in charge of the bill characterized the provisions as tending "greatly to promote careful operation for safety on the highways," and spoke with assurance of the Commission's ability to "formulate a set of reasonable rules . . . including therein maximum labor-hours service on the highway." And in the report of the House Committee a member set out separate views criticizing the delegation of discretion to the Commission and proposing an amendment providing for an eight-hour day for "any employee engaged in the operation of such motor vehicle."

The Commission and the Wage and Hour Division, as we have said, have both interpreted Section 204(a) as relating solely to safety of operation. In any case such interpretations are entitled to great weight. This is peculiarly true here where the interpretations involve "contemporaneous construction of a statute by the men charged with the responsibility of setting its machinery in motion; of making the parts work efficiently and smoothly while they are yet untried and new." Furthermore, the Commission's interpretation gains much persuasiveness from the fact that it was the Commission which suggested the provisions' enactment to Congress.

It is important to remember that the Commission has three times concluded that its authority was limited to securing safety of operation. The first interpretation was made on December 29, 1937, when the Commission stated: ". . . until the Congress shall have given us a more particular and definite command in the premises, we shall limit our regulations concerning maximum hours of service to those employees whose functions in the operation of motor vehicles make such regulations desirable because of safety considerations." This expression was half a year old when Congress enacted the Fair Labor Standards Act with the exemption of Section 13(b) (1). Seemingly the Senate at least was aware of the Commission's investigation of its powers even before its interpretation was announced. Under the circumstances it is unlikely indeed that Congress would not have explicitly overruled the Commission's interpretation had it intended to exempt others than employees who affected safety from the Labor Standards Act. . . . Our conclusion . . . is that "employees" . . . is limited to those . . . whose activities affect the safety of operation. . . .

### *(b) Wages for purpose of statute*

SOCIAL SECURITY BOARD v. NIEROTKO

327 U.S. 358 (1946)

The National Labor Relations Board may order the reinstatement of an improperly discharged employee and direct that the employer pay him the "back pay" that he lost during the period of his wrongful discharge. The benefits obtained under another statute, the Social Security Act, are affected by the amount of wages received by an employee. In this case, the question arose whether the back pay awarded by the National Labor Relations Board should be regarded as "wages" for the purpose of the Social Security Act and whether the employee should be regarded as having been employed during the period from the date of his wrongful discharge until his reinstatement under the order of the board.

OPINION BY REED, J. . . .

The respondent, Joseph Nierotko, was found by the National Labor Relations Board to have been wrongfully discharged for union activity by his employer, the Ford Motor Company, and was reinstated by that Board in his employment with directions for "back pay" for the period February 2, 1937, to September 25, 1939. The "back pay" was paid by the employer on July 18, 1941. Thereafter

Nierotko requested the Social Security Board to credit him in the sum of the "back pay" on his Old Age and Survivor's Insurance account with the Board. In conformity with its minute of formal general action of March 27, 1942, the Board refused to credit Nierotko's "back pay" as wages. . . .

Wages are the basis for the administration of federal old age benefits. . . . Only those who earn wages are eligible for benefits. The periods of time during which wages were earned are important and may be crucial on eligibility under either the original act or the Amendments of 1939. . . . The benefits are financed by payments from employees and employers which are calculated on wages. The Act defines "wages" for Old Age benefits as follows:

"Sec. 210. When used in this title—

"(a) The term 'wages' means all remuneration for employment, including the cash value of all remuneration paid in any medium other than cash, . . ."

Employment is defined thus: "(b) The term 'employment' means any service, of whatever nature, performed within the United States by an employee for his employer, except—."

The tax titles of the Social Security Act have identical definitions of wages and employment. An employee under the Social Security Act is not specifically defined but the individual to whom the Act's benefits are to be paid is one receiving "wages" for "employment" in accordance with § 210(c) and employment is service by an "employee" to an "employer." Obviously a sharply defined line between payments to employees which are wages and which are not is essential to proper administration.

Under the National Labor Relations Act an employee is described as "any individual whose work has ceased . . . because of any unfair labor practice.". . . The enforcement provisions of this Act under which Nierotko received his "back pay" allow the Labor Board to reinstate "employees with or without back pay." § 10(c). The purpose of the "back pay" allowance is to effectuate the policies of the Labor Act for the preservation of industrial peace.

The purpose of the federal old age benefits of the Social Security Act is to provide funds through contributions by employer and employee for the decent support of elderly workmen who have ceased to labor. Eligibility for these benefits and their amount depends upon the total wages which the employee has received and the periods in which wages were paid. While the legislative history of the Social Security Act and its amendments or the language of the enactments themselves do not specifically deal with whether or not "back pay" under the Labor Act is to be treated as wages under the Social Security Act, we think it plain that an individual, who is an employee under the Labor Act and who receives "back pay" for a period of time during which he was wrongfully separated from his job, is entitled to have that award of back pay treated as wages under the Social Security Act definitions which define wages as "remuneration for employment" and employment as "any service . . . performed . . . by an employee for his employer."

Surely the "back pay" is "remuneration." Under Section 10(c) of the Labor Act, the Labor Board acts for the public to vindicate the prohibitions of the Labor Act against unfair labor practices . . . and to protect the right of employees to self-organization which is declared by section 7. It is also true that in requiring reparation to the employee through "back pay" that reparation is based upon the loss of wages which the employee has suffered from the employer's wrong. "Back pay" is not a fine or penalty imposed upon the employer by the Board. Reinstatement and "back pay" are for the "protection of the employees and the redress of their grievances" to make them "whole." . . . A worker is not given "back pay" by the Board equal to what he would have earned with the employer but for the unlawful discharge but is given that sum less any net earnings during the time between discharge and reinstatement.

Since Nierotko remained an employee under the definition of the Labor Act, although his employer had attempted to terminate the relationship, he had "employment" under that Act and we need further only consider whether under the Social Security Act its definition of employment, as "any service . . . performed by an employee for his employer," covers what Nierotko did for the Ford Motor Company. The petitioner urges that Nierotko did not perform any service. It points out that Congress in considering the Social Security Act thought of benefits as related to "wages earned" for "work done." We are unable, however, to follow the Social Security Board in such a limited circumscription of the word "service." The very words "any service . . . performed . . . for his employer," with the purpose of the Social Security Act in mind import breadth of coverage. They admonish us against holding that "service" can be only productive activity. We think that "service" as used by Congress in this definitive phrase means not only work actually done but the entire employer-employee relationship for which compensation is paid to the employee by the employer.

An argument against the interpretation which we give to "service performed" is the contrary ruling of the governmental agencies which are charged with the administration of the Social Security Act. Their competence and experience in this field command us to reflect before we decide contrary to their conclusion. The first administrative determination was apparently made in 1939 by an Office Decision of the Bureau of Internal Revenue on the problem of whether "back pay" under a Labor Board order was wages subject to tax under Titles VIII and IX of the Social Security Act which the Bureau collects. The back pay was held not to be subject as wages to the tax because no service was performed, the employer had tried to terminate the employment relationship and the allowance of back pay was discretionary with the Labor Board. . . . This position is maintained by the Social Security Board by minute of March 27, 1942. It is followed by the National Labor Relations Board which at one time approved the retention by the employer of the tax on the employees' back pay for transmission to the Treasury Department as a tax on wages and later reversed its position on the authority of the Office Decision to which reference has just been made. . . .

The Office Decision seems to us unsound. . . . there is nothing . . . which supports the idea that the "back pay" award differs from other pay. . . .

But it is urged by petitioner that the administrative construction on the question of whether "back pay" is to be treated as wages should lead us to follow the agencies' determination. There is a suggestion that the administrative decision should be treated as conclusive. . . .

The Social Security Board and the Treasury were compelled to decide, administratively, whether or not to treat "back pay" as wages and their expert judgment is entitled, as we have said, to great weight. . . . however, . . . such decisions are only conclusive as to properly supported findings of fact. . . . Administrative determinations must have a basis in law and must be within the granted authority. Administration, when it interprets a statute so as to make it apply to particular circumstances, acts as a delegate to the legislative power. Congress might have declared that "back pay" awards under the Labor Act should or should not be treated as wages. Congress might have delegated to the Social Security Board to determine what compensation paid by employers to employees should be treated as wages. Except as such interpretive power may be included in the agencies' administrative functions, Congress did neither. An agency may not finally decide the limits of its statutory power. That is a judicial function. Congress used a well understood word—"wages"—to indicate the receipts which were to govern taxes and benefits under the Social Security Act. There may be borderline payments to employees on which courts would follow administrative determination as to whether such payments were or were not wages under the act.

We conclude, however, that the Board's interpretation of this statute to exclude back pay goes beyond the boundaries of administrative routine and the statutory limits. This is a ruling which excludes from the ambit of the Social Security Act payments which we think were included by Congress. It is beyond the permissible limits of administrative interpretation.

Petitioner further questions the validity of the decision of the circuit court of appeals on the ground that it must be inferred from the opinion that the "back pay" must be allocated as wages by the Board to the "calendar quarters" of the year in which the money would have been earned, if the employee had not been wrongfully discharged. . . .

. . . We have no doubt that it should be allocated to the periods when the regular wages were not paid as usual. Admittedly there are accounting difficulties which the Board will be called upon to solve but we do not believe they are insuperable.

### *(c) Division of joint carrier rates*

THE NEW ENGLAND DIVISIONS CASE
261 U.S. 184 (1923)

The Interstate Commerce Commission adopted a regulation for the division of joint rates of carriers. The action of the Commission was challenged as exceeding its authority.

OPINION BY BRANDEIS, J.

Transportation Act 1920 . . . authorizes the Commission, upon complaint or upon its own initiative, to prescribe, after full hearing, the divisions of joint rates among carriers parties to the rate. In determining the divisions, the Commission is directed to give due consideration, among other things, to the importance to the public of the transportation service rendered by the several carriers; to their revenues, taxes, and operating expenses; to the efficiency with which the carriers concerned are operated; to the amount required to pay a fair return on their railway property; to the fact whether a particular carrier is an original, intermediate, or delivering line; and to any other fact which would, ordinarily, without regard to the mileage haul, entitle one carrier to a greater or less proportion than another of the joint rate.

Invoking this power of the Commission, the railroads of New England instituted, in August, 1920, proceedings to secure for themselves larger divisions from the freight moving between that section and the rest of the United States. . . . The Commission . . . made an order . . . which directed, in substance, that the divisions, or shares, of the several New England railroads in the joint through freight rates be increased 15 per cent. . . . Since it did not increase any rate, it necessarily reduced the aggregate amounts receivable from each rate by carriers operating west of Hudson river. . . . It was to continue in force only until further order of the Commission. And it left the door open for correction upon application of any carrier in respect to any rate.

Prior to the effective date of that order, there was in force between each of the New England carriers and substantially each of the railroads operating west of the Hudson, a series of contracts providing for the division of all joint class rates upon the basis of stated percentages. These agreements were in the form of express contracts. Section 208(b) of Transportation Act of 1920 provided that all divisions of joint rates in effect at the time of its passage should continue in force until thereafter changed either by mutual agreement between the interested carriers or by state or federal authorities. The second report enjoined upon all parties the necessity for proceeding, as expeditiously as possible, with a revision of divisions upon a more logical and systematic basis, made specific suggestions as to the character of the study to be pursued, and invited carriers to present to the Commission any cases of inability to agree upon such revision. No further application was, however, made to the Commission.

In March, 1922, this suit was commenced in the federal court . . . to enjoin enforcement of the order and to have it set aside as void.

. . . It is contended that the order is void, because its purpose was not to establish divisions just, reasonable, and equitable, as between connecting carriers, but, in the public interest, to relieve the financial needs of the New England lines, so as to keep them in effective operation. The argument is that Congress did not authorize the Commission to exercise its power to accomplish that purpose. An order, regular on its face, may, of course, be set aside if made to accomplish a purpose not authorized. . . . But the order here assailed is not subject to that infirmity.

Transportation Act 1920, introduced into the federal legislation a new railroad policy. . . . Theretofore, the effort of Congress had been directed mainly to the prevention of abuses, particularly those arising from excessive or discriminatory rates. The 1920 act sought to insure, also, adequate transportation service. . . .

. . . It was necessary to avoid unduly burdensome rate increases and yet secure revenues adequate to satisfy the needs of the weak carriers. To accomplish this two new devices were adopted: the group system of rate making and the division of joint rates in the public interest. Through the former, weak roads were to be helped by recapture from prosperous competitors of surplus revenues. Through the latter, the weak were to be helped by preventing needed revenue from passing to prosperous connections. Thus, by marshaling the revenues, partly through capital account, it was planned to distribute augmented earnings, largely in proportion to the carrier's needs. This, it was hoped, would enable the whole transportation system to be maintained, without raising unduly any rate on any line. The provision concerning divisions was, therefore, an integral part of the machinery for distributing the funds expected to be raised by the new rate-fixing sections. It was, indeed, indispensable.

Raising joint rates for the benefit of the weak carriers might be the only feasible method of obtaining currently the needed revenues. Local rates might already be so high that a further increase would kill the local traffic. The through joint rates might be so low that they could be raised without proving burdensome. On the other hand the revenues of connecting carriers might be ample; so that any increase of their earnings from joint rates would be unjustifiable. Where the through traffic would, under those circumstances, bear an increase of the joint rates, it might be proper to raise them, and give to the weak line the whole of the resulting increase in revenue. That, to some extent, may have been the situation in New England, when, in 1920, the Commission was confronted with the duty, under the new section 15a, of raising rates so as to yield a return of substantially 6 per cent. on the value of the property used in the transportation service. . . .

The deficiency in income of the New England lines in 1920 was so great that (even before the raise in wages ordered by the Railroad Labor Board) an increase in freight revenues of 47.40 per cent. was estimated to be necessary to secure to them a fair return. On a like estimate, the increased revenues required to give the same return to carriers in Trunk Line Territory was only 29.76 per cent and to carriers in Central Freight Association Territory 24.31 per cent. To have raised the additional revenues needed by the New England lines wholly by raising the rates within New England—particularly when rates west of the Hudson were raised much less—might have killed New England traffic. Rates there had already been subjected (besides the three general increases mentioned above) to a special increase, applicable only to New England, of about 10 per cent. in 1918. . . . A further large increase in rates local to New England would, doubtless, have provoked more serious competition from auto trucks and water carriers. For hauls are short and the ocean is near. Instead of erecting New England into a separate rate group, the Commission placed it, with the other two subdivisions of Official Classification Territory, into the Eastern Group, and ordered that freight rates in that group be raised 40 per cent. At that rate level the revenues of the carriers in Trunk Line and Central Freight Association territories would, it was asserted, exceed by 1.48 per cent. what they would have received if they had been a separate group. It was estimated that the excess would be about $25,000,000. Substantially that amount (besides the additional revenue to be raised otherwise) was said to be necessary to meet the needs of the New England lines.

Plaintiffs insist . . . that the power conferred upon the Commission is co-extensive only with the duty imposed on the carriers by § 400 of Transportation Act 1920, which declares that they shall establish "in case of joint rates . . . just, reasonable, and equitable divisions thereof as between the carriers subject to this act participating therein which shall not unduly prefer or prejudice any of such participating carriers.". . .

. . . It is contended that if the act be construed as authorizing such apportionment of a joint rate on the basis of the greater needs of particular carriers it is unconstitutional. There is no claim that the apportionment results in confiscatory rates, nor is there in this record any basis for such a contention. The argument is that the division of a joint rate is essentially a partition of property; that the rate must be divided on the basis of the services rendered by the several carriers; that there is no difference between taking part of one's just share of a joint rate and taking from a carrier part of the cash in its treasury; and, thus, that apportionment according to needs is a taking of property without due process. But the argument begs the question. What is its just share? It is the amount properly apportioned out of the joint rate. That amount is to be determined, not by an agreement of the parties or by mileage. It is to be fixed by the Commission; fixed at what that board finds to be just, reasonable, and equitable. Cost of the service is one of the elements in rate making. It may be just to give the prosperous carrier a smaller proportion of the increased rate than of the original rate. Whether the rate is reasonable may depend largely upon the disposition which is to be made of the revenues derived therefrom.

. . . It is asserted that the order is necessarily based upon the theory that, under § 15(6), the Commission has authority to fix divisions as between groups of carriers without considering the carriers individually; that Congress did not confer such authority; and that, hence, the order is void. . . .

. . . Congress intended that a method should be pursued by which the task, which it imposed upon the Commission, could be performed. The number of carriers which might be affected by an order of the Commission, if the power granted were to be exercised fully, might far exceed six hundred; the number of rates involved, many millions. The weak roads were many. The need to be met was urgent. To require specific evidence, and separate adjudication, in respect to each division of each rate of each carrier, would be tantamount to denying the possibility of granting relief. We must assume that Congress knew this; and that it knew, also, that the Commission had been confronted with similar situations in the past and how it had dealt with them.

For many years before the enactment of Transportation Act, 1920, it had been necessary, from time to time, to adjudicate comprehensively upon substantially all rates in a large territory. When such rate changes were applied for, the Commission made them by a single order; and, in large part, on evidence deemed typical of the whole rate structure. This remained a common practice after the burden of proof to show that a proposed increase of any rate was reasonable had been declared, by Act of . . . 1910 . . . to be upon the carrier. Thus, the practice did not have its origin in the group system of rate-making provided for in 1920 by the new § 15(6). It was the actual necessities of procedure and administration which had led to the adoption of that method, in passing upon the reasonableness of proposed rate increases. The necessity of adopting a similar course when multitudes of divisions were to be passed upon was obvious. The method was equally appropriate in such inquiries, and we must assume that Congress intended to confer upon the Commission power to pursue it.

That there is no constitutional obstacle to the adoption of the method pursued is clear. Congress may, consistently with the due process clause, create rebuttable presumptions. . . . and shift the burden of proof. . . . It might, therefore, have declared in terms that, if the Commission finds that evidence introduced is typical of traffic and operating conditions, and of the joint rates and divisions, of the carriers of a group, it may be accepted as *prima facie* evidence bearing upon the proper divisions of each joint rate of every carrier in that group. Congress did so provide, in effect, when it imposed upon the Commission the duty of determining the divisions. For only in that way could the task be performed. . . . Serious injustice to any carrier could be avoided, by availing of the saving clause which allows anyone to except itself from the order, in whole or in part, on proper showing. . . .

## § 34:6. Review of Mixed Questions of Law and Fact

The problem of judicial review of the administrator's findings is further complicated by the classification of certain findings as "mixed questions of law and fact" or "mixed questions." A finding that a businessman has committed a fraudulent practice is both a finding of fact that he has done a fraudulent act and also a finding of law that his conduct is classified as fraudulent. A finding that an employer discharged an employee is at first glance merely a finding of fact, but it is also a finding that the conduct of the employer was such as legally had the effect of severing or terminating the employer-employee relationship. In a very broad sense, virtually every significant finding of fact is also a finding of law.

If the administrator's findings of fact and his findings of law were subject to the same degree of review, no difficulty would arise. The general rule, however, is that his findings of fact will be affirmed if supported by evidence, while his findings of law will be set aside if the court disagrees with them. This difference of the degree of review poses a difficulty when a finding is classified as a mixed finding of law and fact.

As an abstract problem, every question of fact is also a question of law and a mixed question of law and fact. The law generally does recognize this, but it attempts to preserve the artificial and separate compartments of questions of fact, questions of law, and mixed questions. The selection of the particular compartment is to a large extent based on precedent, judicial tradition, and whether the particular question is material to the disposition of the issues involved.

### *(a) Review of tax court decisions*

DOBSON v. COMMISSIONER OF INTERNAL REVENUE
320 U.S. 489 (1943)

The taxpayer purchased stock, part of which he sold in later years. Thereafter the taxpayer learned that the stock was issued in violation of a state blue sky law and began an action against the seller on the ground of fraud. The action was compromised and a sum paid the taxpayer. The Commissioner of Internal Revenue claimed that the portion of the settlement payment which could be charged to the shares already sold by the taxpayer must be included in his tax as taxable income.

OPINION BY JACKSON, J. . . .

With the 1926 Revenue Act, Congress promulgated, and at all times since has maintained, a limitation on the power of courts to review Board of Tax Appeals (now the Tax Court) determinations. ". . . such courts shall have power to affirm or, if the decision of the Board is not in accordance with law, to modify or to reverse the decision of the Board. . . ."

It is more difficult to maintain sharp separation of court and administrative functions in tax than in other fields. One reason . . . why courts have deferred less to the Tax Court than to other administrative tribunals is the manner in which the Tax Court finality was introduced into the law.

The courts have rather strictly observed limitations on their reviewing powers where the limitation came into existence simultaneously with their duty to review administrative action in new fields of regulation. But this was not the history of the tax law. Our modern income tax experience began with the Revenue Act of 1913. The World War soon brought high rates. The law was an innovation, its constitutional aspects were still being debated, interpretation was just beginning, and administrators were inexperienced. The Act provided no administrative review of the Commissioner's determinations. It did not alter the procedure followed under the Civil War income tax by which an aggrieved taxpayer could pay under protest and then sue the Collector to test the correctness of the tax. The courts by force of this situation entertained all manner of tax questions, and precedents rapidly established a pattern of judicial thought and action whereby the assessments of income tax were reviewed without much restraint or limitation. Only after that practice became established did administrative review make its appearance in tax matters.

Administrative machinery to give consideration to the taxpayer's contentions existed in the Bureau of Internal Revenue from about 1918 but it was subordinate to the Commissioner. In 1923, the situation was brought to the attention of Congress by the Secretary of the Treasury, who proposed creation of a Board of Tax Appeals, within the Treasury Department, whose decision was to conclude Government and taxpayer on the question of assessment and leave the taxpayer to pay the tax and then test its validity by suit against the collector. Congress responded by creating the Board of Tax Appeals as "an independent agency in the executive branch of the Government." The Board was to give hearings and notice thereof and "make a report in writing of its findings of fact and decision in each case." But Congress dealt cautiously with finality for the Board's conclusions, going only so far as to provide that in later proceedings the findings should be "prima facie evidence of the facts therein stated." So the Board's decisions first came before the courts under a statute which left them free to go into both fact and law questions. Two years later Congress reviewed and commended the work of the new Board, increased salaries and lengthened the tenure of its members, provided for a direct appeal from the Board's decisions to the circuit courts of appeals or the Court of Appeals of the District of Columbia, and enacted the present provision limiting review to questions of law.

But this restriction upon judicial review of the Board's decisions came only after thirteen years of income tax experience had established a contrary habit. Precedents had accumulated in which courts had laid down many rules of taxation not based on statute but upon their ideas of right accounting or tax practice. It was difficult to shift to a new basis. This Court applied the limitation, but with less emphasis and less forceful resolution of borderline cases in favor of administrative finality than it has employed in reference to other administrative determinations.

That neglect of the congressional instruction is a fortuitous consequence of this evolution of the Tax Court rather than a deliberate or purposeful judicial policy is the more evident when we consider that every reason ever advanced in support of administrative finality applies to the Tax Court.

The court is independent, and its neutrality is not clouded by prosecuting duties. Its procedures assure fair hearings. Its deliberations are evidenced by careful opinions. All guides to judgment available to judges are habitually consulted and respected. It has established a tradition of freedom from bias and pressures. It deals with a subject that is highly specialized and so complex as to be the despair of judges. It is relatively better staffed for its task than is the judiciary. Its members not infrequently bring to their task long legislative or administrative experience in their subject. The volume of tax matters flowing through the Tax Court keeps its members abreast of changing statutes, regulations, and Bureau practices, informed as to the background of controversies and aware of the impact of their decisions on both Treasury and taxpayer. Individual cases are disposed of wholly on records publicly made, in adversary proceedings, and the court has no responsibility for previous handling. Tested by every theoretical and practical reason for administrative finality, no administrative decisions are entitled to higher credit in the courts. Consideration of uniform and expeditious tax administrations require that they be given all credit to which they are entitled under the law.

Tax Court decisions are characterized by substantial uniformity. Appeals fan out into courts of appeal of ten circuits and the District of Columbia. This diversification of appellate authority inevitably produces conflict of decision, even if review is limited to questions of law. But conflicts are multiplied by treating as questions of law what really are disputes over proper accounting. The mere number of such questions and the mass of decisions they call forth become a menace to the certainty and good administration of the law.

To achieve uniformity by resolving such conflicts in the Supreme Court is at best slow, expensive, and unsatisfactory. Students of federal taxation agree that the tax system suffers from delay in getting the final word in judicial review, from retroactivity of the decision when it is obtained, and from the lack of a roundly tax-informed viewpoint of judges.

Perhaps the chief difficulty in consistent and uniform compliance with the congressional limitation upon court review lies in the want of a certain standard for distinguishing "questions of law" from "questions of fact." This is the test Congress has directed, but its difficulties in practice are well known and have been subject of frequent comment. Its difficulty is reflected in our labeling some questions as "mixed questions of law and fact" and in a great number of opinions distinguishing "ultimate facts" from evidentiary facts.

It is difficult to lay down rules as to what should or should not be reviewed in tax cases except in terms so general that their effectiveness in a particular case will depend largely upon the attitude with which the case is approached. However, all that we have said of the finality of administrative determination in other fields is applicable to determinations of the Tax Court. Its decision, of course, must have "warrant in the record" and a reasonable basis in the law. But "the judicial function is exhausted when there is found to be a rational basis for the conclusions approved by the administrative body." . . .

Congress has invested the Tax Court with primary authority for redetermining deficiencies, which constitutes the greater part of tax litigation. This requires it to consider both law and facts. Whatever latitude exists in resolving questions such as those of proper accounting, treating a series of transactions as one for tax purposes, or treating apparently separate ones as single in their tax consequences, exists in the Tax Court and not in the regular courts; when the court cannot separate the elements of a decision so as to identify a clear-cut mistake of law, the decision of the Tax Court must stand. In view of the division of functions between the Tax Court and reviewing courts it is of course the duty of the Tax Court to distinguish with clarity between what it finds as fact and what conclusion it reaches on the law. In deciding law questions courts may properly attach weight to the decision of points of law by an administrative body having special competence to deal with the subject matter. The Tax Court is informed by experience and kept current with tax evolution and needs by the volume and variety of its work. While its decisions may not be binding precedents for courts dealing with similar problems, uniform administration would be promoted by conforming to them where possible.

. . . Where no statute or regulation controls, the Tax Court's selection of the [accounting procedure] to follow is no more reviewable than any other question of fact. . . .[3]

---

[3] The Dobson doctrine was later overruled by statute by providing that the United States Court of Appeals should have exclusive jurisdiction to review decisions of the Tax Court and that it should do so "in the same manner and to the same extent as decisions of the district court in civil actions tried without a jury." 26 U.S.C. § 782. In spite of this statutory repudiation, the Dobson doctrine is still significant as evidencing a high judicial regard for administrative processes and an attitude to which the Supreme Court may adhere when not prohibited by statute from so doing. As stated by Jackson, J., in a dissenting opinion in which Frankfurter, J., concurred: "In spite [of the statutory overruling of the Dobson case], I still think the Tax Court is more competent and steady influence toward a systematic body of tax law than our sporadic omnipotence in a field beset with invisible boomerangs. I should reverse, in reliance upon the Tax Court's judgment more, perhaps, than my own." Arrowsmith v. Commissioner of Internal Revenue, 344 U.S. 6, at page 12 (1952). See also the Motion Picture Advertising Service Company case, § 34:7(a), in which the majority opinion shows the same high regard for the administrative determination as in the Dobson case.

### (b) Appraisal of the Dobson doctrine

BINGHAM'S TRUST v. COMMISSIONER OF INTERNAL REVENUE
325 U.S. 365 (1945)

CONCURRING OPINION BY FRANKFURTER, J.

In *Dobson* v. *Commissioner*, . . . this Court elaborately considered the special function of the Tax Court and the very limited functions of the Circuit Courts of Appeals and of this Court in reviewing the Tax Court. The unanimous opinion in the *Dobson* case was surely a case of much ado about nothing, if it did not emphasize the vast range of questions as to which the Tax Court should have the final say. In making the *Dobson* pronouncement, the Court was not unaware that "questions of fact" and "questions of law" were legal concepts around which dialectic conflicts have been fought time out of mind. The *Dobson* opinion took for granted that they are useful instruments of thought even though not amenable to fixed connotations. The terms are unmanageable and too confusing if it be assumed that unless they have invariant meaning, that is, unless they serve the same purpose for every legal problem in which they are invoked, they can serve no purpose for any problem. The contribution of the *Dobson* case, one had a right to believe, was the restriction of reviewable "questions of law" in tax litigation to issues appropriate for review in relation to the machinery which Congress has designed for such litigation. The *Dobson* case eschewed sterile attempts at differentiation between "fact" and "law" in the abstract. Instead, it found significance in the scheme devised by Congress for adjudicating tax controversies whereby Congress had in the main, centralized in the Tax Court review of tax determinations by the Treasury and had made the decisions of the Tax Court final unless they were "not in accordance with law,". . . with the result that, as a practical matter, only a small percentage of Tax Court decisions gets into the Circuit Courts of Appeals, and a still smaller percentage reaches this Court. Therefore, the decisions of the Circuit Courts of Appeals, and even more so of this Court, are bound to be more or less episodic and dependent upon contingencies that cannot give these appellate courts that feel of the expert which is so important for wise construction of such interrelated and complicated enactments as those which constitute our revenue laws. These factors, so decisive in the stream of tax litigation, weigh heavily in apportioning functions between the Tax Court and the courts reviewing the Tax Court. Accordingly, the vital guidance of the *Dobson* opinion was that a decision of the Tax

Court should stand unless it involves "a clear-cut mistake of law," . . . Considerations that may properly govern what are to be deemed questions of fact and questions of law as between judge and jury, or considerations relevant to the drawing of a line between questions of facts and questions of law on appeal from a court of first instance sitting without a jury, or in determining what is a foreclosed question of fact in cases coming to this Court from State courts on claims of unconstitutionality, may be quite misleading when a decision of the Tax Court is challenged in the various Circuit Courts of Appeals or here as "not in accordance with law."

Certainly, all disputed questions regarding events and circumstances—the raw materials, as it were, of situations which give rise to tax controversies—are for the Tax Court to settle and definitively so. Secondly, there are questions that do not involve disputes as to what really happened—as, for instance, what expenses were incurred or what distribution of assets was made—but instead turn on the meaning of what happened as a matter of business practice or business relevance. Here we are in the domain of financial and business interpretation in relation to taxation as to which the Tax Court presumably is as well informed by experience as are the appellate judges and certainly more frequently enlightened by the volume and range of its litigation. Such issues bring us treacherously near to what abstractly are usually characterized as questions of law, whether the question of division of labor in a litigation is between judges and lay juries, or between judges of first instance and of appellate courts when there is no difference of specialized experience between the two classes of judges. Thus, the construction of documents has for historic reasons been deemed to be a question of law in the sense that the meaning is to be given by judges and not by laymen. But this crude division between what is "law" and what is "fact" is not relevant to the proper demarcation of functions as between the Tax Court and the reviewing courts. To hold that the Circuit Courts of Appeals, and eventually this Court, must make an independent examination of the meaning of every word of tax legislation, no matter whether the words express accounting, business or other conceptions peculiarly within the special competence of the Tax Court, is to sacrifice the effectiveness of the judicial scheme designed by Congress especially for tax litigation to an abstract notion of "law" derived from the merely historic function of courts generally to construe documents, including legislation. More than that. If the appellate courts must make an independent examination of the meaning of every word in tax legislation, on the assumption that the construction of legislative language is necessarily for the appellate courts, how can they reasonably refuse to consider claims that the words have been misapplied in the circumstances of a particular case? Meaning derives vitality from application. Meaning is easily thwarted or distorted by misapplication. If the appellate courts are charged with the duty of giving meaning to words because they are contained in tax legislation, they equally cannot escape the duty of examining independently whether a proper application has been given by the Tax Court.

The specialized equipment of the Tax Court and the trained instinct that comes from its experience ought to leave with the Tax Court the final say also as to matters which involve construction of legal documents and the application of legislation even though the process may be expressed in general propositions, so long as the Tax Court has not committed what was characterized in the Dobson case as a "clear-cut mistake of law."

That serves as a guide for judgment even though no inclusive definition or catalogue is essayed. The Tax Court of course must conform to the procedural requirements which the Constitution and the laws of Congress command. Likewise, in applying the provisions of the revenue laws, the Tax Court must keep within what may broadly be called the outward limits of categories and classifications expressing legislative policy. Congress has invested the Tax Court with primary—and largely with ultimate—authority for redetermining deficiencies. It is a tribunal to which mastery in tax matters must be attributed. The authority which Congress has thus given the Tax Court involves the determination of what really happened in a situation and what it means in the taxing world. In order to redetermine deficiencies the Tax Court must apply technical legal principles. The interpretation of tax statutes and their application to particular circumstances are all matters peculiarly within the competence of the Tax Court. On the other hand, constitutional adjudication, determination of local law questions and common law rules of property, such as the meaning of a "general power of appointment" or the application of the rule against perpetuities, are outside the special province of the Tax Court. . . . Congress did not authorize review of all legal questions upon which the Tax Court passed. It merely allowed modification or reversal if the decision of the Tax Court is "not in accordance with law." But if a statute upon which the Tax Court unmistakably has to pass allows the Tax Court's application of the law to the situation before it as a reasonable one—if the situation could, without violence to language, be brought within the terms under which the Tax Court placed it or be kept out of the terms from which that Court kept it—the Tax Court cannot in reason be said to have acted "not in accordance with law." In short, there was no "clear-cut mistake of law" but a fair administration of it.[4]

### § 34:7. Uncertainty as to Classification as Questions of Fact or Law

Much confusion exists as to the scope of review because of the uncertainty as to whether a given question will be classified by the court as a question of law, or a question of fact, or as a mixed question of law or fact. Some of the conflict may perhaps be explained on the basis that when the court believed that it was dealing with the criteria or standards for reaching decisions generally, it held that a question of law was involved; whereas when it believed that it was dealing with the application of such criteria or standards to the facts of a particular situation, it held that a question of fact was involved.

The effect of foreclosing a review by giving a question the label of "question of fact" may be seen in *Federal Trade Commission* v. *Standard Oil Company,*[5] in which the Company was charged with price discrimination in that it gave lower prices to four buyers. The Company defended on the ground that these four buyers were "jobbers" and not retailers. The Federal Trade Commission sustained this defense, holding that the four buyers were "jobbers" who could be distinguished from the other buyers who were retailers. The Supreme Court refused to review the determination that the four buyers were "jobbers" because it involved a question of fact the determination of which depended upon the "appreciation of standards which admit of different interpretations." As pointed out by the four dissenting Justices, the "jobbers" were merely large retailers who were given that label by the Company to conceal the fact that it was giving the four large retailers a quantity discount which it did not give the small retailers.

In contrast with the result of this case is the decision in *Federal Trade Commission* v. *Morton Salt Company*[6] in which the Morton Salt Company openly published a list of graduated quantity discounts available to all purchasers. This was condemned as a price dis-

---

4 See note 3 to § 34:6(a) as to statutory change.
5 355 U.S. 396 (1958).
6 334 U.S. 37 (1948).

crimination because in actual practice only five buyers purchased in sufficient quantities to be entitled to receive the maximum discount.

### *(a) Classification of "unfair" method of competition*

FEDERAL TRADE COMMISSION v. MOTION PICTURE ADVERTISING SERVICE COMPANY

344 U.S. 392 (1953)

The Motion Picture Advertising Service Company produced and distributed interstate advertising motion pictures to theatre owners. These were distributed under exclusive dealing contracts. The Federal Trade Commission concluded that the exclusive dealing provision was an unfair method of competition unless the contracts were limited to a period of a year. It ordered the Company to so limit its contracts. The Company appealed.

OPINION BY DOUGLAS, J.

. . . An attack is made on that part of the order which restricts the exclusive contracts to one-year terms. It is argued that one-year contracts will not be practicable. It is said that the expenses of securing these screening contracts do not warrant one-year agreements, that investment of capital in the business would not be justified without assurance of a market for more than one year, that theatres frequently demand guarantees for more than a year or otherwise refuse to exhibit advertising films. These and other business requirements are the basis of the argument that exclusive contracts of a duration in excess of a year are necessary for the conduct of the business of the distributors. The Commission considered this argument and concluded that, although the exclusive contracts were beneficial to the distributor and preferred by the theatre owners, their use should be restricted in the public interest. The Commission found that the term of one year had become a standard practice and that the continuance of exclusive contracts so limited would not be an undue restraint upon competition, in view of the compelling business reasons for some exclusive arrangement. The precise impact of a particular practice on the trade is for the Commission, not the courts, to determine. The point where a method of competition becomes "unfair" within the meaning of the Act will often turn on the exigencies of a particular situation, trade practices, or the practical requirements of the business in question. Certainly we cannot say that exclusive contracts in this field should have been banned in their entirety or not at all, that the Commission exceeded the limits of its allowable judgment . . . in limiting their term to one year.

DISSENTING OPINION BY FRANKFURTER, J., in which Burton, J., concurs.

My doubts that the Commission has adequately shown that it has been guided by relevant criteria in dealing with its findings under § 5 of the Federal Trade Commission Act are dispelled neither by those findings nor by the opinion of the Court. The Commission has not explained its conclusion with the "simplicity and clearness" necessary to tell us "what a decision means before the duty becomes ours to say whether it is right or wrong." . . .

My primary concern is that the Commission has not related its analysis of this industry to the standards of illegality in § 5 with sufficient clarity to enable this Court to review the order. Although we are told that respondent and three other companies have exclusive exhibition contracts with three-quarters of the theaters in the country that accept advertising, there are no findings indicating how many of these contracts extend beyond the one-year period which the Commission finds not unduly restrictive. . . .

. . . The Commission merely states a dogmatic conclusion that the use of these contracts constitutes an "unreasonable restraint and restriction of competition." . . . The Court's opinion is merely an echo of this conclusion and states without discussion that such exclusion from a market without more "falls within the prohibitions of the Sherman Act" because, taken with exclusive contracts of other competitors, 75% of the market is shut off. But there is no reliance here on conspiracy or concerted action to foreclose the market, a charge that would of course warrant action under the Sherman Law. . . .

. . . If other factors pertinent to a Sherman Law violation were present here, the Commission could not leave such factors unmentioned and simply ask us to review a broad unexplained finding that there is such a violation. In any event, the Commission has not found any Sherman Law violation.

But we are told, as is of course true, that § 5 of the Federal Trade Commission Act comprehends more than violations of the Sherman Law. The Federal Trade Commission Act was designed, doubtless, to enable the Commission to nip in the bud practices which, when full blown, would violate the Sherman or Clayton Act. But this record does not explain to us how these practices, if full blown, would violate one of those Acts. The Commission has been content to rest on its conclusion that respondent's exclusive contracts unreasonably restrain competition and tend to monopoly. If judicial review is to have a basis for functioning, the Commission must do more than pronounce a conclusion by way of fiat and without explication. This is not a tribunal for investigating an industry. Analysis of practices in the light of definable standards of illegality is for the Commission. It is for us to determine whether the Commission has correctly applied the proper standards and thus exhibited that familiarity with competitive problems which the Congress anticipated the Commission would achieve from its experience. . . .

. . . It is urged that the Commission should be allowed ample discretion in developing the law of unfair methods of competition to meet the exigencies of a particular situation without undue hampering by the Court. But if judicial review is to have any meaning, extension of principle to meet new situations must be based on some minimum demonstration to the courts that the Commission has relied on relevant criteria to conclude that the new application is in the public interest. . . .

It is of great importance to bear in mind that the determination of the scope of the prohibition of "unfair methods of competition" has not been left to the administrative agency as part of its fact-finding authority but is a matter of law to be defined by the courts. . . . The significance of such judicial review may be indicated by the dissimilar treatment of comparable standards entrusted to the enforcement of the Interstate Commerce Commission. In dealing with the provisions of the Interstate Commerce Act requiring reasonableness in rates and practices from carriers subject to the control of the Commerce Commission, we read the Act as making the application of standards of reasonableness a determination of fact by that Commission and not an issue of law for the courts. Unlike the Federal Trade Commission Act, the Interstate Commerce Act dealt with governmental regulation not only of a limited sector of the economy but of economic enterprises that had long been singled out for public control. The range within which the broadly stated concepts of reasonableness moved was confined as well as defined by experience, and application of the concepts was necessarily limited to easily comparable economic activity. On the other hand, the Federal Trade Commission Act gave an administrative agency authority over economic controls of a different sort that began with the Sherman Law—

restrictions upon the whole domain of economic enterprise engaged in interstate commerce. The content of the prohibition of "unfair methods of competition," to be applied to widely diverse business practices, was not entrusted to the Commission for *ad hoc* determination within the interstices of individualized records but was left for ascertainment by this Court.

The vagueness of the Sherman Law was saved by imparting to it the gloss of history. . . . Difficulties with this inherent uncertainty in the Sherman Law led to the particularizations expressed in the Clayton Act. 38 Stat. 730. The creation of the Federal Trade Commission, 38 Stat. 717, made available a continuous administrative process by which fruition of Sherman Law violations could be aborted. But it is another thing to suggest that anything in business activity that may, if unchecked, offend the particularizations of the Clayton Act may now be reached by the Federal Trade Commission Act. The curb on the Commission's power, . . . so as to leave to the courts rather than the Commission the final authority in determining what is an unfair method of competition, would be relaxed, and unbridled intervention into business practices encouraged.

I am not unaware that the policies directed at maintaining effective competition, as expressed in the Sherman Law, the Clayton Act, as amended by the Robinson-Patman Act, and the Federal Trade Commission Act, are difficult to formulate and not altogether harmonious. Therefore, the interpretation of the Acts by the agency which is constantly engaged in construing them should carry considerable weight with courts even in the solution of the legal puzzles these statutes raise. But he is no friend of administrative law who thinks that the Commission should be left at large. In any event, whatever problems would be raised by withholding judicial review from determinations of the Commission are for Congress to face, at least in the first instance. . . . Until Congress chooses to do so, we cannot shirk our duty by leaving determinations of law to the discretion of the Federal Trade Commission. . . . We [must] abstain from approving a mere say-so of the Commission and thus fail to discharge the task implied by judicial review. . . .

## § 34:8. Review of Questions of Policy

Ordinary questions of policy are not reviewable if they come within the area of the administrator's discretion. In some instances, the administrator may even establish the policy when the statute is silent.[7] If a Federal administrator relies solely on his own interpretation of national policy, the Supreme Court will reverse his decision if it does not agree with his conclusion.

### *(a) National policy*

FEDERAL COMMUNICATIONS COMMISSION v. RCA COMMUNICATIONS

346 U.S. 86 (1953)

Mackay Radio and Telegraph Co. applied to the Federal Communications Commission for authorization to provide service to specified foreign countries. The application was opposed by RCA Communications, which was already providing service to those countries. The Federal Communications Commission granted Mackay the authorization because the Commission concluded that the national policy favored competition. RCA appealed from the grant of authority.

OPINION BY FRANKFURTER, J.

. . . In this case, the Court of Appeals has ruled that the Commission was guided by a misinterpretation of national policy, in that it thought that the maintenance of competition is in itself a sufficient goal of federal communications policy so as to make it in the public interest to authorize a license merely because competition, *i.e.*, duplication of existing facilities, was "reasonably feasible." RCAC relies on the holding of the Court of Appeals that the Commission must decide, in the circumstances of the application, that competition is not merely feasible but beneficial.

The Commission has not in this case clearly indicated even that its own experience, entirely apart from the tangible demonstration of benefit for which RCAC contends, leads it to conclude that competition is here desirable. It seems to have relied almost entirely on its interpretation of national policy. Since the Commission professed to dispose of the case merely upon its view of a principle which it derived from the statute and did not base its conclusion on matters within its own special competence, it is for us to determine what the governing principle is. . . .

. . . Had the Commission clearly indicated that it relied on its own evaluation of the needs of the industry rather than on what it deemed a national policy, its order would have a different foundation. There can be no doubt that competition is a relevant factor in weighing the public interest. . . . Our difficulty arises from the fact that

[7] See § 28:3(e) and (f).

while the Commission recites that competition may have beneficial effects, it does so in an abstract, sterile way. Its opinion relies in this case not on its independent conclusion, from the impact upon it of the trends and needs of this industry, that competition is desirable but primarily on its reading of national policy, a reading too loose and too much calculated to mislead in the exercise of the discretion entrusted to it.

To say that national policy without more suffices for authorization of a competing carrier wherever competition is reasonably feasible would authorize the Commission to abdicate what would seem to us one of the primary duties imposed on it by Congress. And since we read the opinion of the Commission as saying precisely that, we think the case must be remanded for its reconsideration. . . . We think it not inadmissible for the Commission, when it makes manifest that in so doing it is conscientiously exercising the discretion given it by Congress, to reach a conclusion whereby authorizations would be granted wherever competition is reasonably feasible. This is so precisely because the exercise of its functions gives it accumulating insight not vouchsafed to courts dealing episodically with the practical problems involved in such determination. Here, however, the conclusion was not based on the Commission's own judgment but rather on the unjustified assumption that it was Congress' judgment that such authorizations are desirable. . . .

In reaching a conclusion that duplicating authorizations are in the public interest wherever competition is reasonably feasible, the Commission is not required to make specific findings of tangible benefit. It is not required to grant authorizations only if there is a demonstration of facts indicating immediate benefit to the public. To restrict the Commission's action to cases in which tangible evidence appropriate for judicial determination is available would disregard a major reason for the creation of administrative agencies, better equipped as they are for weighing intangibles "by specialization, by insight gained through experience, and by more flexible procedure. . . . In the nature of things, the possible benefits of competition do not lend themselves to detailed forecast, . . . but the Commission must at least warrant, as it were, that competition would serve some beneficial purpose such as maintaining good service and improving it. Although we think RCAC's contention that an applicant must demonstrate tangible benefits is asking too much, it is not too much to ask that there be ground for reasonable expectation that competition may have some beneficial effect. Merely to assume that competition is bound to be of advantage, in an industry so regulated and so largely closed as is this one, is not enough. . . .

### § 34:9. Review of Enforcement Method

Under earlier regulatory systems, no discretion was vested in the administrator as to the enforcement method to be followed. Under those statutes a course of action was defined for him once he made the determination necessary to invoke such action. As an example, the health officer with authority to kill diseased cattle had only to determine whether the cattle were or were not diseased. If he determined that they were, his duty to have them destroyed was clear. Under modern regulations, which more frequently include a pattern of control as well as prohibition or destruction of the subject matter regulated, the administrator is frequently given a degree of discretion or latitude in selecting an appropriate method of enforcing or in carrying out his determinations. The general attitude of the modern court is that, so long as the administrator keeps within the confines of the statute giving him authority, the courts will not interfere with his decision as to the particular method of enforcement to be used. The fact that the court might consider that a less or more drastic method of enforcement would be preferable is not sufficient to justify interference with the administrative determination.

#### *(a) Dissolution of holding company*

AMERICAN POWER AND LIGHT CO. v. SECURITIES AND EXCHANGE COMMISSION

329 U.S. 90 (1946)

Under the authority of the Securities and Exchange Act, the Securities and Exchange Commission directed the dissolution of a holding company that it found to serve no useful economic purpose. The objection was made that the policy of the Act could be carried out without going to the extreme of ordering the dissolution of the holding company.

OPINION BY MURPHY, J. . . .

[The] evidence is more than enough to support the finding that American and Electric are but paper companies without legitimate function and purpose. They serve merely as a mechanism by which Bond and Share maintains a pyramided structure containing the seeds of all the attendant evils condemned by the Act. It was reasonable, therefore, for the Commission to conclude that American and Electric are undue and unnecessary complexities in the Bond and Share system and that their existence unfairly and inequitably distributes voting power among the security holders of the system.

The major objection raised by American and Electric relates to the Commission's choice of dissolution as "necessary to insure" that the evils would be corrected and the standard of [the Act] . . . effectuated. Emphasis is placed upon alternative plans which are less drastic in nature and which allegedly would meet the statutory standards.

It is a fundamental principle, however, that where Congress has intrusted an administrative agency with the responsibility of selecting the means of achieving the statutory policy "the relation of remedy to policy is peculiarily a matter for administrative competence.". . . In dealing with the complex problem of adjusting holding company systems in accordance with the legislative standards, the Commission here has accumulated experience and knowledge which no court can hope to attain. Its judgment is entitled to the greatest weight. While recognizing that the Commission's discretion must square with its responsibility, only if the remedy chosen is unwarranted in law or is without justification in fact should a court attempt to intervene in the matter. Neither ground of intervention is present in this instance.

Dissolution of a holding company or a subholding company plainly is contemplated by [the Act] . . . as a possible remedy. . . .

Nor can we say that the Commission's choice of dissolution with respect to American and Electric is so lacking in reasonableness as to constitute an abuse of its discretion. The Commission chose dissolution because it felt such action is calculated to correct the situation most effectively and quickly. . . .

Without attempting to invade the domain of the Commission's discretion, we can readily perceive a factual basis underlying the choice of dissolution in this instance. The Commission reasonably could conclude from the record that American and Electric performed no justifiable function; they are unnecessary complexities enabling Bond and Share to perpetuate its pyramided system. The actual and potential evils resulting from their continued existence may well be said to outweigh any other claimed advantages, especially since many of the latter seem impossible of attainment due to the unsound financial structure of the companies. . . .

We are unimpressed, moreover, by the claim that dissolution is so drastic a remedy as to be unreasonable. Elimination of useless holding companies may be carried out by fair and equitable methods so as to destroy nothing of real value. American and Electric, the Commission found, are little more than a set of books and a portfolio of securities. And we cannot say that the Commission was without basis for its belief that dissolution under these circumstances would harm no one. It may well have considered the fact brought out in the argument before us that "so far as Bond and Share and the public security holders are concerned, dissolution would mean little more than the receipt of securities of the operating companies in lieu of their present shares in American and Electric. Any number of benefits might thereafter accrue to these security holders. Their equities in the Bond and Share system would be materially strengthened by the removal of the useless and costly subholding companies and their voting power would tend to be more in proportion to their investment. The financial weaknesses of the various companies remaining in the system would be easier to correct, with numerous benefits to the consumers and the general public as well as the investors. . . ." These factors [support] the Commission's conclusion that "the dissolution of these companies which . . . never served any useful purpose but have been a medium of much harm will be . . . beneficial to the public interest and . . . investors and consumers. . . ."

In view of the rational basis for the Commission's choice, the fact that other solutions might have been selected becomes immaterial. The Commission is the body which has the statutory duty of considering the possible solutions and choosing that which it considers most appropriate to the effectuation of the policies of the act. Our review is limited solely to testing the propriety of the remedy so chosen from the standpoint of the Constitution and the statute. We would be impinging upon the Commission's rightful discretion were we to consider the various alternatives in the hope of finding one that we consider more appropriate. Since the remedy chosen by the Commission in this instance is legally and factually sustainable, it matters not that American and Electric believe that alternative orders should have been entered. It is likewise irrelevant that they feel that Bond and Share is the principal offender against the statutory standards and that the Commission should merely have required Bond and Share to divest itself of its interests in American and Electric. . . .

### *(b) Hiring with back pay*

PHELPS-DODGE CORP. v. NATIONAL LABOR RELATIONS BOARD
313 U.S. 177 (1941)

The National Labor Relations Board found that the employer had refused to hire certain persons as employees because of their union activity. The board ordered the employer to employ these men and to pay them the wages they would have received had they not been improperly denied employment. The employer attacked the scope of the decree of the board.

OPINION BY FRANKFURTER, J. . . .

The dominating question which this litigation brings here for the first time is whether an employer subject to the National Labor Relations Act may refuse to hire employees solely because of their affiliations with a labor union. . . .

. . . Since the refusal to hire Curtis and Daugherty solely because of their affiliation with the Union was an unfair labor practice under § 8(3), the remedial authority of the Board under § 10(c) became operative. Of course it could issue, as it did, an order "to cease and desist from such unfair labor practice" in the future. Did Congress also empower the Board to order the employer to undo the wrong by offering the men discriminated against the opportunity for employment which should not have been denied them?

Reinstatement is the conventional correction for discriminatory discharges. Experience having demonstrated that discrimination in hiring is twin to discrimination in firing, it would indeed be surprising if Congress gave a remedy for the one which it denied for the other. The powers of the Board as well as the restrictions upon it must be drawn from § 10(c), which directs the Board "to take such affirmative action, including reinstatement of employees with or without back pay, as will effectuate the policies of this Act." It could not be seriously denied that to require discrimination in hiring or firing to be "neutralized" . . . by requiring the discrimination to cease not abstractly but in the concrete victimizing instances, is an "affirmative action" which "will effectuate the policies of this Act." Therefore, if § 10(c), had empowered the Board to "take such affirmative action . . . as will effectuate the policies of this Act," the right to restore to a man employment which was wrongfully denied him could hardly be doubted. Even without such a mandate from Congress this Court compelled reinstatement to enforce the legislative policy against discrimination represented by the Railway Labor Act.

. . . Attainment of a great national policy through expert administration in collaboration with limited judicial review must not be confined within narrow canons for equitable relief deemed suitable by chancellors in ordinary private controversies. . . . To differentiate between discrimination in denying employment and in terminating it, would be a differentiation not only without substance but in defiance of that against which the prohibition of discrimination is directed.

But, we are told, this is precisely the differentiation Congress has made. It has done so, the argument runs, by not directing the Board "to take such affirmative action as will effectuate the policies of this Act," simpliciter, but, instead, by empowering the Board "to take such affirmative action, including reinstatement of employees with or without back pay, as will effectuate the policies of this Act." To attribute such a function to the participial phrase introduced by "including" is to shrivel a versatile principle to an illustrative application. We find no justification whatever for attributing to Congress such a casuistic withdrawal of the authority which, but for the illustration, it clearly has given the Board. The word "including" does not lend itself to such destructive significance. . . .

. . . There remain for consideration the limitations upon the Board's power to undo the effects of discrimination. Specifically, we have the question of the Board's power to order employment in cases where the men discriminated against had obtained "substantially equivalent employment." The Board as a matter of fact found that no such employment had been obtained, but alternatively concluded that, in any event, the men should be offered employment. . . .

. . . Section 10(c) . . . authorizes the Board "to take such affirmative action, including reinstatement of employees with or without back pay, as will effectuate the policies of this Act." The relevant portions of Section 2(3) follow: "The term 'employee' shall include any employee, and shall not be limited to the employees of a particular employer, unless the Act explicitly states otherwise, and shall include any individual whose work has ceased as a consequence of, or in connection with, any current labor dispute or because of any unfair labor practice, and who has not obtained any other regular and substantially equivalent employment.". . .

Denial of the Board's power to order opportunities of employment in this situation derives wholly from an infiltration of a portion of § 2 (3) into § 10(c). The argument runs thus: § 10(c) specifically refers to "reinstatement of employees"; the latter portion of § 2(3) refers to an "employee" as a person "who has not obtained any other regular and substantially equivalent employment"; therefore, there can be no reinstatement of an employee who has obtained such employment. The syllogism is perfect. But this is a bit of verbal logic from which the meaning of things has evaporated. In the first place, we have seen that the Board's power to order an opportunity for employment does not derive from the phrase "including reinstatement of employees with or without back pay," and is not limited by it. . . .

To deny the Board power to neutralize discrimination merely because workers have obtained compensatory employment would confine the "policies of this Act" to the correction of private injuries. The Board was not devised for such a limited function. It is the agency of Congress for translating into concreteness the purpose of safeguarding and encouraging the right of self-organization. The Board, we have held very recently, does not exist for the "adjudication of private rights"; it "acts in a public capacity to give effect to the declared public policy of the Act to eliminate and prevent obstructions to interstate commerce by encouraging collective bargaining." . . . To be sure, reinstatement is not needed to repair the economic loss of a worker who, after discrimination, has obtained an equally profitable job. But to limit the significance of discrimination merely to questions of monetary loss to workers would thwart the central purpose of the Act, directed as that is toward the achievement and maintenance of workers' self-organization. That there are factors other than loss of wages to a particular worker to be considered is suggested even by a meager knowledge of industrial affairs. Thus, to give only one illustration, if men were discharged who were leading efforts at organization in a plant having a low wage scale, they would not unnaturally be compelled by their economic circumstances to seek and obtain employment elsewhere at equivalent wages. In such a situation, to deny the Board power to wipe out the prior discrimination by ordering the employment of such workers would sanction a most effective way of defeating the right of self-organization.

Therefore, the mere fact that the victim of discrimination has obtained equivalent employment does not itself preclude the Board from undoing the discrimination and requiring employment. But neither does this remedy automatically flow from the Act itself when discrimination has been found. A statute expressive of such large public policy as that on which the National Labor Relations Board is based must be broadly phrased and necessarily carries with it the task of administrative application. There is an area plainly covered by the language of the Act and an area no less plainly without it. But in the nature of things Congress could not catalogue all the devices and stratagems for circumventing the policies of the Act. Nor could it define the whole gamut of remedies to effectuate these policies in an infinite variety of specific situations. Congress met these difficulties by leaving the adaptation of means to end to the empiric process of administration. The exercise of the process was committed to the Board, subject to limited judicial review. Because the relation of remedy to policy is peculiarly a matter for administrative competence, courts must not enter the allowable area of the Board's discretion and must guard against the danger of sliding unconsciously from the narrow confines of law into the more spacious domain of policy. On the other hand, the power with which Congress invested the Board implies responsibility—the responsibility of exercising its judgment in employing the statutory powers.

The Act does not create rights for individuals which must be vindicated according to a rigid scheme of remedies. It entrusts to an expert agency the maintenance and promotion of industrial peace. According to the experience revealed by the Board's decisions, the effectuation of this important policy generally requires not only compensation for the loss of wages but also offers of employment to the victims of discrimination. Only thus can there be a restoration of the situation, as nearly as possible to that which would have obtained but for the illegal discrimination. But even where a worker has not secured equivalent employment, the Board, under particular circumstances, may refuse to order his employment because it would not effectuate the policies of the Act. It has, for example, declined to do so in the case of a worker who had been discharged for union activities and had sought re-employment after having offered his services as a labor spy. . . .

From the beginning the Board has recognized that a worker who has obtained equivalent employment is in a different position from one who has lost his job as well as his wages through an employer's unfair labor practice. In early decisions, the Board did not order reinstatement of workers who had secured such equivalent employment. . . . It apparently focussed on the absence of loss of wages in determining the applicable remedy. But other factors may well enter into the appropriateness of ordering the offending employer to offer employment to one illegally denied it. Reinstatement may be the effective assurance of the right of self-organization. Again, without such a remedy industrial peace might be endangered because workers would be resentful of their inability to return to jobs to which they may have been attached and from which they were wrongfully discharged. On the other hand, it may be . . . that, in making such an order for reinstatement the necessity for making room for the old employees by discharging new ones, as well as questions affecting the dislocation of the business, ought to be considered. All these and other factors outside our domain of experience may come into play. Their relevance is for the Board, not for us. In the exercise of its informed discretion the Board may find that effectuation of the Act's policies may or may not require reinstatement. We have no warrant for speculating on matters of fact the determination of which Congress has entrusted to the Board. All we are entitled to ask is that the statute speak through the Board where the statute does not speak for itself.

. . . The court below found, and the Board has not challenged the finding, that the Board left the issue of equivalence of jobs at the Shattuck Denn Company in doubt, and remanded the order to the Board for further findings. Of course, if the Board finds that equivalent employment has not been obtained, it is within its province to require offers of re-employment in accordance with its general conclusion that a worker's loss in wages and in general working conditions must be made whole. Even if it should find that equivalent jobs were secured by the men who suffered from discrimination, it may order employment at Phelps Dodge if it finds that to do so would effectuate the policies of the Act. We believe that the procedure we have indicated will likewise effectuate the policies of the Act by making workable the system of restricted judicial review in relation to the wide discretionary authority which Congress has given the Board.

From the record of the present case we cannot really tell why the Board has ordered reinstatement of the strikers who obtained subsequent employment. The Board first found that the men had not obtained substantially equivalent employment within the meaning of § 2(3); later it concluded that even if they had obtained such employment it would order their reinstatement. It did so, however, as we have noted, merely because it asserted its legal power so to do. When the court below held that proof did not support the Board's finding concerning equivalence of employment at Shattuck Denn and remanded the case to the Board for additional evidence on that issue, the Board took this issue out of the case by expressly declining to ask for its review here.

The administrative process will best be vindicated by clarity in its exercise. Since Congress has defined the authority of the Board and the procedure by which it must be asserted and has charged the federal courts with the duty of reviewing the Board's orders [§ 10(e) and (f)], it will avoid needless litigation and make for effective and expeditious enforcement of the Board's order to require the Board to disclose the basis of its order. We do not intend to enter the province that belongs to the Board, nor do we do so. All we ask of the Board is to give clear indication that it has exercised the discretion with which Congress has empowered it. This is to affirm most emphatically the authority of the Board.

. . . As part of its remedial action against the unfair labor practices, the Board ordered that workers who had been denied employment be made whole for their loss of pay. In specific terms, the Board ordered payment to the men of a sum equal to what they normally would have earned from the date of the discrimination to the time of employment less their earnings during this period. The court below added a further deduction of amounts which the workers "failed without excuse to earn," and the Board here challenges this modification.

Making the workers whole for losses suffered on account of an unfair labor practice is part of the vindication of the public policy which the Board enforces. Since only actual losses should be made good, it seems fair that deductions should be made not only for actual earnings by the worker but also for losses which he willfully incurred. To this the Board counters that to apply this abstractly just doctrine of mitigation of damages to the situations before it, often involving substantial numbers of workmen, would put on the Board details too burdensome for effective administration. Simplicity of administration is thus the justification for deducting only actual earnings and avoiding . . . controversy as to wages that might have been earned.

But the advantages of a simple rule must be balanced against the importance of taking fair account, in a civilized legal system, of every socially desirable factor in the final judgment. The Board, we believe, overestimates administrative difficulties and underestimates its administrative resourcefulness. Here again we must avoid the rigidities of an either-or rule. The remedy of back pay, it must be remembered, is entrusted to the Board's discretion; it is not mechanically compelled by the Act. And in applying its authority over back pay orders, the Board has not used stereotyped formulas but has availed itself of the freedom given it by Congress to attain just results in diverse, complicated situations. . . . The Board has a wide discretion to keep the present matter within reasonable bounds through flexible procedural devices. The Board will thus have it within its power to avoid delays and difficulties incident to passing on remote and speculative claims by employers, while at the same time it may give appropriate weight to a clearly unjustifiable refusal to take desirable new employment. By leaving such an adjustment to the administrative process we have in mind not so much the minimization of damages as the healthy policy of promoting production and employment. This consideration in no way weakens the enforcement of the policies of the Act by exerting coercion against men who have been unfairly denied employment to take employment elsewhere and later, because of their new employment, declaring them barred from returning to the jobs of their choice. This is so because we hold that the power of ordering offers of employment rests with the Board even as to workers who have obtained equivalent employment.

. . .

### *(c) Reinstatement with back pay*

REPUBLIC STEEL CORP. v. NATIONAL LABOR RELATIONS BOARD
311 U.S. 7 (1940)

The National Labor Relations Board ordered the reinstatement of employees improperly discharged by the employer and payment to them of back pay for the period since their improper discharge. The Board directed there be deducted from such back pay the amounts received by the employees from government relief and that such deduction be paid to the government. The authority to direct this deduction was challenged.

OPINION BY HUGHES, C. J. . . .

The National Labor Relations Board, finding that the Republic Steel Corporation had engaged in unfair labor practices in violation of § 8(1), 8(2) and 8(3) of the National Labor Relations Act, ordered the company to desist from these practices, to withdraw recognition from a labor organization found to be dominated by the company, and to reinstate certain employees, with back pay, found to have been discriminatorily discharged or denied reinstatement. The Board, in providing for back pay, directed the company to deduct from the payments to the reinstated employees the amounts they had received for work performed upon "work relief projects" and to pay over such amounts to the appropriate governmental agencies. . . .

The amounts earned by the employees before reinstatement were directed to be deducted from their back pay manifestly because, having already been received, these amounts were not needed to make the employees whole. That principle would apply whether the employees had earned the amounts in public or private employment. Further, there is no question that the amounts paid by the governmental agencies were for services actually performed. Presumably these agencies, and through them the public, received the benefit of services reasonably worth the amounts paid. There is no finding to the contrary.

The Board urges that the work relief program was designed to meet the exigency of large-scale unemployment produced by the depression; that projects had been selected, not with a single eye to costs or usefulness, but with a view to providing the greatest amount of employment in order to serve the needs of unemployed workers in various communities; in short, that the Work Projects Administration has been conducted as a means of dealing with the relief problem. Hence it is contended that the Board could properly conclude that the unfair labor practices of the company had occasioned losses to the Government financing the work relief projects.

The payments to the Federal, State, County, or other governments concerned are thus conceived as being required for the purpose of redressing, not an injury to the employees, but an injury to the public,—an injury thought to be not the less sustained although here the respective governments have received the benefit of the services performed. So conceived, these required payments are in the nature of penalties imposed by law upon the employer,—the Board acting as the legislative agency in providing that sort of sanction by reason of public interest. We need not pause to pursue the application of this theory of the Board's power to a variety of circumstances where community interests might be asserted. The question is,—Has Congress conferred the power upon the Board to impose such requirements?

We think that the theory advanced by the Board proceeds upon a misconception of the National Labor Relations Act. The Act is essentially remedial. It does not carry a penal program declaring the described unfair labor practices to be crimes. The Act does not prescribe penalties or fines in vindication of public rights or provide indemnity against community losses as distinguished from the protection and compensation of employees. Had Congress been intent upon such a program, we cannot doubt that Congress would have expressed its intent and would itself have defined its retributive scheme.

The remedial purposes of the Act are quite clear. It is aimed, as the Act says (§ 1) at encouraging the practice and procedure of collective bargaining and at protecting the exercise by workers of full freedom of association, of self organization and of negotiating the terms and conditions of their employment or other mutual aid or protection through their freely chosen representatives. This right of the employees is safeguarded through the authority conferred upon the Board to require the employer to desist from the unfair labor practices described and to leave the employees free to organize and choose their representatives. They are thus protected from coercion and interference in the formation of labor organizations and from discriminatory discharge. Whether the Act has been violated by the employer—whether there has been an unfair labor practice—is a matter for the board to determine upon evidence. When it does so determine the Board can require the employer to disestablish organizations created in violation of the Act; it can direct the employer to bargain with those who appear to be the chosen representatives of the employees and it can require that such employees as have been discharged in violation of the Act be reinstated with back pay. All these measures relate to the protection of the employees and the redress of their grievances, not to the redress of any supposed public injury after the employees have been made secure in their right of collective bargaining and have been made whole.

As the sole basis for the claim of authority to go further and to demand payments to governments, the Board relies on the language of § 10(c) which provides that if upon evidence the Board finds that the person against whom the complaint is lodged has engaged in an unfair labor practice, the Board shall issue an order—"requiring such person to cease and desist from such unfair labor practice, and to take such affirmative action, including reinstatement of employees with or without back pay, as will effectuate the policies of this Act."

This language should be construed in harmony with the spirit and remedial purposes of the Act. We do not think that Congress intended to vest in the Board a virtually unlimited discretion to devise punitive measures, and thus to prescribe penalties or fines which the Board may think would effectuate the policies of the Act. We have said that "this authority to order affirmative action does not go so far as to confer a punitive jurisdiction enabling the Board to inflict upon the employer any penalty it may choose because he is engaged in unfair labor practices even though the Board be of the opinion that the policies of the Act might be effectuated by such an order." We have said that the power to command affirmative action is remedial, not punitive. . . . We adhere to that construction.

In that view, it is not enough to justify the Board's requirements to say that they would have the effect of deterring persons from violating the Act. That argument proves too much, for if such a deterrent effect is sufficient to sustain an order of the Board, it would be free to set up any system of penalties which it would deem adequate to that end. . . .

In truth, the reasons assigned by the Board for the requirement in question—reasons which relate to the nature and purpose of work relief projects and to the practice and aims of the Works Project Administration—indicate that its order is not directed to the appropriate effectuating of the policies of the National Labor Relations Act, but to the effectuating of a distinct and broader policy with respect to unemployment. The Board has made its requirement in an apparent effort to provide adjustments between private employment and public work relief, and to carry out supposed policies in relation to the latter. That is not the function of the Board. It has not been assigned a rôle in relation to losses conceived to have been sustained by communities or governments in connection with work relief projects. The function of the Board in this case was to assure to petitioner's employees the right of collective bargaining through their representatives without interference by petitioner and to make good to the employees what they had lost through the discriminatory discharge.

We hold that the additional provision requiring the payments to governmental agencies was beyond the Board's authority. . . .

## § 34:10. Review under the Federal Administrative Procedure Act

The Federal Administrative Procedure Act endeavors to restate the substance of the existing law by providing:

"Except so far as (1) statutes preclude judicial review or (2) agency action is by law committed to agency discretion—

. . .

(e) Scope of Review.—So far as necessary to decision and where presented the reviewing court shall decide all relevant questions of law, interpret constitutional and statutory provisions, and determine the meaning or applicability of the terms of any agency action. It shall (A) compel agency action unlawfully withheld or unreasonably delayed; and (B) hold unlawful and set aside agency action, findings, and conclusions found to be (1) arbitrary, capricious, an abuse of discretion, or otherwise not in accordance with law; (2) contrary to constitutional right, power, privilege, or immunity; (3) in excess of statutory jurisdiction, authority, or limitations, or short of statutory right; (4) without observance of procedure required by law; (5) unsupported by substantial evidence in any case subject to the requirements of sections 7 and 8 or otherwise reviewed on the record of an agency hearing provided by statute; or (6) unwarranted by the facts to the extent that the facts are subject to trial de novo by the reviewing court. In making the foregoing determinations the court shall review the whole record or such portions thereof as may be cited by any party, and due account shall be taken of the rule of prejudicial error."

## Questions for Discussion

1. Why does the Court hold that the determination of the administrator is not subject to review on the basis that he has believed all the witnesses of one party and disbelieved all the opposing witnesses?

2. Will the Court review the action of the administrator on the ground that he believed the testimony of one person and disbelieved the testimony of a large number of persons?

3. What is a constitutional fact?

4. What constitutes "substantial evidence?"

5. What is the effect upon the scope of judicial review of administrative action of interpreting "evidence" in the following provision as meaning "substantial evidence:" "The findings of the Board as to the facts, if supported by evidence, shall be conclusive?"

6. Is the substantiality of evidence to be determined solely from an examination of the evidence in support of the disputed finding or may the reviewing court weigh the evidence adverse to it?

7. Is the classification of a buyer as a "jobber" a question of law, a question of fact, or a mixed question?

8. Why is the dissenting opinion in the *Motion Picture Advertising Service Company* case concerned about the failure of the commission to make findings?

9. How is "unfair competition" treated in the *Motion Picture Advertising Service Company* case?

10. Does the *RCA Communications* case restrict or expand the power of the administrator?

11. What are the arguments for and against a judicial review de novo of administrative action?

12. What are the arguments for and against a review of administrative action by which the court forms its own independent judgment on the basis of the record before the administrator?

13. Compare the scope of review of a constitutional fact and an ordinary fact.

14. What social policy is served by the doctrine of jurisdictional fact?

15. Why is there a distinction between a jurisdictional defect that makes legal proceedings everywhere void and other defects that do not have this effect?

16. Is a proceeding in a law court or before an administrator void whenever a wrong decision is made?

17. When does a court or an administrator have jurisdiction over a case?

18. Why did the Court in *Crowell* v. *Benson* conclude that a broader review should be required of those facts on the existence of which federal jurisdiction depended?

19. Does the broadening definition of federal powers beginning with the *Jones & Laughlin Steel Corporation* case, page 205, affect the attitude of the Court to the doctrine of federal jurisdictional fact?

20. What effect does the decision in *Crowell* v. *Benson* have on the work of federal administrators? on the work of the courts? on the costs of the proceedings to the private individual and the government?

21. Compare the majority and the minority opinions in *Crowell* v. *Benson.* Which is more persuasive?

22. What type of review should be provided according to the dissenting opinion in *Crowell* v. *Benson*?

23. Does the due process clause require any particular scope of review of federal jurisdictional facts?

24. To what extent is the Court influenced in *Crowell* v. *Benson* by a fear of bureaucracy?

25. What are the advantages and the disadvantages of a trial de novo by a court reviewing the action of an administrator? Which do you think are more convincing?

26. Does the Court give a literal interpretation to the statute in the *American Trucking* case?

27. What was the basis for the decision of the Court in the *American Trucking* case?

28. What guides does the Court recognize in interpreting a statute?

29. What factors were considered by the Court in interpreting the statute in the *New England Divisions* case?

30. To what extent may an order made by an administrator for an unauthorized purpose be reviewed by the Court?

31. Is the Court influenced by the character or the personnel of the administrator involved?

32. What argument could be made in the *Nierotko* case that the money received by the reinstated worker should not be included as wages for the purpose of the Social Security Act?

33. Does the Court in the *Nierotko* case consider whether the administrator's interpretation of the statute was reasonable?

34. Does custom or judicial habit influence the scope of judicial review of administrative action?

35. What factors relating to the organization and the procedure of the administrator are relevant to the scope of judicial review of the administrator's action?

36. Comment upon the definition and the value of the distinctions between questions of law, questions of fact, and mixed questions of law and fact.

37. To what extent is the choice of the enforcement remedy and procedure by the administrator subject to judicial review?

38. (a) Does the imposition of an unnecessarily drastic enforcement remedy deprive the party affected of property without due process of law? (b) Compare the approach of the Court to this problem with its approach in rate-making cases where the issue of confiscation is raised.

39. Was the enforcement remedy adopted by the administrator in the *Phelps-Dodge* case expressly authorized by the statute?

40. Discuss the practical effect of the decision in the *Phelps-Dodge* case.

41. Does the Court in the *Phelps-Dodge* case attempt to confine the administrator to the granting of traditional forms of relief that had been obtainable from the courts?

42. To what extent is the Court in the *Phelps-Dodge* case influenced by the "public purpose" to be served by the administrator?

43. (a) Does the Court require the administrator to state the basis of his action? (b) Does a recital by the administrator of the reason for his action permit the Court to review the correctness of that reason?

44. Compare the decision in the *Republic Steel Corporation* case with the preceding *Phelps-Dodge* decision. Is there a difference in approach or can the two be reconciled?

45. A state unemployment compensation law provided that no payment could be made unless the employee had in a given year been paid wages of a certain amount, "some part of which amount has been paid in at least two different calendar quarters of such base period." X applied for unemployment compensation. He was refused on the ground that all the wages received by him for that base period had been paid in one calendar quarter. He appealed on the ground that, while payment had been made in one quarter, the wages were owing to him and had become due during two different quarters. The administrator interpreted the law as requiring actual payment within two different quarters. Can X obtain a review of the administrator's decision? Was the administrator correct? *Giammattei v. Eagan*, 135 Conn. 666, 68 A. 2d 129 (1949).

46. (a) What is the judicial attitude to judicial review of administrative action? (b) Has this attitude been the same during the last fifty years? How do you account for your answer?

47. What are the arguments for and against:

(a) Finality of administrative determinations.

(b) Complete review of administrative determinations.

48. Government by regulatory commission is merely another step in carrying out the traditional division of government into separate branches. Government by commission is the opposite of government by divided branches because all powers are combined within the one commission. Is there any foundation for either of these statements? Which one is correct?

49. What is meant by the "Fourth Estate" in American constitutional law?

50. It is inevitable that government by bureauracy replace the ballot. Do you agree with this statement? If you do, is there any remedy or alternative plan?

# APPENDIX

## CONSTITUTION OF THE UNITED STATES

WE THE PEOPLE of the United States, in Order to form a more perfect Union, establish Justice, insure domestic Tranquility, provide for the common defence, promote the general Welfare, and secure the Blessings of Liberty to ourselves and our Posterity, do ordain and establish this CONSTITUTION for the United States of America.

### ARTICLE I

Section. 1. All legislative Powers herein granted shall be vested in a Congress of the United States, which shall consist of a Senate and House of Representatives.

Section. 2. (1) The House of Representatives shall be composed of Members chosen every second Year by the People of the several States, and the Electors in each State shall have the Qualifications requisite for Electors of the most numerous Branch of the State Legislature.

(2) No Person shall be a representative who shall not have attained to the Age of twenty-five Years and been seven Years a Citizen of the United States, and who shall not, when elected, be an Inhabitant of that State in which he shall be chosen.

(3) Representatives and direct Taxes shall be apportioned among the several States which may be included within this Union, according to their respective Numbers, which shall be determined by adding to the whole Number of free Persons, including those bound to Service for a Term of Years, and excluding Indians not taxed, three fifths of all other Persons. The actual Enumeration shall be made within three Years after the first Meeting of the Congress of the United States, and within every subsequent Term of ten Years, in such Manner as they shall by Law direct. The Number of Representatives shall not exceed one for every thirty Thousand, but each State shall have at Least one Representative; and until such enumeration shall be made, the State of New Hampshire shall be entitled to chuse three, Massachusetts eight, Rhode-Island and Providence Plantations one, Connecticut five, New-York six, New Jersey four, Pennsylvania eight, Delaware one, Maryland six, Virginia ten, North Carolina five, South Carolina five, and Georgia three.

(4) When vacancies happen in the Representation from any State, the Executive Authority thereof shall issue Writs of Election to fill such Vacancies.

(5) The House of Representatives shall chuse their Speaker and other Officers; and shall have the sole Power of Impeachment.

Section. 3. (1) The Senate of the United States shall be composed of two Senators from each State, chosen by the Legislature thereof, for six Years; and each Senator shall have one Vote.

(2) Immediately after they shall be assembled in Consequence of the first Election, they shall be divided as equally as may be into three Classes. The Seats of the Senators of the first Class shall be vacated at the Expiration of the second year, of the second Class at the Expiration of the fourth Year, and of the third Class at the Expiration of the sixth Year, so that one-third may be chosen every second Year; and if Vacancies happen by Resignation, or otherwise, during the Recess of the Legislature of any State, the Executive thereof may make temporary Appointments until the next Meeting of the Legislature, which shall then fill such Vacancies.

(3) No Person shall be a Senator who shall not have attained to the Age of thirty Years, and been nine Years a Citizen of the United States, and who shall not, when elected, be an Inhabitant of that State for which he shall be chosen.

(4) The Vice President of the United States shall be President of the Senate, but shall have no Vote, unless they be equally divided.

(5) The Senate shall chuse their other Officers, and also a President pro tempore, in the Absence of the Vice President, or when he shall exercise the Office of President of the United States.

(6) The Senate shall have the sole Power to try all Impeachments. When sitting for that Purpose, they shall be on Oath or Affirmation. When the President of the United States is tried, the Chief Justice shall preside: And no Person shall be convicted without the Concurrence of two thirds of the Members present.

(7) Judgment in Cases of Impeachment shall not extend further than to removal from office, and disqualification to hold and enjoy any Office of honor, Trust or Profit under the United States: but the Party convicted shall nevertheless be liable and subject to Indictment, Trial, Judgment and Punishment, according to Law.

Section. 4. (1) The Times, Places and Manner of holding Elections for Senators and Representatives, shall be prescribed in each State by the Legislature thereof; but the Congress may at any time by Law make or alter such Regulations, except as to the Places of chusing Senators.

(2) The Congress shall assemble at least once in every Year, and such Meeting shall be on the first Monday in December, unless they shall by Law appoint a different Day.

Section. 5. (1) Each House shall be the Judge of the Elections, Returns, and Qualifications of its own Members, and a Majority of each shall constitute a Quorum to do Business; but a smaller Number may adjourn from day to day, and may be authorized to compel the Attendance of absent Members, in such Manner, and under such Penalties as each House may provide.

(3) Each House may determine the Rules of its Proceedings, punish its Members for disorderly Behavior, and, with the Concurrence of two thirds, expel a Member.

(3) Each House shall keep a Journal of its Proceedings, and from time to time publish the same, excepting such Parts as may in their Judgment require Secrecy; and the Yeas and Nays of the Members of either House on any question shall, at the Desire of one fifth of those present, be entered on the Journal.

(4) Neither House, during the Session of Congress, shall, without the Consent of the other, adjourn for more than three days, nor to any other Place than that in which the two Houses shall be sitting.

Section. 6. (1) The Senators and Representatives shall receive a Compensation for their Services, to be ascertained by Law, and paid out of the Treasury of the United States. They shall in all Cases, except Treason, Felony and Breach of the Peace, be privileged from Arrest during their Attendance at the Session of their respective Houses, and in going to and returning from the same; and for any Speech or Debate in either House, they shall not be questioned in any other Place.

(2) No Senator or Representative shall, during the Time for which he was elected, be appointed to any civil Office under the Authority of the United States, which shall have been created, or the Emoluments whereof shall have been encreased during such time; and no Person holding any Office under the United States, shall be a Member of either House during his Continuance in Office.

Section. 7. (1) All bills for raising Revenue shall originate in the House of Representatives; but the Senate may propose or concur with Amendments as on other Bills.

(2) Every Bill which shall have passed the House of Representatives and the Senate, shall, before it become a Law, be presented to the President of the United States; If he approve he shall sign it, but if not he shall return it, with his Objections to that House in which it shall have originated, who shall enter the Objections at large on their Journal, and proceed to reconsider it. If after such Reconsideration two thirds of that House shall agree to pass the Bill, it shall be sent, together with the Objections, to the other House, by which it shall likewise be reconsidered, and if approved by two thirds of that House, it shall become a Law. But in all such Cases the Votes of both Houses shall be determined by Yeas and Nays, and the Names of the Persons voting for and against the Bill shall be entered on the Journal of each House respectively. If any Bill shall not be returned by the President within

ten Days (Sundays excepted) after it shall have been presented to him, the Same shall be a Law, in like Manner as if he had signed it, unless the Congress by their Adjournment prevent its Return, in which Case it shall not be a Law.

(3) Every Order, Resolution, or Vote to which the Concurrence of the Senate and House of Representatives may be necessary (except on a question of Adjournment) shall be presented to the President of the United States; and before the Same shall take Effect, shall be approved by him, or being disapproved by him, shall be repassed by two thirds of the Senate and House of Representatives, according to the Rules and Limitations prescribed in the Case of a Bill.

Section. 8. (1) The Congress shall have Power To lay and collect Taxes, Duties, Imposts and Excises, to pay the Debts and provide for the common Defence and general Welfare of the United States; but all Duties, Imposts and Excises shall be uniform throughout the United States;

(2) To borrow Money on the credit of the United States;

(3) To regulate Commerce with foreign Nations, and among the several States, and with the Indian Tribes;

(4) To establish an uniform Rule of Naturalization, and uniform Laws on the subject of Bankruptcies throughout the United States;

(5) To coin Money, regulate the Value thereof, and of foreign Coin, and fix the Standard of Weights and Measures;

(6) To provide for the Punishment of counterfeiting the Securities and current Coin of the United States;

(7) To establish Post Offices and post Roads;

(8) To promote the Progress of Science and useful Arts, by securing for limited Times to Authors and Inventors the exclusive Right to their respective Writings and Discoveries;

(9) To constitute Tribunals inferior to the supreme Court;

(10) To define and punish Piracies and Felonies committed on the high Seas, and Offenses against the Law of Nations;

(11) To declare War, grant Letters of Marque and Reprisal, and make Rules concerning Captures on Land and Water;

(12) To raise and support Armies, but no Appropriation of Money to that Use shall be for a longer Term than two Years;

(13) To provide and maintain a Navy;

(14) To make Rules for the Government and Regulation of the land and naval Forces;

(15) To provide for calling forth the Militia to execute the Laws of the Union, suppress Insurrections and repel Invasions;

(16) To provide for organizing, arming, and disciplining, the Militia, and for governing such Part of them as may be employed in the Service of the United States, reserving to the States respectively, the Appointment of the Officers, and the Authority of training the Militia according to the discipline prescribed by Congress;

(17) To exercise exclusive Legislation in all Cases whatsoever, over such District (not exceeding ten Miles square) as may, by Cession of particular States, and the Acceptance of Congress, become the Seat of the Government of the United States, and to exercise like Authority over all Places purchased by the consent of the Legislature of the State in which the Same shall be, for the Erection of Forts, Magazines, Arsenals, dock-Yards, and other needful Buildings;—And

(18) To make all Laws which shall be necessary and proper for carrying into Execution the foregoing Powers, and all other Powers vested by this Constitution in the Government of the United States, or in any Department or Officer thereof.

Section. 9. (1) The Migration or Importation of such Persons as any of the States now existing shall think proper to admit, shall not be prohibited by the Congress prior to the Year one thousand eight hundred and eight, but a Tax or duty may be imposed on such Importation, not exceeding ten dollars for each Person.

(2) The Privilege of the Writ of Habeas Corpus shall not be suspended, unless when in Cases of Rebellion or Invasion the public Safety may require it.

(3) No Bill of Attainder or expost facto Law shall be passed.

(4) No Capitation, or other direct, tax shall be laid, unless in Proportion

to the Census or Enumeration herein before directed to be taken.

(5) No Tax or Duty shall be laid on Articles exported from any State.

(6) No Preference shall be given by any Regulation of Commerce or Revenue to the Ports of one State over those of another: nor shall Vessels bound to, or from, one State, be obliged to enter, clear, or pay Duties in another.

(7) No Money shall be drawn from the Treasury, but in Consequence of Appropriations made by Law; and a regular Statement and Account of the Receipts and Expenditures of all public Money shall be published from time to time.

(8) No Title of Nobility shall be granted by the United States: And no Person holding any Office of Profit or Trust under them, shall, without the Consent of the Congress, accept of any present, Emolument, Office, or Title, of any kind whatever, from any King, Prince, or foreign State.

Section. 10. (1) No State shall enter into any Treaty, Alliance, or Confederation; grant Letters of Marque and Reprisal; coin Money; emit Bills of Credit; make any Thing but gold and silver Coin a Tender in Payment of Debts; pass any Bill of Attainder, ex-post facto Law, or Law impairing the Obligation of Contracts, or grant any Title of Nobility.

(2) No State shall, without the Consent of the Congress, lay any Imposts or Duties on Imports or Exports, except what may be absolutely necessary for executing its inspection Laws: and the net Produce of all Duties and Imposts, laid by any State on Imports or Exports, shall be for the Use of the Treasury of the United States; and all such Laws shall be subject to the Revision and Controul of the Congress.

(3) No State shall, without the Consent of Congress, lay any Duty of Tonnage, keep Troops, or Ships of War in time of Peace, enter into any Agreement or Compact with another State, or with a foreign Power, or engage in War, unless actually invaded, or in such imminent Danger as will not admit of delay.

## ARTICLE II

Section. 1. (1) The executive Power shall be vested in a President of the United States of America. He shall hold his Office during the Term of four Years, and, together with the Vice President, chosen for the same Term, be elected, as follows:

(2) Each State shall appoint, in such Manner as the Legislature thereof may direct, a Number of Electors, equal to the whole Number of Senators and Representatives to which the State may be entitled in the Congress: but no Senator or Representative, or Person holding an Office of Trust or Profit under the United States, shall be appointed an Elector.

The electors shall meet in their respective States, and vote by ballot for two Persons, of whom one at least shall not be an Inhabitant of the same State with themselves. And they shall make a List of all the Persons voted for, and of the Number of Votes for each; which List they shall sign and certify, and transmit sealed to the Seat of the Government of the United States, directed to the President of the Senate. The President of the Senate shall, in the Presence of the Senate and House of Representatives, open all the Certificates, and the Votes shall then be counted. The Person having the greatest Number of Votes shall be the President, if such Number be a Majority of the whole Number of Electors appointed; and if there be more than one who have such Majority, and have an equal Number of Votes, then the House of Representatives shall immediately chuse by Ballot one of them for President; and if no Person have a Majority, then from the five highest on the List the said House shall in like Manner chuse the President. But in chusing the President, the Votes shall be taken by States, the Representation from each State having one Vote; A quorum for this Purpose shall consist of a Member or Members from two-thirds of the States, and a Majority of all the States shall be necessary to a Choice. In every Case, after the Choice of the President, the Person having the greatest Number of Votes of the Electors shall be the Vice President. But if there should remain two or more who have equal Votes, the Senate shall chuse from them by Ballot the Vice-President.

(3) The Congress may determine the Time of chusing the Electors, and the Day on which they shall give their

Votes; which Day shall be the same throughout the United States.

(4) No Person except a natural born Citizen, or a Citizen of the United States, at the time of the Adoption of this Constitution, shall be eligible to the Office of President; neither shall any Person be eligible to that Office who shall not have attained to the Age of thirty-five Years, and been fourteen Years a Resident within the United States.

(5) In Case of the Removal of the President from Office, or of his Death, Resignation, or Inability to discharge the Powers and Duties of the said Office, the same shall devolve on the Vice President, and the Congress may by Law provide for the Case of Removal, Death, Resignation, or Inability, both of the President and Vice President, declaring what Officer shall then act as President, and such Officer shall act accordingly, until the Disability be removed, or a President shall be elected.

(6) The President shall, at stated Times, receive for his Services, a Compensation, which shall neither be encreased nor diminished during the Period for which he shall have been elected, and he shall not receive within that Period any other Emolument from the United States, or any of them.

(7) Before he enter on the Execution of his Office, he shall take the following Oath or Affirmation:—"I do solemnly swear (or affirm) that I will faithfully execute the Office of President of the United States, and will to the best of my Ability, preserve, protect and defend the Constitution of the United States."

Section. 2. (1) The President shall be Commander in Chief of the Army and Navy of the United States, and of the Militia of the several States, when called into the actual Service of the United States; he may require the Opinion, in writing, of the principal Officer in each of the executive Departments, upon any Subject relating to the Duties of their respective Offices, and he shall have Power to grant Reprieves and Pardons for Offenses against the United States, except in Cases of Impeachment.

(2) He shall have Power, by and with the Advice and Consent of the Senate, to make Treaties, provided two thirds of the Senators present concur; and he shall nominate, and by and with the Advice and Consent of the Senate, shall appoint Ambassadors, other public Ministers and Consuls, Judges of the supreme Court, and all other Officers of the United States, whose Appointments are not herein otherwise provided for, and which shall be established by Law: but the Congress may by Law vest the Appointment of such inferior Officers, as they think proper, in the President alone, in the Courts of Law, or in the Heads of Departments.

(3) The President shall have Power to fill up all Vacancies that may happen during the Recess of the Senate, by granting Commissions which shall expire at the End of their next Session.

Section. 3. He shall from time to time give to the Congress Information of the State of the Union, and recommend to their Consideration such Measures as he shall judge necessary and expedient; he may, on extraordinary Occasions, convene both Houses, or either of them, and in Case of Disagreement between them, with Respect to the Time of Adjournment, he may adjourn them to such Time as he shall think proper; he shall receive Ambassadors and other public Ministers; he shall take Care that the Laws be faithfully executed, and shall Commission all the Officers of the United States.

Section. 4. The President, Vice President and all civil Officers of the United States, shall be removed from Office on Impeachment for, and Conviction of, Treason, Bribery, or other high Crimes and Misdemeanors.

## ARTICLE III

Section. 1. The judicial Power of the United States, shall be vested in one supreme Court, and in such inferior Courts as the Congress may from time to time ordain and establish. The Judges, both of the supreme and inferior Courts, shall hold their Offices during good Behaviour, and shall, at stated Times, receive for their Services, a Compensation, which shall not be diminished during their Continuance in Office.

Section. 2. (1) The judicial Power shall extend to all Cases, in Law and Equity, arising under this Constitution, the Laws of the United States, and Treaties made, or which shall be made, under their Authority;—to all Cases affecting Ambassadors, other public Ministers and Consuls;—to all Cases of admiralty and maritime Jurisdiction;—to Controversies to which the United States shall be a Party;—to Controversies between two or more States;—between a State and Citizens of another State;—between citizens of different States,—between citizens of the same State claiming Lands under Grants of different States, and between a State, or the Citizens thereof, and foreign States, Citizens or Subjects.

(2) In all Cases affecting Ambassadors, other public Ministers and Consuls, and those in which a State shall be Party, the supreme Court shall have original Jurisdiction. In all the other Cases before mentioned, the supreme Court shall have appellate Jurisdiction, both as to Law and Fact, with such Exceptions, and under such Regulations as the Congress shall make.

(3) The Trial of all Crimes, except in Cases of Impeachment, shall be by Jury; and such Trial shall be held in the State where the said Crimes shall have been committed; but when not committed within any State, the Trial shall be at such Place or Places as the Congress may by Law have directed.

Section. 3. (1) Treason against the United States, shall consist only in levying War against them, or in adhering to their Enemies, giving them Aid and Comfort. No Person shall be convicted of Treason unless on the Testimony of two Witnesses to the same overt Act, or on Confession in open Court.

(2) The Congress shall have Power to declare the Punishment of Treason, but no Attainder of Treason shall work Corruption of Blood, or Forfeiture except during the Life of the Person attainted.

## ARTICLE IV

Section. 1. Full Faith and Credit shall be given in each State to the public Acts, Records, and Judicial Proceedings of every other State. And the Congress may by general Laws prescribe the Manner in which such Acts, Records and Proceedings shall be proved, and the Effect thereof.

Section. 2. (1) The Citizens of each State shall be entitled to all Privileges and Immunities of Citizens in the several States.

(2) A person charged in any State with Treason, Felony, or other Crime, who shall flee from Justice, and be found in another State, shall on Demand of the executive Authority of the State from which he fled, be delivered up to be removed to the State having Jurisdiction of the Crime.

(3) No Person held to Service or Labour in one State, under the Laws thereof, escaping into another, shall, in Consequence of any Law or Regulation therein, be discharged from such Service or Labour, but shall be delivered up on Claim of the Party to whom such Service or Labour may be due.

Section. 3. (1) New States may be admitted by the Congress into this Union; but no new State shall be formed or erected within the Jurisdiction of any other State; nor any State be formed by the Junction of two or more States, or Parts of States, without the Consent of the Legislatures of the States concerned as well as of the Congress.

(2) The Congress shall have Power to dispose of and make all needful Rules and Regulations respecting the Territory or other Property belonging to the United States; and nothing in this Constitution shall be so construed as to Prejudice any Claims of the United States, or of any particular State.

Section. 4. The United States shall guarantee to every State in this Union a Republican Form of Government, and shall protect each of them against Invasion; and on Application of the Legislature, or of the Executive (when the Legislature cannot be convened) against domestic Violence.

## ARTICLE V

The Congress, whenever two thirds of both Houses shall deem it necessary, shall propose Amendments to this Constitution, or, on the Application of the Legislatures of two thirds of the several States, shall call a Convention for proposing Amendments, which, in either Case, shall be valid to all Intents and Purposes, as Part of this Constitution, when ratified by the Legislatures of three fourths of the several States, or by Conventions in three fourths thereof, as the one or the other Mode of Ratification may be proposed by the Congress; Provided that no Amendment which may be made prior to the Year One thousand eight hundred and eight shall in any Manner affect the first and fourth Clauses in the Ninth Section of the first Article; and that no State, without its Consent, shall be deprived of its equal Suffrage in the Senate.

## ARTICLE VI

(1) All Debts contracted and Engagements entered into, before the Adoption of this Constitution, shall be as valid against the United States under this Constitution, as under the Confederation.

(2) This Constitution, and the Laws of the United States which shall be made in Pursuance thereof; and all Treaties made, or which shall be made, under the Authority of the United States, shall be the supreme Law of the Land; and the Judges in every State shall be bound thereby, any Thing in the Constitution or Laws of any State to the Contrary notwithstanding.

(3) The Senators and Representatives before mentioned, and the Members of the several State Legislatures, and all executive and judicial Officers, both of the United States and of the several States, shall be bound by Oath or Affirmation, to support this Constitution; but no religious Test shall ever be required as a Qualification to any Office or public Trust under the United States.

## ARTICLE VII

The Ratification of the Conventions of nine States, shall be sufficient for the Establishment of this Constitution between the States so ratifying the Same.

## Articles in Addition to, and Amendment of, the Constitution of the United States of America, Proposed by Congress, and Ratified by the Legislatures of the Several States Pursuant to the Fifth Article of the Original Constitution

## [ARTICLE I]

Congress shall make no law respecting an establishment of religion, or prohibiting the free exercise thereof; or abridging the freedom of speech, or of the press; or the right of the people peaceably to assemble, and to petition the Government for a redress of grievances.

## [ARTICLE II]

A well regulated Militia, being necessary to the security of a free State, the right of the people to keep and bear Arms, shall not be infringed.

## [ARTICLE III]

No Soldier shall, in time of peace be quartered in any house, without the consent of the Owner, nor in time of war, but in a manner to be prescribed by law.

## [ARTICLE IV]

The right of the people to be secure in their persons, houses, papers, and effects, against unreasonable searches and seizures, shall not be violated, and no Warrants shall issue, but upon probable cause, supported by Oath or affirmation, and particularly describing the place to be searched, and the persons or things to be seized.

## [ARTICLE V]

No person shall be held to answer for a capital, or otherwise infamous crime, unless on a presentment or indictment of a Grand Jury, except in cases arising in the land or naval forces, or in the Militia, when in actual service in time of War or public danger; nor shall any person be subject for the same offense to be twice put in jeopardy of life or limb; nor shall be compelled in any Criminal Case to be a witness against himself, nor be deprived of life, liberty, or property, without due process of law; nor shall private property be taken for public use, without just compensation.

## [ARTICLE VI]

In all criminal prosecutions, the accused shall enjoy the right to a speedy and public trial, by an impartial jury of the State and district wherein the crime shall have been committed, which district shall have been previously ascertained by law, and to be informed of the nature and cause of the accusation; to be confronted with the witnesses against him; to have compulsory process for obtaining Witnesses in his favor, and to have the Assistance of Counsel for his defence.

### [ARTICLE VII]

In suits at common law, where the value in controversy shall exceed twenty dollars, the right of trial by jury shall be preserved, and no fact tried by a jury shall be otherwise re-examined in any Court of the United States, than according to the rules of the common law.

### [ARTICLE VIII]

Excessive bail shall not be required, nor excessive fines imposed, nor cruel and unusual punishments inflicted.

### [ARTICLE IX]

The enumeration in the Constitution, of certain rights, shall not be construed to deny or disparage others retained by the people.

### [ARTICLE X]

The powers not delegated to the United States by the Constitution, nor prohibited by it to the States, are reserved to the States respectively, or to the people.

### [ARTICLE XI]

The Judicial power of the United States shall not be construed to extend to any suit in law or equity, commenced or prosecuted against one of the United States by Citizens of another State or by Citizens or Subjects of any Foreign State.

### [ARTICLE XII]

The Electors shall meet in their respective states, and vote by ballot for President and Vice-President, one of whom, at least, shall not be an inhabitant of the same state with themselves; they shall name in their ballots the person voted for as President, and in distinct ballots the person voted for as Vice-President, and they shall make distinct lists of all persons voted for as President, and of all persons voted for as Vice-President, and of the number of votes for each, which lists they shall sign and certify, and transmit sealed to the seat of the government of the United States, directed to the President of the Senate;—The President of the Senate shall, in the presence of the Senate and House of Representatives, open all the certificates and the votes shall then be counted;—The person having the greatest number of votes for President, shall be the President, if such number be a majority of the whole number of Electors appointed; and if no person have such majority, then from the persons having the highest numbers not exceeding three on the list of those voted for as President, the House of Representatives shall choose immediately, by ballot, the President. But in choosing the President, the votes shall be taken by states, the representation from each state having one vote; a quorum for this purpose shall consist of a member or members from two-thirds of the states, and a majority of all the states shall be necessary to a choice. And if the House of Representatives shall not choose a President whenever the right of choice shall devolve upon them, before the fourth day of March next following, then the Vice-President shall act as President, as in the case of the death or other constitutional disability of the President. The person having the greatest number of votes as Vice-President, shall be the Vice-President, if such number be a majority of the whole number of Electors appointed, and if no person have a majority, then from the two highest numbers on the list, the Senate shall choose the Vice-President; a quorum for the purpose shall consist of two-thirds of the whole number of Senators, and a majority of the whole number shall be necessary for a choice. But no person constitutionally ineligible to the office of President shall be eligible to that of Vice-President of the United States.

### [ARTICLE XIII]

Section 1. Neither slavery nor involuntary servitude, except as a punishment for crime whereof the party shall have been duly convicted, shall exist within the United States, or any place subject to their jurisdiction.

Section 2. Congress shall have power to enforce this article by appropriate legislation.

## [ARTICLE XIV]

Section 1. All persons born or naturalized in the United States, and subject to the jurisdiction thereof, are citizens of the United States and of the State wherein they reside. No State shall make or enforce any law which shall abridge the privileges or immunities of citizens of the United States; nor shall any State deprive any person of life, liberty, or property, without due process of law; nor deny to any person within its jurisdiction the equal protection of the laws.

Section 2. Representatives shall be apportioned among the several States according to their respective numbers, counting the whole number of persons in each State, excluding Indians not taxed. But when the right to vote at any election for the choice of electors for President and Vice President of the United States, Representatives in Congress, the Executive and Judicial officers of a State, or the members of the Legislature thereof, is denied to any of the male inhabitants of such State, being twenty-one years of age, and citizens of the United States, or in any way abridged, except for participation in rebellion, or other crime, the basis of representation therein shall be reduced in the proportion which the number of such male citizens shall bear to the whole number of male citizens twenty-one years of age in such State.

Section 3. No person shall be a Senator or Representative in Congress, or elector of President and Vice President, or hold any office, civil or military, under the United States, or under any State, who, having previously taken an oath, as a member of Congress, or as an officer of the United States, or as a member of any State legislature, or as an executive or judicial officer of any State, to support the Constitution of the United States, shall have engaged in insurrection or rebellion against the same, or given aid or comfort to the enemies thereof. But Congress may by a vote of two-thirds of each House, remove such disability.

Section 4. The validity of the public debt of the United States, authorized by law, including debts incurred for payment of pensions and bounties for services in suppressing insurrection or rebellion, shall not be questioned. But neither the United States nor any State shall assume or pay any debt or obligation incurred in aid of insurrection or rebellion against the United States, or any claim for the loss or emancipation of any slave; but all such debts, obligations and claims shall be held illegal and void.

Section 5. The Congress shall have power to enforce, by appropriate legislation, the provisions of this article.

## [ARTICLE XV]

Section 1. The right of citizens of the United States to vote shall not be denied or abridged by the United States or by any State on account of race, color, or previous condition of servitude.

Section 2. The Congress shall have power to enforce this article by appropriate legislation.

## [ARTICLE XVI]

The Congress shall have power to lay and collect taxes on incomes, from whatever source derived, without apportionment among the several states, and without regard to any census or enumeration.

## [ARTICLE XVII]

The Senate of the United States shall be composed of two Senators from each state, elected by the people thereof, for six years; and each Senator shall have one vote. The electors in each state shall have the qualifications requisite for electors of the most numerous branch of the state legislatures.

When vacancies happen in the representation of any state in the Senate, the executive authority of such state shall issue writs of election to fill such vacancies: Provided, that the legislature of any state may empower the executive thereof to make temporary appointment until the people fill the vacancies by election as the legislature may direct.

This amendment shall not be so construed as to affect the election or term of any Senator chosen before it becomes valid as part of the Constitution.

## [ARTICLE XVIII]

Section 1. After one year from the ratification of this article the manufacture, sale, or transportation of intoxicating liquors within, the importation thereof into, or the exportation thereof from the United States and all territory subject to the jurisdiction thereof for beverage purposes is hereby prohibited.

Section 2. The Congress and the several States shall have concurrent power to enforce this article by appropriate legislation.

Section 3. This article shall be inoperative unless it shall have been ratified as an amendment to the Constitution by the legislatures of the several States, as provided in the Constitution, within seven years from the date of the submission hereof to the States by the Congress.

## [ARTICLE XIX]

The right of citizens of the United States to vote shall not be denied or abridged by the United States or by any State on account of sex.

Congress shall have power to enforce this article by appropriate legislation.

## [AMENDMENT XX]

Section 1. The terms of the President and Vice President shall end at noon on the 20th day of January, and the terms of Senators and Representatives at noon on the 3d day of January, of the years in which such terms would have ended if this article had not been ratified; and the terms of their successors shall then begin.

Section 2. The Congress shall assemble at least once in every year, and such meeting shall begin at noon on the 3d day of January, unless they shall by law appoint a different day.

Section 3. If, at the time fixed for the beginning of the term of the President, the President elect shall have died, the Vice President elect shall become President. If a President shall not have been chosen before the time fixed for the beginning of his term, or if the President elect shall have failed to qualify, then the Vice President elect shall act as President until a President shall have qualified; and the Congress may by law provide for the case wherein neither a President elect nor a Vice President elect shall have qualified, declaring who shall then act as President, or the manner in which one who is to act shall be selected, and such person shall act accordingly until a President or Vice President shall have qualified.

Section 4. The Congress may by law provide for the case of the death of any of the persons from whom the House of Representatives may choose a President whenever the right of choice shall have devolved upon them, and for the case of the death of any of the persons from whom the Senate may choose a Vice President whenever the right of choice shall have devolved upon them.

Section 5. Sections 1 and 2 shall take effect on the 15th day of October following the ratification of this article.

Section 6. This article shall be inoperative unless it shall have been ratified as an amendment to the Constitution by the legislatures of three-fourths of the several States within seven years from the date of its submission.

## [AMENDMENT XXI]

Section 1. The eighteenth article of amendment to the Constitution of the United States is hereby repealed.

Section 2. The transportation or importation into any State, Territory, or possession of the United States for delivery or use therein of intoxicating liquors, in violation of the laws thereof, is hereby prohibited.

Section 3. This article shall be inoperative unless it shall have been ratified as an amendment to the Constitution by conventions in the several States, as provided in the Constitution, within seven years from the date of the submission hereof to the States by the Congress.

## [AMENDMENT XXII]

Section 1. No person shall be elected to the office of the President more than twice, and no person who has held the office of President, or acted as President, for more than two years of a term to which some other person was elected President shall be elected to the office of the President more than once. But this Article shall not apply to any person holding the office of President when this Article was proposed by the Congress, and shall not prevent any person who may be holding the office of President, or acting as President, during the term within which this Article becomes operative from holding the office of President, or acting as President during the remainder of such term.

Section 2. This article shall be inoperative unless it shall have been ratified as an amendment to the Constitution by the legislatures of three-fourths of the several States within seven years from the date of its submission to the States by the Congress.

# INDEX

## A



## B

D



E



F

## T



## U



## V



## W